FUNDAMENTALS OF
COMPUTING
KAMALJEET SANGHERA
SECOND EDITION

First time users must work through the tutorial prior to registration.

During the tutorial you will familiarize yourself with the testing environment and this will help you feel more comfortable with the program prior to starting a real test.

Log In Instructions:

Go to: https://assess.ite.gmu.edu
System Requirements:
Macromedia Authorware Web Player plug-in is required to run the tutorial or a test. On the student test center page, click on the button provided to download the Macromedia Authorware plug-in. Remember this needs to be done prior to running the tutorial or self registering.

To set up a new account you must first Self Register.

To Self Register:

Step 1
• **Click on Self Registration** (Existing Users: Go to **Start Test**)

Step 2
• **Type Your Registration Number** and then click **Submit**. (Existing Users: Enter your **Login Name and Password**)

Step 3
• Click on **Submit Query**

 KENDALL/HUNT PUBLISHING COMPANY
Dubuque, Iowa

YOUR REGISTRATION NUMBER
RH8HB7CD

Fundamentals
of Computing

SECOND EDITION

Kamaljeet Sanghera
George Mason University

KENDALL/HUNT PUBLISHING COMPANY
4050 Westmark Drive   Dubuque, Iowa 52002

Contents

Preface   ix

CHAPTER 1   Windows XP Introduction   1

Getting Started   1

Logging on to Windows XP   1
The Windows XP Desktop   2
Using the Start Menu   4
Moving and Resizing a Window   5
Logging Off of Windows XP   7
Shutting Down a Windows XP Computer   8

Modifying System Settings   9

The Control Panel   9
Changing the System Date and Time   10
Changing the Screen Display   12
Working with Mouse, Keyboard and
    Printer Settings   17

Software   21

Understanding the Operating System   22
History of Operating Systems   22
Operating System Categories   23
Comparing Popular Operating Systems   24
Common Look and Feel   24
Solving Common Operating System
    Problems   24
Software Application Programs   26
Identifying Different Type of Software   27
Selecting Commands in an Office 2003
    Application   28
Word Processing Applications   29
Spreadsheet Applications   30
Presentation Applications   31
Database Applications   31
Graphics and Multimedia Applications   31
Utility Programs   32
Additional Specialized Software   33

Exploring Your Computer   34

Windows Explorer   34
Examining Components of Your
    Computer   35

Managing Your Files   41

Common Problems Associated with
    Working with Files   41
Creating a New Folder   42
Copying a File or Folder   45
Moving a File or Folder   45
Renaming a File or Folder   46
Deleting a File or Folder   47
Finding a File   48

CHAPTER 2   MS Word 2003— Case Study 1   49

Case Study 1—MS Word 2003   50

Getting Started   51

What Is Word?   52
Starting Word   52
The Word Application Window   53
Using the Word Menu System   55
Using Word Toolbars   57
Using Word Task Panes   58

Creating a Document   59

Entering Text into a Document   59
Saving a Document   62
Printing a Document   63
Closing a File   64

Editing a Document (Part 1)   65

Reopening a File   65
Moving the Insertion Point within a
    Document/Selecting Text   67

Inserting the Current Date and Time into a Document **70**

Inserting Text into a Document/Deleting Text from a Document **72**

Reversing an Edit Operation **75**

Editing a Document (Part 2) **77**

Finding Text in a Document **77**

Moving a Text Block **80**

Formatting a Document (Part 1) **82**

Applying Attributes to Text **82**

Applying a New Font and Font Size to Text **84**

Simultaneously Applying Multiple Font Options to Text **85**

Indenting a Paragraph **87**

Resetting Line and Paragraph Spacing in a Document **90**

Formatting a Document (Part 2) **94**

Resetting the Margins of a Document **94**

Creating a Bulleted List **96**

Inserting a Hard Page Break/Creating a Multiple-Page Document **99**

Changing the Zoom Level of a Document **100**

Using the Spelling and Grammar Checker **102**

Using a Word Template to Create a Document **103**

Displaying Help Information **107**

Exiting from Word **111**

Further Practice **111**

CHAPTER 3   MS Word 2003— Case Study 2 **113**

Case Study 2—MS Word 2003 **114**

1. Creating a Multiple-Section Document **116**

Setting up a Table **123**

Inserting a Table into a Document **123**

Formatting a Table **125**

Inserting and Deleting Rows/Columns in a Table **133**

Using Table AutoFormat **137**

Creating Charts and Diagrams **139**

Inserting a Chart into a Document **139**

Modifying a Chart **141**

Creating Newsletter-Style Columns in a Document **146**

Producing a Report **151**

Adding a Border and Shading to Text **151**

Adding a Header/Footer to a Document **153**

Adding Page Numbers to a Document **156**

Further Practice **158**

CHAPTER 4   MS Excel 2003— Case Study 1 **161**

Case Study 1—MS Excel 2003 **161**

Getting Started **162**

What Is Excel? **162**

Start and Open a New Excel Workbook **163**

The Excel Application Window **165**

Using the Excel Menu System **167**

Using Excel Toolbars **169**

Using Excel Task Panes **170**

Modifying an Existing Worksheet **170**

Enter Labels and Values into a Blank Worksheet of the Workbook **170**

Entering a Formula into a Worksheet **174**

Saving a Workbook **180**

Formatting a Worksheet **181**

Resetting the Alignment of Cell Entries **181**

Resetting Font Options for Cell Entries **182**

Adding Borders and Shading to a Worksheet **186**

Adjusting Column Width in a Worksheet **190**

Adjusting Row Height in a Worksheet **192**

Editing a Worksheet 193

Changing Data in a Worksheet 193

Using AutoFill 194

Copying Cells 195

Inserting and Deleting Rows
and Columns 197

Resetting the Number Format
of Cell Entries 201

**Changing the Page Setup for
a Worksheet 208**

Exiting from Excel 214

Displaying Help Information 215

Further Practice 219

**CHAPTER 5 MS Excel 2003—
Case Study 2 225**

Case Study 2—MS Excel 2003 226

**Open a New Workbook and Enter
Information 228**

**Using Absolute Cell Reference
into a Formula 231**

Inserting and Deleting Rows
and Columns 233

Using Excel Functions 237

What Is a Function? 237

Using the MAX and MIN Functions 238

Using the AVERAGE Function 238

Using the SUM Function 238

Using the IF Function 243

Nesting IF Functions 245

Using NOW Function 246

Sorting the Records of a List 247

**Applying Conditional Formatting
to a Worksheet 249**

**Linking Worksheets within a
Workbook 253**

Renaming Worksheets in a Workbook 253

Entering a Formula to Link Related
Worksheets in a Workbook 255

Formatting Multiple Worksheets in One
Operation 259

Using AutoFormat 262

Creating a Chart 265

Creating and Plotting a Chart 265

Using the Spelling Checker 271

Further Practice 273

**CHAPTER 6 MS PowerPoint
2003—Case Study 1 277**

**Case Study 1—MS
PowerPoint 2003 278**

Getting Started 280

What Is PowerPoint? 280

Starting PowerPoint 281

The PowerPoint Application Window 282

Working with PowerPoint Menus
and Toolbars 283

Using PowerPoint Task Panes 285

Creating Text Slides 285

Creating a New Presentation 286

Adding a New Slide to a Presentation 288

Saving a Presentation 292

Editing the Text on a Slide 294

Working in the Slides Tab 296

Working in the Outline Tab 299

Resetting the Line Spacing of Paragraphs
on a Slide 307

Using the Drawing Toolbar 310

Moving a Placeholder 310

Adding an AutoShape to a Slide 312

Adding Text to an AutoShape 315

**Including Clip Art in a
Presentation 319**

Inserting a Clip Art Image into a Slide 319

Entering Additional Text on a Slide 322

Using Design Templates 324

Applying a Design Template to
a Presentation 324

Adding a Footer to Slides 327

Using the Spelling Checker 329

Closing a Presentation File 332

Reopening a Presentation File 333

Printing Slides 334

Displaying Help Information 336

Further Practice 341

CHAPTER 7   MS PowerPoint 2003—Case Study 2 345

Case Study 2—MS PowerPoint 2003 346

Creating a New Presentation from Design Template 349

Saving a Presentation 352

Creating a PowerPoint Table 354

Adding a PowerPoint Table to a Slide 354

Formatting a PowerPoint Table 357

Creating a Powerpoint Chart 364

Adding a PowerPoint Chart to a Slide 364

Modifying the Components of a
   PowerPoint Chart 367

Stacking Autoshapes 370

Producing a Slide Show 374

Running a Slide Show 374

Adding Transition Effects to Slides 379

Adding Animation Effects to Slides 381

Further Practice 385

CHAPTER 8   MS Access 2003—Case Study 1 389

Case Study 1—MS Access 2003 390

Getting Started 392

What Is Access? 392

Starting Access 392

The Access Application Window 393

Working with Access Menus 395

Basic Access Terminology 396

Examining Access Objects 396

Setting up a New Database 397

Designing a New Database 397

Creating a New Database 398

Creating a New Table 400

Entering Records in Datasheet View 408

Printing the Datasheet of a Table 411

Navigating Through Records in
   Datasheet View 413

Closing a Table/Closing a Database File 415

Creating a Form/Modifying and Manipulating Data 416

Reopening a Database File/Reopening
   a Table 416

Creating a Form 419

Navigating Through Records in Form
   View/Closing a Form 421

Reopening a Form 423

Switching Between Form View and
   Datasheet View 423

Entering Records in Form View 425

Editing Records in Datasheet View and in
   Form View/Using the Find Feature 427

Deleting Records in Datasheet View
   and in Form View 430

Modifying the Datasheet View
   of a Table 433

Sorting the Records in a Table 436

Displaying Selected Data 437

Filtering the Records in a Table 437

Creating a Simple Query 440

Creating a Query in Design View 447

Creating a Report 451

Creating a Simple Tabular Report 451

Creating a Grouped Tabular Report 454

Displaying Help Information 458

Exiting from Access 462

Further Practice 462

CHAPTER 9   MS Access 2003—Case Study 2 467

Case Study 2—MS Access 2003 468

Creating a New Database 469

Working with Multiple Tables 472

Creating Two New Tables and Setting Their
   Primary Keys 472

Creating a Relationship Between Two Tables in a Database   477
Displaying and Using a Subdatasheet   481

Intermediate Query Techniques   483

Creating a Query to Extract Information from Multiple Tables   483
Creating a Query to Generate Summary Information   487
Creating a Crosstab Query   491
Creating a Query to Find Unmatched Records in a Table   496
Including Multiple Conditions in a Query   498
Creating a Parameter Query   503

Further Practice   506

CHAPTER 10   Microsoft Internet Explorer Introduction   513

Getting Started   513

Introduction   513
What Is the Internet?   513
What Is the World Wide Web?   514
What Is Internet Explorer?   514
The Components of a URL   514
Connecting to the Internet   515
Starting Internet Explorer   515
The Internet Explorer Window   515
Customizing the Internet Explorer Toolbar   517
Displaying Help Information   517
Exiting from Internet Explorer   521

Browsing the World Wide Web   522

Displaying a Specific Web Page   522
Navigating Through a Web Site   523
Using the History Explorer Bar   525
Setting a New Home Page   526
Adding a Web Page to the Favorites List   528
Adding an Internet Radio Station to the Favorites List   530
Printing a Web Page   531

Searching the World Wide Web   532

Internet Search Services   532
Using the Search Companion   532
Using the Autosearch Feature   534
Using a Major Search Engine   535

Security on the Internet   537

Internet Security Concerns   537
Protecting Your Password   538
Protecting Your E-mail Messages   538
Using Security Certificates and Security Zones   539
Protecting Your Privacy on the Web   542

Further Practice   543

CHAPTER 11   XHTML—Case Study 1   545

Case Study 1—XHTML   546

What Is XHTML?   547

Creating a Web Page Using Notepad   547

Header Section   550
Saving a Document and Viewing in a Browser   551
Body Section   554
Document Formatting Tags   557

Validating Web Pages   575

Further Practice   583

CHAPTER 12   XHTML—Case Study 2   585

Case Study 2—XHTML   586

Tables   593

Images   601
Download an Image from the Web Site   603

Hyperlinks   614

Navigation   622

Further Practice   629

Appendix A: Windows XP—Summary of Keyboard and Toolbar Shortcuts   631

Appendix B: Internet Explorer—Summary of Keyboard and Toolbar Shortcuts   635

Appendix C: MS Word—Summary of Keyboard and Toolbar Shortcuts   639

Appendix D: MS Excel—Summary of Keyboard and Toolbar Shortcuts   645

Appendix E: MS PowerPoint—Summary of Keyboard and Toolbar Shortcuts   651

Appendix F: MS Access—Summary of Keyboard and Toolbar Shortcuts   655

Appendix G: Tags   659

Index   663

Preface

Welcome to *Fundamentals of Computing*. The primary objective of the course is to teach first time computer users the basics of computing, Windows XP, Microsoft Internet Explorer and four applications: Microsoft Word, Microsoft Excel, Microsoft PowerPoint and Microsoft Access. This course is written in a tutorial manner. There are 10 chapters and an appendix containing shortcut techniques covered throughout the course.

Chapter 1—"Windows XP Operations"

The primary objective of chapter 1 is to present the basic operations of Microsoft Windows XP Professional, hereafter referred to as simply "Windows XP". Topics include logging on to Windows XP; using start menu; logging off of Windows; examining different components of computer; creating, copying, moving, renaming, deleting a file or folder; changing system date and time, screen display, mouse and keyboard settings; and displaying help information.

Chapter 2—"Microsoft Word 2003—Case Study 1"

Chapter 2 introduces a user to the basic operations of Microsoft Office Word 2003, hereafter referred to as simply "Word". It begins with a case study. By following step-by-step instructions, user will learn how to start, close, save, reopen, and print Word documents; enter, navigate, edit, move, and delete text in a document; insert the current date and time; find and replace text in a document; apply a new font and font size to text; indent a paragraph, create a bulleted list, insert a hard page break, change the zoom level of a document; use the spelling and grammar checker; use a template to create a document; and display help information.

Chapter 3—"Microsoft Word 2003—Case Study 2"

Chapter 3 introduces a user to the intermediate and advanced operations of Word. By following step-by-step instructions, user will learn how to insert a section break in a document; change the orientation of a page (Portrait/Landscape); create and format a table; delete rows/columns in a table; insert and modify chart into a document; create newsletter-style columns in a document; add a border and shading to text; add a header/footer and page numbers to a document.

Chapter 4—"Microsoft Excel 2003—Case Study 1"

Chapter 4 introduces a user to the basic operations of Microsoft Office Excel 2003, hereafter referred to as simply "Excel". It begins with a case study. By following step-by-step instructions, user will learn how to start open, close, save, and print an Excel file; enter labels and values into a worksheet; enter a formula using both typing and pointing techniques; reset font options for cell entries; realign cell entries; add a border and shading to a worksheet; adjust column width and row height in a worksheet; automatically fill a range; insert and delete rows and columns; reset the number format of cell entries; change the page setup for a worksheet; preview a worksheet; and display help information.

Chapter 5—"Microsoft Excel 2003—Case Study 2"

Chapter 5 introduces a user to the intermediate and advanced operations of Excel. By following step-by-step instructions, user will learn how to enter an absolute cell reference into a formula; use Excel functions (SUM, AVERAGE, MAX, MIN and COUNT), IF function and NOW function; sort the records of a list; apply conditional formatting to a worksheet; filter the records of a list; work on multiple worksheets; renaming worksheets and formatting the worksheet tabs; enter a formula to link related worksheets in a workbook; format multiple worksheets in one operation; use Excel's Auto format feature; plot, modify and enhance chart; and use the spell checker tool.

Chapter 6—"Microsoft PowerPoint 2003—Case Study 1"

Chapter 6 introduces a user to the basic operations of Microsoft Office PowerPoint 2003, hereafter referred to as simply "PowerPoint". It begins with a case study. By following step-by-step instructions, user will learn how to start, create, close, save, and reopen PowerPoint presentation; add new slides and edit existing slides; wok in both Slides and Outline tabs; add an AutoShape and a clip art image into a slide; apply a design template to a presentation; add footer to presentation slides; use the spelling checker; display help information; and print slides.

Chapter 7—"Microsoft PowerPoint 2003—Case Study 2"

Chapter 7 introduces a user to the intermediate and advanced operations of PowerPoint. By following step-by-step instructions, user will learn how to create new Presentation from design templates; add and format PowerPoint table; add and modify PowerPoint chart; stack AutoShapes; run a slide show; add transition effects and animation effects to slides.

Chapter 8—"Microsoft Access 2003—Case Study 1"

Chapter 8 introduces a user to the basic operations of Microsoft Office Access 2003, hereafter referred to as simply "Access". It begins with a case study. By following step-by-step instructions, user will learn how to start access; create a new database and a new table; enter, edit and print records from Datasheet view; create a form; enter and edit records in Form view; sort and filter records in a table; create and modify query; create and modify simple tabular report; and display help information.

Chapter 9—"Microsoft Access 2003—Case Study 2"

Chapter 9 introduces a user to the intermediate and advanced operations of Access. By following step-by-step instructions, user will learn how to create and display multiple tables on the Access desktop; add Primary Key; create a relationship between two tables; display and use a subdatasheet; create a query to extract information from multiple tables, generate summary information, find unmatched records in a table, include multiple conditions in a query; create parameter query, cross-tab query.

Chapter 10—"Microsoft Internet Explorer"

The primary objective of Chapter 10 is to present the basic operations of Microsoft Internet Explorer 6, hereafter referred to as simply "Internet Explorer". Topics include starting Internet Explorer; displaying specific Web page; navigate through a Web site; setting a new home page; adding a Web page to the favorites list; printing a Web page; using major search engine; and using security certificates, security zones and privacy settings.

Chapter 11—"XHTML—Case Study 1"

Chapter 11 introduces a user to XHTML (Extensible HyperText Markup Language). It begins with a case study. By following step-by-step instructions, user will learn the basic rules of XHTML; DocTypes; header elements; formatting elements; ordered, unordered and definition lists; viewing web pages in a browser; and validating web pages.

Chapter 12—"XHTML—Case Study 2"

Chapter 12 introduces a user to the intermediate and advanced tags of XHTML. By following step-by-step instructions, user will learn how to create hyperlinks using both relative and absolute path names; create tables in a web page; insert an image from Internet and Microsoft application; and cite the sources of images used in the web site.

Appendix—"Summary of Keyboard and Toolbar Shortcuts and Tags"

The primary objective of Appendix A to F is to provide a quick reference to keyboard and toolbar shortcuts presented throughout the book. These appendices list the shortcuts for Windows XP, Internet Explorer, Word, Excel, PowerPoint, and Access. Appendix G provides a reference to XHTML tags used in creating web pages.

Course Prerequisites

In this introductory course, no previous experience using Internet Explorer (or any other Web-browser program), web page development, Microsoft Windows XP or Microsoft applications such as Microsoft Word, Microsoft Excel, Microsoft PowerPoint or Microsoft Access is required. It is assumed, however, that you have:

- Knowledge of **personal computer fundamentals**.
- Experience working in the **Microsoft Windows environment**.
- A reasonable degree of **keyboard proficiency**.
- Experience using a **mouse**.

You will also need the following to complete this course:

- A **personal computer** with a **Pentium 233 MHz or higher microprocessor**.
- A minimum of **128 MB** of **random access memory**.
- **Microsoft Internet Explorer 6**, properly installed.
- **Microsoft Windows XP**, **Microsoft Word 2003**, **Microsoft Excel 2003**, **Microsoft PowerPoint 2003**, and **Microsoft Access 2003**, properly installed.
- A **Super VGA (800 X 600) or higher-resolution monitor** with **256 colors**.
- An installed **pointing device** (mouse) that is supported by your operating system.
- An installed **printer** that is supported by your operating system.
- **Internet connection**.

Course Conventions

A number of conventions are used in this manual. Please be sure that you understand them. The course is divided into **sections**. Most sections consist of an **introduction** and various **subsections**.

Most **subsections** include an **overview** of the topic to be presented and an **exercise** headed by the word **Objective**.

Instructions of an exercise may be a combination of selecting a command (or command sequence), typing information and/or pressing one or more keys. Typical examples are given below:

<u>Example 1</u>

Choose the **File** command.

This means that you should select the **File** command on the Menu bar.

<u>Example 2</u>

Choose the **File**, **Open** command.

This means that you should first select the **File** command on the Menu bar and then select the **Open** option on the File menu.

Example 3

When a shortcut button is available for a command sequence, that button is often indicated.

Click on the **Save** button.

This means that you should position the mouse pointer on the **Save** button and then click the mouse button. (When clicking on any command, button or other screen object, or when dragging a screen object, use the **left** mouse button unless otherwise instructed.)

Example 4

Type: **Travel Brochure**
Press [**ENTER**].

This means that you should type the words **Travel Brochure** and then press the [**ENTER**] key. (In such instructions, special keys, such as [**ENTER**], [**ESC**] and [**F1**], can be easily identified because they are always enclosed in square brackets.)

Example 5

When you are required to press two keys at the same time, the **+** sign is used.
Press [**CTRL**] + [**O**].

This means that you should press the [**CTRL**] key and, while holding it down, press the letter **O**.

In the end of each chapter (except for the first chapter), **Further Practice** activity is provided. It has been included to enable you to review techniques you have learned. Again, follow the instructions carefully. If necessary, refer to any notes you may have taken as you work through it.

This course assumes that you are using a mouse. Basic mouse techniques are summarized below.

ACTION	DESCRIPTION
Point	Position the mouse pointer on the specified screen item.
Click	Press and release the **left** mouse button.
Double-click	Press and release the **left** mouse button two times in rapid succession.
Right-click	Press and release the **right** mouse button.
Drag	Move the mouse pointer from its initial position to another area of the screen while holding down the **left** mouse button.

Acknowledgements

The second edition of "Fundamentals of Computing" would not have been possible without the support of Dr. Don Gantz, Chair of Applied Information Technology, and Dr. Sharon Caraballo, Associate Chair of Applied Information Technology department at George Mason University. I am extremely grateful to them.

I want to thank my husband, Paramjeet, for his patience and encouragement that has enabled me to accomplish things I never thought were possible, my son, Bhavjeet, our little bundle of joy and my constant source of inspiration, and my little princess, Suman. I would also like to thank my parents-in-law, Gian and Harbhajan Sanghera, for their love and endless support. Finally, I want to thank my parents, brothers and sister for an upbringing that got me to where I am today.

Thanks to Curtis Ross and Amanda Smith for their help. Thanks to my students and instructors for their suggestions and feedback.

Windows XP Introduction

OBJECTIVES

After successfully completing this chapter, you should be able to:

- Log on to Windows XP
- Use the Start menu
- Move and resize a window
- Modify system settings using Windows XP Control Panel
- Change the system date and time
- Change the screen display
- Change mouse settings

- Change keyboard settings
- View and update the list of installed printers
- Select commands in Office 2003 application
- Use Windows Explorer
- Use Windows Explorer as a file management tool
- Log off of Windows XP

Getting Started

Logging on to Windows XP

Windows XP is your computer's operating system. An **operating system** is a group of programs that provide an interface between application software and hardware, coordinating input and output (the flow of information into, and out of, the computer) and giving hardware devices the instructions they need to carry out the requested tasks at the appropriate time. An operating system also controls the storage of computer data by managing both the storage media (disks) and the various files in which the information is held.

Windows XP is started as soon as you turn on the computer. Before you can begin using the computer, however, you must log on to Windows XP. The procedure for doing this depends on the way your computer is set up—whether it is part of a network domain or a stand-alone computer.

To **log on to Windows XP** (on a computer that is part of a **network domain**):

- When the Welcome to Windows screen appears, press [**CTRL**] + [**ALT**] + [**DEL**]. (Doing this prevents other programs from running on your computer, thereby protecting your user account name and password from being accessed by what are called "Trojan horse" programs.)

- In the Log On to Windows dialog box, which is subsequently displayed:
    - Type your **user account name**.
    - Type your **password**.
    - Select the appropriate **domain name**.
    - Click on the **OK** button.

To **log on to Windows XP** (on a **stand-alone computer**):

- On the Welcome screen, point to your **user account name**, and click the mouse button.
- If the user account is password protected, type your **password**, and click on the **right arrow button**.

Notes

1. If a stand-alone computer has been set up to include only one user account, you are automatically logged on to Windows XP as soon as the computer is booted.
2. If a stand-alone computer was previously connected to a network domain, you log on to Windows XP by using the first method described above. In this case, the information you enter is compared with the information that was stored on the computer the last time you logged on to the network.

Objective

In this exercise, you will **log on to Windows XP**. (Your computer system should be off at this point.) **NOTE:** This exercise assumes that you are using a stand-alone computer that has not been connected to a network domain.

- **Turn on** your **computer system**.

If your computer has been set up to include only one user account, the user profile is loaded, and the Windows XP desktop is displayed. In this case, skip the remaining steps.

- Point to your **user account name**, and click the (left) mouse button.

If the user account is not password-protected, your user profile is loaded, and the Windows XP desktop is displayed. In this case, skip the remaining step.

- Type: (**your password**) Point to the **right arrow button**, and click the mouse button.

The password is entered, your user profile is loaded, and the Windows XP desktop is displayed.

The Windows XP Desktop

The Windows XP **desktop**, which appears when you log on to Windows XP, is the screen from which all operations are initiated. Although the appearance of the desktop may vary from one computer to the next, the following elements are standard:

Icons: These small graphics provide access to programs, folders and special Windows XP tools. Icons that you may see include **My Documents** (a link to a special folder for storing documents with which you are currently working), **My Computer** (a link to a tool for examining the components of your computer), **My Network Places** (a link to a tool for examining the resources—for example, the shared computers, printers, files and folders—on the network to which you are connected), **Internet Explorer** (a link to Windows XP's Web browser), and **Recycle Bin** (a link to an area for temporarily storing deleted files).

Taskbar: This bar at the bottom of the screen is the primary tool for controlling Windows XP. It includes the Start button and Notification area (both described below) and displays icons for windows that are currently open. It may also display the Quick Launch toolbar to the right of the Start button.

Start button: This button provides access to the Start menu, which includes options for initiating the majority of Windows XP operations.

Notification area: This area initially displays the current time. It may also display buttons for accessing other programs that have been installed on your computer. When certain events take place (for example, when you print a document or when you receive an e-mail message), an icon appears temporarily in this area.

WINDOWS XP DESKTOP

Notes

Since Windows XP can be customized in a number of ways, what appears on your screen may sometimes vary from what is shown in this manual. Note that the initial appearance of the Windows XP desktop varies according to whether the operating system was installed on a new computer or on a computer running a previous version of Windows.

Using the Start Menu

Clicking on the Start button displays the **Start menu**—Windows XP's main menu of options. This menu displays the following options:

My Documents: This option opens the My Documents folder, which, as mentioned earlier, is used to store documents with which you are currently working.

My Recent Documents: This option displays a list of the last documents that were opened. You can reopen any document in this list in the application in which it was created by simply selecting its filename.

My Pictures: This option opens the My Pictures folder, which is used to store picture files and perform various operations involving those files.

My Music: This option opens the My Music folder, which is used to store music files and create lists of songs (playlists) that can be played using Windows Media Player.

My Computer: This option is a link to Windows Explorer, which allows you to examine the hardware, files and folders on your computer.

Control Panel: This option is a link to the Control Panel, which allows you to modify system settings and personalize your computer.

Printers and Faxes: This option displays the Printers and Faxes window, which allows you to add a new printer, share a printer, and monitor current print jobs.

Help and Support: This option is a link to the Help and Support Center, which allows you to obtain information about Windows XP features.

Search: This option is a link to the Search Companion, which allows you to search for specific files, folders, computers and individuals.

Run: This option allows you to run a particular application (for example, a setup program) from the command line.

All Programs: This option is a link to all applications (programs) that are installed on your computer.

Log Off: This option is used to log off of Windows XP so that another individual with a different user account can log on.

Turn Off Computer or **Shut Down:** This option is used to shut down or restart your computer.

The name of the current user appears at the top of the Start menu. Below the user name are two areas: one displaying links to favorite (pinned) programs and one displaying links to the most frequently-used programs.

Objective

In this exercise, you will **display the Start menu**. You will then **select options on this menu**.

- Make sure that the **Windows XP desktop** is displayed.
- Point to the **Start** button.
- With the mouse pointer positioned on the **Start** button, click the mouse button.

A small box appears, displaying the text "Click here to begin." This small box is called a ScreenTip. You will notice that a ScreenTip appears when you point to many items on the Windows XP desktop or in a window displayed while using Windows XP. The ScreenTip will display either an instruction, as in this case, or the name or a description of the item to which you are pointing.

- Point to **All Programs** on the Start menu.

The All Programs submenu is displayed.

- Point to **Accessories** on the All Programs submenu.

The Accessories submenu is displayed.

- Point to **System Tools** on the Accessories submenu.

The System Tools submenu is displayed.

- Point to any **empty area** of the **desktop** (any area that does not display a menu or icon), and click the mouse button.

The Start menu and all submenus are closed.

Moving and Resizing a Window

You can easily move a window to any area of the desktop, as well as resize it horizontally and/or vertically.

To **move a window**:

- **Drag** the **Title bar** to the new location.

To **resize a window**:

- **Drag** the **left** or **right border** to increase/decrease the **width** of the window; or
- **Drag** the **top** or **bottom border** to increase/decrease the **height** of the window; or
- **Drag** a **corner border** to simultaneously increase/decrease both the **width** and **height** of the window.

Alternatively, you can display a full-screen view of a window by clicking on the **Maximize** button on the Title bar. Subsequently clicking on the **Restore Down** button (which replaces the Maximize button) restores the window to its previous size. You can also reduce a window to a button on the taskbar, without closing it, by clicking on the **Minimize** button on the Title bar. Subsequently clicking on this button redisplays the window.

Objective

In this exercise, you will **move and resize a window**. To perform these operations, you will use the **Recycle Bin window**.

3.1

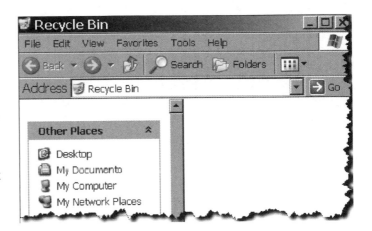

- **Make sure that the Windows XP desktop is displayed.**

- **Point to the Recycle Bin icon, and double-click the mouse button.**

The Recycle Bin window is opened. Notice that a button representing the window appears on the taskbar.

NOTE: *If the window is maximized (fills the screen), click on the **Restore Down** button on the Title bar to reduce its size.*

- **If the Recycle Bin currently contains one or more deleted files, use the File, Empty Recycle Bin command to remove the file(s).**

NOTE: *To do this, click on **File** on the Menu bar, and click on **Empty Recycle Bin** on the File menu. Then click on the **Yes** button when prompted to confirm the operation.*

You will now move the window.

- **Point to the Title bar of the window. Press and hold down the mouse button, and drag the window to another area of the desktop. Then release the mouse button.**

The window is repositioned. You will now resize it.

- **Click on the Maximize ▣ button on the Title bar of the window.**

The window is displayed in its full-screen size.

- **Click on the Restore Down ▣ button (which replaced the Maximize button).**

The window is restored to its previous size.

- **Click on the Minimize ▬ button on the Title bar of the window.**

The window is reduced to a button on the taskbar.

- **Click on the Recycle Bin button on the taskbar.**

The window is redisplayed.

- **Point to the right border of the window.**

The mouse pointer will appear as a double-headed horizontal arrow when it is properly positioned.

- **Press and hold down the mouse button, and drag the right border to the left approximately one-half inch. Then release the mouse button.**

The width of the window is decreased.

- **Point to the bottom border of the window.**

The mouse pointer will appear as a double-headed vertical arrow when it is properly positioned.

- **Press and hold down the mouse button, and drag the bottom border upward approximately one-half inch. Then release the mouse button.**

The height of the window is decreased.

- **Point to the lower-right corner border of the window.**

The mouse pointer will appear as a double-headed diagonally-pointing arrow when it is properly positioned.

- **Press and hold down the mouse button, and drag the corner border diagonally downward and to the right approximately one-half inch. Then release the mouse button.**

Both the width and height of the window are increased.

- **Using the techniques you have learned, continue moving and resizing the Recycle Bin window until it is in a desired location and appears in a size of your choice.**

- **Click on the Close button on the Title bar of the window.**

The Recycle Bin window is closed.

Logging Off of Windows XP

When you are finished using your computer but wish to keep the computer running, you should log off of Windows XP. Doing so ends the computer session for your user account, allowing another person to initiate another session using his or her user account.

   To **log off of Windows XP**:

- Select the **Log Off** option on the **Start menu**.
- In the Log Off Windows dialog box, which is subsequently displayed, click on the **Log Off** button.

Notes

If you are working on a stand-alone computer, you can allow another user to log on to Windows XP without ending your computer session. To do this, click on the **Switch User** button in the Log Off Windows dialog box described above instead of the Log Off button.

Objective

In this exercise, you will **log off of Windows XP**.

- Make sure that the **Windows XP desktop** is displayed.
- Click on the **Start** button.

The Start menu is displayed.

- Click on **Log Off** (at the bottom of the menu).

The Log Off Windows dialog box is displayed.

- Click on the **Log Off** button.

You are logged off of Windows XP.

- **Log on** to **Windows XP** once again.

The Windows XP desktop is redisplayed.

Shutting Down a Windows XP Computer

When you are finished using your computer and wish to turn off the power, it is important that you properly shut down the computer. Doing so closes all open applications and files and ends your Windows XP session. It also shuts down Windows XP, allowing you to safely turn off the power.

To **shut down a Windows XP computer**:

- Select either the **Shut Down** option or the **Turn Off Computer** option on the Start menu.
- In either the Shut Down Windows dialog box or the Turn off computer dialog box, select the desired option:
- **Shut down** (Shut Down Windows dialog box) or **Turn Off** (Turn off computer dialog box)—which simply shuts down the computer.
- **Restart**—which shuts down the computer and then restarts it.
- **Hibernate**—which shuts down the computer but saves the current session (the applications that are running and the files that are open). When the computer is restarted, the session is restored to its previous point. (To display this option in the Turn off computer dialog box, press and hold down [**SHIFT**].)
- **Stand by** (Shut Down Windows dialog box) or **Stand By** (Turn off computer dialog box)—which does not fully shut down the computer. Instead, it maintains the current session, keeping the current data in memory. The computer, however, runs on low power. You can subsequently return to a normal session by pressing [**CTRL**] + [**ALT**] + [**DEL**].
- In the Shut Down Windows dialog box, click on the **OK** button.

Objective

In this exercise, you will **shut down your computer**.

- Make sure that the **Windows XP desktop** is displayed.
- Click on the **Start** button.

The Start menu is displayed.

- Click on either **Shut Down** or **Turn Off Computer** (whichever option appears at the bottom of the menu).

Either the Shut Down Windows dialog box or the Turn off computer dialog box is displayed.

- If the Shut Down Windows dialog box is displayed, make sure that the **Shut down** option appears in the **What do you want the computer to do?** box. (If it does not, click on the **down arrow** at the right side of the box, and click on **Shut down** in the list of options that appears.) Then click on the **OK** button.

After a few moments, a message appears, informing you that you can turn off your computer.

NOTE: Depending on how your computer has been set up, it may have been turned off automatically. If so, skip the remaining steps.

- In the Turn off computer dialog box, click on the **Turn Off** button.

After a few moments, a message appears, informing you that you can turn off your computer.

NOTE: Depending on how your computer has been set up, it may have been turned off automatically. If so, skip the remaining step.

- **Turn off** your **computer**.

Modifying System Settings

The Control Panel

The Windows XP **Control Panel** is a tool for changing hardware and software settings for your computer. Using the Control Panel, you can, for example:

- **Add new hardware** to your computer system.
- **Set up new programs** on your computer.
- **Remove programs** from your computer.
- **Modify** the **date** and **time settings**.
- **Modify** the **display** and **audio settings**.
- **Modify keyboard, mouse** and **printer settings**.
- **Set up network** and **Internet connections**.
- **Set up** and **manage user accounts**.
- **Set passwords** and other **security options**.
- **Configure Windows XP** for special **vision, hearing** and **mobility needs**.

Notes

It is important to note that changes should never be made to system settings unless you are fully aware of how these changes will impact the computer. The computer uses the system settings to recognize hardware and software installed on your computer, security options, communication protocols, etc.

Careless changing of system settings can lead to all kinds of problems. Typical examples of these are listed below:

- If you remove an application, you will no longer be able to access any files associated with that application.
- If you change the mail server information, you may not be able to send or receive e-mails.
- If you change or remove a printer driver, you will not be able to print your documents on your printer.

- If you change the date and time, any files that you save thereafter will have the new date and time. This information is used to track versions of files, dates of transactions in accounting software, etc. If the date and time is set incorrectly, all kinds of accuracy issues could arise. The computer uses its internal clock to determine the date and time.

In some centrally controlled computer networks, permission for access to selected system settings are limited by the system administrator. This prevents users from making changes that could negatively impact the computer and/or network.

6.1

To access the Control Panel:

- **Select the Control Panel option on the Start menu.**

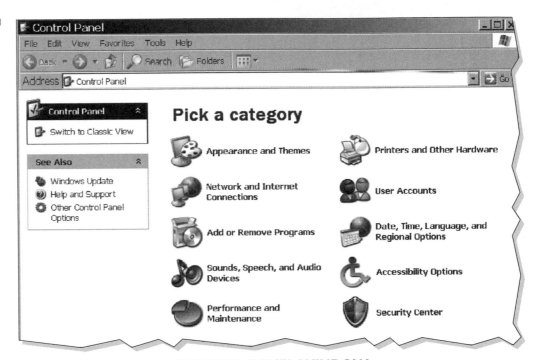

CONTROL PANEL WINDOW

Notes

Windows XP gives you the option of displaying the Control Panel window in the previous version Classic view by selecting the **Switch to Classic View** option. This course assumes that the Control Panel window appears in the default Category view.

Changing the System Date and Time

Control Panel options are grouped into nine categories. The **Date**, **Time**, **Language, and Regional Options** category includes options for changing the date, the time and the time zone settings for your computer.

Objective

In this exercise, you will access the Control Panel. You will then change the system date and time on your computer.

- Make sure that the **Windows XP desktop** is displayed.
- Click on the **Start** button. Then click on **Control Panel** on the Start menu.

The Control Panel window is opened.

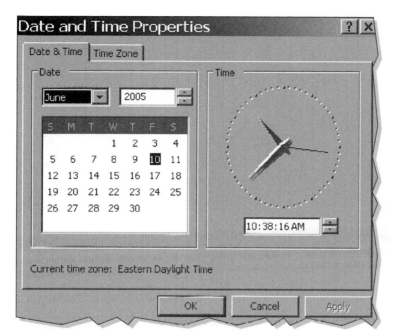

NOTE: *Make sure that the toolbar is displayed.*

- **Click on Date, Time, Language, and Regional Options.**

The Date, Time, Language, and Regional Options window appears, displaying a list of options related to the category you have chosen.

- **Click on Change the date and time.**

The Date & Time panel of the Date and Time Properties dialog box is displayed.

NOTE: *You can also display this dialog box by **right-clicking** on the current time in the Notification area of the taskbar and by selecting the **Adjust Date/Time** option on the shortcut menu, or by selecting the **Date and Time** option in the Date, Time, Language, and Regional Options window.*

- **Click on the down arrow at the right side of the month box.**

The box is expanded, and a list of months is displayed.

NOTE: *The month box is an example of a **drop-down list box** (also called an **expandable list box**).*

- **Click on next month (for example, April if the current month is March).**

The month is increased by one.

- **Click on the up arrow at the right side of the year box.**

The year is increased by one.

- **In the calendar below, click on yesterday's date (for example, 9 if the current day is 10).**

The day is decreased by one.

- **Double-click on the current hour (below the clock).**

The hour is highlighted.

- **Click on the down arrow at the right side of the time box.**

The hour is decreased by one.

- **Change the date and time settings back to the current date and time.**

7.2

• **Click on the Time Zone tab.**

The Time Zone panel of the dialog box is displayed. This panel is used to reset the time zone for your computer. (It is assumed that the correct time zone is currently listed in the time zone box at the top of the panel.)

• **Click on the OK button.**

The dialog box is closed, and the Date, Time, Language, and Regional Options window is redisplayed.

• **Click on the Back button.**

The Control Panel window is redisplayed.

Changing the Screen Display

The **Appearance and Themes** category in the Control Panel window includes options for changing a number of settings that affect the appearance of your screen—for example, the background displayed on the desktop, the screen saver that appears when your computer is on but is not being used, and the style and/or color of dialog box elements.

Objective

In this exercise, you will **change your screen display by selecting both a new background and screen saver**. You will also **reset the style and color of dialog box elements**.

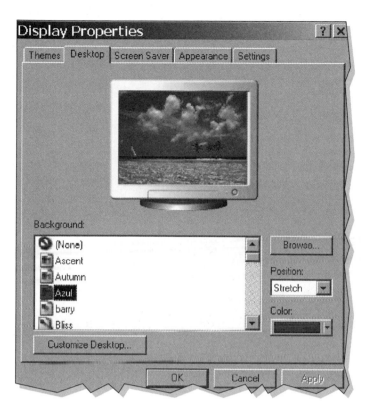

- **Make sure that the Control Panel window is displayed.**
- **Click on Appearance and Themes.**

The Appearance and Themes window appears, displaying a list of options related to the category you have chosen. You will now select a new background for the desktop.

- **Click on Change the desktop background.**

The Desktop panel of the Display Properties dialog box is displayed.

NOTE: *You can also display this dialog box by right-clicking on the Windows XP desktop and by selecting the Properties option on the shortcut menu, or by selecting the Display option in the Appearance and Themes window.*

- **Click on the Help** ❓ **(question mark) button on the Title bar of the dialog box.**

The mouse pointer changes to an upward-pointing arrow and question mark.

- **Click on the monitor that appears in the upper section of the dialog box.**

A description of the monitor appears in a small window.

- **Click in any empty area of the dialog box.**
- **In the Background box, click on Autumn.**

The selected background is displayed on the monitor above.

- **In the Background box, click on Gone Fishing.**

The new background now appears on the monitor. Notice that this background consists of a tiled image (a single image that is repeated many times).

- **Click on the down arrow at the right side of the Position box.**

The box is expanded, and a list of options is displayed.

- **Click on Stretch.**

The monitor now displays a large view of the background image.

- **In the Background box, click on (None).**

The monitor now displays the color that appears in the Color box.

- **Click on the down arrow at the right side of the Color box.**

The box is expanded, and a list of colors is displayed.

- **Click on a color of your choice.**

The monitor now displays the color you have selected.

- **In the Background box, click on Bliss.**

The default Windows XP background is restored. You will now select a new screen saver.

8.2

- **Click on the Screen Saver tab.**

The Screen Saver panel of the dialog box is displayed.

- **Point to the monitor that appears in the upper section of the dialog box, and right-click the mouse button.**

A small button labeled "What's This?" appears.

- **Click on the What's This? button.**

A description of the monitor appears in a small window.

NOTE: *This alternate technique can be used to display information about items in any dialog box that includes a Help button.*

- **Click in any empty area of the dialog box.**

The description window is closed.

- **Click on the down arrow at the right side of the Screen saver box.**

The box is expanded, and a list of screen savers is displayed.

- **Click on 3D Flying Objects.**

The selected screen saver is displayed on the monitor above.

- **Click on the Preview button.**

- **Cancel the display (by moving your mouse).**

The selected screen saver is previewed on your monitor.

NOTE: *Make sure that you do not move your mouse during the preview display. If you do, the display will be cancelled.*

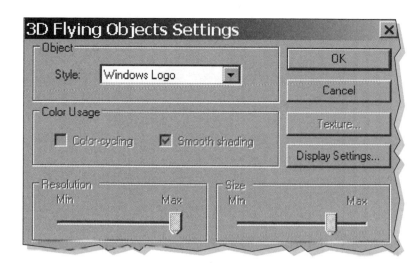

- **Click on the Settings button.**

The 3D Flying Objects Settings dialog box is displayed.

- **Under Object, click on the down arrow at the right side of the Style box.**

The box is expanded, and a list of objects is displayed.

- **Click on an object (style option) of your choice. Then click on the OK button.**

The new style is selected, and the dialog box is closed.

- **Click on the Preview button.**

The modified screen saver is previewed.

- **Cancel the display.**

- **Click on the Settings button. Change the Style option back to Windows Logo. Then click on the OK button.**

The default style is restored.

- **Expand the Screen saver box, and click on Starfield.**

The option is selected.

NOTE: The **Wait** box allows you to reset the number of minutes that must elapse before the screen saver is activated.

8.4

- **Click on the Appearance tab.**

The Appearance panel of the dialog box is displayed.

- **Expand the Color scheme box, and click on Olive Green.**

The new color scheme is applied to the screen elements displayed in the window at the top of the dialog box.

- **Expand the Font size box, and click on Large Fonts.**

The new font size is applied to the screen elements.

- **Expand the Windows and buttons box, and click on Windows Classic style.**

The default Windows Classic style options are applied to the screen elements.

- **Expand the Color scheme box, and click on Maple.**

The new color scheme is applied to the screen elements.

- **Expand the Windows and buttons box, and click on Windows XP style.**

The default Windows XP style options are restored.

8.5

- **Click on the Effects button.**

The Effects dialog box is displayed.

- **Examine the options in the dialog box. Then click on the Cancel button.**

The Display Properties dialog box is redisplayed.

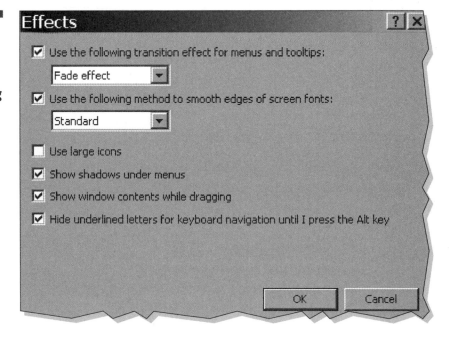

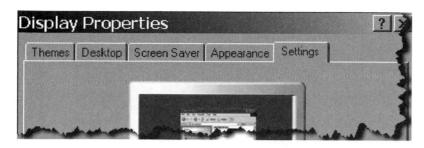

8.6

- **Click on the Settings tab.**

The Settings panel of the dialog box is displayed. Options on this panel allow you to change screen resolution and various other monitor settings.

- **Click on the OK button.**

The dialog box is closed, and the Appearance and Themes window is redisplayed.

- **Click on the Back button.**

The Control Panel window is redisplayed.

Notes

You can also customize your screen display by applying a **theme**—a collection of unique desktop and window elements, including a background and screen saver, and a set of fonts, colors, icons, mouse pointers and sounds. This is accomplished from the **Themes** panel of the Display Properties dialog box. Windows XP initially includes two themes—Windows XP (the default theme) and Windows Classic. Other themes can be downloaded from the Internet.

Working with Mouse, Keyboard and Printer Settings

The **Printers and Other Hardware** category in the Control Panel window includes options for changing a number of settings that affect the way you use your mouse and keyboard. It also includes options for viewing and adding printers.

Objective

In this exercise, you will **reset the double-click rate for your mouse** and **select a different set of mouse pointers**. Then you will **reset the repeat delay/repeat rate for characters typed** and **reset the cursor blink rate**. You will also **list your installed printers** and **review how to update the list of installed printers**.

- Make sure that the **Control Panel window** is displayed.

9.1

- **Click on Printers and Other Hardware.**

The Printers and Other Hardware window appears, displaying a list of options related to the category you have chosen. You will now change your mouse settings.

- **Click on Mouse (in the lower section of the window).**

The Buttons panel of the Mouse Properties dialog box is displayed.

- **In the Double-click speed section of the dialog box, double-click on the folder icon.**

If you double-click at the correct speed, the folder will open. If the folder does not open, double-click again on the folder icon, increasing the speed at which you press and release the mouse button.

- **Point to the lever to the left of the folder icon. Press and hold down the mouse, and drag the lever approximately one-half inch to the left. Then release the mouse button.**

The double-click speed is decreased.

- **Test the new speed by double-clicking on the folder icon.**

If you double-click at the correct speed, the folder will close.

- **Using a procedure similar to that described on the previous page, increase the double-click speed. Then test the new setting by double-clicking on the folder icon.**

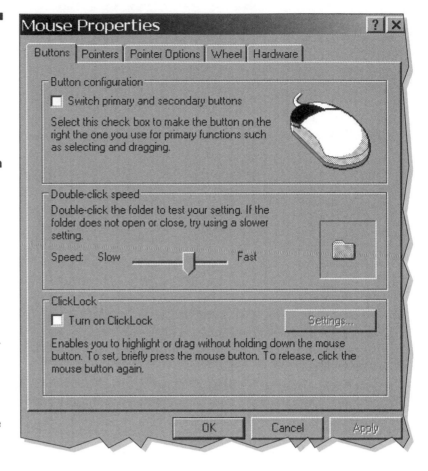

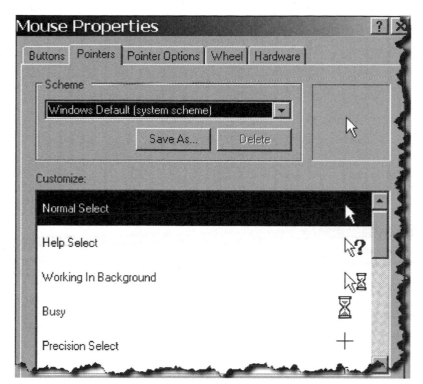

9.2

Next, you will select a different set of mouse pointers.

• **Click on the Pointers tab.**

The Pointers panel of the dialog box is displayed.

• **Click on the down arrow at the right side of the Scheme box.**

The box is expanded, and a list of mouse pointer sets is displayed.

• **Click on Conductor (system scheme).**

The mouse pointers of the selected set are displayed.

• **Expand the Scheme box, and click on Windows Default (system scheme) in the list of mouse pointer sets.**

The default mouse pointers are restored.

• **Click on the Pointer Options tab.**

The Pointer Options panel of the dialog box is displayed.

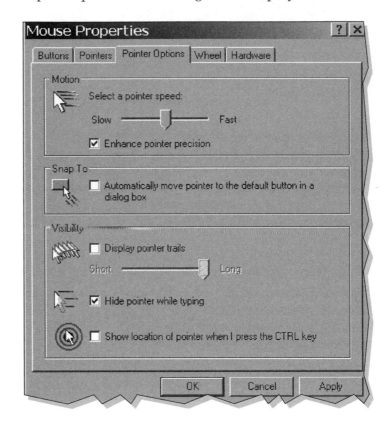

- Examine the options on the current panel of the dialog box. Then click on the **Cancel** button

The dialog box is closed, and the Printers and Other Hardware window is redisplayed. You will now change your keyboard settings.

- Click on **Keyboard** (in the lower section of the dialog box).

The Speed panel of the Keyboard Properties dialog box is displayed.

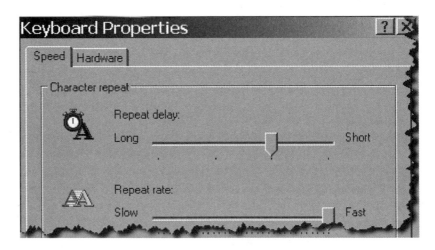

- Click in the **text box** above the **Cursor blink rate** section of the dialog box. Then press and **hold down any key**.

The current repeat delay and repeat rate of a character is indicated in the text box.

- **Delete** the **characters** you have typed by **dragging** the mouse pointer over them and by pressing [**DEL**], or by simply pressing [**BACKSPACE**] the appropriate number of times.
- **Reset** both the **repeat delay** and **repeat rate** of a character by **dragging** the associated **lever**. Then **test** the **new settings** by using the procedure described above.
- **Reset** the **cursor blink rate** by **dragging** the associated **lever**.
- Click on the **Cancel** button.

The Printers and Other Hardware window is redisplayed. You will now list your installed printers.

- Click on the **View installed printers or fax printers** *task*.

A list of installed printers and fax printers that have been installed will be displayed. To delete an installed printer, you can select the printer from the list and then select the Delete this printer choice from the Printer Tasks list. Do **not** do this now!

- Click on the **Back** button.

The Printers and Other Hardware window is redisplayed. You will now review how to Add a printer to your installed printers list.

- Click on the **Add a printer** *task*.

The Add Printer Wizard will be displayed. To complete the installation, you must have a printer connected for the Plug-and-Play option to detect the printer and do the installation automatically. If you do not have the printer connected, you will have to do a manual installation using the Add Printer Wizard. You will have to follow the screen prompts and select the appropriate responses for your system. This will include selecting the port, the printer make and model, specifying if it should be the default printer, whether it should be a shared printer on a network and whether to print a test page. You will not add a printer in this course.

- Click on the **Cancel** button.

The dialog box is closed.

- Click on the **Close** button on the Title bar of the window.

The Printers and Other Hardware window is closed, and the Control Panel is exited.

Software

Software consists of instructions and information that are stored electronically on a computer. Software can be divided into two categories:

- System software: Consists of the computer's "operating system" and the utilities that enable the computer to work.

- Application software: Programs that users use to perform tasks. Examples include word processing, spreadsheets, and database programs.

This section describes how software works on its own and how, together with hardware, it allows users to perform computing tasks.
In this section, you will identify:

- What an operating system is.
- Types of application software and the tasks for which they are suited.
- How software applies rules to process data.
- How software problems (or "bugs") are detected and resolved.
- How to install and run a program.

Understanding the Operating System

The operating system is a software application that starts automatically when the computer is turned on. The operating system manages the computer's hardware and software resources. Examples of resources that the operating system manages include the:

Microprocessor
Random Access Memory (RAM)
Space on the hard disk drive
Mouse or other pointing device

All of these resources compete for the attention of the microprocessor and need memory and storage to operate. The operating system acts as a traffic cop, directing the necessary resources to each application while ensuring that each application coexists with all the other applications on the computer.

The operating system also provides a way for applications to work with the computer's hardware without having to know all the details about the hardware. The operating system also imposes limitations on the computer. For instance, the MS-DOS operating system (which you'll learn about in the next topic) supports only 64 Kb of Random Access Memory (RAM) and allows only eight characters for file names, as opposed to modern Windows operating systems, which support larger amounts of RAM and long file names.

History of Operating Systems

The very first operating systems for personal computers (PCs) were called Control Program for Microcomputers (CPM) and Microsoft Disk Operating System (MS-DOS). Both of these operating systems offered a command-line interface (CLI). With these operating systems, the user sees a command line on the monitor and a prompt that is waiting to accept instructions. The user types a command and the computer acts on that command; then the computer issues a new prompt for the next instruction from the user. Eventually, MS-DOS superseded CP/M as the operating system of choice.

While MS-DOS enjoyed a respectable life, it eventually became insufficient for handling modern computer applications. Microsoft Corporation addressed these problems by developing a replacement operating system called Windows. Windows is now the standard operating system on IBM and IBM-compatible computers.

Unlike MS-DOS, Windows is a graphical-user interface, or "GUI (pronounced "Goo-ee"). A GUI is a program interface that uses the computer's graphics capabilities to make programs easier to use. Well-designed graphical user interfaces can free users from having to learn complex command languages, such as those used with MS-DOS.

GUIs feature the following visual components:

Pointer: A symbol that lets users select objects and commands. Usually, the pointer appears as a small angled arrow on the monitor. In some applications, however, the pointer may appear as a capital I. Users move the pointer using a pointing device such as a mouse or trackball.

Icons: Small pictures that represent commands, files, or windows. By moving the pointer to the icon and pressing (or "clicking") a mouse button once or twice, users can execute a command. Users can move icons around the monitor.

Desktop: The area on the monitor where icons are grouped. This area is referred to as the desktop because the icons are intended to represent real objects on a real desktop.

Windows: Users can divide the monitor into different areas. In each window, users can run a different program or display a different file. Users can move windows around the monitor, and change their shape and size at will.

Menus: Most GUIs let users execute commands by selecting a command from a menu.

In addition to their visual components, GUIs make it easy to move data between applications (such as copying a graph from a spreadsheet program into a document created by a word processing program). Moreover, applications that run under the same GUI have a common look and feel. The menu bar in most Windows applications, for instance, has File as the leftmost menu and Help as the rightmost menu.

Operating System Categories

Operating systems fall into four broad categories, based on the types of computers they control and the types of applications they support.

Single-user, multi-tasking: Allows one computer user to have several programs operating at the same time. For example, a user could write a letter in a word processing application, print an e-mail, and download an audio file from the Internet. This is the type of operating system most people use on their desktop and notebook computers. Examples include Microsoft Windows and Apple Macintosh.

Multi-user: Allows many users to access the computer's resources at the same time. These operating systems must balance the requirements of the various users, and ensure that each program being used has sufficient and separate resources so that a problem with one user doesn't affect the other users. Examples include Unix, VMS, and mainframe operating systems such as MVS.

Real-time operating system (RTOS): Control machinery, scientific instruments, and industrial systems.

Single-user, single task: Manages the computer so that one user can effectively do one thing at a time. The operating system used with Palm handheld computers is an example.

Comparing Popular Operating Systems

Table 1 compares popular operating systems that are currently in use, as well as "legacy" operating systems of the not-too-distant past.

Common Look and Feel

Versions of the Windows operating system starting with Windows 95 share a common look and feel. Some of the consistencies among these operating systems are:

- A Start button at the lower-left side for starting applications.
- The use of folders as repositories for holding files.
- Windows Explorer, which can be used to navigate among files and folders.
- Buttons and icons that can be clicked and double-clicked to perform tasks.
- A garbage can icon for holding files that have been deleted from the hard disk drive.

This consistent look and feel provides users with a familiarity. An operating system that is easy to use often is so because the user has experience with another operating system that works similarly. In this way, consistency and familiarity contribute to the popularity and success of Microsoft Windows operating system. After all, an operating system that is filled with inconsistencies, even minor ones, force users to think about it. The best operating systems allow users to conduct their tasks unimpeded, with attention focused on the job to be done, not on the operating system that permits the job to be done.

Solving Common Operating System Problems

Operating systems provide a variety of options for making work easier and making the computing experience more enjoyable. Sometimes, however, changes made to an operating system cause problems with the computer.

TABLE I	Comparing Operating Systems	
Operating System	**Advantages**	**Disadvantages**
MS-DOS	An older operating system that requires users to type commands at a prompt. Because MS-DOS is old, it runs on older, low-cost PCs.	Because MS-DOS has been around for a while, there is a lot of software available for it but the software usually is not up-to-date.
Microsoft Windows 3.x	The first PC-based operating system to provide a graphical-user interface. As the former standard operating systems, it runs on older and low-cost PCs.	Relegated to being an operating system of the past.
Microsoft Windows 95, 98, ME, XP Home	Provides a graphical-user interface as well as a CLI geared to home users. The later the operating system, the more stable it is.	Windows 95, 98, and ME are no longer supported by Microsoft. Windows XP Home provides stability and built-in features that the other operating systems lack.
Microsoft Windows NT, 2000, XP Professional	Provides a graphical-user interface as well as a CLI geared to companies and professional use. The later the operating system, the more stable it is.	Windows NT and 2000 are still found in many companies. However, Windows XP Professional provides stability and built-in features that the other operating systems lack.
Unix	An extremely powerful operating system that requires users to type commands at a prompt. Unix is old, but still up-to-date, with a growing number of software packages.	The more powerful a command line-based operating system is, the more complicated it gets to be learned. Many books may have to be studied to fully use this operating system.
Linux	A free UNIX derivate that is available for individuals with a low budget.	Same as Unix, with the additional disadvantage that support may not be easily available.
Windows Mobile 2003	Familiarity for traditional Windows users. Tight integration with Microsoft applications.	Not transportable to Palm devices. Limited capability when compared with other operating systems for desktop computers.
PalmOS	Provides a graphical-user interface specifically written for Palm handheld devices.	Not transportable to Windows Mobile devices. Limited capability when compared with other operating systems for desktop computers.
Apple Macintosh	Provides a graphical-user interface geared for Apple Macintosh computers. Unlike the Windows operating systems, there is no CLI available to handle text-oriented programs.	Useful when working with Macintosh data and applications. Mostly used with graphical applications.

For example, Windows comes with the ability to change the Language settings. If this is changed, illegible characters may appear on the monitor. Similarly, some programs (notably games) are required to run at specific monitor resolutions. If the resolution is changed within the operating system, an application that used to run on the computer may not run at all. Sometimes problems arise that can only be resolved by booting up in Safe Mode (a basic default mode), making the necessary setting changes, and then rebooting as normal. For these reasons, changes made through the computer's operating system should only be performed by individuals who understand the system settings and their ramifications.

Sometimes the operating system files become damaged or corrupted, or the computer becomes unstable. If this happens, it is not always possible to use the computer. If the problem is instability, the user need only shut down the computer and reboot, and the problem can usually resolve itself. However, with corrupted or damaged files, the operating system may need to be reinstalled. It is best to let an experienced person deal with the reinstallation of the operating system, or under certain circumstances, an upgrade to a later release of the operating system. An upgrade often also solves stability problems inherent in older operating systems.

Software Application Programs

To perform a task, a computer needs to have a software application program written for it. A software application program provides the computer with step-by-step instructions about what to do to accomplish the intended objective and how it is going to do it. Software is created through a process called development that includes writing instructions, testing and review.

Computer users interact with software applications by issuing instructions. With CLI-based operating systems, these instructions take the form of typed commands. With GUI operating systems such as Windows, users send instructions by pointing and clicking a mouse. Behind the scenes, however, it is computer algorithms that provide the basic technique for getting the job done.

The following example explains how a computer algorithm works. Imagine that you need to get to work. Here are three different algorithms that you might use to get to work.

Car algorithm:	Go to the garage. Get in the car. Start the engine. Drive to work.
Taxi algorithm:	Call for a taxi on the phone. Wait for the taxi. When the taxi arrives, get in it. Give the driver the address for your place of work.
Bus stop algorithm:	Go to the bus stop. Get in the bus when it arrives. Transfer to another bus, if necessary. Get off the bus and walk to work.

All three of these algorithms achieve the same goal, but in completely different ways. Each algorithm also has a different cost and a different travel time. Driving to work, for example, is probably the fastest and least costly way, whereas taking a taxi is the most expensive algorithm. Taking the bus, on the other hand, is less expensive but much slower.

Similarly, computer programs often have different ways—algorithms—to accomplish a task. Each algorithm has advantages and disadvantages in different situations.

Identifying Different Type of Software

Software applications enhance the usability of a computer and extend the capabilities inherent in the computer's operating system. Examples of software applications are:

- Word processing applications
- Spreadsheet applications
- Presentation software
- E-mail applications
- Web browsers

Some applications are created to run on certain operating systems. Internet Explorer, for example, was designed as a Web browser to run on Windows operating systems. Other applications run on different operating systems. Microsoft Word, for example, offers separate versions that run on Windows and Apple Macintosh operating systems.

Software companies periodically release updated software versions full of new capabilities. This software also ensures that the product is compatible with the latest hardware, operating systems and other applications. These updated applications, often called upgrades, come at a price, though. First, the same computer that runs an earlier software version might "choke" on the updated application. Newer computers, however, perform fine with the latest programs. Second, when users in an office start switching to a variety of versions, it can lead to file-sharing problems caused by incompatibility between the different versions of software. Upgrades are usually available on CDs, DVDs and for download from the Internet. Information about the availability of upgrades is provided in manufacturers newsletters, computer publications and often by email to existing registered users. Details of what changes have been made in the upgrade are available from the manufacturer's Web site.

Software companies may combine (or "bundle") individual applications into a "suite" of solutions. Microsoft Corporation, for example, combines its word processing (Word), spreadsheet (Excel), and presentation (PowerPoint) applications into a single suite called Microsoft Office. IBM offers a similar software bundle called Lotus SmartSuite.

Notes

Before performing a task, it is important to select the software application that is suited to handle the job. For example, to keep financial records for a company or family on a computer, use a spreadsheet or financial application that can store, sort, and calculate numbers, instead of a word processing application, whose strength lies in creating documents.

Selecting Commands in an Office 2003 Application

When working in an Office 2003 application, you perform operations by selecting the **commands** (or command sequences) for executing those operations. This can be accomplished with either a **mouse** or the **keyboard** by using the following procedure:

- Choose the primary command on the **Menu bar**. With a mouse, point to the **command**, and click the **left** mouse button; with the keyboard, press and hold down the [**ALT**] key, and press (type) the **underscored letter** of the command.
- Choose the desired option on the **menu** that is subsequently displayed. With a mouse, point to the **option**, and click the **left** mouse button; with the keyboard, press (type) the **underscored letter** of the option. In some cases, selecting a menu option displays a submenu of additional options. In this case, select the desired option on this submenu by using either technique described above.

A menu offers a series of choices related to the Menu bar command you have selected.

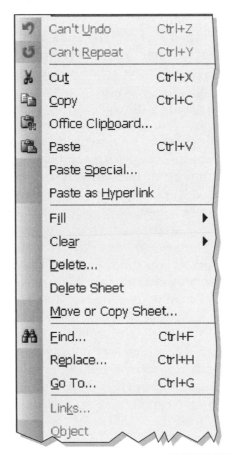

EDIT MENU (MICROSOFT EXCEL)

The illustration above, for example, shows the menu that appears when you select the Edit command in Microsoft Excel.

Note the following:

- If a menu option is dimmed, that option is not relevant at the current time and, therefore, is not available.
- If a command sequence can be accessed with shortcut keys, these are listed at the right side of the menu. For example, pressing [**CTRL**] + [**C**] is equivalent to choosing the **Edit** command and then choosing the **Copy** option on the Edit menu.
- If a menu option is followed by a small wedge-shaped arrow, choosing that option leads to a submenu from which an additional selection must be made.
- If a menu option is followed by three dots (ellipsis), choosing that option displays a **dialog box** in which additional options can be specified.

Most Windows XP applications also provide **shortcut buttons** for performing common operations, allowing you to bypass the menu system. In Microsoft Excel, as well as many other Windows XP applications, for example, the following button can be used in lieu of the Edit, Copy command.

COPY BUTTON

Notes

In the exercises that follow, you will use both the menu system and various shortcut buttons to perform operations. It is assumed that you are using a mouse. Therefore, only the mouse method for selecting commands is indicated in these exercises.

Word Processing Applications

A word processing application is a program that lets users create, edit, format, and print documents using their computer. Essentially, a word processing application can be used for desktop publishing activities. The documents can be short or long. Examples of typical documents are letters, memos, reports, and Web pages. The key advantage that a word processing application has over a typewriter is that users can make changes without retyping the entire document. Examples of word processing applications are Microsoft Word, Corel WordPerfect, and Lotus WordPro.

While word processing applications do vary, most support the following basic features:

Insert text: Allows text to be inserted anywhere in the document.

Delete text: Allows characters, words, lines, and pages to be erased easily.

Cut and paste: Allows sections of text to be removed (cut) from one place in a document and inserted (pasted) at another location in the same document or another document.

Copy: Allows sections of text to be duplicated (copied) from one place in a document and pasted at another location in the same document or another document.

Page size and margins: Allows page sizes and margins to be adjusted.

Search and replace: Searches for a particular word or phrase. Most word processing applications can also replace the word with other words.

Word wrap: Automatically moves the typed characters to the next line when a line has been filled with text. Most word processing applications also readjust text if the margins are changed.

Print: Lets documents be sent to a printer to get a hardcopy.

Fonts: Allows the typefaces, letter size, and styles (bold, italic, underscore) to be used.

Graphics: Allows illustrations and graphs to be embedded into a document. Some word-processing applications let users create illustrations within the application, while others let users import illustrations created in a different program.

Spell checker: A utility that checks the spelling of words.

Tables of contents and indexes: Allows a table of contents and index to be created automatically.

Thesaurus: Lets users search for synonyms without leaving the word processing application.

Spreadsheet Applications

A spreadsheet application (also called a worksheet) is a computer program that lets users record and analyze numbers. A spreadsheet consists of a table of values arranged in rows and columns. Each value is entered in a "cell" and can have a predefined relationship to the other values; this means that if one value is changed, the other values can automatically update. Text, numbers and formulas can be entered into cells.

Most spreadsheet applications let users create graphs and charts from the tabular information. Most spreadsheet applications are "multidimensional." This means you can link one spreadsheet to another. In a 2-dimensional spreadsheet, for example, a change made in one spreadsheet automatically affects the other spreadsheet. Multiple linked spreadsheets are accommodated in a workbook. More powerful spreadsheet applications provide graphics features that can produce charts and graphs from the information in the cells.

Spreadsheets are most commonly used for creating budgets, expense reports, analyzing financial data, creating and managing simple databases, etc. A simple example of a useful spreadsheet application is one that calculates the payments for a leased car. You would define five values:

> Total cost of the car
> Down payment
> Interest rate
> Term of the loan
> Monthly payment

After you define how these values depend on one another, you could enter numbers and try various possibilities. For example, keeping all the other values the same, you could see how different interest rates can affect your monthly payments. In addition to analyzing data, spreadsheets can also be used to sort and filter information.

Examples of spreadsheet applications are Microsoft Excel and Lotus 1-2-3. Like word processing applications, spreadsheet applications are created to run on various operating systems.

Presentation Applications

Presentation software lets users create and communicate information using highly stylized images for slide shows, overhead transparencies, audience handouts, speaker notes and reports. Most presentation software includes features for creating various types of charts and graphs, importing pictures, and inserting text in a variety of fonts. They also include a special kind of slide called a slide master. It controls text characteristics of the slide presentation including font, color, etc., as well as background color, bullet styles and other special effects.

Typical applications of presentation software include giving presentations for business, training and educational purposes on computer screens, using overhead projectors and using the Internet.

Examples of presentation software are Microsoft PowerPoint and Lotus Freelance.

Database Applications

A database application is a form of electronic filing system. It consists of a collection of related objects (tables, forms, queries, reports, etc.) stored in a single database file. It organizes information in such a way that a computer program can quickly select (query) desired pieces of data. One or more tables make up the core of a database. Each table contains information related to a particular subject (for example, employee work history).

All tables are made up of fields and records. A field is a single category of information (for example, name or address); a record is a collection of all fields for one table entity. An example of a database file is a telephone book. It contains a list of records, each of which consists of three fields: name, address, and telephone number.

Databases can be used to maintain large amounts of complex corporate data (for example, a hotel reservation system), and small amounts of private information (for example, personal investments). Examples of database programs are Microsoft Access, dBASE, MySQL, and Oracle. These database programs are called relational databases because the various tables stored in the database file can be related (linked) through key fields. The key fields are fields that are common to two or more tables. This differs from flat-file databases in which the entire database in located in one table. Flat-file databases are not very powerful or flexible and are therefore not used much anymore.

Graphics and Multimedia Applications

Graphics applications (also called Paint and Drawing software) allow users to create, manipulate, change, save, and print drawings. They use different kinds of tools to create the drawings including line tools for drawing lines, curve tools for drawing curves, shape tools for drawing rectangles, triangles, etc., pencil tools for drawing freehand, fill tools for filling a shape with color, and many more. Some graphics applications allow a series of images to be chained to simulate movement. Each image is like a frame in a movie. Together, the series of images create animation.

Other graphics applications, such as Computer Aided Design (CAD), enable architects and engineers to draft designs. These are identified as Drawing products.

Desktop publishing programs are used to create large documents, advertising brochures, etc. Although usually associated primarily with word processing, desktop publishing software includes graphics features and can be used for most generic graphics requirements. Dedicated drawing software is required for specialized applications like CAD, as mentioned previously.

In general, graphics applications require a powerful microprocessor, a large amount of RAM, and a high-resolution video card and monitor. Some graphics applications, such as those designed for creating animation and 3-dimensional graphics, require more computing power than is available on average computers and will run only on powerful workstations or specially designed graphics computers.

Multimedia programs present text, graphics, video, animation, and sound in an integrated way. Until the mid-1990s, multimedia applications were uncommon because they required expensive hardware. However, with increases in performance and falling prices, multimedia has become ubiquitous. The advent of low cost graphic and multimedia software has promoted creativity among adults and children. Nearly all computers can display video, though the resolution available depends on the power of the computer's microprocessor and video card. Because multimedia applications have high storage requirements, the most effective media for distributing these applications is by CD-ROM.

It will become evident later in the course that files are identified with a filename that includes a three character extension, for example, travel.xls. The .xls extension identifies the file as being a Microsoft Excel document. In the same way, there are a number of extensions that identify graphics and multimedia files. Typical extensions include .bmp, .gif and .jpg for graphics files, .wav and .mp3 for audio files, and .mov for video and animation products such as QuickTime.

Utility Programs

Utility programs are applications that perform very specific tasks, usually related to managing system resources. Examples of utility programs include:

- Anti-virus software programs, which protect a computer against viruses.
- Compression software, which stores information in a format that requires less space than usual.
- Disk defragmenter software, which consolidates fragmented files and folders on a computer's hard disk drive, so that each occupies a single, contiguous space on the volume. This allows the computer to access files and folders and save new ones more efficiently. It also consolidates the volume's free space, making it less likely that new files will be fragmented. Disk defragmenter software is included with Microsoft Windows operating systems.

Additional Specialized Software

In addition to the application programs already mentioned, there are many additional specialized software programs. In this category are applications such as contact-management, financial, e-mail programs, Web browsers, Web page authoring and custom specialized software. These applications are described briefly:

Contact-management applications let users store and find contact information, such as names, addresses, and telephone numbers. Sophisticated contact manager applications provide reporting functions and allow several people in a workgroup to access the same database of contacts. Some also provide calendar functions. Examples of contact-management applications include ACT! and AZZ Cardfile.

Financial software allows individuals and businesses to manage their accounts professionally. Quicken, QuickBooks Pro, and Great Plains are examples of increasingly sophisticated accounting packages that are used by individuals, small businesses and medium sized companies.

Electronic mail, or e-mail as it is more commonly known, allows messages and attachments to be transmitted over the Internet from one computer to another. Most e-mail programs include a text editor for typing messages on the keyboard. Users then send the message to the recipient by specifying the recipient's e-mail address. Users can also send the same message to several users at once by specifying the e-mail addresses of all intended recipients. Examples of e-mail programs include Eudora, Microsoft Outlook, and Lotus ccMail.

A Web browser is an application that finds and displays Web pages on the Internet. Examples of Web browsers are Microsoft Internet Explorer and Netscape Navigator. Both of these browsers display graphics and text and present multimedia information including sound, video, and animation.

Browsers parse and render Web pages according to their own logic and rules, so not every browser will provide the same viewing experience of a particular Web page. Older browsers, for example, might not support animation and graphics. Other browsers might not support frames, blinking, and certain fonts.

In addition, there are no guarantees that all browsers will support or have enabled all of the functionality required by a page; for example, if a Web page requires cookies to be enabled, any browser that cannot handle cookies will handle the functionality incorrectly.

Notes

A cookie identifies users to Web sites. When a user enters a Web site using cookies, the user may be asked to fill out a form providing such information as your name and interests. This Web browser stores this information as a cookie for later use. The next time the user goes to the same Web site, the browser sends the cookie to the Web server. The server can use this information to present the user with custom Web pages. So, for example, instead of seeing a generic welcome page, the user might see a welcome page with the user's name on it.

Web page authoring programs are applications that are used to create Web pages. Microsoft FrontPage is an example of a web page authoring program.

The software already discussed in this section is standard, off-the-shelf, readily available product. Another category of software is called custom product. These are sophisticated programs written for dedicated applications. Typical examples include manufacturing plant automation software, investment banking software, airline reservation software, etc.

Exploring Your Computer

This section introduces **Windows Explorer**. In it, you will learn how to:

- **Examine components** of your **computer**.

Windows Explorer

Windows Explorer provides a graphical view of hardware, files and folders on your computer and on other network computers to which you are connected (if you are part of a network). The information is displayed in the two-pane window, which can appear in either of two views:

Folders view: In this view, the window displays a hierarchical (tree) representation of hard disk drives, removable storage devices, other peripherals, and folders in the left pane and lists the contents of the currently-selected item in the right pane.

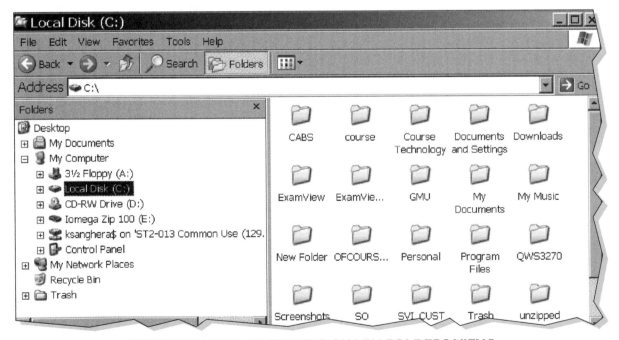

WINDOWS EXPLORER WINDOW (IN FOLDERS VIEW)

Tasks view: In this view, the window lists the contents of the currently-selected item in the right pane, as in Folders view, and a list of tasks and other locations that are relevant to that item in the left pane.

You switch from one view to the other by clicking on the **Folders** button on the toolbar of the Windows Explorer window.

To **start Windows Explorer:**

- Select the **All Programs** option on the **Start menu**, followed by the **Accessories** option on the All Programs submenu.
- Select the **Windows Explorer** option on the Accessories submenu.

Notes

You can also start Windows Explorer in the following ways: by **right-clicking** on the Start button and by selecting the **Explore** option on the shortcut menu, by **double-clicking** on the **My Documents** or **My Computer** icon on the desktop (if the desktop displays either or these icons), by selecting the **My Documents** or **My Computer** option on the Start menu, or by entering the appropriate path on the Address bar (on the taskbar) and by pressing [ENTER].

Examining Components of Your Computer

In Windows Explorer, the components of your computer are represented by various icons. When listing the contents of a disk drive, you will see the following:

 This icon represents a **folder**, which is used to hold related files, as well as other related folders. The icon illustrated here is the standard folder icon. You can, however, choose a different icon to represent a particular folder.

 This icon represents a **file**, the basic unit of storage. Different file types are represented by different icons. The icon illustrated here is the icon for a Microsoft Word file.

Objective

In this exercise, you will **use Windows Explorer to examine the contents of your hard disk**.

- Make sure that the **Windows XP desktop** is displayed.
- Click on the **Start** button. Point to **All Programs** on the Start menu and then to **Accessories** on the All Programs submenu.

The Accessories submenu is displayed.

- Click on **Windows Explorer**.

NOTE: Your view will be different based on the subfolders you have under My Documents.

- **Point in any empty area of the Menu bar, and right-click the mouse button.**

A shortcut menu is displayed.

- If either of the following options is *not* selected (checked), click on it:

Standard Buttons
Address Bar

   NOTE: You will need to redisplay the shortcut menu to select more than one option.

   If you added the **Address bar** to the window and it does not appear below the Standard Buttons toolbar (which displays the Folders button), do the following:

a) Redisplay the above **shortcut menu,** and click on **Lock the Toolbars** if that option is currently selected (to deselect the option and unlock the Address bar).

b) **Drag** the **Address bar** to the area immediately below the Standard Buttons toolbar. (Do this by dragging the dotted line that marks the left border of the Address bar when it is unlocked.)

c) Display the above **shortcut menu** once again, and click on **Lock the Toolbars** (to select that option and once again lock the Address bar).

- In the left pane of the window, click on **My Computer**.

A listing of the hard disk drives and removable storage devices on your computer is displayed in the right pane of the window.
   NOTE: The listing on your screen may also include other items.

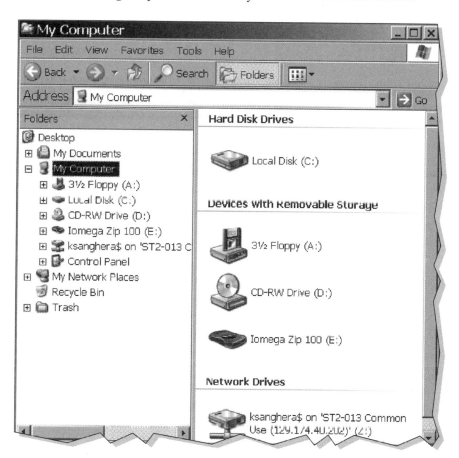

- In the right pane of the window point to the **Local Disk (C:)** icon.

A ScreenTip appears, indicating the amount of used space on the disk (Drive C), as well as the total size of that disk.

- In the left pane of the window, click on **Local Disk (C:)**.

The contents of the **root directory** (also called the **root folder**) of Drive C are listed in the right pane of the window. Notice that the listing includes a folder named **Program Files**, which contains the necessary files for running most of the programs that are installed on your computer, and a folder named **Windows**, which contains the operating system files. (Make sure that you do not delete or otherwise modify either of these folders or any of the files contained in the folders.)
   NOTE: If the above-mentioned contents do not appear, click on **Show the contents of this folder**.

- In the left pane of the window, click on **Documents and Settings**.

The Documents and Settings folder is opened, and its contents are listed. Notice that this folder includes a subfolder for each user account. It also includes a subfolder named **All Users**, which contains files that are available to all users of the computer. You will now display the folder listing in different ways.

- Click on the **Views**  button on the toolbar.

The button is expanded, and a list of views is displayed. The current view is indicated by a dot to the left of that option.

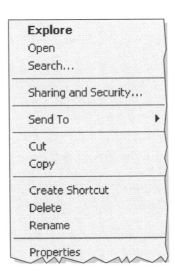

Thumbnails
- Tiles
Icons
List
Details

- If the **Tiles** option is not currently selected in the list, click on that option. Then redisplay the **list** of **views**.
- Click on **Icons**.

The folder listing now appears in Icons view.

- Click on the **Views** button. Then click on **List** in the list of views.

The folder listing now appears in List view.

- Using a procedure similar to that described above, display the **folder listing** in **Details view** and in **Thumbnails view**.

Thumbnails view is appropriate for a folder containing graphic files since its icon displays miniature views of the contents of up to four of those files.

- Using a similar procedure, redisplay the folder listing in **Tiles view**.

Next, you will display the properties of your user profile folder.

- Point to the **icon** for your **user profile folder**, and **right-click** the mouse button.

Explore
Open
Search...

Sharing and Security...

Send To   ▶

Cut
Copy

Create Shortcut
Delete
Rename

Properties

- Click on **Properties**.

The General panel of the Properties dialog box is displayed.

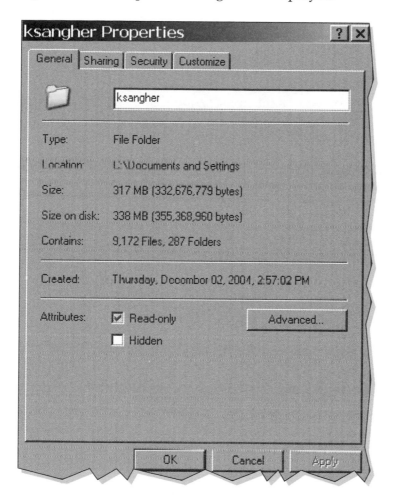

- Click on the **Sharing** tab.

The Sharing panel of the dialog box is displayed.

- Click on the **Customize** tab.

The Customize panel of the dialog box is displayed.

- Click on the **Cancel** button.

The dialog box is closed.

- In the right pane of the window, point to the **icon** for your **user profile folder**, and **double-click** the mouse button.

Your user profile folder is opened, and its contents are listed.
NOTE: This step demonstrates an alternate method for opening a folder.

- In the right pane of the window, point to the **My Documents folder** icon, and **double-click** the mouse button.

The contents of the My Documents folder are listed.

- In the right pane of the window, point to the **My Pictures folder** icon, and **double-click** the mouse button.

The contents of the My Pictures folder are listed.

- In the right pane of the window, point to the **Sample Pictures folder** icon, and **double-click** the mouse button.

The contents of the Sample Pictures folder are listed.
   NOTE: The contents of this folder should appear in **Filmstrip view**.
Notice that each picture contained in the folder is previewed at the bottom of the pane. The first picture also appears in a larger view at the top of the pane.

- In the group of pictures at the bottom of the right pane, click on the **second picture**.

The selected picture now appears at the top of the pane. You will now use buttons on the toolbar to navigate backward and forward through the folder structure.

- Click on the **Back** button on the toolbar.

   NOTE: Click on the button itself and not on the down arrow at the right side of the button.
   The contents of the previous location accessed (the My Pictures folder) are listed.

- Click again on the **Back** button.

The contents of the location accessed prior to the My Pictures folder (the My Documents folder) are listed.

- Click on the **Forward** button on the toolbar.

   NOTE: Again, click on the button itself and not on the down arrow at the right side of the button.
   The contents of the location accessed after the My Documents folder (the My Pictures folder) are listed.

- Click on the **Up** button on the toolbar.

The contents of the level above the current level (the My Documents folder) are listed.

- Click again on the **Up** button.

The contents of the level above the current level (your user profile folder) are listed.

- Click on the **down arrow** at the right side of the **Back** button.

The button is expanded, and a list of the various locations you have accessed is displayed.

- Click on **Local Disk (C:)**.

The contents of the root directory of Drive C are listed. You will now switch to Tasks view.

- Click on the **Folders** button on the toolbar.

The button is deselected, and the Windows Explorer window now appears in Tasks view. Notice that the right pane of the window displays the same information as in Folders view. The left pane, however, displays a list of tasks and other locations that are relevant to the current location (Drive C).

- In the left pane of the window under **Other Places**, click on **My Computer**.

A listing of the hard disk drives and removable storage devices on your computer is redisplayed in the right pane of the window.

- Click again on the **Folders** button.

The button is selected, and the Windows Explorer window once again appears in Folders view.

- Click on the **Close** button on the Title bar of the window.

The Windows Explorer window is closed.

Managing Your Files

It is assumed that you are now familiar with Windows Explorer. This section discusses the use of Windows Explorer as a **file management tool**. In it, you will learn how to:

- **Create** a **new folder**.
- **Copy** a **file**.
- **Move** a **file**.
- **Rename** a **file** or **folder**.
- **Delete** a **file** or **folder**.

Common Problems Associated with Working with Files

It is important that you always take precautions when working with files. It is very easy to "lose" a file if you delete it by accident, or move it to the wrong location, or rename it using the incorrect extension, and so on. These problems can usually be avoided, and often fixed.

- Be extra careful before deleting a file. Make sure that you do not need the file any longer as you may not be able to retrieve it after deletion. If however, you do accidentally delete a file, provided that it is a file on your hard drive, you can usually recover the file by restoring it from the Recycle Bin. If the file was on your floppy diskette, it cannot be recovered. Removing unused files and programs is important to avoid **"Disk Full"** messages.
- When renaming a file, be sure that you are not creating a problem that causes the associated application to not recognize the file format. This is important especially with the file extension. File extensions should not be

changed under normal circumstances. If you are working with a Word document, it will have a **.doc** extension. If you change or delete the extension, Word will not recognize the format, and you will not be able to open it.

- Be aware of the location of files that you are moving or copying. You don't want to get into a situation where you cannot find the files when you need them. If you inadvertently copy or move a file to the wrong place, you can usually **Undo** the process provided that it had just been done. Most applications have an **Edit**, **Undo** command, or **Undo** icon. If you know the name of the file, you can usually do a **Search** or **Find** exercise to locate it.

- The naming of files and folders is an important exercise. It is similar to setting up a manual filing system. Everything needs to be named and filed logically so that you can locate documents as you need them.

- Storage media and devices can fail. When this happens, it can result in a catastrophic loss of data. You must always be prepared for these eventualities, by making regular **Backups** of your data. The easiest way to do this is to copy your files onto floppy diskettes or CD's.

- Remember to **Save** your work regularly as you develop documents, worksheets, etc. Interruption of power to your PC can result in the loss of documents not saved. Avoid having to redo work already done!

- If you get a "**Denied file access**" or similar message, it usually means that you require a password or you do not have the required permission to use the file. This often requires the assistance of your system administrator to change the permissions to give you access.

Creating a New Folder

A **folder**, as you know, is used to store related files, as well as other related folders. The first step in setting up a folder is that of creating it.

- To **create a new folder**:
- With the appropriate location open in Tasks view of the Windows Explorer window, select the **Make a new folder** option.
- Type a **name** for the folder, and press [**ENTER**].

Notes

You can also create a new folder by **right-clicking** in the appropriate folder listing and by selecting the **New** option on the shortcut menu, followed by the **Folder** option on the submenu. (This technique is demonstrated in the next subsection.)

Every Windows XP folder has a specific folder type associated with it. When a new folder is created, that folder is assigned the default folder type of Documents, which is appropriate for storing all types of files. Windows XP also provides six other folder types, which are appropriate for storing the corresponding type of file:

- Pictures
- Photo Album
- Music
- Music Artist
- Music Album
- Videos

By storing specific types of files in a related type of folder, you are given access to features that are relevant to those files. A Pictures or Photo Album folder, for example, includes Filmstrip view, which displays preview images of graphic files in the folder listing.

To **change the folder type**:

- Point to the **icon** for the folder, and **right-click** the mouse button.
- On the shortcut menu that appears, select the **Properties** option.
- On the Customize panel of the Properties dialog box which is subsequently displayed, select the desired **file type** in the **Use this folder type as a template** box.
- Click on the **OK** button.

Notes

From the Customize panel of the Properties dialog box (described above), you can also change the icon for a folder. (The procedure for doing this is demonstrated in the next exercise.)

Objective

In this exercise, you will **create a new folder**. You will also **change the folder icon**.

- Make sure that the **Windows XP desktop** is displayed. (All windows should be closed.)
- **Start Windows Explorer.**
- List the contents of **Drive C** (the local disk) in the Windows Explorer window. (The listing should appear in **Folders view**.)
- Click on the **Folders** button.

The window appears in Tasks view.

- In the left pane under **File and Folder Tasks**, click on **Make a new folder**.

A new folder icon is displayed, and the default folder name (New Folder) is highlighted.

- Type: **Adocs**
  Press [**ENTER**].

The name you have entered replaces the default folder name.

- Click on the **Folders** button.

The window appears in Folders view. You will now change the folder icon.

- Point to the **icon** for your **new folder**, and **right-click** the mouse button. Then click on **Properties** on the shortcut menu that appears.

The Adocs Properties dialog box is displayed.

- Click on the **Customize** tab.

The Customize panel of the dialog box is displayed. Notice that the Use this folder type as a template box displays Documents, the default folder type. In this case, you will leave the folder type as is since the folder will be used to store different types of files.

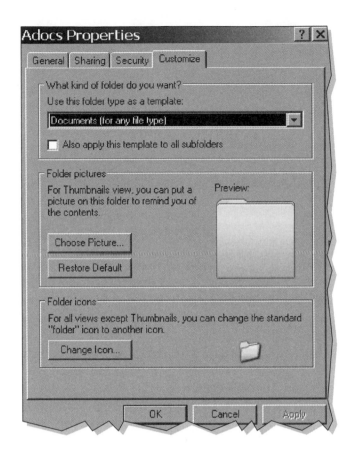

- Under **Folder icons**, click on the **Change Icon** button.

The Change Icon for Adocs Folder dialog box is displayed.

- Click on the **right arrow** button on the **scroll bar** at the bottom of the dialog box to scroll through the list of icons. Then click on any **icon** of your choice.

The icon is selected.

- Click on the **OK** button.

The Adocs Properties dialog box is redisplayed.

- Click on the **OK** button. Click in any **empty area** of the **folder listing** to deselect the folder icon.

The Adocs Properties dialog box is closed. Notice the new icon for the Adocs folder.

Copying a File or Folder

Windows XP provides several methods for copying a file from one folder to another or a folder to another folder. For example, you can use Windows Explorer's **Tasks view menu** or you can use a technique called **drag and drop**.
    To **copy one or more files** (using Windows Explorer's **Tasks view menu**):

- In the **source folder**, select the file(s) that is/are to be copied.
- Select the **Copy this file** or **Copy the selected items** option on the Tasks view menu.
- In the Copy Items dialog box, which is subsequently displayed, select the **destination folder**.
- Click on the **Copy** button.

To **copy one or more files/folders** (using **drag and drop**):

- In the **source folder**, select the file(s) that is/are to be copied, or select the folder(s) that is/are to be copied.
- **Drag** the selected **file(s)/folder(s)** to the **destination folder** using the **right** mouse button.
- On the shortcut menu that appears when you release the mouse button, select the Copy Here option.

Notes

1. You can also copy the contents of an entire folder by using procedures similar to those described above.
2. Windows XP, by default, does not display file extensions when listing the contents of a folder. If you wish to have file extensions displayed, you can do so by choosing the **Tools, Folder Options** command from the Windows Explorer window, by deselecting the **Hide extensions for known file types** option on the View panel of the Folder Options dialog box and by clicking on the **OK** button. (In this section, files will be identified by their filenames only. For example, the file named Auto Sales.xls will be identified as simply Auto Sales.)

When either pane of the Windows Explorer window includes more information than can be accommodated by the pane, a scroll bar will appear at the right side and/or bottom of the pane. You can display the additional information by clicking on the **up arrow** and **down arrow** buttons (at the top and bottom of a vertical scroll bar) or the **left arrow** and **right arrow** buttons (at the left side and right side of a horizontal scroll bar) to scroll the pane in the respective direction.

3. List the **contents** of the **Adocs** folder. **Adjust** the **column width** so that all filenames are fully displayed.

Moving a File or Folder

Windows XP also provides several methods for moving a file from one folder to another, or moving a folder on the desktop. Again, the operation can be performed using Windows Explorer's **Tasks view menu** or by using a **drag and drop** procedure.

To **move one or more files** (using Windows Explorer's **Tasks view menu**):

- In the **source folder**, select the file(s) that is/are to be moved.
- Select the **Move this file** or **Move the selected items** option on the Tasks view menu.
- In the Move Items dialog box, which is subsequently displayed, select the **destination folder**.
- Click on the **Move** button.

To **move one or more files** (using **drag and drop**):

- In the **source folder**, select the file(s) that is/are to be moved.
- **Drag** the selected **file(s)** to the **destination folder** using the **left** mouse button.
- On the shortcut menu that appears when you release the mouse button, select the **Move Here** option.

To move a folder (or icon) into another folder (using **drag and drop**):

- Select the source folder to be moved.
- Drag the selected folder to the destination folder **or required desktop position** using the **right** mouse button.
- On the shortcut menu that appears when you release the mouse button, select the **Move Here** option.

Notes

You can also move the contents of an entire folder by using procedures similar to those described above.

Renaming a File or Folder

If necessary, you can easily rename any file or folder from Windows Explorer.
To **rename a file or folder** (using Windows Explorer's **Tasks view menu**):

- Select the file/folder that is to be renamed.
- Select the **Rename this file** or **Rename this folder** option on the Tasks view menu.
- Type the **new name**, and press [**ENTER**].

To **rename a file or folder** (using the **shortcut menu**):

- Point to the file/folder that is to be renamed, and **right-click** the mouse button.
- On the shortcut menu that appears, select the **Rename** option.
- Type the **new name**, and press [**ENTER**].

Objective

In this exercise, you will **rename your Adocs folder**.

- Point to the **Adocs folder** icon, and **right-click** the mouse button.

The folder is selected, and a shortcut menu is displayed.

- Click on **Rename**.

The current folder name is highlighted.

- Type: **Course Docs**
  Press [**ENTER**].

Deleting a File or Folder

From time to time, it is sometimes necessary to delete files, as well as folders, that are no longer needed. Keeping files unnecessarily on your computer only serves to clutter the hard disk which eventually runs out of space. Deleting files and folders is easily accomplished from Windows Explorer.

Deleting a file or folder, by default, moves that file/folder into the Recycle Bin. Since the contents of the Recycle Bin are not deleted until the bin is emptied, you can often restore a file or folder that has been deleted in error.

To **delete one or more files/folders** (using Windows Explorer's **Tasks view menu**):

- Select the file(s)/folder(s) that is/are to be deleted.
- Select the **Delete this file**, **Delete this folder** or **Delete the selected items** option on the Tasks view menu.
- In the prompt box that appears, click on the **Yes** button to confirm the operation.

To **delete one or more files/folders** (using the **shortcut menu**):

- Select the appropriate files/folders (if you are deleting more than one item).
- Point to any file/folder that is to be deleted and **right-click** the mouse button.
- On the shortcut menu that appears, select the **Delete** option.
- In the prompt box that appears, click on the **Yes** button to confirm the operation.

Notes

You can also delete a file or folder by selecting it and by pressing [DEL], or by simply dragging it either to the Recycle Bin icon on the desktop or into the Recycle Bin window.

To **restore one or more files/folders**:

- In the Recycle Bin, select the file(s)/folder(s) that is/are to be restored.
- Choose the **File**, **Restore** command, or select the **Restore** option on the shortcut menu.

Notes

You can also restore a deleted file/folder by dragging it from the Recycle Bin window into the Windows Explorer window.

Finding a File

The **Search** option on the Start menu allows you to quickly locate a particular file (or folder). You can perform the search by specifying a number of different criteria, including filename, specific text contained in the file, file size, last modification date, location of file, and more. If you know only part of a name, you can use **wildcard characters** to locate files or folders that include that part of the name. For example, *Rep.* will find **Sales Rep.doc** and **Sal??.doc** will find **Sales.doc**. The asterisk (*) substitutes for any number of characters, and the question mark (?) substitutes for a single character.

To **find a file**:

- Select the **Search** option on the Start menu, or the **Search** button, followed by the **All files and folders** option in the **Search Results** window.
- In the window which is subsequently displayed, set the **search criteria**.
- Click on the **Search** button.
- Choose the appropriate response when prompted on completion of the search.

Notes

A Search operation, by default, is not case sensitive. For example, searching for the text **sales** will match **sales**, **Sales**, **SALES**, etc.

MS Word 2003
Case Study 1

OBJECTIVES

After successfully completing this case study, you should be able to:

- Start, close, save, reopen, and print Word documents
- Use the Word menu system, the Word toolbars and Word task panes
- Enter, edit, and delete text in a document
- Insert the current date and time into the document
- Navigate through the document
- Find and replace text in a document
- Move text using the cut, copy and paste features
- Apply attributes to text
- Apply a new font and font size to text
- Indent a paragraph

- Reset line and paragraph spacing in a document
- Reset paragraph alignment in a document
- Reset the margins of a document
- Create a bulleted list
- Inserting a Hard Page Break
- Change the zoom level of a document
- Use the Spelling and Grammar Checker
- Use a template to create a document
- Display help information

Case Study 1—MS Word 2003

Assume that you work for the KS Travel Agency. You are asked to create a travel brochure for Western Caribbean ports. Some of your customers want the brochure to be faxed. Your boss has asked you to create a fax cover page and the Caribbean travel brochure for one of the customers named Luisa Lopez.

The desired fax cover page and travel brochure are:

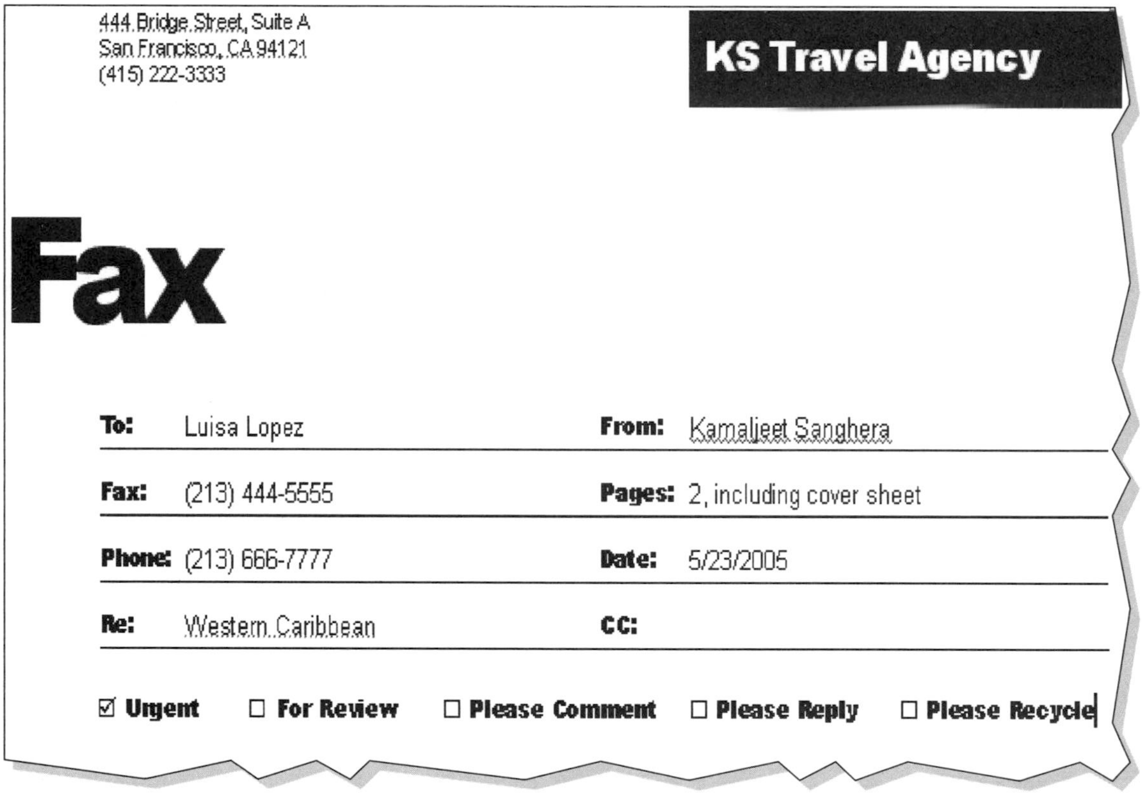

444 Bridge Street, Suite A
San Francisco, CA 94121
(415) 222-3333

KS Travel Agency

Fax

To:	Luisa Lopez	**From:**	Kamaljeet Sanghera
Fax:	(213) 444-5555	**Pages:**	2, including cover sheet
Phone:	(213) 666-7777	**Date:**	5/23/2005
Re:	Western Caribbean	**CC:**	

☒ **Urgent**   ☐ **For Review**   ☐ **Please Comment**   ☐ **Please Reply**   ☐ **Please Recycle**

FAX COVER PAGE

May 27, 2005

WESTERN CARIBBEAN

The Western Caribbean is a popular destination for cruise ships departing from Miami or Tampa, Florida. Like all cruise destinations, this area includes a number of diverse ports of call. Four of these ports of call are discussed below.

- **Key West**

  Key West, in the Florida Keys, is a city with a colorful history. Today it is both stylish and funky, with something for everyone. In Old Town, the most charming part of Key West, you will find unique shops and world-class restaurants, as well as a number of art galleries and museums.

- **Montego Bay**

  Montego Bay is Jamaica's second largest city. Although much of it looks new today, the city is more than 200 years old! Strolling through the town center of Montego Bay, you can enjoy calypso music and sample a Jamaican specialty, such as jerk chicken. Driving east on the road to Ocho Rios, you will see beautiful beaches and luxury resorts.

- **Cozumel**

  Cozumel is part of the Mexican Caribbean. Once a sleepy town, this resort city now hosts visitors from all over the world. In addition to diving, for which it is well known, Cozumel offers you fine shopping and dining, all with a special Mexican flavor.

- **George Town**

  George Town is the capital of the Cayman Islands. It is also a leading financial center in the region. In George Town, you will find many diversions, from first-class shops and restaurants to submarine dives to view the famous reefs that surround the island.

TRAVEL BROCHURE

Getting Started

This section discusses various **Word fundamentals**. In it, you will learn how to:

- **Start Word.**
- **Identify** the **elements** of the **Word Application window**.
- **Use** the **Word menu system**.
- **Use Word toolbars.**
- **Use Word task panes.**

What Is Word?

Microsoft Word is a leading **word processing** application for personal computers. Using this program, you can create a variety of documents, from a simple letter to a multiple-column newsletter combining text and graphics.

Starting Word

You start Word by clicking on the **Start** button on the Windows taskbar, by pointing to **All Programs** (if you are running Windows XP) or to **Programs** (if you are running Windows 2000), by selecting the **Microsoft Office** option on the All Programs or Programs menu, and by selecting the **Microsoft Office Word 2003** option on the subsequent submenu.

Objective

In this exercise, you will **start Word and display the opening Word Application window**.

1.1

- **Click on the Start button on the Windows taskbar.**

- **Point to All Programs (if you are running Windows XP) or to Programs (if you are running Windows 2000).**

- **Point to Microsoft Office on the menu.**

- **Click on Microsoft Office Word 2003 on the submenu.**

NOTE: If the Start menu includes a Microsoft Office Word 2003 shortcut icon, you can start Word by simply clicking on this icon. If the Windows desktop includes a Microsoft Office Word 2003 shortcut icon, you can start Word by double-clicking on this icon.

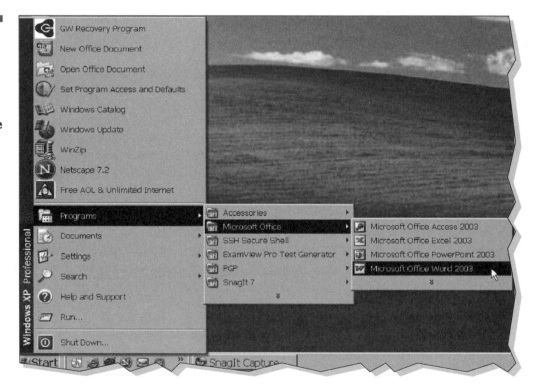

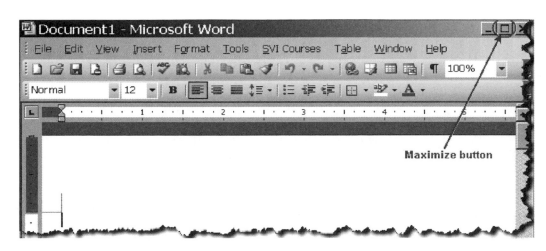

1.2

- **If the Word Application window is not maximized, click on the Maximize button on the Title bar of the window.**

Maximize button

The Word Application Window

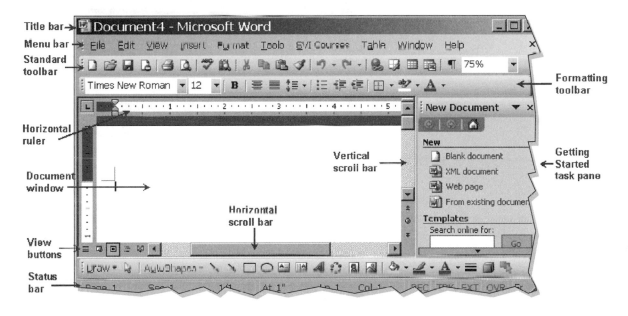

Notes

What appears on your screen may sometimes vary slightly from what is shown in this manual.

The initial **Word Application window** includes the following elements:

Title bar	This displays the name of the program, as well as the name of the current document if it has been saved. (If the document has not been saved, it is identified by a number—for example, Document1.) The standard Windows Control-menu box and window sizing buttons appear at the left end and right end of the bar, respectively.
Menu bar	This displays Word's primary commands.
Standard/Formatting toolbars	These display a number of shortcut buttons and boxes for performing common Word operations. When you point to one of these buttons or boxes, the name of the button/box appears in a small window (ScreenTip) next to the mouse pointer. The Standard and Formatting toolbars, by default, appear side-by-side. On your screen, however, one toolbar may appear above the other.
Getting Started task pane	This displays options for accessing Microsoft Office Online, a Web site for users of Microsoft Office products, as well as options for opening an existing document file and for creating a new document. The program includes several other task panes. Each pane includes options for performing a specific task (for example, inserting a picture into a document or setting document protection).
Horizontal ruler	This provides shortcuts for setting margins, tab stops and indents. (If a document appears in Print Layout view, Word also displays a Vertical ruler down the left side of the screen.)
Document window	This is the area in which you create your documents. The insertion point (the flashing vertical bar) indicates the location in which the next character typed will appear. The end mark (the horizontal bar) identifies the end of the document.
Vertical/Horizontal scroll bars	These are used to scroll the Document window vertically/ horizontally through a document.
View buttons	These allow you to change the way you view a document.
Status bar	This displays helpful information (for example, the current location of the insertion point) as you use the program.

Using the Word Menu System

The Word **menu system** is one means of communicating with the program. You can access the menu system by using a **mouse** (the most efficient method) or by using the **keyboard**. In either case, the procedure is as follows:

- Select a **command** on the **Menu bar**. With a mouse, point to the command, and click the **left** mouse button; with the keyboard, press and hold down [**ALT**], and press (type) the **underscored letter** of the command.
- Select an **option** on the **menu** that is subsequently displayed. With a mouse, point to the option, and click the **left** mouse button; with the keyboard, press (type) the **underscored letter** of the option. (Selecting an option on a Word menu sometimes leads to a submenu. In this case, use the procedure described above to select the appropriate option on this submenu.)

A menu offers a series of options for the command you have chosen. If you choose the **Edit** command, for example, a menu similar to that illustrated below is displayed.

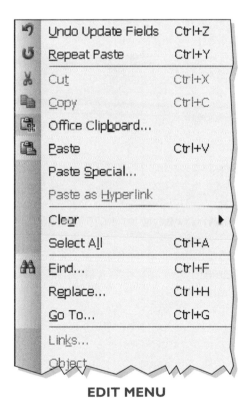

EDIT MENU

Note the following:

- If a menu option is dimmed, that option is not relevant at the current time and, therefore, is not available.
- If a command sequence (a command, followed by a specific option) can be accessed with shortcut keys, these keys appear to the right of the relevant option. For example, pressing [**CTRL**] + [**C**] is equivalent to choosing the **Edit** command, followed by the **Copy** option.

- If a command sequence can be accessed with a shortcut button, that button appears to the left of the relevant option.
- If a menu option is followed by a wedge-shaped arrow, selecting that option displays a submenu of additional options.
- If a menu option is followed by three dots (ellipsis), choosing that option displays a **dialog box** in which additional options can be specified. An example of a dialog box is illustrated on the following page:

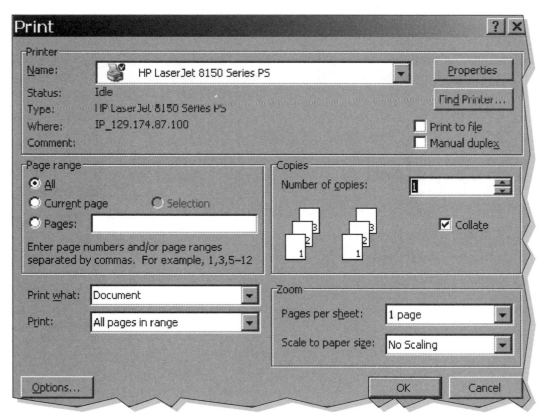

PRINT DIALOG BOX

The menus that you initially access from the Menu bar are called short menus since they include only a basic set of commonly-used options. You can expand a short menu and display the full menu—that is, one that includes additional options, by clicking on the chevron (the two down arrows) at the bottom of the menu. (Note that a menu will expand automatically if you continue pointing for a few seconds to the command that displayed it.) Any option selected on this expanded menu is added to the basic set of options, thereby creating a personalized menu that reflects your needs. The same option is removed from the basic set of options after a period of time if you no longer use it.

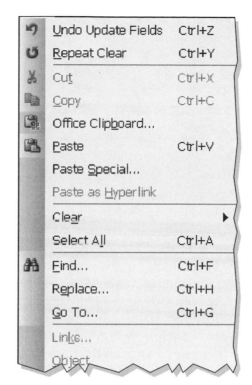

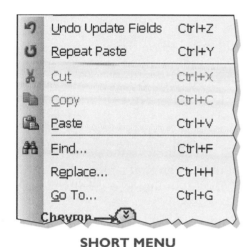

SHORT MENU   **FULL MENU**

Notes

If you prefer to work only with full menus, you can do so by choosing the **Tools**, **Customize** command and by selecting the **Always show full menus** option in the Customize dialog box. You can also restore personalized menus (and toolbars) to their original state by clicking on the **Reset menu and toolbar usage data** button in the same dialog box.

To help you work even more efficiently, Word also provides a number of shortcut menus. A **shortcut menu** includes options that are relevant to a particular screen element or area of a document and is displayed by clicking the **right** mouse button.

Using Word Toolbars

The **Standard** and **Formatting toolbars** include shortcuts for bypassing the menu system. You will generally use these bars, in lieu of the menu system, to perform operations when they contain relevant options.

The Standard and Formatting toolbars are initially "docked" side-by-side and include only a subset of the available buttons and boxes. You can display a list of additional options by clicking on the **Toolbar Options** button at the right side of either toolbar. Any button/box selected in the Toolbar Options list is added to the associated toolbar. To make room for the new option, a button/box not used recently is moved to the Toolbar Options list.

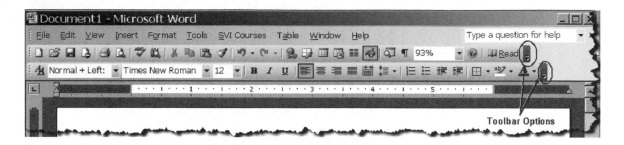

Notes

1. If you prefer to have more buttons/boxes displayed on the Standard and Formatting toolbars, you can do so by moving either one to a different row or to another part of the screen. This can be done either by choosing the **Tools**, **Customize** command and by selecting the **Show Standard and Formatting toolbars on two rows** option in the Customize dialog box, or by pointing to the **Move handle** (which displays a dotted vertical bar) at the left side of the toolbar and by dragging the toolbar to the new location. (Dragging a toolbar to an area of the screen that is not adjacent to the window border creates a "floating" toolbar—that is, a small window in which the various buttons/boxes appear.)

2. You can increase or decrease the width of the Standard and Formatting toolbars when they appear side-by-side by dragging the Move handle of the toolbar on the right. (Dragging this handle to the left, increases the width of the toolbar on the right while decreasing the width of the toolbar on the left; dragging this handle to the right, decreases the width of the toolbar on the right while increasing the width of the toolbar on the left.)

Word also provides a number of other toolbars with shortcuts related to specific tasks. You can display any of these toolbars by choosing the **View**, **Toolbars** command (or by **right-clicking** on any visible toolbar) and by selecting the toolbar name on the submenu that appears. You can also hide any toolbar by deselecting the toolbar name on the same submenu.

Using Word Task Panes

The **Getting Started task pane** is opened when you start Word, displaying options for accessing Microsoft Office Online, for opening an existing document file, and for creating a new document. Other task panes appear when you initiate relevant operations.

Notes

You can manually display a different task pane by clicking on the **Other Task Panes** button at the top of the current pane and by selecting the desired pane in the list that appears.

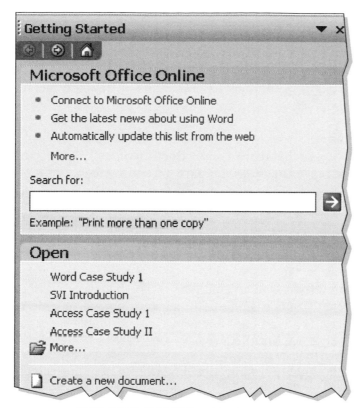

GETTING STARTED TASK PANE

Creating a Document

This section discusses the methods for **creating a new document from a blank Document window**. In it, you will learn how to:

- **Enter text** into a **document**.
- **Save a document**.
- **Print** a **document**.
- **Close** a **file**.

Entering Text into a Document

You enter text into a document by simply positioning the insertion point, if necessary, and by typing the information. As with all other word processing programs, it is not necessary to press **[ENTER]** at the end of a line since Word automatically moves the insertion point from line to line. Press **[ENTER]** only to:

- End a short line (for example, Dear Sir:).
- End a paragraph.
- Insert one or more blank lines.

Notes

A new (blank) document appears automatically when you start Word. You can display a blank document after closing the current document (or when another document is open) either by choosing the **File, New** command and by selecting the **Blank document** option in the New Document task pane, or by clicking on the **New Blank Document** button on the Standard toolbar. In either case, the document is based on Word's **Normal** template, which includes a number of predefined format settings (for example, margins, line spacing and tab stops).

Objective

In this exercise, you will **create a short document by entering text into the blank document that currently appears on your screen**.

Notes

As you enter text in the Document window, you may from time to time see the effect of Word's **AutoCorrect** feature. The AutoCorrect feature automatically corrects common spelling errors, as well as certain grammatical errors. It also performs various "format-as-you-type" tasks, such as converting a single- or double-hyphen (- or --) to an en dash (–). The background Spelling and Grammar Checker flags possible spelling errors, as well as grammatical errors, by displaying a wavy red line under questionable words and a wavy green line under grammatically incorrect text.

- **Type** the following, pressing **[ENTER]** only where indicated:

WESTERN CARIBBEAN **[ENTER] [ENTER]**

The Western Caribbean is a popular destination for cruise ships departing from Miami or Tampa, Florida. Like all cruise destinations, this area includes a number of diverse ports of call. Four of these ports of call are discussed below. **[ENTER] [ENTER]**

Key West **[ENTER]**

Key West, in the Florida Keys, is a city with a colorful history. Today it is both stylish and funky, with something for everyone. In Old Town, the most charming part of Key West, you will find unique shops and restaurants, as well as a number of art galleries and museums. **[ENTER] [ENTER]**

Montego Bay **[ENTER]**

Montego Bay is Jamaica's second largest city. Although much of it looks new today, the city is more than 200 years old! Strolling through the town center of Montego Bay, you can enjoy calypso music and sample a Jamaican specialty, such as jerk chicken. Driving east on the road to Ocho Rios, you will see beautiful beaches and luxury resorts. **[ENTER] [ENTER]**

George Town **[ENTER]**

George Town is the capital of the Cayman Islands. It is also a leading financial center in the region. In George Town, you will find many diversions, from first-class shops and restaurants to submarine dives to view the famous reefs that surround the island. **[ENTER] [ENTER]**

Cozumel **[ENTER]**

Cozumel is part of the Mexican Caribbean. Once a sleepy town, this resort city now hosts visitors from all over the world. In addition to diving, for which it is well known, Cozumel offers you fine shopping and dining, all with a special Mexican flavor.

- Make sure that **Normal View** is selected on the task pane.
- When you are finished, the document should appear as illustrated on the following page.

Ignore the wavy red line that appears in the document.

NOTE: If Word's background **Spelling and Grammar Checker** is enabled (as it is, by default), the program checks the spelling and grammar of text automatically as it is entered, and displays a wavy red line under questionable words and a wavy green line under grammatically incorrect text. If you find this feature distracting, you can disable it by choosing the **Tools, Options** command and by deselecting the **Check spelling as you type** and **Check grammar as you type** options on the Spelling & Grammar panel of the Options dialog box. You will perform a spelling and grammar check on an entire document once it is completed.

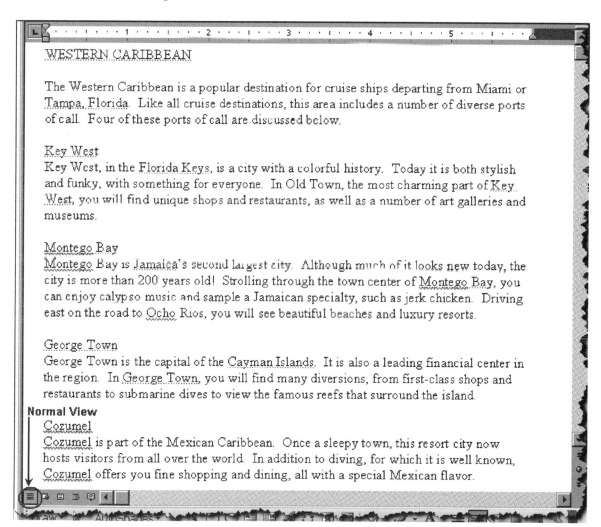

Saving a Document

To avoid losing what appears on the screen due to an unexpected occurrence, such as a power failure, it is important that you frequently save a document as you work.

To **save a document** (for the **first time**):

- Choose the **File**, **Save** command, or click on the **Save** button on the Standard toolbar.
- In the Save As dialog box, enter a **name** for the file in which the document is to be saved.
- If you wish to store the file in a folder other than the working folder, switch to that **folder**.
- Click on the **Save** button (in the dialog box).

To **resave a document**:

- Choose the **File**, **Save** command, or click on the **Save** button on the Standard toolbar.

You can save a previously-saved document in a new location (for example, in a different folder on the hard drive or on a floppy diskette) and/or under a different filename by choosing the **File**, **Save As** command and by specifying the new location/new filename in the Save As dialog box. You will then have two copies of the document—the original version saved in the original file and a second version saved in the new file. From the Save As dialog box, you can also save a document in a different format (for example, one that can be used with an earlier version of Word or one that can be used by another word processing program) by expanding **Save as type** box and by selecting the new file type in the list that appears.

Objective

In this exercise, you will **save your new document**.

3.1

- **Click on the Save button on the Standard toolbar.**

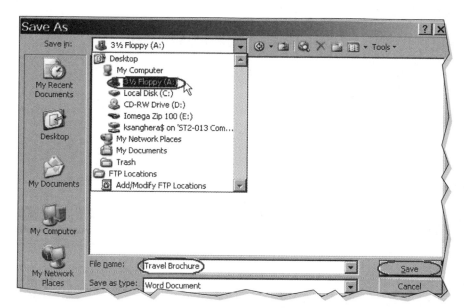

3.2

The Save As dialog box is displayed.

- **Expand Save in box and select 3½ Floppy (A:).**

Notice also that the document heading (WESTERN CARIBBEAN) appears as the default filename.

- **Type: Travel Brochure for File name.**

The filename is entered.

NOTE: The program will add the default extension (doc) to the filename. This extension may or may not appear in file listings on your screen.

- **Choose the Save button (In the dialog box).**

NOTE: You can "choose" a button either by clicking on it or by pressing [**ENTER**].

The dialog box is closed, and the document is saved in a file named Travel Brochure.doc.

Printing a Document

Word offers a number of options for printing a document. For example, you can print a single copy or multiple copies of a document; you can print all or specific pages (of a multiple-page document); and you can select a particular printer to perform the operation if you have more than one printer installed.

To **print a document**:

- Choose the **File**, **Print** command, or click on the **Print** button on the Standard toolbar.
- If you click on the Print button, the print operation begins immediately. If you choose the File, Print command, the Print dialog box is displayed. In this case, set any necessary **print options**, and then click on the **OK** button.

PRINT BUTTON

Objective

In this exercise, you will **print your new document**.

 4.1

- **Click on the Print button on the Standard toolbar.**

The document is printed.

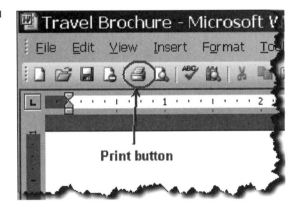

Print button

Closing a File

When you are finished working with a document, you can close the file either by choosing the **File**, **Close** command or by clicking on the **Close Window** button for the Document window. If you have not saved changes in the document, Word will prompt you to indicate whether or not you want to save those changes before closing the file.

Objective

In this exercise, you will **close the current file**.

 5.1

- **Choose the File, Close command.**

The file is closed, and the document is cleared from the screen.

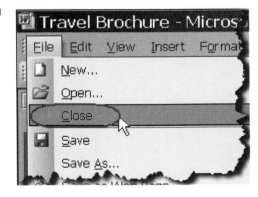

Editing a Document (Part 1)

This section begins a discussion of **basic document editing techniques**. In it, you will learn how to:

- **Reopen** a **file**.
- **Move** the **insertion point** within a document.
- **Select text.**
- **Insert** the **current date** and **time** into a document.
- **Insert text** into a document.
- **Delete text** from a document.
- **Reverse** an **edit operation**.

Reopening a File

Once you have saved a document and cleared it from the screen, you can reopen the file and redisplay the document at any time.

To **reopen a file**:

- Choose the **File**, **Open** command, click on the **Open** button on the Standard toolbar, or select the **More** option in the Getting Started task pane.
- In the Open dialog box, switch to the appropriate **folder** if the file is stored in a folder other than the working folder.
- Select the **filename**.

Do one of the following:

- To simply open the file in edit mode, click on the **Open** button (in the dialog box); or
- To open the file in non-edit (read-only) mode, expand the **Open** button (by clicking on the down arrow at the right side of the button), and select the **Open Read-Only** option in the list that appears; or
- To open a copy of the file in edit mode, expand the **Open** button, and select the **Open as Copy** option in the list that appears.

OPEN BUTTON

Notes

1. Both the File menu and the Getting Started task pane include a list of recently-opened files. You can reopen in edit mode any file listed on this menu or in this task pane by simply selecting the filename.
2. If you cannot find a particular file, you can use Word's **File Search** feature to locate it. This feature can be accessed by expanding the **Tools** button on the toolbar of the Open dialog box and by selecting the **Search** option in the list that appears.

Objective

In this exercise, you will **reopen an existing file**.

6.1

- **Make sure that the Word Application window is displayed.**

- **Click on the Open button on the Standard toolbar.**

6.2

The Open dialog box is displayed.

- **Make sure that 3½ floppy (A:) appears in the Look in box.**

- **In the list of filenames, click on Travel Brochure.**

*NOTE: File extensions may or may not appear in file listings on your screen. The above file, for example, may be listed as **Travel Brochure.doc***

- **Click on the Open button (in the dialog box).**

NOTE: Click on the button itself, not on the down arrow at the right side of the button.

The dialog box is closed, and the selected file is opened.

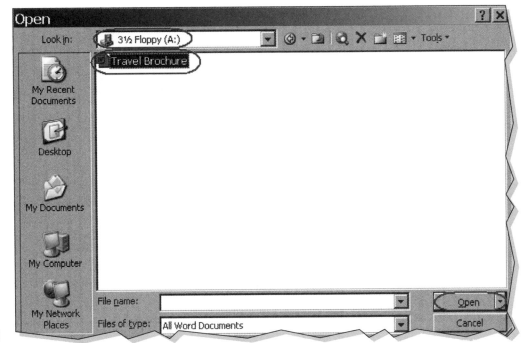

Moving the Insertion Point within a Document/Selecting Text

To edit a document, you must either move the insertion point to the location where the change is to be made or select the text that is to be affected by the change. There are several ways in which this can be done.

To move the insertion point with a **mouse**, simply click in the location in which it is to appear. To display an area of the document that is not visible, use the **Vertical** and/or **Horizontal scroll bar** to scroll the Document window.

To move the insertion point with the **keyboard**, use the methods summarized below.

To Move the Insertion Point:	Press:
One character to the right	[RIGHT ARROW]
One character to the left	[LEFT ARROW]
One word to the right	[CTRL] + [RIGHT ARROW]
One word to the left	[CTRL] + [LEFT ARROW]
One line up	[UP ARROW]
One line down	[DOWN ARROW]
To the beginning of the current line	[HOME]
To the end of the current line	[END]
To the beginning of the document	[CTRL] + [HOME]
To the end of the document	[CTRL] + [END]

Notes

You can also use the **Edit, Go To** command to move to a specific line, to a specific page (in a multiple-page document), as well as to other locations in a document.

To select specific text, use the methods summarized below:

To select:	Do the following:
A single word	Double-click on the word.
Multiple words	Drag the mouse pointer from the first word to the last word.
A single line	Click in the selection bar (the area to the left of the text) to the left of the line.
Multiple lines	Drag in the selection bar from the first line to the last line.
A single sentence	Hold down [CTRL], and click anywhere in the sentence.
Multiple sentences	Drag from the beginning of the first sentence to the end of the last sentence.
A paragraph	Double-click in the selection bar to the left of the paragraph.
Multiple paragraphs	Drag in the selection bar from the first line to the last line.
The entire document	Press [CTRL] + [A], or hold down [CTRL] and click anywhere in the selection bar.
Any block of text (keyboard method)	Move the insertion point to the first character, hold down [SHIFT], and press the appropriate [ARROW] key(s) to highlight the block.
Any block of text (mouse method)	Drag from the beginning of the block to the end of the block.

Notes

1. Word normally selects all characters of a word when you drag through any part of the word. You can disable this feature (which will allow you to select only specific characters in a word) by choosing the **Tools, Options** command and by deselecting the **When selecting, automatically select entire word** option on the Edit panel of the Options dialog box.
2. You can select non-contiguous text (for example, a word or sentence in one paragraph and a word or sentence in another paragraph) by holding down [CTRL] while selecting each individual text block.

Objective

In this exercise, you will **move the insertion point within the current document and select specific text**. You will use both your **mouse** and the **keyboard** to do this.

- **Left Click the mouse button to the immediate left of the W in the word WESTERN.**

- **Press [RIGHT ARROW] six times.**

The insertion point moves six characters to the right.

- **Press [LEFT ARROW] three times.**

The insertion point moves three characters to the left.

- **Press [CTRL] + [RIGHT ARROW] two times.**

The Insertion point moves two words to the right.

- **Press [CTRL] + [LEFT ARROW] one time.**

The insertion point moves one word to the left.

- **Press [END].**

The insertion point moves to the end of the line.

- **Press [HOME].**

The insertion point moves to the beginning of the line.

- **Press [CTRL] + [END].**

The insertion point moves to the end of the document.

- **Press [CTRL] + [HOME].**

The insertion point moves to the beginning of the document.

Key West

Key West, in the Florida Keys, is a city with a colorful history. Today it is both stylish and funky, with something for everyone. In Old Town, the most charming part of Key West, you will find unique shops and restaurants, as well as a number of art galleries and museums.

Montego Bay

Montego Bay is Jamaica's second largest city. Although much of it looks new today, the city is more than 200 years old! Strolling through the town center of Montego Bay, you can enjoy calypso music and sample a Jamaican specialty, such as jerk chicken. Driving east on the road to Ocho Rios, you will see beautiful beaches and luxury resorts.

Down arrow at the bottom of vertical scroll bar →

- **Point to the down arrow at the bottom of the Vertical scroll bar, and click the mouse button several times.**

The Document window is scrolled downward.

- **Point to the Vertical scroll bar in an area above the scroll box, and click the mouse button (once).**

The Document window is scrolled upward to the beginning of the document. You will now practice selecting specific text in the document.

NOTE: *The techniques demonstrated in this step and in the previous step are most useful in large (for example, multiple-page) documents.*

7.3

- **Point to the first word (The) of the first body paragraph. Then double-click the mouse button.**

The first word of the first body paragraph is selected.

- **Click anywhere in the text of the document.**

The selection is cancelled.

- **Press and hold down [CTRL]. Point to the first word of the first body paragraph. Click the mouse button. Then release [CTRL].**

The first sentence of the first body paragraph is selected.

- **Click anywhere in the text of the document.**

The selection is cancelled.

- **Point to left of the first word of the first body paragraph.**

The mouse pointer will appear as an upward-pointing arrow when it is properly positioned.

NOTE: *The area to the left of the text is called the selection bar.*

- **Click the mouse button three times.**

The entire paragraph is selected.

- **Cancel the selection.**

- **Press [CTRL] + [A].**

The entire document is selected.

- **Cancel the selection.**

- **Point to the beginning of the first body paragraph (to the immediate left of the T in the word The). Press and hold down the mouse button, and drag the mouse pointer over the words The and Western. Then release the mouse button.**

The first two words of the paragraph are selected.

- **Press [CTRL] + [HOME].**

The insertion point moves to the beginning of the document, and the selection is cancelled.

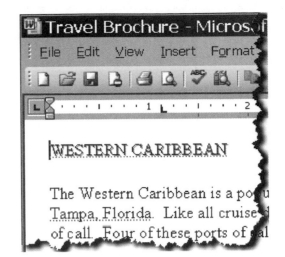

Inserting the Current Date and Time into a Document

With Word, you can automatically insert both the **system date** and **system time** (the date and time that are stored in your computer) into a document, saving you the time it would take to manually enter them.

To **insert the current date and/or time into a document**:

- Move the insertion point to the location in which the date/time is to appear.
- Choose the **Insert, Date and Time** command.

- In the Date and Time dialog box, select the desired **date/time format**.
- To insert the date/time as a field that is updated as the system date/time changes, select the **Update automatically** option (if it is not currently selected).
- Click on the **OK** button.

Objective

In this exercise, you will **insert the current date and time into the current document**.

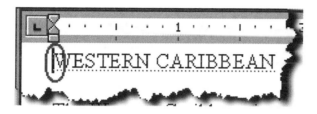

8.1

- **Make sure that the insertion point is located at the beginning of the document.**

- **Press [ENTER] two times.**

Two blank lines are inserted, and the text is moved down.

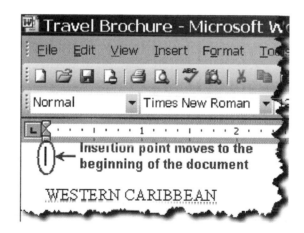

8.2

- **Press [CTRL] + [HOME].**

The insertion point moves back to the beginning of the document.

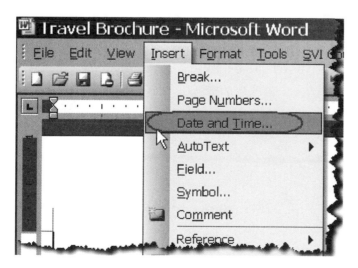

8.3

- **Choose the Insert, Date and Time command.**

8.4

The Date and Time dialog box is displayed.

- **In the list of date and time formats, click on the format which is of the type month/day/year hours:minutes AM/PM (the twelfth option).**

The date and time format is selected.

- **Click on Update automatically if that option is not currently selected.**

The date and time will be inserted as a field that is updated as the system date and time changes.

- **Click on the OK button.**

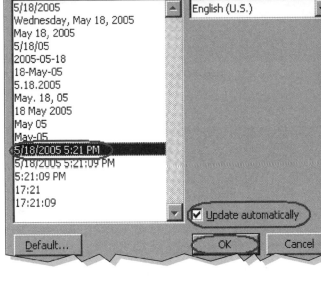

8.5

The dialog box is closed, and the date and time are inserted.

- **Click on the Save button.**

The changes are saved.

NOTE: *Fields, such as those representing the date and time, may or may not appear shaded on your screen, or they may appear shaded only when selected.*

Inserting Text into a Document/Deleting Text from a Document

One of the major advantages of using a word processing program, such as Word, is the ease in which text can be inserted into or deleted from a document.

To **insert text into a document**:

- Move the insertion point to the location in which the new text is to appear.
- **Type** the **new character(s)**.

To **delete text from a document**:

- Press **[DEL]** to delete the character to the **right** of the insertion point; or
- Press **[BACKSPACE]** to delete the character to the **left** of the insertion point.

Notes

1. You can simultaneously delete an entire word and insert another by **double-clicking** on the original word and by typing the new word.

2. Word, by default, is in **Insert** mode, which allows you to insert one or more characters into existing text. You can switch to **Overtype** mode, which allows you to replace one character with another, by **double-clicking** on the **OVR** indicator on the Status bar.

Objective

In this exercise, you will **insert text into and delete text from the current document**.

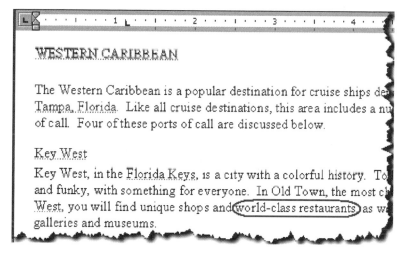

9.1

- **Move the insertion point to the immediate left of the r in the word restaurants (in the second body paragraph).**

- **Type: world-class** *Press* **[SPACEBAR].**

The word "world-class" and a space are inserted.

9.2

You will now delete the word "four" and insert the word "three."

- **Point to the word Four (in the first body paragraph), and double-click the mouse button.**

The word is selected.

- **Type: Three**

The word "Four" is replaced by the word "Three."

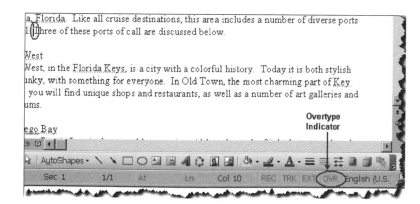

Overtype Indicator

9.3

You will now switch to Overtype mode and replace one word with another.

- **Move the insertion point to the immediate left of the T in the word Three (in the first body paragraph).**

- **Double-click on the OVR indicator on the Status bar.**

NOTE: *This indicator is initially dimmed.*

Overtype mode is activated, and the OVR indicator appears darker.

9.4

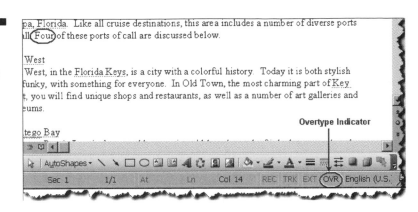

Overtype Indicator

- **Type: Four**

The previous characters are overwritten by the new characters.

- **Press [DEL] one time.**

The extra character is deleted.

- **Double-click on the OVR indicator.**

Overtype mode is deactivated.

You will now replace the current date/time field with a field in a different format.

9.5

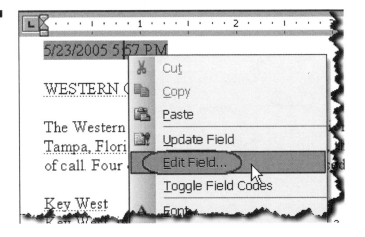

- **Point to any part of the date/time field, and right-click the mouse button.**

NOTE: *If date/time field is not highlighted, make sure that Normal View is selected on above the status bar.*

- **Click on Edit Field...**

9.6

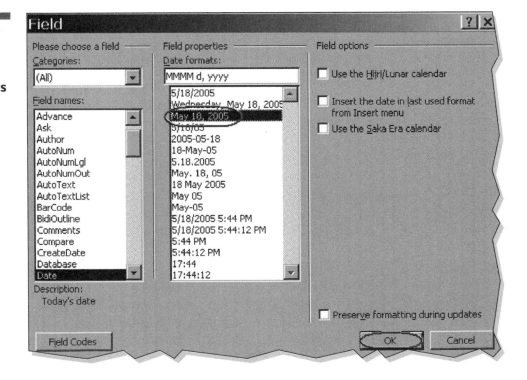

The Field dialog box is displayed.

- **In the Date formats box, click on the month day, year (the third) option. Then click on the OK button.**

The dialog box is closed, and the new date field replaces the previous date/time field.

- **Click on the Save button.**

Reversing an Edit Operation

Word's **Undo** and **Redo** features allow you to reverse one or more edit operations and restore a document to its previous state. They are useful when you find that you have accidentally deleted the wrong text or have performed some other operation that has erroneously modified your document.

To **reverse the previous edit operation**:

- Choose the **Edit, Undo** command, or click on the **Undo** button on the Standard toolbar.

To **reverse the previous undo operation**:

- Choose the **Edit, Redo** command, or click on the **Redo** button on the Standard toolbar.

UNDO / REDO BUTTONS

Notes

1. You can simultaneously undo or redo a series of edit operations by expanding the Undo or Redo button and by selecting an option in the list that appears. Doing this reverses the selected edit operation and all subsequent edit operations.
2. The Undo and Redo buttons, as well as the Undo and Redo commands on the Edit menu, always reflect the last edit operation performed. For example, if you enter text, the Undo button/Undo command will appear as "Undo Typing." If you subsequently undo the typing operation, the Redo button/Redo command will appear as "Redo Typing."

Objective

In this exercise, you will **reverse (undo and redo) edit operations in the current document**.

10.1

- **Select the word Four (in the first body paragraph) by double-clicking on it.**

Type: Five

- **Select the word popular (in the first body paragraph) by double-clicking on it. Then press [DEL].**

The word is deleted. You will now undo the changes you have just made.

- **Click on the Undo button on the Standard toolbar.**

NOTE: *The Undo button reflects the last edit operation performed (Clear).*

NOTE: *Click on the button itself, not on the down arrow at the right side of the button.*

The last edit operation is reversed, and the word "popular" is restored in the first body paragraph.

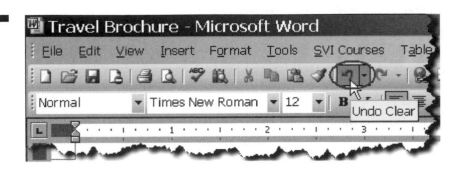

10.2

- **Click again on the Undo button.**

The previous edit operation is reversed, and the word "Four" is restored in the second body paragraph.

- **Click on the Redo button on the Standard toolbar.**

NOTE: *Again, click on the button itself, not on the down arrow at the right side of the button.*

The last undo operation is reversed, and the word "Five" is restored in the first body paragraph.

- **Click on the Undo button.**

The word "Four" is once again restored in the first body paragraph.

- **Cancel the selection. Then click on the Save button.**

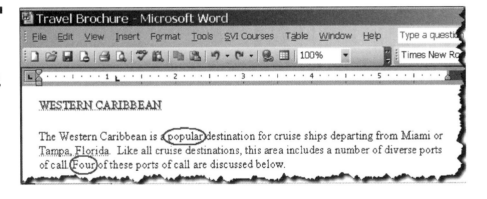

Editing a Document (Part 2)

This section continues the discussion of **basic document editing techniques**. In it, you will learn how to:

- **Find text** in a document.
- **Move** a **text block**.
- **Copy** a **text block**.

Finding Text in a Document

Word's **Find** feature can be used to find a particular word or phrase, making it an alternate method for moving from one part of a document to another.
   To **find text in a document**:

- Choose the **Edit, Find** command.
- On the Find panel of the Find and Replace dialog box, enter the **search text** (the word or phrase you wish to find).
- Optionally, expand the dialog box by clicking on the **More** button, and select any necessary **search options**. For example:

  - To search only for an exact match with regard to case, select the **Match case** option.
  - To search only for whole words, select the **Find whole words only** option.
  - To include the ? and/or * wildcard in the search text, select the **Use wildcards** option. (The question mark represents any single character; the asterisk represents 0 or more consecutive characters.)
  - To change the direction of the search from the location of the insertion point, expand the **Search** box, and select the desired option (**Down**, **Up** or **All**). (The default direction is All, which searches the entire document.)

- Click on the **Find Next** button to highlight the **first occurrence** of the **search text**. Continue clicking on this button to highlight subsequent occurrences of the text.
- To close the dialog box at any time, click on the **Cancel** or **Close** button.

Notes

1. You can also highlight all occurrences of the specified search text in one operation by selecting the **Highlight all items found in** option and by clicking on the **Find All** button (in the Find and Replace dialog box).
2. The Find and Replace dialog box can also be displayed by clicking on the **Find** button on the Standard toolbar. To add this button to the Standard toolbar, click on the **Toolbar Options** button (on the toolbar), select the **Add or Remove Buttons** option in the list that appears, followed by the **Standard** option. Then, in the list of available buttons, click on **Find**.

Objective

In this exercise, you will **find specific words in a document**. You will begin by finding all occurrences of the word "**restaurant.**"

 11.1

- **Choose the Edit, Find command.**

The Find panel of the Find and Replace dialog box is displayed.

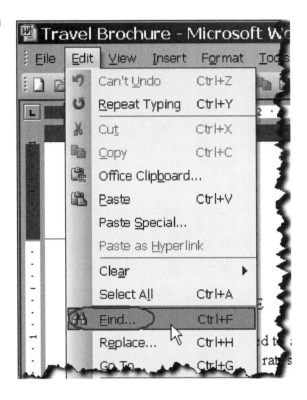

11.2

- **Type: restaurant**

NOTE: *Since case will not be considered, any occurrence of the text will be included in the search, whether it includes uppercase characters, lowercase characters, or a combination of uppercase and lowercase characters.*

- **Click on the Find Next button.**

The first occurrence of the search text (restaurant) is highlighted in the second body paragraph.

NOTE: *If necessary, you can move the dialog box to another area of the screen by dragging its Title bar.*

- **Click again on the Find Next button.**

The second occurrence of the search text is highlighted.

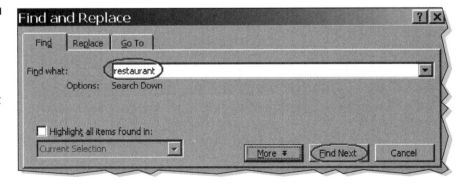

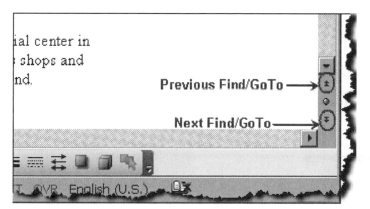

- **Continue clicking on the Find Next button until the search text is no longer found. Then click on the OK button in the message box that appears.**

You will use the navigation buttons at the bottom of the Vertical scroll bar to highlight the search text.

NOTE: *The above buttons are normally used to display the previous and next pages of a multiple-page document. After using the Edit, Find command, however, they become the Previous Find/GoTo and Next Find/GoTo buttons and can be used to highlight the previous and next occurrences, respectively, of the search text specified in the Find and Replace dialog box. Notice that the buttons are currently blue.*

- **Make sure that the insertion point is located at the beginning of the document. Then click on the Next Find/Go To ⬇ button.**

The first occurrence of the current search text (Restaurant) is highlighted.

- **Click again on the Next Find/GoTo button.**

The next occurrence of the search text is highlighted.

- **Click on the Previous Find/GoTo ⬇ button.**

The previous occurrence of the search text is once again highlighted.

- **Cancel the selection.**

You will now highlight all occurrences of the current search text in one operation.

11.5

Next, you will perform another Find operation. This time, however, you will limit the search to the word "Restaurant" (with an uppercase "R").

- **Make sure that the current search text (restaurant) is highlighted in the Find what box of the dialog box. Type: Restaurant**

NOTE: *Make sure that you include the uppercase "R" in the above entry.*

- **Click on the More button.**

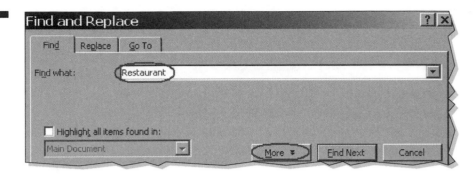

11.6

- **Under Search Options, click on Match case. Click on the Less button.**

- **Click on the Find Next button.**

NOTE: *Since the document does not contain any restaurant word with upper-case "R", Find Next button will not find the search text.*

- **Click on the OK button in the message box that appears.**

- **Click on the Cancel button.**

The dialog box is closed.

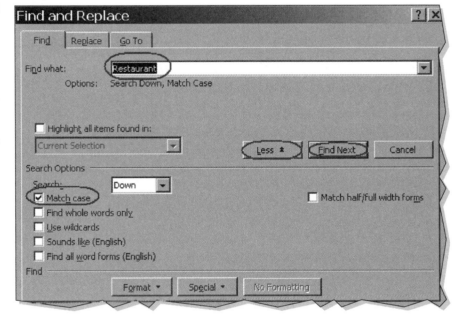

Moving a Text Block

Word provides two methods for moving a block of text from one location in a document to another. One method uses the standard Windows **cut and paste** technique; the other uses a **drag and drop** technique.

To **move a text block** (using **cut and paste**):

- Select the text that is to be moved.
- Choose the **Edit, Cut** command, or click on the **Cut** button on the Standard toolbar. Doing this deletes the text from the document and places it on the Windows Clipboard.
- Move the insertion point to the location in which the text is to appear.

- Choose the **Edit, Paste** command, or click on the **Paste** button on the Standard toolbar. Doing this inserts the text on the Windows Clipboard into the document at the insertion point location.

To move a text block (using drag and drop):

- Select the text that is to be moved. Then point to the selection.
- Press and **hold down** the mouse button, and **drag** the mouse pointer to the new location. The insertion point moves with the pointer as you drag. The text will appear at the insertion point location when you release the mouse button.

Notes

When you use the Edit, Cut command or the Cut button to move text (or when you use the Edit, Copy command or the Copy button to copy text), the text is placed on both the **Windows Clipboard** (also called the System Clipboard) and the **Office Clipboard**, two temporary storage areas. Although the Windows Clipboard and the Office Clipboard are separate entities, they are used for similar purposes. The Windows Clipboard, however, can hold only one item (selection) at a time and can, therefore, be used to store and paste only single items. The Office Clipboard, on the other hand, can hold up to 24 items and can, as a result, be used to collect and paste multiple items, from the same or from different Microsoft Office programs. The contents of the Office Clipboard appear in the Clipboard task pane, which can be displayed by choosing the **Edit**, **Office Clipboard** command.

Objective

In this exercise, you will **move a block of text** by using the **cut and paste** techniques.

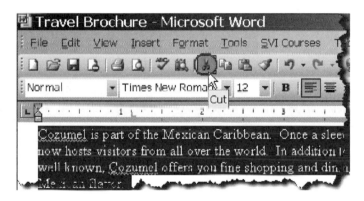

12.1

- **Point to the left of the word Cozumel (heading of the fourth port). Press and hold down the mouse button, and drag the mouse pointer to the last word of the fourth line (flavor). Then release the mouse button.**

- **Click on the Cut button on the Standard toolbar. A copy of the selection is placed on the Windows Clipboard.**

12.2

- **Click on the left of letter "G" of George Town.**
- **Click on the Paste button on the Standard toolbar.**

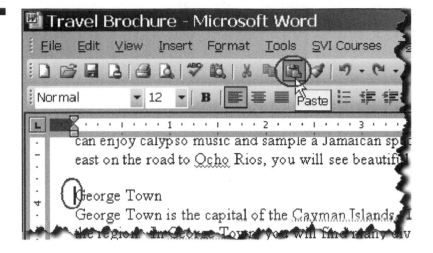

12.3

The text previously copied is inserted at the location of the insertion point.

- **Press [ENTER] two times so George Town port is on a new line after a blank line.**
- **Save the document.**

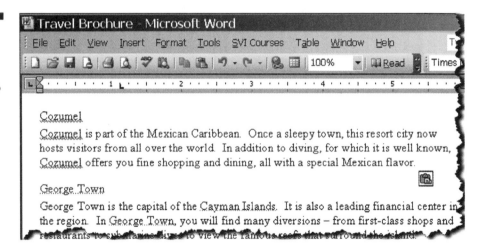

Formatting a Document (Part 1)

This section begins a discussion of **basic document formatting techniques**. In it, you will learn how to:

- **Apply attributes** to text.
- **Apply** a new **font** and **font size** to text.
- **Simultaneously apply multiple font options** to text.
- **Indent** a **paragraph**.
- **Reset line** and **paragraph spacing** in a document.

Applying Attributes to Text

With Word, you can apply a number of **attributes** to text in a document. Three of the most common attributes are **bold**, **italic** and **underline**, which are turned on and off with the associated button on the Formatting toolbar.

BOLD / ITALIC / UNDERLINE BUTTONS

Notes

You can also use the "format-as-you-type" feature of **AutoCorrect** to apply the bold and italic attributes to text. Simply enter an asterisk (*) before and after the text to bold it (for example, *This text is bolded.*) or enter a single underline (_) before and after the text to italicize it (for example, _This text is italicized._). (Note that to accomplish the above, the **"Bold" and _italic_ with real formatting** option, under Replace as you type, must be selected on the AutoFormat As You Type panel of the AutoCorrect dialog box.)

Objective

In this exercise, you will **apply bold, italic and underline attributes to text**.

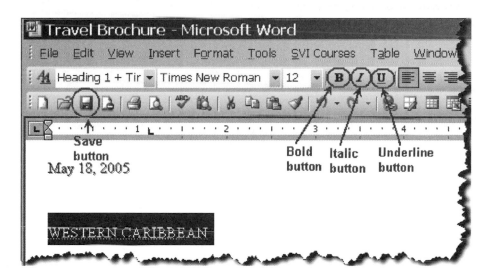

13.1

- **Select WESTERN CARIBBEAN text.**

- **Click on the Bold button on the Formatting toolbar. Click on the Italic button and then click on the Underline button**

The selected text is bolded, italicized and underlined.

- **Click again on the Underline button.**

The Underline attribute is cancelled.

- **Cancel the selection by clicking anywhere in the document.**

13.2

- **Click on the Save button.**

Applying a New Font and Font Size to Text

In addition to attributes, you can also apply a new **font** and **font size** to text. To do this, simply expand the **Font** box and the **Font Size** box, respectively, on the Formatting toolbar, and select the desired option in each list that appears.

FONT / FONT SIZE BOXES

Notes

You can also reset the font size by clicking in the Font Size box or by typing the new setting and by pressing [ENTER].

Objective

In this exercise, you will **apply a new font and font size to text**.

14.1

• **Select WESTERN CARIBBEAN** text.

• **Click on the down arrow at the right side of the Font box on the Formatting toolbar.**

The box is expanded, and a list of available fonts is displayed.

• **Click on Arial.**

The new font is selected.

• **Click on the down arrow at the right side of the Font Size box on the Formatting toolbar.**

The box is expanded, and a list of available font sizes is displayed.

• **Click on 14.**

The new font size (14 points) is selected.

NOTE: *One point is equal to 1/72 of an inch.*

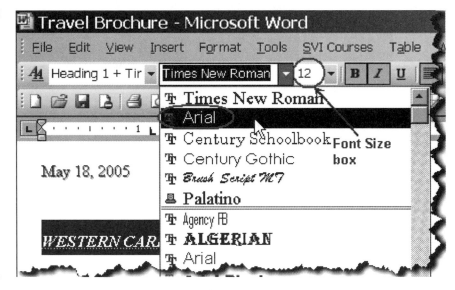

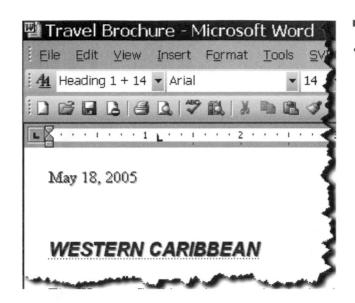

14.2

- **Save the document.**

Simultaneously Applying Multiple Font Options to Text

The **Font dialog box**, which is displayed either by choosing the **Format**, **Font** command or by selecting the **Font** option on the shortcut menu, allows you to simultaneously apply multiple font options (for example, a new font and font size, along with selected attributes) to text in a document.

Objective

In this exercise, you will **use the Font dialog box to apply font options**.

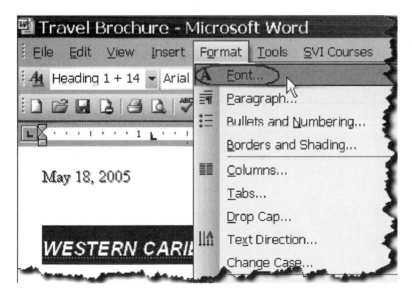

15.1

- **Select WESTERN CARIBBEAN text.**
- **Choose the Format, Font command.**

15.2

The Font panel of the Font dialog box is displayed.

- **In the Font box, click on Century Schoolbook. In the Size box, click on 16.**

A new font and font size are selected.

- **In the Font style box, click on Bold.**

The bold attribute is turned on.

- **Click on the down arrow at the right side of the Underline style box.**

The box is expanded, and a list of options is displayed.

- **Click on the first double line option.**

The double-line attribute is turned on.

- **Click on the down arrow at the right side of the Font color box.**

The box is expanded, and a palette of colors is displayed.

- **Click on the Blue option (the sixth option in the second row of the color palette).**

The new color is selected.

- **Click on the OK button.**

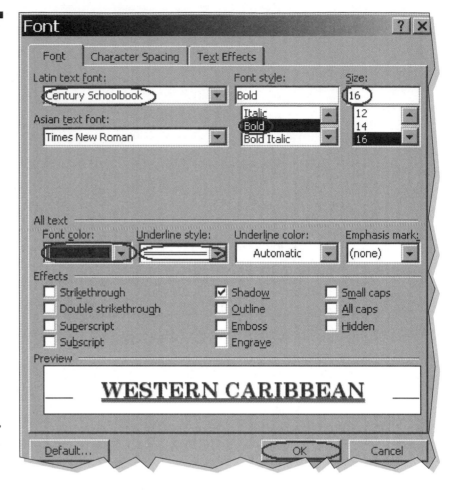

15.3

The dialog box is closed.

- **Save the document.**

Indenting a Paragraph

Word allows you to indent a paragraph from the **left margin**, from the **right margin**, or from the **left and right margins**. You may want to use indentation to set off special text, such as a quote.

To **indent a paragraph** (using the **menu system**):

- Choose the **Format**, **Paragraph** command, or select the **Paragraph** option on the shortcut menu.
- On the Indents and Spacing panel of the Paragraph dialog box, specify the desired **indentation**.
- Click on the **OK** button.

To **indent a paragraph** (using the **Horizontal ruler**):

- Drag any of the following along the ruler:
- **First Line Indent marker**—to set left margin indentation for the first line of a paragraph.
- **Hanging Indent marker**—to set left margin indentation for all lines of a paragraph except for the first line.
- **Left Indent marker**—to set left margin indentation for all lines of a paragraph.
- **Right Indent marker**—to set right margin indentation for all lines of a paragraph.

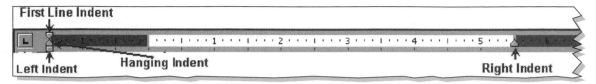

INDENT MARKERS ON THE HORIZONTAL RULER

Alternatively, you can use the **Increase Indent** and **Decrease Indent** buttons on the Formatting toolbar to indent a paragraph to the next tab stop and to the previous tab stop, respectively.

INCREASE INDENT / DECREASE INDENT BUTTONS

Objective

In this exercise, you will use **Indent markers on the horizontal ruler** and **Increase/Decrease Indent** buttons on the Formatting toolbar to indent a paragraph to the next tab stop.

 16.1

• **Click on the left of "W" of WESTERN.**

• **Point to the First Line Indent marker on the Horizontal ruler.**

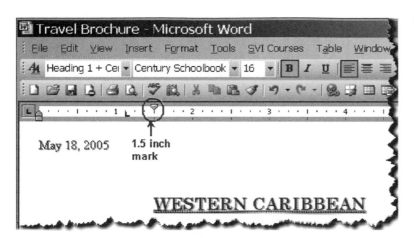

May 18, 2005   1.5 inch mark

WESTERN CARIBBEAN

16.2

- **Press and hold down the mouse button, and drag the marker to the 1.5-inch mark on the ruler. Then release the mouse button.**

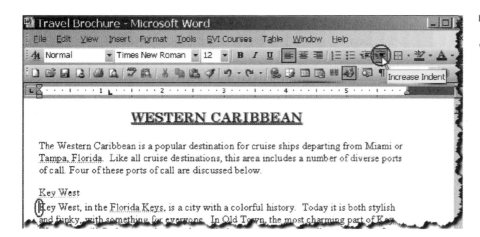

16.3

- **Click on the "K" of Key West paragraph and click on the Increase Indent button on the Formatting toolbar.**

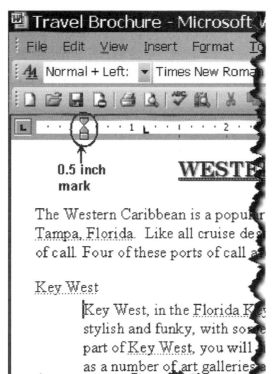

0.5 inch mark

WESTE

16.4

The insertion point moves to the first tab stop (one half inch from the left margin).

16.5

- **Using the procedure explained above, indent the paragraph body of Montego Bay, Cozumel and George Town.**

- **Save the document.**

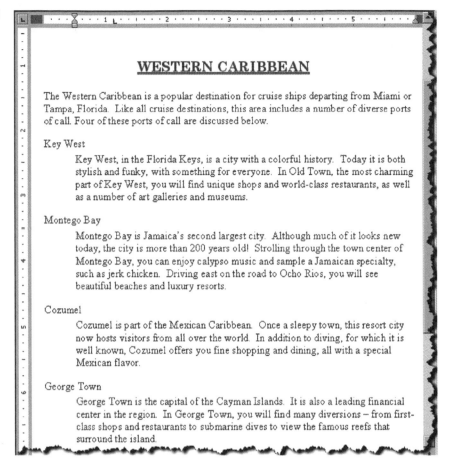

WESTERN CARIBBEAN

The Western Caribbean is a popular destination for cruise ships departing from Miami or Tampa, Florida. Like all cruise destinations, this area includes a number of diverse ports of call. Four of these ports of call are discussed below.

Key West

> Key West, in the Florida Keys, is a city with a colorful history. Today it is both stylish and funky, with something for everyone. In Old Town, the most charming part of Key West, you will find unique shops and world-class restaurants, as well as a number of art galleries and museums.

Montego Bay

> Montego Bay is Jamaica's second largest city. Although much of it looks new today, the city is more than 200 years old! Strolling through the town center of Montego Bay, you can enjoy calypso music and sample a Jamaican specialty, such as jerk chicken. Driving east on the road to Ocho Rios, you will see beautiful beaches and luxury resorts.

Cozumel

> Cozumel is part of the Mexican Caribbean. Once a sleepy town, this resort city now hosts visitors from all over the world. In addition to diving, for which it is well known, Cozumel offers you fine shopping and dining, all with a special Mexican flavor.

George Town

> George Town is the capital of the Cayman Islands. It is also a leading financial center in the region. In George Town, you will find many diversions – from first-class shops and restaurants to submarine dives to view the famous reefs that surround the island.

Resetting Line and Paragraph Spacing in a Document

Text in a document is **single-spaced**, by default. You can, however, increase or decrease the line spacing of paragraphs, as necessary, anywhere in a document.

To **reset line spacing in a document**:

- Expand the **Line Spacing** button on the Formatting toolbar.
- In the list of options that appears, do one of the following:

  - Select a **line spacing** option; or
  - Select the **More** option, specify the **new line spacing** on the Indents and Spacing panel of the Paragraph dialog box, and click on the **OK** button.

LINE SPACING BUTTON

Using options in the Paragraph dialog box you can also control the spacing between paragraphs of a document.

To **reset paragraph spacing in a document**:

- Choose the **Format, Paragraph** command, or select the **Paragraph** option on the shortcut menu.
- On the Indents and Spacing panel of the Paragraph dialog box, specify the **amount of space** that is to appear **above** and/or **below** a paragraph.
- Click on the **OK** button.

Objective

In this exercise, you will **reset the spacing of lines and paragraphs in a document**.

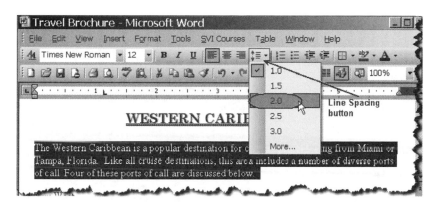

17.1

- **Select the first paragraph.**
- **Click on the down arrow at the right side of the Line Spacing button on the Formatting toolbar.**

The button is expanded, and a list of options is displayed.

- **Click on 2.0.**

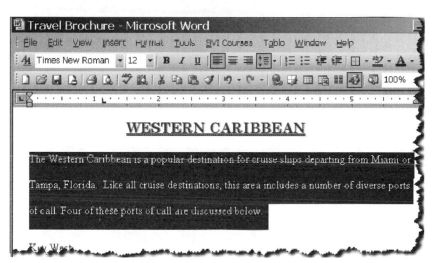

17.2

The selected paragraph is displayed with double-line spacing.

- **Click on the Line Spacing button on the Formatting toolbar.**

NOTE: *Click on the button itself, not on the down arrow.*

The new line spacing is cancelled, and the paragraphs are displayed with the default single-line spacing.

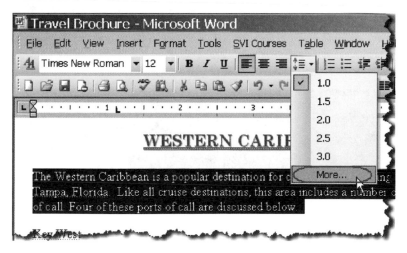

17.3

- **Make sure that the first paragraph is still selected. Then expand the Line Spacing button, and click on More.**

17.4

The Indents and Spacing panel of the Paragraph dialog box is displayed.

- **Under Spacing, expand the Line spacing box, and click on Double. Then click on the OK button.**

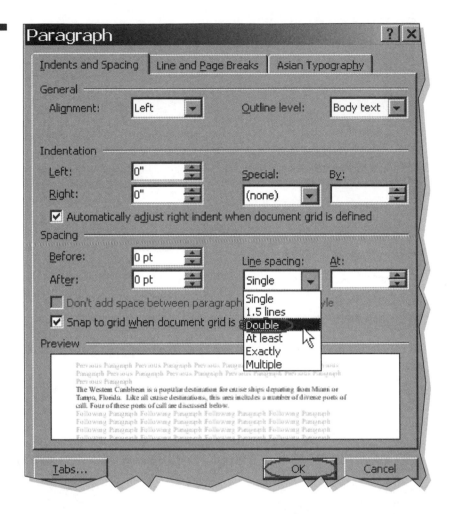

17.5

- **The paragraph is displayed with the new line spacing.**

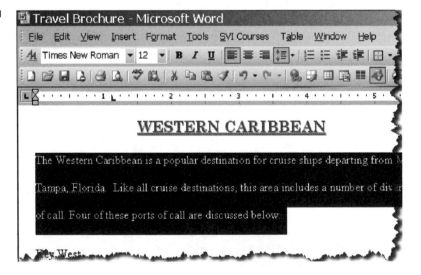

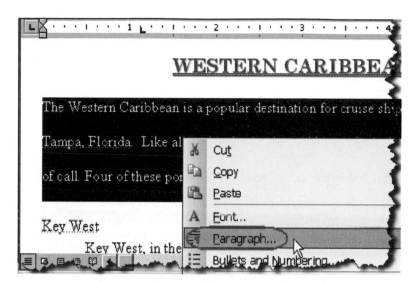

17.6

- **Right click on the selected paragraph and click on Paragraph... on the short cut menu.**

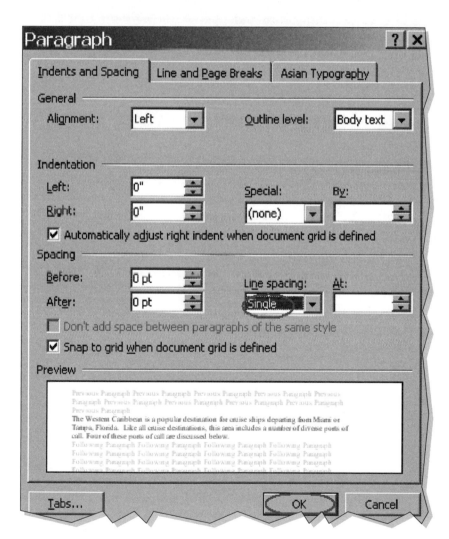

17.7

The Indents and Spacing panel of the Paragraph dialog box is redisplayed.

- **Under Spacing, expand the Line spacing box, and click on Single. Then click on the OK button.**

The default line spacing is restored.

- **Save the document.**

Formatting a Document (Part 2)

This section continues the discussion of **basic document formatting techniques**. In it, you will learn how to:

- **Reset** the **margins** of a document.
- **Create** a **bulleted/numbered list**.
- **Insert** a **hard page break** into a document.

Resetting the Margins of a Document

Word sets default **left** and **right margins** of **one and one-quarter inches** and default **top** and **bottom margins** of **one inch**. You can, however, increase or decrease these margins if the default settings are not appropriate for a particular document.

To **reset one or more margins of a document**:

- Choose the **File**, **Page Setup** command.
- On the Margins panel of the Page Setup dialog box, specify the **new margin(s)**.
- Click on the **OK** button.

Objective

In this exercise, you will **reset the left and right margins of a document**.

18.1

- **Choose the File, Page Setup command.**

The Margins panel of the Page Setup dialog box is displayed.

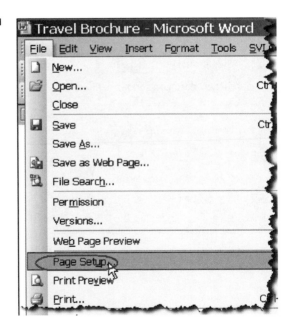

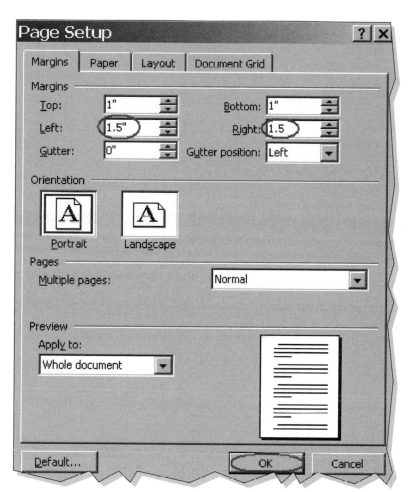

18.2

- **Select the current Left setting (1.250") and Type: 1.5**

  Press [TAB]. The left margin is reset to 1.5 inches, and the current Right setting is selected.

- **Type: 1.5**

The right margin is also reset to 1.5 inches.

- **Choose the OK button. The dialog box is closed, and the text of the document is reformatted to reflect the new margins.**

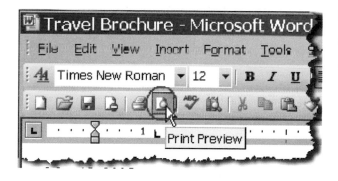

18.3

- **Save the document.**

- **Click on the Print Preview button on the Standard toolbar.**

18.4

- **A full-page view of the document is displayed in the Print Preview window.**

- **Click on the Close Preview button on the toolbar of the Print Preview window.**

The Print Preview window is closed.

- **Save the document.**

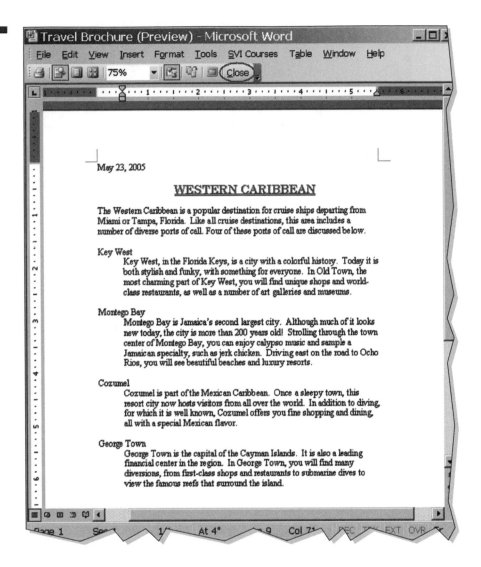

Creating a Bulleted List

Word's **Bullets** and **Numbering** features automatically insert a variety of **bullet characters** and a sequentially-incremented **series of numbers**, respectively, into a document. These features, used individually or in combination, allow you to create lists of items.

To **create a bulleted/numbered list**:

- Move the insertion point to the location in which the list is to appear.
- Choose the **Format**, **Bullets and Numbering** command, or select the **Bullets and Numbering** option on the shortcut menu.
- In the Bullets and Numbering dialog box, select the desired **bullet character** or **number format**.
- Optionally, click on the **Customize** button, and modify the default settings in the dialog box that appears.

- Click on the **OK** button.
- Type the list items, pressing **[ENTER]** at the end of each item. (List items can be single- or multiple-line entries.)

Alternatively, you can use the **Bullets** or **Numbering** button on the Formatting toolbar to insert the default bullet or number, respectively.

BULLETS/NUMBERING BUTTONS

Notes

You can also use the "format-as-you-type" feature of **AutoCorrect** to create a bulleted or numbered list. Simply type an asterisk (*) and press **[TAB]** to begin a bulleted list, or type the first number and press **[TAB]** to begin a numbered list. Each time you press **[ENTER]**, the next bullet or number is inserted automatically. (Note that to accomplish the above, the **Automatic bulleted lists** and **Automatic numbered lists** options, under Apply as you type, must be selected on the AutoFormat As You Type panel of the AutoCorrect dialog box.) To cancel the bullet or number, press **[BACKSPACE]**, or press **[ENTER]** a second time, to delete it.

Objective

In this exercise, you will use **Bullets button** and will **add bullets in front of four listed ports**.

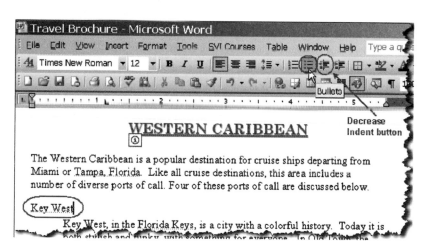

19.1

- **Click anywhere on the first port Key West and click on Bullets button on the toolbar.**

- **Click on the Decrease Indent button on the Formatting toolbar.**

19.2

- **Select Key West and click on Bold button.**

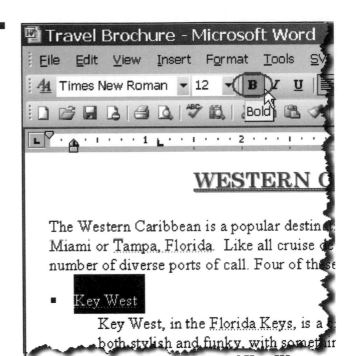

19.3

- **Using the above procedure, add bullets in front of Montego Bay, Cozumel, and George Town and then bold them.**

- **Save your document.**

WESTERN CARIBBEAN

The Western Caribbean is a popular destination for cruise ships departing from Miami or Tampa, Florida. Like all cruise destinations, this area includes a number of diverse ports of call. Four of these ports of call are discussed below.

- **Key West**

    Key West, in the Florida Keys, is a city with a colorful history. Today it is both stylish and funky, with something for everyone. In Old Town, the most charming part of Key West, you will find unique shops and world-class restaurants, as well as a number of art galleries and museums.

- **Montego Bay**

    Montego Bay is Jamaica's second largest city. Although much of it looks new today, the city is more than 200 years old! Strolling through the town center of Montego Bay, you can enjoy calypso music and sample a Jamaican specialty, such as jerk chicken. Driving east on the road to Ocho Rios, you will see beautiful beaches and luxury resorts.

- **Cozumel**

    Cozumel is part of the Mexican Caribbean. Once a sleepy town, this resort city now hosts visitors from all over the world. In addition to diving, for which it is well known, Cozumel offers you fine shopping and dining, all with a special Mexican flavor.

- **George Town**

    George Town is the capital of the Cayman Islands. It is also a leading financial center in the region. In George Town, you will find many diversions — from first-class shops and restaurants to submarine dives to

Inserting a Hard Page Break / Creating a Multiple-Page Document

Your document consists of one page. Word begins a new page automatically when the insertion point reaches the bottom margin. (In this case, the program also inserts a **soft page break** at the end of the full page of text.) Often, however, you may want to move to a new page before typing a complete page. You can do this by inserting a **hard page break**.

To **insert a hard page break**:

- Choose the **Insert**, **Break** command.
- In the Break dialog box, click on the **OK** button.

  OR

- Simply press [CTRL] + [ENTER].

Objective

In this exercise, you will **insert a hard page break**.

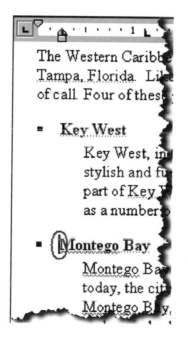

20.1

- **Click on the left of letter "M" of the second Port "Montego Bay."**

- **Make sure that the Normal View is selected above the status bar and then press [CTRL] + [ENTER].**

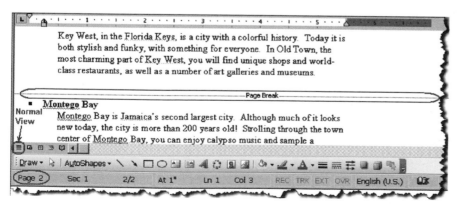

20.2

A hard page break is inserted, and the insertion point moves to the beginning of a new page (2).

- **Click on the page break line. Then press [DEL].**

20.3

The page break is deleted, and the entire document appears on one page.

- **Save the document**

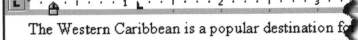

> The Western Caribbean is a popular destination f
> Tampa, Florida. Like all cruise destinations, this
> of call. Four of these ports of call are discussed be
>
> ■ **Key West**
>
> > Key West, in the Florida Keys, is a city wi
> > stylish and funky, with something for eve
> > part of Key West, you will find unique sho
> > as a number of art galleries and museums.
>
> ■ **Montego Bay**
>
> > Montego Bay is Jamaica's second largest c
> > today, the city is more than 200 years old!
> > Montego Bay, you can enjoy calypso musi
> > such as jerk chicken. Driving east on the

Changing the Zoom Level of a Document

A document is normally displayed at the default **zoom level** (screen size) of **100%**. You can, however, increase or decrease the screen size, as necessary, to suit the particular document you are viewing and/or editing.

To **change the zoom level of a document**:

- Choose the **View, Zoom** command.
- In the Zoom dialog box, specify the desired **magnification** option.
- Click on the **OK** button.

Alternatively, you can change the zoom level by expanding the **Zoom**

`75% ▾` box on the Standard toolbar and by selecting a magnification option in the list that appears.

Objective

In this exercise, you will **change the zoom level of your document**.

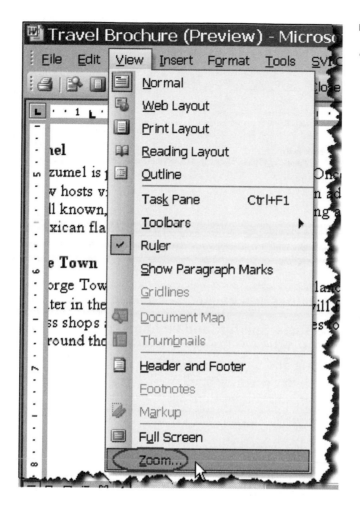

- **Choose the View, Zoom command.**

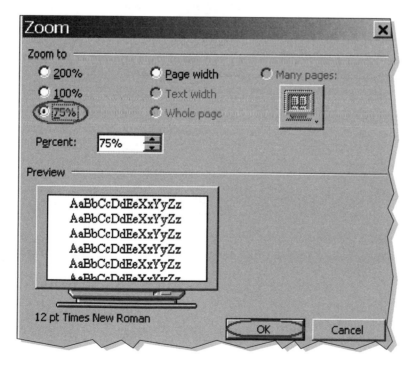

The Zoom dialog box is displayed.

- **Click on 75%.**

The new zoom level is selected.

NOTE: *Notice that you can enter your own setting in the* **Percent** *box.*

- **Click on the OK button.**

The dialog box is closed, and the document appears at 75% of the default screen size.

21.3

- **Click on the down arrow at the right side of the Zoom box on the Standard toolbar.**

The box is expanded, and a list of magnification options is displayed.

- **Click on 100%.**

NOTE: *Modifying the screen size of a document does not affect the actual (printed) size of the document.*

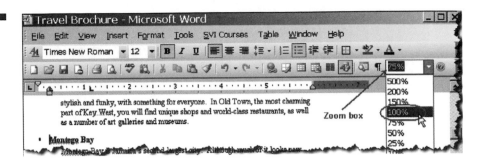

Using the Spelling and Grammar Checker

To **perform a spelling and grammar check** (on a **completed document**):

- Choose the **Tools, Spelling and Grammar** command, or click on the **Spelling and Grammar** button on the Standard toolbar.
- In the Spelling and Grammar dialog box, which is subsequently displayed when a possible spelling or grammatical error is encountered, choose the appropriate option:

  - **Ignore Once**—which skips the flagged entry.
  - **Ignore All**—which skips the flagged entry and all other occurrences of that entry. (This option is available only when a possible spelling error is encountered.)
  - **Ignore Rule**—which skips the flagged entry and all other occurrences of that entry. (This option is available only when a grammatical error is encountered.)
  - **Next Sentence**—which skips the flagged entry and continues by checking the next sentence. (This option is available only when a grammatical error is encountered.)
  - **Change**—which replaces the flagged entry with the alternate entry you have selected or typed.
  - **Change All**—which replaces the flagged entry and all other occurrences of that entry with the alternate entry you have selected or typed. (This option is available only when a possible spelling error is encountered.)
  - **Add to Dictionary**—which skips the flagged entry and adds the entry to a specific Spelling dictionary. (This option is available only when a possible spelling error is encountered.)
  - **AutoCorrect**—which replaces the flagged entry with the alternate entry you have selected or typed and adds the entry to the AutoCorrect dictionary. (This option is available only when a possible spelling error is encountered.)
  - **Delete**—which deletes the flagged entry. (This option is available only when a repeated word is encountered.)

SPELLING AND GRAMMAR BUTTON

Objective

In this exercise, you will **use the Spelling and Grammar Checker to correct spelling and grammatical errors in an existing document**. (In this case, it will not be necessary for you to disable the Spelling and Grammar Checker, if it is enabled, since you will only correct text in the document. You will not enter any new text.)

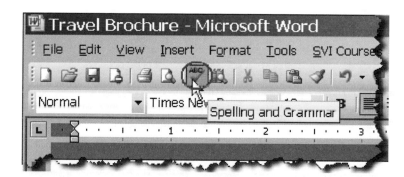

22.1

- **Click on the Spelling and Grammar button on the Standard toolbar.**

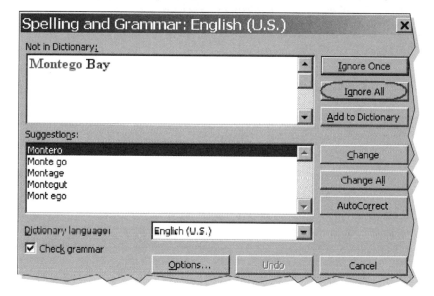

22.2

The Spelling and Grammar dialog box is displayed and "Montego" is flagged. Notice that the possible correct words are listed in the Suggestions box. Since this word is correct, you will not change it.

- **Click on the Ignore All button.**

- **Using the procedure above, check the entire document and make sure that you have not mistyped any word.**

- **When a message box appears, informing you that the operation is complete, click on the OK button.**

- **Save the document**

Using a Word Template to Create a Document

A **template** is a preformatted model on which other documents are based. Word provides a number of templates for setting up business letters, faxes, memos, and many other types of documents in a number of visually-pleasing formats. These templates cannot only simplify, and therefore speed up, the document creation process; they can help you maintain a standard format for each type of document you produce.

[Click here and type return address and phone and fax numbers]

Company Name Here

To: [Click here and type name]   **From:**   [Click here and type name]

Fax: [Click here and type fax number]   **Pages:** [Click here and type # of pages]

Phone: [Click here and type phone number]   **Date:**   5/22/2005

Re: [Click here and type subject of fax]   **CC:**   [Click here and type name]

☐ **Urgent**   ☐ **For Review**   ☐ **Please Comment**   ☐ **Please Reply**   ☐ **Please Recycle**

● **Comments:** To save changes to this template for future use, on the File menu, click **Save As**. In the **Save As Type** box, choose **Document Template** (the filename extensions should change from *.doc* to *.dot*) and save the template. Next time you want to use the updated template, on the **File** menu, click **New**. In the **New Document** task pane, under **Templates**, click **On my computer**. In the **Templates** dialog, your updated template will appear on the General tab.

WORD TEMPLATE

If no template is specified when you begin a new document (for example, when you click on the New Blank Document button), the program bases the document on the default **Normal** (Blank Document) template.

To **base a new document on a template** (other than the default template):

- Choose the **File**, **New** command.
- In the New Document task pane (under **Templates**), select the **On my computer** option.
- On the appropriate panel of the Templates dialog box, select the desired **template**.
- Click on the **OK** button.

Notes

1. In addition to templates, the Templates dialog box includes a number of Word **wizards**. A wizard is similar to a template in that it produces a custom, ready-to-complete, document. Wizards, however, allow you to choose from various layout options and prompt you for document content, while templates merely provide a preset layout.
2. The Microsoft Office Online Web site also provides a number of templates from which you can choose. To access these templates, select the **Templates on Office Online** option in the New Document task pane.

Objective

In this exercise, you will **use a Word template to create a fax**.

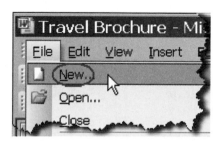

23.1

- **Choose the File, New command.**

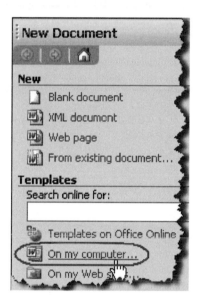

23.2

If you have task pane, choose View, Task Pane and then click on Create a new document.

- **Under Templates, click on On my computer.**

The Templates dialog box is displayed.

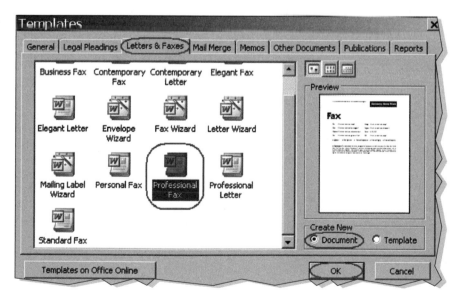

23.3

- **Click on the Letters & Faxes tab.**

- **Make sure that Document (under Create New) is selected.**

- **Click on the Professional Fax icon and then click on the OK button.**

*The dialog box is closed, and the template is opened in Print Layout view. Notice that the template includes several **placeholders** for text. You will create the actual fax by entering text into these placeholders.*

23.4

- **Select the text Company Name Here.**

  Type: KS Travel Agency

The placeholder text is replaced with the company name.

- **Click in the placeholder that reads Click here and type return address and phone and fax numbers.**

  Type: 444 Bridge Street, Suite A and press [ENTER].

  Type: San Francisco, CA 94121 and press [ENTER].

  Type: (415) 222-3333

The placeholder text is replaced with the company address and telephone number.

- **Using a procedure similar to that described above, replace the following placeholders as indicated:**

To:	**Luisa Lopez**
Fax:	**(213) 444-5555**
Phone:	**(213) 666-7777**
Re:	**Western Caribbean**
From:	**(Enter your name)**
Pages:	**2, including cover sheet**

NOTE: *The Date placeholder should display today's date.*

- **Select the CC placeholder (the label and the placeholder text). Then press [DEL].**

The CC placeholder is deleted.

- **Select the Comments placeholder (the bullet, the label and the placeholder text). Then press [DEL].**

The Comments placeholder is also deleted.

- **Point to the Urgent check box, and double-click the mouse button.**

The Urgent check box is selected, and the cover sheet is now complete.

- **Click on the Save button and save it as KS FAX.**

- **Close the file.**

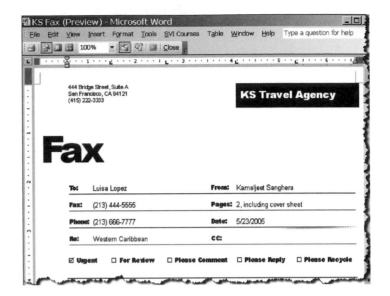

Displaying Help Information

If you encounter a problem or just need additional information while using Word, there are a number of ways in which you can obtain help.

The program itself includes an extensive **Help system**, which can be accessed in the following ways:

- By choosing the **Help, Microsoft Office Word Help** command or by clicking on the **Microsoft Office Word Help** button on the Standard toolbar. Doing this displays the Word Help task pane in which you enter one or more keywords and click on the **Start searching** button.
- By entering a request in the **Type a question for help** box and by pressing **[ENTER]**.

**MICROSOFT OFFICE WORD HELP BUTTON /
TYPE A QUESTION FOR HELP BOX**

You can also get help:

- By clicking on the **Table of Contents** option in the Word Help task pane. Doing this displays a list of Help topics in a table of contents format.
- By clicking on the **Connect to Microsoft Office Online** option in the Word Help task pane. Doing this displays the Microsoft Office Online Home page (assuming you have access to the Internet).

Notes

1. The Microsoft Office Online Web site provides a number of resources for users of Microsoft Office products, including "how-to" articles to assist the user in performing various tasks, interactive training tutorials to help the user become more familiar with the programs he or she is running, and various downloads (for example, templates, clip art and product upgrades).

2. The Office Assistant, which is displayed by choosing the **Help, Show the Office Assistant** command, can provide tips and other helpful information as you work. When the Office Assistant has a tip, a light bulb will appear. To display the tip, simply click on this light bulb. To control the type of information the Office Assistant provides, click on the Office Assistant icon, and click on the **Options** button in the balloon that appears. Then, on the Options panel of the Office Assistant dialog box, select/deselect the relevant options, and click on the **OK** button.

Objective

In this exercise, you will **access the Word Help system and display help information for various topics**.

24.1

- **Click on the Microsoft Office Word Help** 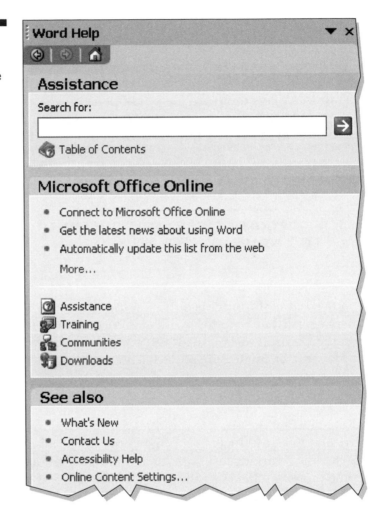 **button on the Standard toolbar.**

- **Type: Indent a paragraph**

- **Click on the Start searching** ➔ **button.**

A list of topics is displayed in Search Results task pane.

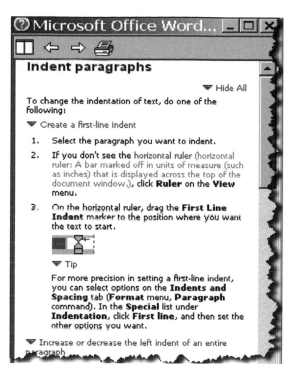

- **Click on Indent paragraphs.**

The Microsoft Office Word Help window is opened, displaying a list of subtopics.

NOTE: *If the Search Results task pane no longer appears, click on the **Auto Tile** button on the toolbar of the Microsoft Office Word Help window. If necessary, resize the two open windows.*

- **Click on Create a first-line indent.**

The selected subtopic is expanded, and instructions for performing the selected operation are displayed.

- **In the help information, click on the words horizontal ruler (which appear in blue).**

The definition of "horizontal ruler" is displayed.

- **Click again on the words horizontal ruler.**

The definition of "horizontal ruler" no longer appears.

- **Click on Show All (in the upper-right corner of the Microsoft Office Word Help window).**

All subtopics are expanded.

NOTE: *You can print the current help information by using the **Print** button on the toolbar of the Microsoft Office Word Help window.*

- **Scroll through the help information by clicking on the down arrow on the scroll bar of the Microsoft Office Word Help window.**

The Application window is reactivated.

24.3

- **Click in any empty area of the Application window.**

- **Click on the Back button at the top of the Search Results task pane.**

The Word Help task pane is redisplayed.

- **Click on the Close button on the Title bar of the Microsoft Office Word Help window.**

- **Click in the Type a question for help box (which appears in the upper-right corner of the Application window).**

An insertion point appears in the box.

- **Type: Print a document Press [ENTER].**

A list of topics is displayed in the Search Results task pane.

NOTE: *Notice that you did not enter an actual question in the Type a question for help box. Instead, you simply entered the action "Print a document." (You could have entered the question "How do I print a document?" Doing so, however, would have displayed the same list of topics.)*

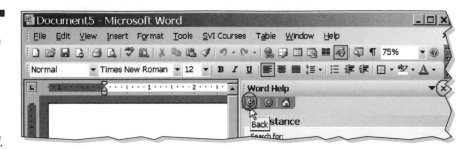

24.4

- **Click on Print a document.**

- **Click in any empty area of the Application window.**

- **In the task pane, click on Print an envelope that is attached to a document.**

- **Click on the Back button on the toolbar of the Microsoft Office Word Help window.**

- **Click on the Close button on the Title bar of the Microsoft Office Word Help window.**

- **Click on the Close button at the top of the Search Results task pane.**

Exiting from Word

When you are finished using Word, you can exit from the program either by choosing the **File**, **Exit** command or by clicking on the **Close** button on the Title bar of the Application window. If you have not saved changes in a document, you will be prompted to indicate whether or not you want to save those changes before exiting.

Objective

In this exercise, you will **exit from Word**.

- Choose the **File**, **Exit** command.

A prompt box appears, asking you if you want to save the changes in the document.

- Click on the **Yes** button, if you want to save the changes.

The program is exited, and the Windows desktop is redisplayed.

Congratulations! You have completed the Case Study.

Conclusion

You have just completed **Microsoft Office Word 2003—Case Study 1**. In the case study, you were introduced to many techniques. To reinforce your understanding of these techniques, it is recommended that you read and work through it once again.

Further Practice

The following Case Study will give you the opportunity to review and practice many of the Word features you have learned.

1. Make sure that all documents are closed. Then display a **blank document**.
2. **Reset** both the **left margin** and **right margin** to **1.5"**.
3. Press [**ENTER**] **six** times to insert six blank lines. **Reset** the **font size** to **18**. Then type the following and **bold** and **horizontally center** the **title**:

> CAREFREE TRAVEL
> EUROPEAN VACATION

4. **Restore** the default **font size** (**12**). Then **insert** a **hard page break**.
5. Type the following on a **second page**, paying close attention to attributes that have been applied as well as to the alignment of text:

WEEK ONE

The first week of your vacation will be spent in London. Please note that the cost will depend on the particular hotel and number of optional tours you choose.

The following hotels are available:

Hotel	Location	Price Per Night
King George	Mayfair	$350.00
Buckingham	Westminster	$200.00
Regents	Earls Court	$140.00
Budget Inn	Fulham	$95.00

The following optional tours are available:

Boat Cruise

Cruise the Thames River from *Westminster Pier* to *Hampton Court*. The tour includes a *light lunch*. Cost: $54.00

London by Day

Spend the day seeing the city's *major sights*. The tour includes admission to the *Tower of London* and *Westminster Abbey*. Cost: $75.00

London by Night

Spend an evening dining in one of the city's *major restaurant*s. The tour includes a ticket to a *West End production* and *after-theater refreshments*. Cost: $125.00

---

6. **Save** the **document** in a file named **European Vacation.doc**.
7. **Insert** a **hard page break**. Then type the following on the **third page**:

Terms and Conditions

This tour is subject to the following terms and conditions:

- Payment must be received at least thirty days prior to departure.
- Cancellation within one week of departure will be subject to a 10% charge.
- Travel insurance is available as an optional extra.
- Carefree Travel is not responsible for flight delays or other changes in travel arrangements.

---

8. **Save** the **changes**.
9. **Preview**, and then **print** the **document**.
10. **Close** the **file**.

MS Word 2003
Case Study 2

After successfully completing this case study, you should be able to:

- Insert a section break in a document
- Change the orientation of a page (Portrait/ Landscape)
- Create and format a table
- Delete rows/columns in a table
- Insert a chart into a document

- Modify a created chart
- Create newsletter-style columns in a document
- Add a border and shading to text
- Add a header/footer and page numbers to a document

Case Study 2—MS Word 2003

Assume that you work in the Sales department of an auto-parts company. You are asked to create an annual report for the department meeting next week. The report should include each model's sales performance in the USA and the Company's news on new products.

The desired annual report is one page long with a cover page:

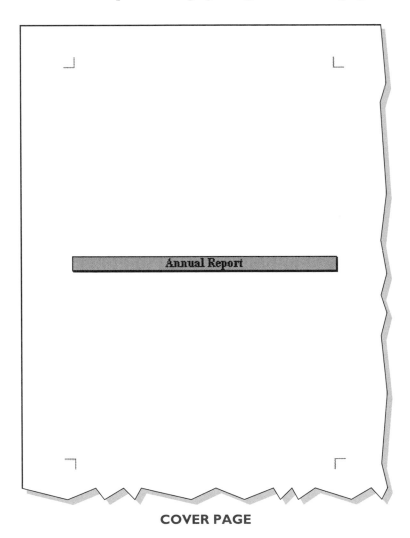

COVER PAGE

The following table shows an increase in sales:

USA SALES

	NORTH	SOUTH	EAST
Model A	340	390	430
Model AA	350	420	470
Model B	360	450	490
Model C	400	480	530
Model D	410	525	580

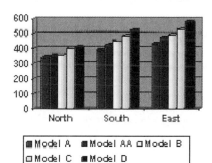

Company News

NEW PRODUCTS

During the next two months we plan to introduce several new products.

Each of these products will be supported by an extensive newspaper, television and advertising campaign. More information will follow.

WORLDWIDE SALES

Our company has experienced record worldwide sales in the second and third quarters.

Congratulations to the entire staff, who will receive a well-deserved bonus at the end of the year!

I. Creating a Multiple-Section Document

When you begin a new document, that document initially consists of one **section**. All page settings (for example, margins, paper size and page orientation) affect the entire document.

There may be times, however, when you will want to apply particular page settings to specific paragraphs, or to a specific page, of a document. For example, you may wish to have a table printed in landscape orientation but retain the default portrait orientation for printing the remainder of the document. This can be accomplished by inserting one or more **section breaks** to divide the document into multiple sections.

To **insert a section break into a document**:

- Choose the **Insert**, **Break** command.
- In the Break dialog box, select the desired **section break** option:

  - **Next page**—which begins the new section on a new page.
  - **Continuous**—which begins the new section on the same page.
  - **Even page**—which begins the new section on the next even-numbered page. If the current page is even-numbered, a blank page is inserted before the break.
  - **Odd page**—which begins the new section on the next odd-numbered page. If the current page is odd-numbered, a blank page is inserted before the break.

- Click on the **OK** button.

Objective

In this exercise, you will **create a document containing two sections by inserting a section break**. You will then **apply different page settings on those two sections**.

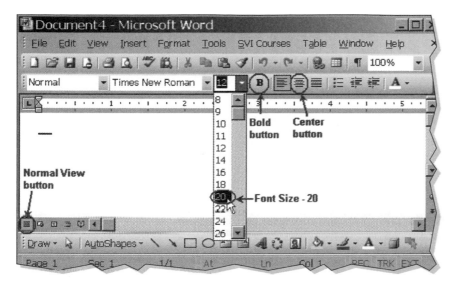

- **Click on the Start button on the Windows taskbar.**
- **Point to All Programs (if you are running Windows XP) or to Programs (if you are running Windows 2000).**
- **Point to Microsoft Office on the menu.**
- **Click on Microsoft Office Word 2003 on the submenu.**

A blank document is displayed.

- **Click on the Normal View button above the Status bar.**

You will now create a title page.

- **Click on the down arrow at the right side of the Font Size box on the Formatting toolbar. Then click on 20 in the list of font sizes.**

The font size is increased.

- **Click on the Bold button on the Formatting toolbar.**

The bold attribute is turned on.

- **Click on the Center button on the Formatting toolbar.**

The insertion point moves to the center of the line.

- **Type: Annual Report Press [ENTER].**

A large bolded and centered title is entered, and the insertion point moves to the next line.

- **Expand the Font Size box, and click on 12.**
- **Click on the Bold button to turn off the bold attribute.**
- **Click on the Align Left button on the Formatting toolbar.**

The insertion point moves back to the left margin.

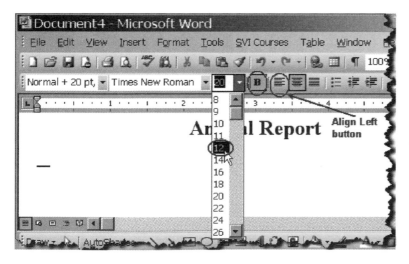

1.3

You will now insert a section break.

- **Choose the Insert, Break command.**

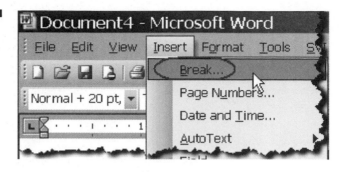

1.4

The Break dialog box is displayed.

- **Under Section break types, click on Next page. Then click on the OK button.**

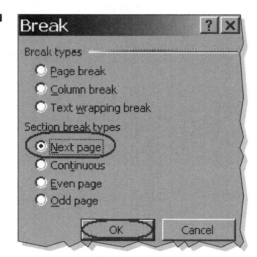

1.5

- **Type: The following table shows an increase in sales:**

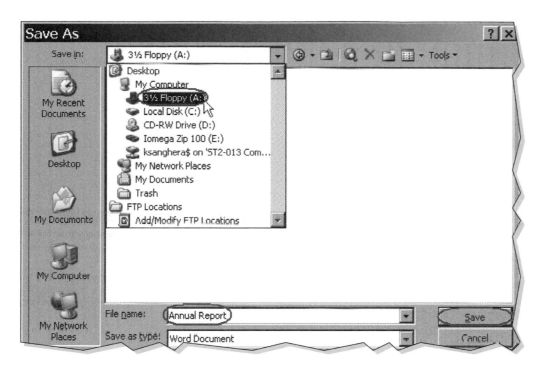

- **Click on the Save button on the Standard toolbar.**

The Save As dialog box is displayed.

- **Expand Save in box and select 3½ Floppy (A:).**

- **Type: Annual Report for File name.**

The filename is entered.

NOTE: *The program will add the default extension (doc) to the filename. This extension may or may not appear in file listings on your screen.*

- **Choose the Save button (in the dialog box).**

NOTE: *You can "choose" a button either by clicking on it or by pressing [**ENTER**].*

The dialog box is closed, and the document is saved in a file named Annual Report.doc.

- **Press [CTRL] + [HOME].**

The insertion point moves to the beginning of page 1. You will now set the necessary option to vertically center the title on this page.

1.7

- **Choose the File, Page Setup command.**

The Page Setup dialog box is displayed.

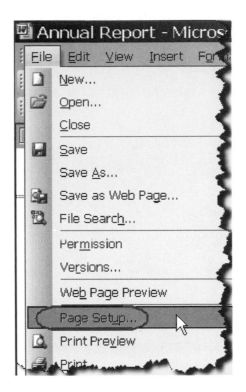

1.8

- **Click on the Layout tab.**

The Layout panel of the dialog box is displayed.

- **Under Page, expand the Vertical alignment box, and click on Center. Then click on the OK button.**

The new alignment is selected, and the dialog box is closed.

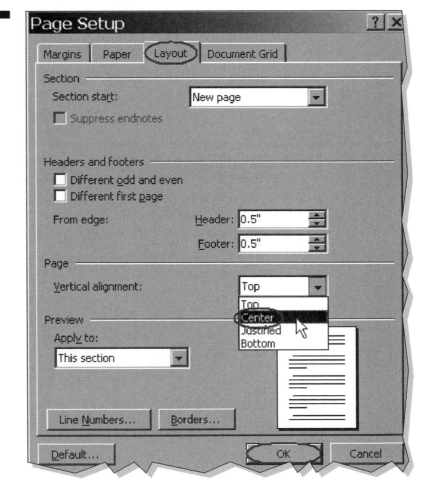

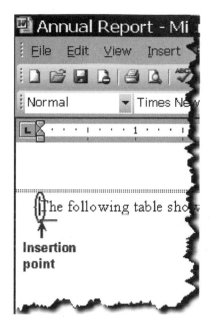

Insertion point

1.9

The section break divides a page into two pages.

- **Move the insertion point to the beginning of page 2.**

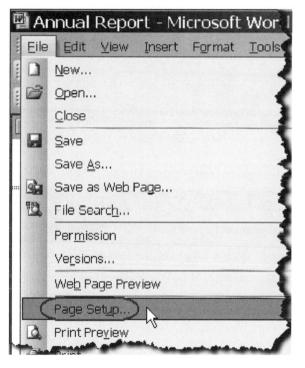

1.10

You will now set the necessary option to print this page in landscape orientation.

- **Choose the File, Page Setup command.**

1.11

The Page Setup dialog box is redisplayed.

- **Click on the Margins tab.**

The Margins panel of the dialog box is displayed.

- **Under Orientation, click on the Landscape option. Then click on the OK button.**

The new orientation is selected, and the dialog box is closed.

- **Save the document.**

- **Press [CTRL] + [HOME].**

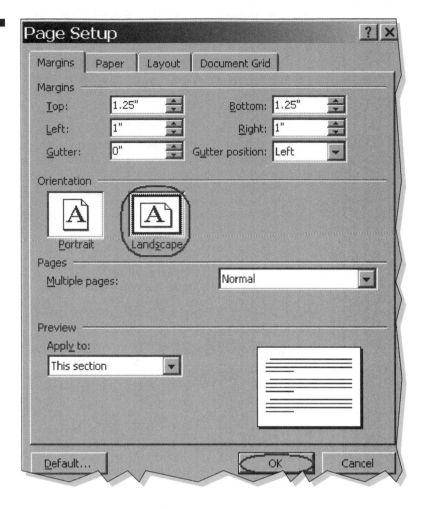

1.12

The insertion point moves back to the beginning of page 1. You will now preview the document.

- **Click on the Print Preview button on the Standard toolbar.**

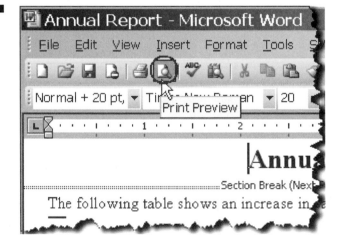

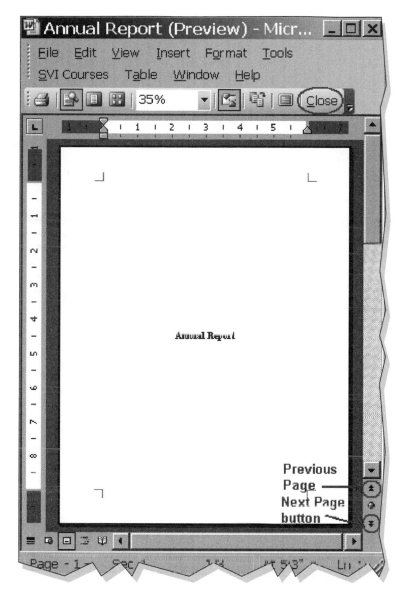

1.13

A full-page view of page 1 is displayed in the Print Preview window. Notice the horizontal and vertical centering of the text.

NOTE: *If more than one page appears in this window, click on the One Page*

button on the toolbar of the Print Preview window.

- **Click on the Next Page button at the bottom of the Vertical scroll bar.**

A full-page view of page 2 is displayed.

- **Click on the Previous Page button at the bottom of the Vertical scroll bar**

Page 1 is redisplayed.

- **Click on the Close Preview button on the toolbar of the Print Preview window.**

The Print Preview window is closed.

Setting up a Table

This section discusses Word's **Table** feature. In it, you will learn how to:

- **Insert** a **table** into a document.
- **Format** a **table**.
- **Insert** and **delete rows/columns** in a table.
- **Use Table AutoFormat**.

Inserting a Table into a Document

You should already be familiar with one method for creating a table—that of aligning information on tab stops. Word's **Table** feature provides an alternate and more powerful means of creating a table. Using this feature, you can display information in a tabular (row/column) arrangement similar to that of a spreadsheet.

To **insert a table into a document**:

- Choose the **Table, Insert, Table** command.
- In the Insert Table dialog box, specify the number of **columns** and **rows** the table is to include.
- Click on the **OK** button.
- Enter the information into the empty table that appears.

Alternatively, you can insert an empty table by clicking on the **Insert Table** button on the Standard toolbar and by dragging the mouse pointer over the grid that appears to select the desired number of columns and rows.

INSERT TABLE BUTTON

Objective

In this exercise, you will **create a table of numeric information**.

2.1

- **Press [CTRL] + [END].**

The insertion point moves to the end of page 2.

- **Press [ENTER] two times.**

- **Click on the Bold button.**

- **Type: USA SALES**
  Press [ENTER]. Then click again on the Bold button to turn off the bold attribute.

- **Choose the Table, Insert command, followed by Table.**

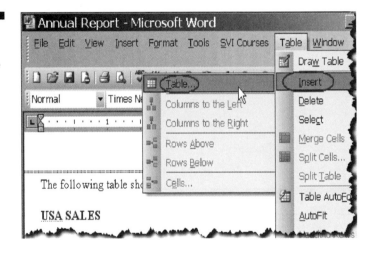

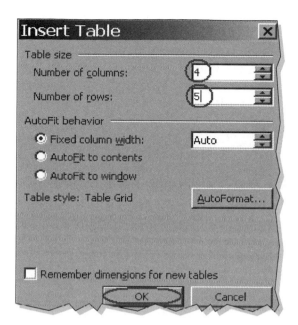

The Insert Table dialog box is displayed.

- **Type: 4 in the text box for number of columns. Press [TAB].**

- **Type: 5 in the text box for number of rows**

- **Choose the OK button.**

NOTE: You can "choose" a button either by clicking on it or by pressing [**ENTER**].

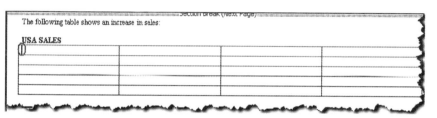

The dialog box is closed, and an empty table with four columns and five rows is displayed. The insertion point should be located in the first cell.

- **Enter the table information illustrated in the screen shot, and save the document.**

NOTE: You can move from cell to cell by pressing [**TAB**] or the [**ARROW**] keys. You can also move to a specific cell by clicking in that cell. **Do not** press [**ENTER**] when entering data into the table.

Formatting a Table

Word provides a number of options for formatting both the entries in a table and the structure of the table itself. These options can not only add visual interest to a table, they can also make the information easier to read and understand.

The methods for applying attributes (for example, bold and italic) to table entries are same as the methods for performing those operations on text in any other part of a document. Formatting the structure of a table (for example, adjusting the column width and/or row height, modifying the table borders and shading cells) is accomplished by using the methods described below.

To **adjust the width of one or more columns in a table**:

- Select the column(s) that is/are to be adjusted.
- Choose the **Table**, **Table Properties** command, or select the **Table Properties** option on the shortcut menu.
- On the Column panel of the Table Properties dialog box, specify the **new column width**.
- Click on the **OK** button.

Notes

You can also adjust the width of a single column by **dragging** the column border.

To **adjust the height of one or more rows in a table**:

- Select the row(s) that is/are to be adjusted.
- Choose the **Table**, **Table Properties** command, or select the **Table Properties** option on the shortcut menu.
- On the Row panel of the Table Properties dialog box, specify the **new row height**.
- Click on the **OK** button.

Notes

You can also adjust the height of a single row by **dragging** the row border. (To use this method, the table must appear in Print Layout view.)

In addition to the above methods, you can have Word automatically adjust column width and/or row height in a table by using the **Table, AutoFit** command. Choosing this command displays a submenu of options that include **AutoFit to Contents**, which increases or decreases the width of all columns to accommodate the longest entry in each column, **Distribute Columns Evenly**, which applies the same width to all or selected columns while retaining the overall width of those columns, and **Distribute Rows Evenly**, which applies the same height to all or selected rows while retaining the overall height of those rows.

To **modify the borders of a table**:

- Select the table, or simply position the insertion point in any cell in the table.
- Choose the **Format**, **Borders and Shading** command, or select the **Borders and Shading** option on the shortcut menu.
- On the Borders panel of the Borders and Shading dialog box, select the **border type**. Then select a **style**, **color** and **width** for that type.
- Click on the **OK** button.

Notes

You can also use the above method to modify the borders of individual cells in a table. In this case, you should select the cell(s) that is/are to be formatted before displaying the Borders and Shading dialog box.

To **shade one or more cells in a table**:

- Select the cell(s) that is/are to be shaded.
- Choose the **Format, Borders and Shading** command, or select the **Borders and Shading** option on the shortcut menu.
- On the Shading panel of the Borders and Shading dialog box, select a **fill color** and **pattern**.
- Click on the **OK** button.

Objective

In this exercise, you will **format your new table**. Specifically, you will 1) bold and align various entries, 2) decrease the width of each column, 3) increase the height of the first row, 4) modify the table borders, and 5) shade various cells.

This exercise also demonstrates the use of the **Edit, Repeat…** command, which repeats the last edit operation performed in a document.

The following table shows an increase in sales.

USA SALES

	North	South
Model A	340	390
Model B	360	450
Model C	400	480
Model D	410	525

3.1

- **Point to the first cell (in the upper-left corner of the table). Press and hold down the mouse button, and drag the mouse pointer to the last cell of the first column. Then release the mouse button.**

USA SALES

Model A
Model B
Model C
Model D

3.2

- **Click on the Bold button.**

The column headings are bolded.

USA SALES

	North	South	East
Model A	340	390	430
Model B	360	450	490
Model C	400	480	530
Model D	410	525	580

3.3

You will now bold the column headings.

- **Point to the first cell (in the upper-left corner of the table). Press and hold down the mouse button, and drag the mouse pointer to the last cell of first row. Then release the mouse button.**

3.4

- **Choose the Edit, Repeat Bold command.**

The previous edit operation is repeated, and the row headings are also bolded.

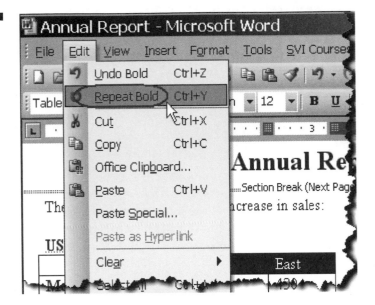

3.5

You will now center the column headings.

*Make sure that **column headings** are still selected.*

- **Point to the selected headings and right-click the mouse button. Then point to Cell Alignment on the shortcut menu that appears.**

A list of alignment options is displayed.

- **Click on the Middle Center Align option.**

The column headings are centered in their respective cells.

NOTE: *You can also use the Center button on the Formatting toolbar to horizontally center table entries. Using the Cell Alignment, Middle Center Align option sequence, however, centers table entries both horizontally and vertically. The vertical centering will become apparent when you increase the row height in a later step.*

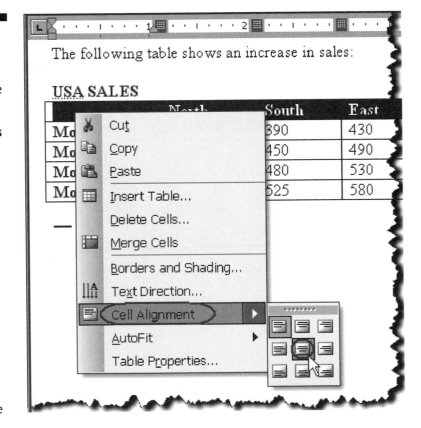

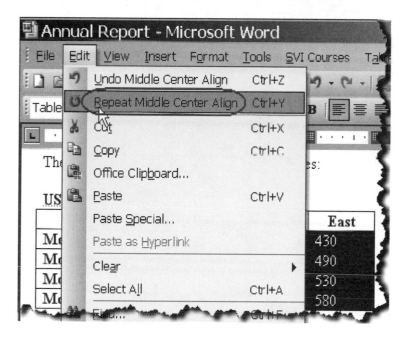

USA SALES

	North	South	East
Model A	340	390	430
Model B	360	450	490
Model C	400	480	530
Model D	410	525	580

3.6

You will now center the numeric entries.

- **Using the above procedure, select the numeric entries in the table.**

3.7

- **Choose the Edit, Repeat Middle Center Align command.**

The numeric entries are also centered.

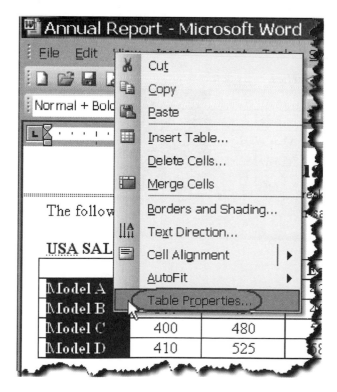

3.8

You will now decrease the width of the first column.

- **Select the first column of the table.**

- **Right click on the selected columns and click on Table Properties.**

3.9

The Tables Properties dialog box is displayed.

- **Click on the Column tab.**

The Column panel of the dialog box is displayed.

- **Under Column 1, make sure that the check box for the Preferred Width is checked.**

- **Click on the down arrow at the right side of the Preferred width box until the setting reads 1". Then click on the OK button.**

The dialog box is closed, and the width of the selected column is decreased.

- **Cancel the selection (by clicking the left mouse button anywhere in the page).**

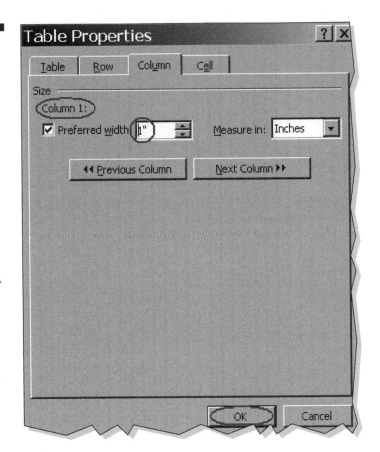

3.10

You will now simultaneously decrease the width of the three remaining columns.

- **Select the second, third and fourth columns of the table. Point to the selected columns and right-click the mouse button. Then click on Table Properties on the shortcut menu that appears.**

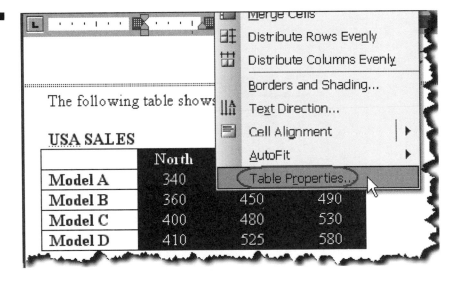

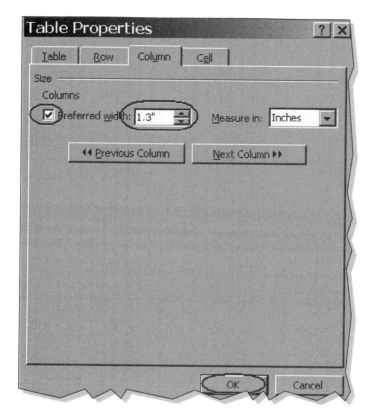

The Table Properties dialog box is redisplayed.

- **Under Columns tab, click on the Preferred width check box and then click on the down arrow at the right side of the Preferred width box until the setting reads 1.3".**

NOTE: You can also type the preferred width in the box (for example, type 1.3 in the Preferred width box). Then click on the OK button.

The dialog box is closed, and the width of each of the selected columns is decreased.

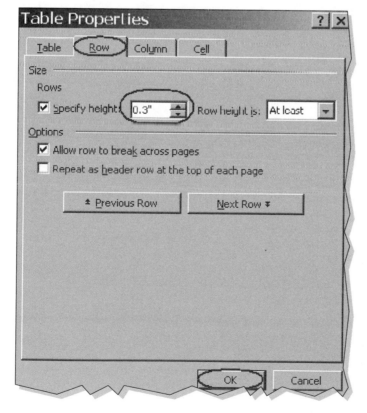

You will now increase the height of the first row.

- **Select the first row of the table. Point to the selected row and right-click the mouse button. Then click on Table Properties on the shortcut menu that appears.**

The Table Properties dialog box is once again displayed.

- **Click on the Row tab.**

*Make sure that the check box for the **Specify Height** is checked.*

- **Click on the up arrow at the right side of the Specify height box until the setting reads 0.3". Then click on the OK button.**

The dialog box is closed, and the height of the selected row is increased. You will now modify the table borders.

3.13

- **Select the entire table. Then choose the Format, Borders and Shading command.**

The Borders panel of the Borders and Shading dialog box is displayed.

NOTE: *Notice that the All option (under Setting) is selected, by default. Therefore, all gridlines of the table, including the outer border, will be affected.*

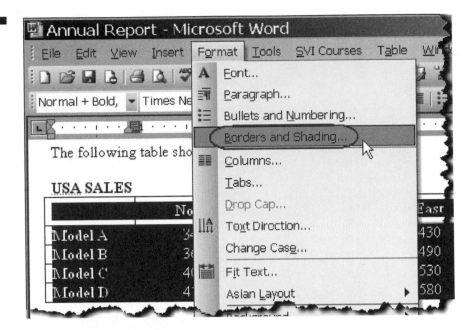

3.14

- **Expand the Width box, and click on the 1½ pt line. Then click on the OK button.**

The dialog box is closed, and the width of the table borders is increased.

- **Cancel the selection.**

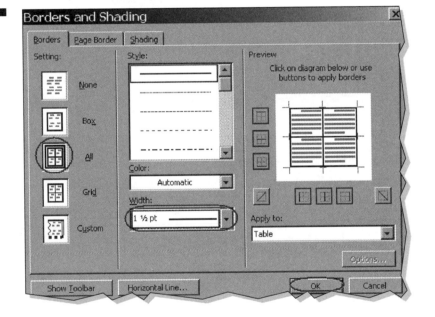

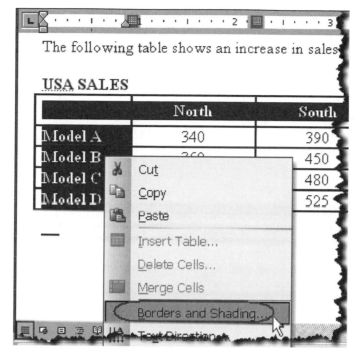

3.15

You will now shade the cells in which the column and row headings appear.

- **Select the column headings. Press and hold down [CTRL]. Select the row headings. Then release [CTRL].**

Two blocks of cells are selected.

NOTE: *This step demonstrates the [CTRL] key method for selecting multiple blocks of cells in a table. You can also use this method to select individual cells that are non-contiguous.*

- **Point to any of the selected entries, and right-click the mouse button. Then click on Borders and Shading on the shortcut menu that appears.**

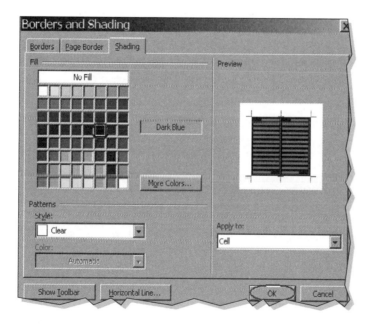

3.16

The Borders and Shading dialog box is redisplayed.

- **Click on the Shading tab.**

The Shading panel of the dialog box is displayed.

- **In the palette of Fill options, click on the Dark Blue option (the sixth option in the fourth row). Then click on the OK button.**

The dialog box is closed, and the shading is applied to the selected cells.

- **Cancel the selection.**
- **Save the document.**

Inserting and Deleting Rows/Columns in a Table

You can also modify the structure of a table by inserting and deleting both rows and columns.

To **insert a row at the end of a table** (below the last row):

- Move the insertion point to the **last cell** in the table.
- Press [**TAB**].

To **insert one or more rows within a table**:

- Select the number of rows you wish to insert. The selection should be immediately above or below where the new row(s) is/are to appear.
- Do one of the following:

  - Choose the **Table, Insert, Rows Above** command, or click on the **Insert Rows** button on the Standard toolbar, to insert the new row(s) immediately above the selected row(s); or
  - Choose the **Table, Insert, Rows Below** command to insert the new row(s) immediately below the selected row(s).

INSERT ROWS BUTTON

To **insert one or more columns within a table**:

- Select the number of columns you wish to insert. The selection should be immediately to the right of or to the left of where the new column(s) is/are to appear.
- Do one of the following:

  - Choose the **Table, Insert, Columns to the Left** command, or click on the **Insert Columns** button on the Standard toolbar, to insert the new column(s) to the immediate left of the selected column(s); or
  - Choose the **Table, Insert, Columns to the Right** command to insert the new column(s) to the immediate right of the selected column(s).

INSERT COLUMNS BUTTON

To **delete one or more rows or columns from a table**:

- Select the row(s) or column(s) that is/are to be deleted.
- Choose the **Table, Delete, Rows** command or the **Table, Delete, Columns** command.

Objective

In this exercise, you will **insert a new row and a new column into a table**. You will then **delete the new column**. You will also delete, and then restore, a row.

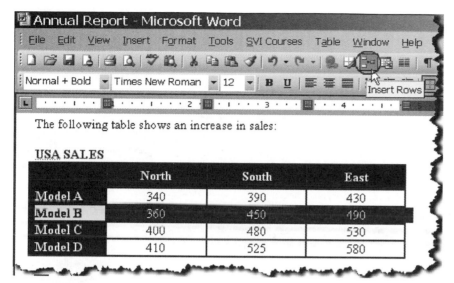

4.1

- **Select the third row of the table (which includes information for Model B). You will now insert a new row immediately above this row.**

- **Click on the Insert Rows button on the Standard toolbar.**

ALTERNATIVE: You can choose Table, Insert, Rows Above from the menu bar.

4.2

A blank row is inserted.

- **Click in the first cell in the new row.**
  Type: Model AA
  Press [TAB].
  Type: 350
  Press [TAB].
  Type: 420
  Press [TAB].
  Type: 470

Data is entered into the new row. Notice that each new entry includes the same formatting as other entries in the column.

- **Select the fourth column of the table (which includes information for the East region).**

4.3

You will now insert a column to the right of the selected column.

- **Choose the Table, Insert command, followed by Columns to the Right.**

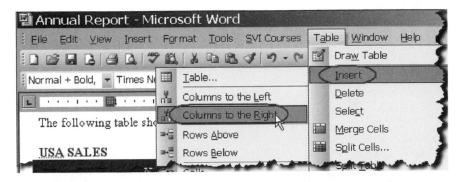

4.4

A blank column is inserted.

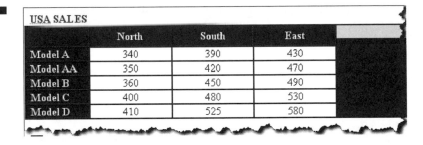

USA SALES	North	South	East	
Model A	340	390	430	
Model AA	350	420	470	
Model B	360	450	490	
Model C	400	480	530	
Model D	410	525	580	

4.5

You will now delete the blank column.

- **Make sure that the new column is still selected. Then choose the Table, Delete command, followed by Columns.**

The selected column is deleted.

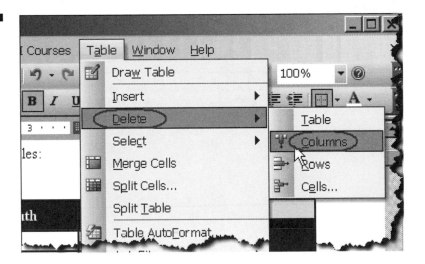

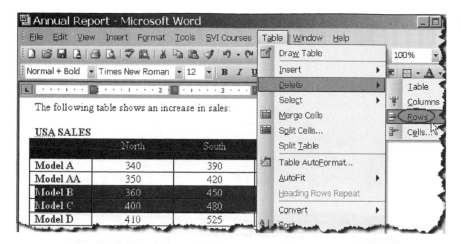

4.6

You will now delete, and then restore a row.

- **Select the fourth and fifth rows of the table (which include information for Models B and C). Then choose the Table, Delete command, followed by Rows.**

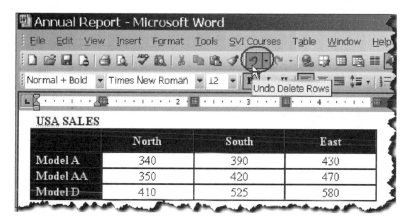

4.7

The selected rows are deleted.

- **Click on the Undo button, and Cancel the selection.**

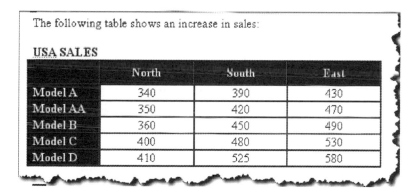

4.8

The deleted rows are restored.

- **Save the document.**

Using Table AutoFormat

Word's **Table AutoFormat** feature allows you to apply, in one operation, a predefined group of format options (for example, border, shading and other enhancement settings) to a table. The feature is accessed with the **Table, Table AutoFormat** command or the **Table AutoFormat** option on the shortcut menu.

Objective

In this exercise, you will **use Table AutoFormat to format the current table**.

5.1

- **Select the entire table.**

- **Point to any cell in the table, and right-click the mouse button. Then click on Table AutoFormat on the shortcut menu that appears.**

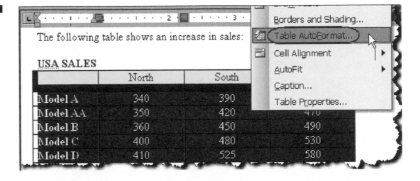

5.2

The Table AutoFormat dialog box is displayed.

- **In the Table styles box, click on Table Elegant.**

The table style is selected and is previewed in the area below the Table styles box.

- **Under Apply special formats to, click on Last row and on Last column to deselect those options.**

The special formatting that has been applied to the last column and last row is removed. This formatting is unnecessary since your table does not include a total row or total column.

- **Click on the Apply button.**

The dialog box is closed, and the selected table style is applied to the table.

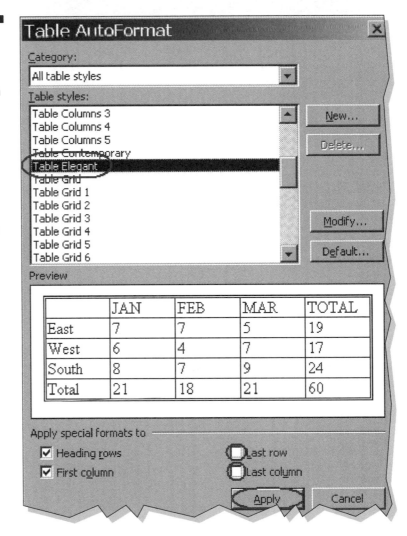

5.3

- **Cancel the selection.**

- **Save the document.**

USA SALES

	NORTH	SOUTH	EAST
Model A	340	390	430
Model AA	350	420	470
Model B	360	450	490
Model C	400	480	530
Model D	410	525	580

Creating Charts and Diagrams

This section discusses **additional ways in which you can visually enhance your documents**. In it, you will learn how to:

- **Insert** a **chart** into a document.
- **Modify** a **chart**.

Inserting a Chart into a Document

Included with Word is a program called **Microsoft Graph**, which allows you to graphically represent data in the form of a **chart**. Charts are often used to provide a visual picture of the information.

To **insert a chart into a document** (to represent **data of a Word table**).

- Select the table entries that are to be represented.
- Choose the **Insert**, **Picture**, **Chart** command. Doing this displays the chart in the Microsoft Graph window. A datasheet showing the selected entries also appears.
- Optionally, **modify** the **datasheet**. Then click on the **Close** button in the datasheet window.

Notes

1. You can also access Microsoft Graph by choosing the **Insert**, **Object** command and by selecting the **Microsoft Graph Chart** option in the Object dialog box.
2. You can also create a chart that represents data other than that in a Word table. To do this, choose the **Insert**, **Picture**, **Chart** command, and manually enter the appropriate data into the datasheet that appears.

Objective

In this exercise, you will **create a chart representing data in a Word table**.

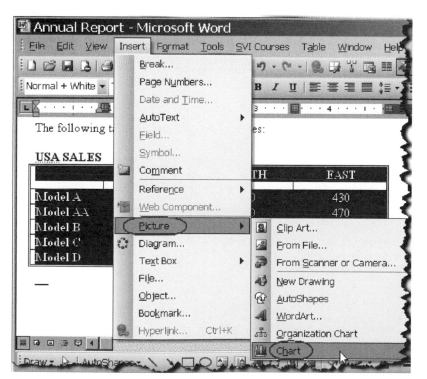

6.1

- **Select the entire table.**

  The information that is to be represented in the chart is selected.

- **Choose the Insert, Picture command, followed by Chart.**

6.2

The chart is displayed in the Microsoft Graph window (the hatched border). The selected table entries also appear in a datasheet.

- **Click on the Close button on the Title bar of the datasheet window.**

The datasheet is closed.

6.3

- **Point to the lower-right sizing handle of the Microsoft Graph window (the small black square in the lower-right corner of the hatched border).**

The mouse pointer will appear as a double-headed arrow when it is properly positioned.

- **Press and hold down the mouse button, and drag the sizing handle diagonally downward and to the right approximately one-half inch. Then release the mouse button.**

Both the height and the width of the chart are increased.

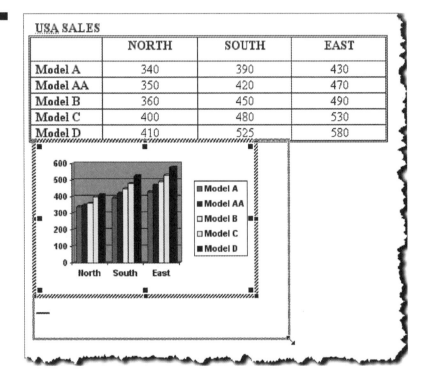

⊞ C:\GMU\IT 103\SVI\Word\Ann... - Datasheet [X]				
		A	B	C	D
		North	South	East	Close button
1	Model A	340	390	430	
2	Model B	360	450	490	
3	Model AA	350	420	470	
4	Model C	400	480	530	
5	Model D	410	525	580	

USA SALES

	NORTH	SOUTH	EAST
Model A	340	390	430
Model AA	350	420	470
Model B	360	450	490
Model C	400	480	530
Model D	410	525	580

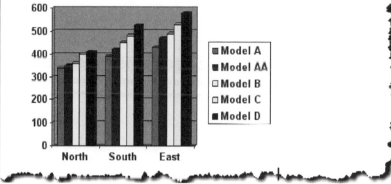

USA SALES

	NORTH	SOUTH	EAST
Model A	340	390	430
Model AA	350	420	470
Model B	360	450	490
Model C	400	480	530
Model D	410	525	580

6.4

- **Click outside the Microsoft Graph window.**

The hatched border is no longer displayed.

- **Save the document.**

Modifying a Chart

After inserting a chart, you may wish to change the **chart type** and/or reformat the various **chart components** (data markers, axes, legend, etc.).

To **change the chart type**:

- Double click on the chart area, so that you can see the chart area with the hatched border.
- With the chart displayed in the Microsoft Graph window, choose the **Chart, Chart Type** command, select the **Chart Type** option on the shortcut menu, or expand the **Chart Type** button on the Standard toolbar.
- Select the **new chart type** and, optionally, a **new chart subtype** (if you used the Chart, Chart Type command or the Chart Type option on the shortcut menu).
- Click on the **OK** button (if you used the Chart, Chart Type command or the Chart Type option on the shortcut menu).

To **reformat a chart component**:

- Double click on the chart area, so that you can see the hatched border surrounding it.
- With the chart displayed in the Microsoft Graph window, point to the **component**, **right-click** the mouse button, and select the **Format . . .** option on the shortcut menu that appears; or

Simply **double-click** on the component.

- In the dialog box that is subsequently displayed, make the necessary **change(s)**.
- Click on the **OK** button.

Objective

In this exercise, you will **modify your new chart**. Specifically, you will 1) change the chart type, 2) change the color of the data makers representing one data series, and 3) reposition the legend.

 7.1

- **Point to the chart, and double-click the mouse button.**

The chart is once again displayed in the Microsoft Graph window.

- **Right-click on the chart area (in the upper-right corner of the Microsoft Graph window). Then click on Chart Type on the shortcut menu that appears.**

Notice that when you point to a chart component, the name of that component appears in a ScreenTip next to the mouse pointer.

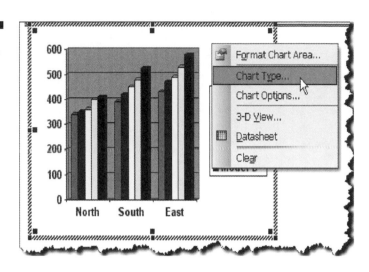

 7.2

- **In the Chart type box, click on Cylinder.**

The new chart type is selected.

- **Point to the button labeled Press and Hold to View Sample.**

The dialog box displays a preview of how your data will appear when formatted as a 3-D area chart.

- **Release the mouse button.**

- **Click on the OK button.**

The dialog box is closed, and the chart is displayed in a cylindrical column format.

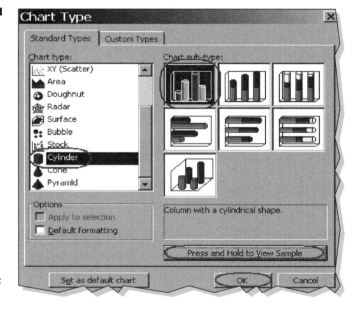

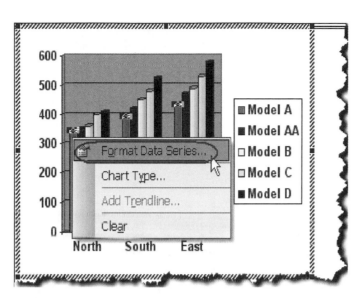

You will now change the color of the data markers representing the first data series.

- **Click on the first data marker (representing Model A), and then right-click the mouse button. Then click on Format Data Series on the shortcut menu that appears.**

The Patterns panel of the Format Data Series dialog box is displayed.

- **In the color palette, click on the seventh option in the second row.**

The new color is selected.

NOTE: The **Fill Effects** button can be used to add a pattern to the data marker.

- **Click on the OK button.**

The dialog box is closed, and the selected color is applied to the first data marker.

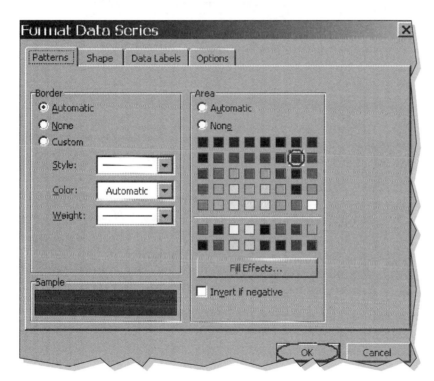

7.5

You will now reposition the legend.

- **Point to the legend, and double-click the mouse button.**

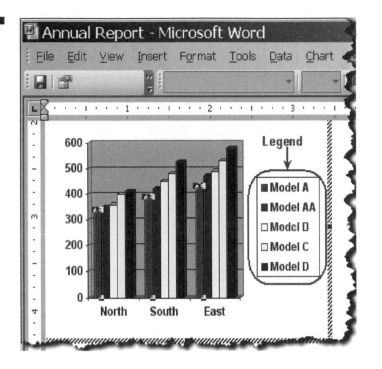

7.6

- **Click on the Placement tab.**

- **Click on Bottom. Then click on the OK button.**

The dialog box is closed, and the legend is displayed at the bottom of the chart area.

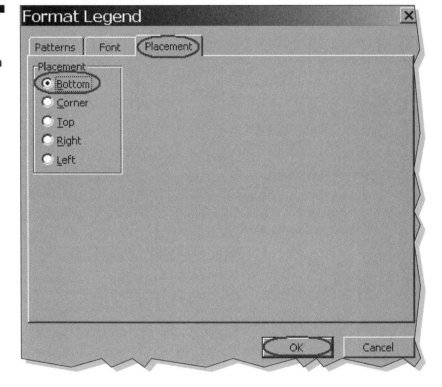

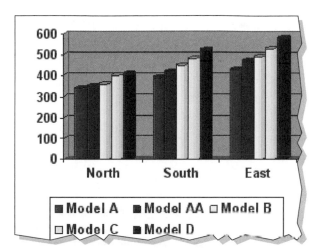

7.7

- **Click outside the Microsoft Graph window.**

The hatched border is no longer displayed. You will now reposition the chart in the document.

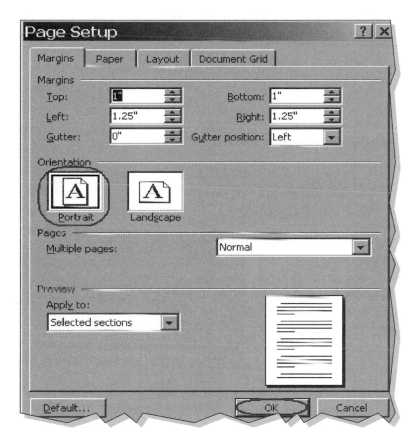

7.8

- **Choose the File, Page Setup command.**

The Page Setup dialog box is displayed.

- **Click on the Margins tab.**

- **Under Orientation, click on Portrait. Then click on the OK button.**

The new alignment is selected, and the dialog box is closed.

- **Save the document.**

Creating Newsletter-Style Columns in a Document

In **newsletter-style columns**, text flows down one column and then to the top of the next column, as in a newspaper or magazine article. Text in one column is related to text in another column only when a particular story or article spans multiple columns.

To **create newsletter-style columns in a document**:

- Move the insertion point to the location in which the columns are to begin.
- Choose the **Format**, **Columns** command.
- In the Columns dialog box, set the desired number of **columns**.
- Optionally, reset the **column width** and/or the **column spacing**.
- Optionally, select the **Line between** option to include a vertical line between the columns.
- Expand the **Apply to** box, and select the **This point forward** option. (Selecting this option is unnecessary if the column definition is being applied at the beginning of the document.)
- Click on the **OK** button.
- Type the column text.

Notes

You can also apply a newsletter-style column definition to existing text. To do this, move the insertion point to the beginning of the first line of the text, and then choose the Format, Columns command.

Alternatively, you can apply a newsletter-style column definition to an entire document (or to a specific section if the document contains more than one section), either before or after typing the column text, by positioning the insertion point anywhere in the document (or section), by clicking on the **Columns** button on the Standard toolbar and by selecting the desired number of columns in the grid that appears. You can also apply the column definition to a specific block of existing text by selecting that text before using the Columns button.

COLUMNS BUTTON

Objective

In this exercise, you will **include two newsletter-style columns**.

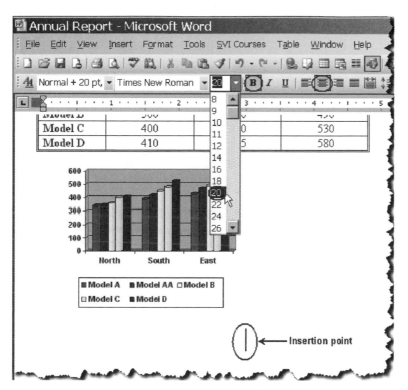

- **Click outside the chart on the right.**

- **Press [ENTER] twice.**

- **Expand the Font Size box, and click on 20.**

- **Click on the Bold button and on the Center button.**

The bold attribute is turned on, and the insertion point moves to the center of the line.

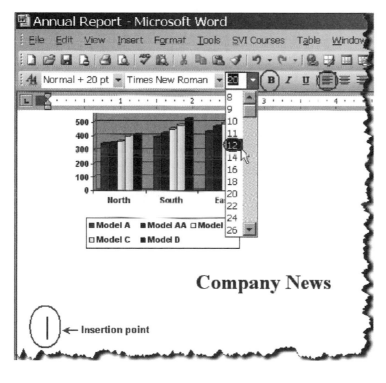

- **Type: Company News Press [ENTER] two times.**

A large bolded and centered heading is entered, and the insertion point moves two lines down.

- **Expand the Font Size box, and click on 12.**

- **Click on the Bold button to turn off the bold attribute. Then click on the Align Left button to restore the default text alignment.**

8.3

You will now define the columns.

- **Choose the Format, Columns command.**

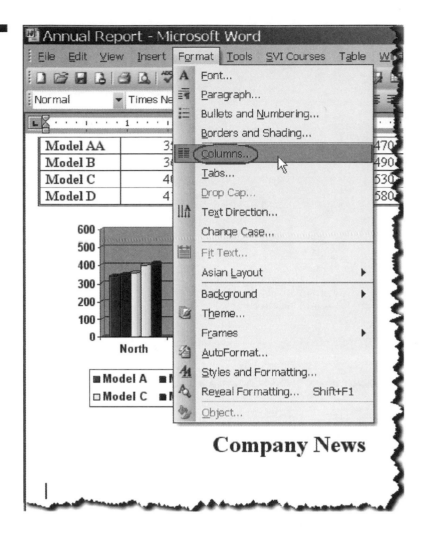

8.4

The Columns dialog box is displayed.

- **Under Presets, click on the Two option. Then click on Line between check box.**

The number of columns is selected. They will be separated by a vertical line.

- **Expand the Apply to box, and click on This point forward.**

The program will insert a section break before the columns, thereby creating a new section for the column text. All page settings for this new section will be independent of page settings for the previous section (containing the document heading).

- **Click on the OK button.**

The dialog box is closed, and the document appears in Print Layout view.

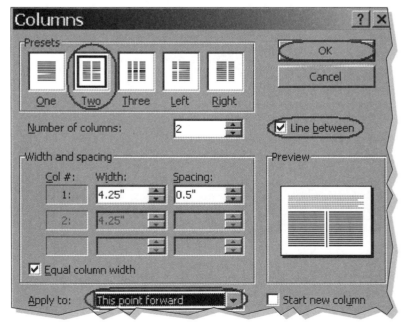

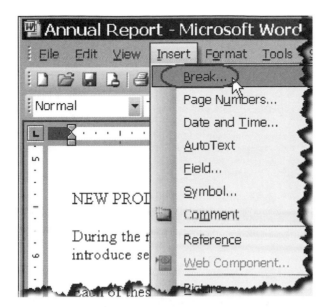

8.5

You will now enter text into the first column.

- **Type the following, pressing [ENTER] only where indicated:**

*NEW PRODUCTS [**ENTER**] two times*

*During the next two months we plan to introduce several new products. [**ENTER**] two times*

Each of these products will be supported by an extensive newspaper, television, and advertising campaign. More information will follow.

- **Choose the Insert, Break command.**

The Break dialog box is displayed.

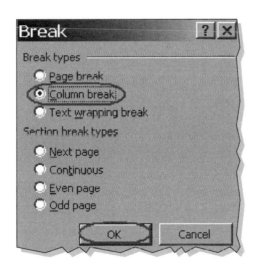

8.6

You will now insert a column break so that subsequent text is entered into the second column.

- **Click on Column break. Then click on the OK button.**

The dialog box is closed, and the column break is inserted. Notice that the insertion point now appears at the top of the second column.

8.7

- **Type the following, pressing [ENTER] only where indicated:**

WORLDWIDE SALES [ENTER] two times

Our company has experienced record worldwide sales in the second and third quarters. **[ENTER] two times**

Congratulations to the entire staff, who will receive a well-deserved bonus at the end of the year!

8.8

- **Select NEW PRODUCTS and click on the Bold button.**

- **Select WORLDWIDE SALES and click on the Bold button.**

- **Select the two body paragraphs in the first column. Then click on the Justify button on the Formatting toolbar.**

The selected paragraphs are aligned on the left and right margins of the column.

8.9

- **Using a procedure similar to that described above, justify the two body paragraphs in the second column. Then cancel the selection.**

- **Save the document.**

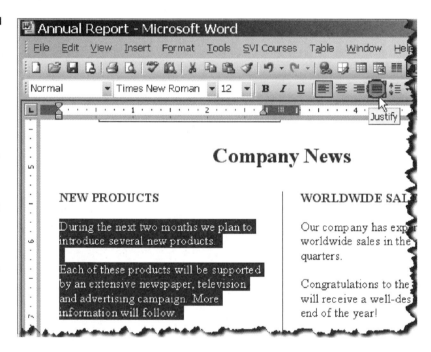

Producing a Report

This section discusses features that are useful in **reports and other multiple-page documents**. In it, you will learn how to:

- **Add** a **border** and **shading** to text.
- **Add** a **header/footer** to a document.
- **Add page numbers** to a document.

Adding a Border and Shading to Text

With Word's **Borders and Shading** feature, you can add visual interest to your documents, as well as call attention to important information, by adding borders and/or shading to paragraphs and other blocks of text.

To **add borders and/or shading to text**:

- Choose the **Format**, **Borders and Shading** command.
- On the Borders panel of the Borders and Shading dialog box, select the **border type** and a **style**, **color** and **width** for that type; and/or

On the Shading panel of the dialog box, select a **fill color** and **pattern**.

- Make sure that the correct option (**Paragraph** or **Text**) appears in the **Apply to** box.
- To reset the default spacing between the border and the text, click on the **Options** button (on the Borders panel), and set the appropriate options in the Border and Shading Options dialog box. Then click on the **OK** button to return to the Borders and Shading dialog box. (This button is available only when a border is to be applied to one or more paragraphs.)
- Click on the **OK** button.

Objective

In this exercise, you will **add a shaded border to the text on the title page of a document**.

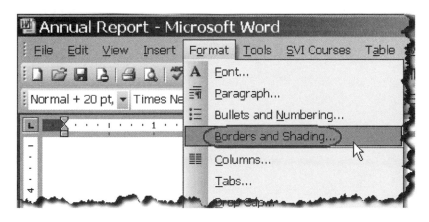

9.1

- **On page 1, select Annual Report text. Then choose the Format, Borders and Shading command.**

9.2

The Borders and Shading dialog box is displayed.

NOTE: *If the Borders panel does not appear in the dialog box, click on the Borders tab.*

- **Click on the Shadow option. Then expand the Width box, and click on the 1 pt line (unless that option is already selected). Make sure that Paragraph appears in the Apply to box.**

The border type and border width are selected.

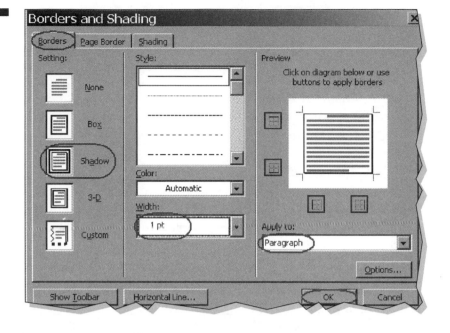

9.3

You will now shade the area inside the border.

- **Click on the Shading tab.**

The Shading panel of the dialog box is displayed.

- **In the Fill palette, click on the Gray-20% option (the sixth option in the first row).**

The shading is selected.

- **Click on the OK button.**

The dialog box is closed, and the border and shading are applied to the selected paragraphs.

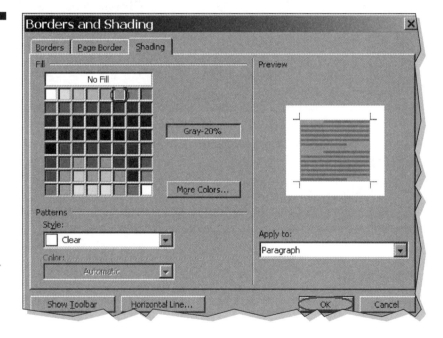

- Cancel the selection (by clicking anywhere on page 1).
- Save the document.

Adding a Header/Footer to a Document

In a multiple-page document, you may want to include a **header** (information that appears at the top of each page) and/or footer (information that appears at the bottom of each page). Headers and footers in a Word document can include both text (for example, the document title or filename) and graphics (for example, a company logo).

To **add a header and/or footer to a document**:

- Choose the **View, Header and Footer** command. Doing this displays the Header box. To switch to the Footer box, click on the **Switch Between Header and Footer** button on the Header and Footer toolbar, which appears in the Application window.
- Enter the **header/footer text** and/or **graphics**, applying any necessary formatting.
- To eliminate the header/footer on the first page, click on the **Page Setup** button on the Header and Footer toolbar, and select the **Different first page** option in the Page Setup dialog box. Then click on the **OK** button to close the dialog box.
- To close the Header/Footer box, click on the **Close Header and Footer** button on the Header and Footer toolbar.

Notes

1. The **Insert AutoText** button on the Header and Footer toolbar can be used to insert common items (for example, the filename, the author's name, or a running total of page numbers) into a header or footer.
2. You can create an **alternating header/footer** (one header/footer that appears on odd pages and another header/footer that appears on even pages) by selecting the **Different odd and even** option in the Page Setup dialog box (described above). Doing this, displays Odd Page Header/ Odd Page Footer boxes and Even Page Header/Even Page Footer boxes in which you then enter the appropriate information.

Objective

In this exercise, you will **add a right-aligned header to the current document**.

10.1

- **Make sure that the insertion point is located on page 1. Then choose the View, Header and Footer command.**

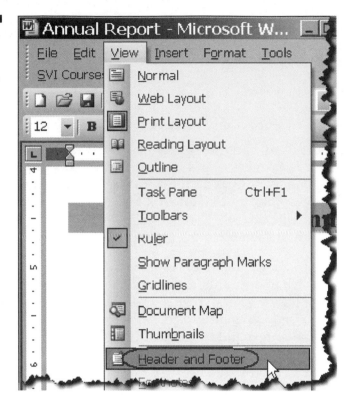

10.2

A Header box and the Header and Footer toolbar are displayed

- **Press [TAB] two times in the header box.**

The insertion point moves to the right margin of the Header box.

- **Click on the Bold button.**

The bold attribute is turned on.

- **Type: Annual Report Press [ENTER].**

The header text is entered, and the insertion point moves to the next line.

- **Press [TAB] two times. Then click on the Insert Date button on the Header and Footer toolbar.**

The current date is inserted.

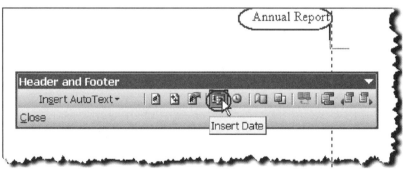

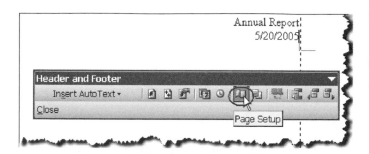

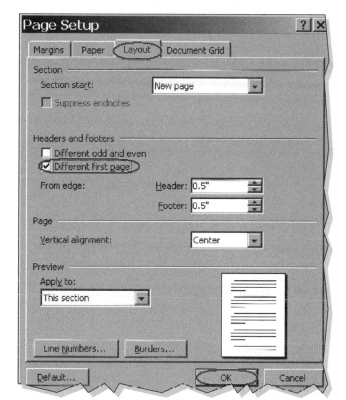

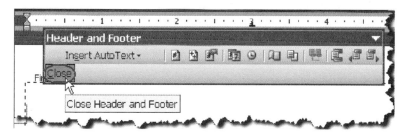

10.3

You will now eliminate the header from the first page.

- **Click on the Page Setup button on the Header and Footer toolbar.**

10.4

The Page Setup dialog box is displayed.

- **Click on the Layout tab.**

The Layout panel of the dialog box is displayed.

- **Under Headers and footers, click on Different first page. Then click on the OK button.**

The option is selected, and the dialog box is closed. A new First Page Header box is displayed.

NOTE: You could include a different header on page 1 by entering the information into this box. In this case, however, you will leave the box empty, thereby creating a blank header on page 1.

10.5

- **Click on the Close Header and Footer button on the Header and Footer toolbar.**

10.6

The Header and Footer toolbar and the Header box are both closed.

- **Click on the Next Page button (at the bottom of the Vertical scroll bar).**

The second page of the document is displayed. Notice the header at the top of this page.

- **Save the document.**

Adding Page Numbers to a Document

In a multiple-page document, you may also want to include a **page number** at the top or bottom of each page. Page numbers in a Word document are placed in either a header or footer and can be aligned on the left or right margin or centered between the left and right margins. (They can also be aligned relative to the inside and outside edges when pages are to be bound.)

To **add page numbers to a document**:

- Choose the **Insert, Page Numbers** command.
- In the Page Numbers dialog box, select the desired **position** and **alignment** for the numbers.
- To eliminate the number from the first page, deselect the **Show number on first page** option, if necessary.
- To reset the page number format, click on the **Format** button, and select the desired **number format** in the Page Number Format dialog box. Then click on the **OK** button to return to the Page Numbers dialog box.
- Click on the **OK** button.

Notes

You can manually enter page numbers into a header or footer by using the **Insert Page Number** and **Insert AutoText** buttons on the Header and Footer toolbar. You can manually enter the current page number anywhere in a document by pressing [**ALT**] + [**SHIFT**] + [**P**].

Objective

In this exercise, you will **add a page number to the current document**. It will appear at the **bottom** of the **second page**.

- **Choose the Insert, Page Numbers command.**

The Page Numbers dialog box is displayed.

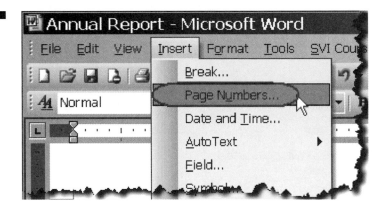

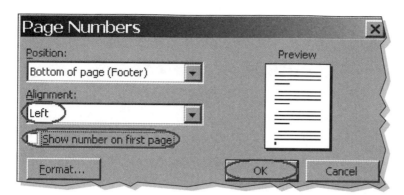

11.2

You will accept the default Position option, Bottom of page (Footer).

- **Expand the Alignment box, and click on Left.**

The alignment of the numbers is selected.

- **Make sure that the Show number on first page option is not selected.**

The first (title) page will not include a page number.

- **Click on the OK button.**

11.3

The dialog box is closed.

- **Scroll through the document, and note the page number is at the bottom of page 2.**

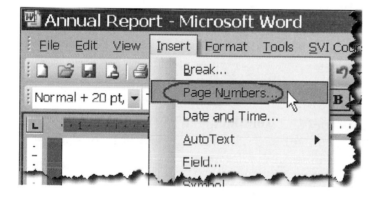

11.4

Next, you will change the position of the page number and reset the page number format.

- **Move the insertion point back to the beginning of the document. Then choose the Insert, Page Numbers command.**

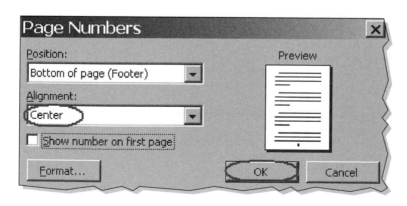

11.5

The Page Numbers dialog box is redisplayed.

- **Expand the Alignment box, and click on Center.**

The alignment of the numbers is reset.

- **Click on the OK button.**

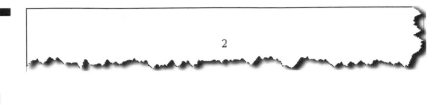

11.6

- **The dialog box is closed.**
- **Scroll through the document once again, and note that the page number is now centered at the bottom of page 2.**
- **Save the document.**

Congratulations! You have completed the Case Study.

Conclusion

You have just completed **Microsoft Office Word 2003—Case Study 2**. In the case study, you were introduced to many intermediate and advanced techniques. To reinforce your understanding of these techniques, it is recommended that you read and work through it once again.

Further Practice

The following Case Study will give you the opportunity to review and practice many of the Word features you have learned.

1. Make sure that the Document window is clear. Then display a **blank document**.
2. Create a **title page** that includes the following **centered** and **bolded text**:

CAREFREE TRAVEL
MONTHLY REPORT

3. **Apply** a **border** and **shading** to the above **text**.
4. **Save** the **document** in a file named **Monthly Report.doc**. (As you continue working on the document, make sure that you periodically **save** your **changes**.)
5. **Insert** a **hard page break** below the title.
6. Type the following:

NEW AIRFARES

FLIGHT	FROM	TO	FARE
AB008	New York	Honolulu	$700.00
AB009	New York	Seattle	$450.00
AB010	New York	Denver	$300.00
AB011	New York	Chicago	$250.00
AB012	New York	Atlanta	$100.00

7. Press **[ENTER] two** times. Then, using the **Table** feature, create a **table**, and enter the following **information**:

8. **Enhance** the **appearance** of the **table** in ways of your choice. You may, for example, wish to bold and/or realign various entries.

9. Move the insertion point to the blank line below the table, and press **[ENTER]**. Then type the following:

> **Fare Notes:**
>
> The fares quoted are for round-trip travel and are based on a one-week advance purchase of tickets.
>
> Fare information is current as of press time, but is subject to change without notice.

10. **Bold** the **NEW AIRFARES** heading.

11. **Apply** the **List Bullet** style to the **first informational paragraph** (which begins "The fares quoted . . ."). Then **apply** the **same style** to the **second informational paragraph** (which begins with "Fare information is current . . .").

12. **Move** the **insertion point** to the **beginning** of the **current page** (2). Then **apply** a **two-column** definition to the page.

13. **Insert** the appropriate **column break** so that the text **Fare Notes:** and the **two informational paragraphs** appear in the **second column**.

14. **Insert** another **hard page break** below the informational paragraphs.

15. **Restore** the default **one-column** definition on the **current page** (3).

16. Type the following:

> **Carefree Travel** has been providing vacations, both domestically and internationally, for almost half a century! We believe that our service is second to none. As a result, our business continues to grow, as indicated below.

17. Press **[ENTER] two** times. Then type the following:

> **Number of Individuals Served (During the Latest Four-Year Period)**

18. Press [ENTER] two times. Then, using the **Table** feature, create another **table**, and enter the following **information**:

	2000	2001	2002	2003
USA	7500	7900	8500	9800
Europe	8000	7600	8200	8800
Australia	3000	3200	3100	3900

19. **Decrease** the **width** of each **column** of the table to **1 inch**.
20. **Enhance** the **appearance** of the **table** in other ways of your choice.
21. **Center** the **table horizontally**. (**HINT:** On the Table panel of the Table Properties dialog box, select the **Center** alignment option.)
22. **Move** the **insertion point** to the **beginning** of the document. Then **add page numbers** to the document, beginning on, and **centered** at the **bottom** of, **page 2**.
23. **Preview**, and then **print**, the entire **document**.
24. **Save** the **document**, and then **close** the **file**.

MS Excel 2003
Case Study 1

OBJECTIVES

After successfully completing this case study, you should be able to:

- Start Excel
- Use the Excel menu system, toolbars and task panes
- Open, close, save, and print a file
- Enter labels and values into a worksheet
- Enter a formula using both typing and pointing techniques
- Reset font options for cell entries
- Realign cell entries
- Add a border and shading to a worksheet

- Adjust column width and row height in a worksheet
- Automatically fill a range
- Insert and delete rows and columns
- Reset the number format of cell entries
- Change the page setup for a worksheet
- Preview a worksheet
- Display help information

Case Study I—MS Excel 2003

Assume that you work in the Sales Department of an ice cream company. Your company is considering introducing a new flavor, Pineapple Coconut, and has commissioned market research.

You start a worksheet to present the information and will produce a projection over a five-year period to analyze the viability of this project.

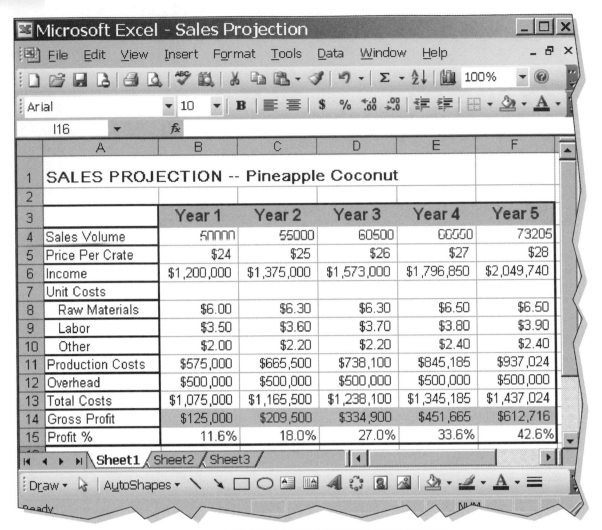

SALES PROJECTION IN MICROSOFT EXCEL

Getting Started

This section begins with a discussion of **Excel and the tools it provides**. It then covers various **program fundamentals**. In this section, you will learn how to:

- **Start Excel.**
- **Identify** the **elements** of the **Excel Application window**.
- **Use** the **Excel menu system.**
- **Use Excel toolbars.**
- **Use Excel task panes.**

What Is Excel?

Excel is a popular spreadsheet program designed for use on a personal computer. Although it has many applications, Excel is used primarily as a **financial modeling package** for such purposes as budgeting, cash flow forecasting, sales reporting, and the preparation of profit and loss statements.

The advantages of using a program such as Excel are immediately apparent if you have used a strictly manual procedure to perform spreadsheet operations. Not only does the program make it easier for you to enter information, it can save you countless hours in calculating and recalculating information. In addition, it allows you to quickly obtain answers to what are called **"what-if" scenarios**.

For example, suppose you wish to predict the income from the sale of a particular product over a period of time. Using Excel, you can set up the appropriate model and then test various assumptions—for example, "What if our costs rise by 5%?" or "What if actual sales fall short of projections by 10%?"

Excel provides three main types of **modeling tools**—worksheets, charts and lists.

Worksheets	A worksheet, Excel's term for a spreadsheet, is used to store numeric data, calculations involving that data, as well as descriptive text. The information is arranged in columns and rows in a format similar to an accountant's ledger. Related worksheets are saved in a **workbook**, which can be thought of as an electronic binder. An example of a worksheet might be a departmental budget.
Charts	A chart is used to graphically represent the data contained in a worksheet. For example, a pie chart could be generated to show how a budget is allocated between different areas of expenditure.
Lists	A list, sometimes called a database, serves as an electronic filing system. The information can be manipulated (for example, sorted and filtered) to suit a user's specific needs. An example of a list might be a detailed listing of company employees, including their names, addresses, titles, salaries, and so on.

Start and Open a New Excel Workbook

You start Excel by clicking on the **Start** button on the Windows taskbar, by pointing to **All Programs** (if you are running Windows XP) or to **Programs** (if you are running Windows 2000), by selecting the **Microsoft Office** option on the All Programs or Programs menu, and by selecting the **Microsoft Office Excel 2003** option on the subsequent submenu.

If the Start menu includes a Microsoft Office Excel 2003 shortcut icon, you can start Excel by simply clicking on this icon. If the Windows desktop includes a Microsoft Office Excel 2003 shortcut icon, you can start Excel by double-clicking on this icon.

You can **open a new workbook** by following any of three options:

- Choose the **File**, **New**… command.
  - In the New Workbook task pane, select the **Blank workbook** option.
- Simply click on the **New** button [ ] on the Standard toolbar.

Notes

The procedure described opens a workbook containing three blank worksheets. Excel also provides a number of pre-designed workbooks, called **templates**, which can be used to set up common types of worksheets—for example, expense statements and sales invoices.

You can also create a new workbook that is based on an existing workbook. To do this, select the **From existing workbook** option (under **New**) in the New Workbook task pane. Then, in the New from Existing Workbook dialog box, select the filename of the workbook to be used, and click on the **Create New** button.

- Click on the **Start** button on the Windows taskbar.
- Point to **Programs**.
- Point to **Microsoft Office** on the menu.
- Click on **Microsoft Office Excel 2003** on the submenu.

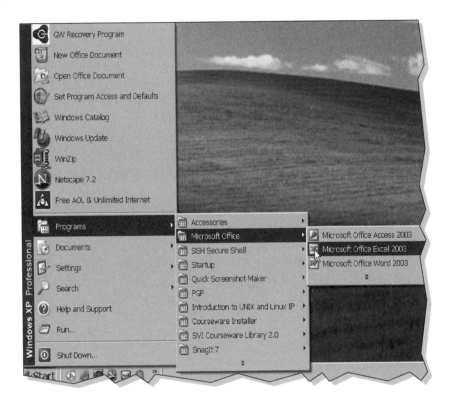

Excel is started, and the Excel Application window appears, displaying a blank workbook.

A new workbook is opened. You will now enter data into Sheet1 of this workbook.

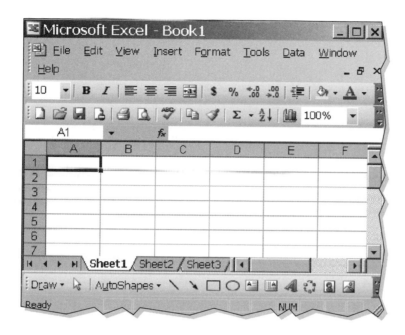

The Excel Application Window

What appears on your screen may sometimes vary slightly from what is shown in the following screen:

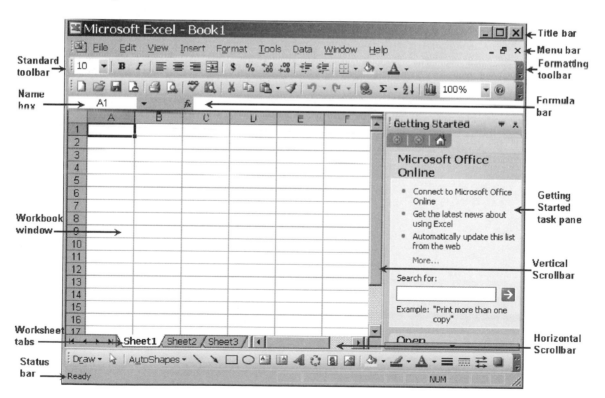

The initial **Excel Application window** includes the following elements:

Title bar	This displays the name of the **program**, as well as the name of the current **workbook** if it has been saved. (If the workbook has not been saved, it is identified by a number—for example, Book1). The standard Windows Control-menu box and window sizing buttons appear at the left end and right end of the bar, respectively.
Menu bar	This displays Excel's **primary commands**.
Formula bar	This displays the contents of the active cell, if any. As you will soon learn, it is also used to enter the formulas that specify calculations in a worksheet.
Status bar	This displays helpful information as you use the program. The "Ready" indicator that currently appears lets you know that the program is ready for data input.
Standard or Formatting toolbars	These display a number of **shortcut buttons** and **boxes** for performing common Excel operations. When you point to one of these buttons or boxes, the name of the button/box appears in a small window (**Screen-Tip**) next to the mouse pointer. The Standard and Formatting toolbars, by default, appear side-by-side. On your screen, however, one toolbar may appear above the other.
Name box	This identifies the active cell (described later).
Getting Started task pane	This displays options for accessing Microsoft Office Online, a Web site for users of Microsoft Office products, as well as options for opening an existing workbook file and for creating a new workbook. The program includes several other task panes. Each pane includes options for performing a specific task (for example, inserting a picture into a worksheet).
Workbook window	This window, which occupies the majority of the screen, displays an Excel **workbook**. A workbook initially contains three **worksheets**, which are saved in a single file. Each worksheet consists of a series of **columns** (identified by the letters A, B, C, etc., which appear across the top of the window) and a series of **rows** (identified by the numbers 1, 2, 3, etc., which appear down the left side of the window). Since an entire Excel worksheet contains 256 columns and 65,536 rows, only a small part appears in this window at one time.
	Columns and rows of a worksheet intersect to form **cells**. Each cell is identified by its column/row coordinates, or **cell reference** (for example, B5). Notice that cell A1 is currently surrounded by a border. This border, or **cell pointer**, identifies the **active cell**—that is, the cell in which any information entered from the keyboard will be stored.
Vertical/Horizontal scroll bars	These are used to scroll the Workbook window vertically/horizontally through a worksheet.
Worksheet tabs	These identify the various worksheets in a workbook, and allow you to move from one worksheet to another.

Using the Excel Menu System

The Excel **menu system** is one means of communicating with the program. You can access the menu system by using a **mouse** (the most efficient method) or by using the **keyboard**. In either case, the procedure is as follows:

- Select a **command** on the **Menu bar**. To do this with a mouse, point to the command, and click the **left** mouse button. To do this with the keyboard, press and hold down [**ALT**], and press (type) the **underscored letter** of the commands on the menu bar.
- Select an **option** on the **menu** that is subsequently displayed. To do this with a mouse, point to the option, and click the **left** mouse button; To do this with the keyboard, press (type) the **underscored letter** of the option. (Selecting an option on an Excel menu sometimes leads to a submenu. In this case, use the procedure described above to select the appropriate option on this submenu.)

A menu, as mentioned above, offers a series of options for the command you have chosen.

Notes

If a menu option is dimmed, that option is not relevant at the current time and, therefore, is not available.

If a command sequence (a command, followed by a specific option) can be accessed with shortcut keys, these keys appear to the right of the relevant option. For example, pressing [**CTRL**] + [**C**] is equivalent to choosing the **Edit** command, followed by the **Copy** option.

If a command sequence can be accessed with a shortcut button, that button appears to the left of the relevant option.

If a menu option is followed by a wedge-shaped arrow, selecting that option displays a submenu of additional options.

If a menu option is followed by three dots (ellipsis), choosing that option displays a **dialog box** in which additional options can be specified.

The menus that you initially access from the Menu bar are called **short menus** since they include only a basic set of commonly-used options. You can expand a short menu and display the **full menu** by clicking on the chevron (the two down arrows) at the bottom of the menu. (Note that a menu will expand automatically if you continue pointing for a few seconds to the command that displayed it.) Any option selected on this expanded menu is added to the basic set of options, thereby creating a personalized menu that reflects your needs. The same option is removed from the basic set of options after a period of time if you no longer use it.

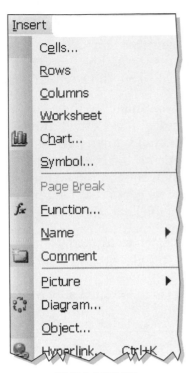

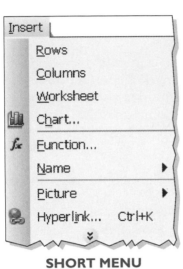

SHORT MENU   **FULL MENU**

If you prefer to work only with full menus, you can do so by choosing the **Tools, Customize** command and by selecting the **Always show full menus** option in the Customize dialog box. You can also restore personalized menus (and toolbars) to their original state by clicking on the **Reset menu and toolbar usage data** button in the same dialog box.

To help you work even more efficiently, Excel also provides a number of shortcut menus. A **shortcut menu** includes options that are relevant to a particular screen element or area of a worksheet and is displayed by clicking the **right** mouse button. For example, if you position the mouse pointer in a worksheet and right-click the mouse button, the following shortcut menu is displayed:

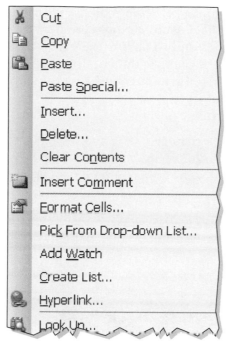

SHORTCUT MENU

Using Excel Toolbars

The **Standard** and **Formatting toolbars**, as mentioned earlier, include shortcuts for bypassing the menu system. You generally use these bars, in lieu of the menu system, to perform operations when they contain relevant options.

The Standard and Formatting toolbars initially are "docked" side-by-side and include only a subset of the available buttons and boxes. You can display a list of additional options by clicking on the **Toolbar Options** button at the right side of either toolbar. Any button/box selected in the Toolbar Options list is added to the associated toolbar. To make room for the new option, a button/box not used recently is moved to the Toolbar Options list.

Notes

1. If you prefer to have more buttons/boxes displayed on the Standard and Formatting toolbars, you can do so by moving one or the other either to a different row or to another part of the screen. This can be done either by choosing the **Tools, Customize** command and by selecting the **Show Standard and Formatting toolbars on two rows** option in the Customize dialog box, or by pointing to the **Move handle** (which displays a dotted vertical bar) at the left side of the toolbar and by dragging the toolbar to the new location. (Dragging a toolbar to an area of the screen that is not adjacent to the window border creates a "floating" toolbar—that is, a small window in which the various buttons/boxes appear.)

2. You can increase or decrease the width of the Standard and Formatting toolbars when they appear side-by-side by dragging the Move handle of the toolbar on the right. (Dragging this handle to the left, increases the width of the toolbar on the right while decreasing the width of the toolbar on the left; dragging this handle to the right, decreases the width of the toolbar on the right while increasing the width of the toolbar on the left).

Excel also provides a number of other toolbars with shortcuts related to specific tasks. You can display any of these toolbars by choosing the **View, Toolbars** command (or by **right-clicking** on any visible toolbar) and by selecting the toolbar name on the submenu that appears. You can also hide any toolbar by deselecting the toolbar name on the same submenu.

Using Excel Task Panes

The **Getting Started task pane**, as you have seen, is opened when you start Excel, displaying options for accessing Microsoft Office Online, for opening an existing workbook file, and for creating a new workbook. Other task panes appear when you initiate relevant operations.

Notes

You can manually display a different task pane by clicking on the **Other Task Panes** button at the top of the current pane and by selecting the desired pane in the list that appears.

Modifying an Existing Worksheet

This section discusses **basic worksheet techniques**. In it, you will learn how to:

- **Add data** to a worksheet.
- **Move** the **cell pointer**.
- **Enter** a **formula** into a worksheet.
- **Save** a **workbook**.

Enter Labels and Values into a Blank Worksheet of the Workbook

To enter data into a cell or to change a cell's contents, you must first select the cell by moving the **cell pointer** to it. This can be done with either a **mouse** or the **keyboard**.

To enter the new information into the worksheet, just select a cell and type in the information, press [**ENTER**] to subsequently move to the cell below, press any of the [**ARROW**] keys to subsequently move to the adjacent cell in the respective direction, or click in any other cell to subsequently move to that cell.

Using the keyboard:

To Move the Cell Pointer:	Press:
Down one cell	[DOWN ARROW]
Up one cell	[UP ARROW]
Right one cell	[RIGHT ARROW] or [TAB]
Left one cell	[LEFT ARROW] or [SHIFT] + [TAB]
Down one screen	[PG DN]
Up one screen	[PG UP]
To the beginning of the current row	[HOME]
To the first cell in the worksheet (AI)	[CTRL] + [HOME]

Data in a worksheet falls into three general classifications:

Labels   These include entries consisting of text only (for example, INCOME) or a combination of text and numbers (for example, Year 1). You can input an entry consisting solely of numbers (for example, a zip code) as a label by preceding the entry with an apostrophe (for example, '94105).

Values   These include entries consisting of numbers only and entries that display a date and/or time.

Formulas   These specify the calculations that are to be performed in a worksheet.

Objective

In this exercise, you will **enter labels and values into a blank worksheet**.

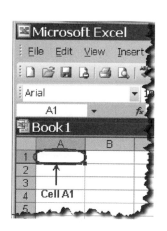

• **Click in cell AI**

NOTE: *Cell AI becomes the active cell.*

1.2

- **Type: SALES PROJECTION and Press [ENTER].**

NOTE: If you make a mistake while typing, use [BACKSPACE] to delete the incorrect character(s).

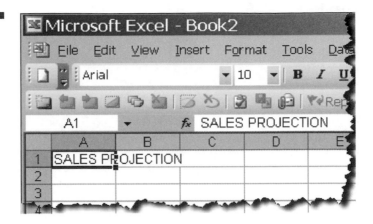

1.3

- **Click in cell B3.**

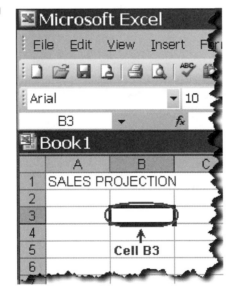

1.4

- **Type: Year 1**
- **Press [ENTER].**
- **Click in cell A4.**
- **Type: Sales Volume and Press [ENTER].**

Cell A5 becomes active.

NOTE: *Do not be concerned if various entries are truncated. You will adjust the column width in a later step.*

- **Type: Price Per Crate in Cell A5 and press [ENTER].**
- **Type: Income in Cell A6 and press [ENTER].**
- **Type: Raw Material in Cell A7 and press [ENTER].**
- **Type: Labor in Cell A8 and press [ENTER].**
- **Type: Other in Cell A9 and press [ENTER].**
- **Type: Production Costs in Cell A10 and press [ENTER].**
- **Type: Overhead in Cell A11 and press [ENTER].**
- **Type: Total Costs in Cell A12 and press [ENTER].**
- **Type: Gross Profit in Cell A13 and press [ENTER].**

1.5

- **Click in cell B4.**

- **Type: 50000 and Press [ENTER].**

Cell B5 becomes active.

NOTE: *Do not be concerned if various entries are truncated. You will adjust the column width in a later step.*

- **Type: 24 in Cell B5 and Press [ENTER].**

- **Using down Arrow Key, select cell B7.**

- **Type: 6 in Cell B7 and Press [ENTER].**

- **Type: 3.5 in cell B8 and Press [ENTER].**

- **Type: 2 in Cell B9 and Press [ENTER].**

- **Using down Arrow Key, skip cell B10 and select cell B11.**

- **Type: 500000 in Cell B11 and Press [ENTER].**

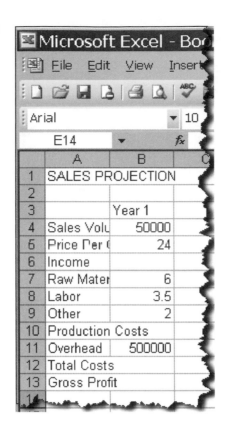

Entering a Formula into a Worksheet

Formulas specify the calculations that are to be performed in a worksheet. A formula consists of two elements: operands and one or more operators. An **operand** represents an item of data that is to be used in the calculation and can include constants (for example, 30 or 1.75) and/or cell references (for example, C20); an **operator** indicates what is to be done with the various operands and can include any of the following:

^	**(Exponentiation)**
*	**(Multiplication)**
/	**(Division)**
+	**(Addition)**
-	**(Subtraction)**

To **enter a formula into a worksheet**:

- Select the cell in which the formula is to appear.
- Type = (an equal sign). Doing this activates the Formula bar and displays an equal sign in that bar and in the current cell.
- Specify a **constant** or **operator** by **typing** it.
- Specify a **cell reference**:

  - By **typing** the **column/row coordinates** (for example, B5); or
  - By **pointing** (moving the cell pointer) to it and left clicking in it.

- Click on the **Enter** button next to the Formula bar, or press [**ENTER**]. (If necessary, you can cancel the formula before entering it by clicking on the **Cancel** button next to the Formula bar or by pressing [**ESC**].)

FORMULA BAR

If you include more than one operator in a formula, you should consider **operator precedence**—that is, the order in which Excel carries out the various operations. Considering the five operators mentioned on the previous page:

- **Exponentiation (^)** is performed first.
- **Multiplication (*) or division (/)** is performed next.
- **Addition (+) or subtraction (-)** is performed last.
- In the case of two operators of the same precedence (for example, multiplication and division), the operations are performed in a left-to-right order.

You can override the default operator precedence by enclosing the appropriate operands and operator in parentheses. For example:

$3 + 4 / 2 = 5$
$(3 + 4) / 2 = 3.5$
$7 * 6 - 2^2 = 38$
$7 * (6 - 2^2) = 14$
$7 * (6 - 2)^2 = 112$

Formulas can also be used to compare values and to join text strings. In this section, however, you will use formulas only to perform mathematical operations.

Objective

In this exercise, you will **enter simple formulas into the current worksheet** by using both the **pointing** and **typing** methods. This exercise also demonstrates the use of the **Go To** feature to identify all worksheet cells containing a formula.

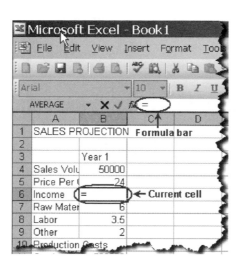

2.1

- **Double click in cell B6.**

- **Type: =**

The Formula bar is activated, and an equal sign is displayed in both the current cell and the Formula bar.

2.2

- **Click in cell B4.**

The cell is surrounded by a thin moving border, called a marquee, and the cell reference (B4) is added to the formula.

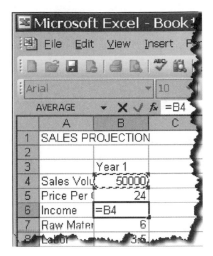

2.3

- **Type: ***

The multiplication operator is added to the formula.

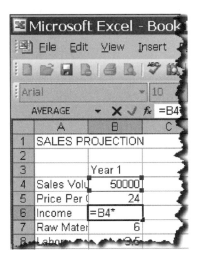

2.4

- **Click in cell B5.**

The cell reference (B5) is added to the formula, which is now complete.

- **Click on the Enter ☑ button to the left of the Formula bar.**

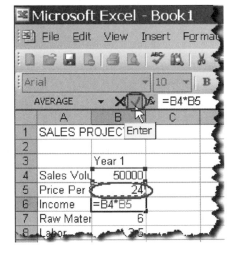

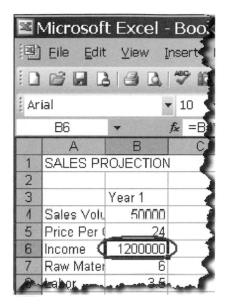

2.5

The formula is entered, and the result of the calculation (1200000) is displayed in cell B6.

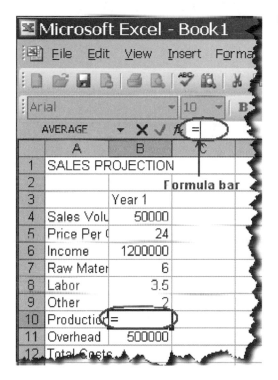

2.6

- **Click in cell B10 and type: = in the formula bar**

The Formula bar is activated.

2.7

*You are now ready to begin building the second formula (**B7+B8+B9)*B4**). This time you will use the keyboard to point to the operands.*

- **Type: (B7+B8+B9)*B4**

NOTE: *Cell references can be entered into a formula in either uppercase or lowercase characters. The above, for example, can also be entered as* ***(b7+b8+b9)*b4***.

Notice that each operand of the formula (B7, B8, B9 and B4) appears in a different color. Notice also that the corresponding cell of each operand is surrounded by a border of the same color.

Microsoft Excel - Book1

File   Edit   View   Insert   Format   Tools   D

Arial   10   B I U

AVERAGE   X √ fx   =(B7+B8+B9)*B4

	A	B	C	D
1	SALES PROJECTION			
2				
3		Year 1		
4	Sales Volu	50000		
5	Price Per (	24		
6	Income	1200000		
7	Raw Mater	6		
8	Labor	3.5		
9	Other	2		
10	Production	+B9)*B4		
11	Overhead	500000		
12	Total Costs			
13	Gross Profit			

2.8

- **Press [ENTER] key or click on the Enter ☑ button to the left of the Formula bar.**

The formula is entered, and the result of the calculation (575000) is displayed in cell B10.

	A	B
1	SALES PROJECTION	
2		
3		Year 1
4	Sales Volu	50000
5	Price Per (	24
6	Income	1200000
7	Raw Mater	6
8	Labor	3.5
9	Other	2
10	Production	575000
11	Overhead	500000
12	Total Costs	
13	Gross Profit	

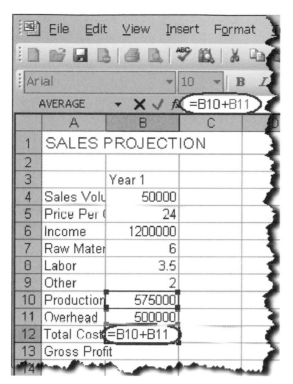

2.9

- **Click in cell B12**
- **Type: =B10+B11 in the formula bar.**
  - **Press [ENTER] or click on the Enter ☑ button to the left of the Formula bar.**

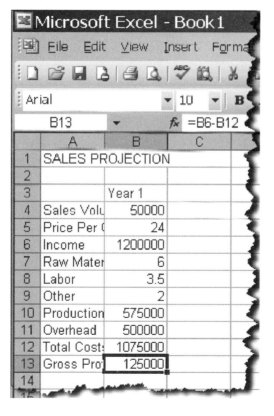

2.10

- **Click in cell B13**
- **Type: =B6-B12 in the formula bar.**
- **Press [ENTER] or click on the Enter (check mark) ☑ button to the left of the Formula bar.**

The formulas are entered, and the results of the calculation are displayed in cell B12 and B13.

Saving a Workbook

To avoid losing what appears on the screen due to an unexpected occurrence, such as a power failure, it is important that you periodically save a workbook as you work.

To **save a workbook** (for the **first time**):

- Choose the **File, Save** command, or click on the **Save** button on the Standard toolbar.
- In the Save As dialog box, enter a **name** for the file in which the workbook is to be saved.
- If you wish to store the file in a folder other than the working folder, switch to that **folder**.
- Click on the **Save** button (in the dialog box).

To **resave a workbook**:

- Choose the **File, Save** command, or click on the **Save** 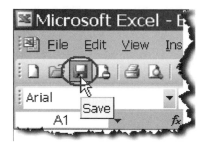 button on the Standard toolbar or using shortcut key **Ctrl+S**

You can save a previously-saved workbook in a new location (for example, in a different folder on the hard drive or on a floppy diskette) and/or under a different filename by choosing the **File, Save As** command and by specifying the new location/new filename in the Save As dialog box. You will then have two copies of the workbook—the original version saved in the original file and a second version saved in the new file. From the Save As dialog box, you can also save a workbook in a different format (for example, one that can be used with an earlier version of Excel or one that can be used by another program) by expanding **Save as type** box and by selecting the new file type in the list that appears.

Notes

Excel includes an **AutoRecover** feature that periodically saves the open workbook in a special recovery file. If you do lose power or, for some other reason, are unable to save the workbook, you can use this recovery file. AutoRecover, however, should not be used in place of the normal save procedure since a recovery file is only a temporary file. (The AutoRecover feature is enabled/disabled with the **Tools, Options** command.)

Objective

In this exercise, you will **save the current workbook**. You will then **close** the file.

3.1

- **Insert floppy disk in drive A.**

- **Click on the Save 🖫 button on the Standard toolbar or choose the File, Save command.**

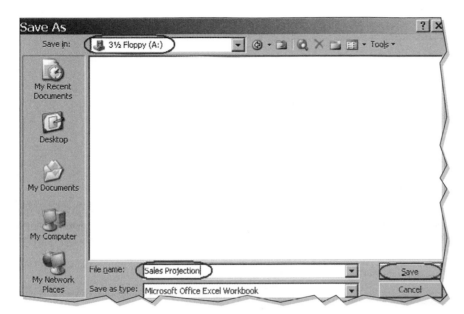

3.2

A Save As dialog box opens.

- **In a Save As dialog box, enter File name as Sales Projection and select 3½ Floppy (A:) in the Save in list.**

- **Click on Save button.**

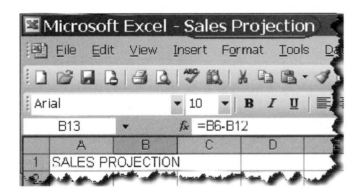

3.3

The new file name (Sales Projection) is displayed in the title bar.

Formatting a Worksheet

This section discusses techniques for **enhancing the contents of an Excel worksheet**. In it, you will learn how to:

- **Reset** the **alignment** of cell entries.
- **Reset font options** for cell entries.
- **Add borders** and **shading** to a worksheet.
- **Adjust Column width** in a worksheet.
- **Adjust Row width** in a worksheet.

Resetting the Alignment of Cell Entries

By default, labels are **left-aligned** in a cell while values are **right-aligned**.

Using the **Align Left** , **Center** and **Align Right** buttons on the Formatting toolbar, however, you can easily reset the alignment of entries in single cells as well as in ranges of cells.

Objective

In this exercise, you will **center** the entry in cell **B3**.

4.1

- **Select the cell B3.**
- **Click on the Center** **button on the Formatting toolbar.**

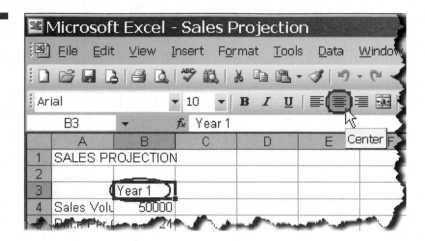

4.2

Cell B3 is centered.

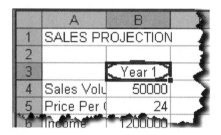

Resetting Font Options for Cell Entries

The ability to use different font options to display and print cell entries is one of the most important features for enhancing the appearance of data in a worksheet.

To **reset font options for one or more cell entries**:

- Select the cell(s) in which the new font options are to be applied.
- **Click on Format in the Menu bar then click on the Cells** command, or select the **Format Cells** option on the shortcut menu (using right click of the mouse).
- On the Font panel of the Format Cells dialog box, select the desired **options**.
- Click on the **OK** button.

Alternatively, you can use the various buttons and boxes on the Formatting toolbar to reset font options. For example, the **Font** and **Font Size** boxes allow you to apply a new font and font size, respectively, to cell entries, while the **Bold, Italic** and **Underline** buttons allow you to apply the corresponding attribute to cell entries.

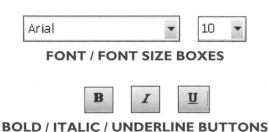

FONT / FONT SIZE BOXES

BOLD / ITALIC / UNDERLINE BUTTONS

Objective

In this exercise, you will **reset font options for cell B3** by using the **Format Cells dialog box.**

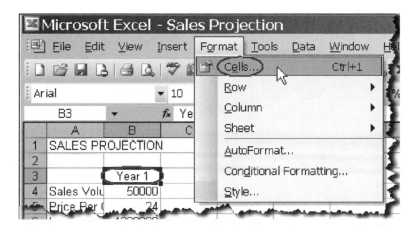

5.1

- **Select cell B3.**

- **Click on Format and then click on Cells . . . command.**

Alternative: Right click on cell B3 and click on Format Cells on the shortcut menu that appears.

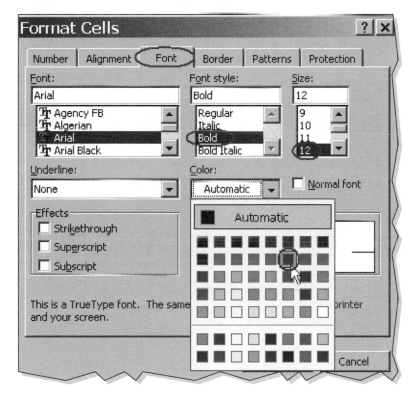

5.2

The Format Cells dialog box is displayed.

- **Click on the Font tab.**

The Font panel of the dialog box is displayed.

- **In the Font style box, click on Bold. Then, in the Size box, click on 12.**

The bold attribute is turned on, and the font size is increased.

- **Expand the Color box by clicking on little downward pointing arrow, and click on the Blue option (the sixth option in the second row of the color palette).**

The new color is selected.

5.3

• **Click on the OK button.**

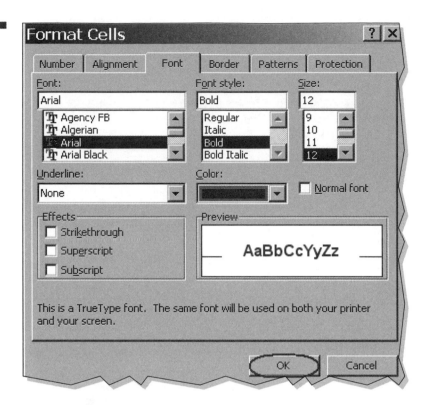

5.4

The dialog box is closed, and the selected font options are applied to cell B3.

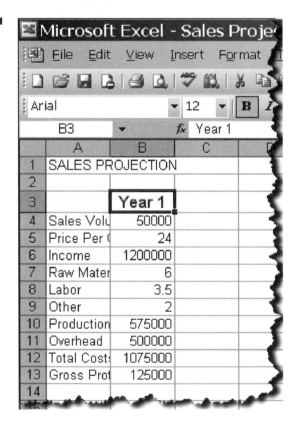

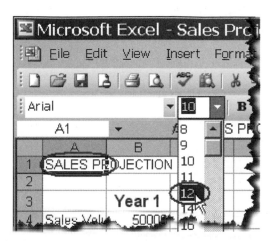

5.5

- **Select the cell A1.**
- **Click on the down arrow at the right side of the Font size box on the Formatting toolbar.**

The box is expanded, and a list of available font sizes is displayed.

- **Click on 12.**

The new font size is applied to the cell A1.

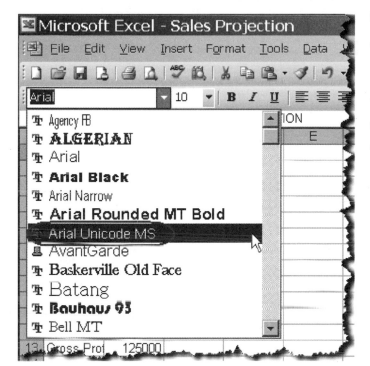

5.6

- **Click on the down arrow at the right side of the Font box on the Formatting toolbar.**

The box is expanded, and a list of available fonts is displayed.

- **Click on Arial Unicode MS.**

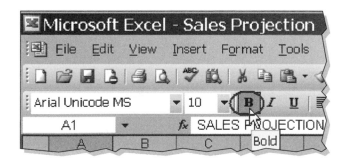

5.7

- **Click on the Bold** **button on the formatting toolbar.**

5.8

Now cell A1 font is Arial Unicode MS, font size is 12, and the text is bolded.

- **Save the document.**

Adding Borders and Shading to a Worksheet

One or more borders can add visual interest to a worksheet, as well as make the data easier to read and understand. Shading can also visually enhance a worksheet, as well as call attention to important information.

To **add a border to a worksheet**:

- Select the range that is to include the border.

A **range** is a contiguous group of cells in a worksheet. When editing (or formatting) a worksheet, you often must select a specific range prior to performing a particular operation.

The methods for selecting a range are summarized below.

To Select:	Do the Following:
A single column	Click on the column heading.
Two or more adjacent columns	Drag from the column heading for the first column to the column heading for the last column.
A single row	Click on the row heading.
Two or more adjacent rows	Drag from the row heading for the first row to the row heading for the last row.
A rectangular block of cells (keyboard method)	Select the first cell of the block (the cell in the upper-left corner), hold down [**SHIFT**], and use the appropriate [**ARROW**] key(s) to extend the selection to the last cell of the block (the cell in the lower-right corner).
A rectangular block of cells (mouse method)	Drag from the first cell of the block to the last cell of the block.
The entire worksheet	Click on the **Select All** button (in the upper-left corner of the worksheet frame).

- Choose the **Format, Cells** command, or select the **Format Cells** option on the shortcut menu.
- On the Border panel of the Format Cells dialog box, select the desired **style, color** and **position** for the border.
- Click on the **OK** button.

Alternatively, you can use the **Borders** button on the Formatting toolbar to add a border to a worksheet.

To **add shading to a worksheet**:

- Select the cell(s) in which the shading is to appear.
- Choose the **Format, Cells** command, or select the **Format Cells** option on the shortcut menu.

- On the Patterns panel of the Format Cells dialog box, select the desired **color** and **pattern** for the shading.
- Click on the **OK** button.

The above procedure allows you to apply both a color and pattern when shading cells.

If you wish to apply only a color, you can alternatively use the **Fill Color**

 button on the Formatting toolbar to add shading to cells.

Objective

In this exercise, you will **add borders and shading** to a worksheet.

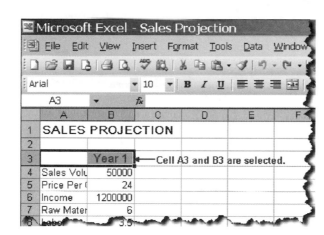

Cell A3 and B3 are selected.

6.1

- **Click on cell A3.**
- **Hold down [SHIFT].**
- **Press the [RIGHT ARROW] key once.**
- **While holding down [SHIFT] key, click on cell B13.**

Cell A3 to B13 are selected.

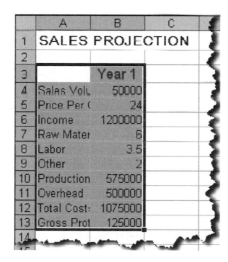

6.2

- Point to the selected cells and right-click the mouse button. Then click on Format Cells on the shortcut menu that appears.

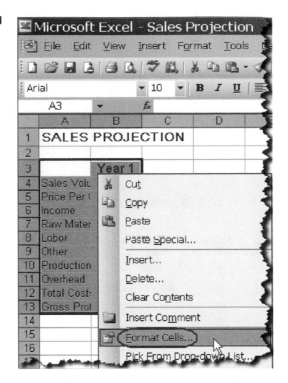

6.3

The Format Cells dialog box is displayed.

- Click on the Border tab.

- In the Style box, click on the medium thick line (the fifth option down in the second column).

The border style is selected.

- Under Presets, click on the Inside button. Then click on the Outline button.

- Click on the OK button.

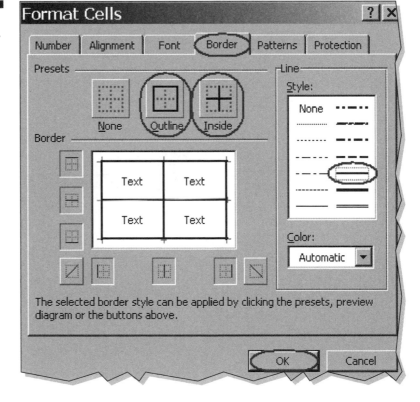

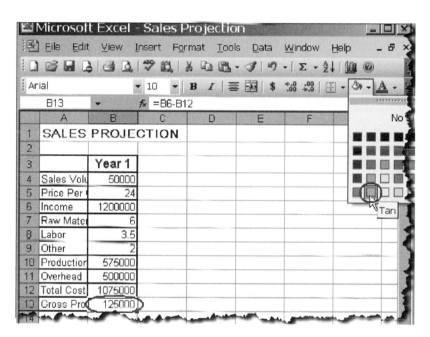

6.4

The dialog box is closed, and an outline border is drawn around the selected cells.

NOTE: You will need to cancel the selection to actually see the border. To cancel the selection, click on any cell outside the selection.

6.5

- **Select cell B13.**
- **Click on the down arrow at the right side of the Fill Color button on the Formatting toolbar.**
- **Click on the Tan option (fifth option down in the second column).**

6.6

The color is selected and the shading is added to the selected cells.

6.7

- **Make sure cell B13 is selected.**

- **Choose Edit, Undo Format Cells to undo cell B13 formatting.**

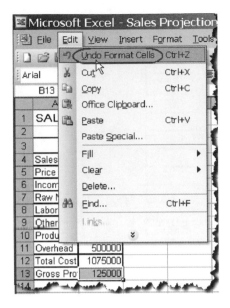

6.8

- **Save the document.**

Adjusting Column Width in a Worksheet

As you notice, entries that are too long to fit within the width of a cell are truncated when the adjacent cell to the right is filled. This problem can be easily corrected by adjusting the column width to correctly display the entries in that column. There are several ways to do this.

To **adjust column width an exact amount** (using the **menu system**):

- Select the column that is to be adjusted by clicking on the **column heading**.
- Choose the **Format, Column, Width** command, or select the **Column Width** option on the shortcut menu.
- In the Column Width dialog box, enter the **new width**.
- Click on the **OK** button.

To **adjust column width an exact amount** (using a **mouse**):

- Point to the **right border** of the **column heading**.
- Drag the **border** to the **right** (to increase the width) or to the **left** (to decrease the width).

To **adjust column width to accommodate the longest entry**:

- Select the column that is to be adjusted.
- Choose the **Format, Column, AutoFit Selection** command.

OR

- Simply **double-click** on the **right border** of the **column heading** when the mouse cursor change to double arrow cross pointer.

You can simultaneously adjust the width of multiple columns by selecting the columns and by performing the adjustment operation on any one column.

Objective

In this exercise, you will increase the **width** of column **A** so that all labels are fully displayed.

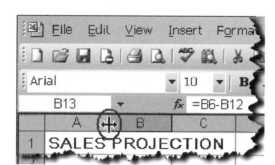

7.1

- **Point to the border (vertical line) between the column A and column B headings.**

The mouse pointer will appear as a double-arrow cross when it is properly positioned.

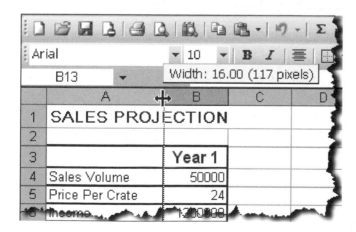

7.2

- **Press and hold down the (left) mouse button, and drag the border to the right until the column is approximately Width: 16.00 (117 pixels). Then release the mouse button.**

The entries in column A should be fully displayed.

Notice that the new column width appears in a ScreenTip above the mouse pointer as you drag the border.

- **Save the document.**

Alternative: Point to the border (vertical line) between the column A and column B headings. Right-click the mouse button. Click on Column Width. Change the Column width in the Column Width dialog box. Click OK.

Adjusting Row Height in a Worksheet

At times, you may want to adjust the height of one or more worksheet rows. For example, you may wish to increase the height of rows in which certain data (for example, the worksheet title, worksheet headings and/or summary information) appears to add visual interest to the sheet.

To **adjust row height an exact amount** (using the **menu system**):

- Select the row that is to be adjusted by clicking on the **row heading**.
- Choose the **Format, Row, Height** command, or select the **Row Height** option on the shortcut menu.
- In the Row Height dialog box, enter the **new height**.
- Click on the **OK** button.

To **adjust row height an exact amount** (using a **mouse**):

- Point to the **bottom border** of the **row heading**.
- Drag the **border downward** (to increase the height) or **upward** (to decrease the height).

To **adjust row height to accommodate the tallest entry**:

- Select the row that is to be adjusted.
- Select the **Format, Row, AutoFit** command.

OR

- Simply double-click on the bottom border of the row heading.

You can simultaneously adjust the height of multiple rows by selecting the rows and by performing the adjustment operation on any one row.

Objective

In this exercise, you will **increase the height of row 1** in the current worksheet.

 8.1

- **Point to the border (horizontal line) between the row 1 and row 2 headings.**

The mouse pointer will appear as a double-arrow cross when it is properly positioned.

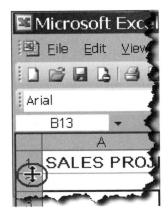

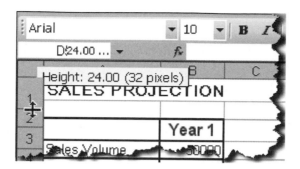

- **Press and hold down the mouse button, and drag the border downward until the row height is increased to 24.00 (32 pixels). Then release the mouse button.**

- **Save the document.**

Notice that the new row height appears in a ScreenTip above the mouse pointer as you drag the border.

Alternative: Point to the row I heading, and right-click the mouse button.

Row I is selected, and a shortcut menu is displayed. Click on Row Height. The Row Height dialog box is displayed. Type: 24

Choose the OK button. The dialog box is closed, and the height of the row is increased to 24.00.

Editing a Worksheet

This section discusses additional techniques for **modifying a worksheet**, along with various **worksheet shortcuts**. In it, you will learn how to:

- **Change data** in a worksheet.
- **Use AutoFill**.
- **Copy cells**.
- **Insert** and **delete rows** and **columns**.
- **Reset the Number format** of cell entries.

Changing Data in a Worksheet

To change a cell's contents, simply select the cell, and type the new information.

Objective

In this exercise, you will **edit the entry** in A1 to read SALES PROJECTION—Pineapple Coconut.

As you enter data, you may from time to time see the effect of Excel's **AutoCorrect** and **AutoComplete** features. The various tasks of the AutoCorrect feature are enabled/disabled with the **Tools, AutoCorrect Options** command; the AutoComplete feature is enabled/disabled with the **Tools, Options** command. The AutoCorrect feature corrects common spelling errors as you type; the AutoComplete feature repeats a label that appears in a cell above when you begin typing a new label with the same initial characters. (To accept a label displayed by AutoComplete, press [**ENTER**] or an [**ARROW**] key; to enter a different label, continue typing. To delete additional characters entered by AutoComplete, press [**DEL**].)

9.1

- Double click in the cell A1.

- Using arrow key, move your cursor to the end of **SALES PROJECTION** and type: - - Pineapple Coconut (in bold).

- Press [ENTER].

- Save the document.

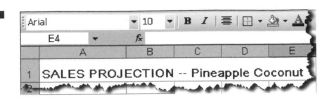

Using AutoFill

With Excel's **AutoFill** feature, you can quickly fill a range either with a series of labels or values or with copies of a particular value or formula. The result of an AutoFill operation is determined by the contents of the first cell or cells in the range. For example, the single label "January" generates the series "January, February, March, April, May," etc., while the values "10" and "20" generate the series "10, 20, 30, 40, 50," etc. A single value or a formula, on the other hand, is simply copied into adjacent cells. In the case of a formula, column/row coordinates are adjusted to reflect the columns/rows in which the new formulas appear.

To **use AutoFill**:

- Enter the first **entry or entries** of the range, and then select the cell(s) in which that information appears.
- **Drag** the **fill handle** (in the lower-right corner of the selection), and extend the selection until it includes the entire range that is to be filled.

You can also fill any range with the same entry by selecting the range, by entering the label or value that is to be repeated into the active cell, and by pressing [**CTRL**] + [**ENTER**].

Objective

In this exercise, you will **use AutoFill to enter column headings** into the range C3:F3 (These headings should read Year 2, Year 3, etc.)

10.1

- Click on cell B3.

- Point to the fill handle (the small black square) in the lower-right corner of cell B3. The mouse pointer appears to be like a thick **+** sign.

- Drag the fill handle (in the lower-right corner of the selection), and extend the selection to cell F3 that is to be filled with Year 5.

- Release the mouse button.

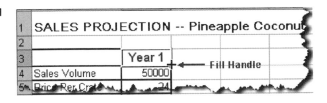

	A	B	C	D	E	F
1	SALES PROJECTION -- Pineapple Cocunut					
2						
3		Year 1	Year 2	Year 3	Year 4	Year 5
4	Sales Volume	50000				

10.2

The mouse pointer will appear as a thin black cross when it is properly positioned.

- **Save the document.**

Copying Cells

In the previous subsection, you used AutoFill to copy values and formulas into adjacent cells. You can also copy any cell entry into any worksheet location by using either the standard Windows **copy and paste** technique or a **drag and drop** technique.

To **copy one or more cells** (using **copy and paste**):

- Select the cell(s) that is/are to be copied.

- Choose the **Edit, Copy** command, or click on the **Copy** button on the Standard toolbar. Doing this places a copy of the selected cell(s) on the Windows Clipboard. (See the second note below.)

- Select the **paste range** (the cell(s) in which the information is to appear). If you are copying more than one cell, you can simply select the first (upper-left) cell of this range.

- Choose the **Edit, Paste** command, or click on the **Paste** button on the Standard toolbar. Doing this inserts the cell(s) on the Windows Clipboard into the paste range.

Notes

1. When you perform a copy and paste operation, the cells that are copied normally replace any existing cells in the paste range. You can, if necessary, insert those cells without replacing existing cells by using either the **Insert, Copied Cells** command or the **Insert Copied Cells** option on the shortcut menu (instead of the Edit, Paste command or the Paste button) and by specifying the direction in which the existing cells are to be moved.

2. When you use the Edit, Copy command or the Copy button to copy cells (or when you use the Edit, Cut command or the Cut button to move cells, as described in the next subsection), the information is placed on both the **Windows Clipboard** (also called the System Clipboard) and the **Office Clipboard**, two temporary storage areas. Although the Windows Clipboard and the Office Clipboard are separate entities, they are used for similar purposes. The Windows Clipboard, however, can hold only one item (selection) at a time and can, therefore, be used to store and paste only single items. The Office Clipboard, on the other hand, can hold up to 24 items and can, as a result, be used to collect and paste multiple items,

from the same or from different Microsoft Office programs. The contents of the Office Clipboard appear in the Clipboard task pane, which can be displayed by choosing the **Edit, Office Clipboard** command.

To **copy one or more cells** (using **drag and drop**):

- Select the cell(s) that is/are to be copied.
- Point to the **border** of the selection. Then press and **hold down** both [**CTRL**] and the mouse button.
- **Drag** the mouse pointer to the **new location** (the first cell of the range if you are copying more than one cell). Then **release** the mouse button and [**CTRL**].

Objective

In this exercise, you will **copy a cell in a worksheet** by using **drag and drop** technique.

- **Select cell C4.**
- **Click in the formula bar.**
- **Type: =B4*1.1**
- **Press [ENTER].**

Cell C4 data is changed to 55000.

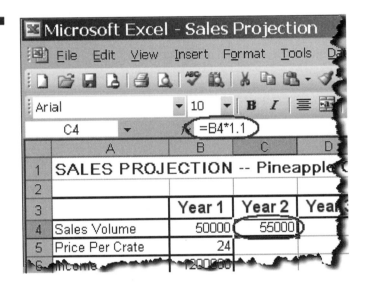

11.2

- **Click on cell C4.**
- **Point to the fill handle (the small black square) in the lower-right corner of cell C4.**
- **Drag the fill handle (in the lower-right corner of the selection), and extend the selection to cell F4.**
- **Release the mouse button.**

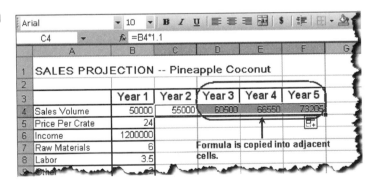

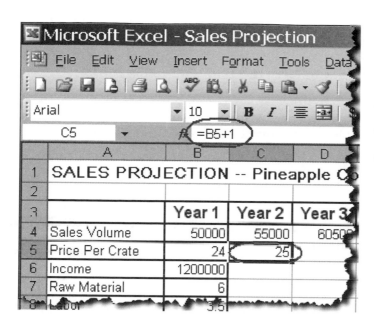

11.3

- **Select cell C5.**
- **Click in the formula bar.**
- **Type: =B5+1**
- **Press [ENTER].**

Cell C5 data is changed to 25.

11.4

- **Click on cell C5.**
- **Point to the fill handle (the small black square) in the lower-right corner of cell C5.**
- **Drag the fill handle (in the lower-right corner of the selection), and extend the selection to cell F5.**
- **Release the mouse button.**

11.5

- **Select cell B6.**
- **Point to the fill handle (the small black square) in the lower-right corner of cell B6.**
- **Drag the fill handle (in the lower-right corner of the selection), and extend the selection to cell F6.**
- **Release the mouse button.**
- **Save the document.**

Inserting and Deleting Rows and Columns

With Excel, you can quickly insert new rows and columns, as well as delete existing rows and columns, anywhere in a worksheet. When you do so, existing or remaining rows/columns are adjusted automatically—rows are moved down and columns are moved to the right to open up space for an inserted row/column; rows are moved up and columns are moved to the left to close up space left by a deleted row/column.

To **insert one or more rows/columns into a worksheet**:

- Select the area in which the row(s) or column(s) is/are to be inserted by selecting the row or column heading(s).
- Choose the **Insert**, **Rows** or **Insert**, **Columns** command, or select the **Insert** option on the shortcut menu.

To **delete one or more rows/columns from a worksheet**:

- Select the row(s) or column(s) that is/are to be deleted.
- Choose the **Edit**, **Delete** command, or select the **Delete** option on the shortcut menu.

Objective

In this exercise, you will **insert a new row into a worksheet**. You will then **enter data into this row** to complete the worksheet.

12.1

- **Click on the row 7 heading.**

Row 7 is selected. You will now insert a new row into the selected area.

	A	B	C	D
1	SALES PROJECTION -- Pineapple C			
2				
3		Year 1	Year 2	Year 3
4	Sales Volume	50000	55000	60500
5	Price Per Crate	24	25	26
6	Income	1200000	1375000	1573000
7	Raw Material	6		
8	Labor	3.5		
9	Othe Row 7 heading	2		
10	Production Costs	575000		

12.2

- **Choose the Insert, Rows command.**

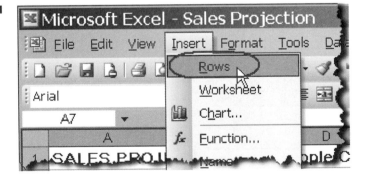

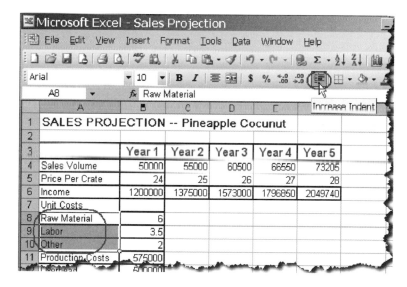

	A	B	C	D	E	F
1	SALES PROJECTION -- Pineapple Cocunut					
2						
3		Year 1	Year 2	Year 3	Year 4	Year 5
4	Sales Volume	50000	55000	60500	66550	73205
5	Price Per Crate	24	25	26	27	28
6	Income	1200000	1375000	1573000	1796850	2049740
7						
8	Raw Material	6				
9	Labor	3.5				
10	Other	2	New row is inserted			
11	Production Costs	575000				

12.3

A new row is inserted.

	A	B
1	SALES PROJECTION	
2		
3		Year 1
4	Sales Volume	50000
5	Price Per Crate	24
6	Income	1200000
7	Unit Costs	
8	Raw Material	6
9	Labor	3.5

12.4

- **Select cell A7.**
- **Type: Unit Costs**

Microsoft Excel - Sales Projection

File   Edit   View   Insert   Format   Tools   Data   Window   Help

Arial   10   B I $ %   Increase Indent

A8   Raw Material

	A	B	C	D	E	F
1	SALES PROJECTION -- Pineapple Cocunut					
2						
3		Year 1	Year 2	Year 3	Year 4	Year 5
4	Sales Volume	50000	55000	60500	66550	73205
5	Price Per Crate	24	25	26	27	28
6	Income	1200000	1375000	1573000	1796850	2049740
7	Unit Costs					
8	Raw Material	6				
9	Labor	3.5				
10	Other	2				
11	Production Costs	575000				

12.5

- **Click on cell A8.**
- **Press Shift key.**
- **Holding Shift key, click on cell A10.**
- **Release Shift Key.**
- **Click on Increase Indent button on the Formatting toolbar.**

12.6

- **Enter the Unit costs over the five-year period as indicated in the screen shot.**

	A	B	C	D	E	F	G
1	SALES PROJECTION -- Pineapple Cocunut						
2							
3		Year 1	Year 2	Year 3	Year 4	Year 5	
4	Sales Volume	50000	55000	60500	66550	73205	
5	Price Per Crate	24	25	26	27	28	
6	Income	1200000	1375000	1573000	1796850	2049740	
7	Unit Costs						
8	Raw Material	6	6.3	6.3	6.5	6.5	
9	Labor	3.5	3.6	3.7	3.8	3.9	
10	Other	2	2.2	2.2	2.4	2.4	
11	Production Costs	575000					
12	Overhead	500000		Enter this data into			
13	Total Costs	1075000		the worksheet			
14	Gross Profit	125000					
15							

12.7

- **Select cell B12.**

- **Point to the fill handle (the small black square) in the lower-right corner of cell B12.**

- **Drag the fill handle (in the lower-right corner of the selection), and extend the selection to cell F12.**

- **Release the mouse button.**

	A	B	C	D	E	F	G
7	Unit Costs						
8	Raw Material	6	6.3	6.3	6.5	6.5	
9	Labor	3.5	3.6	3.7	3.8	3.9	
10	Other	2	2.2	2.2	2.4	2.4	
11	Production Costs	575000					
12	Overhead	500000	500000	500000	500000	500000	
13	Total Costs	1075000					
14	Gross Profit	125000	Formula is copied to				
15			adjacent cells				

12.8

- **Select cell B11.**

- **Point to the fill handle (the small black square) in the lower-right corner of cell B11.**

- **Drag the fill handle (in the lower-right corner of the selection), and extend the selection to cell F11.**

- **Release the mouse button.**

- **Repeat the same for cells B13 and B14.**

	A	B	C	D	E	F
4	Sales Volume	50000	55000	60500	66550	73205
5	Price Per Crate	24	25	26	27	28
6	Income	1200000	1375000	1573000	1796850	2049740
7	Unit Costs					
8	Raw Material	6	6.3	6.3	6.5	6.5
9	Labor	3.5	3.6	3.7	3.8	3.9
10	Other	2	2.2	2.2	2.4	2.4
11	Production Costs	575000	665500	738100	845185	937024
12	Overhead	500000	500000	500000	500000	500000
13	Total Costs	1075000	1165500	1238100	1345185	1437024
14	Gross Profit	125000	209500	334900	451665	612716
15						

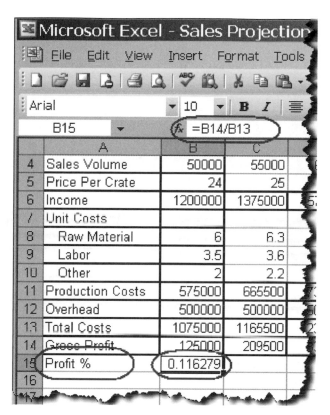

■ 12.9 ■

- **Select cell A15.**
- **Type: Profit %**
- **Select cell B15**
- **Click on the formula bar.**
- **Type: =B14/B13**
- **Press [ENTER].**
- **Save the document.**

Resetting the Number Format of Cell Entries

Excel assigns the appropriate format to a number if you include a numeric symbol (for example, dollar sign or comma) when entering it. Numbers entered without a numeric symbol are assigned the default **General** format.

To **reset the number format of one or more cell entries:**

- Select the cell(s) in which the new number format is to be applied.
- Choose the **Format, Cells** command, or select the **Format Cells** option on the shortcut menu.
- On the Number panel of the Format Cells dialog box, select the **new number format**.
- Click on the **OK** button.

Alternatively, you can use the **Currency Style** $\boxed{\$}$, **Percent Style** $\boxed{\%}$ and **Comma Style** $\boxed{,}$ buttons on the Formatting toolbar to apply the corresponding numeric style to cell entries.

The Increase Decimal $\boxed{{}^{\leftarrow.0}_{.00}}$ and Decrease Decimal $\boxed{{}^{.00}_{\rightarrow.0}}$ buttons can be used to respectively add and remove decimal places to and from an entry.

Objective

In this exercise, you will **format** cell **B15** so that the entry is displayed as a **percentage** with **1** decimal place.

13.1

- **Select cell B15.**

- **Click on the Percent Style**

  % **button on the Formatting toolbar.**

The selected entries are displayed as percentages.

Microsoft Excel - Sales Projection

File   Edit   View   Insert   Format   Tools   Data   Window   Help

B15   =B14/B13

	A	B	C	D	E
4	Sales Volume	50000	55000	60500	66550	73205
5	Price Per Crate	24	25	26	27	28
6	Income	1200000	1375000	1573000	1796850	2049740
7	Unit Costs					
8	Raw Material	6	6.3	6.3	6.5	6.5
9	Labor	3.5	3.6	3.7	3.8	3.9
10	Other	2	2.2	2.2	2.4	2.4
11	Production Costs	575000	665500	738100	845185	937024
12	Overhead	500000	500000	500000	500000	500000
13	Total Costs	1075000	1165500	1238100	1345185	1437024
14	Gross Profit	125000	209500	334900	451665	612716
15	Profit %	0.116279				
16						

13.2

- **Make sure cell B15 is selected.**

- **Click on the Increase Decimal**

  button on the Formatting toolbar.

A decimal place is added to cell B15.

Microsoft Excel - Sales Projection

File   Edit   View   Insert   Format   Tools   Data   Window   Help

B15   =B14/B13

	A	B	C	D	E	G
4	Sales Volume	50000	55000	60500	66550	73205	
5	Price Per Crate	24	25	26	27	28	
6	Income	1200000	1375000	1573000	1796850	2049740	
7	Unit Costs						
8	Raw Material	6	6.3	6.3	6.5	6.5	
9	Labor	3.5	3.6	3.7	3.8	3.9	
10	Other	2	2.2	2.2	2.4	2.4	
11	Production Costs	575000	665500	738100	845185	937024	
12	Overhead	500000	500000	500000	500000	500000	
13	Total Costs	1075000	1165500	1238100	1345185	1437024	
14	Gross Profit	125000	209500	334900	451665	612716	
15	Profit %	12%					
16							

13.3

- **Select cell B15.**

- **Point to the fill handle (the small black square) in the lower-right corner of cell B15.**

- **Drag the fill handle (in the lower-right corner of the selection), and extend the selection to cell F15.**

- **Release the mouse button.**

	A	B	C	D	E	F
4	Sales Volume	50000	55000	60500	66550	73205
5	Price Per Crate	24	25	26	27	28
6	Income	1200000	1375000	1573000	1796850	2049740
7	Unit Costs					
8	Raw Material	6	6.3	6.3	6.5	6.5
9	Labor	3.5	3.6	3.7	3.8	3.9
10	Other	2	2.2	2.2	2.4	2.4
11	Production Costs	575000	665500	738100	845185	937024
12	Overhead	500000	500000	500000	500000	500000
13	Total Costs	1075000	1165500	1238100	1345185	1437024
14	Gross Profit	125000	209500	334900	451665	612716
15	Profit %	11.6%	18.0%	27.0%	33.6%	42.6%
16						

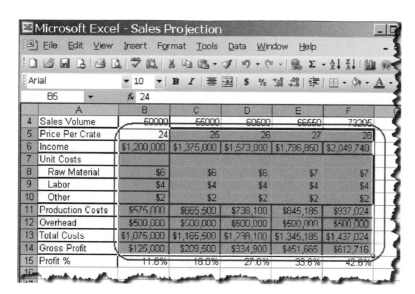

- **Save the document.**
- **Select cell B5.**
- **Hold down [SHIFT].**
- **Select cell F14.**

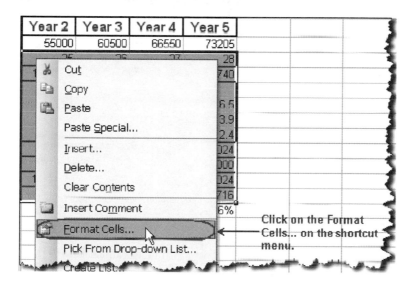

Click on the Format Cells... on the shortcut menu.

- **Point to the selected cells and right-click the mouse button.**
- **Click on Format Cells... on the shortcut menu that appears.**

13.6

The Format Cells dialog box is displayed.

- **Click on the Number tab.**

The Number panel of the dialog box is displayed (as illustrated on the right).

- **In the Category box, click on Custom.**

- **Select $#,##0_);($#,##0) choice in the Type box.**

- **Click on the OK button.**

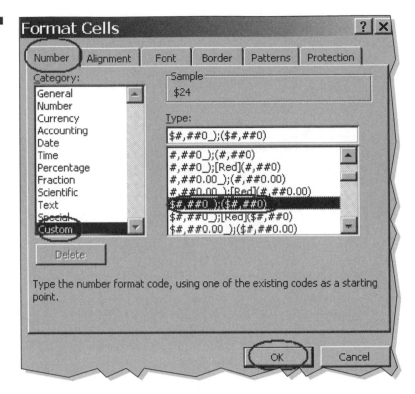

13.7

The dialog box is closed, and the dollar signs and commas are added to the selected entries. Notice that the entries have 0 decimal places.

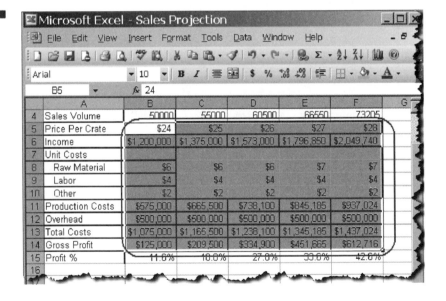

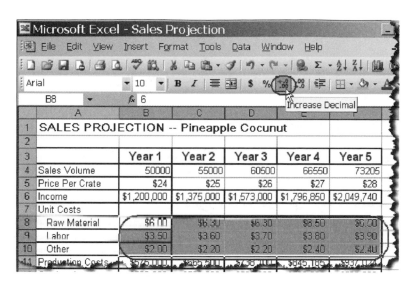

- **Select cell B8.**
- **Hold down [SHIFT].**
- **Select cell F10.**
- **Click two times on the**

  Increase Decimal **button.**

The selected entries are displayed with 2 decimal places.

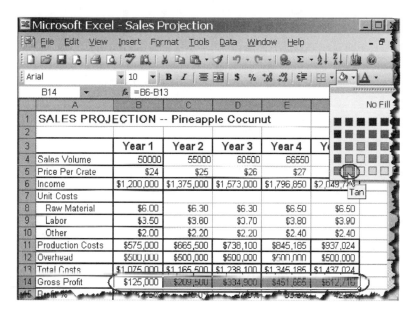

13.9

- **Save the document.**
- **Select cell B14.**
- **Hold down [SHIFT].**
- **Select cell F14.**
- **Click on the down arrow at the right side of the Fill Color**

  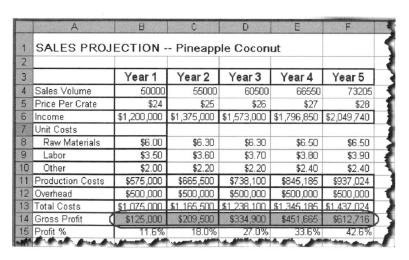 **button on the Formatting toolbar.**
- **Click on the Tan option (fifth option down in the second column).**

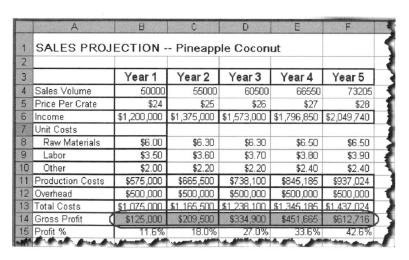

13.10

The color is selected and the shading is added to the selected cells.

■ 13.11

- Select cell B3.

- Hold down [SHIFT].

- Select cell F3.

- Click on the down arrow at the right side of the Fill Color button on the Formatting toolbar.

- Click on the Gold option (fourth option down in the second column).

The color is selected and the shading is added to the selected cells.

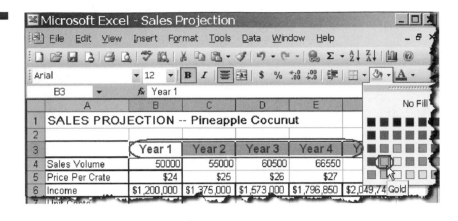

■ 13.12

- Select cell A3.

- Hold down [SHIFT].

- Click on cell F15, the cells A3 through F15 are selected. Leave the shift button.

- Right click on the selected cells.

- Click on Format Cells...

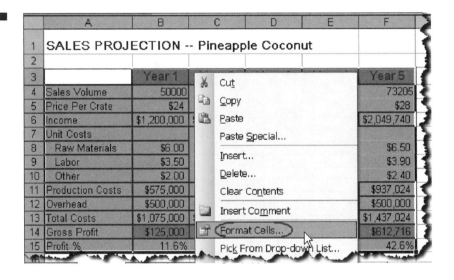

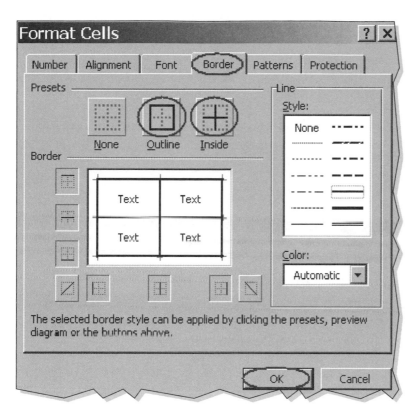

- **Select the Border tab.**

- **Click on the Outline button to select the outline for the selected cells.**

- **Click on the Inside button to include inside vertical and horizontal lines.**

- **Click OK.**

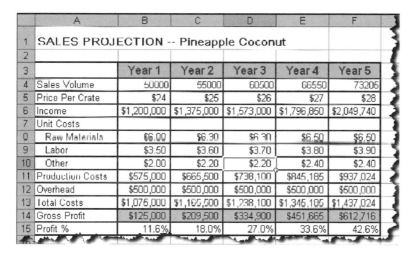

The Format cells dialog box is closed and you have added outside and inside border on the selected cells.

	A	B	C	D	E	F
1	SALES PROJECTION -- Pineapple Coconut					
2						
3		Year 1	Year 2	Year 3	Year 4	Year 5
4	Sales Volume	50000	55000	60500	66550	73205
5	Price Per Crate	$24	$25	$26	$27	$28
6	Income	$1,200,000	$1,375,000	$1,573,000	$1,796,850	$2,049,740
7	Unit Costs					
8	Raw Materials	$6.00	$6.30	$6.30	$6.50	$6.50
9	Labor	$3.50	$3.60	$3.70	$3.80	$3.90
10	Other	$2.00	$2.20	$2.20	$2.40	$2.40
11	Production Costs	$575,000	$665,500	$738,100	$845,185	$937,024
12	Overhead	$500,000	$500,000	$500,000	$500,000	$500,000
13	Total Costs	$1,075,000	$1,165,500	$1,238,100	$1,345,185	$1,437,024
14	Gross Profit	$125,000	$209,500	$334,900	$451,665	$612,716
15	Profit %	11.6%	18.0%	27.0%	33.6%	42.6%

13.15

- **Make sure that the Border tab is selected.**
- **Select cell B3.**
- **Hold down [SHIFT].**
- **Select cell F15.**
- **Right click on the selected cells.**
- **Click on Format Cells...**

- **Click on the Inside** Inside **button.**
- **Click on** **border.**
- **Click on**  **border.**
- **Click OK.**

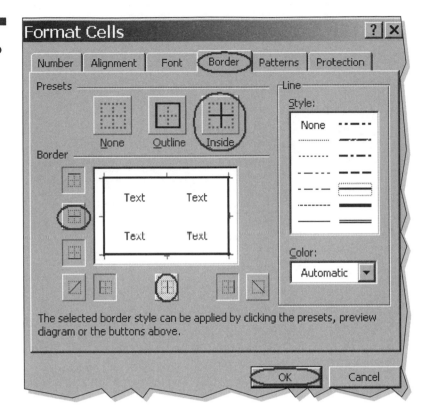

13.16

The Format cells dialog box is closed. Your worksheet should appear similar to that illustrated in the screen shot.

- **Save the document.**

	A	B	C	D	E	F
1	SALES PROJECTION -- Pineapple Coconut					
2						
3		Year 1	Year 2	Year 3	Year 4	Year 5
4	Sales Volume	50000	55000	60500	66550	73205
5	Price Per Crate	$24	$25	$26	$27	$28
6	Income	$1,200,000	$1,375,000	$1,573,000	$1,796,850	$2,049,740
7	Unit Costs					
8	Raw Materials	$6.00	$6.30	$6.30	$6.50	$6.50
9	Labor	$3.50	$3.60	$3.70	$3.80	$3.90
10	Other	$2.00	$2.20	$2.20	$2.40	$2.40
11	Production Costs	$575,000	$665,500	$738,100	$845,185	$937,024
12	Overhead	$500,000	$500,000	$500,000	$500,000	$500,000
13	Total Costs	$1,075,000	$1,165,500	$1,238,100	$1,345,185	$1,437,024
14	Gross Profit	$125,000	$209,500	$334,900	$451,665	$612,716
15	Profit %	11.6%	18.0%	27.0%	33.6%	42.6%

Changing the Page Setup for a Worksheet

All page setup options for printing a worksheet are accessed with the **File, Page Setup** command. Selecting this command displays the Page Setup dialog box, which includes the following panels:

Page　　　　This panel includes options for defining page characteristics, such as orientation (portrait or landscape), paper size and print quality. It also includes a **Fit to** option, which can be used to automatically scale down the font, if necessary, to ensure that the worksheet is printed on a specified number of pages.

Margins This panel includes options for resetting the various margins, as well as options for centering the page between the left and right and/or top and bottom margins.

Header/Footer This panel includes options for including a header and/or footer on each page of a multiple-page printout. A header (which appear at the top of a page) or footer (which appears at the bottom of a page) can include such information as the worksheet name, the filename, the page number, the date and/or the time.

Sheet This panel includes options for printing a specific area of the worksheet, as well as options for including cell gridlines and the worksheet frame (row and column headings) in the printout.

Objective

In this exercise, you will **change various page setup options for a worksheet**. Specifically, you will begin by setting the necessary options to 1) print the entire worksheet on one page, 2) include a custom header and a custom footer at the top and bottom of the page, and 3) include cell gridlines in the printout. You will then redisplay the same worksheet and set the necessary options to 1) print the worksheet in landscape orientation, and 2) center the worksheet on the page.

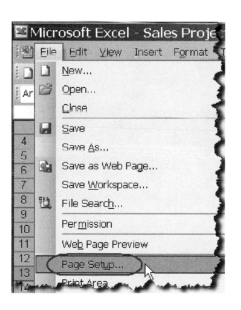

14.1

- **Choose the File, Page Setup command.**

14.2

The Page panel of the Page Setup dialog box is displayed.

- **Under Scaling, click on Fit to and select 1.**

This option ensures that the entire worksheet will be printed on one page.

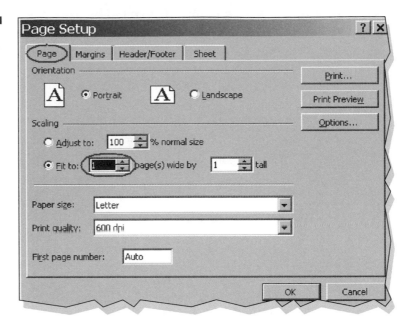

14.3

- **Click on the Margins tab.**

The Margins panel of the dialog box is displayed.

- **Click on the up arrow at the right side of the Top box until the setting reads 2.**

The top margin of the worksheet is increased to two inches.

- **Under Center on page, click on Horizontally and on Vertically.**

The worksheet will be centered on the page (between the left and right margins, as well as between the top and bottom margins).

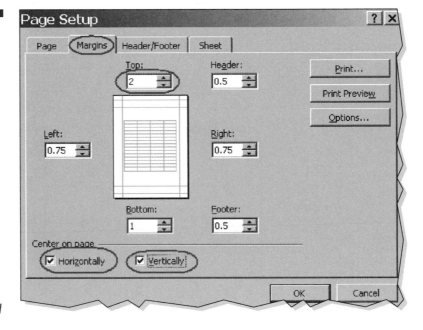

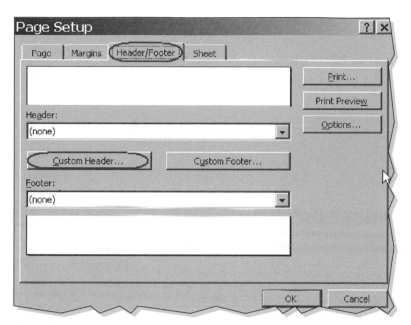

14.4

- **Click on the Header/Footer tab.**

The Header/Footer panel of the dialog box is displayed. You will now define a header and footer.

NOTE: *The Header and Footer boxes include a list of suggested headers and footers, respectively. In this case, however, you will create your own custom header and footer.*

- **Click on the Custom Header button.**

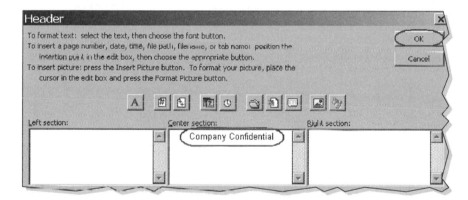

14.5

The Header dialog box is displayed.

- **Press [TAB].**

- **In the Center section box, Type: Company Confidential**

The header text is entered. This text will be centered at the top of the page.

- **Click on the OK button.**

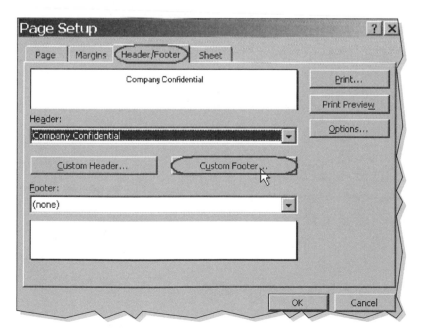

14.6

The Page Setup dialog box is redisplayed.

- **Click on the Custom Footer button.**

The Footer dialog box is displayed.

14.7

- **Press [TAB] two times. The insertion point moves to the Right section box.**

- **Click on the Date  button.**

A date code is inserted.

- **Click on the OK button.**

The Page Setup dialog box is redisplayed.

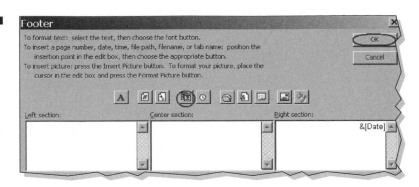

14.8

- **Click on the Sheet tab.**

The Sheet panel of the dialog box is displayed.

- **Under Print, click on Gridlines.**

Cell gridline will be included in the printout. You are now ready to print the worksheet with the new settings.

- **Click on the Print button (in the dialog box).**

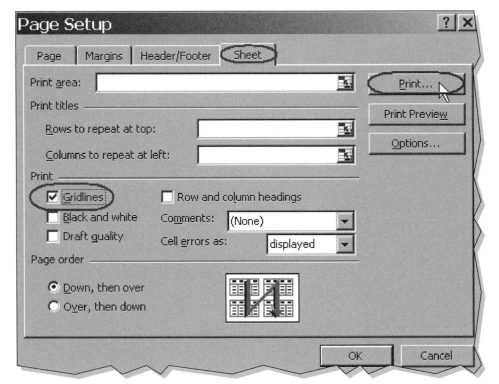

14.9

The Print dialog box is displayed.

NOTE: *Note that when a printout includes gridlines, any special borders and/or shading that have been applied to cells appear instead of the cell gridlines.*

- **On a Print dialog box, click on Properties.**

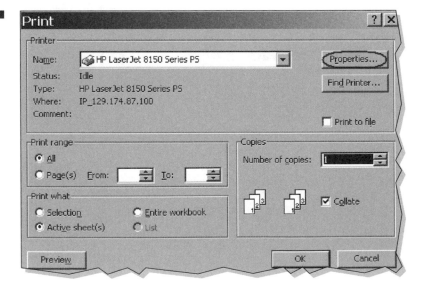

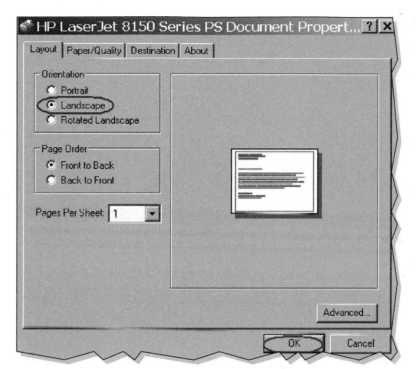

14.10

- **Select Layout tab.**
- **Under Orientation, click on Landscape.**

The page orientation is reset.

- **Click OK.**

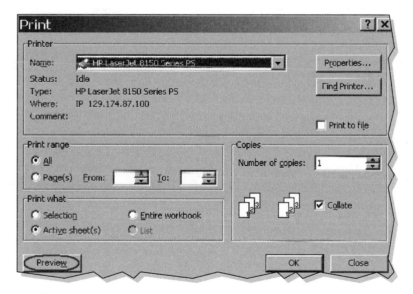

14.11

- **On the Print dialog box, click on Preview.**

Alternative: Click on the Print Preview button on the Standard toolbar.

The Print Preview window is opened, displaying the full-page view of the worksheet. Notice that since the worksheet includes more columns than the width of the page can accommodate, only columns A through G appear on this page and the remaining columns will appear on another page.

14.12

NOTE: *From the Print Preview window, you can make any necessary adjustments to the page setup, thereby saving time and paper.*

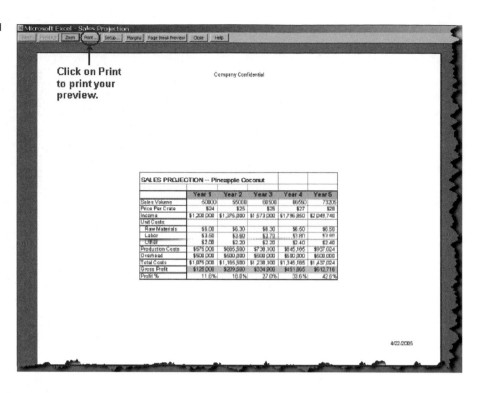

Click on Print to print your preview.

Exiting from Excel

When you are finished using Excel, you can exit from the program either by choosing the **File**, **Exit** command or by clicking on the **Close** button on the Title bar of the Application window. If you have not saved changes in a workbook, you will be prompted to indicate whether or not you want to save those changes before exiting.

Objective

In this exercise, you will **exit from Excel**.

15.1

• **Choose the File, Exit command.**

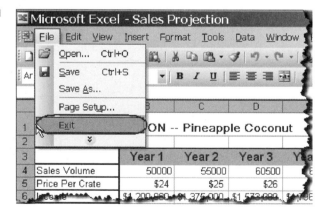

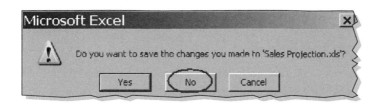

15.2

- **A prompt box appears, asking you if you want to save the changes in the workbook.**
- **Click on the No button.**

The program is exited, and the Windows desktop is redisplayed.

Displaying Help Information

If you encounter a problem or just need additional information while using Excel, there are a number of ways in which you can obtain help.

The program itself includes an extensive **Help system**, which can be accessed in the following ways:

- By choosing the **Help → Microsoft Excel Help** command or by clicking on the **Microsoft Excel Help** button on the Standard toolbar. Doing this displays the Excel Help task pane in which you enter one or more keywords and click on the **Start searching** button.
- By entering a request in the **Type a question for help** box (in the upper right corner of the Application window) and by pressing **[ENTER]**.

You can also get help:

- By clicking on the **Table of Contents** option in the Excel Help task pane. Doing this displays a list of Help topics in a table of contents format.
- By clicking on the **Connect to Microsoft Office Online** option in the Excel Help task pane. Doing this displays the Microsoft Office Online Home page (assuming you have access to the Internet).

1. The Microsoft Office Online Web site provides a number of resources for users of Microsoft Office products, including "how-to" articles to assist the user in performing various tasks, interactive training tutorials to help the user become more familiar with the programs he or she is running, and various downloads (for example, templates, clip art and product upgrades).
2. The Office Assistant, which is displayed by choosing the **Help, Show the Office Assistant** command, can provide tips and other helpful information as you work. When the Office Assistant has a tip, a light bulb will appear. To display the tip, simply click on this light bulb. To control the type of information the Office Assistant provides, click on the Office Assistant icon, and click on the **Options** button in the balloon that appears. Then, on the Options panel of the Office Assistant dialog box, select/deselect the relevant options, and click on the **OK** button.

Objective

In this exercise, you will **access the Excel Help system and display help information for various topics**.

16.1

- **Click on the Help and then click on Microsoft Excel Help button.**

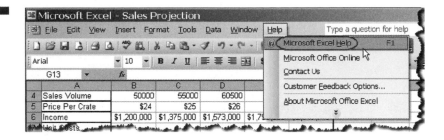

16.2

- **In the Excel Help task pane, type: Print a worksheet and then click on the Start searching button.**

A list of topics is displayed in Search Results task pane.

NOTE: *Notice that you did not enter an actual question in the Search for help box. Instead, you simply entered the action "Print a worksheet." (You could have entered the question "How do I print a worksheet?" Doing so, however, would have displayed the same list of topics.)*

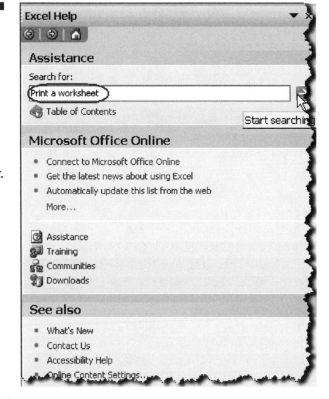

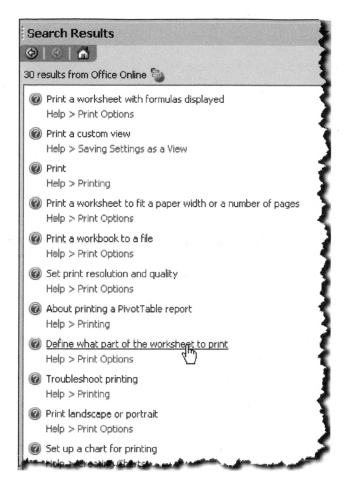

16.3

- **Click on Define what part of the worksheet to print.**

The Microsoft Excel Help window is reopened, displaying a list of subtopics.

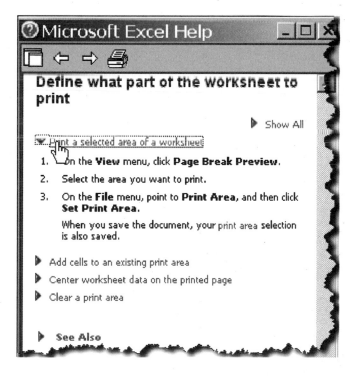

16.4

- **Click on Print a selected area of a worksheet.**

The subtopic is expanded, and instructions for performing the selected operation are displayed.

16.5

- **Click on the Close button on the Title bar of the Microsoft Excel Help window.**

The Microsoft Excel Help window is closed.

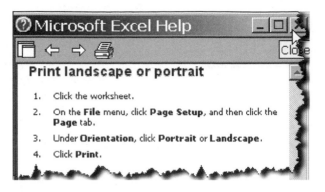

16.6

- **Click on the Close button at the top of the Search Results task pane.**

The task pane is closed.

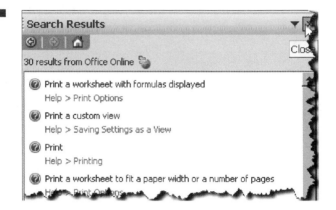

Additional methods for obtaining help: (A screenshot is needed for this)

1. Click on the **Microsoft Excel Help** button. Then, in the Excel Help task pane, click on **Table of Contents** to display a list of main help topics. (Note that you can display the latest help information by clicking on **For the best content, view the online Table of Contents** at the top of the Excel Help task pane, assuming you have access to the Internet. In this case, however, you will simply view the current help information.)
2. In the task pane, click on a **help topic** of your choice to display a list of subtopics. Click on a **subtopic** of your choice in the current list and in any subsequent list until the desired help information is displayed in the Microsoft Excel Help window.
3. **Close** both the **Microsoft Excel Help window** and the **Excel Help task pane**.

Congratulations! You have completed the Case Study.

Conclusion

You have just completed **Microsoft Office Excel 2003—Case Study 1**. In the case study, you were introduced to many techniques. To reinforce your understanding of these techniques, it is recommended that you read and work through it once again.

Further Practice

The following Case Study will give you the opportunity to review and practice many of the Excel features you have learned. It is divided into several steps.

Step 1

Make sure that all documents are closed. Then display a **blank document**.

Step 2

Enter the data as shown in the following screen-shot:

	A	B
1	Sales Summary	
2		
3		Jan
4	Sales Volume	4,600
5	Unit Price	25
6	Income	
7	Unit Cost	11
8	Sales Cost	
9	Fixed Cost	50000
10	Total Cost	
11	Gross Profit	
12	Tax Rate	0.25
13	Tax Due	
14	Net Profit	

Increase the **width** of column **A** so that all labels are fully displayed.
Increase the **font size** of the **worksheet title** (in cell **A1**).
Bold the entries in cells **A4:A14**.
Bold and **centered** the entry in cell **B3**.
Add shading to the entry in cell **B3**.

	A	B
1	Sales Summary	
2		
3		Jan
4	Sales Volume	4,600
5	Unit Price	$25
6	Income	
7	Unit Cost	$11
8	Sales Cost	
9	Fixed Cost	$50,000
10	Total Cost	
11	Gross Profit	
12	Tax Rate	25%
13	Tax Due	
14	Net Profit	

Step 3

Enter **column headings** into the range **C3:G3.** (These headings should read **Feb, Mar, Apr,** etc.)

    Enter the data as shown in the following screen-shot for Sales Volume:

	A	B	C	D	E	F	G
1	Sales Summary						
2							
3		Jan	Feb	Mar	Apr	May	Jun
4	Sales Volume	4,600	4,800	5,000	5,200	5,400	5,600
5	Unit Price	25					
6	Income						
7	Unit Cost	11					
8	Sales Cost						
9	Fixed Cost	50000					
10	Total Cost						
11	Gross Profit						
12	Tax Rate	0.25					
13	Tax Due						
14	Net Profit						

Step 4

The Unit Price, Unit Cost, Fixed Cost, and Tax Rate are forecasted to remain same till June.

    Copy the data value of Unit Price, Unit Cost, Fixed Cost, and Tax Rate into the appropriate cells.

    Save the workbook as **Sales Summary**.

	A	B	C	D	E	F	G
1	Sales Summary						
2							
3		Jan	Feb	Mar	Apr	May	Jun
4	Sales Volume	4,600	4,800	5,000	5,200	5,400	5,600
5	Unit Price	25	25	25	25	25	25
6	Income						
7	Unit Cost	11	11	11	11	11	11
8	Sales Cost						
9	Fixed Cost	50000	50000	50000	50000	50000	50000
10	Total Cost						
11	Gross Profit						
12	Tax Rate	0.25	0.25	0.25	0.25	0.25	0.25
13	Tax Due						
14	Net Profit						

Step 5

In cell B6, enter the following formula for Income:
=B4*B5
Copy this **formula** into the appropriate cells.

	A	B	C	D	E	F	G
1	Sales Summary						
2							
3		Jan	Feb	Mar	Apr	May	Jun
4	Sales Volume	4,600	4,800	5,000	5,200	5,400	5,600
5	Unit Price	25	25	25	25	25	25
6	Income	115000	120000	125000	130000	135000	140000
7	Unit Cost	11	11	11	11	11	11
8	Sales Cost						
9	Fixed Cost	50000	50000	50000	50000	50000	50000
10	Total Cost						
11	Gross Profit						
12	Tax Rate	0.25	0.25	0.25	0.25	0.25	0.25
13	Tax Due						
14	Net Profit						

Step 6

In cell B8, enter Sales Cost formula as =B4*B7
In cell B10, enter Total Cost formula as =B8+B9
In cell B11, enter Gross Profit formula as =B6-B10
In cell B13, enter Tax Due formula as =B11*B12
In cell B14, enter Net Profit formula as =B11-B13

The formulas for **Sales Cost, Total Cost, Gross Profit, Tax Due, Net Profit** are the same till June. **Copy** these **formulas** into the appropriate cells.

	A	B	C	D	E	F	G
2							
3		Jan	Feb	Mar	Apr	May	Jun
4	Sales Volume	4600	4,800	5,000	5,200	5,400	5,600
5	Unit Price	25	25	25	25	25	25
6	Income	115000	120000	125000	130000	135000	140000
7	Unit Cost	11	11	11	11	11	11
8	Sales Cost	50600	52800	55000	57200	59400	61600
9	Fixed Cost	50000	50000	50000	50000	50000	50000
10	Total Cost	100600	102800	105000	107200	109400	111600
11	Gross Profit	14400	17200	20000	22800	25600	28400
12	Tax Rate	0.25	0.25	0.25	0.25	0.25	0.25
13	Tax Due	3600	4300	5000	5700	6400	7100
14	Net Profit	10800	12900	15000	17100	19200	21300

Step 7

Format cells **B4:G14** so that the entries have dollar-sign ($) currency with **no** decimal place.

    Format cells **B12:G12** so that the entries are displayed as a **percentage** with **1** decimal place.

	A	B	C	D	E	F	G
2							
3		Jan	Feb	Mar	Apr	May	Jun
4	Sales Volume	$4,600	$4,800	$5,000	$5,200	$5,400	$5,600
5	Unit Price	$25	$25	$25	$25	$25	$25
6	Income	$115,000	$120,000	$125,000	$130,000	$135,000	$140,000
7	Unit Cost	$11	$11	$11	$11	$11	$11
8	Sales Cost	$50,600	$52,800	$55,000	$57,200	$59,400	$61,600
9	Fixed Cost	$50,000	$50,000	$50,000	$50,000	$50,000	$50,000
10	Total Cost	$100,600	$102,800	$105,000	$107,200	$109,400	$111,600
11	Gross Profit	$14,400	$17,200	$20,000	$22,800	$25,600	$28,400
12	Tax Rate	25%	25%	25%	25%	25%	25%
13	Tax Due	$3,600	$4,300	$5,000	$5,700	$6,400	$7,100
14	Net Profit	$10,800	$12,900	$15,000	$17,100	$19,200	$21,300

Save the **workbook** once again.

Step 8

Your worksheet is now complete, but the presentation could still be improved.

    Use the available **format options** to enhance the appearance of the **numeric data**.

    Use other available **format options** to make further enhancements (for example, reset the font, add borders and shading, etc.).

Step 9

Set **print options** of your choice (for example, add a header and/or footer, center the data horizontally, etc.).

    Preview and then **print**, the worksheet.

    (Your worksheet should appear similar to that illustrated on next page. The formatting will vary, of course, depending on the options you have chosen.)

Step 10

Save the **workbook** once again, and then **close** the **file**.

	A	B	C	D	E	F	G
1	**Sales Summary**						
2							
3		**Jan**	**Feb**	**Mar**	**Apr**	**May**	**Jun**
4	**Sales Volume**	$4,600	$4,800	$5,000	$5,200	$5,400	$5,600
5	**Unit Price**	$25	$25	$25	$25	$25	$25
6	**Income**	$115,000	$120,000	$125,000	$130,000	$135,000	$140,000
7	**Unit Cost**	$11	$11	$11	$11	$11	$11
8	**Sales Cost**	$50,600	$52,800	$55,000	$57,200	$59,400	$61,600
9	**Fixed Cost**	$50,000	$50,000	$50,000	$50,000	$50,000	$50,000
10	**Total Cost**	$100,600	$102,800	$105,000	$107,200	$109,400	$111,600
11	**Gross Profit**	$14,400	$17,200	$20,000	$22,800	$25,600	$28,400
12	**Tax Rate**	25%	25%	25%	25%	25%	25%
13	**Tax Due**	$3,600	$4,300	$5,000	$5,700	$6,400	$7,100
14	**Net Profit**	$10,800	$12,900	$15,000	$17,100	$19,200	$21,300
15							

MS Excel 2003
Case Study 2

OBJECTIVES

After successfully completing this case study, you should be able to:

- Enter an absolute cell reference into a formula
- Use Excel functions (SUM, AVERAGE, MAX, MIN and COUNT)
- Use the IF function
- Use the NOW function
- Sort the records of a list
- Apply conditional formatting to a worksheet
- Filter the records of a list
- Work on multiple worksheets

- Renaming worksheets and formatting the worksheet tabs
- Enter a formula to link related worksheets in a workbook
- Format multiple worksheets in one operation
- Use Excel's Auto format feature
- Plot a chart
- Modify and enhance a chart
- Use the spell checker tool

Case Study 2—MS Excel 2003

Assume that you work in the HR department of Priceless Shoe Company. You are asked to calculate bonuses for your sales employees for 2004 and 2005. Bonus is awarded to sales employees who exceed their sales targets. It is calculated as a percentage of the amount by which they exceed their targets. The bonus rate was 10% and 12% for the years 2004 and 2005 respectively.

Your boss would also like to see a summary worksheet based on year 2004 and year 2005. In addition, he wants to see a chart comparing the target sales and actual sales for each employee.

The desired worksheets are:

Priceless Shoe Store
BONUS REPORT
4/29/05 5:34 PM

Bonus Rate: 10%

	Target Sales	Actual Sales	Difference	Bonus	Percent Target Achieved	Performance
Bill	$ 55,000	$ 63,000	$ 8,000	$ 800	114.5%	Above Expectation
Mary	$ 43,000	$ 43,000	$ -	$ -	100.0%	Meets Expectation
Steve	$ 21,750	$ 28,000	$ 6,250	$ 625	128.7%	Above Expectation
Sue	$ 34,000	$ 30,000	$ (4,000)	$ -	88.2%	Below Expectation
Tom	$ 27,500	$ 32,000	$ 4,500	$ 450	116.4%	Above Expectation
Highest	$ 55,000	$ 63,000	$ 8,000	$ 800	128.7%	
Lowest	$ 21,750	$ 28,000	$ (4,000)	$ -	88.2%	
Total	$ 181,250	$ 196,000	$ 14,750	$ 1,875	547.9%	
Average	$ 36,250	$ 39,200	$ 2,950	$ 375	109.6%	

BONUS WORKSHEET FOR YEAR 2004

Priceless Shoe Store
BONUS REPORT
4/29/05 5:34 PM

Bonus Rate: 12%

	Target Sales	Actual Sales	Difference	Bonus	Percent Target Achieved	Performance
Bill	$ 105,000	$ 125,000	$ 20,000	$ 2,400	119.0%	Above Expectation
Mary	$ 105,000	$ 43,000	$ (62,000)	$ -	41.0%	Below Expectation
Steve	$ 105,000	$ 131,000	$ 26,000	$ 3,120	124.8%	Above Expectation
Sue	$ 105,000	$ 30,000	$ (75,000)	$ -	28.6%	Below Expectation
Tom	$ 105,000	$ 107,500	$ 2,500	$ 300	102.4%	Above Expectation
Highest	$ 105,000	$ 131,000	$ 26,000	$ 3,120	124.8%	
Lowest	$ 105,000	$ 30,000	$ (75,000)	$ -	28.6%	
Total	$ 525,000	$ 436,500	$ (88,500)	$ 5,820	415.7%	
Average	$ 105,000	$ 87,300	$ (17,700)	$ 1,164	83.1%	

BONUS WORKSHEET FOR YEAR 2005

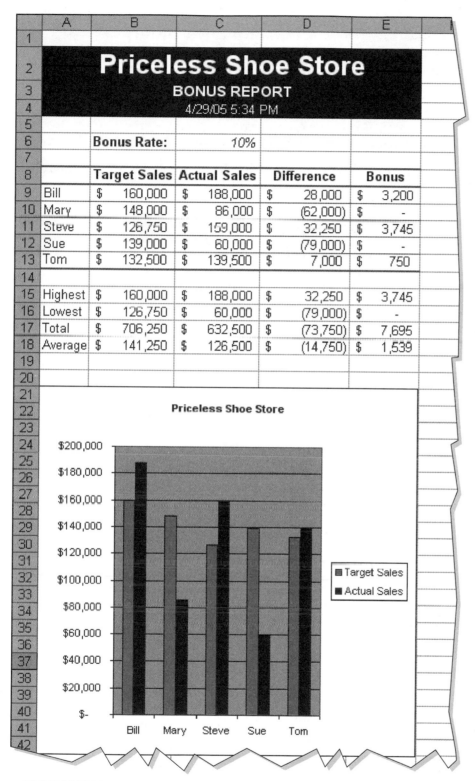

	Target Sales	Actual Sales	Difference	Bonus
Priceless Shoe Store				
BONUS REPORT				
4/29/05 5:34 PM				
Bonus Rate:	10%			
Bill	$ 160,000	$ 188,000	$ 28,000	$ 3,200
Mary	$ 148,000	$ 86,000	$ (62,000)	$ -
Steve	$ 126,750	$ 159,000	$ 32,250	$ 3,745
Sue	$ 139,000	$ 60,000	$ (79,000)	$ -
Tom	$ 132,500	$ 139,500	$ 7,000	$ 750
Highest	$ 160,000	$ 188,000	$ 32,250	$ 3,745
Lowest	$ 126,750	$ 60,000	$ (79,000)	$ -
Total	$ 706,250	$ 632,500	$ (73,750)	$ 7,695
Average	$ 141,250	$ 126,500	$ (14,750)	$ 1,539

SUMMARY WORKSHEET BASED ON YEAR 2004 AND YEAR 2005

Open a New Workbook and Enter Information

You can **open a new workbook** by following any of three options:

- Choose the **File**, **New**... command.
- In the New Workbook task pane, select the **Blank workbook** option.
- Simply click on the **New** button ▢ on the Standard toolbar.

To **enter data** into a cell, you must first select the cell by moving the **cell pointer** to it.

To **enter a formula** into a worksheet:

- Select the cell in which the formula is to appear
- Type = (an equal sign). Doing this activates the Formula bar and displays an equal sign in that bar and in the current cell.
- Specify a **constant** or **operator** by **typing** it.
- Specify a **cell reference**:

  - By **typing** the **column/row coordinates** (for example, B5); or
  - By **pointing** (moving the cell pointer) to it.

- Click on the **Enter** button next to the Formula bar, or press **[ENTER]**. (If necessary, you can cancel the formula before entering it by clicking on the **Cancel** button next to the Formula bar or by pressing **[ESC]**.)

Objective

In this exercise, you will **enter labels, values and formulas in a new worksheet**.

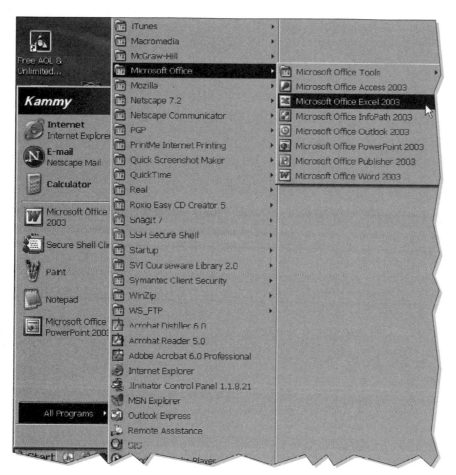

1.1

- **Click on the Start button on the Windows taskbar.**

- **Point to Programs.**

- **Point to Microsoft Office on the menu.**

- **Click on Microsoft Office Excel 2003 on the submenu.**

Excel is started, and the Excel Application window appears, displaying a blank workbook.

1.2

- In cell **A1**, type **BONUS REPORT**

*NOTE: If you made a mistake while typing, use [**BACKSPACE**] to delete the incorrect character(s). If you find a mistake in a typed cell, point the cell and type correct information again.*

- In cell **B3**, type **Bonus Rate**

- In cell **C3**, type **10%**

- In cell **B5, C5, D5, and E5** type **Target Sales, Actual Sales, Difference, and Bonus** respectively.

- In cell **A6, B6, C6** type **Tom, 27500, and 32000** respectively.

- In cell **A7, B7, and C7** type **Sue, 34000 and 30000** respectively.

- In cell **A8, B8, and C8** type **Steve, 21750 and 28000** respectively.

- In cell **A9, B9, and C9** type **Mary, 43000, and 43000** respectively.

- In cell **A10, B10, and C10** type **Bill, 55000, and 63000** respectively.

	A	B	C	D	E
1	BONUS REPORT				
2					
3		Bonus Rat	10%		
4					
5		Target Sal	Actual Sal	Difference	Bonus
6	Tom	27500	32000		
7	Sue	34000	30000		
8	Steve	21750	28000		
9	Mary	43000	43000		
10	Bill	55000	63000		

1.3

- In cell **D6**, type **=C6-B6** and press **[ENTER]**.

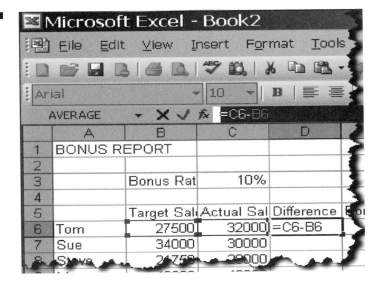

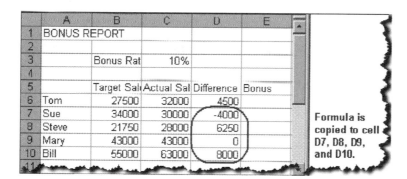

 1.4

The formula is entered, and the result of the calculation (4500) is displayed in cell D6.

- **Click on cell D6 and point to the fill handle (the small black square) in the lower-right corner of cell D6.**

*Drag the **fill handle** (in the lower-right corner of the selection), and extend the selection to cell D10.*

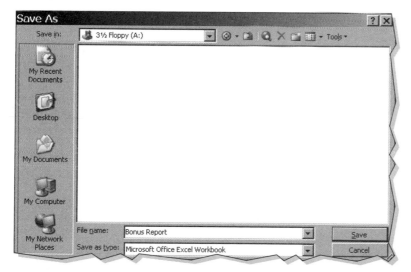

Formula is copied to cell D7, D8, D9, and D10.

 1.5

- **Release the mouse button.**

The formula is copied to cells D7, D8, D9, and D10 and the corresponding results are displayed.

1.6

- **Insert floppy disk in drive A.**
- **Click on the Save 🖫 button on the Standard toolbar or choose the File, Save command.**
- **In a Save As dialog box, enter file name as Bonus Report and select 3½ Floppy (A:) in the Save in list.**
- **Click on Save button.**

Using Absolute Cell Reference into a Formula

You have seen how cell references are adjusted when a formula is copied. The formula =**C6-B6** in cell **D6**, for example, normally appears as =**C7-B7** when copied into cell **D7**, as =**C8-B8** when copied into cell **D8**, and so on. C6 and B6, in this case, are called **relative cell references** since their row coordinates vary according to the row into which the formula is copied.

There may be times, however, when you will not want the column and/or row coordinates of a cell reference to be adjusted when a formula is copied. In the worksheet illustrated below, for example, cell C3 contains the bonus rate of 10% (a constant value). Normally the formula to calculate the bonus for the individual in E6 would be **=D6*C3**. Copying this formula down the column to calculate the bonuses for the other individuals in column E, however, would produce invalid results since the row coordinate for the second operand would vary from row to row, and the operand, therefore, would no longer refer to the bonus rate. To produce the correct results, you would want the formula to continue referring to cell C3 when copied into cell E7, when copied into cell E8, and so on.

	A	B	C	D	E
1	BONUS REPORT				
2					
3		Bonus Rat	10%		
4					
5		Target Sal	Actual Sal	Difference	Bonus
6	Tom	27500	32000	4500	450
7	Sue	34000	30000	-4000	-400
8	Steve	21750	28000	6250	625
9	Mary	43000	43000	0	0
10	Bill	55000	63000	8000	800

WORKSHEET WITH A CONSTANT VALUE IN CELL C3

To "anchor" a cell, you must change its reference from relative to **absolute** while building or editing the formula in which it appears. This can be done in either of the following ways:

- By typing a **dollar sign** before each coordinate (for example, C3); or
- By pressing the **[F4]** key.

Objective

In this exercise, you will **build a formula that includes an absolute cell reference**.

You will begin by entering a formula to calculate the bonus for the first individual.

- **Select cell E6.
  Type: =D6*C3**

- **Press [ENTER]**

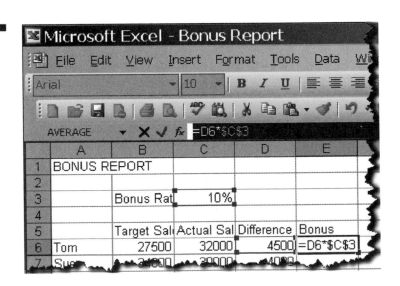

	A	B	C	D	E	F
1	BONUS REPORT					
2						
3		Bonus Rat	10%			
4						
5		Target Sal	Actual Sal	Difference	Bonus	
6	Tom	27500	32000	4500	450	
7	Sue	34000	30000	-4000	-400	
8	Steve	21750	28000	6250	625	
9	Mary	43000	43000	0	0	
10	Bill	55000	63000	8000	800	
11						

Formula is copied to cell E7, E8, E9, and E10.

2.2

The formula is entered, and the result of the calculation (450) is displayed in cell E6.

- **Click on cell E6.**

- **Point to the fill handle.**

- **Drag the fill handle and extend the selection to cell E10.**

The formula is copied to cells E7, E8, E9, and E10 and the corresponding results will be displayed.

NOTE: *Select various cells in the above range, and notice that the formula in each contains the cell reference **C3**. The absolute cell reference was not adjusted when the formula was copied.*

- **Save the document.**

Inserting and Deleting Rows and Columns

With Excel, you can quickly insert new rows and columns, as well as delete existing rows and columns, anywhere in a worksheet. When you do so, existing or remaining rows/columns are adjusted automatically—rows are moved down and columns are moved to the right to open up space for an inserted row/column; rows are moved up and columns are moved to the left to close up space left by a deleted row/column.

To **insert one or more rows/columns into a worksheet**:

- Select the area in which the row(s) or column(s) is/are to be inserted by selecting the row or column heading(s).
- Choose the **Insert**, **Rows** or **Insert**, **Columns** command, or select the **Insert** option on the shortcut menu.

To **delete one or more rows/columns from a worksheet**:

- Select the row(s) or column(s) that is/are to be deleted.
- Choose the **Edit**, **Delete** command, or select the **Delete** option on the shortcut menu.

Objective

In this exercise, you will **insert both a new row and a new column into a worksheet**. You will then **enter data into this row and column** to complete the worksheet.

3.1

- **Click on the row1 heading.**

Row1 is selected. You will now insert a new row into the selected area.

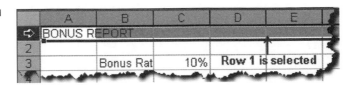

3.2

- **Choose the Insert, Rows command.**

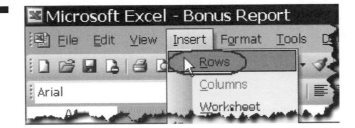

3.3

A new row is inserted.

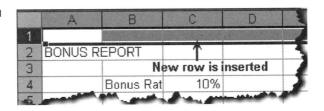

3.4

- **Click in the cell A1.**
- **Type: Priceless Shoe Store**

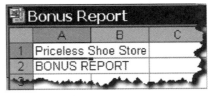

3.5

- **Using the above procedure, click on the row1 heading and insert a new row above it.**

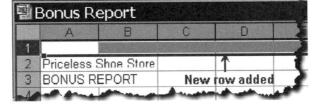

3.6

- **Click in the cell F7.**
- **Type: Performance**

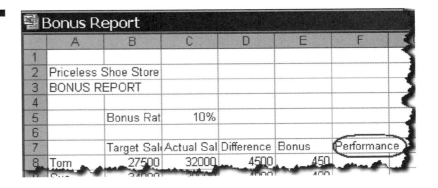

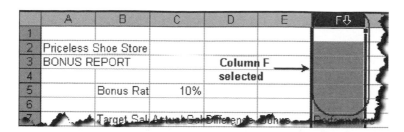

3.7

- **Click on the column F heading.**

Column F is selected.

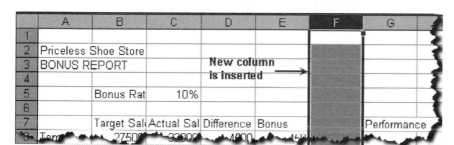

3.8

You will now insert a new column into the selected area.

- **Point to the selected column and right-click the mouse button.**

A shortcut menu is displayed.

3.9

- **Click on Insert.**

A new column is inserted between Bonus and Performance.

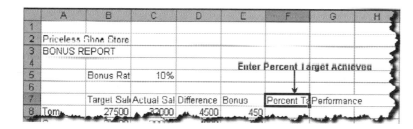

3.10

- **Click in cell F7.**
- **Type: Percent Target Achieved and press [ENTER].**

3.11

- **Click in cell F8.**
- **Type: =C8/B8**

3.12

- **Press [ENTER].**
- **Click on cell F8 and point to the fill handle of cell F8.**
- **Drag the fill handle and extend the selection to cell F12**

The formula is copied to cells F9, F10, F11, and F12 and the corresponding results will be displayed.

6						
7		Target Sal	Actual Sal	Difference	Bonus	Percent Ta	Perfo
8	Tom	27500	32000	4500	450	1.163636
9	Sue	34000	30000	-4000	-400	0.882353
10	Steve	21750	28000	6250	625	1.287356
11	Mary	43000	43000	0	0	1
12	Bill	55000	63000	8000	800	1.145455

3.13

- **Select cell F8.**
- **Hold Shift key and click on F12.**
- **Click on the Percent Style button on the Formatting toolbar.**

The selected entries are displayed as percentages.

3.14

- **While range F8 to F12 is selected, click on the Increase Decimal button on the Formatting toolbar.**

A decimal place is added.

- **Save the document.**

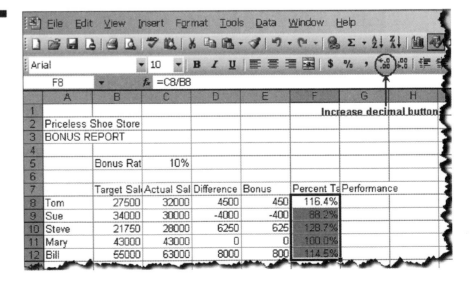

Using Excel Functions

This section is an introduction to **Excel functions**. In it, you will learn how to:

- Use the **SUM** function to compute **subtotals** and **grand totals**.
- Use the **AVERAGE** function to compute the **arithmetic mean** of a group of numeric entries.
- Use the **MAX** function to compute the **maximum** of a group of numeric entries.
- Use the **MIN** function to compute the **minimum** of a group of numeric entries.
- Use the **COUNT** function to compute the **number** of **numeric entries** in a range.

You will also learn how to use the following **logical and time functions**:

- **Use** the **IF** function.
- **Nest IF** functions.
- **NOW** function.

What Is a Function?

A **function** is a special type of formula that produces, or "returns," a specific result. Excel provides more than 300 functions for use in any worksheet, allowing you to perform calculations that would otherwise be difficult, if not impossible, to achieve. These functions fall into several categories including:

Math	This category includes functions for computing totals, square roots, logarithms, tangents, etc.
Statistical	This category includes functions for computing averages, maximums, minimums, variances, etc.
Financial	This category includes functions for computing loan repayments, rates of return, depreciation, etc.
Date and Time	This category includes functions for computing the number of days in a specific date interval, the number of hours in a specific time interval, etc.

All functions are made up of two elements: the function name and an argument list. The **function name** is simply the name assigned to the function (for example, **SUM**). The **argument list** usually includes one or more operands (arguments), enclosed in parentheses, which the function uses to produce its result. An **argument** can be any item of information that is appropriate for the function in which it appears—for example, a text or numeric constant, a formula, another function, a single cell reference, or multiple cell references (for example, a range).

Since a function is a formula, it must be preceded by an equal sign (=), as follows:

=FUNCTION NAME(ARGUMENT)

OR

=FUNCTION NAME(ARGUMENT1, ARGUMENT2, . . .)

Notes

1. The function name and arguments can be entered in either uppercase or lowercase characters.
2. Multiple arguments must be separated by commas. Spaces separating arguments are optional.
3. Certain functions do not require arguments. However, it is still necessary to include an "empty" argument list—for example, ( ).

Using the MAX and MIN Functions

The **MAX** and **MIN** functions return the **maximum** and **minimum value**, respectively, in their list of numeric arguments. The MAX and MIN functions can be entered into a worksheet either manually or by expanding the AutoSum button and by selecting the appropriate option (in this case, Max or Min) in the list that appears.

Using the AVERAGE Function

The **AVERAGE** function returns the **arithmetic mean** (average value) of its list of numeric arguments. It can be entered into a worksheet either manually or by expanding the AutoSum button and by selecting the **Average** option in the list that appears.

Using the SUM Function

The **SUM** function returns the **total** of its list of numeric arguments. It can be entered into a worksheet either manually or by clicking on the AutoSum button on the Standard toolbar. Using the AutoSum button is generally the preferred method since it allows you to quickly compute either a subtotal or grand total (the sum of subtotals) in a single row or column, as well as in multiple rows or columns.

To **compute a subtotal** (using the **AutoSum** button):

- Select the **range of entries** that are to be totaled (including the cell in which the subtotal is to appear).

- Click on the **AutoSum** Σ ▾ button.

To **compute a grand total** (using the **AutoSum** button):

- Select all **subtotal ranges** (including the cell in which the grand total is to appear).

- Click on the **AutoSum** Σ ▾ button.

Objective

In this exercise, you will **use the MAX, MIN AVERAGE, and SUM functions** to compute the **maximum**, **minimum**, **average and sum** respectively, of a range of numeric entries.

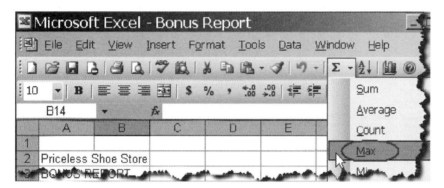

4.1

- **Click in cell A14.**

Type: **Highest**

4.2

- **Select cell B14. Do not double click in cell B14.**
- **Expand the AutoSum** **button by clicking on the little down pointing arrow, and then click on Max.**

4.3

- **Point to cell B8. Press and hold down the mouse button, and drag the mouse pointer to cell B12. Then release the mouse button.**

The range you have selected appears in the argument list of the function.

4.4

• **Press [ENTER].**

The MAX function is entered, and the result (55000) is displayed in cell B14.

		Target Sal	Actual Sal	Difference
7		Target Sal	Actual Sal	Difference
8	Tom	27500	32000	4500
9	Sue	34000	30000	-400
10	Steve	21750	28000	625
11	Mary	43000	43000	
12	Bill	55000	63000	800
13				
14	Highest	55000		
15				

4.5

• **Click in cell A15.**

• **Type: Lowest**

• **Select cell B15.**

• **Expand the AutoSum** ∑ ▾ **button by clicking on the little down pointing arrow, and click on Min.**

• **Point to cell B8. Press and hold down the mouse button, and drag the mouse pointer to cell B12. Then release the mouse button.**

The range you have selected appears in the argument list of the function.

	A	B	C	D	
1					
2	Priceless Shoe Store				
3	BONUS REPORT				
4					
5		Bonus Rat	10%		
6					
7		Target Sal	Actual Sal	Difference	B
8	Tom	27500	32000	4500	
9	Sue	34000	30000	-4000	
10	Steve	21750	28000	6250	
11	Mary	43000	43000	0	
12	Bill	55000	63000	8000	
13					
14	Highest	55000			
15	Lowest	=MIN(B8:B12)			
16		MIN(**number1**, [number2], ...)			
17					

4.6

• **Press [ENTER].**

The MIN function is entered, and the result (21750) is displayed in cell B15.

	A	B	C	D	
1					
2	Priceless Shoe Store				
3	BONUS REPORT				
4					
5		Bonus Rat	10%		
6					
7		Target Sal	Actual Sal	Difference	B
8	Tom	27500	32000	4500	
9	Sue	34000	30000	-4000	
10	Steve	21750	28000	6250	
11	Mary	43000	43000	0	
12	Bill	55000	63000	8000	
13					
14	Highest	55000			
15	Lowest	21750			
16					

		Target Sal	Actual Sal	Difference	Bo
6					
7		Target Sal	Actual Sal	Difference	Bo
8	Tom	27500	32000	4500	
9	Sue	34000	30000	-4000	
10	Steve	21750	28000	6250	
11	Mary	43000	43000	0	
12	Bill	55000	63000	8000	
13					
14	Highest	55000			
15	Lowest	21750			
16	Total	=SUM(B8:B12)			
17		SUM(**number1**, [number2], ...)			

4.7

- **Save the document.**
- **Click in cell A16.**
- **Type: Total**
- **Select cell B16.**

  Σ ▾

- **Expand the AutoSum button by clicking on the little down pointing arrow, and then click on Sum.**
- **Point to cell B8. Press and hold down the mouse button, and drag the mouse pointer to cell B12. Then release the mouse button.**

The range you have selected appears in the argument list of the function.

4.8

- **Press [ENTER].**

The Sum function is entered, and the result (181250) is displayed in cell B16.

4.9

- Save the document.
- Click in cell A17.
- Type: Average
- Select cell B17.
- Expand the AutoSum button by clicking on the little down pointing arrow, and then click on Average.
- Point to cell B8. Press and hold down the mouse button, and drag the mouse pointer to cell B12. Then release the mouse button.

The range you have selected appears in the argument list of the function.

		Target Sal	Actual Sal	Difference	Bonu
7					
8	Tom	27500	32000	4500	
9	Sue	34000	30000	-4000	
10	Steve	21750	28000	6250	
11	Mary	43000	43000	0	
12	Bill	55000	63000	8000	
13					
14	Highest	55000			
15	Lowest	21750			
16	Total	181250			
17	Average	=AVERAGE(B8:B12)			
18		AVERAGE(number1, [number2]			

4.10

- Press [ENTER].

The Average function is entered, and the result (36250) is displayed in cell B17.

14	Highest	55000
15	Lowest	21750
16	Total	181250
17	Average	36250
18		

4.11

- Click on cell B14.
- Press [SHIFT] Key.
- While [SHIFT] Key is pressed, click on cell B17.

13		
14	Highest	55000
15	Lowest	21750
16	Total	181250
17	Average	36250

4.12

- Drag the fill handle and extend the selection to cell F14, F15, F16, and F17.

	A	B	C	D	E	F	G
7		Target Sal	Actual Sal	Difference	Bonus	Percent Ta	Performance
8	Tom	27500	32000	4500	450	116.4%	
9	Sue	34000	30000	-4000	-400	88.2%	
10	Steve	21750	28000	6250	625	128.7%	
11	Mary	43000	43000	0	0	100.0%	
12	Bill	55000	63000	8000	800	114.5%	
13							
14	Highest	55000					
15	Lowest	21750					
16	Total	181250					
17	Average	36250					
18							

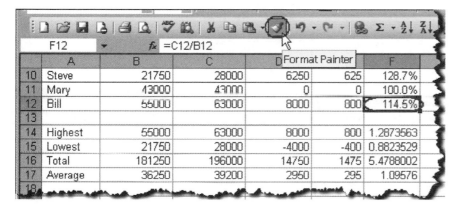

The formula is copied to adjacent cells and the corresponding values are displayed.

You will now apply F12 formatting to F14, F15, F16, and F17 cells.

- **Click on cell F12.**

- **Click on Format Painter button.**

- **Point to cell F14. Press and hold down the mouse button, and drag the mouse pointer to cell F17. Then release the mouse button.**

Cell F12 Formatting (percentage with decimal format) is applied to range F14 to F17.

- **Save the document.**

Using the IF Function

The **IF** function is used to test a certain condition and return one of two entries, depending on whether the result of the test is true or false.

The syntax of the IF function is as follows:

=IF(Logical_Test, Value_If_True, Value_If_False)

The **Value_If_True** and **Value_If_False** arguments can be a text or numeric constant, the reference for a cell containing a text or numeric constant, or a formula/function that returns a text or numeric constant.

The **Logical_Test** argument can be any conditional statement and can include any of the following **comparison operators**:

Operator	Meaning
=	Equal to
<>	Not equal to
>	Greater than
> =	Greater than or equal to
<	Less than
<=	Less than or equal to

Objective

In this exercise, you will **use the IF function** to evaluate a condition.

You will enter an IF function that determines whether or not Priceless Sales employees are exceeding their sales target. If they are exceeding their sales target, you calculate Bonus else no bonus is calculated.

5.1

- **Select cell E8.**

- **In the formula bar, edit your current formula as following:**

=IF(D8>0, D8*C5, 0)

5.2

- **Press [ENTER].**

- **Select cell E8.**

- **Point to the fill handle of cell E8.**

- **Drag the fill handle and extend the selection to cell E12.**

The formula is copied to cell E9, E10, E11, and E12.

- **Save the document.**

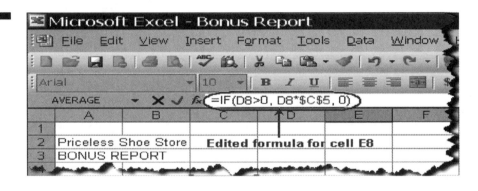

Nesting IF Functions

By **nesting** (combining) IF functions, you can set up a conditional statement that returns one of several messages. You can include up to seven nested IF functions within the Value_If_True and/or Value_If_False argument of an IF function.

Objective

In this exercise, you will **nest IF functions** to evaluate **two conditions** and return **one of three messages**.

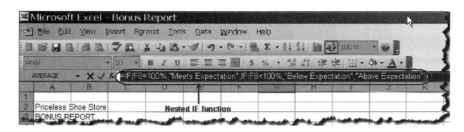

6.1

- **Select cell G8.**

- **Type:**

=IF(F8=100%,"Meets Expectation",IF(F8<100%,"Below Expectation","Above Expectation"))

Difference	Bonus	Percent Ta	Performance
4500	450	116.4%	Above Expectation
-4000	0	88.2%	
6250	625	128.7%	
0	0	100.0%	
8000	800	114.5%	
8000	800	128.7%	
-4000	0	88.2%	
14750	1875	547.9%	
2950	375	109.6%	

6.2

- **Press [ENTER].**

The function is entered, and the result is displayed.

	A	B	C	D	E	F	G	H
1								
2	Priceless Shoe Store							
3	BONUS REPORT							
4								
5		Bonus Rat	10%					
6								
7		Target Sal	Actual Sal	Difference	Bonus		Percent Ta	Performance
8	Tom	27500	32000	4500	450	116.4%	Above Expectation	
9	Sue	34000	30000	-4000	0	88.2%	Below Expectation	
10	Steve	21750	28000	6250	625	128.7%	Above Expectation	
11	Mary	43000	43000	0	0	100.0%	Meets Expectation	
12	Bill	55000	63000	8000	800	114.5%	Above Expectation	
13								
14	Highest	55000	63000	8000	800	128.7%		
15	Lowest	21750	28000	-4000	0	88.2%		
16	Total	181250	196000	14750	1875	547.9%		
17	Average	36250	39200	2950	375	109.6%		

6.3

- **Select cell G8.**

- **Point to the fill handle of cell G8.**

- **Drag the fill handle and extend the selection to cell G12.**

The formula is copied to cells G9, G10, G11, and G12 and the corresponding values are displayed.

- **Save the document.**

Using NOW Function

The **NOW** function is used to display the current date and time. Although it does not require an argument, it does require an "empty" argument list—that is, a left parenthesis, followed by a right parenthesis.

Notes

The NOW function returns a serial number. This number is automatically formatted as the actual date and time when a single NOW function is entered.

Excel also provides a **TODAY** function, which is similar to the NOW function except that it returns only the current date.

Objective

In this exercise, you will **use the NOW function** to enter the current date and time into the current worksheet.

7.1

• **Select cell A4.**

Type: =NOW()

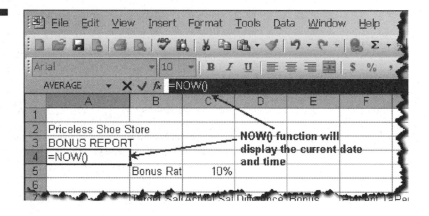

7.2

• **Press [ENTER].**

The function is entered, and the result is displayed.

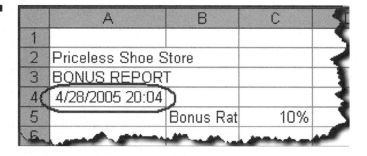

7.3

You will now reformat the result.

• **Point to cell A4, and right-click the mouse button. Then click on Format Cells on the shortcut menu that appears.**

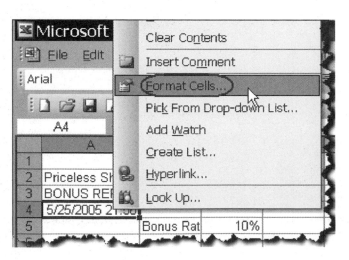

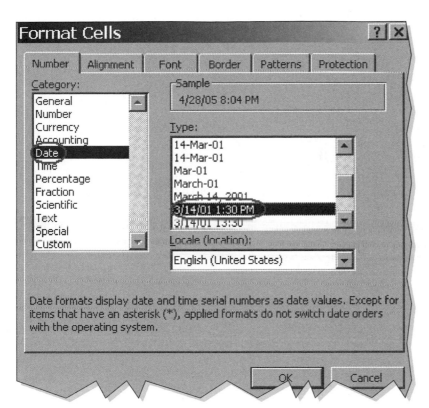

7.4

- **Click on the Number tab.**
- **In the Category box, click on Date.**

The list of date formats appears in the Type box.

- **In the list of formats, click on the 3/14/01 1:30 PM option. Then click on the OK button.**

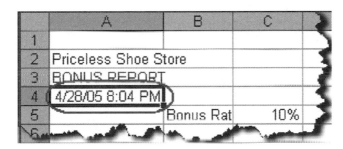

7.5

The dialog box is closed, and the new format is applied to the date and time in cell A4.

- **Save the document.**

Sorting the Records of a List

An Excel **list** (sometimes called a database) can be thought of as an electronic filing system. With it, you can store small or large amounts of information, organized anyway you wish. You can also use the program's powerful list management features to quickly retrieve that information and manipulate it in numerous ways.

A list is made up of two components: fields and records. A **field** is one category of information, such as an individual's name, job title or salary; a **record** is the collection of all related fields for each list entity. Since the column/row structure of a worksheet is similar to the field/record structure of a list, the worksheet is used for storing list information. Thus, all of the operations you have learned in connection with worksheets are available for setting up, editing, and formatting a list.

You can **sort** the records of a list on the basis of information in a **single field**, as well as on the basis of information in **multiple fields**.

To **sort the records of a list by the entries in one field**:

- Select **any cell** in the **field** by which the list is to be sorted.
- Click on the Sort Ascending ▲↓ or Sort Descending ▲↓ button on the Standard toolbar.

To sort the records of a list by the entries in two or more fields:

- Select **any cell** in the **list**.
- Choose the **Data**, **Sort** command.
- In the Sort dialog box, select the **first sort field** in the **Sort by** list of field names.
- Select the **second sort field** and, if necessary, the **third sort field** in the **Then by** list(s) of field names.
- Optionally, change the **sort order** for any sort field.
- Click on the **OK** button.

Notes

The **Data**, **Sort** command can also be used to sort the records of a list by the entries in a single field.

Objective

In this exercise, you will **sort the records of an Excel list** by the entries in **seven fields**.

8.1

- **Click in cell A8.**

- **Press [SHIFT] key.**

- **While SHIFT key is still pressed, click in cell G12.**

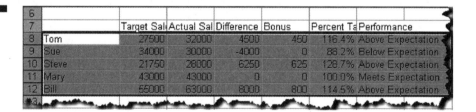

		Target Sal	Actual Sal	Difference	Bonus		Percent Ta	Performance
8	Tom	27500	32000	4500	450		116.4%	Above Expectation
9	Sue	34000	30000	-4000	0		88.2%	Below Expectation
10	Steve	21750	28000	6250	625		128.7%	Above Expectation
11	Mary	43000	43000	0	0		100.0%	Meets Expectation
12	Bill	55000	63000	8000	800		114.5%	Above Expectation

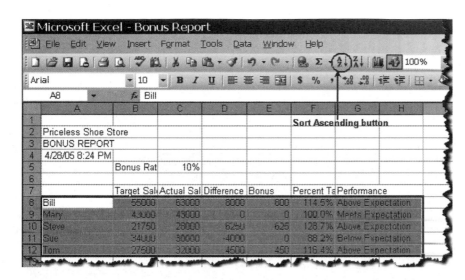

8.2

- **Click on the Sort Ascending**

  button on the Standard toolbar.

The records are sorted in ascending order by name.

- **Save the document.**

Applying Conditional Formatting to a Worksheet

Excel's **Conditional Formatting** feature allows you to specify a format (for example, a new font color or shading) that is to be applied to specific worksheet cells when one or more conditions are met. It is an important data-tracking tool since it can help identify worksheet entries that exceed, or fall short of, a particular amount.

To **apply conditional formatting to a worksheet**:

- Select the cell(s) that is/are to be affected.
- Choose the **Format**, **Conditional Formatting** command.
- In the Conditional Formatting dialog box, which is subsequently displayed, define the first **condition**. Then click on the **Format** button.
- In the Format Cells dialog box, which is then displayed, specify the **format option(s)** that is/are to be applied when the specified condition is met. Then click on the **OK** button to return to the Conditional Formatting dialog box.
- To define another condition, click on the **Add >>** button, and repeat the previous two steps. (You can define up to three conditions.)
- When you are finished, click on the **OK** button.

Objective

In this exercise, you will **apply conditional formatting to a worksheet**.

Bonus	Percent Ta	Performance
800	114.5%	Above Expectation
0	100.0%	Meets Expectation
625	128.7%	Above Expectation
0	88.2%	Below Expectation
450	116.4%	Above Expectation

9.1

- **Click in cell G8.**
- **Press [SHIFT] key.**
- **While [SHIFT] key is pressed, click on cell G12.**

9.2

• **Choose the Format, Conditional Formatting command.**

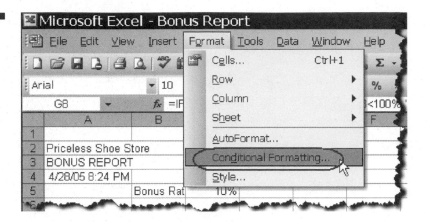

9.3

The Conditional Formatting dialog box is displayed. You will now specify the first condition.

9.4

• **Expand the operator box (which currently displays the entry between), and click on equal to.**

• **Click in the box to the right. Type: Above Expectation**

• **Click on the Format... button.**

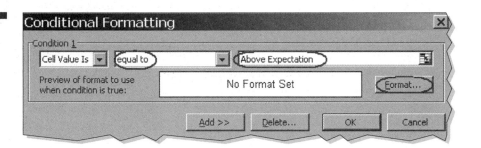

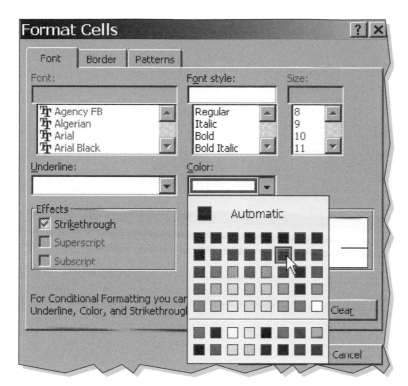

9.5

The Font panel of the Format Cells dialog box is displayed.

- **In the Color box, click on Blue (sixth option in the second row).**

- **Click OK on Format Cells dialog box.**

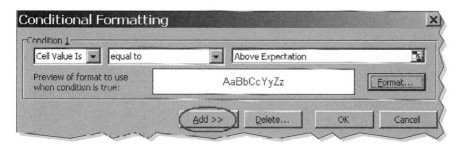

9.6

- **On Conditional Formatting, click on Add>> to format other messages.**

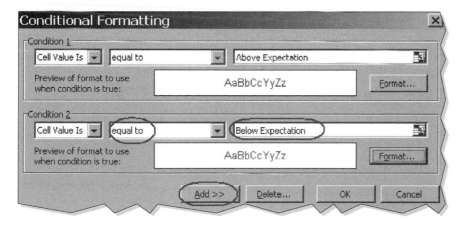

9.7

- **Expand the operator box for Condition 2 and click on equal to.**

- **Click in the box to the right. Type: Below Expectation.**

- **Click on the Format... button.**

The Font panel of the Format Cells dialog box is displayed.

- **In the Format Cells dialog box, select Red (first option in the third row) for Color box.**

- **Click OK on Format Cells dialog box.**

9.8

- **On Conditional Formatting, click on Add>> to format "Meets Expectation" message.**

- **Expand the operator box for Condition 3 and click on equal to.**

- **Click in the box to the right. Type: Meets Expectation.**

- **Click on the Format… button.**

The Font panel of the Format Cells dialog box is displayed.

- **In the Format Cells dialog box, select Olive Green (third option in the first row) for Color box.**

- **Click OK on Format Cells dialog box.**

- **Click OK on Conditional Formatting dialog box.**

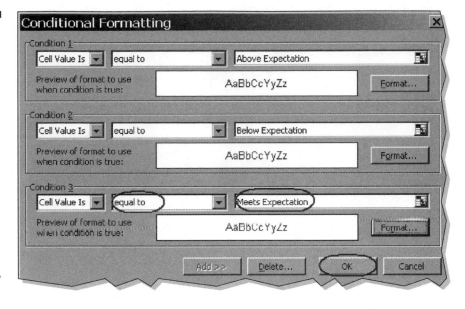

9.9

Conditional formatting is applied to G8, G9, G10, G11, and G12 cells.

- **Save the document.**

	A	B	C	D	E	F	G	H
1								
2	Priceless Shoe Store							
3	BONUS REPORT							
4	4/28/05 8:24 PM							
5		Bonus Rat	10%					
6								
7		Target Sal	Actual Sal	Difference	Bonus		Percent Ta	Performance
8	Bill	55000	63000	8000	800		114.5%	Above Expectation
9	Mary	43000	43000	0	0		100.0%	Meets Expectation
10	Steve	21750	28000	6250	625		128.7%	Above Expectation
11	Sue	34000	30000	-4000	0		88.2%	Below Expectation
12	Tom	27500	32000	4500	450		116.4%	Above Expectation
13								
14	Highest	55000	63000	8000	800		128.7%	
15	Lowest	21750	28000	-4000	0		88.2%	
16	Total	181250	196000	14750	1875		547.9%	
17	Average	36250	39200	2950	375		109.6%	

Linking Worksheets within a Workbook

One of the most powerful features of Excel is its ability to link two or more worksheets. In this section, you will learn how to:

- **Rename worksheets** in a workbook.
- **Enter** a **formula** to **link related worksheets** in a workbook.
- **Format multiple worksheets** in one operation.

Renaming Worksheets in a Workbook

An Excel workbook initially contains three worksheets, labeled **Sheet1**, **Sheet2** and **Sheet3**.

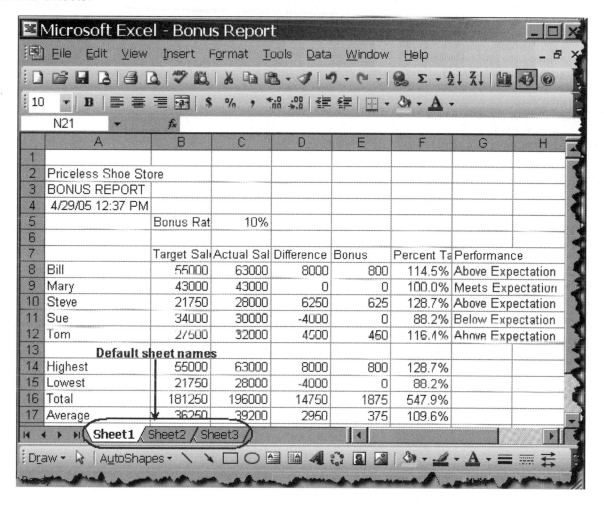

Although the various worksheets in a single workbook can contain dissimilar information, they are generally used to store related data—for example, expense details for regional offices or sales figures for consecutive months. This data can be linked through one or more formulas, thereby allowing you to compare information from different sources, as well as consolidate that information in order to produce summary reports.

You can rename a worksheet in a workbook by simply double-clicking on the worksheet tab (or by right-clicking on the tab and by selecting the **Rename** option on the shortcut menu), by typing the new name and by pressing **[ENTER]**.

Objective

In this exercise, you will examine related worksheets in a workbook. You will then rename the worksheets. This exercise also demonstrates the procedure for **applying a color to worksheet tabs**.

10.1

- **Double-click on the Sheet1 tab.**

The current worksheet name (Sheet1) is highlighted.

10.2

- **Type: Year2004**
- **Make sure that you type Year2004 as one word.**
- **Press [ENTER].**

The new worksheet name (Year2004) replaces the previous name.

10.3

- **Using a procedure similar to that described above, rename Sheet2 as Year2005 and rename Sheet3 as Summary.**

When you are finished, the worksheet tabs should appear as an image on the right. Next, you will apply a unique color to each of the worksheet tabs.

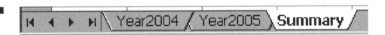

10.4

- **Point to the Year2004 tab, and right-click the mouse button. Then click on Tab Color on the shortcut menu that appears.**

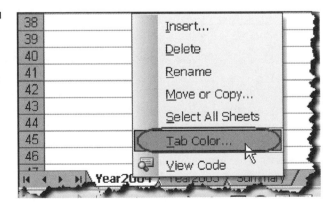

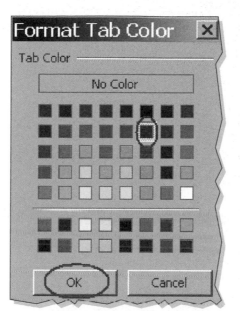

10.5

The Format Tab Color dialog box is displayed.

- **In the color palette, click on the Blue option (the sixth option in the second row). Then click on the OK button.**

*Alternative: You can also display this dialog box by choosing the **Format, Sheet, Tab Color** command.*

10.6

The dialog box is closed, and the Blue color is applied to the Year2004 tab.

10.7

- **Click on the Year2005 tab. The color applied to the Year2004 tab is now visible.**

10.8

- **Using a procedure similar to that described above, apply dark red color (the first option in the second row) to Year2005 and Pink color (the first option in the fourth row) to Summary tabs**

- **Save the document.**

Entering a Formula to Link Related Worksheets in a Workbook

Related worksheets in a workbook can be linked through **formulas**. When entering a formula that references another worksheet, you must include the appropriate worksheet name (and exclamation point) with the cell coordinates, for example:

=Year2004!B5+Year2005!B5

Objective

In this exercise, you will **summarize the data in the current workbook by entering formulas that link the worksheets**. The summary information will be entered in the Summary worksheet. This exercise also demonstrates the use of the **Office Clipboard** to copy and paste worksheet entries.

11.1

- **Make sure Year2004 sheet is selected.**

- **Click in cell A1.**

- **Press [SHIFT] key.**

- **While pressing [SHIFT] key, click on cell G17.**

- **Right-click on the selection and select Copy command.**

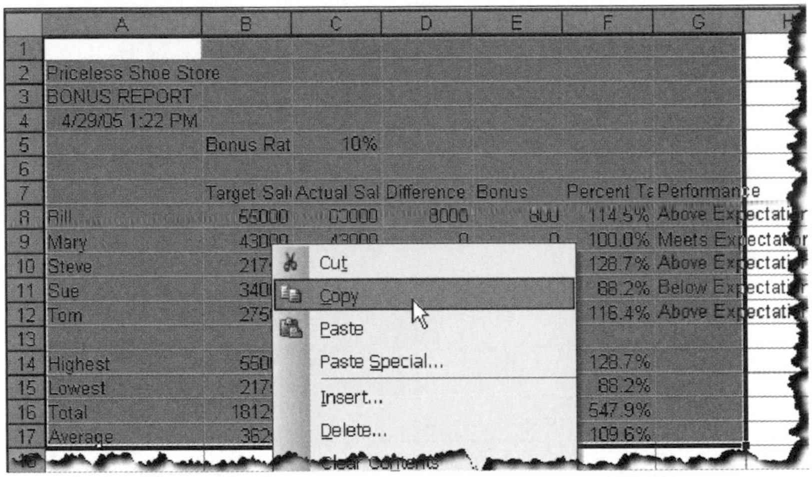

	A	B	C	D	E	F	G	H
1								
2	Priceless Shoe Store							
3	BONUS REPORT							
4	4/29/05 1:22 PM							
5		Bonus Rat	10%					
6								
7		Target Sal	Actual Sal	Difference	Bonus		Percent Ta	Performance
8	Bill	55000	63000	8000	800		114.5%	Above Expectati
9	Mary	43000	43000	0	0		100.0%	Meets Expectat
10	Steve	217					128.7%	Above Expectati
11	Sue	340					88.2%	Below Expectati
12	Tom	275					116.4%	Above Expectati
13								
14	Highest	550					128.7%	
15	Lowest	217					88.2%	
16	Total	1812					547.9%	
17	Average	362					109.6%	

(Right-click menu showing: Cut, Copy, Paste, Paste Special..., Insert..., Delete..., Clear Contents)

11.2

- **Click on Year2005 worksheet tab.**

- **Click in cell A1 of Year2005 tab.**

- **Right-click and select Paste command.**

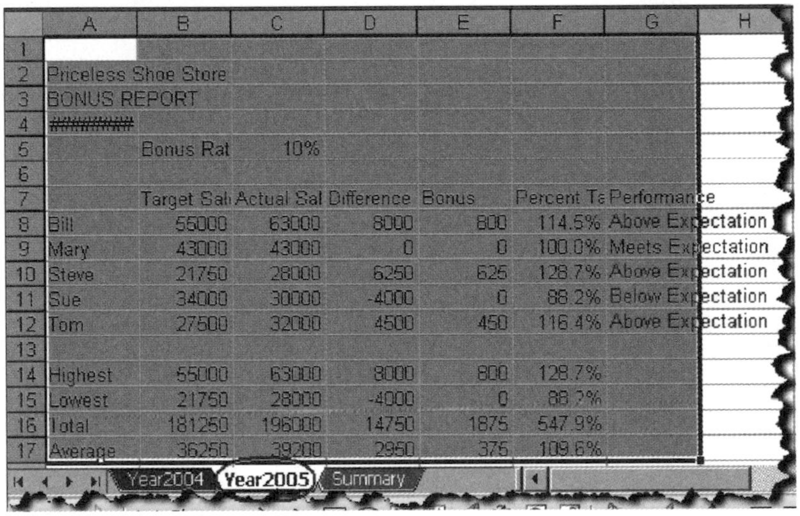

	A	B	C	D	E	F	G	H
1								
2	Priceless Shoe Store							
3	BONUS REPORT							
4	########							
5		Bonus Rat	10%					
6								
7		Target Sal	Actual Sal	Difference	Bonus		Percent Ta	Performance
8	Bill	55000	63000	8000	800		114.5%	Above Expectation
9	Mary	43000	43000	0	0		100.0%	Meets Expectation
10	Steve	21750	28000	6250	625		128.7%	Above Expectation
11	Sue	34000	30000	-4000	0		88.2%	Below Expectation
12	Tom	27500	32000	4500	450		116.4%	Above Expectation
13								
14	Highest	55000	63000	8000	800		128.7%	
15	Lowest	21750	28000	-4000	0		88.2%	
16	Total	181250	196000	14750	1875		547.9%	
17	Average	36250	39200	2950	375		109.6%	

Year2004 / **Year2005** / Summary

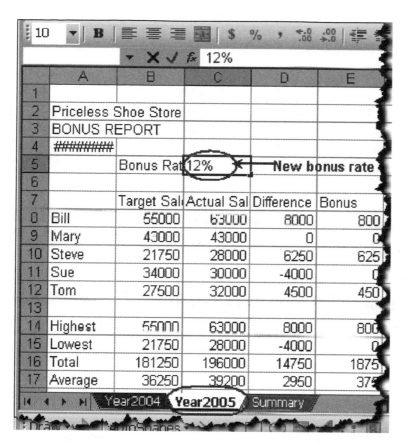

11.3

- Using a procedure similar to that described above, paste Year2004 selected ranges in Summary worksheet.

- Open Year2005 worksheet by clicking on Year 2005 tab.

- Change the bonus rate from 10% to 12%.

- Press [ENTER].

11.4

- Make sure that Year2005 worksheet is active.

- Select cell B8.

- Type: 105000

- Point to the fill handle of cell B8.

- Drag the fill handle and extend the selection to cell B12.

The new targeted sale is copied in cell B9, B10, B11, and B12.

- Enter 125000 in cell C8. Press [ENTER].

- Enter 131000 in cell C10. Press [ENTER].

- Enter 107500 in cell C12. Press [ENTER].

11.5

You will now calculate employees'
combined target sales for last two years.

- **Select Summary worksheet.**

- **Select cell B8.**

- **Type: =Year2004!B8+
  Year2005!B8**

NOTE: *Make sure that you enter all of
the indicated exclamation points.*

- **Press [ENTER].**

*The formula is entered, and the result
(160000) is displayed.*

11.6

- **Select cell B8.**

- **Point to the fill handle of cell
  B8.**

- **Drag the fill handle and extend
  the selection to cell E8.**

The formula is copied to cell E8.

11.7

- **Make sure cells B8 to E8 are
  selected.**

- **Point to the fill handle.**

- **Drag the fill handle and extend
  the selection to cell B12 and
  E12.**

*The formula is copied on the selected
range of cells and the corresponding
values will be displayed.*

- **Save the document.**

Formatting Multiple Worksheets in One Operation

You can simultaneously apply the same formatting to two or more related worksheets in a workbook, saving you the time it would take to individually format each of those worksheets. To do this, select all worksheets that are to be changed, and then apply the necessary format options to the current (displayed) worksheet.

To **select two or more** *non-consecutive* **worksheets**:

- Click on the **tab** of each worksheet while holding down [**CTRL**].

To **select two or more** *consecutive* **worksheets**:

- Click on the **tab** of the **first** worksheet and then on the **tab** of the **last** worksheet while holding down [**SHIFT**].

Notes

You can select all worksheets in a workbook by pointing to any worksheet tab, by **right-clicking** the mouse button and by selecting the **Select All Sheets** option on the shortcut menu.

Objective

In this exercise, you will **apply the same formatting to the three worksheets**.

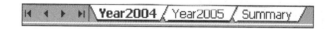

12.1

- **Select Year2004 worksheet tab.**

- **Press and hold down [SHIFT].**

- **Click on the Summary tab. Then release [SHIFT].**

All three worksheets are selected.

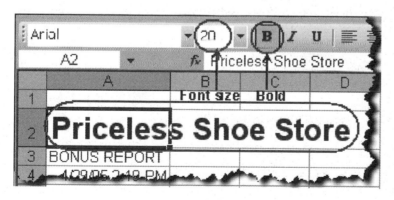

12.2

- **Select cell A2.**

- **Select 20 for Font Size.**

- **Click on Bold button.**

The row label is bolded and the font size is changed to 20.

12.3

- **Select cell A3.**
- **Select 11 for Font Size.**
- **Click on Bold button.**

The row label is bolded and the font size is changed to 11.

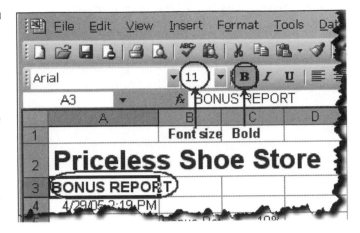

12.4

- **Click on the row 5 heading.**

Row 5 is selected. You will now insert a new row into the selected area.

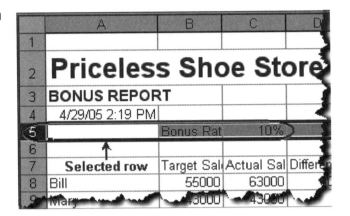

12.5

- **Choose the Insert, Rows command.**

A new row is inserted.

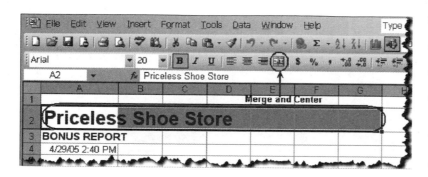

12.6

- **Select cell A2.**
- **Press and hold down [SHIFT].**
- **Click on cell G2 and release [SHIFT].**

The range A2:G2 is selected.

- **Click on Merge and Center button on the toolbar.**

12.7

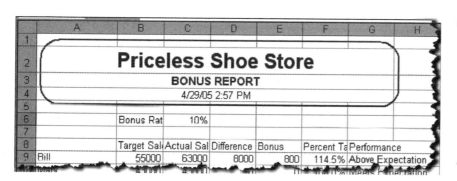

- **Using a procedure similar to that described above, select cells A3 to G3 and click on Merge and Center button on the toolbar.**

- **Select cells A4 to G4 and click on Merge and Center button on the toolbar.**

When you are finished, the worksheet should look similar to the figure shown on the left.

12.8

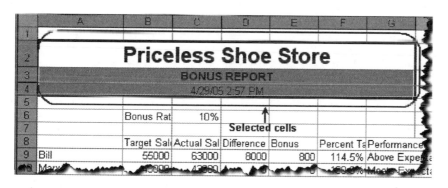

- **Click on Priceless Shoe Store.**
- **Press and hold down [SHIFT].**
- **Click on the date and release [SHIFT].**

The range A2:G4 is selected.

12.9

- Click on small down pointing

  arrow in Fill Color  button. In the color palette, click on the **Dark Blue** option (the sixth option in the first row).

- Click on small down pointing

  arrow in Font Color button. In the color palette, click on the **White** option (last option in the last row).

12.10

- **Select cell B6 and click on bold button.**

- **Select cell C6 and click on Italic button.**

- **Save the document.**

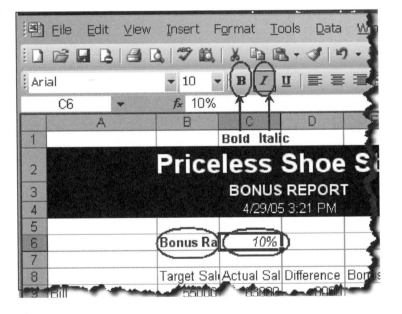

Using AutoFormat

Excel's **AutoFormat** feature allows you to apply, in one operation, a predefined group of format options (for example, border, shading and other enhancement settings) to selected cells in a worksheet. The feature is accessed with the **Format**, **AutoFormat** command.

Objective

In this exercise, you will **use AutoFormat to format data in a worksheet**.

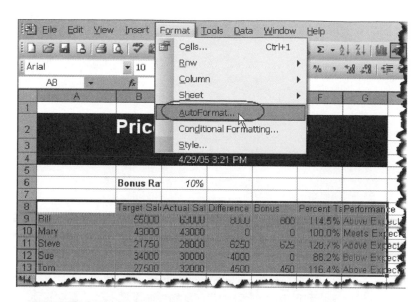

13.1

- **Click on A8.**
- **Press and hold down [SHIFT].**
- **Click on cell G13 and release [SHIFT].**

The range A8:G13 is selected.

- **Choose the Format, AutoFormat command.**

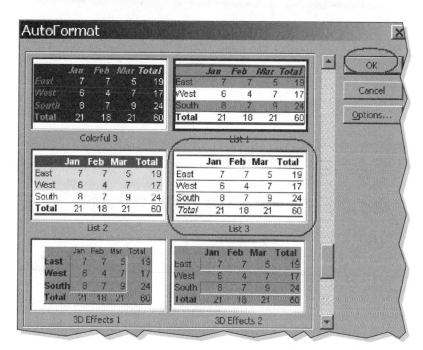

13.2

The AutoFormat dialog box is displayed.

- **Scroll down and click on the List 3 option.**
- **Click on the OK button.**

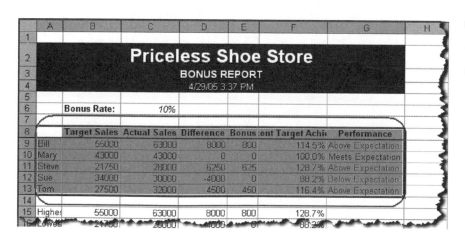

13.3

The dialog box is closed, and the table appears in the selected format.

13.4

- **Right click on the selected cells.**
- **Select Format Cells...**
- **If the Alignment tab is not selected, click on the Alignment tab.**
- **Under Text control, select Wrap text.**
- **Click on the OK button.**

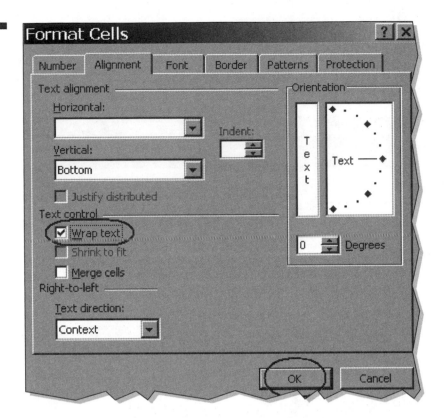

13.5

- **Select cells B9 to E18.**
- **Click on Currency Style button.**
- **Click two times on Decrease Decimal button.**

The selected entries are displayed without decimal places.

- **Increase the width of your worksheet columns so that all cell entries are fully displayed.**

Formatting changes are applied to all worksheets.

- **Save the document.**

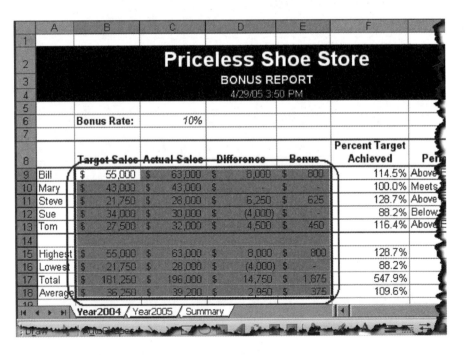

Creating a Chart

This section discusses the methods for **representing worksheet data in an Excel chart**. In it, you will learn how to:

- **Plot** a **chart**.
- **Modify** and **enhance** a **chart**.

Creating and Plotting a Chart

A **chart** is a graphic representation of worksheet data. Presenting information in the form of a chart is often one of the best ways to analyze data, as well as call attention to specific entries.

With Excel, you can create several types of charts. Some of the most common chart types include:

Column	In a column chart, values are represented by vertical bars. This type of chart can be used to compare data either across various categories (for example, regions) or over a specific period of time.
Bar	In a bar chart, values are represented by horizontal bars. This type of chart, like a column chart, can be used to compare data either across various categories or over a specific period of time.
Line	In a line chart, values are represented by points on one or more lines. This type of chart can be used to compare data across various categories or over a specific period of time to identify a trend.
Area	In an area chart, values are represented by shaded areas. This type of chart can also be used to compare data across various categories or over a specific period of time to identify a trend.
XY (Scatter)	In an xy (scatter) chart, two sets of values are represented by points, usually on two lines. This type of chart can be used to determine the correlation between sets of data.
Pie	In a pie chart, values are represented by slices of a pie-shaped figure. This type of chart can be used to show what part of the whole each value in a single data set represents.
Doughnut	In a doughnut chart, values are represented by slices of a doughnut-shaped figure. This type of chart can be used for the same purpose as a pie chart, except that more than one data set can be included in the chart.
Cylinder	A cylinder chart is actually a column or bar chart in which values are represented by cylindrical-shaped figures.
Cone	A cone chart is actually a column or bar chart in which values are represented by cone-shaped figures.
Pyramid	A pyramid chart is actually a column or bar chart in which values are represented by pyramid-shaped figures.

A chart is made up of a number of components. The column chart includes the following:

Chart title	This identifies the overall data that is represented in the chart.
Category axis	This horizontal line, which appears at the bottom of the plot area (the area in which the chart data is represented), lists the various categories of the chart. (In the illustration, these categories are New York, Sydney, London and Milan.) The Category axis is also called the X axis.
Value axis	This vertical line, which appears at the left side of the plot area, displays a list of values. (In the illustration, these values range from 0 to 600.) The Value axis is also called the Y axis.
Data markers	These represent the various data points in the chart. (In this case, the data markers are bars since the chart is a column chart.) Each data point represents a particular value from the associated worksheet. Related data points are called a **series**. In a column chart, the bars of each data series are the same color.
Legend	This identifies the various data series in the chart.
Gridlines	These horizontal lines, one for each value on the Y axis, help to identify the value each data marker represents. (In addition to horizontal gridlines, a chart can also include vertical gridlines.)

Using Excel's **Chart Wizard**, you can quickly plot a chart on either the worksheet containing the source data or a separate chart sheet.

To **plot a chart** (using the **Chart Wizard**):

- Select the data that is to be represented. The selection should include any labels that describe the data (for example, row and column headings).

- Choose the **Insert**, **Chart** command, or click on the **Chart Wizard** 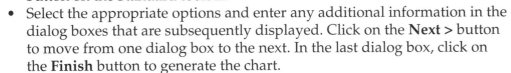 button on the Standard toolbar.
- Select the appropriate options and enter any additional information in the dialog boxes that are subsequently displayed. Click on the **Next >** button to move from one dialog box to the next. In the last dialog box, click on the **Finish** button to generate the chart.

Objective

In this exercise, you will **plot a column chart**.

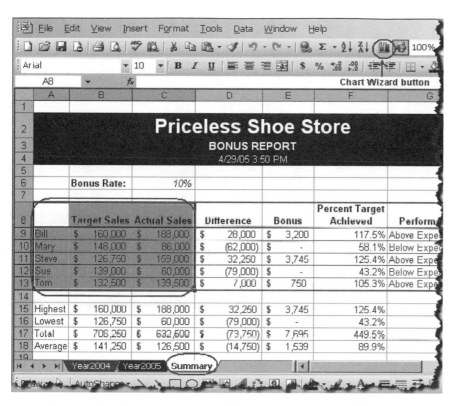

- **Select Summary worksheet.**
- **Select the range A8:C13.**

The chart data range is selected. Notice that the range includes both the column headings and the row headings, which will be used to identify the data in the chart.

- **Click on the Chart Wizard button on the Standard toolbar.**

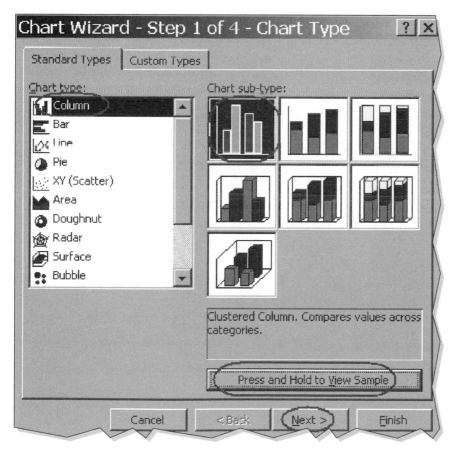

The first Chart Wizard dialog box is displayed. Notice that the Column option is selected, by default, in the Chart type box.

- **Select Clustered column chart subtype (first option in first row).**
- **Point to the button labeled Press and Hold to View Sample.**
- **Press and hold down the mouse button.**
- **Release the mouse button.**
- **Click on the Next > button.**

14.3

The second Chart Wizard dialog box is displayed. Notice that the chart data range is listed in the **Data range** box.

- **Make sure that the Series in: Columns option is selected.**

- **Click on the Next > button.**

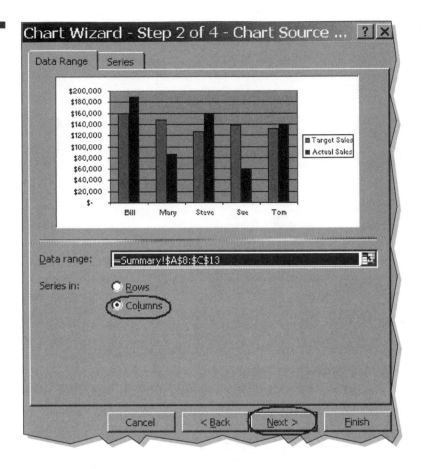

14.4

The third Chart Wizard dialog box is displayed.

- **Click in the Chart title box.**

- **Type: Priceless Shoe Store**

A chart title is entered.

- **Click on the Next > button.**

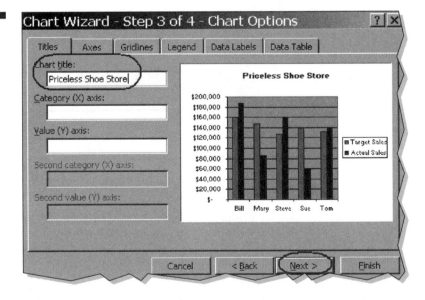

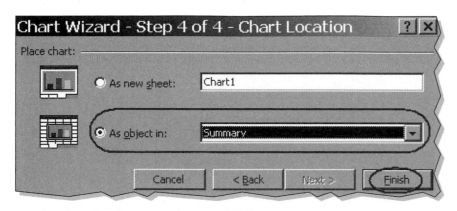

■■■14.5■■■■■■■■■■■

The last Chart Wizard dialog box is displayed.

- **Make sure that the As object in: Summary option is selected.**

The new chart will appear as an embedded object on the current worksheet.

- **Click on the Finish button.**

■■■14.6■■■■■■■■■■■

The dialog box is closed, and the chart is displayed on the worksheet. Notice that it is surrounded by eight sizing handles (small black squares), indicating that it is selected.

NOTE: *When the chart is selected, the* **Chart toolbar** *should appear in the Application window. If it does not appear, choose the* **View, Toolbars, Chart** *command.*

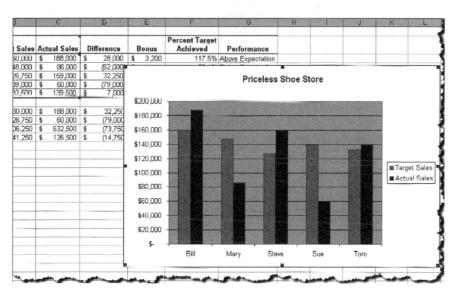

14.7

You will now reposition and resize the chart.

- **Point in the upper-right corner of the chart (in the chart area).**

NOTE: *Notice that when you point to a chart component (for example, chart area, plot area or legend), the name of that component appears in a ScreenTip next to the mouse pointer.*

- **Press and hold down the mouse button, and drag the chart downward and to the left. When the upper-left corner of the chart is located in the upper-left corner of cell A21, release the mouse button.**

NOTE: *As you drag, an outline of the chart box will move with the mouse pointer.*

- **Point to the sizing handle in the lower-right corner of the chart.**

The mouse pointer will appear as a double-headed arrow when it is properly positioned.

- **Press and hold down the mouse button, and drag the sizing handle to the lower-right corner of cell E42. Then release the mouse button.**

The chart is resized.

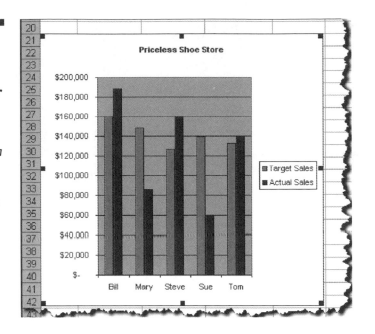

14.8

- **Click on the column F heading.**

Column F is selected. You will now delete column F.

- **Right-click and select Delete.**

Column F is deleted.

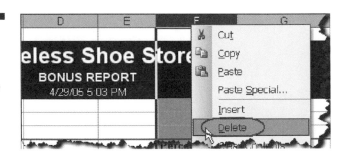

	Target Sales	Actual Sales	Difference	Bonus
Bill	$ 160,000	$ 188,000	$ 28,000	$ 3,200
Mary	$ 148,000	$ 86,000	$ (62,000)	$ -
Steve	$ 126,750	$ 159,000	$ 32,250	$ 3,745
Sue	$ 139,000	$ 60,000	$ (79,000)	$ -
Tom	$ 132,500	$ 139,500	$ 7,000	$ 750
Highest	$ 160,000	$ 188,000	$ 32,250	$ 3,745
Lowest	$ 126,750	$ 60,000	$ (79,000)	$ -
Total	$ 706,250	$ 632,500	$ (73,750)	$ 7,695
Average	$ 141,250	$ 126,500	$ (14,750)	$ 1,539

Priceless Shoe Store

Legend: Target Sales, Actual Sales

14.9

- **Using a procedure similar to that described above, delete column G (now labeled as F).**

When you are finished, your worksheet should look similar to the figure shown on the left.

- **Save the document.**

Using the Spelling Checker

The Excel **Spelling Checker** can help you find and correct misspelled words in a worksheet.

To **use the Spelling Checker**:

- To check only a portion of a worksheet, select the appropriate **cells**; or

  To check the entire worksheet, select **any cell**.

- Choose the **Tools**, **Spelling** command, or click on the **Spelling** button on the Standard toolbar.

- In the Spelling dialog box, which is displayed when a possible spelling error is encountered, choose the appropriate option:
  - **Ignore Once**—which skips the flagged entry.
  - **Ignore All**—which skips the flagged entry and any subsequent occurrence of that entry.
  - **Change**—which replaces the flagged entry with the entry you have selected or typed.
  - **Change All**—which replaces the flagged entry and any subsequent occurrence of that entry with the entry you have selected or typed.
  - **Add to Dictionary**—which skips the flagged entry and adds the entry to a specified dictionary.
  - **AutoCorrect**—which replaces the flagged entry with the entry you have selected or typed and adds the entry to the AutoCorrect dictionary.
  - **Delete**—which deletes the flagged entry. (This option is available only when the program encounters a repeated entry.)

Objective

In this exercise, you will **use the Spelling Checker to correct spelling errors in a worksheet**.

15.1

- **Make sure that cell A1 is selected. Then click on the Spelling button on the Standard toolbar.**

*The Spelling dialog box is displayed. The spelling error is flagged, if it found any. Click on the **Change** button to accept the suggested replacement.*

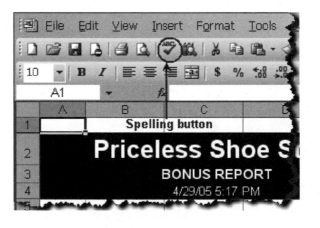

15.2

- **If Spelling Checker could not find any spelling errors, a message box will appears, informing you that the operation is complete.**

- **Click on the OK button.**

Congratulations! You have completed the Case Study.

Conclusion

You have just completed **Microsoft Office Excel 2003—Case Study 2**. In the case study, you were introduced to many intermediate and advanced techniques. To reinforce your understanding of these techniques, it is recommended that you read and work through it once again.

Further Practice

The following two exercises will give you the opportunity to review and practice many of the Excel features you have learned. It is divided into several steps

Exercise One

Step 1

Make sure that all documents are closed. Then display a **blank document**.

Step 2

Enter the data as shown in the following screen-shot:

	A	B	C	D	E
1	First Semester Report				
2					
3	Name	Dept	Score	Comments	Result
4	Smith, J.	Arts	75	Is a hard working student who demonstrates leadership.	Pass
5	King, L.	Science	34	Has missed three of his final examinations.	Fail
6	Wong, W.	Arts	68	Is consistently prompt in handing in assignments.	Pass
7	Moore, H.	Arts	81	Has missed two weeks of lectures due to ill health.	Pass
8	Brandt, P.	Science	65	Has shown considerable improvement this semester.	Pass
9	Dupont, D.	Arts	42	Was four times late handing in assignments.	Fail
10	Fitzpatrick, M.	Science	86	Is one of the most promising students in this institution.	Pass
11	Harris, R.	Arts	92	Finished top of the class for the second consecutive year.	Pass
12	Thomas, T.	Science	37	Lacks confidence and needs encouragement.	Fail
13	George, J.	Science	78	Is a quiet but hardworking and conscientious student.	Pass

16.1

The message box is closed.

- **Save the document.**

- **Choose the File, Exit command.**

The program is exited, and the Windows desktop is redisplayed.

Step 3

Create the **bar chart** illustrated on the following page on a separate sheet.
Rename the **Chart sheet** as FirstSemesterChart.

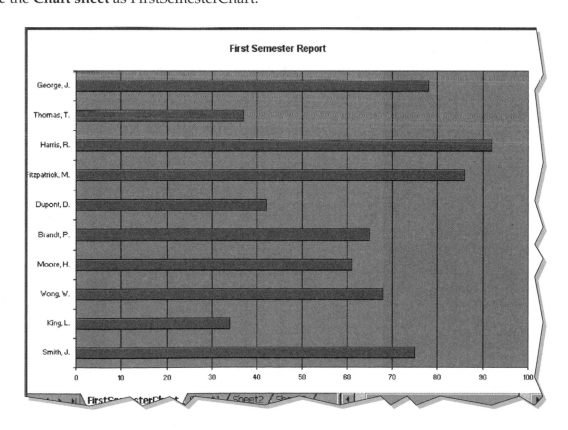

Step 4

Rename Sheet1 as **FirstSemesterReport**.

Save the **workbook** as First Semester Report.

Step 5

Sort the **Dept** records in **ascending** order.

Under column Result, change the **font color of "Fail" to red**. **You must use conditional formatting for this.**

Spell check the document.

Format the **worksheet data** so that it appears similar to that illustrated on the next page.

Save the **workbook** once again, and then **close** the **file**.

	A	B	C	D	E
1	First Semester Report				
2					
3	Name	Dept	Score	Comments	Result
4	Smith, J.	Arts	75	Is a hard working student who demonstrates leadership.	Pass
5	Wong, W.	Arts	68	Is consistently prompt in handing in assignments.	Pass
6	Moore, H.	Arts	61	Has missed two weeks of lectures due to ill health.	Pass
7	Dupont, D.	Arts	42	Was four times late handing in assignments.	Fail
8	Harris, R.	Arts	92	Finished top of the class for the second consecutive year.	Pass
9	King, L.	Science	34	Has missed three of his final examinations.	Fail
10	Brandt, P.	Science	65	Has shown considerable improvement this semester.	Pass
11	Fitzpatrick, M.	Science	86	Is one of the most promising students in this institution.	Pass
12	Thomas, T.	Science	37	Lacks confidence and needs encouragement.	Fail
13	George, J.	Science	78	Is a quiet but hardworking and conscientious student.	Pass

Exercise Two

Step 1

Make sure that all documents are closed. Then display a **blank document**.

Step 2

Enter and format the **data** as shown in the following screen-shot in Sheet1:

	A	B	C	D	E	F	G
1	Sales for Europe						
2							
3		Year 1	Year 2	Year 3	Year 4	Year 5	Year 6
4	United Kingdom	615	650	670	640	690	720
5	France	535	550	540	560	585	575
6	Italy	430	435	480	450	425	430
7	Germany	590	650	660	690	670	675

Step 3

Enter and format the **data** as shown in the following screen-shot in Sheet2:

	A	B	C	D	E	F	G
1	**Sales for North America**						
2							
3		Year 1	Year 2	Year 3	Year 4	Year 5	Year 6
4	Canada	370	330	320	360	385	380
5	United States	880	900	970	990	950	980
6							
7	Total						

Change the names of **Sheet1, Sheet2 and Sheet3** to **Europe, NorthAmerica,** and **Summary** respectively.

On the **Summary** worksheet, enter the necessary **labels** and **formulas** to summarize the total sales in the **Europe** and **NorthAmerica** worksheets.

Enhance the **appearance** of the **three worksheets** in ways of your choice.

Save the **workbook as** International Forecast.

Close the **file**.

MS PowerPoint 2003 Case Study 1

OBJECTIVES

After successfully completing this case study, you should be able to:

- Start, create, close, save, and reopen PowerPoint presentation
- Use the PowerPoint menu system, the PowerPoint toolbars and PowerPoint task panes
- Add new slides in the PowerPoint presentation
- Edit existing slides
- Work in both Slides and Outline tabs
- Add an AutoShape to a slide
- Add text to an AutoShape

- Insert a clip art image into a slide
- Change the color scheme for clip art image
- Apply a design template to a presentation
- Add footer to presentation slides
- Use the Spelling Checker
- Display help information
- Print slides

Case Study 1—MS PowerPoint 2003

Assume that you work for a school named ABC Computer Education which is offering new IT courses in the fall and winter semesters. Your task is to produce a presentation that summarizes your school's new courses. This presentation includes five slides.

POWERPOINT SLIDE 1

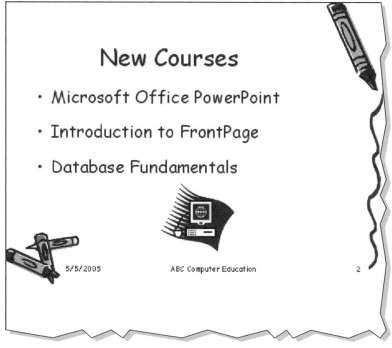

POWERPOINT SLIDE 2

Microsoft Office PowerPoint

- Create a new presentation
- Add tables, charts and clip art to slides
- Apply a design template to a presentation
- Produce a slide show

5/5/2005   ABC Computer Education   3

POWERPOINT SLIDE 3

Introduction to FrontPage

- Use FrontPage interface elements
- Add text and images
- Create text links, hotspots and graphic links
- Create tables
- Add frames
- Post and test your Website

5/5/2005   ABC Computer Education   4

POWERPOINT SLIDE 4

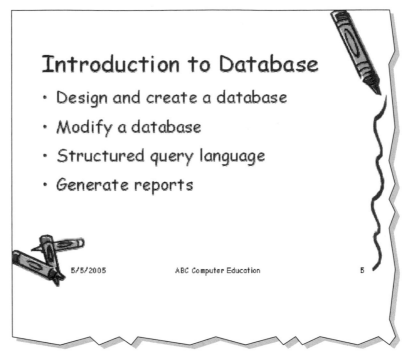

POWERPOINT SLIDE 5

Getting Started

This section begins with a discussion of **PowerPoint and its uses**. It then covers various **program fundamentals**.

In this section, you will learn how to:

- **Start PowerPoint.**
- **Identify** the **elements** of the **PowerPoint Application window**.
- **Work** with **PowerPoint menus** and **toolbars**.
- **Use PowerPoint task panes.**

What Is PowerPoint?

PowerPoint: A sophisticated **presentation graphics program** which provides all of the necessary tools for creating a high-quality, visually-pleasing presentation of information. With PowerPoint, you can produce the following:

Slides: These are the actual images that illustrate the information you wish to present. Slides can include text, drawn objects, tables, charts, clip art, as well as visuals created with other applications. They can appear on a computer screen, or they can be projected as either overhead transparencies or 35mm slides.

Handouts: These are smaller, printed versions of slides. Handouts, which are usually provided to audience members to support a presentation, can include additional text, such as a company name and the date.

Notes: These are smaller, printed versions of slides, along with relevant text. Notes usually include information a speaker wishes to convey to his or her audience during a presentation.

Notes

In PowerPoint, the term **presentation** refers to the entire collection of related elements (for example, slides, handouts, notes, etc.), stored in a single file.

Starting PowerPoint

You start PowerPoint by clicking on the **Start** button on the Windows taskbar, by pointing to **All Programs** (if you are running Windows XP) or to **Programs** (if you are running Windows 2000), by selecting the **Microsoft Office** option on the All Programs or Programs menu, and by selecting the **Microsoft Office PowerPoint 2003** option on the subsequent submenu.

Objective

In this exercise, you will **start PowerPoint and display the opening PowerPoint Application window**.

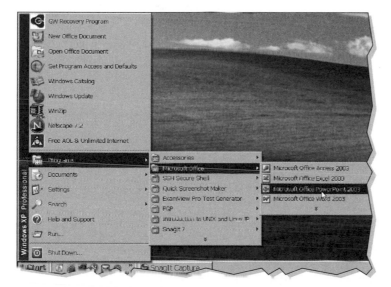

1.1

- **Click on the Start button on the Windows taskbar.**

- **Point to All Programs (if you are running Windows XP) or to Programs (if you are running Windows 2000).**

- **Point to Microsoft Office on the menu.**

- **Click on Microsoft Office PowerPoint 2003 on the submenu.**

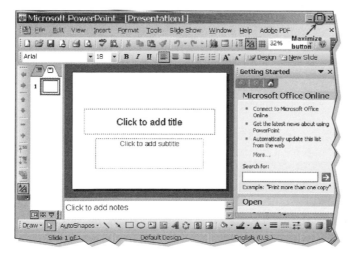

1.2

PowerPoint is started, and the PowerPoint Application window is displayed.

- **If the PowerPoint Application window is not maximized, click on the Maximize button on the Title bar of the window.**

The PowerPoint Application Window

The initial **PowerPoint Application window** includes the following elements:

Title bar	This displays the name of the **program**, as well as the name of the current **presentation** if it has been saved. (If the presentation has not been saved, it is identified by a number—for example, Presentation1.) The standard Windows Control-menu box and window sizing buttons appear at the left end and right end of the bar, respectively.
Menu bar	This displays PowerPoint's **primary commands**.
Standard/Formatting toolbars	These display a number of **shortcut buttons** and **boxes** for performing common PowerPoint operations. When you point to one of these buttons or boxes, the name of the button/box appears in a small window (**Screen-Tip**) next to the mouse pointer. The Standard and Formatting toolbars, by default, appear side-by-side. On your screen, however, one toolbar may appear above the other.
Getting Started task pane	This displays options for accessing Microsoft Office Online, a Web site for users of Microsoft Office products, as well as options for opening an existing presentation file and for creating a new presentation. The program includes several other task panes. Each pane includes options for performing a specific task (for example, changing the layout of a slide or applying a design template to a presentation).
Presentation window	This window, which occupies the majority of the screen, is the area in which you create your presentations.
View buttons	These are used to switch from one PowerPoint view to another. The Presentation window currently appears in **Normal view**. Notice that in this view, the Presentation window is divided into three panes: the **Slide pane** in which a blank slide currently appears, the **Notes pane** (below the Slide pane) in which you can enter notes for the current slide, and the **Outline/ Slides Tab pane** (to the left of the Slide pane) in which either the text, or a thumbnail image of each slide of a presentation is displayed.

Drawing toolbar	This displays a number of **buttons** for adding various graphic objects to your slides.
Status bar	This displays helpful information (for example, the current slide number) as you use the program.

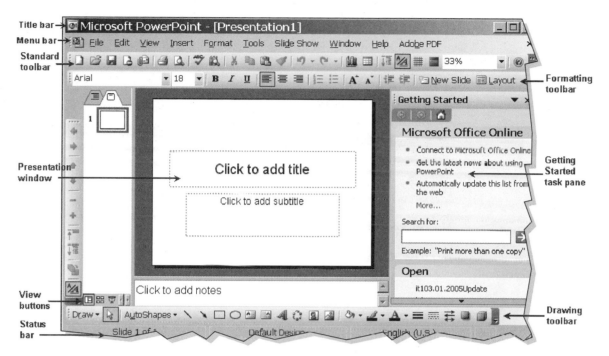

POWERPOINT APPLICATION WINDOW

Notes

What appears on your screen may sometimes vary slightly from what is shown in this manual.

Working with PowerPoint Menus and Toolbars

The menus that you initially access from the Menu bar are called **short menus** since they include only a basic set of commonly-used options. You can expand a short menu and display the **full menu**—that is, one that includes additional options, by clicking on the chevron (the two down arrows) at the bottom of the menu. (Note that a menu will expand automatically if you continue pointing for a few seconds to the command that displayed it.) Any option selected on this expanded menu is added to the basic set of options, thereby creating a personalized menu that reflects your needs. The same option is removed from the basic set of options after a period of time if you no longer use it.

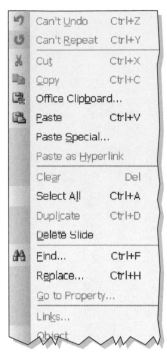

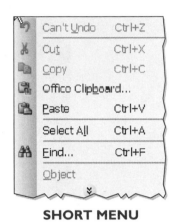

SHORT MENU   **FULL MENU**

Notes

If you prefer to work only with full menus, you can do so by choosing the **Tools, Customize** command and by selecting the **Always show full menus** option in the Customize dialog box. You can also restore personalized menus (and toolbars) to their original state by clicking on the **Reset menu and toolbar usage data** button in the same dialog box.

To help you work even more efficiently, PowerPoint also provides a number of shortcut menus. A **shortcut menu** includes options that are relevant to a particular screen element or area of a slide and is displayed by clicking the **right** mouse button. For example, if you position the mouse pointer in a slide and right-click the mouse button, the following shortcut menu is displayed:

SHORTCUT MENU

The Standard and Formatting toolbars initially are "docked" side-by-side and include only a subset of the available buttons and boxes. You can display a list of additional options by clicking on the **Toolbar Options** button at the right side of either toolbar. Any button/box selected in the Toolbar Options list is added to the associated toolbar. To make room for the new option, a button/box not used recently is moved to the Toolbar Options list.

Notes

1. If you prefer to have more buttons/boxes displayed on the Standard and Formatting toolbars, you can do so by moving either one to a different row or to another part of the screen. This can be done by choosing the **Tools, Customize** command and by selecting the **Show Standard and Formatting toolbars on two rows** option in the Customize dialog box, or by pointing to the **Move handle** (which displays a dotted vertical bar) at the left side of the toolbar and by dragging the toolbar to the new location. (Dragging a toolbar to an area of the screen that is not adjacent to the window border creates a "floating" toolbar—that is, a small window in which the various buttons/boxes appear.)

2. You can increase or decrease the width of the Standard and Formatting toolbars when they appear side-by-side by dragging the Move handle of the toolbar on the right. (Dragging this handle to the left, increases the width of the toolbar on the right while decreasing the width of the toolbar on the left; dragging this handle to the right, decreases the width of the toolbar on the right while increasing the width of the toolbar on the left.)

PowerPoint also provides a number of other toolbars with shortcuts related to specific tasks. You can display any of these toolbars by choosing the **View, Toolbars** command (or by **right-clicking** on any visible toolbar) and by selecting the toolbar name on the submenu that appears. You can also hide any toolbar by deselecting the toolbar name on the same submenu.

Using PowerPoint Task Panes

The **Getting Started task pane**, as you have seen, is opened when you start PowerPoint, displaying options for accessing Microsoft Office Online, for opening an existing presentation file, and for creating a new presentation. Other task panes appear when you initiate relevant operations.

Notes

You can manually display a different task pane by clicking on the **Other Task Panes** button at the top of the current task pane and by selecting the desired pane in the list that appears.

Creating Text Slides

This section discusses methods for **creating slides that consist primarily of text**. In it, you will learn how to:

- **Create** a **new presentation**.
- **Add** a **new slide** to a presentation.
- **Save** a **presentation**.
- **Edit** the **text** on a slide.
- **Work** in the **Outline tab**.
- **Work** in the **Slides tab**.
- **Reset** the **line spacing** of **paragraphs** on a slide.

Creating a New Presentation

The New Presentation task pane (which is displayed by choosing the **File, New** command if the pane has been closed) includes the following options for creating a new presentation:

Blank presentation: This option allows you to create a presentation that uses the program's default font and color scheme settings. Slides of a blank presentation include only basic design elements (for example, bullets) and initially have no color applied to them.

From design template: This option allows you to select a design template (a custom set of fonts, color schemes and design elements) that is applied automatically to all new slides.

From AutoContent wizard: This option prompts you for the type of presentation you wish to create, the output for the presentation, as well as the text that appears on the title slide. It then displays a series of slides with sample text, which you can modify to suit your individual needs. The AutoContent wizard is a convenient method for setting up a quick presentation.

Notes

1. In addition to selecting the Blank presentation option in the New Presentation task pane, you can create a presentation that uses the program's default font and color scheme settings in the following ways: 1) by using the blank slide that appears in the Presentation window when PowerPoint is started, or 2) by clicking on the **New** button on the Standard toolbar and by using the blank slide that is subsequently displayed. (Clicking on the New button is equivalent to selecting the Blank presentation option in the New Presentation task pane.)
2. You can also create a new presentation that is based on an existing presentation. To do this, select the **From existing presentation** option in the New Presentation task pane. Then, in the New from Existing Presentation dialog box, select the appropriate filename, and click on the **Create New** button.
3. The **Photo album** option in the New Presentation task pane can be used to create a special type of presentation, called a photo album—that is, a collection of favorite photos and other pictures. For more information about photo albums, see the PowerPoint Help system.

In this subsection, you will start a new presentation by entering text into the blank slide that should currently appear in the Presentation window. This slide displays what is called **Title Slide** layout since the program assumes that you want a presentation to begin with a **title slide**.

PowerPoint includes a number of other layouts that can be applied to any slide of a presentation. Each layout (except for the Blank layout) includes one or more **placeholders** in which you enter the various elements that are to appear on the slide. Notice that the Title Slide layout includes two placeholders—one for a **main title** and one for a **subtitle**.

Notes

PowerPoint's **AutoLayout** feature automatically adjusts the layout of a slide to accommodate an element that does not "fit" a particular placeholder (for example, a table inserted into a text place-holder). You can override the adjustment by clicking on the **Automatic Layout Options** button that appears in the lower-right corner of the placeholder and by selecting the **Undo Automatic Layout** option in the list that is displayed.

Objective

In this exercise, you will **create a title slide for a new presentation**.

PowerPoint includes an **AutoCorrect** feature, which automatically corrects common spelling errors, as well as an **automatic spell checking** feature, which flags other possible spelling errors by displaying a wavy red line under the text. Since it is assumed these features are currently enabled, you may see their effect from time to time as you enter text throughout this course. (The AutoCorrect feature is enabled/disabled with the **Tools, AutoCorrect Options** command; the automatic spell checking feature is enabled/disabled with the **Tools, Options** command.)

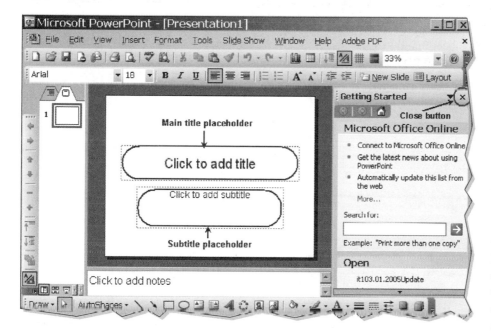

2.1

- **Click in the main title placeholder.**

The placeholder is selected, and an insertion point appears in the center of the placeholder.

*NOTE: When selected, a placeholder is surrounded by eight **sizing handles** (small white circles). Notice also that the current placeholder also includes a hatched border. Any placeholder for text (for example, a main title, subtitle or table placeholder) displays a hatched border and an insertion point when you click inside the placeholder. This allows you to enter or edit text within the placeholder. If you subsequently click on the hatched border, it changes to a dotted border, and the insertion point no longer appears. This allows you to perform operations on the entire contents of the placeholder.*

- **The Getting Started task pane is displayed on the right. Close the Getting Started task pane.**

2.2

- **Type: ABC Computer Education**

The main title is entered.

- **Click in the subtitle placeholder.**

The placeholder is selected, and an insertion point appears in the center of the first line of the placeholder.

- **Type: Fall and Winter Courses**

The subtitle is entered.

- **Click outside the subtitle placeholder (in any empty area of the slide).**

The placeholder is deselected.

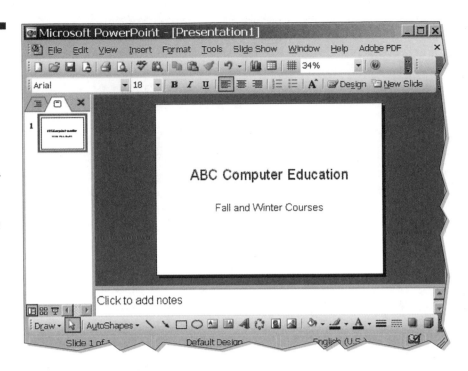

Adding a New Slide to a Presentation

The second slide in your presentation will be a **bulleted list slide**—that is, a slide that displays a title and two or more bulleted items. This type of slide is often used to summarize major discussion points or to list subtopics under a main topic.

> To **add a new slide to a presentation**:
> Do one of the following:

- Choose the **Insert, New Slide** command, or click on the **New Slide** button on the Formatting toolbar; or
- With the insertion point located in either the **Slides tab** or the **Outline tab** of Normal view, press [**ENTER**].
- Optionally, select (click on) a **different layout option** in the Slide Layout task pane.

NEW SLIDE BUTTON

Notes

1. You can also add a new slide to a presentation by choosing the **Format, Slide Layout** command to display the Slide Layout task pane, if necessary, by pointing to the desired layout in the task pane, by clicking on the down arrow that appears, and by selecting the **Insert New Slide** option in the list that is displayed.

2. At any time, you can change the layout that has been applied to one or more slides by simply selecting the new layout in the Slide Layout task pane. (To simultaneously change the layout of multiple slides, you must select those slides before selecting the new layout. You can do this by clicking on each slide (in the Slides tab of Normal view or in Slide Sorter view) while holding down [**CTRL**].)

Objective

In this exercise, you will **create a bulleted list slide for your new presentation**.

3.1

- **Click on the New Slide button on the Formatting toolbar.**

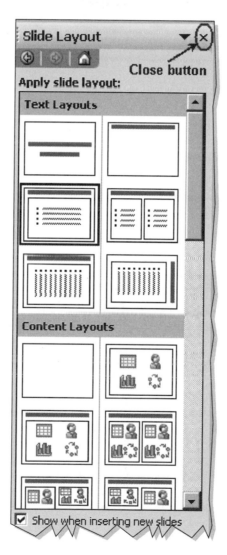

3.2

The Slide Layout task pane is displayed and a new slide appears in the Presentation window. Notice that the Title and Text layout, which is selected in the task pane, has been applied to the new slide. This layout, like the Title Slide layout, includes two placeholders—one for a title and one for text. At this point, you could apply a different layout to the new slide. In this case, however, the current slide layout is the correct layout for a bulleted list slide. (Notice that the first bullet already appears in the text placeholder.)

NOTE: *You can, if necessary, remove the default bullet in a text placeholder by deselecting (clicking on) the Bullets button on the Formatting toolbar.*

- **Close the Slide Layout task pane.**

3.3

- **Click in the Title placeholder.**

  Type: New Courses

The title is entered.

- **Click in the text placeholder.**

  Type: Microsoft Office PowerPoint
  Press [ENTER].

The first bulleted item is entered, and the insertion point moves to the next line. Notice that a second bullet has been inserted automatically.

- **Type: Intro to FrontPage**
  Press [ENTER].

- **Type: Database Fundamentals**

Two more bulleted items are entered.

- **Click outside the text placeholder (in any empty area of the slide).**

The placeholder is deselected. The slide should now appear as illustrated on the right side.

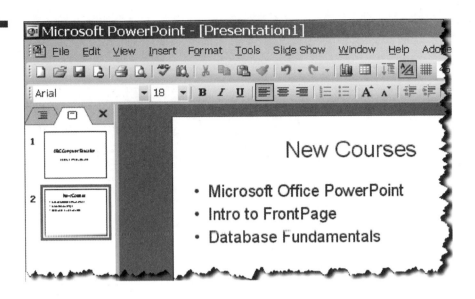

3.4

- **Choose the Format, Slide Layout command.**

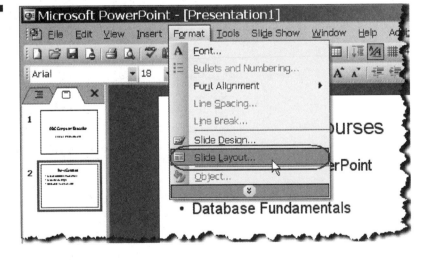

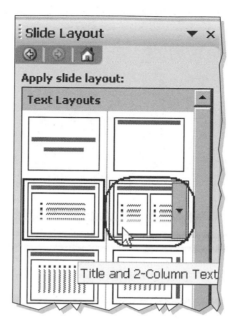

3.5

The Slide Layout task pane is redisplayed.

• **In the task pane, click on the Title and 2-Column Text** 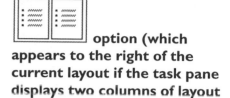 **option (which appears to the right of the current layout if the task pane displays two columns of layout options).**

3.6

The new layout is applied to the current slide. Notice that this layout includes two text placeholders, allowing you to enter text into two columns.

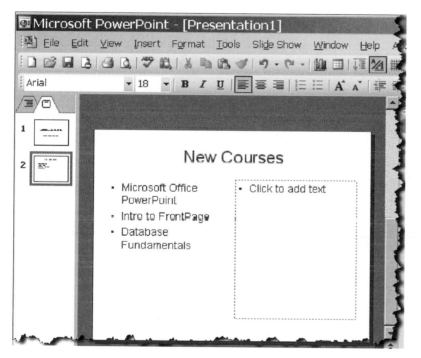

3.7

You will now restore the original (one-column) layout.

- **In the task pane, click on the Title and Text option.**

The original layout is reapplied to the current slide.

- **Close the Slide Layout task pane.**

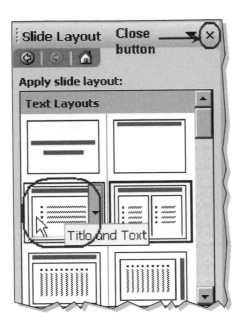

Saving a Presentation

To avoid losing what you have input due to an unexpected occurrence, such as a power failure, it is important that you periodically save a presentation as you work.

To **save a presentation** (for the first time):

- Choose the **File**, **Save** command, or click on the **Save** button on the Standard toolbar.
- In the Save As dialog box, enter a **name** for the **file** in which the presentation is to be saved.
- If you wish to store the file in a folder other than the working folder, switch to that **folder**.
- Click on the **Save** button (in the dialog box).

To **resave a presentation**:

- Choose the **File**, **Save** command, or click on the **Save** button on the Standard toolbar.

SAVE BUTTON

You can save a previously-saved presentation in a new location (for example, in a different folder on your hard disk or on a floppy diskette) and/or under a different filename by choosing the **File**, **Save As** command and by specifying the new location/new filename in the Save As dialog box. You will then have two copies of the presentation—the original version saved in the original file and a second version saved in the new file. From the Save As dialog box, you can also save a presentation in a different format (for example, one that can be used with an earlier version of PowerPoint) by expanding the **Save as type** box and by selecting the new file type in the list that appears.

Notes

PowerPoint includes an **AutoRecover** feature that periodically saves the open presentation in a special recovery file. If you do lose power or, for some other reason, are unable to save the presentation, you can use this recovery file. AutoRecover, however, should not be used in place of the normal save procedure since a recovery file is only a temporary file. (The AutoRecover feature is enabled/disabled with the **Tools**, **Options** command.)

Objective

In this exercise, you will **save your presentation on a floppy disk**.

4.1

- **Insert floppy disk in drive A.**
- **Click on the Save button on the Standard toolbar or choose the File, Save command.**

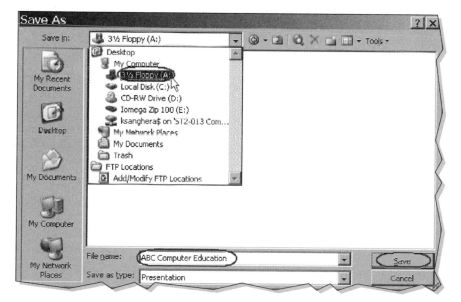

4.2

A Save As dialog box opens.

- **In a Save As dialog box, enter a name for the file–ABC Computer Education and select 3½ Floppy (A:) in the Save in list.**
- **Click on Save button.**

4.3

*The new file name (**ABC Computer Education**) is disp293layed in the title bar.*

Editing the Text on a Slide

While creating a slide, you can easily edit any text you have typed. Simply move the insertion point to the appropriate location in the text, if necessary, and use the standard editing techniques. For example:

To:	Do the following:
Insert one or more characters	Type the new character(s).
Delete one or more characters	Press [DEL] or [BACKSPACE].
Delete one or more words	Select the word(s), and press [DEL].
Replace one or more words	Select the word(s), and type the new text.

Objective

In this exercise, you will **edit the text on Slide #2 of the current presentation**.

5.1

- **Position the mouse pointer (I-beam) to the immediate right of the letter o in the word Intro, and click the mouse button.**

The insertion point is positioned.

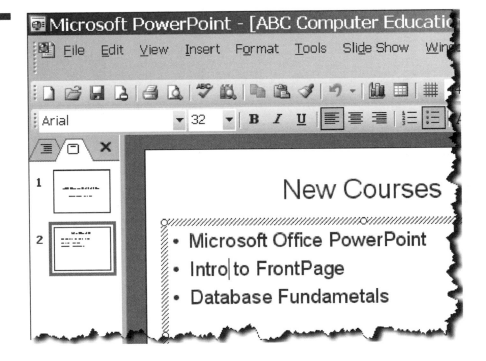

5.2

- **Type: duction**

The word now reads "Introduction."

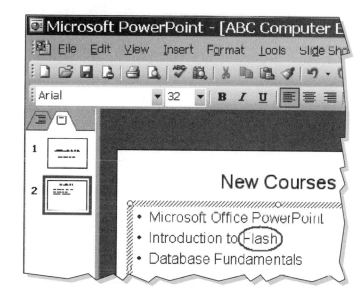

5.3

- **Double-click on the word FrontPage.**

The word is selected.

- **Type: Flash**

The selected word is changed to "Flash."

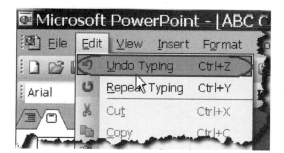

5.4

- **Choose Edit, Undo Typing.**

5.5

The original word (FrontPage) is restored.

- **Choose Edit, Redo Typing.**

The Undo operation is reversed, and the correction (Flash) is restored.

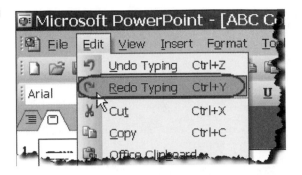

5.6

- **Choose Edit, Undo Typing.**

The original word (FrontPage) is restored.

- **Click outside the text placeholder (in any empty area of the slide).**

The placeholder is deselected.

- **Click on the Save button.**

Working in the Slides Tab

The **Slides tab** of Normal view displays a thumbnail image of each slide of a presentation. Using this tab, you can move from slide to slide, reorder the slides and, if necessary, delete one or more slides.

Objective

In this exercise, you will **work in the Slides tab**.

6.1

- **In the Slides tab, click on Slide #1.**

Slide #1 is displayed.

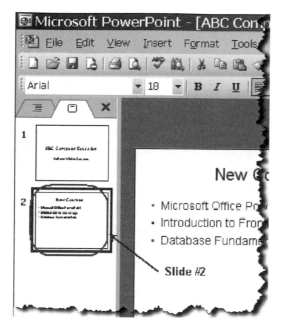

- **In the same tab, click on Slide #2.**

Slide #2 is redisplayed. You will now change the order of the two slides.

- **In the same tab, point to Slide #2. Press and hold down the mouse button, and drag the mouse pointer upward until the placement indicator (the thin horizontal line that moves with the mouse pointer) appears above Slide #1. Then release the mouse button.**

*NOTE: You can also move from slide to slide by clicking on the up and down arrows on the Vertical scroll bar, by dragging the scroll box along the Vertical scroll bar, and by clicking on the **Next Slide** and **Previous Slide** buttons at the bottom of the Vertical scroll bar.*

The two slides are reordered.

6.4

- **Choose Edit, Undo Drag and Drop**

The original slide order is restored.

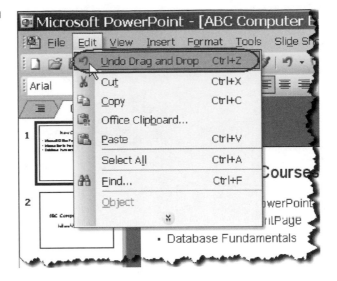

6.5

- **Make sure that Slide #2 is still selected (surrounded by the dark border) in the Slides tab. Then press [DEL].**

Slide #2 is deleted.

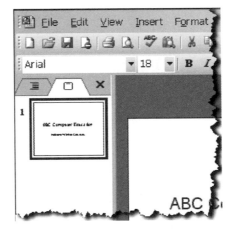

6.6

- **Choose Edit, Undo Delete Slide**

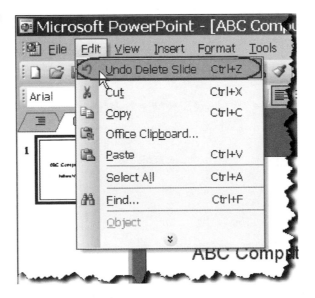

6.7

Slide #2 is restored.

Notes

Slide Sorter view (which is displayed by choosing the **View, Slide Sorter** command or by clicking on the **Slide Sorter View** button above the Drawing toolbar) also shows a thumbnail image of each slide of a presentation. From Slide Sorter view, you can perform some of the same operations performed in the Slides tab. (For example, you can reorder and delete slides.)

Working in the Outline Tab

The **Outline tab** of Normal view displays the text on slides of a presentation in outline format. Using this tab, you can perform the operations you performed in the Slides tab, as well as add new slides and edit existing slides.

Objective

In this exercise, you will **work in the Outline tab.**

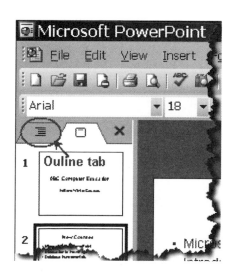

7.1

- **Click on the outline tab.**

7.2

- **In the Outline tab, click anywhere in the Slide #1 listing.**

Slide #1 is displayed.

- **In the same tab, click anywhere in the Slide #2 listing.**

Slide #2 is redisplayed.

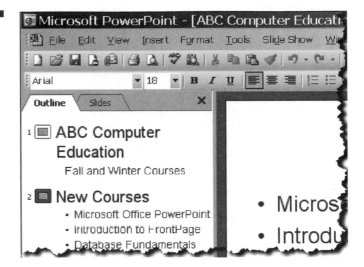

7.3

- **Choose the View, Toolbars command.**

A submenu of toolbar names is displayed.

- **If the Outlining toolbar is not already check marked, click on Outlining.**

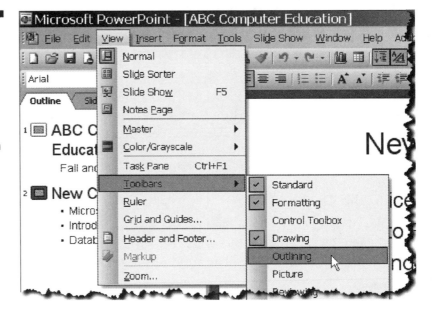

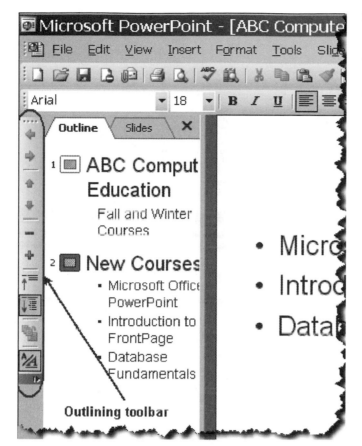

7.4

The Outlining toolbar is displayed down the left side of the Presentation window. You will now use several buttons on this toolbar.

7.5

- **Make sure that Slide #2 is still displayed. Then click on the Collapse** [—] **button on the Outlining toolbar.**

The bulleted items on Slide #2 are hidden in the Outline tab.

7.6

- **Click on the Collapse All button on the Outlining toolbar.**

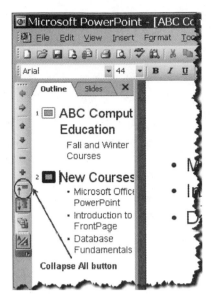

7.7

The subtitle of Slide #1 and the bulleted items on Slide #2 are hidden in the Outline tab.

- **Click on the Expand All button on the Outlining toolbar.**

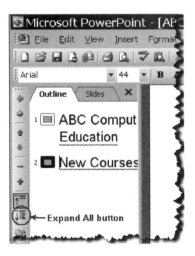

7.8

All items on Slides #1 and #2 are once again displayed in the Outline tab.

- **Make sure that the insertion point is still located in the Slide #2 listing. Then press [CTRL] + [END].**

The insertion point moves to the end of the last item on Slide #2.

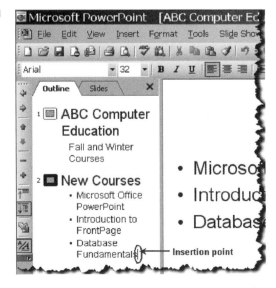

- **Press [ENTER].**

A fourth bullet is displayed. You will now use the Promote button to add another slide to the presentation.

- **Click on the Promote button on the Outlining toolbar.**

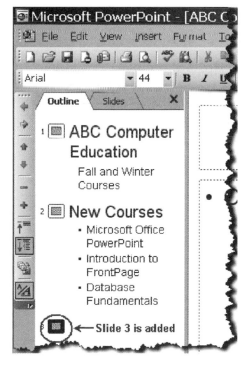

Another slide (#3) is added to the Outline tab.

7.11

You will now enter a title for this slide.

• **Type: Microsoft Office PowerPoint**

The title is entered.

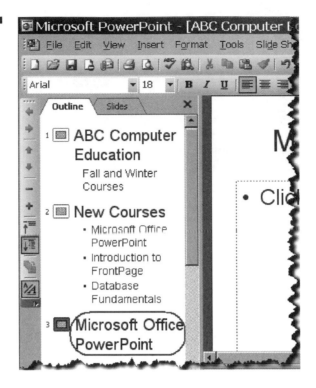

7.12

• **Press [ENTER].**

A fourth slide is added to the display. You will now use the Demote button to return to the previous slide.

• **Click on the Demote button on the Outlining toolbar.**

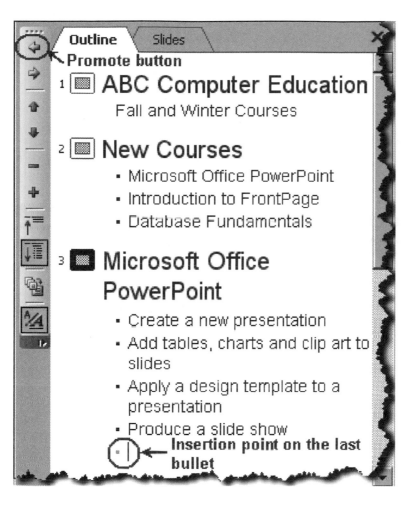

The insertion point is indented, and a bullet is displayed below the title of Slide #3.

- **Type: Create a new presentation and press [ENTER].**

- **Type: Add tables, charts and clip art to slides and press [ENTER].**

- **Type: Apply a design template to a presentation and press [ENTER].**

- **Type: Produce a slide show and press [ENTER].**

Four bulleted items are entered, followed by a fifth bullet. You will now add another slide to the presentation.

- **Make sure that the insertion point is located to the right of the last bullet. Then click on the Promote button.**

7.14

Another slide (#4) is added to the Outline tab.

- **Type: Introduction to FrontPage and press [ENTER].**

The title is entered.

- **Press [TAB].**

The insertion point is indented, and a bullet is displayed below the title of Slide #4.

- **Type: Use FrontPage interface elements and press [ENTER].**

- **Type: Add text and images and press [ENTER].**

- **Type: Create text links, hotspots and graphic links and press [ENTER].**

- **Type: Create tables and press [ENTER].**

- **Type: Add frames and press [ENTER].**

- **Type: Post and test your website and press [ENTER].**

- **Press [SHIFT] + [TAB].**

NOTE: *The insertion point is moved to the first-level bullet.*

- **Type: Introduction to Database and press [ENTER].**

The title is entered.

- **Press [TAB].**

The insertion point is indented, and a bullet is displayed below the title of Slide #5.

- **Type: Design and create a database and press [ENTER].**

- **Type: Modify a database and press [ENTER].**

- **Type: Structured query language and press [ENTER].**

- **Type: Generate reports and press [ENTER].**

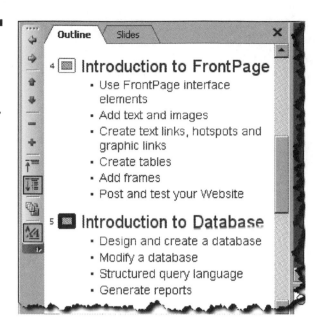

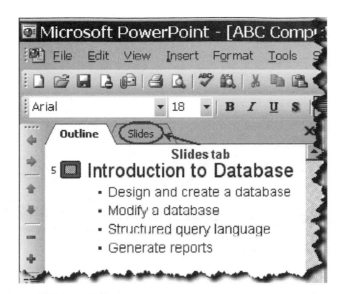

- **At the left side of the Presentation window, click on the word Slides at the top of the Slides tab.**

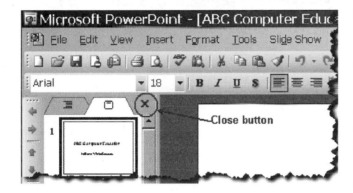

The Slides tab is redisplayed.

- **Click on the Close button (which displays the letter "X") to the right of the Slides tab.**

NOTE: *You can subsequently redisplay these tabs by clicking on the **Normal View** button above the Drawing toolbar.*

- **Click on the Save button.**

Resetting the Line Spacing of Paragraphs on a Slide

In PowerPoint, a **paragraph** is any of the following:

- A title
- A subtitle
- A single bulleted or numbered item
- Any other text that ends with a hard return (inserted by pressing [**ENTER**])

Paragraphs on a PowerPoint slide, by default, include single-line spacing. Most paragraphs, also by default, are preceded by a small amount of space (for example, two-tenths, or five-tenths, of a line).

To **reset the line spacing of one or more paragraphs on a slide**:

- Select the paragraph(s) that is/are to be affected.
- Choose the **Format**, **Line Spacing** command.
- In the Line Spacing dialog box, specify the **new line spacing**, as well as the **new spacing before and/or after paragraphs**, as necessary.
- Click on the **OK** button.

Objective

In this exercise, you will **reset the line spacing on the bulleted list slides** of your presentation.

8.1

- **Display slide #2.**

- **Select the text of the three bulleted items by dragging the mouse pointer over them.**

NOTE: Begin by pointing to the immediate left of the letter "M" in the word "Microsoft."

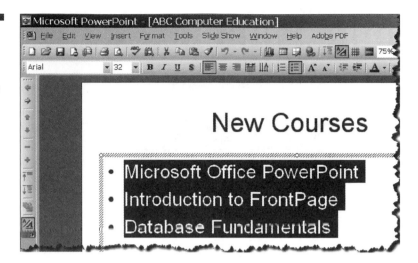

8.2

- **Choose the Format, Line Spacing command.**

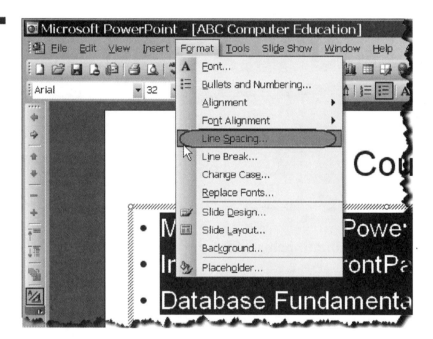

8.3

The Line Spacing dialog box is displayed.

- **Make sure that the current entry (1) in the Line spacing box is selected.**

  Type: 1.5

The line spacing is increased to 1.5 lines.

- **Click on the Preview button.**

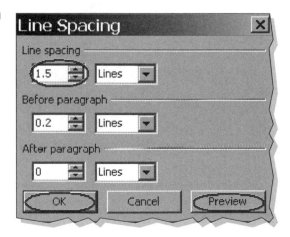

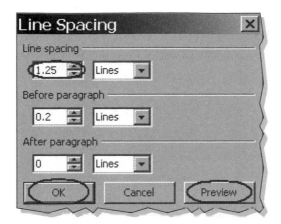

8.4

The new line spacing is previewed on the slide.

NOTE: *You can reposition the dialog box, if necessary, by dragging its Title bar.*

- **Click on the OK button.**

The dialog box is closed, and the new line spacing is applied to the bulleted items.

- **Display Slide #3. Then select the text of all bulleted items.**

- **Choose the Format, Line Spacing command.**

The Line Spacing dialog box is redisplayed.

- **Type: 1.25**
  Click on the OK button.

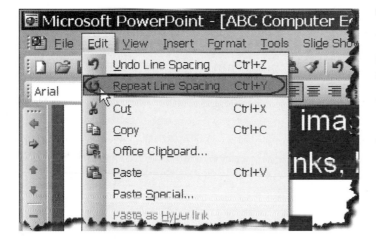

8.5

The dialog box is closed, and the spacing between each of the bulleted items is increased.

- **Display Slide #4. Then select the text of all bulleted items.**

- **Choose the Edit, Repeat Line Spacing command.**

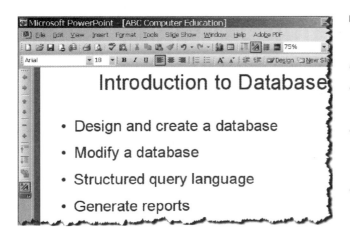

8.6

The spacing between each of the bulleted items is increased.

- **Repeat the last step for Slide #5.**

- **Click outside the text placeholder (in any empty area of the slide).**

- **Click on the Save button.**

Using the Drawing Toolbar

This section discusses the **use of options on PowerPoint's Drawing toolbar to enhance your slides**. In it, you will learn how to:

- **Move** a **placeholder** on a slide.
- **Add** an **AutoShape** to a slide.
- **Add text** to an **AutoShape**.

Moving a Placeholder

In the next section, you will add an AutoShape to the current (title) slide. Before doing this, however, you will reposition the two placeholders on this slide to create additional space for the AutoShape.

To **move a placeholder**:

- Select the placeholder (by clicking within it).

Do one of the following:

- **Drag** the **border** of the **placeholder** to the new location; or
- Press any of the [**ARROW**] keys to nudge the placeholder (move it by small increments) in the respective direction.

Notes

1. You can **resize** a placeholder by selecting it and by dragging any of the **sizing handles** that surround it. If necessary, you can also **delete** a placeholder by selecting it and by pressing [**DEL**].
2. After changing the layout of a slide (for example, after moving or resizing a placeholder or after resetting the line spacing in a placeholder), you can restore the original layout by displaying the Slide Layout task pane, if necessary, by pointing to the layout option (in the task pane), by clicking on the down arrow that appears, and by selecting the **Reapply Layout** option in the list that is displayed.

Objective

In this exercise, you will **move the two placeholders on the title slide** of the current presentation.

9.1

- **Display Slide #1 and click on the main title.**

- **Click on the border of the selected placeholder.**

The mouse pointer will appear as a four-headed arrow when it is properly positioned.

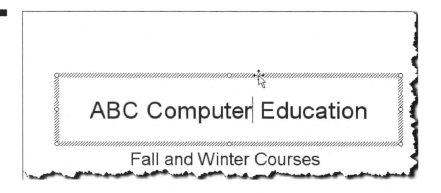

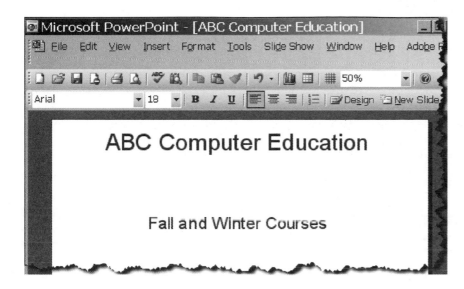

- **Press and hold down the mouse button, and drag the placeholder upward until the top border of the placeholder is approximately half inch from the top of the slide. Then release the mouse button.**

NOTE: Do not reposition the placeholder horizontally. (It should remain centered between the left and right edges of the slide.) You may wish to hold down [SHIFT] while dragging the placeholder. Doing this allows you to move a placeholder (or other object) vertically (or horizontally) in a straight line.

- **Make sure that the main title placeholder is still selected.**

NOTE: The placeholder should now be surrounded by a dotted border (instead of a hatched border), and the insertion point should no longer appear in the placeholder. (If the placeholder still displays a hatched border, click on the border to display the dotted border.)

- **Press [DOWN ARROW] five times and press [UP ARROW] ten times.**

The placeholder is moved downward by small increments and then moved upward by small increments.

- **Click on the subtitle. Point to the border of the selected placeholder. Press and hold down the mouse button, and drag the placeholder upward until the top border of the placeholder is approximately one-half inch below the text of the main title. Then release the mouse button.**

The subtitle is repositioned.

- **Click outside the subtitle placeholder (in any empty area of the slide).**

The placeholder is deselected.

- **Click on the Save button.**

Adding an AutoShape to a Slide

PowerPoint includes a number of tools for adding AutoShapes (rectangles, ellipses, arrows, stars, etc.) to your slides. These tools are available by clicking on the AutoShapes button on the Drawing toolbar and by selecting an option in the list of AutoShape categories that subsequently appears.

DRAWING TOOLBAR

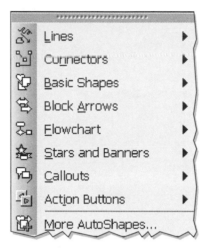

AUTOSHAPE CATEGORIES

Notes

Some AutoShape tools (for example, the rectangle, oval, line and arrow tools) can also be accessed by clicking on the associated buttons on the Drawing toolbar.

To **draw an AutoShape**:

*   Select the appropriate **tool**.
*   **Drag** the **mouse pointer** until the object is the desired size and shape.

To **resize/reposition an AutoShape**:

*   If necessary, select the AutoShape. Doing this, displays sizing handles around the object.
*   To resize the object, **drag** any of the **sizing handles**. (Dragging the top or bottom sizing handle increases the height of the object; dragging the left or right sizing handle increases the width of the object; dragging a corner sizing handle increases both the height and width of the object.)
*   To reposition the object, **drag it** to the new location, or press any of the [**ARROW**] keys to nudge the object in the respective direction.

To **change the fill color of an AutoShape**:

*   If necessary, select the AutoShape.
*   Expand the **Fill Color** button on the Drawing toolbar (by clicking on the down arrow at the right side of the button), and select the **new fill color** in the list that appears.

To **change the line color of an AutoShape**:

- If necessary, select the AutoShape.
- Expand the **Line Color** button on the Drawing toolbar, and select the **new line color** in the list that appears. (To remove the line, select the **No Line** option.)

To **change the line style of an AutoShape**:

- If necessary, select the AutoShape.
- Click on the **Line Style** button on the Drawing toolbar, and select the **new line style** (line thickness) in the list that appears.

To **add a shadow to an AutoShape**:

- If necessary, select the AutoShape.
- Click on the **Shadow Style** button on the Drawing toolbar, and select the desired **shadow position** in the list that appears. (To remove the shadow, select the **No Shadow** option.)

Objective

In this exercise, you will **add an AutoShape (star) to the title slide of the current presentation**.

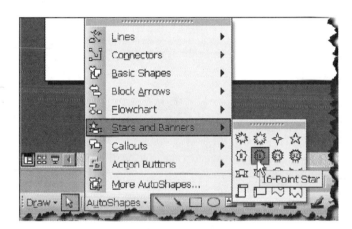

10.1

- **Click on the AutoShapes button on the Drawing toolbar.**

The button is expanded, and a menu of AutoShape categories is displayed.

- **Point to Stars and Banners.**

A list of the available tools for the selected category is displayed.

- **Click on the 16-Point Star** **option.**

The tool is selected.

10.2

- **Point in the left of the slide. Press and hold down the mouse button. Drag the mouse pointer (the cross hair) diagonally downward and to the right until the star drawn is the size and shape of that illustrated on the right side. Then release the mouse button.**

*NOTE: The illustration shows the star as it should appear when the mouse button has been released. You may wish to hold down [**SHIFT**] while dragging the mouse pointer. Doing this allows you to create a star of equal proportions.*

When you release the mouse button, the star should be surrounded by eight sizing handles (small white circles), indicating that it is selected. You will now use various buttons on the Drawing toolbar to reformat the object. First, you will change its fill color.

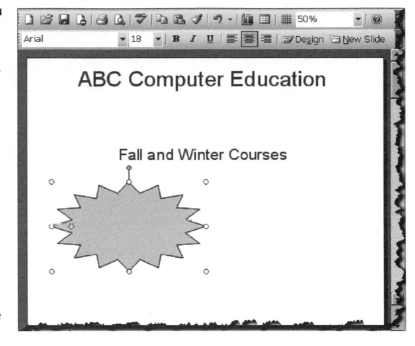

10.3

- **Make sure that the star is still selected. (If it is not, click on it to redisplay the sizing handles.) Then click on the down arrow at the right side of the Fill Color 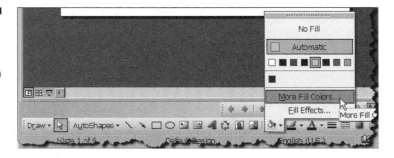 button on the Drawing toolbar.**

The button is expanded, and a list of fill colors is displayed.

- **Click on More Fill Colors…**

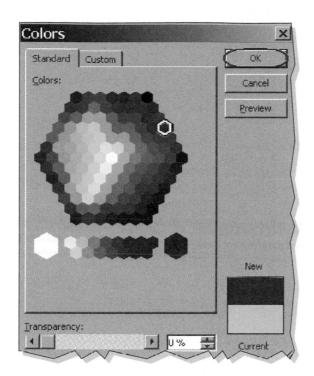

The Custom panel of the Colors dialog box is displayed.

- **Click on the Standard tab.**

The Standard panel of the dialog box appears, displaying a palette of fill colors.

- **Click on the purple color option indicated in the illustration on the right side.**

- **Click on the OK button.**

The dialog box is closed, and the color of the star is changed to purple.

- **Click on the Save button.**

Adding Text to an AutoShape

You can add text to an AutoShape by selecting the object, if necessary, and by simply typing the information. The text you type is automatically centered in the AutoShape and becomes part of that object.

Slide with an AutoShape Containing Text

To **change the attributes of AutoShape text**:

- If necessary, select the AutoShape.
- To change the **color** of the text, use the **Font Color** button on either the Formatting toolbar or the Drawing toolbar; or

To change **other attributes**, use the appropriate **buttons/boxes** on the Formatting toolbar.

Objective

In this exercise, you will **add text to the star on the current slide**.

11.1

- **Select the AutoShape (if it is not currently selected).**

- **Type: Tops in**
  Press [ENTER].
  Type: Training!
  Click outside the star (in any empty area of the slide).

The text is added to the star.

11.2

- **Select the AutoShape.**

NOTE: *Click on the star itself, not on the text.*

You will now use several buttons on the Formatting toolbar to change font attributes of the text.

- **Click four times on the Increase Font Size button on the Formatting toolbar.**

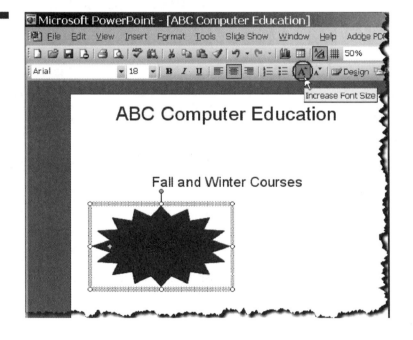

11.3

The size of the text is increased.

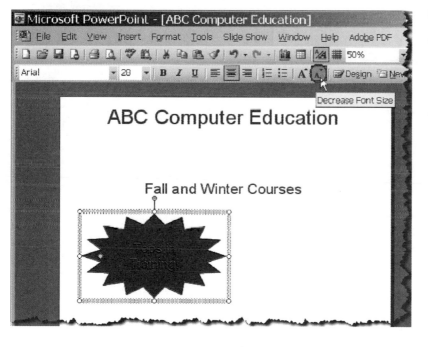

11.4

- **Click one time on the Decrease Font Size** button on the **Formatting toolbar.**

The size of the text is decreased.

11.5

- **Click on the Bold [B] button on the Formatting toolbar.**

The text is bolded.

- **Click on the Italic [I] button on the Formatting toolbar.**

The text is also italicized.

- **Click again on the Italic [I] button.**

The italic attribute is removed, and the text is now only bolded. Finally, you will change the color of the text.

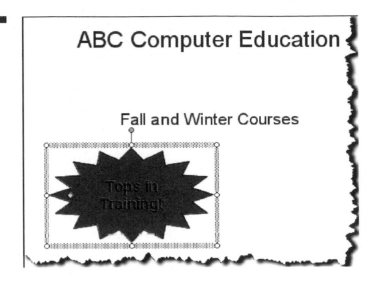

11.6

- **Click on the down arrow at the right side of the Font Color [A ▾] button on either the Formatting toolbar or the Drawing toolbar.**

The button is expanded, and a list of font colors is displayed.

- **Click on the white option.**

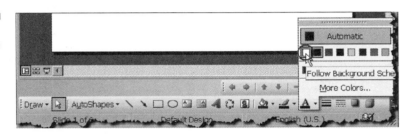

11.7

The color of the text is changed to white.

- **Click outside the star (in any empty area of the slide).**

The star is deselected.

- **Click on the Save button.**

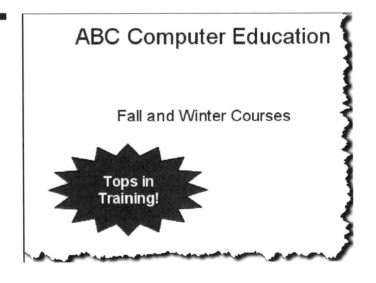

Including Clip Art in a Presentation

This section discusses the **use of the Microsoft Clip Organizer to enhance your slides**. In it, you will learn how to:

- **Insert** a **clip art image** into a slide.
- **Enter additional text** on a slide.

Inserting a Clip Art Image into a Slide

The **Microsoft Clip Organizer** contains a number of professionally-created clip art images. These images provide a convenient way to add visual interest to a presentation.

To **insert a clip art image (from the Microsoft Clip Organizer) into a slide**:

- In a layout that includes a **clip art placeholder**, **double-click** in the placeholder to display the Select Picture dialog box; or

In a layout that includes a **content placeholder**, click on the **Insert Clip Art** button to display the Select Picture dialog box; or

In other layouts, choose the **Insert**, **Picture**, **Clip Art** command, or click on the **Insert Clip Art** button on the Drawing toolbar, to display the Clip Art task pane.

- Do one of the following:
- In the Select Picture dialog box, enter a **keyword** into the **Search text** box, and click on the **Go** button to display related images. Then, in the search results, click on the desired **clip**, and click on the **OK** button to insert the image.

  OR

- In the Clip Art task pane, enter a **keyword** into the **Search for** box, and click on the **Go** button to display related images. Then, in the search results, click on the desired **clip** to insert the image.

Objective

In this exercise, you will **include a clip art image**.

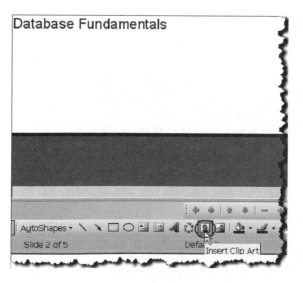

12.1

- **Display Slide #2.**

- **Click on the Insert Clip Art button on the Drawing toolbar.**

12.2

The Clip Art task pane is displayed.

- **Delete any entry that currently appears in the Search for box.**

- **Make sure that the insertion point appears in the Search for box.**

  Type: computer

A keyword is entered. In this case, the program will display Microsoft Clip Organizer clips that are related to computers.

- **Click on the Go button.**

The search results are displayed.

- **Click on the clip art image that is shown in the figure on the right.**

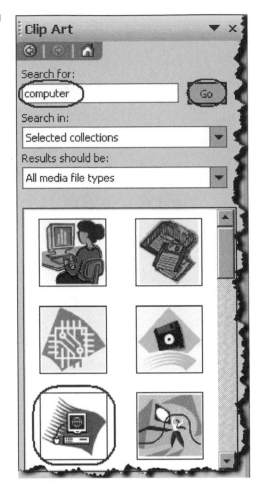

12.3

The image is inserted into the slide.

- **Close the Clip Art task pane.**

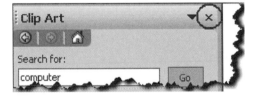

12.4

You will now resize and reposition the image.

- **Point to the clip art image. Press and hold down the mouse button, and drag the image downward and to the center until it is positioned in the lower-center area of the slide. Then release the mouse button.**

12.5

- **Make sure that the clip art image is still selected.**

NOTE: *If the **Picture toolbar** is not displayed, point to the **clip art image**, **right-click** the mouse button, and click on **Show Picture Toolbar** on the shortcut menu that appears.*

- **Click on the Recolor Picture button on the Picture toolbar.**

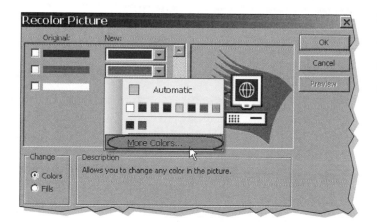

12.6

The Recolor Picture dialog box is displayed.

- **Under New, expand the middle list box (which currently displays the default blue image color), and click on the More Colors...**

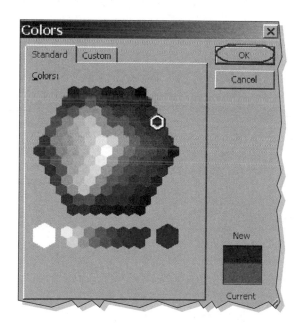

12.7

The Custom panel of the Colors dialog box is displayed.

- **Click on the Standard tab.**

The Standard panel of the dialog box appears, displaying a palette of fill colors.

- **Click on the purple color option indicated in the illustration on the left side.**

- **Click on the OK button on Colors dialog box.**

■ 12.8 ■

- **Click on the OK button on Recolor Picture dialog box.**

The dialog box is closed, and the new color is applied to the image.

- **Save the presentation.**

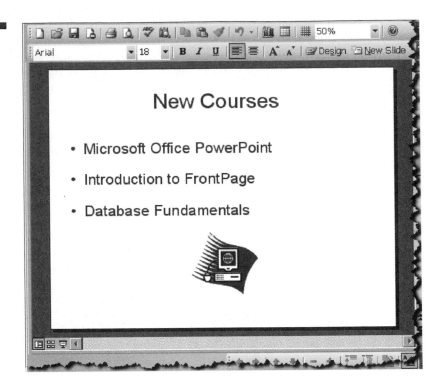

Entering Additional Text on a Slide

The **Text Box** button on the Drawing toolbar provides an additional means of entering a block of text on a slide.

There are two ways in which the Text Box button can be used. After selecting the button, you can drag the mouse pointer to create a text box and then type the text with the insertion point positioned inside the box. The text, in this case, will be wrapped within the text box if it includes more than one line. Alternatively, you can simply click anywhere on a slide and type the text. The text, in this case, will appear on a single line (unless you press [ENTER] to move the insertion point to a new line).

Objective

In this exercise, you will **enter another block of text on the current slide**.

■ 13.1 ■

- **Display Slide #1.**
- **Click on the Text Box button on the Drawing toolbar.**

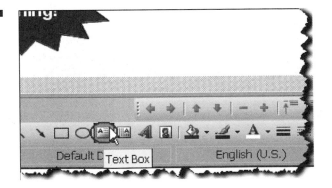

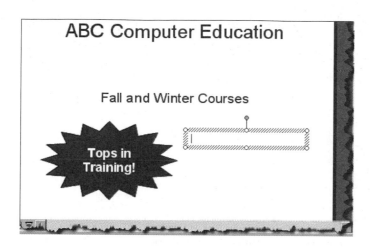

13.2

The button is selected.

- **Point in the area to the right of the AutoShape.**

- **Press and hold down the mouse button, and drag the mouse pointer diagonally downward and to the right to draw a text box that is approximately the size and shape of that illustrated on the left side. Then release the mouse button.**

NOTE: *The illustration shows the text box as should appear when the mouse button has been released.*

13.3

You will now enter a block of text.

- **Make sure that the insertion point is located inside the text box.**

  Type: In the last 5 years, we have trained more than 500,000 individuals in our training centers across the country!

- **Click on the border of the text box.**

The text box should now be surrounded by a dotted border, and the insertion point should no longer appear. This will allow you to treat the entire text block as one entity.

13.4

- **Click on the Bold button. Then click on the Italic button.**

The text is bolded and italicized.

- **Click on the Increase Font Size button.**

The text appears in a larger font size.

- **Resize and/or reposition the text block, as necessary.**

NOTE: *To resize the text block, drag any of the sizing handles that surround the text box when it is selected. To reposition the text block, drag the border of the text box, or press any of the [ARROW] keys to nudge the text box.*

- **Save the presentation.**

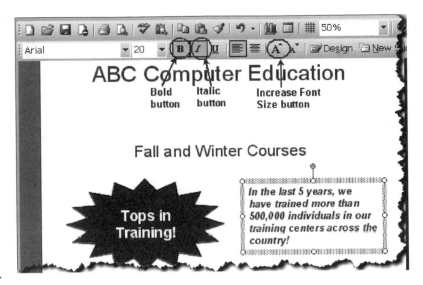

Using Design Templates

This section discusses the **use of design templates to give your presentations a professional appearance**. In it, you will learn how to:

- **Apply** a **design template** to a presentation.
- **Add** a footer to **slides**.

Applying a Design Template to a Presentation

A **design template** is a custom set of fonts, color schemes and design elements that, when applied to a presentation, gives the slides of that presentation a consistent and unique appearance.

You can apply a design template either before or after you create the slides of a presentation. Furthermore, after applying one design template, you can always change your mind and apply another design template to the same presentation.

In most cases, you will probably want to apply only one design template to any one presentation. You do, however, have the option of using more than one design template in a single presentation, which allows you to give different parts of a presentation (especially a large presentation) different looks.

To **apply a design template to a presentation**:

- In the Slides tab of Normal view or in Slide Sorter view, select the **slide(s)** to which the design template is to be applied (by clicking on each while holding down [**CTRL**]). If you wish to apply the design template to all slides, you can simply select or display any slide.
- Choose the **Format**, **Slide Design** command, or click on the **Slide Design** button on either the Formatting toolbar or the Slide Sorter toolbar.

- In the Slide Design task pane, do one of the following:

  - To apply a design template to one slide, point to the desired **design template option**, click on the **down arrow** that appears, and select the **Apply to Selected Slides** option in the list that is displayed; or
  - To apply a design template to two or more slides or to all slides, click on the desired **design template option**.

Objective

In this exercise, you will **apply a design template to an existing presentation**.

14.1

- **Click on the Slide Sorter View button above the Drawing toolbar.**

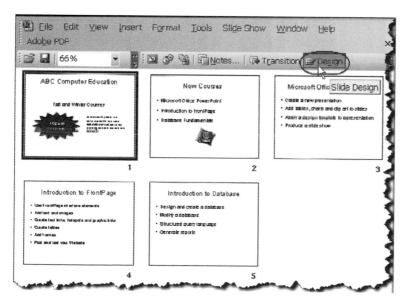

14.2

The presentation appears in Slide Sorter view. Notice that this view, like the Slides tab of Normal view, displays a thumbnail image of each slide. You will now apply a design template to the entire presentation.

- **Click on the Slide Design button on the Slide Sorter toolbar.**

14.3

The Slide Design task pane is displayed.

- **In the list of design templates, click on the Crayons**

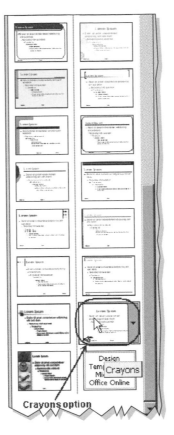

option.

The selected design template is applied to all slides.

14.4

- **Click on the Normal View button above the Status bar.**

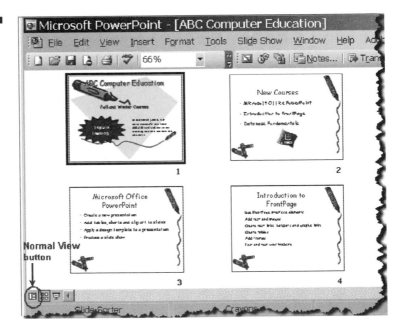

14.5

The presentation is redisplayed in Normal view, allowing you to view the color scheme of the design template in more detail. You will now adjust various elements on the title slide.

If necessary, display **Slide #1**. Then **reposition** the **main title placeholder** and the **AutoShape** (star) so that the slide appears as illustrated in the figure on the left.

• **Save the presentation.**

Adding a Footer to Slides

Slides of a presentation can optionally include a **footer** (text that appears at the bottom of each slide). This footer can include the date, the time, the slide number and/or user-specified text.

To **add a footer to slides**:

- In the Slides tab of Normal view or in the Slide Sorter view, select the **slides** on which the footer is to appear. (This step is unnecessary if you wish to add the footer to all slides or to all slides except for the title slide.)
- Choose the **View, Header and Footer** command.
- On the Slide panel of the Header and Footer dialog box, set the desired **footer option(s)**.
- Click on either the **Apply** button (to add the footer to selected slides) or the **Apply to All** button (to add the footer to all slides).

Objective

In this exercise, you will **add footer to all slides (except for the title slide) of a presentation**.

15.1

- **Choose the View, Header and Footer command.**

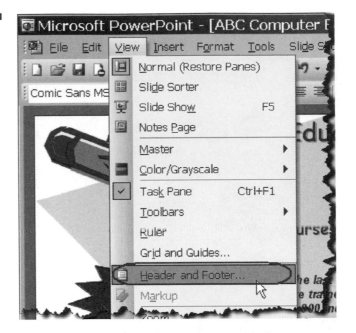

15.2

The Slide panel of the Header and Footer dialog box is displayed.

- **Under Date and time, click on Update automatically.**

NOTE: *The footer will include the date, which will be updated automatically from day to day. You will accept the default date/time format, which does not include the time.*

- **Click on Slide number.**

The footer will also include the slide number, which will appear in the lower-left corner of the slide.

- **Click in the Footer box.**

   Type: ABC Computer Education

The footer will also include the specified text (the company name), which will appear in the lowerright corner of the slide.

- **Click on Don't show on title slide.**

The footer will not appear on the title slide.

- **Click on the Apply to All button.**

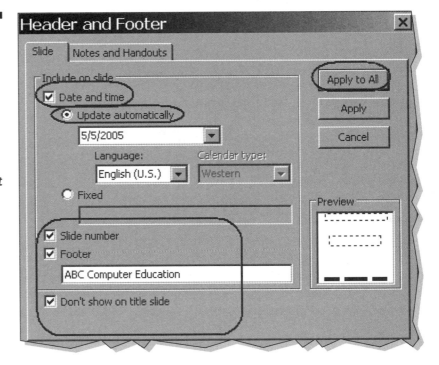

15.3

The dialog box is closed, and Slide #1 is redisplayed in Normal view. Notice that this slide does not include footer.

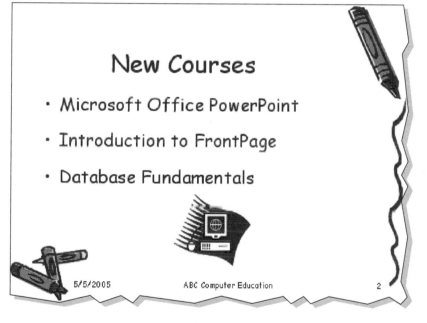

15.4

- **Display Slide #2.**

Notice the footer at the bottom of this slide.

- **Display the remaining slides of the presentation.**

Notice the footer at the bottom of these slides.

- **Save the presentation.**

Using the Spelling Checker

It is assumed that you are familiar with PowerPoint's **automatic spell checking** feature, which flags common spelling errors as you enter text on a slide. If you find this feature distracting, you can disable it and use the program's **Spelling Checker** instead to proof your slides when you have completed a presentation.

To **use the Spelling Checker:**

- With the appropriate presentation open, choose the **Tools, Spelling** command, or click on the **Spelling** button on the Standard toolbar.

- In the Spelling dialog box, which is displayed when a possible spelling error is encountered, choose the appropriate option:

  - **Ignore**—which skips the flagged word.
  - **Ignore All**—which skips the flagged word and any subsequent occurrence of that word.
  - **Change**—which replaces the flagged word with the alternate word you have selected or entered.
  - **Change All**—which replaces the flagged word and any subsequent occurrence of that word with the alternate word you have selected or entered.
  - **Add**—which skips the flagged word and adds it to the specified dictionary.
  - **Suggest**—which displays suggested corrections when the "Always suggest corrections" option has been disabled. (This option is enabled/disabled with the **Tools**, **Options** command.)
  - **AutoCorrect**—which replaces the flagged word with the alternate word you have selected or entered, and adds the error and its correction to the AutoCorrect dictionary.
  - **Delete**—which deletes the second occurrence of two repeated words.

Objective

In this exercise, you will **disable the automatic spell checking feature**. You will then **use the Spelling Checker to proof your presentation**.

- **Choose the Tools, Options… command.**

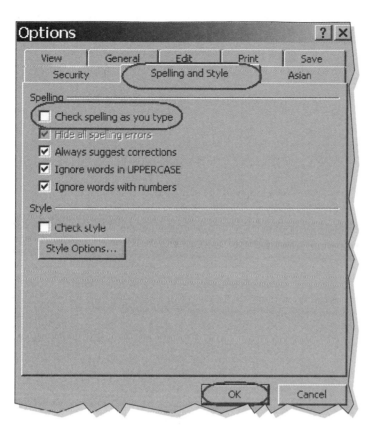

16.2

The Options dialog box is displayed.

- **Click on the Spelling and Style tab (unless the Spelling and Style panel already appears in the dialog box).**

- **Under Spelling, click on Check spelling as you type to remove the check mark and deselect the option. NOTE: If this option is already deselected, skip this step.**

- **Click on the OK button.**

16.3

The dialog box is closed, and the automatic spell checking feature is turned off. You will now create several intentional spelling errors in the current presentation.

- **On Slide #1, change the word Computer to Computter. Also, change the word Winter to Winer.**

16.4

- **Display Slide #1.**

You will now use the Spelling Checker.

- **Click on the Spelling button on the Standard toolbar.**

16.5

The Spelling Checker is activated, and the spelling error "Computter" is flagged in the Spelling dialog box. Notice that the correct spelling is highlighted in the Change to and Suggestions boxes.

- **Click on the Change button to accept the suggested correction.**

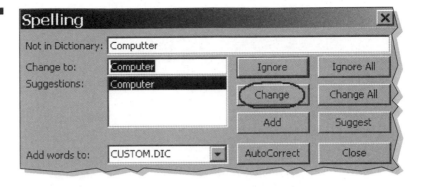

16.6

The correction is made, and the spelling error "Winer" is flagged.

- **In the Suggestions box, click on Winter. Then click on the Change button.**

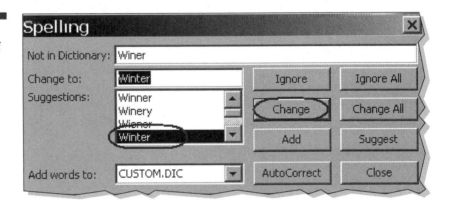

16.7

The correction is made, and a message box appears, informing you that the operation is complete.

NOTE: This step assumes that there are no spelling errors on the various notes pages. If any additional errors are flagged, continue the spell checking operation until the above-mentioned message box appears.

- **Click on the OK button.**

The message box is closed.

- **Save the presentation**

Closing a Presentation File

When you are finished working with a presentation, you can close the file either by choosing the **File**, **Close** command or by clicking on the **Close Window** button for the Presentation window. If you have not saved changes in the presentation, PowerPoint will prompt you to indicate whether or not you wish to save those changes before closing the file.

Objective

In this exercise, you will **close the current presentation file**.

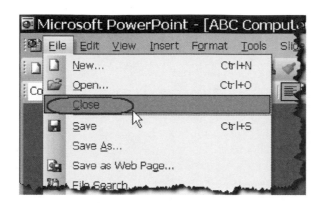

- **Choose the File, Close command.**

The file is closed, and the presentation is cleared from the screen.

Reopening a Presentation File

Once you have saved a presentation and cleared it from the screen, you can reopen the file and redisplay the presentation at any time.

To **reopen a presentation file**:

- Choose the **File, Open** command, click on the **Open** button on the Standard toolbar, or select the **More** option in the Getting Started task pane.
- In the Open dialog box, switch to the folder in which the presentation file is stored (if it is not stored in the working folder).
- Select the **presentation filename**.
- Do one of the following:

  - To simply open the file in edit mode, click on the **Open** button (in the dialog box); or
  - To open the file in non-edit (read-only) mode, expand the **Open** button (by clicking on the down arrow at the right side of the button), and select the **Open Read-Only** option in the list that appears; or
  - To open a copy of the file in edit mode, expand the **Open** button, and select the **Open as Copy** option in the list that appears.

Notes

1. Both the File menu and the Getting Started task pane include a list of recently-open files. You can reopen in edit mode any file listed on this menu or in this task pane by simply selecting the filename.
2. If you cannot find a particular file, you can use PowerPoint's **File Search** feature to locate it. This feature is accessed by expanding the **Tools** button on the toolbar of the Open dialog box and by selecting the **Search** option in the list that appears.

Objective

In this exercise, you will **reopen an existing presentation file**.

18.1

- **Click on the Open button on the Standard toolbar.**

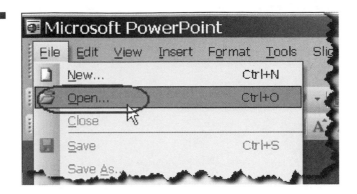

18.2

*NOTE: Clicking on the **My Recent Documents** icon in the Places bar displays a list of files and folders that were recently open.*

The Open dialog box is displayed.

- **Make sure that 3½ Floppy (A:) appears in the Look in box.**

- **In the list of filenames, click on ABC Computer Education**

*NOTE: File extensions may or may not appear in file listings on your screen. The above file, for example, may be listed simply as **ABC Computer Education**.*

*Click on the **Open** button (in the dialog box).*

NOTE: Click on the button itself, not on the down arrow at the right side of the button.

The dialog box is closed, and Slide #1 of the presentation is displayed in Normal view.

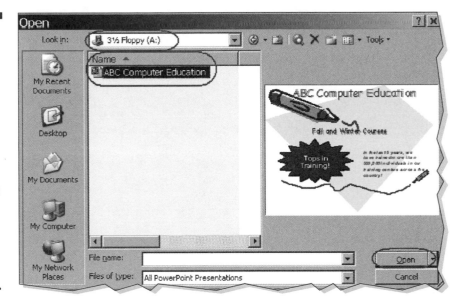

Printing Slides

PowerPoint includes a number of options for printing your slides. For example, you can print a single slide, a range of slides, selected slides, or all slides, of a presentation.

To **print one or more slides**:

- Choose the **File, Print** command, or click on the **Print** button on the Standard toolbar.
- If you click on the Print button, the print operation begins immediately. If you choose the File, Print command, the Print dialog box is displayed. In this case, specify the **slide(s)** you wish to print (the default is all slides), and click on the **OK** button.

Objective

In this exercise, you will **print the grayscale handouts of your presentation**.

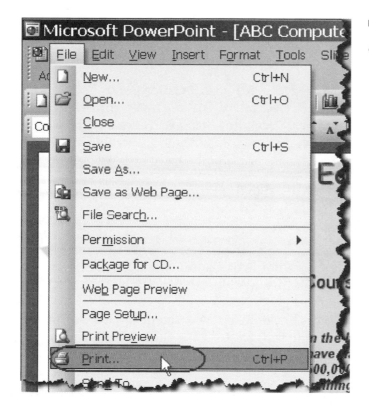

19.1

- **Choose the File, Print... command.**

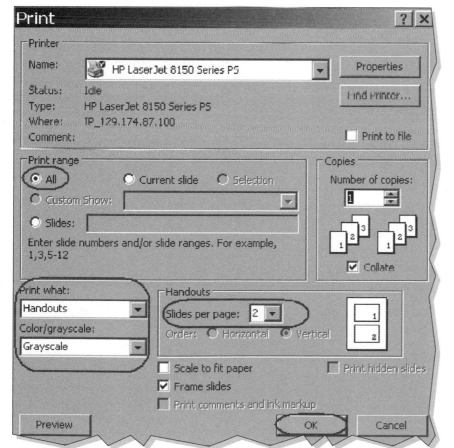

19.2

The Print dialog box is displayed.

- **Under Print range, click on All.**

- **Under Print what, select Handouts.**

- **Under Handouts, select 2.**

- **Under Color/grayscale, select Grayscale.**

- **Click on the OK button.**

The dialog box is closed and all slides are printed in grayscale and handout format (2 slides per page).

Displaying Help Information

If you encounter a problem or just need additional information while using PowerPoint, there are a number of ways in which you can obtain help.

The program itself includes an extensive **Help system**, which can be accessed in the following ways:

- By choosing the **Help, Microsoft Office PowerPoint Help** command or by clicking on the **Microsoft Office PowerPoint Help** button on the Standard toolbar. Doing this displays the PowerPoint Help task pane in which you enter one or more keywords and click on the **Start searching** button.

- By entering a request in the **Type a question for help** box and by pressing [**ENTER**].

You can also get help:

- By clicking on the **Table of Contents** option in the PowerPoint Help task pane. Doing this displays a list of Help topics in a table of contents format.
- By clicking on the **Connect to Microsoft Office Online** option in the PowerPoint Help task pane. Doing this displays the Microsoft Office Online Web site (assuming you have access to the Internet).

Notes

1. The Microsoft Office Online Web site provides a number of resources for users of Microsoft Office products, including "how-to" articles to assist the user in performing various tasks, interactive training tutorials to help the user become more familiar with the programs he or she is running, and various downloads (for example, templates, clip art and product upgrades).
2. The Office Assistant, which is displayed by choosing the **Help, Show the Office Assistant** command, can provide tips and other helpful information as you work. When the Office Assistant has a tip, a light bulb will appear. To display the tip, simply click on this light bulb. To control the type of information the Office Assistant provides, click on the Office Assistant icon, and click on the **Options** button in the balloon that appears. Then, on the Options panel of the Office Assistant dialog box, select/deselect the relevant options, and click on the **OK** button.

Objective

In this exercise, you will **access the PowerPoint Help system and display help information for various topics**.

• **Click on the Microsoft Office PowerPoint Help button on the Standard toolbar.**

NOTE: *If the above button does not currently appear on the Standard toolbar, click on the **Toolbar Options** button at the right side of the toolbar to display the list of additional buttons.*

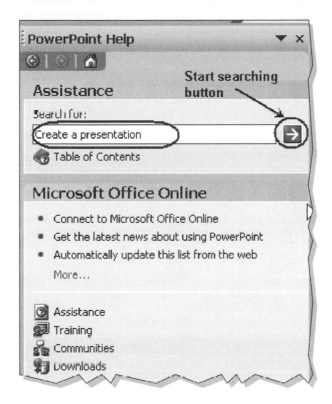

20.2

The PowerPoint Help task pane is displayed.

• **Type: Create a presentation**

• **Click on the Start searching button.**

20.3

A list of topics is displayed in the Search Results task pane.

- **Click on Create a presentation using a design template.**

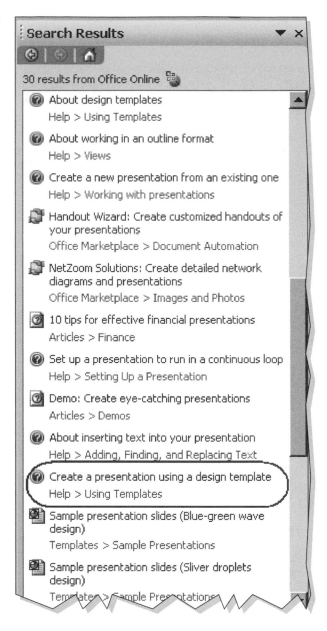

20.4

The Microsoft Office PowerPoint Help window is opened, displaying instructions for performing the selected operation.

- **Click on Show All (in the upper-right corner of the Microsoft Office PowerPoint Help window).**

All subtopics are expanded.

NOTE: *You can print the current help information by using the **Print** button on the toolbar of the Microsoft Office PowerPoint Help window.*

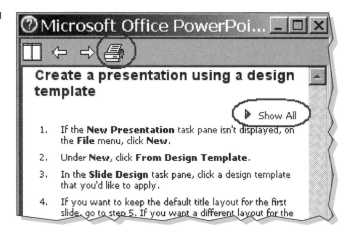

20.5

- **Click on the Close button on the Title bar of the Microsoft Office PowerPoint Help window.**

20.6

The Microsoft Office PowerPoint Help window is closed, and the Application window is expanded. You will now access the Help system through the Type a question for help box.

- **Click in the Type a question for help box (which appears in the upper-right corner of the Application window).**

- **Type: Print a slide Press [ENTER].**

A list of topics is displayed in the Search Results task pane.

20.7

NOTE: *Notice that you did not enter an actual question in the Type a question for help box. Instead, you simply entered the action "Print a slide." (You could have entered the question "How do I print a slide?" Doing so, however, would have displayed the same list of topics.)*

- **Click on Print slides.**

20.8

The Microsoft Office PowerPoint Help window is reopened, displaying information for the selected topic.

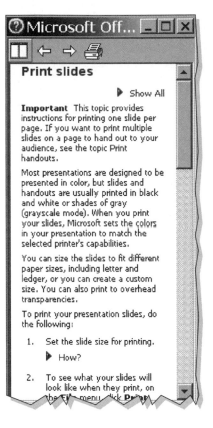

20.9

- **Click on the Title bar of the Application window.**

- **In the task pane, click on Print handouts.**

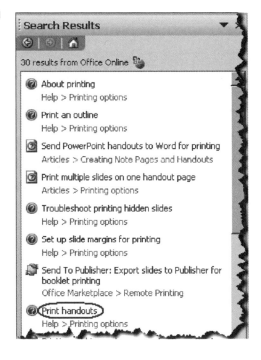

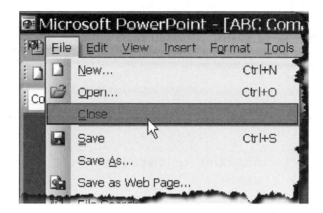

20.10

- **Click on the Back button on the toolbar of the Microsoft Office PowerPoint Help window.**

The previous help information is redisplayed.

20.11

- **Click on the Close button on the Title bar of the Microsoft Office PowerPoint Help window.**

The Microsoft Office PowerPoint Help window is closed.

- **Click on the Close button at the top of the Search Results task pane.**

The task pane is closed.

- **Choose the File, Close command.**

The file is closed, and the presentation is cleared from the screen.

Congratulations! You have completed the Case Study.

Conclusion

You have just completed **Microsoft Office PowerPoint 2003—Case Study 1**. In the case study, you were introduced to many techniques. To reinforce your understanding of these techniques, it is recommended that you read and work through it once again.

Further Practice

The following Case Study will give you the opportunity to review and practice many of the PowerPoint techniques you have learned.

Notes

PowerPoint, as you have seen, provides an extensive number of tools for creating a presentation. How these tools are used, however, depends on the imagination and creativity of the user. This exercise, therefore, gives you considerable flexibility in creating your presentation. Feel free to experiment with the many options that are available.

1. Click on the **New** button on the Standard toolbar.
2. Create the following **title slide**:

Main title: **International Computer Co.**
Subtitle: **Summary Report**

International Computer Co.

Summary Report

3. Create the following **bulleted list slide**:
Worldwide Markets
- **North America**
- **Europe**
- **Australia**

Worldwide Markets

· North America
· Europe
· Australia

4. **Save** the **presentation** in a file named **Summary Report.ppt**.
5. Using the **Outline tab**, create the following three **bulleted list slides**:

North America
- **Canada**
  - **Montreal**
  - **Toronto**
- **United States**
  - **New York**
  - **Chicago**
  - **Los Angeles**

Europe
- **England**
  - **London**
  - **Liverpool**
- **France**
  - **Paris**
- **Italy**
  - **Rome**
  - **Milan**

Australia
- **New South Wales**
  - **Sydney**
  - **Newcastle**
- **Queensland**
  - **Brisbane**
    -**Cairns**

6. Display the **Slides tab**.
7. **Save** the **presentation** once again.
8. **Add** the following **AutoShapes** and **text** to the appropriate slides:

9. **Save** the **presentation**.
10. **Apply** a **design template** of your choice to the presentation.
11. **Change** the **color scheme** for **all** and/or **selected slides**. (Feel free to experiment with the many options that are available.)

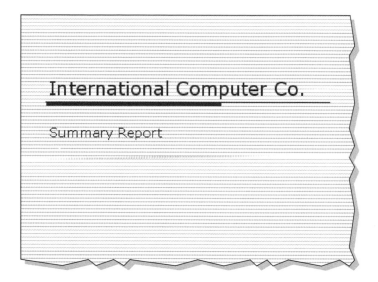

12. **Save** the **presentation**.
13. **Close** the **Slide Design task pane**.
14. **Add** a **footer** to **all slides** (**except** for the **title slide**) that includes:

- **Date**
- **Slide number**
- **Footer text**: **Summary Report**

15. **View** each **slide**, and examine the changes your have made.
16. **Adjust** the **placement** of **text** and **other elements** on the slides, as necessary.
17. Use the **Spelling Checker to proof** your presentation.
18. **Save** the presentation and then **close** the file.

MS PowerPoint 2003
Case Study 2

OBJECTIVES

After successfully completing this case study, you should be able to:

- Create new Presentation from Design Templates
- Add a PowerPoint table to a slide
- Format a PowerPoint table
- Add a PowerPoint chart to a slide
- Modify the components of a PowerPoint chart

- Stack AutoShapes
- Run a slide show
- Add transition effects to slides
- Add animation effects to slides

Case Study 2—MS PowerPoint 2003

Assume that you work for a company named XYZ Travel Company, which is headquartered in New York, London, Paris, Tokyo and Sydney. This company specializes in providing vacations in Europe, the United States and Australia.

Your company has experienced healthy growth over the last few years, as evidenced by the following data, which represents the number of customers for each of the company's locations:

	2000	2001	2002	2003
New York	50,000	56,000	59,000	63,000
London	23,000	28,000	34,000	42,000
Paris	31,000	29,000	37,000	40,000
Tokyo	45,000	58,000	65,000	78,000
Sydney	19,000	26,000	23,000	31,000

Over the same period, your company's worldwide profits have varied, as indicated by the following data, which represents sales in millions of dollars:

	2000	2001	2002	2003
Profits	50.4	43.2	53.6	61.8

Your task is to produce a **corporate presentation** that contains four **slides**.

POWERPOINT SLIDE 1

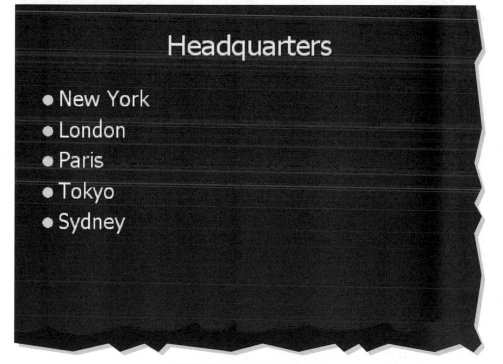

POWERPOINT SLIDE 2

Customer Data

	2000	2001	2002	2003
New York	50000	56000	59000	63000
London	23000	28000	34000	42000
Paris	31000	29000	37000	40000
Tokyo	45000	58000	65000	78000
Sydney	19000	26000	23000	31000

POWERPOINT SLIDE 3

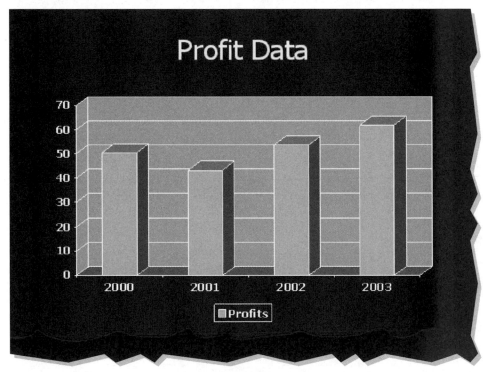

POWERPOINT SLIDE 4

Creating a New Presentation from Design Template

The New Presentation task pane (which is displayed by choosing the **File**, **New** command if the pane has been closed) includes the following options for creating a new presentation:

Blank presentation This option allows you to create a presentation that uses the program's default font and color scheme settings. Slides of a blank presentation include only basic design elements (for example, bullets) and initially have no color applied to them.

From design template This option allows you to select a design template (a custom set of fonts, color schemes and design elements) that is applied automatically to all new slides.

From AutoContent wizard This option prompts you for the type of presentation you wish to create, the output for the presentation, as well as the text that is to appear on the title slide. It then displays a series of slides with sample text, which you can modify to suit your individual needs. The AutoContent wizard is a convenient method for setting up a quick presentation.

Objective

In this exercise, you will **select a design template** (a custom set of fonts, color schemes and design elements) **that is applied automatically to all new slides**. You will **enter information in the first two slides** of your presentation.

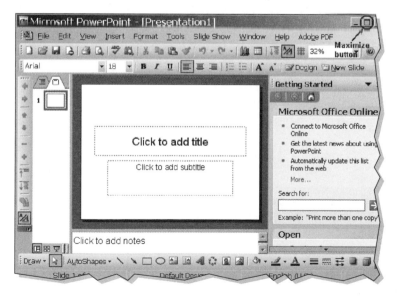

1.1

• **Click on the Start button on the Windows taskbar.**

• **Point to All Programs (if you are running Windows XP) or to Programs (if you are running Windows 2000).**

• **Point to Microsoft Office on the menu.**

• **Click on Microsoft Office PowerPoint 2003 on the submenu.**

PowerPoint is started, and the PowerPoint Application window is displayed.

• **If the PowerPoint Application window is not maximized, click on the Maximize button on the Title bar of the window.**

1.2

- **Move the mouse pointer to the Getting Started task pane and click on Create a new presentation.**

Notice that the mouse pointer changes to a small hand and Create a new presentation option is underlined.

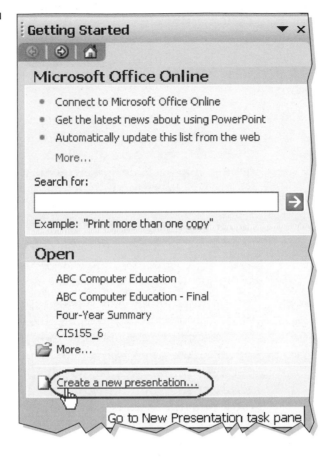

1.3

The New Presentation task pane is displayed.

- **Click on the From design template under New Presentation task pane**

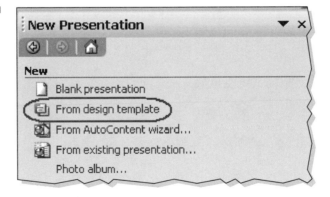

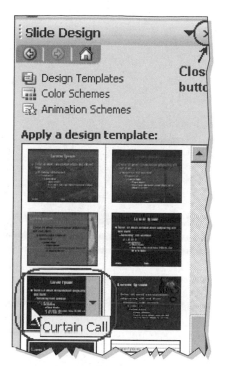

1.4

The Slide Design task pane is displayed.

- **In the list of design templates, click on the Curtain Call**

 option.

The selected design template will be applied to all slides.

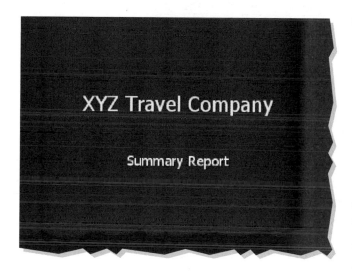

1.5

- **Close Slide Design task pane.**
- **Type: XYZ Travel Company in the main title box**

The main title is entered.

- **Click in the subtitle placeholder.**

The placeholder is selected, and an insertion point appears in the center of the first line of the placeholder.

- **Type: Summary Report**

The subtitle is entered.

- **Click outside the subtitle placeholder (in any empty area of the slide).**

The placeholder is deselected.

1.6

- **Click on the New Slide**
   button on the Formatting toolbar.

The Slide Layout task pane is displayed and a new slide appears in the Presentation window.

- **Close the Slide Layout task pane.**

- **Type: Headquarters in the main title box**

The main title is entered.

- **Click in the subtitle placeholder.**

The placeholder is selected, and an insertion point appears in the center of the first line of the placeholder.

- **Type: New York and press [ENTER].**

- **Type: London and press [ENTER].**

- **Type: Paris and press [ENTER].**

- **Type: Tokyo and press [ENTER].**

- **Type: Sydney and press [ENTER].**

Click outside the subtitle placeholder (in any empty area of the slide).

The placeholder is deselected.

Headquarters

- New York
- London
- Paris
- Tokyo
- Sydney

Saving a Presentation

To avoid losing what you have input due to an unexpected occurrence, such as a power failure, it is important that you periodically save a presentation as you work.

To **save a presentation** (for the first time):

- Choose the **File, Save** command, or click on the **Save** button on the Standard toolbar.
- In the Save As dialog box, enter a **name** for the **file** in which the presentation is to be saved.

- If you wish to store the file in a folder other than the working folder, switch to that **folder**.
- Click on the **Save** button (in the dialog box).

To **resave a presentation**:

- Choose the **File**, **Save** command, or click on the **Save** button on the Standard toolbar.

Objective

In this exercise, you will **save your presentation on a floppy disk**.

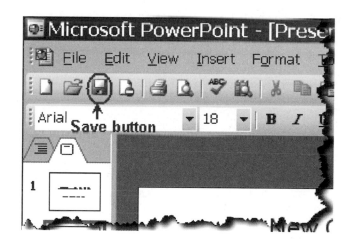

2.1

- **Insert floppy disk in drive A.**

- **Click on the Save** **button on the Standard toolbar or choose the File, Save command.**

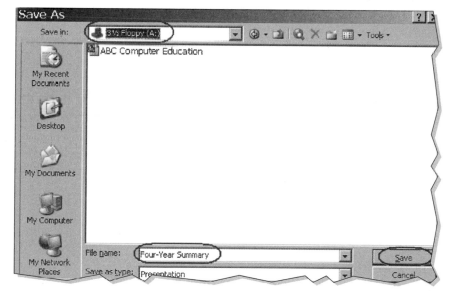

2.2

A Save As dialog box opens.

- **In a Save As dialog box, enter a name for the file—Four-Year Summary and select 3½ Floppy (A:) in the Save in list.**

- **Click on Save button.**

2.3

*The new file name (**Four-Year Summary**) is displayed in the title bar.*

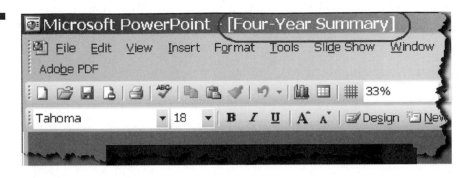

Creating a PowerPoint Table

This section discusses the methods for **displaying tabular information on a slide**. In it, you will learn how to:

- **Add** a **PowerPoint table** to a slide.
- **Format** a **PowerPoint table**.

Adding a PowerPoint Table to a Slide

Including one or more **tables** in a presentation is often one of the best ways to show and analyze certain types of information.

To **add a PowerPoint table to a slide**:

- In the **Title and Table** layout of the slide layout task pane, **double-click** in the **table placeholder**; or

In a layout that includes a **content placeholder** (which can be used to display one of several types of elements—for example, a table, a chart, or a clip art image), click on the **Insert Table** button; or

In other layouts, choose the **Insert**, **Table** command, or click on the **Insert Table** button on the Standard toolbar.

- Do one of the following:
  - If you have clicked on the Insert Table button on the Standard toolbar, drag the mouse pointer over the grid that appears to specify the number of **columns** and **rows** the table is to include; otherwise
  - In the Insert Table dialog box, specify the number of **columns** and **rows** the table is to include. Then click on the **OK** button.
- Enter the **table entries** into the empty table that appears.

Objective

In this exercise, you will **create a slide that includes a PowerPoint table**.

3.1

- **Click on the New Slide**

 button.

A new slide is inserted, and the Slide Layout task pane is displayed. You will now select a new layout.

- **Scroll through the list of slide layouts, until the Other Layouts section appears. Then click on the Title and Table**

 option.

3.2

- **Close the Slide Layout task pane.**

The selected layout is applied to the new slide. Notice that the slide now includes a placeholder for a title and a placeholder for a table.

3.3

- **Click in the title placeholder. Type: Customer Data**

The title is entered. You will now insert a five-column by six-row table into the table placeholder.

- **Double-click in the table placeholder.**

3.4

The Insert Table dialog box is displayed.

- **Type: 5 for number of columns Press [TAB].**

The number of rows is entered.

- **Type: 6 for number of rows**

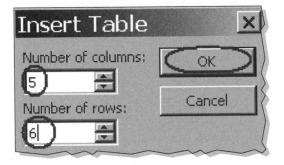

3.5

- **Click on the OK button.**

The dialog box is closed, and an empty table with five columns and six rows is displayed.

- **Enter the information into the table as shown in the figure on the right.**

NOTE: *You can move from cell to cell by pressing [**TAB**] or any of the [**ARROW**] keys. You can also move to a specific cell by clicking in that cell. Do not press [**ENTER**] when entering data into the table.*

- **Save the presentation.**

Customer Data

	2000	2001	2002	2003
New York	50000	56000	59000	63000
London	23000	28000	34000	42000
Paris	31000	29000	37000	40000
Tokyo	45000	58000	65000	78000
Sydney	19000	26000	23000	31000

Notes

If necessary, you can add one or more rows or columns to an existing table by selecting the number of rows or columns you wish to add (the row(s)/column(s) should be adjacent to where the new row(s)/column(s) is/are to appear), by clicking on the **Table** button on the Tables and Borders toolbar, and by selecting the appropriate option (**Insert Rows Above, Insert Rows Below, Insert Columns to the Left,** or **Insert Columns to the Right**) on the menu that appears. (To select a row, drag across the row; to select a column, drag down the column.)

Formatting a PowerPoint Table

After setting up a PowerPoint table, you can enhance its appearance by formatting both the table entries and the table structure (for example, the table and cell borders). This is accomplished with buttons on the **Formatting toolbar,** the **Drawing toolbar** and the **Tables and Borders toolbar.**

Objective

In this exercise, you will **format your new table.** Specifically, you will 1) apply a fill color to the entire table, 2) decrease the font size for all table entries, 3) center the table entries both horizontally and vertically, 4) increase the font size and change the color of the column and row headings, and 5) apply a different fill color to the cells in which the column and row headings appear. You will also remove one cell from the table.

Customer Data

	2000	2001	2002	2003
New York	50000	56000	59000	63000
London	23000	28000	34000	42000
Paris	31000	29000	37000	40000
Tokyo			65000	78000
Sydney			23000	31000

No Fill

Automatic

More Fill Colors...

Fill Effects...

4.1

- **Make sure that the table placeholder is selected. If it is not, click anywhere in the table. Then click on the border of the table placeholder.**

The placeholder should now be surrounded by a dotted border, and the insertion point should no longer appear in the table. This will allow you to treat the entire table as one entity. You will begin by applying a fill color to all cells of the table.

- **Click on the down arrow at the right side of the Fill Color button.**

NOTE: Notice that the Fill Color button appears on both the Tables and Borders toolbar and the Drawing toolbar.

The button is expanded, and a list of fill colors is displayed.

- **Click on More Fill Colors...**

4.2

The Custom panel of the Colors dialog box is displayed.

- **Click on the Standard tab.**

The Standard panel of the dialog box appears, displaying a palette of fill colors.

- **Click on the light yellow color option indicated in the illustration.**

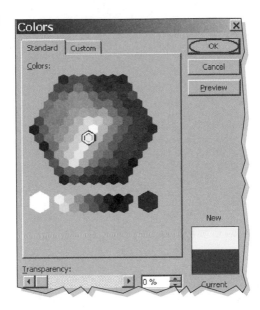

4.3

- **Click on the OK button.**

The dialog box is closed, and the selected color is applied to all cells.

- **Click on the down arrow at the right side of the Font Size** `28 ▼` **box on the Formatting toolbar.**

The box is expanded, and a list of font sizes is displayed.

- **Click on 20.**

The font size for all entries is decreased to 20 points. You will now center the entries.

- **Click on the Center** ≣ **button on the Formatting toolbar.**

All entries are centered horizontally in their respective cells.

- **Click on the Center Vertically** ▤ **button on the Tables and Borders toolbar.**

All entries are centered vertically in their respective cells. You will now reformat the column headings.

NOTE: *If you don't have Tables and Borders toolbar, choose View, Toolbars, and then Tables and Borders.*

Customer Data

	2000	2001	2002	2003
New York	50000	56000	59000	63000
London	23000	28000	34000	42000
Paris	31000	29000	37000	40000
Tokyo	45000	58000	65000	78000
Sydney	19000	26000	23000	31000

4.4

- **Select the column headings by dragging the mouse pointer over them.**

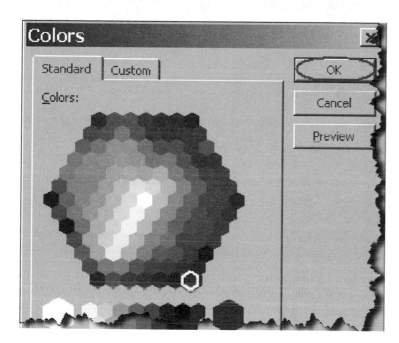

4.5

- **Click on the Increase Font Size button.**

4.6

- **Click on the Bold button.**

The selected entries are bolded.

- **Expand the Font Color button and click on the More Colors option.**

A list of font colors is displayed.

- **Apply the color option indicated in the illustration.**

- **Click on the OK button.**

4.7

The dialog box is closed, and the selected color is applied to all cells.

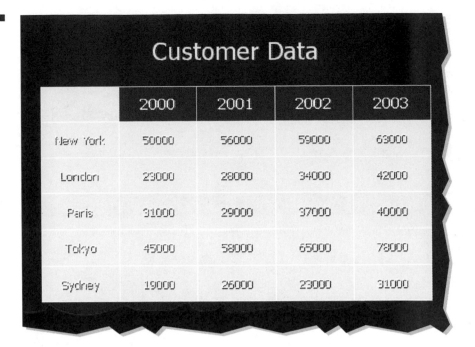

4.8

Next, you will apply the same formatting to the row headings.

- **Select the row headings by dragging the mouse pointer over them.**

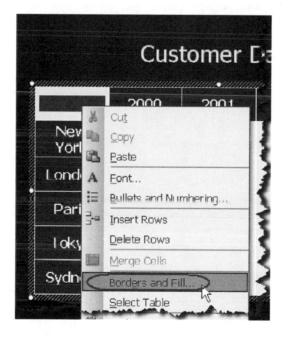

4.9

- **Click on the Increase Font Size button.**
- **Click on the Bold button.**
- **Click on the Font Color button. Then click on the Fill Color button and not on its drop down icon.**
- **Click outside the table to cancel the selection.**

4.10

You will now remove the first (upper-left) cell from the table.

- **Point to the first cell and right-click the mouse button.**
- **Click on Borders and Fill...**

4.11

A shortcut menu is displayed.

The Borders panel of the Format Table dialog box is displayed.

- **In the diagram (at the right side of the dialog box), click on the buttons given on the following page.**

The top border and the left border are removed from the diagram (which represents the current cell).

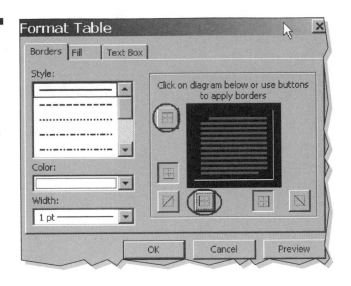

4.12

- **Click on the Fill tab.**

The Fill panel of the dialog box is displayed.

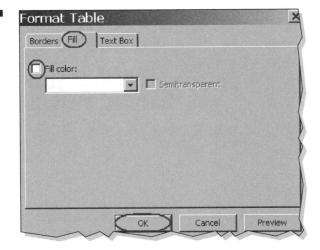

4.13

- **Click on Fill color to remove the check mark and deselect the option. Then click on the OK button.**

The dialog box is closed, and the first cell no longer appears.

NOTE: *In this case, you hid the first cell by removing its top and left borders and by removing the fill color.*

- **Select the customer data entries (all cells except column and row headings) by dragging the mouse pointer over them.**

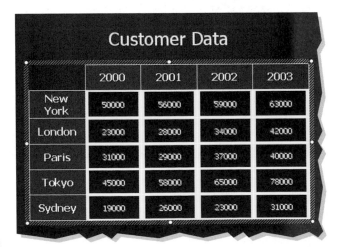

Customer Data				
	2000	2001	2002	2003
New York	50000	56000	59000	63000
London	23000	28000	34000	42000
Paris	31000	29000	37000	40000
Tokyo	45000	58000	65000	78000
Sydney	19000	26000	23000	31000

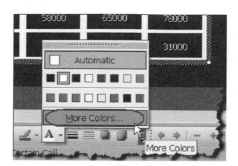

4.14

- **Expand the Font Color button and click on More Colors...**

4.15

The Custom panel of the Colors dialog box is displayed.

- **Click on the Standard tab.**
- **Click on the dark green color option indicated in the illustration.**

4.16

- **Click on the OK button.**

The dialog box is closed, and the selected color is applied to all cells.

*Make sure that the **table placeholder** is still selected. Then **resize** and **reposition** the **table** so that the slide appears similar to that illustrated on the left.*

NOTE: *To resize the table, drag any of the sizing handles that appear when the table placeholder is selected. To reposition the table, drag the border of the table placeholder, or press any of the [**ARROW**] keys to nudge the table.*

- **Save the presentation.**

Creating a PowerPoint Chart

This section discusses the use of **Microsoft Graph**, a supplementary application included with Microsoft Office products, to **create a PowerPoint chart**. In it, you will learn how to:

- **Add** a **PowerPoint chart** to a slide.
- **Modify** the **components** of a **PowerPoint chart**.

Adding a PowerPoint Chart to a Slide

A **PowerPoint chart** is a graphic representation of data. PowerPoint charts not only add visual interest to a presentation, they are often one of the best ways to call attention to specific information.

Slide with a PowerPoint Chart

The first step in creating a PowerPoint chart is that of accessing **Microsoft Graph**. This can be done in several ways.

To **access Microsoft Graph**:

- In the **Title and Chart** layout, **double-click** in the **chart placeholder**; or
- In a layout that includes a **content placeholder**, click on the **Insert Chart**
  button; or
- In other layouts, choose the **Insert**, **Chart** command, or click on the **Insert Chart** button on the Standard toolbar.

To **plot a PowerPoint chart** (from the Microsoft Graph window):

- **Enter** the **data** that is to be represented in the chart by **overwriting** the **sample data** in the datasheet.
- Optionally, **modify** the **chart components**. (The methods for doing this are discussed in the next subsection.)

Objective

In this exercise, you will **create a slide that includes a PowerPoint chart**.

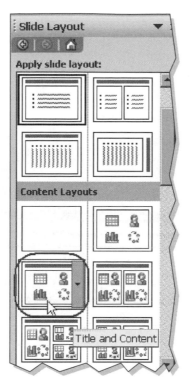

5.1

- **Make sure that you are on the third slide and then click on the New Slide button.**

The Slide Layout task pane is displayed, and a new slide appears in the Presentation window.

- **In the Content Layouts section of the task pane, click on the**

Title and Content option.

5.2

The selected layout is applied to the new slide.

- **Close the Slide Layout task pane.**

- **Click in the title placeholder. Type: Profit Data**

The title is entered. You will now access Microsoft Graph.

- **In the content placeholder, click on the Insert Chart button.**

5.3

A sample chart appears in the Microsoft Graph window (the hatched border). A datasheet also appears. You will now modify the chart by overwriting the sample data in the datasheet.

NOTE: *Notice that when the Microsoft Graph window is active, the Menu bar and toolbars display different options.*

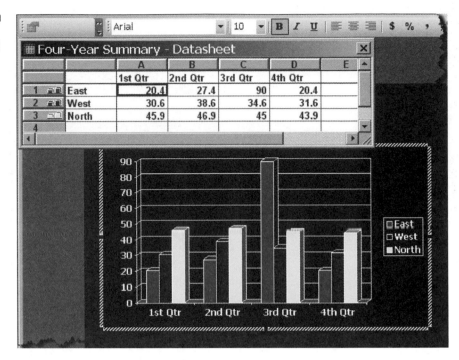

5.4

- **Click in the cell that displays 1st Qtr**
  Type: 2000
  Press [RIGHT ARROW].

- **Using a procedure similar to that described above, change the 2nd Qtr entry to 2001, change the 3rd Qtr entry to 2002, and change the 4th Qtr entry to 2003.**

		A	B	C	D	E
		2000	2001	2002	2003	
1	East	20.4	27.4	90	20.4	
2	West	30.6	38.6	34.6	31.6	
3	North	45.9	46.9	45	43.9	
4						

5.5

- **Right click on the row 1 heading (the box that displays the letter "1").**

The entire column is highlighted.

- **Click on Delete**

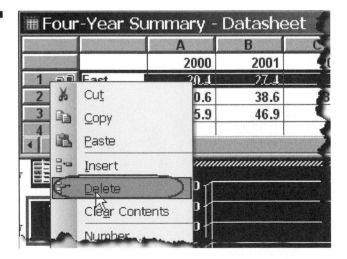

Four-Year Summary - Datasheet

		A	B	C	D	E
		2000	2001	2002	2003	
1	Profits	50.4	43.2	53.6	61.8	
2					Close button	
3						
4						

5.6

Row 1 is deleted.

- **Using a procedure similar to that described above, delete the new row 1 heading.**

- **Replace the last row label and numeric entries with the data illustrated on the left.**

5.7

- **Click on the Close button on the Title bar of the Datasheet window.**

The datasheet is closed.

- **Click outside the Microsoft Graph window.**

Microsoft Graph is exited, and the PowerPoint Menu bar and toolbar options are restored.

- **Save the presentation.**

Modifying the Components of a PowerPoint Chart

After creating a PowerPoint chart, you can easily modify any of its components (for example, category axis, value axis, legend and data markers). To do this, you must first redisplay the chart in the Microsoft Graph window if you have exited from Microsoft Graph.

To **redisplay a PowerPoint chart in the Microsoft Graph window**:

- **Double-click** on the **chart**.

To **modify a PowerPoint chart component**:

- Point to the component, **right-click** the mouse button, and select the **Format** . . . option on the shortcut menu that appears; or

Simply **double-click** on the component.

- In the dialog box that is subsequently displayed, make the necessary **change(s)**.
- Click on the **OK** button.

Notes

From the Microsoft Graph window, you can also change the chart type by using either the **Chart**, **Chart Type** command or the **Chart Type** button on the Standard toolbar. The default chart, as you have seen, appears in a three-dimensional column format. You can select from a number of other chart types (for example, line, area, bar and cylinder), as well as from a number of formats for each type.

Objective

In this exercise, you will **redisplay your PowerPoint chart in the Microsoft Graph window**. You will then **modify several components of the chart**. Specifically, you will 1) change the color of the data markers, 2) change the color of the chart walls, and 3) reposition the legend.

6.1

- **Point to the chart, and double-click the mouse button.**

- **Point to the first data marker (representing Year 2000 profit), and right-click the mouse button. Then click on Format Data Series... on the shortcut menu that appears.**

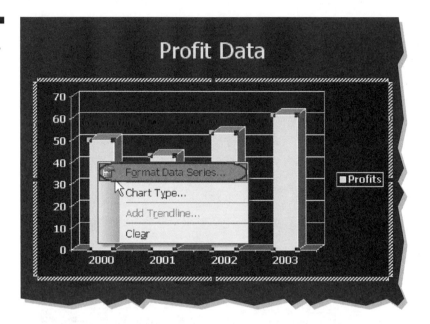

6.2

- **In the color palette, click on the tan option (the second option in the fifth row).**

The new color is selected.

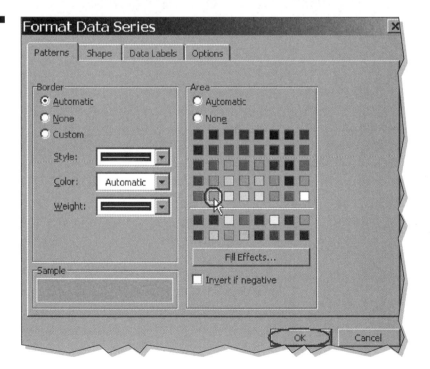

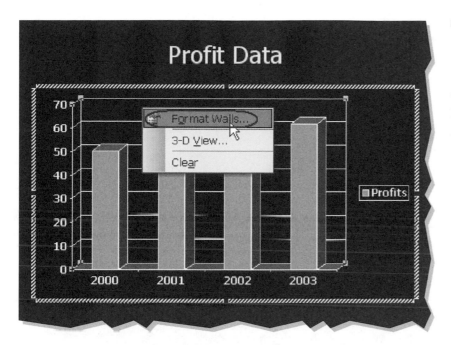

- **Click on the OK button.**

The dialog box is closed, and the new color is applied to all markers for the first data series.

- **Right click between gridlines and click on Format Walls on the shortcut menu that appears.**

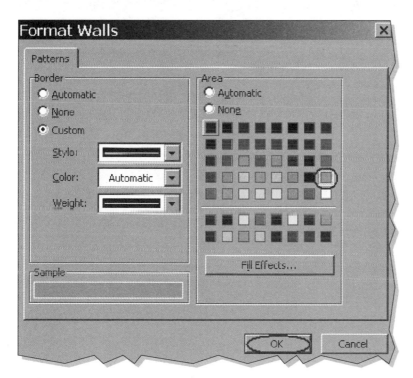

- **Click on the light gray option (the last option in the fourth row of the color palette). Then click on the OK button.**

The dialog box is closed, and the new color is applied to the chart walls. You will now reposition the legend.

6.5

- **Point to the legend** 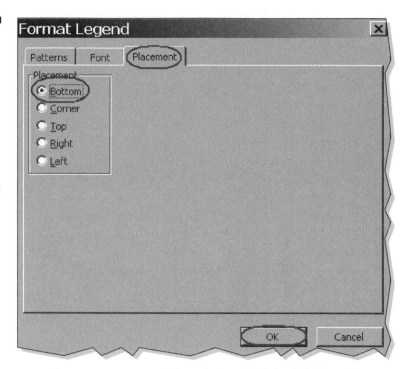 **Profits, and double-click the mouse button.**

The Format Legend dialog box is displayed.

- **Click on the Placement tab.**

The Placement panel of the dialog box is displayed.

6.6

- **Click on Bottom. Then click on the OK button.**

- **Save the presentation.**

The changes are saved.

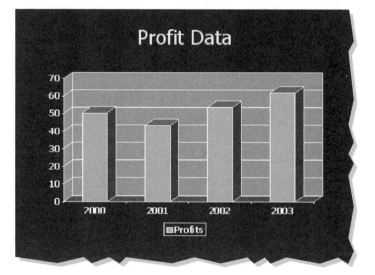

Stacking Autoshapes

In the last case study, you used PowerPoint's Drawing toolbar to add an AutoShape to a slide. In this subsection, you will use this toolbar to draw multiple AutoShapes that are stacked (overlapped).

Objective

In this exercise, you will **create the design illustrated in the beginning of this case study**.

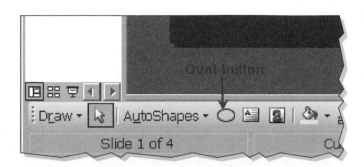

- **Display Slide #1.**
- **Click on the Oval button on the Drawing toolbar.**

- **Point in the center-left area of the slide after Summary Report. Press and hold down both [SHIFT] and the mouse button. Drag the mouse pointer diagonally downward and to the right until the circle drawn is approximately one inch in diameter. Release the mouse button. Then release [SHIFT].**

7.3

- **Make sure that the circle is selected. Then expand the Fill Color button, and click on the red option in the list of fill colors.**

The new fill color is applied to the circle.

- **Type: A**

- **Click on the circle.**

NOTE: *Click in an empty area of the circle, not on the character.*

- **Expand the Font box, and click on Times New Roman in the list of fonts.**

The new font is applied to the AutoShape character.

- **Expand the Font Size box, and click on 48 in the list of font sizes.**

The new font size is applied to the AutoShape character.

- **Click on the Bold button.**

The character is bolded.

- **Expand the Font Color button, and click on the white option in the list of font colors.**

The character is now white. You will now copy the AutoShape.

7.4

- **Make sure that the AutoShape is still selected. Then click on the Copy button on the Standard toolbar.**

- **Click on the Paste button on the Standard toolbar.**

*A copy of the AutoShape is inserted into the slide. You will now reposition this copy. Point to the **second circle** (not to the character in the circle). Press and **hold down** the mouse button, and **drag** the **circle** to the location shown in the illustration. Then **release** the mouse button.*

7.5

- **Change the fill color of the second circle to blue. Also, change the character displayed in this circle to the letter B. Then click outside the circles to cancel the selection.**

NOTE: *To change the character, select the current character, and type the new character.*

7.6

- **Click on the Paste button.**

A copy of the AutoShape is inserted into the slide. You will now reposition this copy.

- **Point to the third circle. Press and hold down the mouse button, and drag the circle to the location shown in the illustration. Then release the mouse button.**

7.7

- **Change the fill color of the third circle to green. Also, change the character displayed in this circle to the letter C. Then click outside the circles to cancel the selection.**

- **Save the presentation.**

Producing a Slide Show

This section discusses the methods for **producing an on-screen slide show** of your completed presentations. In it, you will learn how to:

- **Run** a **slide show**.
- **Add transition effects** to slides.
- **Add animation effects** to slides.

Running a Slide Show

The slides of a PowerPoint presentation can be displayed in several ways. In a formal presentation, they are often projected as overhead transparencies or as 35mm slides. In an informal presentation, they can be displayed electronically on a computer screen in what is called a **slide show**.

To **run a slide show**:

- In Normal view, display the slide with which the presentation is to begin, or in Slide Sorter view, select that slide. (This step is unnecessary if the slide show is to begin with the first slide.)

Do one of the following:

- To begin the slide show with the first slide of the presentation, choose either the **View**, **Slide Show** command or the **Slide Show**, **View Show** command, or
- To begin the slide show with the slide that is currently displayed or selected, click on the **Slide Show from current slide** 🖳 button.

Objective

In this exercise, you will **run a slide show of a presentation**.

8.1

- **Display Slide #1.**

- **Click on the Slide Show from current slide button above the Drawing toolbar.**

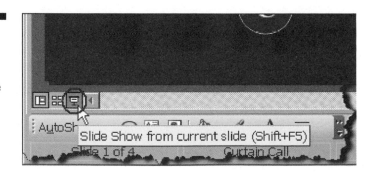

8.2

The slide show begins, and the first slide appears in full-screen display.

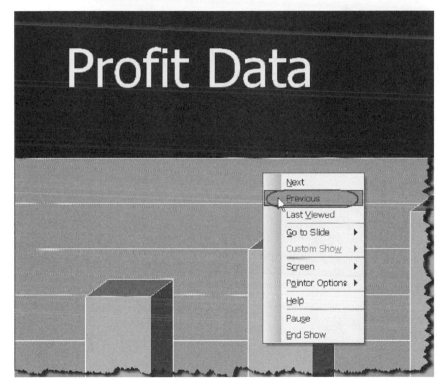

8.3

- **Click the (left) mouse button.**

The second slide is displayed.

- **Continue clicking the mouse button until the last slide (#4) is displayed.**

- **Right-click the mouse button.**

A shortcut menu is displayed (as shown in the figure on the left).

- **Click on Previous.**

■ 8.4

The previous slide (#3) is redisplayed.

NOTE: *You can also display the previous and next slides by clicking on the* ***Previous*** *and* ***Next*** *buttons (which display left arrow and right arrow icons, respectively) on the Slide Show toolbar in the lower-left corner of the screen. (If the default* ***Automatic*** *setting is in effect, this toolbar, as well as the arrow mouse pointer, are hidden when the mouse is idle for three seconds. To redisplay both the toolbar and mouse pointer, simply move your mouse. To have the toolbar and mouse pointer displayed at all times during a slide show, select the* ***Pointer Options, Arrow Options, Visible*** *option sequence from the above shortcut menu.)*

• **Right-click the mouse button.**

The shortcut menu is once again displayed.

• **Point to Pointer Options.**

A submenu is displayed.

NOTE: *You can change the color of the marker (pen or highlighter) by using the* ***Ink Color*** *option on this submenu.*

• **Click on Ballpoint Pen.**

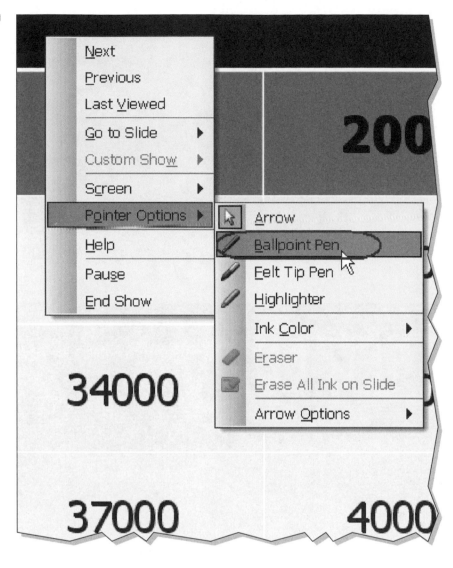

■ 8.5

The mouse pointer changes to a small square dot.

• **Drag the mouse pointer around the number 37000 in the text block in Year 2002.**

The number is encircled.

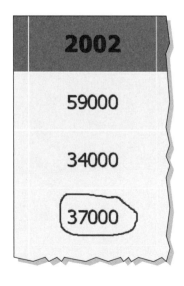

8.6

- **Click on the Pointer button on the Slide Show toolbar (in the lower-left corner of the screen).**

NOTE: If the Slide Show toolbar is no longer displayed, move your mouse until the toolbar buttons reappear.

- **Click on Highlighter.**

8.7

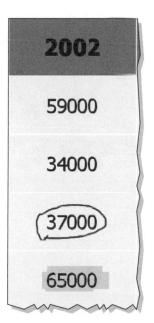

- **Drag the mouse pointer over the number 65000 under Year 2002.**

8.8

- **Click again on the Pointer button, and then click on Erase All Ink on Slide on the menu of annotation options.**

8.9

All annotations are removed from the slide.

- **Click once again on the Pointer button, and then click on Arrow on the menu of annotation options.**

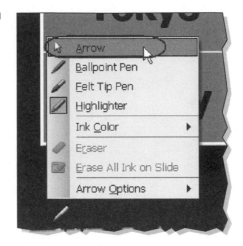

8.10

- **Press [F1].**

A list of slide show keyboard shortcuts is displayed. Notice that the shortcut for ending a slide show is [**ESC**].

- **Choose the OK button.**

The list is closed.

- **Press [ESC].**

The slide show is ended, and the presentation once again appears in Normal view. You will now run another slide show. This time, however, you will begin with a different slide.

- **Display Slide #4. Then click on the Slide Show from current slide button.**

Slide #4 appears in full-screen display.

- **Type: p**

The previous slide (#3) is displayed.

- **Type: 1**
  Press [ENTER].

Slide #1 is displayed.

- **Press [ESC].**

The slide show is ended.

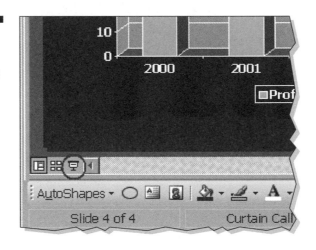

Adding Transition Effects to Slides

Up to this point, your slide shows have simply displayed one slide after another. You can add visual interest to a slide show by including a **transition effect** to introduce each slide.

To **add a transition effect to one or more slides**:

- In the Slides tab of Normal view or in Slide Sorter view, select the **slide(s)** to which the transition effect is to be added.
- Choose the **Slide Show**, **Slide Transition** command, or click on the **Slide Transition** ![Transition] button on the Slide Sorter toolbar.
- In the Slide Transition task pane, select the desired **transition effect**.
- Optionally, change the **speed** at which the transition is to occur, and/or select a **sound** that is to accompany the effect.

Notes

From the Slide Transition task pane, you also can automate a slide show by specifying **slide timings** (the amount of time each slide is to appear on the screen).

Objective

In this exercise, you will **add transition effects to the slides of the current presentation**.

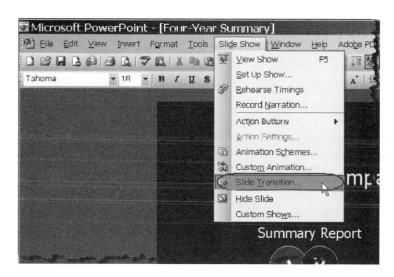

9.1

- **Click on Slide #1.**
- **Choose Slide Show, Slide Transition...**

9.2

The Slide Transition task pane is displayed.

- **Make sure that the AutoPreview option is selected.**

- **In the Apply to selected slides box, click on Blinds Vertical.**

The selected transition effect is previewed in the slide thumbnail.

- **Under Modify transition, expand the Speed box, and click on Medium.**

The same transition effect is once again previewed at the new speed.

- **Click Apply to All Slides button.**

*NOTE: You can preview the current transition effect once again by clicking on the **Play** button in the Slide Transition task pane.*

- **Click on Slide #1. Then click on the Slide Show from current slide 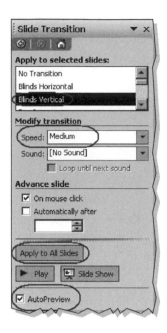 button located on the View bar.**

NOTE: Notice that this button appears both above the Status bar and in the Slide Transition task pane.

The slide show begins with Slide #1. Notice the transition effect that introduces this slide.

- **Click the mouse button.**

Slide #2 is displayed.

- **Display the remaining slides of the presentation. Then return to Slide Sorter view.**

- **Close the Slide Transition task pane. Then switch back to Normal view.**

- **Save the presentation.**

The changes are saved.

Adding Animation Effects to Slides

PowerPoint provides a number of features for visually enhancing a slide show. You can, for example, use one of the program's pre-designed **animation schemes** to display the title and other elements (for example, bulleted text) on each slide. You can also create your own **custom animation effects** to display various elements.

To **add an animation scheme to one or more slides**:

- In the Slides tab of Normal view or in Slide Sorter view, select the **slide(s)** to which the animation scheme is to be added.
- Choose the **Slide Show**, **Animation Schemes** command, or select the **Animation Schemes** option on the shortcut menu (from Slide Sorter view).
- In the Animation Schemes section of the Slide Design task pane, select the desired **animation scheme**.

To **add one or more custom animation effects to a slide**:

- With the slide displayed in Normal view, choose the **Slide Show**, **Custom Animation** command. Doing this displays the Custom Animation task pane.
- Select the element to which the animation effect is to be added.
- In the task pane, click on the **Add Effect** button. Point to the appropriate **animation effect category** on the subsequent menu, and select the desired **animation effect** on the submenu that appears. To add another animation effect to the same element, repeat this step.
- Repeat the previous two steps for any other slide element.

Objective

In this exercise, you will **add animation effects to slides of a presentation**. You will do this by adding an **animation scheme** to each slide and by adding a **custom animation effect** to an AutoShape.

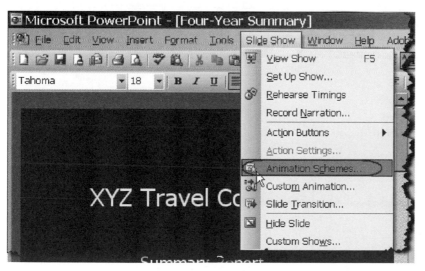

10.1

- **Make sure that slide 1 is selected.**

- **Choose the Slide Show, Animation Schemes command.**

10.2

The Animation Schemes section of the Slide Design task pane is displayed. Notice that the various animation schemes in the Apply to selected slides box are divided into three categories— Subtle, Moderate and Exciting.

- **Make sure that the AutoPreview option is selected.**

- **In the Apply to selected slides box under Moderate, click on Compress.**

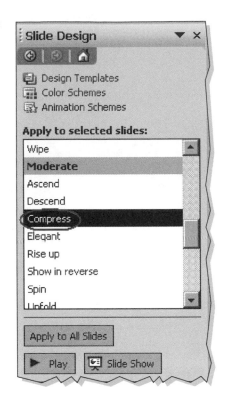

10.3

The animation scheme is applied to the selected slide and is previewed in the slide thumbnail.

NOTE: *You can preview the current animation scheme once again by clicking on the Play button at the bottom of the task pane.*

- **Display Slide #1.**

- **In the Apply to selected slides box, click on No Animation (under the No Animation heading).**

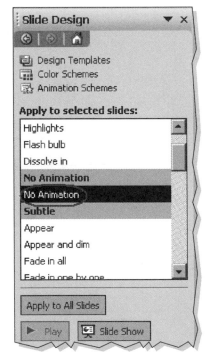

10.4

The animation scheme is removed from the slide.

- **Select one AutoShape circle, press SHIFT and click on the other two circles.**

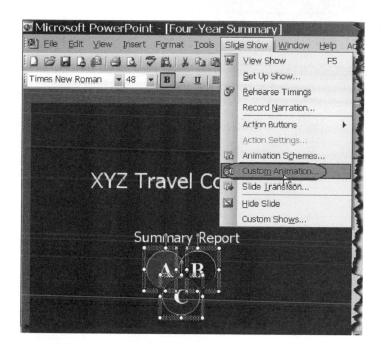

10.5

- **Choose Slide Show, Custom Animation...**

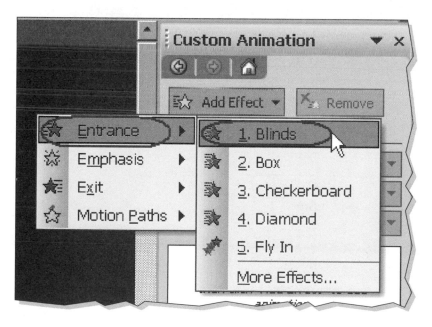

10.6

- **In the task pane, click on the Add Effect button.**

The button is expanded, and a menu of animation effect categories is displayed.

- **Point to Entrance. Then click on 1. Blinds on the submenu that appears.**

10.7

The selected animation effect is added to the star, and the effect is previewed on the slide.

- **Click again on the Add Effect button. Point to Emphasis on the menu that appears. Then click on 5. Spin on the submenu.**

Another animation effect is added and the effect is previewed on the slide.

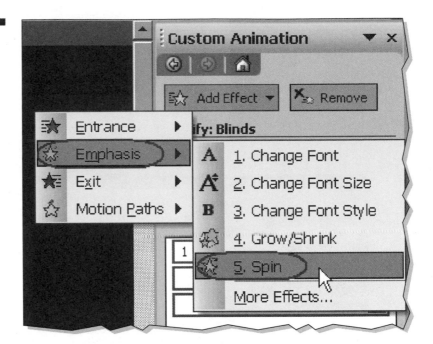

10.8

- **In the task pane, make sure that animation effect number 2 (the Spin effect) is selected. Then click on the Remove** Remove **button.**

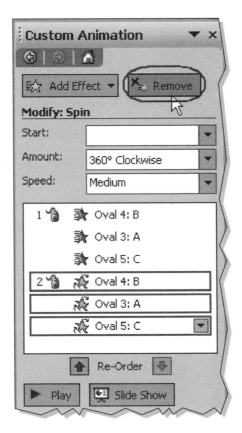

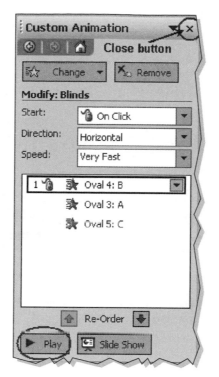

10.9

The selected animation effect is removed from the star.

- **In the task pane, click on the Play** 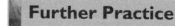 **button.**

The effect is previewed on the slide #1.

- **Close the Custom Animation task pane.**

- **Run another slide show of the presentation.**

- **When the slide show is completed, return to Normal view.**

- **Save the presentation, and then close the file.**

Congratulations! You have completed the Case Study.

Conclusion

You have just completed **Microsoft Office PowerPoint 2003—Case Study 2**. In the case study, you were introduced to many intermediate and advanced techniques of creating and representing slides. To reinforce your understanding of these techniques, it is recommended that you read and work through it once again.

Further Practice

The following Case Study will give you the opportunity to review and practice many of the PowerPoint techniques you have learned. It gives you considerable flexibility in creating your presentation. Therefore, feel free to experiment with the many options that are available.

NOTE: In this case study, you will continue to work on **Summary Report.ppt file** created in the PowerPoint Case Study 1—Further Practice.

1. **Open** the **file** named **Summary Report.ppt**.
2. Create a **new slide (sixth)** that includes the title **Total Sales (All Regions)** and a **table** that includes the following **sales data**:

	North America	Europe	Australia
IC7500	525,000	369,000	282,000
IC8500	546,000	443,000	235,000
IC9500	618,000	397,000	296,000

3. **Save** the **presentation**.
4. **Format** the **table** in ways of your choice.
5. Optionally, **resize** and **reposition** the **table**.

6. **Save** the **presentation**.
7. Create a **new slide** that includes the title **Sales (by Computer Model)** and a **PowerPoint chart** representing the following sales data:

	IC7500	IC8500	IC9500
North America	525,000	546,000	618,000
Europe	369,000	443,000	397,000
Australia	282,000	235,000	296,000

8. **Modify** one or more **chart components** (for example, change the color of the data markers, reformat the value and/or category axis, and reposition the legend).

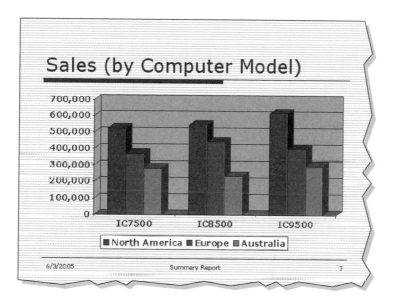

9. **Save** the **presentation**.
10. Create a slide that includes a **three-dimensional AutoShape**. This slide should list your company's **goals for the next six months**.
11. Optionally, **reorder one** or **two slides** of the presentation.
12. **Add** a **transition effect** of your choice to **each slide**.
13. **Add animation effects** and **timings** to **all slides** of the presentation.
14. **Run** a **slide show** of the presentation.
15. **Save** the **changes** you have made in the presentation, and then **close** the **file**.

MS Access 2003 Case Study 1

OBJECTIVES

After successfully completing this case study, you should be able to:

- Start Access
- Create a new database and a new table
- Enter records in Datasheet view
- Print the datasheet of a table
- Create a form
- Enter records in Form view
- Edit records in Datasheet view and in Form view
- Use the Find feature
- Delete records in Datasheet view and in Form view
- Modify the Datasheet view of a table

- Sort the records in a table
- Filter the records in a table
- Create a simple query
- Create a query in Design view
- Modify a query
- Create a simple tabular report
- Create a grouped tabular report
- Modify a report
- Display help information

Case Study 1—MS Access 2003

Assume that you are working as an intern in the HR department of a manufacturing company. Your boss has asked you to use Access to maintain and retrieve staff information.

You will store staff information in Access tables, create Forms to view the information, extract information using Queries and generate Access Reports.

STAFF INFORMATION IN ACCESS TABLE

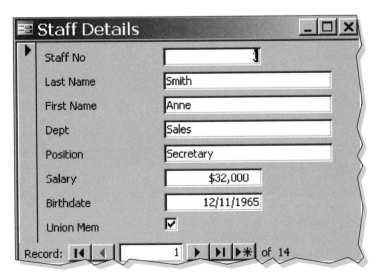

**TABLE INFORMATION (ONE RECORD AT A TIME)
IN ACCESS FORM**

Admin Dept : Select Query

Last Name	First Name	Salary	Dept
Adams	Kyle	$31,000	Admin
Brown	Bill	$19,000	Admin
Crisp	Helen	$19,500	Admin
Potter	Peter	$24,000	Admin
Thomas	Lisa	$23,750	Admin
Wong	Lee	$27,500	Admin

Record: 1 of 6

**SALARY INFORMATION (BY ADMIN DEPARTMENT)
EXTRACTED USING QUERIES**

Staff Listing

Dept	Last Name	First Name	Position	Salary
Admin				
	Adams	Kyle	Secretary	$31,000
	Brown	Bill	Clerk	$19,000
	Crisp	Helen	Clerk	$19,500
	Potter	Peter	Clerk	$24,000
	Thomas	Lisa	Clerk	$23,750
	Wong	Lee	Secretary	$27,500
Sales				
	Bell	Harry	Secretary	$20,000
	Green	Sue	Secretary	$27,000
	Hill	Tony	Clerk	$21,500
	Lewis	Helen	Clerk	$22,500
	Moore	Donna	Clerk	$20,000
	Smith	Anne	Secretary	$32,000
	Wells	Betty	Manager	$48,750

STAFF INFORMATION IN ACCESS REPORT

Getting Started

This section begins with a brief discussion of **Access and its uses**. It then covers various **program fundamentals**.

In this section, you will learn how to:

- **Start Access**.
- **Identify** the **elements** of the **Access Application window**.
- **Work** with **Access menus**.
- **Examine Access objects**.

What Is Access?

Access is a powerful, yet easy-to-use, **database management program** designed for use on a personal computer. Its primary purpose is to provide an efficient system for storing large amounts of data—a system in which any one piece of information can be quickly located.

Besides being merely a data storage and retrieval system, however, Access includes many features for manipulating the information that is stored. Using the program, you can, for example:

- Sort and reorganize the information.
- Extract and work with subsets of the information.
- Design custom **forms** for entering and viewing the information.
- Produce sophisticated **reports** for presenting the information.

Starting Access

You start Access by clicking on the **Start** button on the Windows taskbar, by pointing to **All Programs** (if you are running Windows XP) or to **Programs** (if you are running Windows 2000), by selecting the **Microsoft Office** option on the All Programs or Programs menu, and by selecting the **Microsoft Office Access 2003** option on the subsequent submenu.

Objective

In this exercise, you will **start Access and display the opening Access Application window**.

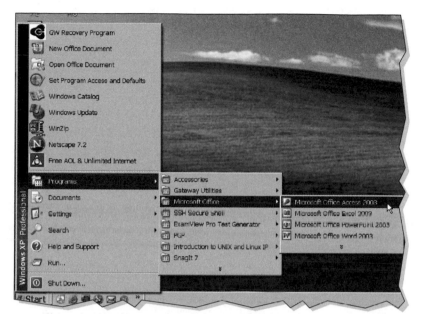

- **Click on the Start button on the Windows taskbar.**
- **Point to All Programs (if you are running Windows XP) or to Programs (if you are running Windows 2000).**
- **Point to Microsoft Office on the menu.**
- **Click on Microsoft Office Access 2003 on the submenu.**

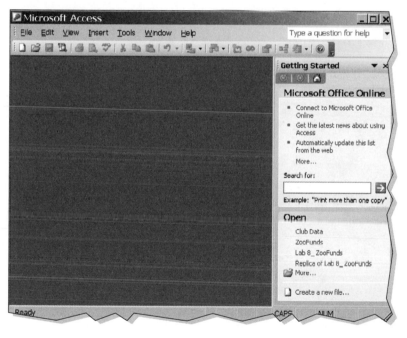

Access is started, and the Access Application window is displayed.

- **If the Access Application window is not maximized, click on the Maximize button on the Title bar of the window.**

The Access Application Window

The initial **Access Application window** includes the following elements:

Title bar
This displays the name of the **program**. The standard Windows Control-menu box and window sizing buttons appear at the left end and right end of the bar, respectively.

Menu bar
This displays the program's **primary commands**. The available options depend on the particular object with which you are working as well as the particular task you are performing. (Objects are described later in this section.)

Toolbar
This displays a number of **shortcut buttons** for performing common Access operations. When you point to one of these buttons, the name of the button appears in a small window

(**ScreenTip**) next to the mouse pointer. The toolbar that appears depends on the object with which you are working as well as the particular task you are performing. In some cases, more than one toolbar may be displayed. (The toolbar that currently appears is called the Database toolbar.)

Getting Started task pane	This displays options for accessing Microsoft Office Online, a Web site for users of Microsoft Office products, as well as options for opening an existing database file and for creating a new database. The program includes several other task panes. Each pane includes options for performing a specific task (for example, searching for a file or displaying help information).
Desktop	This area, which occupies the majority of the screen, is used to display the various objects of your databases.
Status bar	This displays helpful information (for example, the current view) as you use the program. The "Ready" indicator, which currently appears at the left side of the Status bar, lets you know that the program is ready for user action.

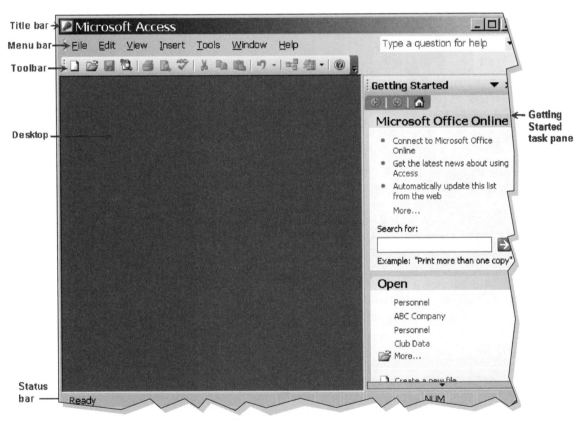

ACCESS APPLICATION WINDOW

Notes

1. In this course, the Database toolbar, as well as any other toolbar that appears at the top of the Access Application window, is identified as simply the Application window toolbar.
2. What appears on your screen may sometimes vary slightly from what is shown in this manual.

Working with Access Menus

The menus that you initially access from the Menu bar are called **short menus** since they include only a basic set of commonly-used options. You can expand a short menu and display the **full menu**—that is, one that includes additional options, by clicking on the chevron (the two down arrows) at the bottom of the menu. (Note that a menu will expand automatically if you continue pointing for a few seconds to the command that displayed it.) Any option selected on this expanded menu is added to the basic set of options, thereby creating a personalized menu that reflects your needs. The same option is removed from the basic set of options after a period of time if you no longer use it.

**PERSONALIZED
(SHORT) MENU**

FULL MENU

If you prefer to work only with full menus, you can do so by choosing the **Tools**, **Customize** command and by selecting the **Always show full menus** option in the Customize dialog box. You can also restore personalized menus (and toolbars) to their original state by clicking on the **Reset menu and toolbar usage data** button in the same dialog box.

To help you work even more efficiently, Access also provides a number of shortcut menus. A **shortcut menu** includes options that are relevant to a particular object or area of the screen and is displayed by clicking the **right** mouse button. For example, if you position the mouse pointer in a table and right-click the mouse button, the following shortcut menu is displayed:

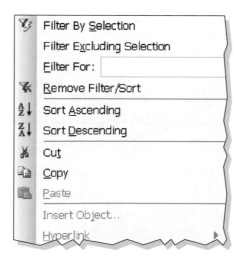

SHORTCUT MENU

Basic Access Terminology

Before you begin using Access, it is important that you understand several important Access terms.

A **database**, in general, is defined as a collection of related information. An Access database, likewise, is a collection of related **objects** (tables, forms, queries, reports, etc.), stored in a single file.

One or more **tables** make up the core of any Access database. Each table contains information related to a particular subject (for example, employee work history or customer orders), organized in a particular way.

All tables are made up of two components: fields and records. A **field** is one category of information (for example, name, job title or salary); a **record** is the collection of all fields for one table entity.

One of the most familiar examples of a table is a telephone directory. The directory listing below includes three fields—**NAME**, **ADDRESS** and **TELEPHONE NO**—with field information displayed vertically in three columns. It also includes six records—for **Adams**, **Bell**, **Lewis**, **Potter**, **Thomas** and **Wells**—displayed horizontally in six rows.

NAME	ADDRESS	TELEPHONE NO
Adams, Kyle	54 Lemon Street	555-4532
Bell, Harry	6 George Avenue	403-2125
Lewis, Helen	51 Beach Road	332-1909
Potter, Peter	125 First Avenue	456-8895
Thomas, Lisa	7 King Street	667-9890
Wells, Betty	87 Sunset Drive	909-6768

Examining Access Objects

An Access database, as mentioned earlier, is made up of various **objects**. These objects include:

Tables: These contain the actual database information, arranged in tabular (column/row) format.

Forms: These are used to view the information in a table, one record at a time.

Queries: These are questions asked about the information in a table, which are used to extract specific data from the table.

Reports: These are custom layouts, which are used to print the information in a table.

Macros: These allow you to automate repetitive tasks, such as entering and printing data.

Modules: These are collections of declarations and procedures written in the Microsoft Visual Basic programming language, which also are used to automate various tasks.

Notes

Access also includes one other type of object: **data access pages**—special Web pages that allow you to work with data via the Internet or an intranet. Unlike other Access objects, however, which are stored in a single database file, data access pages are stored in external HTML files.

Setting up a New Database

This section discusses the methods for **setting up your own Access database**. In it, you will learn how to:

- **Design** a **new database**.
- **Create** a **new database**.
- **Create** a **new table**.
- **Enter records** in **Datasheet view**.
- **Print** the **datasheet** of a table.
- **Navigate** through **records** in **Datasheet view**.
- **Close** a **table**.
- **Close** a **database file**.

Designing a New Database

One of the most important tasks in setting up a new Access database is that of designing the database—that is, planning the various objects that are to make up the database. This should be done before using Access to actually create those objects.

In designing a database, you must first determine its purpose by answering such questions as "What information will I and/or others want to retrieve from this database?" and "How will this information be used?" This initial step is important since it helps you determine the types of output you will require from the database, which, in turn, helps you determine the types of records you will need to input into the database, as well as the details (fields) those records must include.

The next step in designing a database is that of determining the necessary forms and reports for inputting and outputting information, respectively. To do this, you should examine forms and reports you may currently use to record and present information. You should also draft examples of forms you wish to use to enter and view your database information and reports you wish to generate from the information.

The next and probably most difficult step in designing a database is that of determining the necessary tables for storing the actual information. Although a database need contain only a single table, you should avoid including too much information in any one table. It is better to break up one large table into two or more smaller tables and relate those tables by common fields.

Creating a New Database

With Access, you can create a new database in one of two ways:

- By creating a **blank database** and by adding the necessary tables, forms, reports and other database objects to the database.
- By using the **Database Wizard** to create in one operation the necessary tables, queries, forms and reports for a specific type of database.

To **create a new blank database**:

- Display the New File task pane by choosing the **File**, **New** command, or by clicking on the **New** button on the Application window toolbar, or by clicking on the **Create a new file** option in the Getting Started task pane.
- In the task pane, select the **Blank database** option.
- In the File New Database dialog box, enter a **name** (and, if necessary, a **new storage location**) for the database file. Then click on the **Create** button.

To **create a new database using the Database Wizard**:

- Display the New File task pane by choosing the **File**, **New** command, or by clicking on the **New** button on the Application window toolbar, or by clicking on the **Create a new file** option in the Getting Started task pane.
- In the task pane, select the **On my computer** option.
- On the Databases panel of the Templates dialog box, select the **icon** for the type of database you wish to create. Then click on the **OK** button.
- In the File New Database dialog box, enter a **name** (and, if necessary, a **new storage location**) for the database file. Then click on the **Create** button.
- Follow the directions in the Database Wizard dialog boxes that appear. To move from one dialog box to the next, click on the **Next >** button. In the last dialog box, click on the **Finish** button to complete the operation.

NEW BUTTON

Notes

You can also create a new database that is based on an existing database. To do this, select the **From existing file** option in the New File task pane. Then, in the New from Existing File dialog box, select the appropriate filename, and click on the **Create New** button.

Objective

In this exercise, you will **create a new blank database**. This database will be used to store employee information.

Make sure that the **Access Application window** is displayed. (It is assumed that the **Getting Started task pane** appears in the Application window. If this task pane is not displayed, choose the **View**, **Toolbars** command, and select the **Task Pane** option on the submenu that appears. If another task pane is displayed, click on the **Home** button at the top of the pane to display the Getting Started task pane.)

2.1

- **At the bottom of the Getting Started task pane, click on Create a new file.**

2.2

- **In the task pane under New, click on Blank database.**

2.3

The File New Database dialog box is displayed.

- **Type: Personnel**

The database filename is entered.

NOTE: *The program will add the default extension (mdb) to the filename.*

- **Make sure that 3½ Floppy A: appears in the Save in box and Microsoft Office Access Database appears in Save as type.**

- **Click on the Create button.**

NOTE: *You can "choose" a button either by clicking on it or by pressing [ENTER].*

The dialog box is closed, and the Database window is displayed.

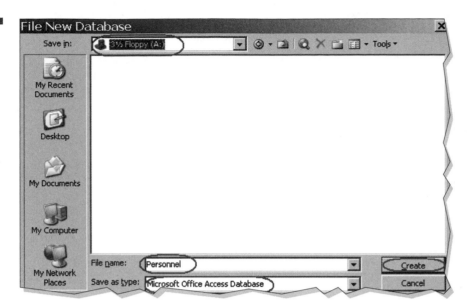

Creating a New Table

After creating a database file, the next step in setting up a database is that of creating the table or tables for storing your information. This is accomplished from the Database window, which currently appears on the Access desktop.

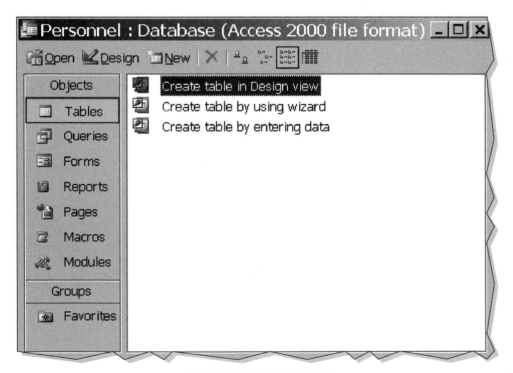

DATABASE WINDOW

One of the easiest methods for creating a table, whether you are setting up a business-related database or a database for your own personal use, is that of using the **Table Wizard**.

To **create a table** (using the **Table Wizard**):

- In the Database window, display the **Tables panel** (if that panel does not currently appear), by clicking on the **tables** option on the Objects bar.
- Do one of the following:

  - Click on the **New** button on the Database window toolbar, select the **Table Wizard** option in the New Table dialog box, and click on the **OK** button; or
  - Simply **double-click** on **Create table by using wizard**.

- Follow the directions in the Table Wizard dialog boxes that appear. In these dialog boxes, you specify the type of table you wish to create, the fields that are to be included in the table and a name for the table. To move from one dialog box to the next, click on the **Next >** button. In the last dialog box, click on the **Finish** button to complete the operation.

Notes

You can also access the New Table dialog box by expanding the **New Object** button on the Application window toolbar and by selecting the **Table** option in the list that appears.

A field in an Access table can be assigned any of nine **data types**, depending on the information that is to be stored in the field:

Text:	This type is used for fields containing alphanumeric data—that is, entries consisting of pure text (for example, names) or entries consisting of text and numbers (for example, addresses). Fields containing pure numeric data that is not used in calculations (for example, zip codes) can also be defined as Text fields.
Memo:	This type is used for fields containing large amounts (up to 65,536 characters) of alphanumeric data.
Number:	This type is used for fields containing numeric (excluding monetary) data on which calculations can be performed.
Currency:	This type is used for fields containing monetary data.
Date/Time:	This type is used for fields containing date or time entries.
AutoNumber:	This type is used for fields that require a unique numeric value (for example, ID number) in each record. This value is automatically calculated and entered by the program.
Yes/No (Boolean):	This type is used for fields containing true or false data.
OLE Object:	This type is used for fields containing linked or embedded objects, such as Microsoft Office Excel data or graphic illustrations.
Hyperlink:	This type is used for fields containing hyperlink text/graphics. (A hyperlink allows you to "jump" to another location in the current file, to another file, or to a Web page on either the World Wide Web or an intranet.)

Notes

The data type list for a field also lists a tenth option—**Lookup Wizard**. Selecting this option starts the Lookup Wizard, which creates a field that allows you to choose an entry from another table or query or from a list of predefined options. The actual data type for the field is determined by the wizard and depends on the information that is to be stored in the field.

Each field in an Access table also has specific **field properties** associated with it. These properties control the appearance (for example, length and format) of the field entries, determine whether or not the field entries are indexed and limit the data that can be entered into the field.

Objective

In this exercise, you will **use the Table Wizard to create a table in your new Personnel database**.

3.1

- **Click on the New**  **button on the Database window toolbar.**

3.2

The New Table dialog box is displayed.

- **Click on Table Wizard. Then click on the OK button.**

The first Table Wizard dialog box is displayed. You will use this dialog box to select the type of table you wish to create and to select the fields that are to be included in the table.

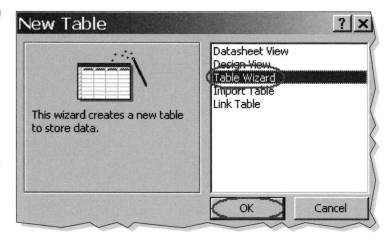

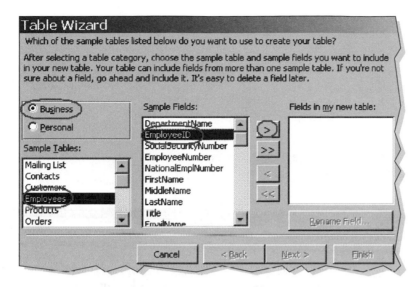

3.3

- **Make sure that the Business option is selected. Then, in the Sample Tables box, click on Employees.**

- **In the Sample Fields box, click on EmployeeID. Then click on the right arrow $\boxed{>}$ button.**

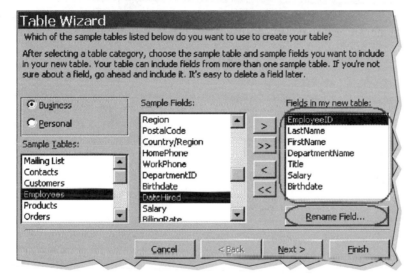

3.4

The EmployeeID field is added to the table.

NOTE: *You can remove a field from the table after adding it by selecting it and by clicking on the **left arrow** button. The double right arrow and double left arrow buttons allow you to respectively add and remove all fields in one operation.*

- **In the same list, click on LastName. Then click on the right arrow button.**

The LastName field is added to the table.

*Using a procedure similar to that described above, **add** the following **fields** to the table (in the indicated order):*

> **FirstName**
> **DepartmentName**
> **Title**
> **Salary**
> **Birthdate**

- **In the Fields in my new table box, click on EmployeeID. Then click on the Rename Field button.**

3.5

The Rename field dialog box is displayed.

3.6

- **Type: StaffNo**
  Click on the OK button.

The field is renamed.

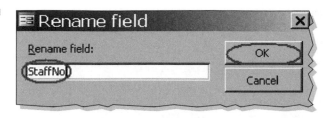

3.7

- **Using a procedure similar to that described above, change the name of the DepartmentName field to Dept and Title field to Position.**

- **Click on the Next > button.**

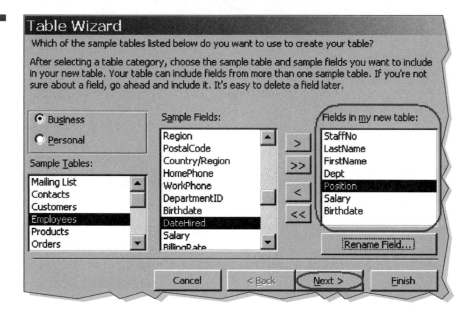

3.8

The next Table Wizard dialog box is displayed and you are prompted to name the table.

- **Type: Staff Details**

*Make sure that the **Yes, set a primary key for me** option is selected.*

The table name is entered.

NOTE: *A **primary key** is a field or combination of fields that uniquely identifies each record in a table. In this case, the StaffNo field will be used as the primary key since it will contain unique values. Records, by default, are displayed in primary key order.*

- **Click on the Next > button.**

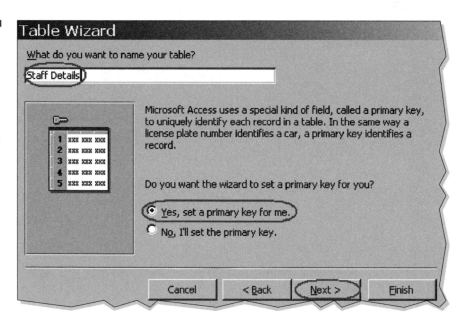

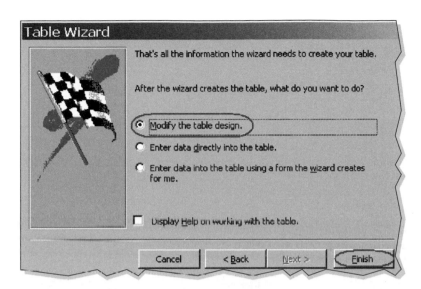

3.9

The last Table Wizard dialog box is displayed, and you are prompted to indicate what you would like to do next.

- **Click on Modify the table design. Then click on the Finish button.**

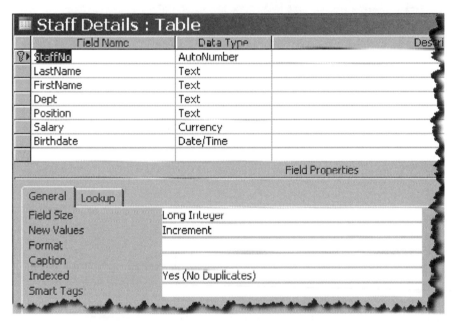

3.10

The dialog box is closed, and the Table window is displayed in Design view. This view allows you to modify the default design that has been set up for you. In this case, you will 1) change the field caption for the StaffNo field, 2) change various field sizes (since the default field size is often larger than what is actually needed), 3) reset the number of decimal places for the Salary field, and 4) add a new field.

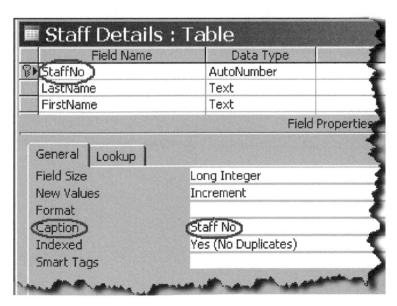

3.11

- **In the Field Name column, make sure that StaffNo is selected. Then, in the Field Properties section, click on Caption.**

- **Type: Staff No**

NOTE: *Make sure that you include the indicated space. Although the field name will be stored as one word (StaffNo) the field caption (heading) will appear as two words. This is consistent with the way Access treats other fields in the table (for example, LastName and FirstName).*

3.12

The new field caption is entered.

- **In the Field Name column, click on LastName.**

The field is selected. Notice that a right-pointing triangle appears in the small button to the left of the field name, and the properties of the LastName field are now listed in the Field Properties section of the window.

NOTE: *The small square button mentioned above is called the row selector.*

- **In the Field Properties section, click on Field Size.**

The current field size (50) is selected.

- **Type: 15**

3.13

The field size is decreased.

Using a procedure similar to that described above, change the Field Size of the FirstName to 12, Dept Field Size to 10 and Position Field Size to 15.

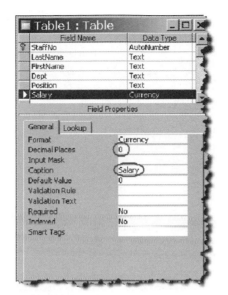

3.14

- **In the Field Name column, click on Salary.**

- **In the Field Properties section, click on Decimal Places.**

A down arrow appears at the right side of the Decimal Places box.

- **Click on the down arrow.**

- **Click on 0.**

3.15

The number of decimal places for Salary field entries is reset to zero. You will now add a new field to the table.

- **In the Field Name column, click in the space immediately below Birthdate.**

  Type: UnionMem
  Press [TAB].

The new field name is entered, and the insertion point moves to the Data Type column. A down arrow appears at the right side of the entry box.

- **Click on the down arrow.**

The box is expanded, and a list of data types is displayed.

- **Click on Yes/No.**

The field data type is selected.

- **In the Field Properties section, click on Caption.**

  Type: Union Mem

NOTE: *Again, make sure that you include the indicated space.*

- **Click on the Save** 🖫 **button on the Application window toolbar.**

Entering Records in Datasheet View

You can enter records directly into the datasheet of a table in what is called **Datasheet view**, or you can create and use a special **form** to enter the records. This subsection discusses the method for entering records into the datasheet itself.

To **switch to Datasheet view**:

- From Design view, choose the **View**, **Datasheet View** command, or click on the **View** button on the Application window toolbar; or
- In the Database window, select the **table name**, and click on the **Open** button on the Database window toolbar.

To **enter records into the datasheet of a table**:

- Type the appropriate **entry** in each field, using **[TAB]** or **[ENTER]** to move from field to field. A record is saved automatically as soon as you move to the next record or close the table.
- If you need to make changes in the table design, choose the **View**, **Design View** command, or click on the **View** button on the Application window toolbar, to return to Design view.

Objective

In this exercise, you will **enter records directly into the datasheet of your Staff Details table**.

4.1

- **Click on the View** button on the **Application window toolbar.**

NOTE: *Click on the button itself, not on the down arrow at the right side of the button.*

4.2

The datasheet of the table is displayed. At this point, of course, it is empty.

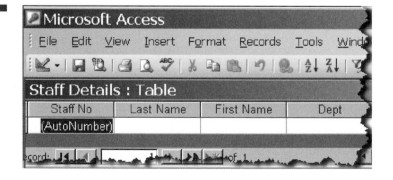

Staff No	Last Name	First Name	Dept	Position	Salary	Birthdate	Union Mem
1	Smith	Anne	Sales	Secretary	$32,000	12/11/1965	☑
AutoNumber							▣

Staff Details : Table

4.3

• **Press [TAB].**

The insertion point moves to the LastName field.

NOTE: *You can also use [**ENTER**] to move from one field to the next.*

• **Type: Smith**

The last name is entered. Notice that the staff number also has been entered automatically by the program.

• **Press [TAB].**

The insertion point moves to the FirstName field.

• **Type: Anne
  Press [TAB].**

The first name is entered, and the insertion point moves to the Dept field.

• **Type: Sales
  Press [TAB].**

The department is entered, and the insertion point moves to the Position field.

• **Type: Secretary
  Press [TAB].**

The position is entered, and the insertion point moves to the Salary field.

• **Type: 32000
  Press [TAB].**

The salary is entered, and the insertion point moves to the Birthdate field.

NOTE: *Notice that a dollar sign and comma have been included automatically in the Salary entry.*

• **Type: 121165
  Press [TAB].**

• **Press [SPACEBAR]. Then press [TAB].**

4.4

A check mark is entered into the field, indicating a "Yes" entry, and the insertion point moves to the StaffNo field of the second record. The first record has been saved.

Staff No	Last Name	First Name	Dept	Position	Salary	Birthdate	Union Mem
1	Smith	Anne	Sales	Secretary	$32,000	12/11/1965	☑
2	King	John	Admin	Manager	$45,000	9/8/1957	☐
3	Lewis	Helen	Sales	Clerk	$22,500	4/10/1973	☑
4	Potter	Peter	Admin	Clerk	$24,000	7/6/1970	☑
5	Wells	Betty	Sales	Manager	$48,750	2/12/1956	☐
6	Brown	Bill	Admin	Clerk	$19,000	10/24/1979	☑
7	Green	Sue	Sales	Secretary	$27,000	6/5/1971	☐
8	Hill	Tony	Sales	Clerk	$21,500	9/19/1977	☐
9	Adams	Kyle	Admin	Secretary	$31,000	12/1/1968	☑
10	Crisp	Helen	Admin	Clerk	$18,000	1/6/1981	☐
11	Bell	Harry	Sales	Secretary	$28,000	5/14/1970	☑
12	Thomas	Lisa	Admin	Clerk	$23,750	8/7/1972	☑
(AutoNumber)							

- **Using a procedure similar to that described above, enter the remaining records listed in the figure on the right.**

NOTE: To correct an entry after typing it, simply click in the entry, reposition the insertion point, if necessary, by using the [ARROW] keys, and make the necessary change(s). You do not have to enter the slashes in the Birthdate field entries. They have been included here to make the entries easier to read. To enter a "Yes" value into the UnionMem field, press [SPACEBAR]; to enter a "No" value into this field, simply press [TAB] (or [ENTER]) to move to the next record.

LastName:	King	Lewis	Potter
FirstName:	John	Helen	Peter
Dept:	Admin	Sales	Admin
Position:	Manager	Clerk	Clerk
Salary:	45000	22500	24000
Birthdate:	09/08/57	04/10/73	07/06/70
UnionMem:	No	Yes	Yes

LastName:	Wells	Brown	Green
FirstName:	Betty	Bill	Sue
Dept:	Sales	Admin	Sales
Position:	Manager	Clerk	Secretary
Salary:	48750	19000	27000
Birthdate:	02/12/56	10/24/79	06/05/71
UnionMem:	No	Yes	No

LastName:	Hill	Adams	Crisp
FirstName:	Tony	Kyle	Helen
Dept:	Sales	Admin	Admin
Position:	Clerk	Secretary	Clerk
Salary:	21500	31000	18000
Birthdate:	09/19/77	12/01/68	01/06/81
UnionMem:	No	Yes	No

LastName:	Bell	Thomas
FirstName:	Harry	Lisa
Dept:	Sales	Admin
Position:	Secretary	Clerk
Salary:	28000	23750
Birthdate:	05/14/70	08/07/72
UnionMem:	Yes	Yes

- **Click on the Save button on the Application window toolbar.**

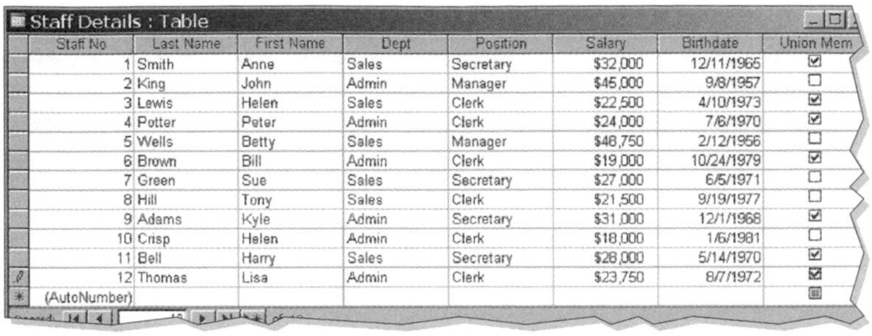

Printing the Datasheet of a Table

You can obtain a quick printout of the records in a table by printing the table's datasheet.

To **print the datasheet of a table**:

- With the datasheet displayed, choose the **File**, **Print** command, or click on the **Print** button on the Application window toolbar.
- If you click on the Print button, the print operation begins immediately. If you choose the File, Print command, the Print dialog box is displayed. In this case, set any necessary **print options**, and then click on the **OK** button.

Objective

In this exercise, you will **print the datasheet of your Staff Details table**. This exercise also demonstrates the methods for 1) **previewing a printout** before beginning the actual print operation, and 2) **resetting the page orientation for a datasheet printout.**

5.1

- **Click on the Print Preview button on the Application window toolbar.**

5.2

A full-page view of the page appears in the Print Preview window.

- **Point to any area of the datasheet and click the mouse button.**

An enlarged view of the datasheet is displayed.

- **If necessary, use the scroll bar at the bottom of the Print Preview window to display the right side of the datasheet.**

Notice that the page does not include the Birthdate and UnionMem fields.

Staff Details   5/10/2005

Staff No	Last Name	First Name	Dept	Position	Salary
1	Smith	Anne	Sales	Secretary	$32,000
2	King	John	Admin	Manager	$45,000
3	Lewis	Helen	Sales	Clerk	$22,500
4	Potter	Peter	Admin	Clerk	$24,000
5	Wells	Betty	Sales	Manager	$48,750
6	Brown	Bill	Admin	Clerk	$19,000
7	Green	Sue	Sales	Secretary	$27,000
8	Hill	Tony	Sales	Clerk	$21,500
9	Adams	Kyle	Admin	Secretary	$31,000
10	Crisp	Helen	Admin	Clerk	$18,000
11	Bell	Harry	Sales	Secretary	$28,000
12	Thomas	Lisa	Admin	Clerk	$23,750

5.3

- **Click on the Two Pages**
  button on the Print Preview
  window toolbar.

5.4

A second page is added to the window.
Both pages now appear in full-page view.

- **Click on the down arrow at**
  the right side of the View

  button on the
  Application window toolbar.

The button is expanded, and a list of
views is displayed.

- **Click on Datasheet View.**

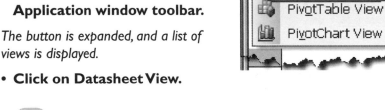

5.5

The Print Preview window is closed, and
the table is redisplayed in Datasheet
view. You will now change the page
orientation so that the entire datasheet
is printed on one page.

- **Choose the File, Page Setup**
  command.

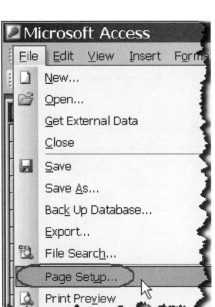

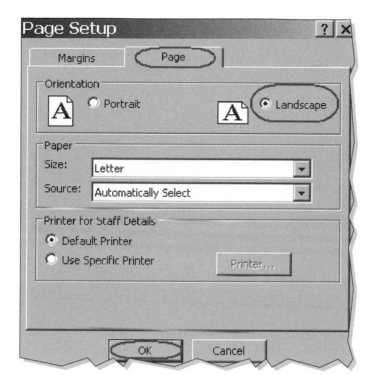

5.6

The Page Setup dialog box is displayed.

• **Click on the Page tab.**

The Page panel of the dialog box is displayed.

• **Under Orientation, click on Landscape. Then click on the OK button.**

5.7

NOTE: *This step assumes that your printer can print in landscape orientation.*

The new page orientation is set, and the dialog box is closed. You will now print the datasheet.

• **Click on the Print button on the Application window toolbar.**

The datasheet is printed.

Navigating Through Records in Datasheet View

In Datasheet view, you can move from record to record and from field to field by using either a **mouse** or the **keyboard**, as summarized on the following page.

To Move to:	(Mouse Method)	(Keyboard Method)
The **next record** (same field)	Click on the **Next Record** button.	Press [**DOWN ARROW**].
The **previous record** (same field)	Click on the **Previous Record** button.	Press [**UP ARROW**].
The **last record** (same field)	Click on the **Last Record** button.	Press [**CTRL**] + [**DOWN ARROW**].
The **first record** (same field)	Click on the **First Record** button.	Press [**CTRL**] + [**UP ARROW**].
A **specific record** (same field)	Select the current record number at the bottom of the Table window, type the new record number, and press [**ENTER**].	Press [**F5**], type the new record number, and press [**ENTER**].
The **next field** (same record)	Click or double-click in that **field**.	Press [**RIGHT ARROW**] or [**TAB**].
The **previous field** (same record)	Click or double-click in that **field**.	Press [**LEFT ARROW**] or [**SHIFT**] + [**TAB**].
The **first field** (same record)	Click or double-click in that **field**.	Press [**HOME**].
The **last field** (same record)	Click or double-click in that **field**.	Press [**END**].
The **first field** (first record)	Click or double-click in that **field**.	Press [**CTRL**] + [**HOME**].
The **last field** (last record)	Click or double-click in that **field**.	Press [**CTRL**] + [**END**].

Objective

In this exercise, you will **navigate through the records in your Staff Details table**.

6.1

- **Make sure that the Staff Details table is displayed in Datasheet view.**
- **If the StaffNo field entry of record #1 is not selected, double-click on that entry.**
- **Click on the Next Record button.**

*A right-pointing triangle appears in the **record selector** to the left of the second record, indicating that record #2 is now current. Notice that the StaffNo field entry is selected (as it was in record #1).*

- **Click on the Next Record button.**

Record #3 is now current.

- **Click on the Previous Record button.**

Record #2 is once again current.

- **Click on the Last Record button.**

Record #12 is now current.

- **Click on the First Record button.**

Record #1 is once again current.

Staff Details : Table

Staff No	Last Name	First Name
1	Smith	Anne
2	King	John
3	Lewis	Helen
4	Potter	Peter
5	Wells	Betty
6	Brown	Bill
7	Green	Sue
8	Hill	Tony
9	Adams	Kyle
10	Crisp	Helen
11	Bell	Harry
12	Thomas	Lisa
*	(AutoNumber)	

Record: [◄◄] [◄] 1 [►] [►►] [►*] of 12

Closing a Table / Closing a Database File

When you are finished working with a table, you can close the Table window either by choosing the **File**, **Close** command or by clicking on the **Close** button on the Title bar of the window. Likewise, when you are finished working with a particular database, you can close the Database window (and the Database file) either by choosing the **File**, **Close** command or by clicking on the **Close** button on the Title bar of the window.

Objective

In this exercise, you will **close your Staff Details table**. You will then **close the database file**.

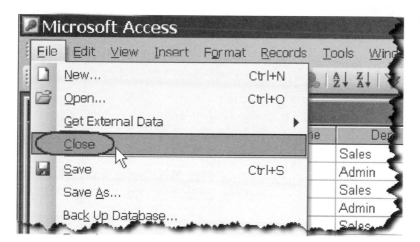

7.1

*Make sure that the **Staff Details table** is open and that it appears in the foreground.*

- **Choose the File, Close command.**

7.2

The table is closed, and the Database window is redisplayed. Notice that your new table is now listed on the Tables panel.

- **Click on the Close button on the Title bar of the Database window.**

The database file is closed, and the Access desktop is cleared.

Creating a Form / Modifying and Manipulating Data

This section discusses methods for **creating and using an Access form**, as well as methods for **modifying and manipulating the data in an Access table**. In it, you will learn how to:

- **Reopen** a **database file**.
- **Reopen** a **table**.
- **Create** a **form**.
- **Navigate** through **records** in **Form view**.
- **Close** a **form**.
- **Reopen** a **form**.
- **Switch** between **Form view** and **Datasheet view**.
- **Enter records** in **Form view**.
- **Edit records** in **Datasheet view** and in **Form view**.
- **Use** the **Find** feature.
- **Delete records** in **Datasheet view** and in **Form view**.
- **Modify** the **Datasheet view** of a table.
- **Sort** the **records** in a table.

Reopening a Database File / Reopening a Table

After closing a table, you can easily reopen it to view or edit records. If you have also closed the database in which the table is stored, you must first reopen the database file.

To **reopen a database file**:

- Choose the **File, Open** command, or click on the **Open** button on the Application window toolbar.
- In the Open dialog box, switch to the folder in which the database file is stored (if it is not stored in the current folder).
- Select the **database filename**.
- Do one of the following:

  - To simply open the file for single access (which allows you as a single-user to view and edit the information) or to open the database for shared access (which allows you and others in a multi-user environment to view and edit the information), click on the **Open** button (in the dialog box); or
  - To open the file for read-only access (which allows you to view, but not edit, the information), expand the **Open** button (by clicking on the down arrow at the right side of the button), and select the **Open Read-Only** option in the list that appears; or
  - To open the file for exclusive access (which prevents others in a multi-user environment from opening the same file), expand the **Open** button, and select the **Open Exclusive** option in the list that appears; or
  - To open the file for exclusive read-only access, expand the **Open** button, and select the **Open Exclusive Read-Only** option in the list that appears.

Notes

1. Both the File menu and the Getting Started task pane include a list of recently-open database files. You can reopen any file listed on this menu or in this pane by simply selecting its filename. (Selecting a database filename on the File menu, opens that database in the mode in which it was last open; selecting a database filename in the Getting Started task pane, opens that database in shared access mode.)

2. If you cannot find a particular file, you can use the **Search** feature to locate it. This feature can be accessed in two ways: 1) by expanding the **Tools** button on the toolbar of the Open dialog box and by selecting the **Search** option in the list that appears, and 2) by using the **Basic File Search** and **Advanced File Search task panes**.

To **reopen a table**:

- In the Database window, display the **Tables panel** (if that panel does not currently appear).
- Select the **table name**.
- Click on the **Open** button on the Database window toolbar.

Objective

In this exercise, you will **open a database file**. You will then **open a table of the database**.

8.1

- **Click on the Open button on the Application window toolbar.**

The Open dialog box is displayed.

NOTE: *Clicking on the **My Recent Documents** icon in the Places bar displays a list of files and folders that were recently open.*

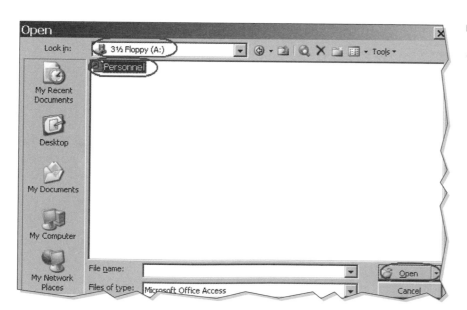

8.2

- **Make sure that 3½ Floppy (A:) appears in the Look in box.**

8.3

• **In the list of filenames, double-click on Personnel.mdb (or Personnel).**

NOTE: Double-clicking on a dialog box option is equivalent to clicking once on the option and then clicking on the default (in this case, Open) button.

The dialog box is closed. A message box should appear, displaying a warning about the safety of the file and asking if you would like to open the file or cancel the operation.

*NOTE: If another message box appears instead, displaying a warning about unsafe expressions not being blocked and asking if you would like to open the file, click on the **Yes** button.*

• **Click on the Open button.**

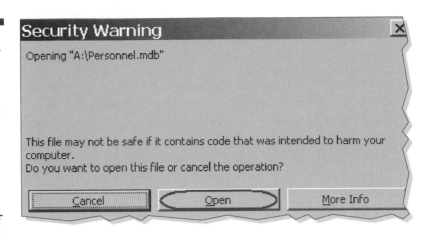

8.4

The Database window is displayed. The Staff Details table should be selected on the Tables panel of the window.

• **Click on the Open button on the Database window toolbar.**

8.5

The table is opened.

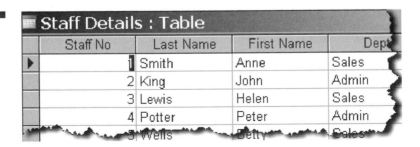

Creating a Form

An Access **form** allows you to display the information in a table one record at a time. Entering, editing and/or viewing data in **Form view** is often the preferred method because:

- All fields of a record can be seen at the same time. In Datasheet view, you often must scroll the window to reveal certain data, especially when a table includes a large number of fields.
- Fields can be arranged anyway you wish. This can facilitate data entry and prevent typing errors.
- A form can include additional text and graphics, as well as other effects, such as colors and shading. These elements can add visual interest to the data display.

You can quickly create a simple form by letting the **AutoForm Wizard** generate it for you.

To **create a form** (using the **AutoForm Wizard**):

- In the Database window, select the appropriate **table**; or

  Open the **table** in **Datasheet view**.

- Expand the **New Object** button on the Application window toolbar.
- In the list of options that appears, do one of the following:

  - Select the **AutoForm** option (to create a form in a single-column format); or
  - Select the **Form** option. In the New Form dialog box, select the **AutoForm: Columnar** option (to create a form in the same single-column format as a form created with the AutoForm option), the **AutoForm: Tabular** option (to create a form in a column/row format) or the **AutoForm: Datasheet** option (to create a form in the same column/row format as a table). Then click on the **OK** button.

NEW OBJECT BUTTON

Objective

In this exercise, you will **use the AutoForm Wizard to create a form for the current table**.

9.1

- **Make sure that the Staff Details table is open.**

- **Point to the New Object button on the Application window toolbar.**

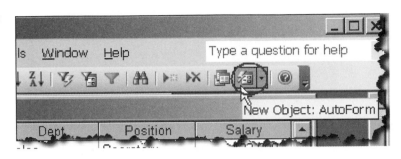

The ScreenTip, which appears next to the mouse pointer, displays "New Object: AutoForm." This indicates that AutoForm is the default option for this button.

- **Click on the New Object button.**

NOTE: *Click on the button itself, not on the down arrow at the right side of the button.*

9.2

A form appears, displaying the first record in the table. You will now save it.

9.3

- **Click on the Save button.**

The Save As dialog box is displayed. You will accept the default form name, Staff Details.

- **Click on the OK button.**

The form is saved, and the dialog box is closed.

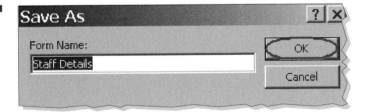

Navigating Through Records in Form View / Closing a Form

In Form view, as in Datasheet view, you can move from record to record and from field to field by using either a **mouse** or the **keyboard**, as summarized below. (The Next Record, Previous Record, Last Record and First Record buttons appear at the bottom of the Form window.)

To Move to:	(Mouse Method)	(Keyboard Method)
The **next record** (same field)	Click on the **Next Record** button.	Press [PG DN].
The **previous record** (same field)	Click on the **Previous Record** button.	Press [PG UP].
The **last record** (same field)	Click on the **Last Record** button.	Press [CTRL] + [DOWN ARROW].
The **first record** (same field)	Click on the **First Record** button.	Press [CTRL] + [UP ARROW].
A **specific record** (same field)	Select the current record number at the bottom of the Form window, type the new record number, and press [ENTER].	Press [F5], type the new record number, and press [ENTER].
The **next field** (same record)	Click or double-click in that **field**.	Press [DOWN ARROW] or [TAB].
The **previous field** (same record)	Click or double-click in that **field**.	Press [UP ARROW] or [SHIFT] + [TAB].
The **first field** (same record)	Click or double-click in that **field**.	Press [HOME].
The **last field** (same record)	Click or double-click in that **field**.	Press [END].
The **first field** (first record)		Press [CTRL] + [HOME].
The **last field** (last record)		Press [CTRL] + [END].

When you are finished working with a form, you can close the Form window either by choosing the **File**, **Close** command or by clicking on the **Close** button on the Title bar of the window.

Objective

In this exercise, you will **use the current form to display various records in the associated table**. You will then **close the form**.

10.1

- **Make sure that the Staff Details form is open. (The StaffNo field entry of record #1 should be selected. If it is not, double-click in the field.)**

You will begin by using the buttons at the bottom of the Form window to navigate through the Staff Details table.

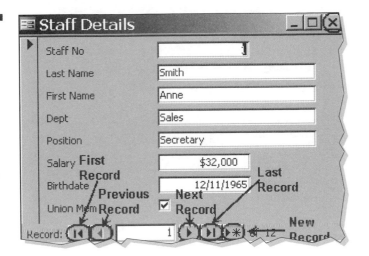

10.2

- **Click on the Next Record button.**

Record #2 is displayed. Notice that the StaffNo field entry is selected (as it was in record #1).

- **Click on the Next Record button.**

Record #3 is displayed.

- **Click on the Previous Record button.**

Record #2 is redisplayed.

- **Click on the Last Record button.**

Record #12 is displayed.

- **Click on the First Record button.**

Record #1 is redisplayed.

- **Click on the Close button on the Title bar of the Form window.**

The form is closed, and the Table window is redisplayed in the foreground.

- **Click on the Close button on the Title bar of the Table window.**

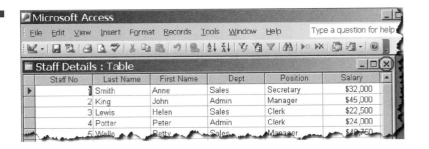

Reopening a Form

After closing a form, you can easily reopen it at any time.
To **reopen a form**:

- In the Database window, display the **Forms panel** (if that panel does not currently appear).
- Select the **form name**.
- Click on the **Open** button on the Database window toolbar.

Objective

In this exercise, you will **reopen the Staff Details form**.

11.1

- **On the Objects bar, click on Forms.**

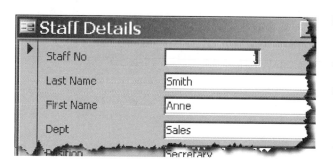

11.2

The Forms panel of the Database window is displayed.

- **Click on Staff Details. Then click on the Open button on the Database window toolbar.**

The form is opened.

Switching Between Form View and Datasheet View

While working in the Form window, you can quickly switch to **Datasheet view** to display all records and then switch back to **Form view** to display one record at a time.
To **switch to Datasheet view** (from **Form view**):

- Choose the **View, Datasheet View** command; or
- Expand the **View** button on the Application window toolbar, and select the **Datasheet View** option in the list that appears.

To **switch back to Form view** (from **Datasheet view**):

* Choose the **View**, **Form View** command; or
* Expand the **View** button, and select the **Form View** option in the list that appears.

Objective

In this exercise, you will **switch from Form view to Datasheet view**. You will then **return to Form view**. This exercise also demonstrates the **method for previewing and printing records** in **Form view**.

12.1

* **Click on the down arrow at the right side of the View button on the Application window toolbar.**

The button is expanded, and a list of views is displayed.

* **Click on Datasheet View.**

12.2

The datasheet of the Staff Details table is displayed in the Form window. You will now return to Form view.

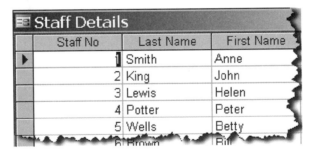

Staff No	Last Name	First Name
1	Smith	Anne
2	King	John
3	Lewis	Helen
4	Potter	Peter
5	Wells	Betty
6	Brown	Bill

12.3

* **Expand the View button, and click on Form View in the list of views.**

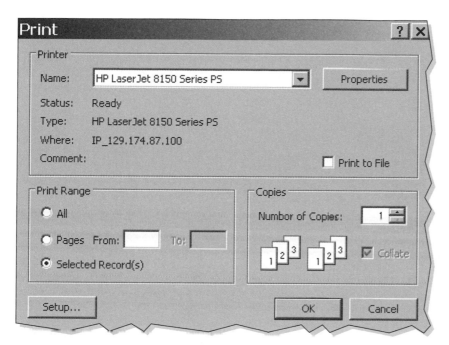

12.4

The Staff Details form is redisplayed in the Form window.

You will now print the first record.

- **Choose the File, Print command.**

The Print dialog box is displayed

- **Under Print Range, click on Selected Records(s). Then click on the OK button.**

The dialog box is closed, and the current record is printed.

Entering Records in Form View

The method for entering records in Form view is essentially the same as that for entering records in Datasheet view. You can display a **blank record** either by choosing the **Insert, New Record** command or by clicking on the **New Record** button, which appears both on the Application window toolbar and in the Form window.

Objective

In this exercise, you will **use the current form to enter records into the associated table**.

13.1

- **Click on the New Record button on the Application window toolbar.**

13.2

A blank record is displayed in the form.

- **Press [TAB]. (The Staff No is filled automatically by the AutoNumber option).**

The insertion point moves to the LastName field.

NOTE: *You can also use* ***[ENTER]*** *to move from one field to the next.*

- **Type: Wong Press [TAB].**

The last name is entered, and the insertion point moves to the FirstName field.

- **Using a procedure similar to that described on the previous page, enter the specified information into the following fields:**

FirstName: Lee
Dept: Admin
Position: Secretary
Salary: 27500
Birthdate: 110374

- **Click in the check box for the UnionMem field.**

The check box is selected, indicating a field entry of "Yes."

NOTE: *You can also select a check box by moving to the field and by pressing* ***[SPACEBAR]*** *(as in a datasheet).*

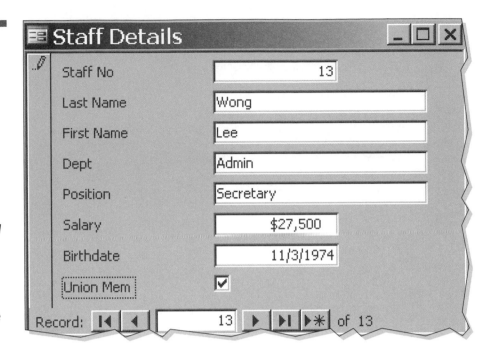

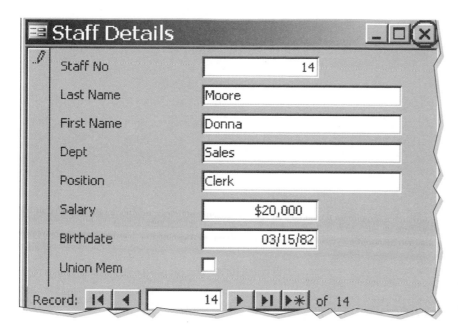

- **Press [TAB] or [ENTER] to display another blank record.**

Create another new record by entering the specified information into the following fields:

LastName:	Moore
FirstName:	Donna
Dept:	Sales
Position:	Clerk
Salary:	20000
Birthdate:	031582

NOTE: *Do not select the **UnionMem** check box.*

- **Click on the Close button on the Title bar of the Form window.**

The form is closed, the record is saved, and the Database window is redisplayed.

Editing Records in Datasheet View and in Form View / Using the Find Feature

Just as you can enter records in either Datasheet view or Form view, you can edit records in either view. Simply move the insertion point to the appropriate field, and insert, delete and/or replace characters, as necessary, or select the entire field entry, and type a new entry. Any changes you make are saved automatically as soon as you move to another record (or close the table or form).

To help you locate the particular record that needs revision, Access provides a **Find** feature, which searches through a table and displays records containing a specific field entry. This feature can be especially useful in a large table or when displaying data one record at a time in a form.

To **use the Find feature**:

- Select or click in **any entry** in the **search field** (the field you wish to search).
- Choose the **Edit, Find** command, or click on the **Find** button on the Application window toolbar.
- On the Find panel of the Find and Replace dialog box, enter the **search value** (the field entry that is to be found).

NOTE: The shortcut for Find and Replace is Ctrl + F.

- Optionally, select any necessary **search options**. For example:

  - To search for any occurrence of the search value, expand the **Match** box, and select the **Any Part of Field** option. (The default Match option is **Whole Field**, which matches only those entries that include only the search value. For example, the search value "Roberts" will match "Roberts," but not "Robertson." The Match box also includes a **Start of Field** option, which matches only those entries that include the search value at the beginning of the field. For example, the search value "anders" will match "Anderson," but not "Sanders.")

- To search only for an exact case match of the search value, select the **Match Case** option. (If this option is not selected, the program will find any occurrence of the search value, regardless of case. For example, the search value "sales" will match "sales," as well as "Sales," "SALES," etc.)

- Click on the **Find Next** button until the desired record is located.
- Click on the **Cancel** button to close the dialog box.

Objective

In this exercise, you will **edit records in the Staff Details table**.

14.1

- **Make sure that the Staff Details form is selected on the Forms panel of the Database window. Then click on the Open button.**

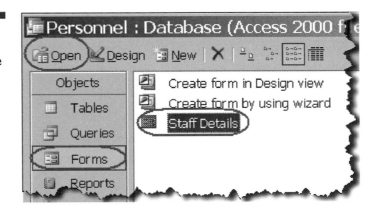

14.2

The Staff Details form is opened. You will now edit the record for employee King. You will use the Find feature to locate the record.

- **Click in the LastName field entry.**

The search field is set.

- **Click on the Find button on the Application window toolbar.**

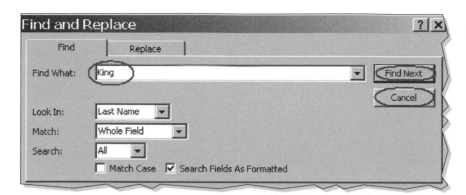

14.3

The Find panel of the Find and Replace dialog box is displayed.

- **Type: King**

The search value is entered.

- **Click on the Find Next button.**

14.4

The record is located.

- **Click on the Cancel button.**

The dialog box is closed.

NOTE: *Notice that the Match Case option, by default, is not selected. Therefore, the case of the search value is not relevant. The program will find any occurrence of the search value (for example, King, king or KING).*

- **Press [TAB] four times to move to the Salary field.**

The Salary field entry is selected.

- **Type: 48000**
  Press [TAB].

The selected field entry is replaced by the new entry ($48,000).

- **Click on the Next Record button at the bottom of the Form window.**

The next record is displayed in the form, and the change is saved. You will now edit a record in Datasheet view.

14.5

- **Expand the View button, and click on Datasheet View in the list of views.**

■ **14.6** ■

The datasheet of the table is displayed in the Form window.

- **Using your mouse, increase the width of the Form window by dragging the right border two or three inches to the right.**

A scroll bar is displayed at the bottom of the window.

NOTE: *You can use this scroll bar to display fields that are not initially visible.*

■ **14.7** ■

- **Drag the mouse pointer over the Salary field entry ($18,000) for Helen Crisp.**

The Salary field entry is selected.

- **Type: 19500**
  Press [TAB].

The selected field entry is replaced by the new entry ($19,500).

- **Close the datasheet view.**

Deleting Records in Datasheet View and in Form View

You also can delete one or more records in either Datasheet view or Form view.

To **delete a single record** (in Datasheet view or Form view):

- Select or click in **any field** of the record that is to be deleted (in Datasheet view) or display the record (in Form view).
- Choose the **Edit, Delete Record** command, or click on the **Delete Record** button on the Application window toolbar.
- In the prompt box that appears, click on the **Yes** button to confirm the operation.

To **delete two or more consecutive records** (in Datasheet view only):

- **Drag** the mouse pointer over the **record selectors** for the records that are to be deleted.
- Choose the **Edit, Delete Record** command, or click on the **Delete Record** button on the Application window toolbar.
- In the prompt box that appears, click on the **Yes** button to confirm the operation.

Notes

You should exercise caution when deleting a record since it cannot be restored once it has been removed from a table.

Objective

In this exercise, you will **delete a record from the Staff Details table**. You will begin by deleting a record in Form view.

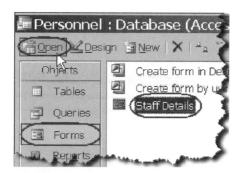

15.1

- **Make sure that the Staff Details form is selected on the Forms panel of the Database window. Then click on the Open button.**

The Staff Details form is opened.

15.2

You will now delete the record of employee King.

- **Click on the Next Record button so Staff No 2 (King John) record is displayed.**

15.3

- **Make sure that the Staff No 2 record still appears in the form. Then click on the Delete Record button on the Application window toolbar.**

You are prompted to confirm the operation.

- **Click on the Yes button.**

15.4

The record is deleted. You will now initiate a delete operation in Datasheet view.

- **Expand the View button, and click on Datasheet View in the list of views.**

15.5

The datasheet of the table is displayed in the Form window. Notice that the record you deleted does not appear.

- **Scroll the Form window upward until the StaffNo fields of the records for Green, Hill and Adams are visible.**

NOTE: You may wish to increase the size of the window.

- **Point to the record selector (the square button to the left of the StaffNo field) for the record for employee Green.**

The mouse pointer will appear as a right-pointing arrow when it is properly positioned.

- **Press and hold down the mouse button, and drag the mouse pointer downward to select (highlight) the records for employees Green, Hill and Adams. Then release the mouse button.**

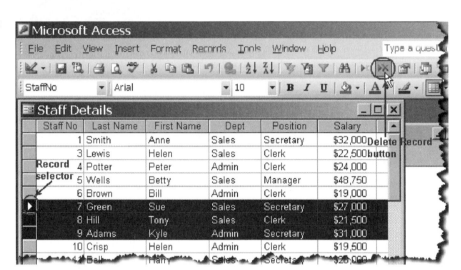

15.6

- **Click on the Delete Record button.**

- **When prompted to confirm the operation, click on the No button.**

The operation is cancelled.

Modifying the Datasheet View of a Table

In addition to changing the actual information in a table, Access allows you to modify the **Datasheet view** by resizing and/or repositioning fields.

To **resize a field**:

- Point to the **right border** of the **field selector**.
- To **increase** the field width, **drag** the **border** to the **right**; or
  To **decrease** the field width, **drag** the **border** to the **left**; or

  To have the program automatically resize the field to fit the field data, **double-click** on the **border**.

To **reposition a field**:

- Click on the **field selector** for the field. Doing this selects the field.
- **Drag** the **field selector** to the new location.

Notes

1. You can also resize a field an exact amount by selecting it, by choosing the **Format, Column Width** command (or by right-clicking on the field and by selecting the **Column Width** option on the shortcut menu), by entering the desired width in the Column Width dialog box, and by clicking on the **OK** button.

2. With Access, there are several additional ways in which you can modify the Datasheet view. For example, you can resize all records (that is, decrease or increase the height of all rows of a table) either by using the **Format, Row Height** command or by dragging the bottom border of the record selector for any row up (to decrease the row height) or down (to increase the row height). You can reset the overall font, as well as the overall font size, style and/or color of field entries, by using the **Format, Font** command. You can also modify the background and/or the gridlines of the datasheet itself by using the **Format, Datasheet** command.

Objective

In this exercise, you will **modify the Datasheet view of the Staff Details table**. Specifically, you will 1) decrease the width of various fields so that all fields can be viewed in the Table window, and 2) move the Position field so that it appears before the Dept field.

16.1

You will begin by decreasing the width of the first field.

- **Make sure that the Staff Details table is open.**

- **Point to the right border of the field selector (the rectangular button that displays the caption) for the StaffNo field.**

The mouse pointer will appear as a double-arrow cross when it is properly positioned.

- **Press and hold down the mouse button, and drag the border approximately one-quarter inch to the left. Then release the mouse button.**

16.2

The width of the StaffNo field is decreased.

- **Point to the right border of the LastName field selector. Then double-click the mouse button.**

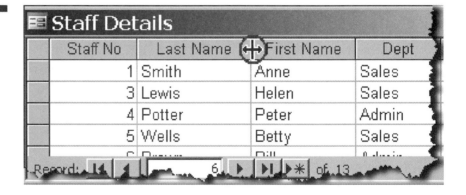

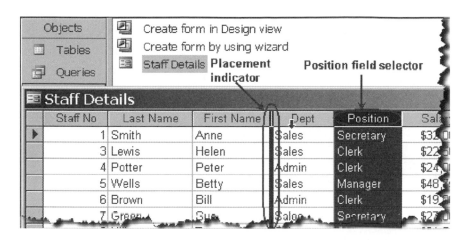

Placement indicator
Position field selector

16.3

The width of the LastName field is decreased to fit the field data.

- **Point to the right border of the FirstName field selector. Then double-click the mouse button.**

The width of the FirstName field is also decreased to fit the field data.

- **Click on the Position field selector.**

The entire field is selected.

- **Point to the Position field selector. Press and hold down the mouse button, and drag the field selector to the left until the placement indicator (the thick vertical line that moves with the mouse pointer) appears to the immediate left of the Dept field. Then release the mouse button.**

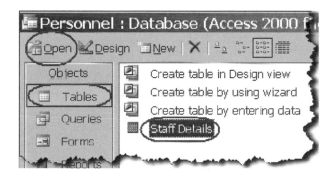

16.4

The Position field now appears to the left of the Dept field.

- **Click on the Save button and close the table.**
- **Open the Staff Details table.**

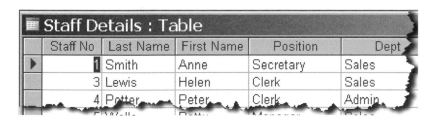

16.5

Notice that the new field widths and field order are still in effect.

Notes

The changes you have made affect only the Datasheet view of the Table window. Similar changes, however, can be made to the Datasheet view of the Form window.

Sorting the Records in a Table

Access normally displays records in **primary key** order. In the Staff Details table, for example, records are listed in ascending order by staff number.

There may be times, however, when you will want the information in a table organized in a different way—by last name or by department, for example, referring to the Staff Details table. This can be accomplished by **sorting** the records.

To **sort the records in a table**:

*   Select or click in **any entry** in the **sort field** (the field by which all records are to be ordered).
*   To sort the records in **ascending order**, choose the **Records, Sort, Sort Ascending** command, select the **Sort Ascending** option on the shortcut menu, or click on the **Sort Ascending** button on the Application window toolbar; or

To sort the records in **descending order**, choose the **Records, Sort, Sort Descending** command, select the **Sort Descending** option on the shortcut menu, or click on the **Sort Descending** button on the Application window toolbar.

SORT ASCENDING / SORT DESCENDING BUTTONS

Notes

You can also sort the Datasheet view of a table by entries in two or more adjacent fields. To do this, select the sort fields by dragging the mouse pointer over the field selectors. Then use the appropriate command or button. In this case, records are initially sorted by entries in the first sort field. Records containing the same entry in that field are then resorted by entries in the second sort field, and so on.

Objective

In this exercise, you will **sort the records in the Staff Details table**. You will begin by sorting the records in ascending order by last name.

*   **Click in the LastName field entry of first record.**
*   **Click on the Sort Ascending button on the Application window toolbar.**

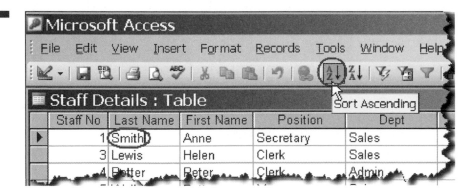

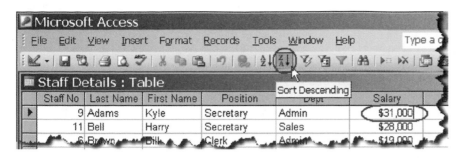

17.2

The records are sorted. You will now sort the records in descending order by salary.

- **Click in the Salary field entry of any record.**
- **Click on the Sort Descending button on the Application window toolbar.**

17.3

The records are resorted.

- **Click on the Print button.**

The records are printed in the order in which they are currently sorted.

- **Click on the Save button.**

The change in the sort order is saved.

Displaying Selected Data

This section discusses the methods for **extracting selected information from an Access table**. In it, you will learn how to:

- **Filter** the **records** in a table.
- **Create** a **simple query**.
- **Create** a **query** in **Design view**.
- **Modify** a **query**.

Filtering the Records in a Table

At times, you may want to view, and work with, only specific records in a table—for example, those for employees in a particular department or those for sales of a certain product. One means of accomplishing this is that of creating a **filter** to display the subset of records containing a specific entry in one or more fields.

Access provides a **Filter By Selection** method and a **Filter By Form** method for filtering records. Filter By Selection is the quickest method when the records you wish to display must satisfy only one condition (contain a particular entry in only one field). Filter By Form, on the other hand, can be used when the records must satisfy multiple conditions.

To **filter the records in a table** (using the **Filter By Selection** method):

- Select or click in the **field entry** that is to be matched (the entry that is to appear in all records).
- Choose the **Records, Filter, Filter By Selection** command, select the **Filter By Selection** option on the shortcut menu, or click on the **Filter By Selection** button on the Application window toolbar.

- To remove the filter, choose the **Records, Remove Filter/Sort** command, select the **Remove Filter/Sort** option on the shortcut menu, or click on the **Remove Filter** button on the Application window toolbar.

To **filter the records in a table** (using the **Filter By Form** method):

- Choose the **Records, Filter, Filter By Form** command, or click on the **Filter By Form** button on the Application window toolbar.
- In the Filter By Form window, enter the **filter condition(s)**.
- Choose the **Filter, Apply Filter/Sort** command, select the **Apply Filter/Sort** option on the shortcut menu, or click on the **Apply Filter** button on the Application window toolbar.
- To remove the filter, choose the **Records, Remove Filter/Sort** command, select the **Remove Filter/Sort** option on the shortcut menu, or click on the **Remove Filter** button on the Application window toolbar.

Notes

Access also provides two other methods for filtering records: **Filter For Input** and **Filter Excluding Selection**. The Filter For Input method is similar to Filter By Selection since it is used to display records that satisfy one condition. (This method is demonstrated later in this section.) The Filter Excluding Selection method, on the other hand, is the opposite of Filter By Selection since it displays all records *except* those containing a specific entry. To use this type of filter, select the appropriate entry and choose the **Records, Filter, Filter Excluding Selection** command (or select the **Filter Excluding Selection** option on the shortcut menu).

Objective

In this exercise, you will **use both the Filter By Selection and Filter By Form methods to filter the records in a table**.

- **Make sure that the Staff Details table is open.**

- **Double-click on the Dept field entry (Admin) of record #3.**

The field entry is selected.

- **Click on the Filter By Selection button on the Application window toolbar.**

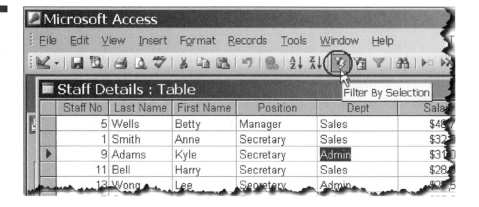

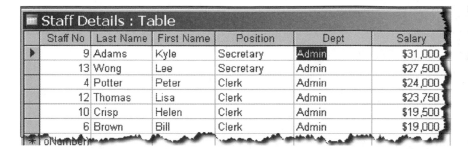

18.2

The records are filtered, and the selected records are displayed.

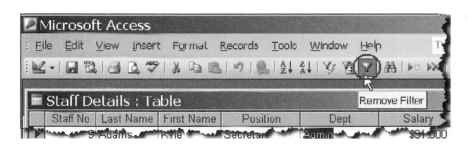

18.3

- **Click on the Remove Filter button on the Application window toolbar.**

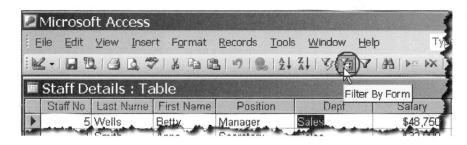

18.4

All records are redisplayed. You will now use the Filter By Form method to display the records for secretaries in the Sales department.

- **Click on the Filter By Form button on the Application window toolbar.**

18.5

The Filter by Form window is displayed. Notice that the previous condition (Admin) appears in the Dept field.

- **Click on the down arrow in the Dept field box.**

The box is expanded, and a list of the Dept field entries is displayed.

- **Click on Admin.**

The first filter condition is entered.

18.6

- **Click in the Position field box, and then click on the down arrow that appears.**

NOTE: *If you click near the right edge of the Position field box, the box will expand automatically. (In this case, you will not need to click on the down arrow.)*

The box is expanded, and a list of the Position field entries is displayed.

- **Click on Secretary.**

- **The second filter condition is entered.**

NOTE: *In this case, you have specified two **AND** conditions. Only those records containing "Sales" in the Dept field and "Secretary" in the Position field will be selected.*

- **Click on the Apply Filter button on the Application window toolbar.**

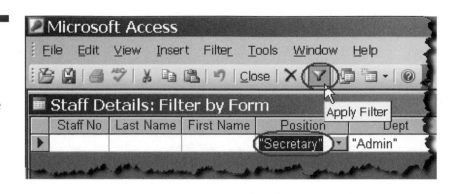

18.7

The records are filtered, and the selected records are displayed. You will now display the records for secretaries in the Sales department, along with the records for all managers.

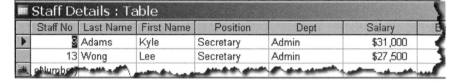

18.8

- **Click on the Remove Filter button and then on the Save button on the Application window toolbar.**

Creating a Simple Query

Another method for limiting the display of table information is that of creating a **query**. Like the filters created in the previous subsection, a query can be used to extract the subset of records containing a specific entry in one or more fields. In addition, a query can also be used to display only selected fields of all or selected records.

You can create a quick query that displays selected fields of all records in a table by using the **Simple Query Wizard**.

To **create a query** (using the **Simple Query Wizard**):

- In the Database window, select the appropriate **table**; or

Open the **table** in **Datasheet view**.

- Expand the **New Object** button on the Application window toolbar, and select the **Query** option in the list that appears.
- In the New Query dialog box, select the **Simple Query Wizard** option. Then click on the **OK** button.
- Follow the directions in the Simple Query Wizard dialog boxes that appear. To move from one dialog box to the next, click on the **Next >** button. In the last dialog box, click on the **Finish** button to complete the operation.

Notes

1. You can also access the Simple Query Wizard by double-clicking on the **Create query by using wizard** option on the Queries panel of the Database window.
2. If you accept the **Open the query to view information** option in the last Simple Query Wizard dialog box, the query is run automatically as soon as you click on the Finish button. You can also run the query by following the procedure described in the next subsection.
3. The queries created in this section are called **select queries** since they are used to extract selected information from a table. With Access, you can also create several types of **action queries** that allow you to perform in one operation various tasks involving records in one or more tables.

Objective

In this exercise, you will **use the Simple Query Wizard to create two queries of the records in the Staff Details table**.

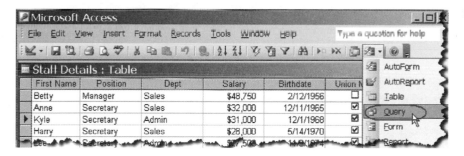

19.1

- **Click on the down arrow at the right side of the New Object button on the Application window toolbar.**

The button is expanded, and a list of objects is displayed.

- **Click on Query.**

19.2

The New Query dialog box is displayed.

- **Click on Simple Query Wizard. Then click on the OK button.**

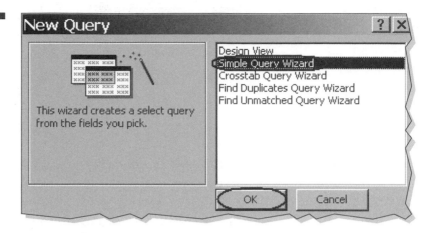

19.3

The first Simple Query Wizard dialog box is displayed. Notice that the fields of the Staff Details table appear in the Available Fields box. You will now specify the fields that are to be displayed by the query.

- **In the Available Fields box, double-click on the following fields (in the indicated order):**

  LastName
  FirstName
  Position
  Salary

The fields are added to the Selected Fields box.

- **Click on the Next > button.**

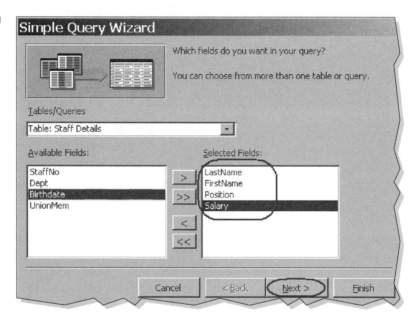

19.4

The next Simple Query Wizard dialog box is displayed, and you are asked if you would like to create a detail or summary query. In this case, you will accept the default option (Detail), which simply displays the selected fields of all records.

NOTE: Selecting the Summary option allows you to summarize numeric data for groups of records. You will use this option later in this exercise.

- **Click on the Next > button.**

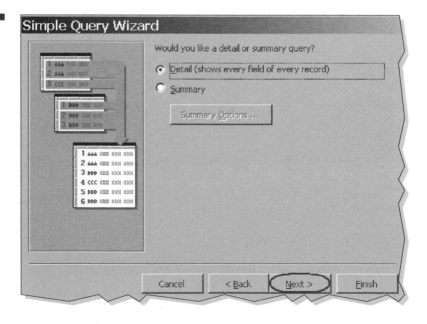

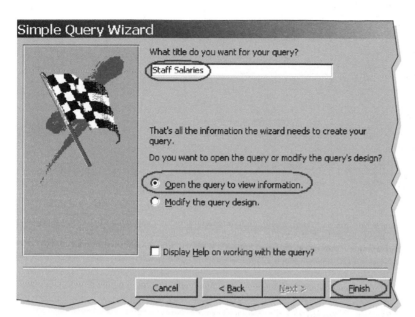

The last Simple Query Wizard dialog box is displayed, and you are prompted to enter a title (name) for the query.

- **Make sure that the default query name (Staff Details Query) is selected. Type: Staff Salaries**

The new query name is entered.

- **Make sure that the Open the query to view information option is selected. Then click on the Finish button.**

The dialog box is closed, the query is run, and the selected fields are displayed.

NOTE: Since the information extracted by a query is stored in a datasheet, you can navigate through the information by using the methods for navigating through the datasheet of any table. You can increase the height of the Query window to fully display all entries by dragging the top or bottom border of the window.

- **Click on the Print button.**

The selected field entries are printed.

19.7

- **Click on the Close button on the Title bar of the Query window.**

The query is closed, and the Database window is redisplayed. Notice that the new query is now listed on the Queries panel of this window.

- **Display the Tables panel of the Database window.**

You will now create a query that summarizes the salaries of individuals in the Staff Details table.

NOTE: *The New Object button currently displays the Query icon since Query was the last option selected in the New Object list. Therefore, you can redisplay the New Query dialog box by simply clicking on this button. (The alternate method of expanding the New Object button and selecting Query in the list of options can, of course, be used as well.)*

- **Click on the New Object button and select Query.**

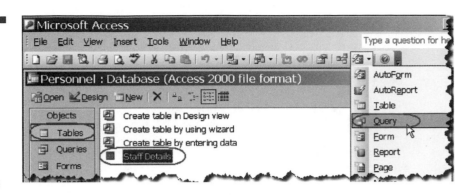

19.8

- **In the New Query dialog box, click on Simple Query Wizard. Then click on the OK button.**

The first Simple Query Wizard dialog box is redisplayed.

- **In the Available Fields box, double-click on the following fields (in the indicated order):**

  Dept
  Position
  Salary

The fields are added to the Selected Fields box.

- **Click on the Next > button.**

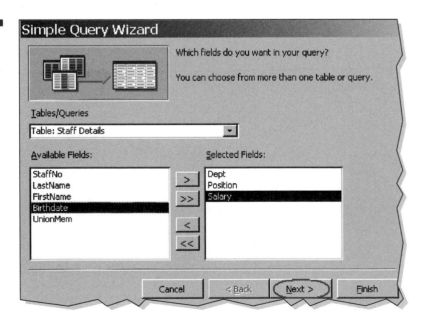

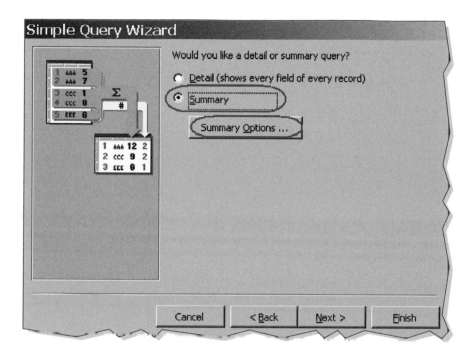

19.9

The second Simple Query Wizard dialog box is displayed.

- **Click on Summary. Then click on the Summary Options button.**

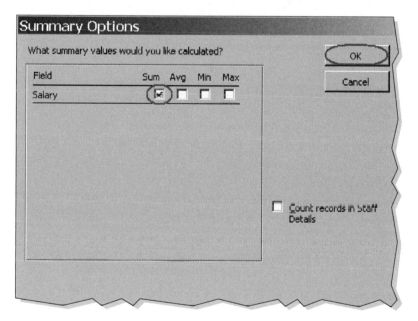

19.10

- **Click in the check box for the Sum option.**

The option is selected. In this case, the Salary field entries for each position within each department will be totaled.

- **Click on the OK button.**

19.11

The Simple Query Wizard dialog box is redisplayed.

- **Click on the Next > button.**

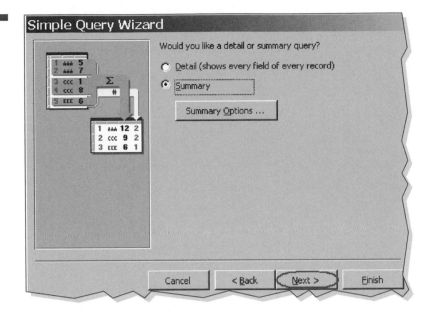

19.12

The last Simple Query Wizard dialog box is displayed.

- **Type: Staff Totals (by Position)**

The query name is entered.

- **Click on the Finish button.**

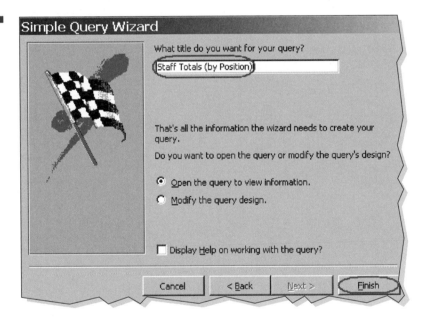

19.13

The dialog box is closed, the query is run, and the summary information is displayed.

- **Close the query.**

Dept	Position	Sum Of Salary
Admin	Clerk	$86,250.00
Admin	Secretary	$58,500.00
Sales	Clerk	$64,000.00
Sales	Manager	$48,750.00
Sales	Secretary	$87,000.00

Record: 1 of 5

Creating a Query in Design View

Although the Simple Query Wizard is a convenient method for quickly extracting information from a table, its use is somewhat limited. In **Design view**, however, you can create a more sophisticated query—for example, one that displays selected fields of selected records, sorted by the entries in one or more fields.

To **create a query** (in **Design view**):

* In the Database window, select the appropriate **table**; or

  Open the **table** in **Datasheet view**.

* Expand the **New Object** button on the Application window toolbar, and select the **Query** option in the list that appears.
* In the New Query dialog box, make sure that the **Design View** option is selected. Then click on the **OK** button.
* In Design view of the Query window, select the **fields** that are to be included in the query results datasheet.
* Optionally, select a **sort order** for any field.
* Enter the **query condition(s)** under the appropriate field(s).

Notes

You can also display Design view of the Query window by double-clicking on the **Create query in Design view** option on the Queries panel of the Database window. In this case, you must add the relevant table (or tables) to the Query window.

To **run a query**:

* From the Query window (in Design view), choose the **Query**, **Run** command, or click on the **Run** button on the Application window toolbar; or
* In the Database window, select the **query name**, and click on the **Open** button on the Database window toolbar.

Objective

In this exercise, you will **create another query of the records in the Staff Details table**—this time in **Design view**. You will then **run the query**.

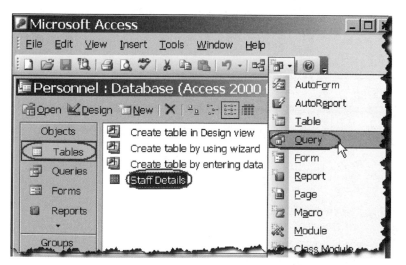

20.1

* **Make sure that the Staff Details table is selected on the Tables panel of the Database window.**

* **Click on the New Object button and select Query.**

20.2

The New Query dialog box is displayed.

- **Make sure that the Design View option is selected. Then click on the OK button.**

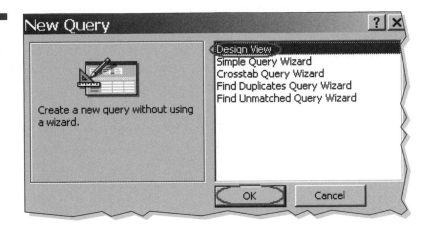

20.3

The Query window is displayed in Design view. You will now create a query that displays the records for employees in the Administration department. The listing will include only the LastName, FirstName, Salary and Dept fields and will be sorted in ascending order by last name.

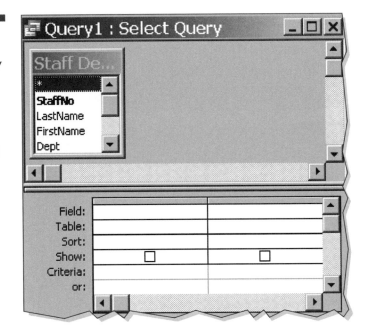

20.4

- **In the field list in the upper-left area of the window, double-click on LastName.**

The LastName field is entered into the Field row in the lower section of the window.

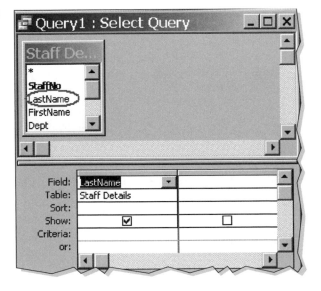

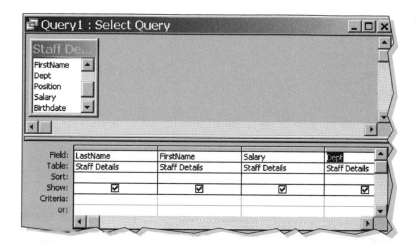

20.5

- **Using a procedure similar to that described above, add the following fields to the Field row (in the indicated order):**

  **FirstName
  Salary
  Dept**

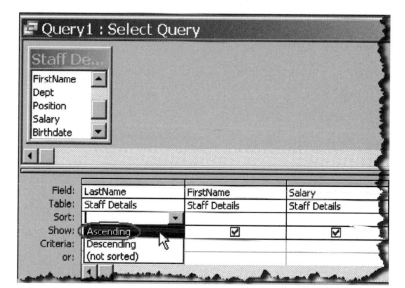

20.6

- **Click in the first Sort box (under the LastName field). Then click on the down arrow that appears.**

The box is expanded, and a list of options is displayed.

- **Click on Ascending.**

The sort field is selected. In this case, selected records will be sorted in ascending order by entries in the LastName field.

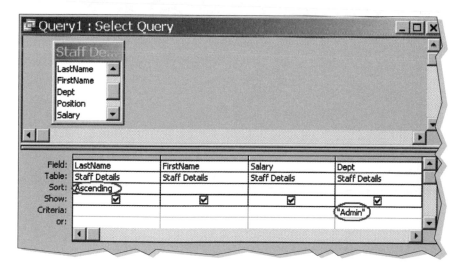

20.7

- **Click in the Criteria box (under the Dept field). Type:"Admin"**

The query condition is entered. The window should now appear as illustrated in the figure on the left.

NOTE: *Notice that a text condition must be enclosed in quotation marks. (These quotation marks are entered automatically by the program if you neglect to include them.)*

20.8

• **Click on the Save button.**

The Save As dialog box is displayed.

• **Type: Admin Dept**
  Choose the OK button.

20.9

The query is saved, and the dialog box is closed.

• **Click on the Run button on the Application window toolbar.**

20.10

The query is run and the selected records are displayed.

• **Click on the Close button on the Title bar of the Query window.**

	Last Name	First Name	Salary	Dept
▶	Adams	Kyle	$31,000	Admin
	Brown	Bill	$19,000	Admin
	Crisp	Helen	$19,500	Admin
	Potter	Peter	$24,000	Admin
	Thomas	Lisa	$23,750	Admin
	Wong	Lee	$27,500	Admin
*				

Record: ◀◀ ◀ 1 ▶ ▶◀ ▶* of 6

20.11

The query is closed, and the Database window is redisplayed. You will now run the Admin Dept query from this window.

• **On the Objects bar, click on Queries.**

• **Click on Admin Dept. Then click on the Open button on the Database window toolbar.**

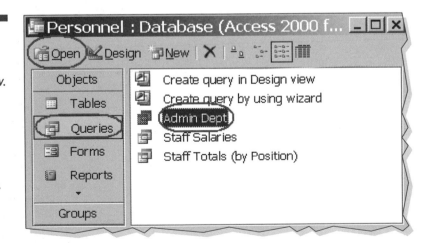

20.12

The query is run, and the selected records are once again displayed.

• **Close the query.**

Creating a Report

This section discusses the methods for **presenting Access data in hard copy form**. In it, you will learn how to:

• **Create a simple tabular report**
• **Create a grouped tabular report**.

Creating a Simple Tabular Report

An Access **report** is a custom layout that is used in printing records. While you can produce a hard copy of the information in a table or query by simply printing the datasheet of that table/query, creating a report is usually the preferred method since:

• The printout can include all or selected fields, arranged anyway you wish.
• Field entries can be grouped and/or sorted.
• Group totals, grand totals and percentages of totals can be calculated.
• Additional information, such as customized field captions, can appear.
• Different fonts and other print enhancements can be used

You can quickly create a simple report of all information in a table or query by letting the **AutoReport Wizard** generate it for you.
   To **create a report** (using the **AutoReport Wizard**):

• In the Database window, select the appropriate **table** or **query**; or

   Open the **table** or **query** in **Datasheet view**.

• Expand the **New Object** button on the Application window toolbar.
• In the list that appears, do one of the following:

   • Select the **AutoReport** option (to create a report in single-column format); or
   • Select the **Report** option. In the New Report dialog box, select either the **AutoReport: Columnar** option (to create a report in a single-column format that is different from the one created with the AutoReport option) or the **AutoReport: Tabular** option (to create a report in column/row format). Then click on the **OK** button.

Objective

In this exercise, you will **use the AutoReport Wizard to create a simple tabular report**.

21.1

- **Make sure that the Staff Details table is selected under Tables Objects panel.**

- **Click on the down arrow at the right side of the New Object button.**

- **Click on Report.**

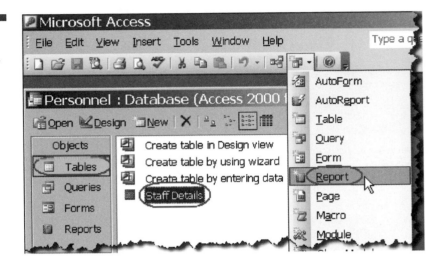

21.2

The New Report dialog box is displayed.

- **Click on AutoReport: Tabular. Make sure that Staff Details appears in the box below. Then click on the OK button.**

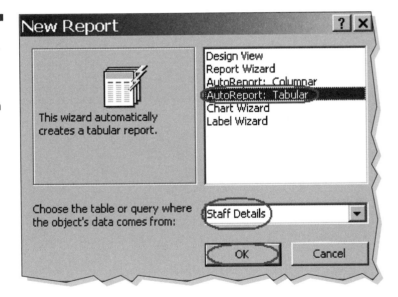

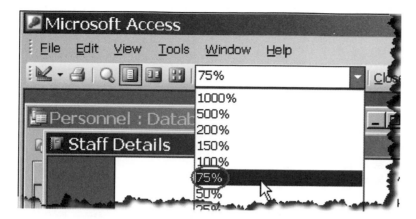

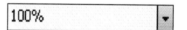

The report is generated, and after a few moments, it is displayed in Print Preview.

- **Point to any area of the report, and click the mouse button.**

A full-page view of the report is displayed.

- **Point to any area of the report, and click the mouse button again.**

The enlarged view of the report is redisplayed.

- **Click on the down arrow at the right side of the Zoom box on the Application window toolbar.**

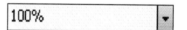

The box is expanded, and a list of magnification options is displayed.

- **Click on 75% or type 75.**

21.4

The report is displayed at 75% of the default (100%) view.

- **Click on the Print button.**

The report is printed.

- **Click on the Close button on the Title bar of the Report window.**

You are asked if you want to save the report design.

- **Click on the No button.**

The report is closed, and the Database window is redisplayed.

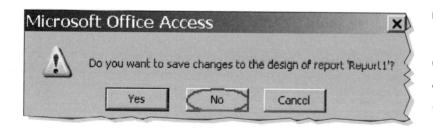

Creating a Grouped Tabular Report

Although the AutoReport Wizard is a convenient method for generating a quick report, there may be times when you will want to present your data in a more sophisticated manner. Using the **Report Wizard**, you can create a report that includes all or selected fields. The information can be grouped and/or sorted and can appear in a number of different layouts and styles.

To **create a report** (using the **Report Wizard**):

- In the Database window, select the appropriate **table** or **query**; or

  Open the **table** or **query** in **Datasheet view**.

- Expand the **New Object** button on the Application window toolbar, and select the **Report** option in the list that appears.
- In the New Report dialog box, select the **Report Wizard** option. Then click on the **OK** button.
- Follow the directions in the Report Wizard dialog boxes that appear. In these dialog boxes, you specify the fields that are to be included on the report, the way records are to be grouped and/or sorted, and the layout, style and title for the report. To move from one dialog box to the next, click on the **Next >** button. In the last dialog box, click on the **Finish** button to complete the operation.

Notes

You can also access the Report Wizard by double-clicking on the **Create report by using wizard** option on the Reports panel of the Database window.

Objective

In this exercise, you will **use the Report Wizard to create a grouped tabular report**.

22.1

Notice that the New Object button currently displays the Report icon since Report was the last option selected in the New Object list. Therefore, you can redisplay the New Report dialog box by simply clicking on this button. (The alternate method of expanding the New Object button and selecting Report in the list of options can, of course, be used as well.)

- **Make sure that the Staff Details table is selected under Tables Objects panel.**

- **Click on the New Object button, and select report.**

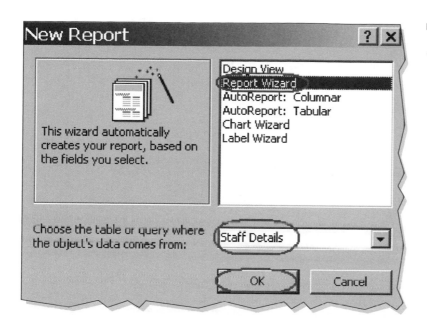

- **Click on Report Wizard. Then click on the OK button.**

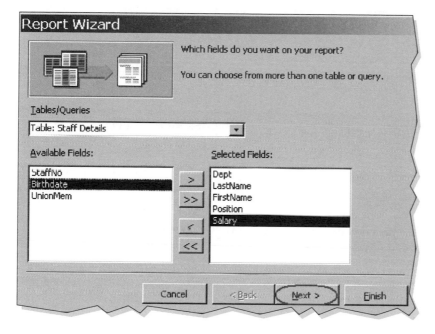

The first Report Wizard dialog box is displayed. Notice that the fields of the Staff Details table are listed in the Available Fields box.

- **In the Available Fields box, double-click on the following fields (in the indicated order):**

  Dept
  LastName
  FirstName
  Position
  Salary

- **Click on the Next > button.**

22.4

The next Report Wizard dialog box is displayed. You are prompted to specify any grouping levels.

- **In the field list, double-click on Dept.**

The group field is selected.

- **Click on the Next > button.**

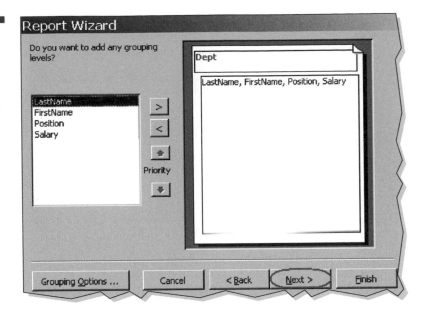

22.5

The next Report Wizard dialog box is displayed. You are prompted to specify the sort order and any summary information for detail records. You can select up to four sort fields. In this report, however, you will use only one sort field.

- **Click on the down arrow to the right of the first (upper) list box, and then click on LastName in the list of field names that appears.**

The sort field is selected.

NOTE: You can change the default sort order (ascending) to descending by clicking on the Ascending button to the right of the sort field. In this case, however, you will accept the default sort order.

- **Click on the Next > button.**

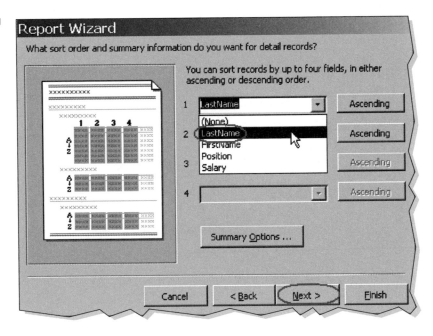

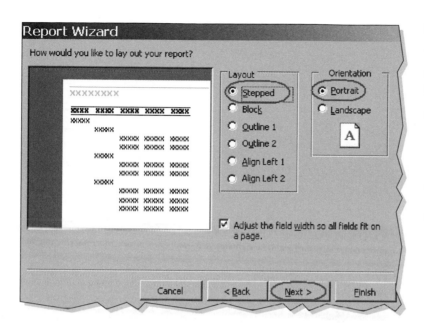

22.6

The next Report Wizard dialog box is displayed. You are prompted to specify a layout for the report.

- **Select the Stepped option and the Portrait option if either or both are not currently selected.**

The layout is specified.

- **Click on the Next > button.**

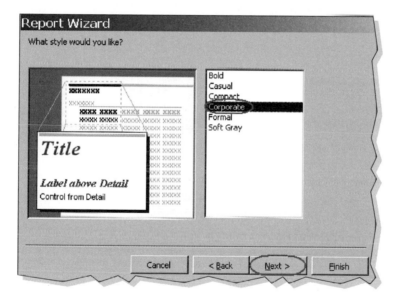

22.7

The next Report Wizard dialog box is displayed. You are prompted to specify a style for the report.

- **Select the Corporate option if it is not currently selected.**

The style is specified.

- **Click on the Next > button.**

22.8

The last Report Wizard dialog box is displayed. You are prompted to enter a title for the report.

- **Type: Staff Listing**

The title is entered.

- **Make sure that the Preview the report option is selected. Then click on the Finish button.**

22.9

The report is generated and is displayed in Print Preview.

NOTE: *A report created with the Report Wizard is automatically saved under the same name as the report title (in this case, Staff Listing).*

- **Click on the Print button and then close the report.**

The report is printed.

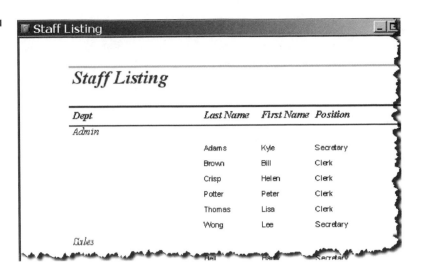

Displaying Help Information

If you encounter a problem or just need additional information while using Access, there are a number of ways in which you can obtain help.

The program itself includes an extensive **Help system**, which can be accessed in the following ways:

- By choosing the **Help, Microsoft Office Access Help** command or by clicking on the **Microsoft Office Access Help** button on the Application window toolbar. Doing this displays the Access Help task pane in which you enter one or more keywords and click on the **Start searching** button.
- By entering a request in the **Type a question for help** box and by pressing [**ENTER**].

MICROSOFT OFFICE ACCESS HELP BUTTON / TYPE A QUESTION FOR HELP BOX

You can also get help:

- By clicking on the **Table of Contents** option in the Access Help task pane. Doing this displays a list of Help topics in a table of contents format.
- By clicking on the **Connect to Microsoft Office Online** option in the Access Help task pane. Doing this displays the Microsoft Office Online Web site (assuming you have access to the Internet).

Notes

1. The Microsoft Office Online Web site provides a number of resources for users of Microsoft Office products, including "how-to" articles to assist the user in performing various tasks, interactive training tutorials to help the user become more familiar with the programs he or she is running, and various downloads (for example, templates, clip art and product upgrades).

2. The Office Assistant, which is displayed by choosing the **Help, Show the Office Assistant** command, can provide tips and other helpful information as you work. When the Office Assistant has a tip, a light bulb will appear. To display the tip, simply click on this light bulb. To control the type of information the Office Assistant provides, click on the Office Assistant icon, and click on the **Options** button in the balloon that appears. Then, on the Options panel of the Office Assistant dialog box, select/deselect the relevant options, and click on the **OK** button.

Objective

In this exercise, you will **access the Access Help system and display help information for various topics**.

23.1

• **Click on the Microsoft Office Access Help button on the Application window toolbar.**

The Access Help task pane is displayed.

• **Type: Enter a record**

• **Click on the Start searching** 🡒 **button.**

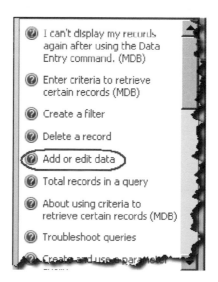

23.2

• **A list of topics is displayed in the Search Results task pane.**

• **Click on Add or edit data.**

▬ 23.3 ▬

The Microsoft Office Access Help window is opened, displaying a list of subtopics.

- **In the list of subtopics, click on Add or edit data in a datasheet or form.**

The subtopic is expanded, and instructions for performing the operation are displayed

- **In the help information, click on the words Form view (which appears in blue).**

The definition of "Form view" is displayed.

- **Click again on the words Form view.**

The definition of "Form view" no longer appears.

- **Click on Show All (in the upper-right corner of the Microsoft Office Access Help window).**

All subtopics are expanded.

▬ 23.4 ▬

NOTE: *You can print the current help information by using the **Print** button on the toolbar of the Microsoft Office Access Help window.*

- **Scroll through the help information by clicking on the down arrow on the scroll bar of the Microsoft Office Access Help window.**

- **Click on the Title bar of the Application window.**

NOTE: *Click in an empty area of the Title bar; do not click on any of the window sizing buttons.*

The Application window is reactivated.

- **Click on the Close button on the Title bar of the Microsoft Office Access Help window.**

The Microsoft Office Access Help window is closed, and the Application window is expanded. You will now access the Help system through the Type a question for help box.

- **Click in the Type a question for help box (which appears in the upper-right corner of the Application window).**

- **Type: Print a datasheet Press [ENTER].**

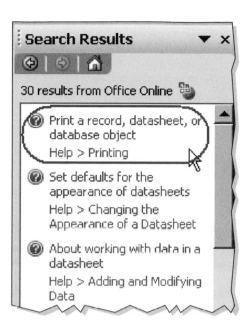

23.5

A list of topics is displayed in the Search Results task pane.

NOTE: Notice that you did not enter an actual question in the Type a question for help box. Instead, you simply entered the action "Print a datasheet." (You could have entered the question "How do I print a datasheet?" Doing so, however, would have displayed the same list of topics.)

- **Click on Print a record, datasheet, or database object.**

The Microsoft Office Access Help window is reopened, displaying a list of subtopics.

- **In the list of subtopics, click on Print the datasheet of a table, query, or form.**

The subtopic is expanded, and instructions for performing the operation are displayed.

- **Click on the Title bar of the Application window.**

The Application window is reactivated.

- **In the task pane, click on Preview a database object.**

Information for the selected topic appears in the Microsoft Office Access Help window.

- **Click on the Back button on the toolbar of the Microsoft Office Access Help window.**

The list of subtopics for the main topic "Print a record, datasheet, or database object" is redisplayed.

- **Click on the Close button on the Title bar of the Microsoft Office Access Help window.**

The Microsoft Office Access Help window is closed.

- **Click on the Close button at the top of the Search Results task pane.**

The task pane is closed.

Exiting from Access

When you are finished using Access, you can exit from the program either by choosing the **File**, **Exit** command or by clicking on the **Close** button on the Title bar of the Application window. If you have not saved changes in any database object, you will be prompted to indicate whether or not you wish to save those changes before exiting.

Objective

In this exercise, you will **exit from Access**.

- Choose the **File**, **Exit** command.

The program is exited, and the Windows desktop is redisplayed.
  Congratulations! You have completed the Case Study.

Conclusion

You have just completed **Microsoft Office Access 2003–Case Study 1**. In the case study, you were introduced to many techniques. To reinforce your understanding of these techniques, it is recommended that you read and work through it once again.

Further Practice

The following Case Study will give you the opportunity to review and practice many of the Access techniques you have learned.
  Assume that you are the secretary of a social club. You have decided to use Access to create a database to help you maintain membership records.

1. Create a **database** named **Club Data.mdb**.
2. In the Club Data database, use the **Table Wizard** to create a **table**, named **Member Details**, that includes the fields listed below. To determine the data type for each field, refer to step 3, which shows the records that are to be entered into the new table.

MemberNo, LastName, FirstName, Category, Fee, Activity

3. **Enter** the following **records** into the datasheet of the **Member Details table**:

Member No	Last Name	First Name	Category	Fee	Activity
I	Robinson	Roberta	Associate	$45.00	Tennis
2	Adams	Allen	Full	$100.00	Swimming
3	Potter	Polly	Associate	$45.00	Tennis
4	Brown	Barbara	Associate	$45.00	Golf
5	Hanson	Harry	Full	$100.00	Swimming
6	Miles	Marion	Associate	$45.00	Golf
7	Greenhill	Gary	Full	$100.00	Tennis
8	Turner	Terrilyn	Full	$100.00	Swimming
9	Jones	Jimmy	Associate	$45.00	Golf
10	Simmons	Steve	Full	$100.00	Golf

4. **Print** the **datasheet** of the table.

	MemberNo	LastName	FirstName	Category	Fee	Activity
	1	Robinson	Roberta	Associate	$45.00	Tennis
	2	Adams	Allen	Full	$100.00	Swimming
	3	Potter	Polly	Associate	$45.00	Tennis
	4	Brown	Barbara	Associate	$45.00	Golf
	5	Hanson	Harry	Full	$100.00	Swimming
	6	Miles	Marion	Associate	$45.00	Golf
	7	Greenhill	Gary	Full	$100.00	Tennis
	8	Turner	Terrilyn	Full	$100.00	Swimming
	9	Jones	Jimmy	Associate	$45.00	Golf
	10	Simmons	Steve	Full	$100.00	Golf
*	(AutoNumber)					

Member Details : Table

Record: 10 of 10

5. Using the **AutoForm Wizard,** create a **form** for the **Member Details table.** **Save** the **form** under the name of **Member Details.**

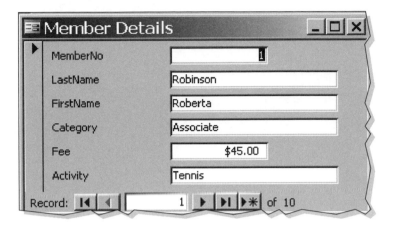

6. **Jimmy Jones** has stopped playing golf and has taken up **swimming.** **Harry Hanson** has stopped swimming and has taken up **tennis. Marion Miles** has become a **full** member and her fees are now **$100.00.** Using the **Member Details form, edit** the **records** for those individuals to update the field information.

7. Create a **query** that displays the records for members who play **tennis.** Include the **MemberNo, LastName, FirstName** and **Category** fields in the listing, and **sort** the records by **last name. Save** the **query** under the name of **All Tennis.**
8. **Run** the **query,** and **print** the **selected records.**

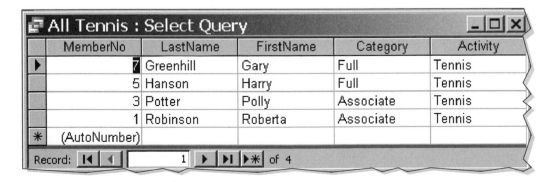

9. Create a **query** that displays the records for **full** category members who play **tennis**. Include the **MemberNo**, **LastName** and **FirstName** fields in the listing, and **sort** the records by **last name**. **Save** the **query** under the name of **Full Tennis**.

10. **Run** the **query**, and **print** the **selected records**.

Full Tennis : Select Query				
MemberNo	LastName	FirstName	Category	Activity
7	Greenhill	Gary	Full	Tennis
5	Hanson	Harry	Full	Tennis
(AutoNumber)				

Record: 1 of 2

11. Using the **Report Wizard**, create a **report**, named **Member Fees** that includes all fields of the **Member Details table** except MemberNo. **Group** the records by **category**, and **sort** them by **last** name.

12. **Print** the **report**.

Member Fees

Category	LastName	FirstName	Fee	Activity
Associate				
	Brown	Barbara	$45.00	Golf
	Jones	Jimmy	$45.00	Swimming
	Potter	Polly	$45.00	Tennis
	Robinson	Roberta	$45.00	Tennis
Full				
	Adams	Allen	$100.00	Swimming
	Greenhill	Gary	$100.00	Tennis
	Hanson	Harry	$100.00	Tennis
	Miles	Marion	$100.00	Golf
	Simmons	Steve	$100.00	Golf
	Turner	Terrilyn	$100.00	Swimming

13. **Close** the **database file**.

MS Access 2003
Case Study 2

After successfully completing this case study, you should be able to:

- Create and display multiple tables on the Access desktop
- Add Primary Key in tables
- Create a relationship between two tables in a database
- Display and use a subdatasheet
- Create a query to extract information from multiple tables
- Create a query to generate summary information
- Create a crosstab query
- Create a query to find unmatched records in a table
- Include multiple conditions in a query
- Create a parameter query and run the query

Case Study 2—MS Access 2003

Your boss is very happy with your first project performance (Case Study I). He wants you work on another assignment with him. In the new assignment, you will create multiple tables (Employee list, Absences) and relate them through common fields. You will also create several queries that extract information from related tables.

Ref No	Emp No	Away	Returned	Reason
1	109	2/2/2004	2/6/2004	Flu
2	105	2/11/2004	2/12/2004	Allergy
3	108	2/20/2004	2/23/2004	Cold
4	105	3/2/2004	3/4/2004	Bronchitis
5	102	3/11/2004	3/16/2004	Flu
6	106	3/22/2004	3/24/2004	Migraine
7	104	3/25/2004	3/26/2004	Backache
8	110	3/30/2004	4/2/2004	Flu
9	103	4/6/2004	4/8/2004	Cold
10	105	4/12/2004	4/16/2004	Tonsillitis
11	108	4/23/2004	4/26/2004	Bronchitis
12	102	4/28/2004	4/29/2004	Toothache
13	101	5/3/2004	5/5/2004	Allergy

Record: |◄ ◄ 1 ► ►| ►* of 13

ABSENCES TABLE

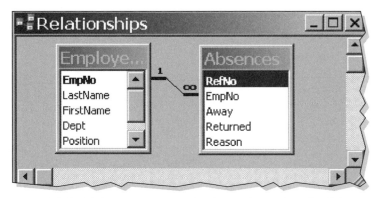

EMPLOYEE LIST AND ABSENCES TABLES IN ONE-TO-MANY RELATIONSHIP

Employee List : Table

	Emp No	Last Name	First Name	Dept	Position	Salary
⊟	101	Smith	Sarah	Admin	Manager	$54,000

	Ref No	Away	Returned	Reason
▶	13	5/3/2004	5/5/2004	Allergy
✱	(AutoNumber)			

	Emp No	Last Name	First Name	Dept	Position	Salary
⊞	102	Benson	Bill	Sales	Clerk	$25,200
⊞	103	Fry	Fred	Admin	Clerk	$21,900
⊞	104	Thomas	Tina	Admin	Secretary	$28,700
⊞	105	Garcia	Gary	Sales	Manager	$48,000
⊞	106	Davies	Diana	Admin	Clerk	$23,400
⊞	107	Peterson	Paul	Sales	Secretary	$27,300
⊞	108	Lewis	Lenny	Sales	Secretary	$25,900
⊞	109	Jones	Julie	Admin	Clerk	$22,600

Record: 1 of 1

EMPLOYEE LIST TABLE RELATED TO ABSENCES TABLE

Absences List : Select Query

	Ref No	Emp No	Last Name	Dept	Away	Returned	Re
▶	13	101	Smith	Admin	5/3/2004	5/5/2004	Allergy
	5	102	Benson	Sales	3/11/2004	3/16/2004	Flu
	12	102	Benson	Sales	4/28/2004	4/29/2004	Tooth:
	9	103	Fry	Admin	4/6/2004	4/8/2004	Cold
	7	104	Thomas	Admin	3/25/2004	3/26/2004	Backa
	2	105	Garcia	Sales	2/11/2004	2/12/2004	Allergy
	4	105	Garcia	Sales	3/2/2004	3/4/2004	Bronc

QUERY OF INFORMATION IN MULTIPLE TABLES (EMPLOYEE LIST AND ABSENCES)

Absent on/after 4/1/2004 : Sel...

	Dept	Last Name	Away	Reason
▶	Admin	Fry	4/6/2004	Cold
	Admin	Smith	5/3/2004	Allergy
	Sales	Benson	4/28/2004	Toothache
	Sales	Garcia	4/12/2004	Tonsillitis
	Sales	Lewis	4/23/2004	Bronchitis
✱				

Record: 1 of 5

**QUERY OF INFORMATION IN MULTIPLE TABLES
(EMPLOYEES ABSENT ON OR AFTER 4/1/2004)**

Creating a New Database

With Access, you can create a new database in one of two ways:

• By creating a **blank database** and by adding the necessary tables, forms, reports and other database objects to the database.

- By using the **Database Wizard** to create in one operation the necessary tables, queries, forms and reports for a specific type of database.

To **create a new blank database**:

- Display the New File task pane by choosing the **File, New** command, by clicking on the **New** button on the Application window toolbar, or by clicking on the **Create a new file** option in the Getting Started task pane.
- In the task pane, select the **Blank database** option.
- In the File New Database dialog box, enter a **name** (and, if necessary, a **new storage location**) for the database file. Then click on the **Create** button.

To **create a new database using the Database Wizard**:

- Display the New File task pane by choosing the **File, New** command, or by clicking on the **New** button on the Application window toolbar, or by clicking on the **Create a new file** option in the Getting Started task pane.
- In the task pane, select the **On my computer** option.
- On the Databases panel of the Templates dialog box, select the **icon** for the type of database you wish to create. Then click on the **OK** button.
- In the File New Database dialog box, enter a **name** (and, if necessary, a **new storage location**) for the database file. Then click on the **Create** button.
- Follow the directions in the Database Wizard dialog boxes that appear. To move from one dialog box to the next, click on the **Next >** button. In the last dialog box, click on the **Finish** button to complete the operation.

Objective

In this exercise, you will **create a new blank database**. This database will be used to store employee information.

 1.1

- **Click on the Start button on the Windows taskbar.**

- **Point to All Programs (if you are running Windows XP) or to Programs (if you are running Windows 2000).**

- **Point to Microsoft Office on the menu.**

- **Click on Microsoft Office Access 2003 on the submenu.**

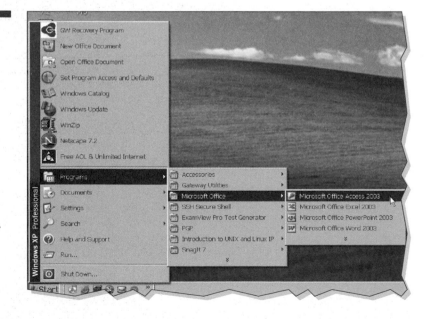

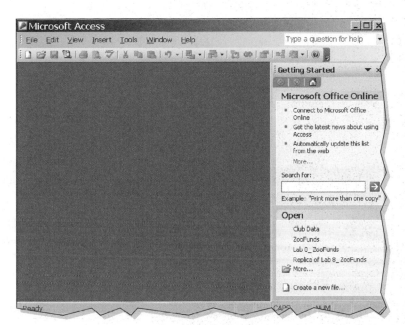

1.2

Access is started, and the Access Application window is displayed.

- **If the Access Application window is not maximized, click on the Maximize button on the Title bar of the window.**

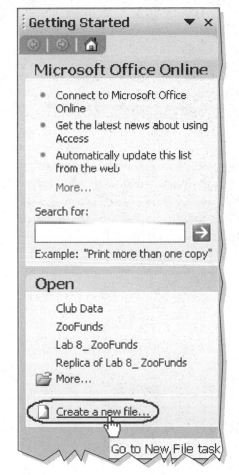

1.3

- **At the bottom of the Getting Started task pane, click on Create a new file.**

1.4

- **In the task pane under New, click on Blank database.**

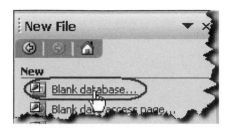

1.5

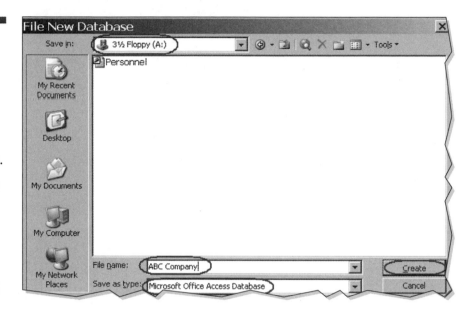

The File New Database dialog box is displayed.

- **Type: ABC Company**

The database filename is entered.

NOTE: *The program will add the default extension (mdb) to the filename.*

- **Make sure that 3½ Floppy (A:) appears in the Save in box.**

- **Click on the Create button.**

NOTE: *You can "choose" a button either by clicking on it or by pressing [ENTER]. The dialog box is closed, and the Database window is displayed.*

Working with Multiple Tables

This section discusses the methods for **working with more than one table on the Access desktop**. In it, you will learn how to:

- Create **multiple** tables.
- Set a **Primary Key** for a table.
- **Create** a **relationship** between **two tables** in a database.
- **Display** and **use** a **subdatasheet**.

Creating Two New Tables and Setting Their Primary Keys

After creating a database file, the next step in setting up a database is that of creating the table or tables for storing your information. This is accomplished from the Database window, which currently appears on the Access desktop.

A **primary key** is a field that uniquely identifies each record in a table. Records, by default, are displayed in primary key order.

In using the Table Wizard to create a new table, you can have the wizard set a primary key for you. If you wish to set a primary key yourself, or if you wish to reset the primary key set by the wizard, you can easily do so.

To **set a primary key for a table**:

- With the table displayed in Design view, select the **primary key field** (by clicking anywhere in the row that defines the field).
- Click on the **Primary Key** button on the Application window toolbar.

Notes

1. If a table does not include a field with unique entries (for example, an AutoNumber field), you can specify two or more fields as the primary key as long as the combined entries in those fields are unique. To select multiple fields in Design view of the Table window, click on the **row selectors** (to the left of the Field Name column) while holding down [**CTRL**].
2. To reset a primary key, follow the procedure described above.

Objective

In this exercise, you will **use Design view to create two tables**. Also, you will **set a primary key for both tables**.

2.1

- **Click on the New** New **button on the Database window toolbar.**

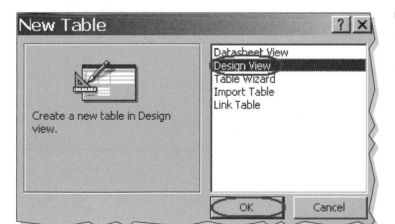

2.2

The New Table dialog box is displayed.

- **Click on Design View. Then click on the OK button.**

2.3

The first Table Wizard dialog box is displayed. You will use this dialog box to select the type of table you wish to create and to select the fields that are to be included in the table.

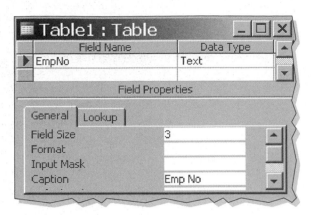

- **In the Design view of the table window, you will add the following field, its respective Data Type and field property:**

Field Name: EmpNo
Data Type: Text
Field size: 3
Caption: Emp No

2.4

- **Using the procedure above, add the following fields, their respective Data Types and field properties:**

Field Name: LastName
Data Type: Text
Field size: 15
Caption: Last Name
Required: Yes

Field Name: FirstName
Data Type: Text
Field size: 12
Caption: First Name

Field Name: Dept
Data Type: Text
Field size: 10
Default Value: "Admin"

Field Name: Position
Data Type: Text
Field size: 15
Default Value: "Clerk"

Field Name: Salary
Data Type: Currency
Decimal Places: 0

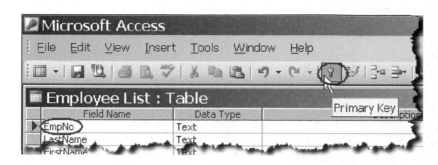

2.5

- **In the Field Name column, click on EmpNo.**

You will now assign primary key status to this field.

- **Click on the Primary Key button on the Application window toolbar.**

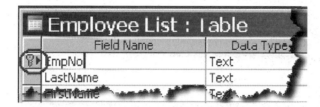

2.6

A small key appears to the left of the field name, indicating that the field is the table's primary key.

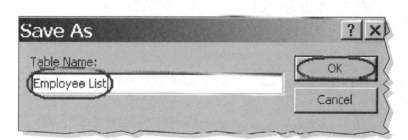

2.7

- **Click on the Save button.**

The Save As dialog box is displayed.

- **Type: Employee List**

  Choose the OK button.

2.8

The table is saved, and the dialog box is closed.

- **Click on the View button on the Application window toolbar.**

NOTE: *Click on the button itself, not on the down arrow at the right side of the button.*

2.9

- Enter the records in Employee List table as shown in the figure on the right.

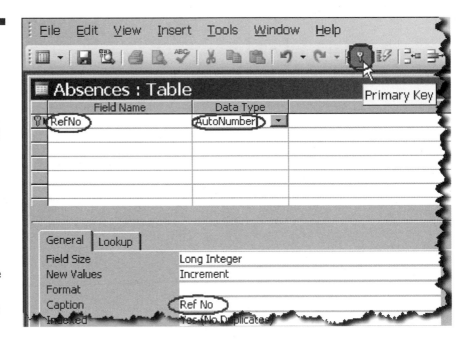

Emp No	Last Name	First Name	Dept	Position	Salary
101	Smith	Sarah	Admin	Manager	$54,000
102	Benson	Bill	Sales	Clerk	$25,200
103	Fry	Fred	Admin	Clerk	$21,900
104	Thomas	Tina	Admin	Secretary	$28,700
105	Garcia	Gary	Sales	Manager	$48,000
106	Davies	Diana	Admin	Clerk	$23,400
107	Peterson	Paul	Sales	Secretary	$27,300
108	Lewis	Lenny	Sales	Secretary	$25,900
109	Jones	Julie	Admin	Clerk	$22,600
110	Hartley	Harriet	Sales	Clerk	$23,000
111	Nicholson	Norm	Admin	Secretary	$26,000
			Admin	Clerk	

Record: 12 of 12

2.10

- **Click on the Save button.**
- **Close Employee List table.**
- **Using a procedure similar to that described above, create a new table called Absences and add the following field, its respective Data Type and field property:**

  Field Name: RefNo
  Data Type: AutoNumber
  Caption: Ref No

- **Click on the RefNo field in the Field Name column and click on the Primary Key button on the application window toolbar for this field.**

Absences : Table

Field Name	Data Type
RefNo	AutoNumber

Primary Key

General | Lookup

Field Size	Long Integer
New Values	Increment
Format	
Caption	Ref No
Indexed	Yes (No Duplicates)

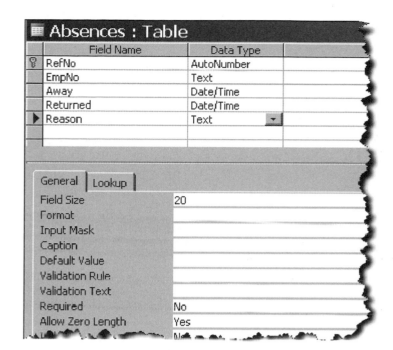

2.11

- **Using the procedure above, add the following fields, their respective Data Types and field properties:**

  Field Name: EmpNo
  Data Type: Text
  Field size: 3
  Caption: Emp No
  Required: Yes

  Field Name: Away
  Data Type: Date/Time
  Format: Short Date
  Input Mask: 99/99/0000;0

  Field Name: Returned
  Data Type: Date/Time
  Format: Short Date
  Input Mask: 99/99/0000;0

  Field Name: Reason
  Data Type: Text
  Field size: 20

2.12

- **Enter the records in Absences table as listed on the left.**

- **Click on the Save button.**

- **Close Absences List table.**

Ref No	Emp No	Away	Returned	Reason
1	109	2/2/2004	2/6/2004	Flu
2	105	2/11/2004	2/12/2004	Allergy
3	108	2/20/2004	2/23/2004	Cold
4	105	3/2/2004	3/4/2004	Bronchitis
5	102	3/11/2004	3/16/2004	Flu
6	108	3/22/2004	3/24/2004	Migraine
7	104	3/25/2004	3/26/2004	Backache
8	110	3/30/2004	4/2/2004	Flu
9	103	4/6/2004	4/8/2004	Cold
10	105	4/12/2004	4/16/2004	Tonsillitis
11	108	4/23/2004	4/26/2004	Bronchitis
12	102	4/28/2004	4/29/2004	Toothache
13	101	5/3/2004	5/5/2004	Allergy
	(AutoNumber)			

Record: 13 of 13

Creating a Relationship Between Two Tables in a Database

Access is a **relational** database management program, which means that the various tables stored in a database can be related through common fields.

With Access, you can create three types of relationships:

One-to-many In this, the most common type of relationship, entries in one field (the common field) in one table (Table 1) must be unique, but may appear any number of times in the matching field in another table (Table 2). The common field in Table 1 is usually that table's **primary key**. However, it can also be any field that has a **unique index**—that is, a field with an **Indexed** property set to **Yes (No Duplicates)**. (In a one-to-many relationship, the common field in Table 2 is called the **foreign key**.)

Many-to-many   In this type of relationship, common field entries may appear any number of times in both Table 1 and Table 2. A many-to-many relationship is actually two one-to-many relationships with a third table (called the **junction table**).

One-to-one   In this type of relationship, common field entries must be unique in both Table 1 and Table 2.

To **create a relationship between two tables in a database**:

- From the Database window, choose the **Tools**, **Relationships** command, or click on the **Relationships** button on the Application window toolbar.
- In the Relationships window, choose the **Relationships**, **Show Table** command, or click on the **Show Table** button on the Application window toolbar. (This step is unnecessary if you are creating a relationship for the first time in the database since the Show Table dialog box is displayed automatically when you select the Tools, Relationships command or click on the Relationships button.)
- In the Show Table dialog box, select the **tables** that are to be related (clicking on the **Add** button after selecting each). Then click on the **Close** button to redisplay the Relationships window.
- **Drag** the **common field** from the **field list** of one table to the **field list** of the related table.
- In the Edit Relationships dialog box, optionally **set/reset** any of the **relationship options**.

RELATIONSHIPS / SHOW TABLE BUTTONS

- Click on the **Create** button.

Objective

In this exercise, you will **create a one-to-many relationship between two tables in a database**.

    You will relate the Employee List table to the Absences table. These tables share the common field, EmpNo. When related, Employee List will be the table on the "one" side of the relationship since it contains unique values in the common field (the primary key of the table); Absences will be the table on the "many" side of the relationship since it contains duplicate values in the common field.

3.1

- **Click on the Relationships button on the Application window toolbar.**

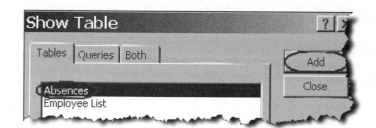

3.2

The Relationships window is opened, and the Show Table dialog box is displayed.

- **Click on Employee List. Then click on the Add button.**

The Employee List table is added to the Relationships window.

- **Click on Absences. Then click on the Add button.**

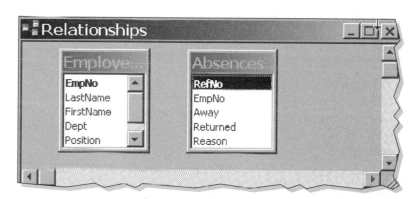

3.3

The Absences table is added to the Relationships window.

- **Click on the Close button.**

The Show Table dialog box is closed.

3.4

- **In the Employee List field list, point to EmpNo. Press and hold down the mouse button, and drag this field to EmpNo in the Absences field list. Then release the mouse button.**

The Edit Relationships dialog box is displayed, listing the common field, EmpNo (as illustrated in the figure on the right).

- **Click on Enforce Referential Integrity.**

The option is selected.

NOTE: *Selecting the Enforce Referential Integrity option ensures that a record will not be entered into the related table (in this case, Absences) unless a matching record exists in the primary table (in this case, Employee List). Normally, it also prevents you from either changing a primary key field in the primary table or deleting a record from the primary table when a matching record exists in the related table. You can, however, override these restrictions by selecting the **Cascade Update Related Fields** option (which updates corresponding entries in the related table when you change a primary key field entry in the primary table) and/or the **Cascade Delete Related Records** option (which deletes related records in the related table when you delete a record from the primary table).*

- **Click on the Create button.**

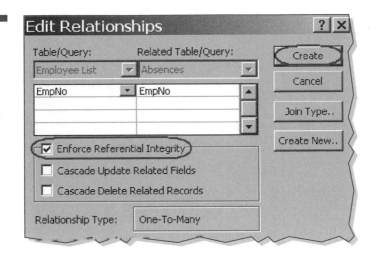

3.5

The relationship is created, and the common fields are connected by a relationship line.

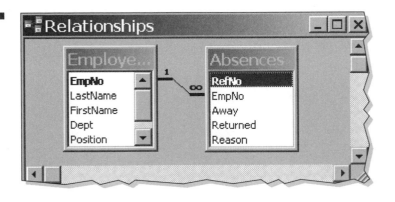

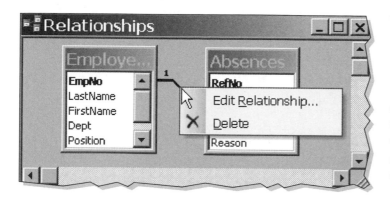

3.6

- **Point to the center of the relationship line, and right-click the mouse button.**

A shortcut menu is displayed. Notice that this menu includes options for editing the relationship (redisplaying the Edit Relationships dialog box) and for deleting the relationship.

- **Click in any empty area of the Relationships window.**

The menu is closed.

- **Click on the Save button.**

*Click on the **Close** button on the Title bar of the Relationships window.*

Displaying and Using a Subdatasheet

When you establish a one-to-many relationship between two tables, Access creates a **subdatasheet** in Table 1 (the table on the "one" side of the relationship). This subdatasheet shows the associated information in Table 2 (the table on the "many" side of the relationship) for each record in Table 1. A new column is added to the left of the first field in Table 1, providing a means of displaying and hiding the subdatasheets.

To **display the subdatasheet for a single record**:

- Click on the **expand indicator** (which displays a **plus sign**) to the left of the appropriate record.

To **hide the subdatasheet for a single record**:

- Click again on the **expand indicator** (which displays a **minus sign**).

To **display the subdatasheet for all records**:

- Choose the **Format, Subdatasheet, Expand All** command.

To **hide the subdatasheet for all records**:

- Choose the **Format, Subdatasheet, Collapse All** command.

Notes

1. The program also creates a subdatasheet for both tables, by default, when you establish a one-to-one relationships between two tables.

2. If a table has a one-to-many relationship with two or more tables, clicking on the expand indicator displays the **Insert Subdatasheet dialog box** in which you select the table that is to provide the subdatasheet information. You can also display this dialog box and use it to add a subdatasheet to any table or query by using the **Insert**, **Subdatasheet** command.

3. You can remove a subdatasheet from a table by choosing the **Format**, **Subdatasheet**, **Remove** command. Doing so does not affect any relationship that has been established between tables.

Objective

In this exercise, you will **display and hide the subdatasheet for records in the Employee List table**. You will then **use this subdatasheet to edit a record in the related Absences table**.

- **Open the Employee List table.**

- **Click on the expand indicator (which displays a plus sign) to the left of record #1 (for employee Smith).**

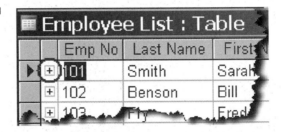

4.2

The subdatasheet for the first record is displayed. Notice that it includes the related information in the Absences table.

- **Click again on the expand indicator (which now displays a minus sign) to the left of record #1.**

The subdatasheet is hidden.

- **Click on the expand indicator for record #2 (for employee Benson). Then click on the expand indicator for record #4 (for employee Thomas).**

The subdatasheet for each record is displayed.

- **Click again on the expand indicators for record #2 and record #4.**

The subdatasheet for each record is hidden.

- **Close the table.**

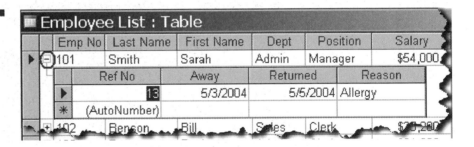

Intermediate Query Techniques

You should be familiar with the methods for creating and running simple Access queries. This section discusses **additional query techniques**. In it, you will learn how to:

- **Create** a **query** to **extract information** from **multiple tables**.
- **Create** a **query** to **generate summary information**.
- **Create** a **Crosstab query**.
- **Create** a **query** to **find unmatched records** in a table.
- **Include multiple conditions** in a query.
- **Create a Parameter query.**

Creating a Query to Extract Information from Multiple Tables

A query can extract and display information not only from a single table, but from multiple tables as well, assuming those tables contain related information.

To **create a query to extract information from multiple tables**:

- With the **Queries** panel of the Database window displayed, click on the **New** button on the Database window toolbar.
- In the New Query dialog box, make sure that the **Design View** option is selected. Then click on the **OK** button.
- In the Show Table dialog box, select the **tables** that are to be included in the query (clicking on the **Add** button after selecting each). Then click on the **Close** button to display the Query window in Design view.
- Specify the **fields** that are to appear in the listing, the **sort order** and the **query condition(s)** in the usual way.

If you have established a relationship between two tables, that relationship will be indicated in the Query window. If you have not established a relationship (and Access cannot determine the relationship), you must join the tables before running the query.

To **join two tables in the Query window**:

- **Drag the common field** from the **field list** of one table to the **field list** of the related table.

Objective

In this exercise, you will **create a query that extracts information from two related tables**. This exercise also demonstrates the methods for **reformatting a query datasheet**.

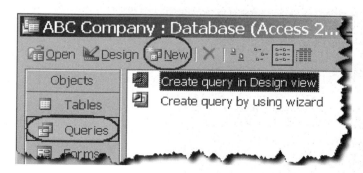

5.1

- **Make sure that the ABC Company database is opened.**
- **Display the Queries panel of the Database window.**
- **Click on the New button on the Database window toolbar.**

5.2

The New Query dialog box is displayed.

- **Make sure that the Design View option is selected. Then click on the OK button.**

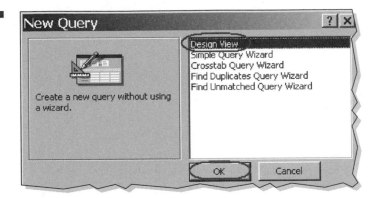

5.3

The Query window is opened, and the Show Table dialog box is displayed.

- **Double-click on Absences.**

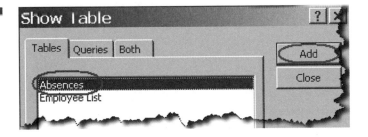

5.4

The Absences table is added to the Query window.

- **Double-click on Employee List.**

The Employee List table is added to the Query window.

- **Click on the Close button.**

The dialog box is closed. The Query window appears. Notice that the two tables are linked by their common field, EmpNo, since a relationship was previously established between the tables.

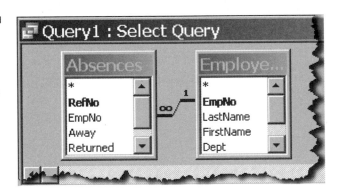

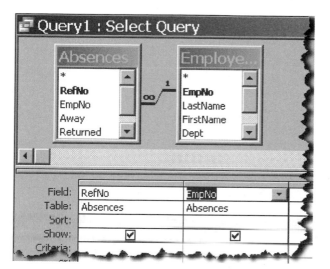

5.5

- **In the Absences field list, double-click on the following fields (in the indicated order):**

  RefNo
  EmpNo

The fields are added to the Field row.

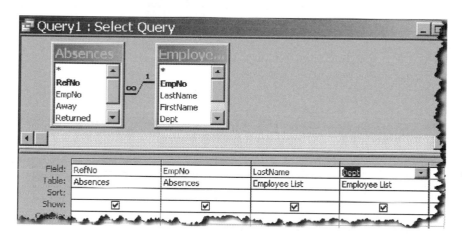

5.6

- **In the Employee List field list, double-click on the following fields (in the indicated order):**

  LastName
  Dept

The additional fields are added to the Field row.

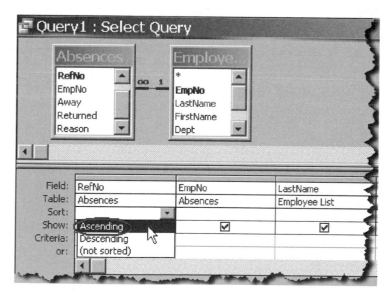

5.7

- **In the Absences field list, double-click on the following fields (in the indicated order):**

  Away
  Returned
  Reason

The additional fields are added to the Field row.

- **Click in the first Sort box (under the RefNo field). Then click on the down arrow that appears.**

NOTE: *If you click near the right edge of the Sort box, it will expand automatically. (In this case, you will not need to click on the down arrow.)*

- **Click on Ascending.**

5.8

- **Click on the Save button.**

The Save As dialog box is displayed.

- **Type: Absences List
  Choose the OK button.**

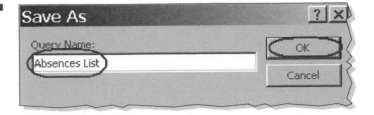

5.9

The query name is entered, and the dialog box is closed.

You will now run the query.

- **Click on the Run** ![Run button] **button on the Application window toolbar.**

The query is run, and the selected information is displayed. You will now reformat the query datasheet.

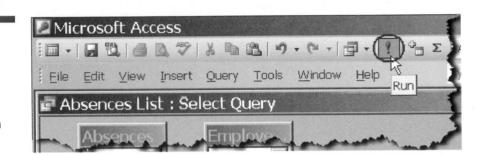

5.10

- **Choose Format, Datasheet command.**

The Datasheet Formatting dialog box is displayed.

- **Expand the Background Color box, and click on the Silver option.**

A new background color for the datasheet is selected.

- **Expand the Gridline Color box, and click on the White option.**

A new gridline color for the datasheet is selected.

- **Under Gridlines Shown, click on Vertical to deselect the option.**

The datasheet will not display vertical gridlines.

- **Click on the OK button.**

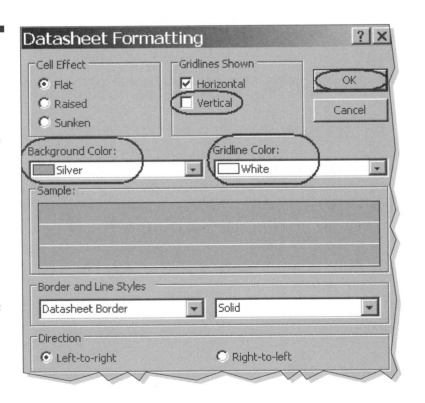

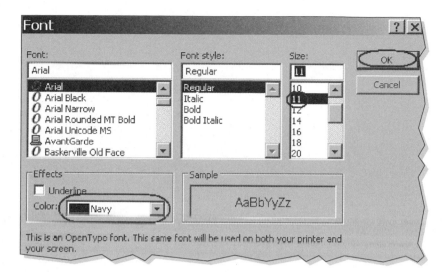

5.11

The dialog box is closed.

- **Choose the Format, Font command.**

The Font dialog box is displayed.

- **In the Size box, click on 11.**

A new font size for the datasheet entries is selected.

- **Expand the Color box, and click on the Navy option.**

A new font color for the datasheet entries is selected.

- **Click on the OK button.**

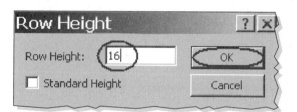

5.12

The dialog box is closed. You will now increase the vertical separation between records by increasing the row height.

- **Choose the Format, Row Height command**

The Row Height dialog box is displayed.

- **Type: 16**

Click on the OK button.

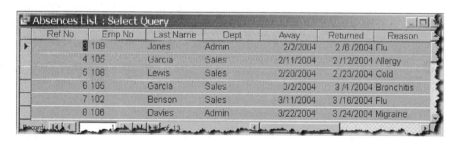

5.13

The new row height is entered, and the dialog box is closed.

- **Click on the Save button and then Close the Absences List query.**

Creating a Query to Generate Summary Information

Although queries are generally used to extract specific entries from a table, they can also be used to generate **summary information** for records in a table. The following **aggregate functions** can be applied either to records as a whole or to records grouped by entries in a particular field:

Function:	Computes:
Sum	The total of values in a field
Avg	The average of values in a field
Min	The smallest value in a field
Max	The largest value in a field
Count	The number of values in a field
StDev	The standard deviation of values in a field
Var	The variance of values in a field

To **create a query to generate summary information**:

- With the Query window displayed in Design view, add the **field(s)** that is/are to be **summarized** to the Field row. Optionally, add the **field** by which records are to be **grouped**.
- Choose the **View**, **Totals** command, or click on the **Totals** button on the Application window toolbar. (Doing this adds a Total row to the Query window.)
- Enter the appropriate **aggregate function(s)** into the Total row.

$$\Sigma$$

TOTALS BUTTON

Objective

In this exercise, you will **create and run a query that generates summary information for records in a table**.

- **Select the Employee List table on the Tables panel of the Database window.**
- **Expand the New Object button, and click on Query in the list of objects.**

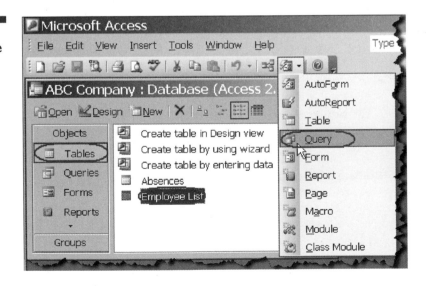

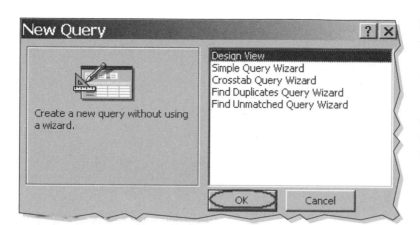

6.2

The New Query dialog box is displayed.

• **Click on the OK button.**

The Query window is displayed. You will now create a query that summarizes the number of employees, and the salaries of employees, in each department.

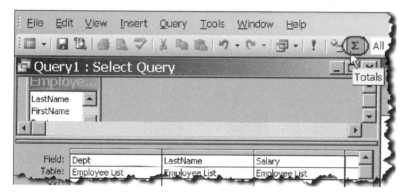

6.3

• **In the field list, double-click on the following fields (in the indicated order):**

Dept
LastName
Salary

The selected fields are added to the Field row.

• **Click on the Totals button on the Application window toolbar.**

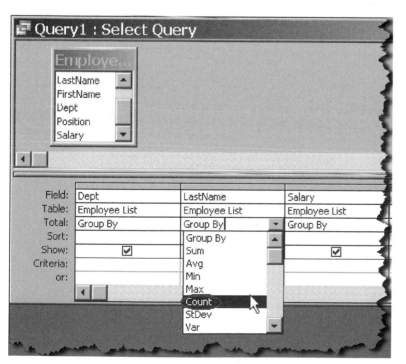

6.4

A Total row is added to the window. Notice that the default entry for each Total field is Group By. Since records, in this case, will be grouped by entries in the Dept field, you will leave the Total entry for that field as is. You will, however, need to change the Total entry for the LastName and Salary fields.

• **Click in the second Total box (under the LastName field). Then click on the down arrow that appears.**

A list of functions is displayed.

• **Click on Count.**

The listing will include the number of entries in the LastName field.

• **Click in the third Total box (under the Salary field). Click on the down arrow that appears. Then click on Sum in the list of functions.**

The listing will include the sum of the entries in the Salary field.

• **Click on the Run button.**

6.5

The summary information is displayed

NOTE: *You may wish to increase the width of the second column (as in the illustration).*

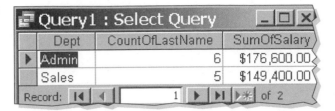

6.6

- **Click on the Save button.
  Type: Department Summary**

  Choose the OK button.

6.7

The query is saved.

- **Click on the View button.**

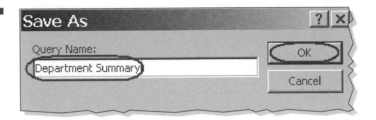

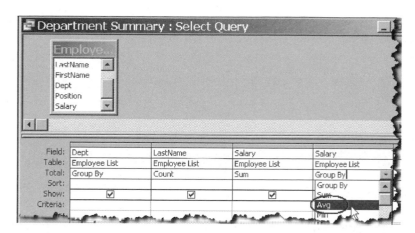

6.8

The Query window is redisplayed in Design view. You will now add an additional field to the query.

- **In the field list, double-click on Salary.**

A second Salary field is added to the Field row.

- **Click in the Total box (under the second Salary field). Click on the down arrow that appears. Then click on Avg in the list of functions.**

The listing will also include the average of the entries in the Salary field.

6.9

- **Click on the Run button.**

The summary information is displayed

- **Save the query, and then close it.**

Creating a Crosstab Query

The **Crosstab Query Wizard** provides an additional method for summarizing the information in an Access table. This wizard sets up a datasheet in which the entries in one field appear as column headings, while the entries in one or more other fields appear as row headings. In the intersection of each column/row, the query calculates a summary total (for example, a sum, average, maximum or minimum) for the column/row grouping. The datasheet illustrated on the next page, for example, shows the total salaries for clerks, managers and secretaries in both the Administration and Sales departments.

Objective

In this exercise, you will **use the Crosstab Query Wizard**.

7.1

- **Select the Employee List table on the Tables panel of the Database window.**
- **Expand the New Object button, and click on Query in the list of objects.**

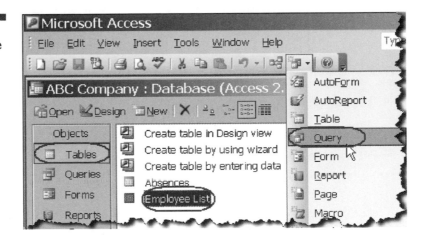

7.2

- **Click on Crosstab Query Wizard. Then click on the OK button.**

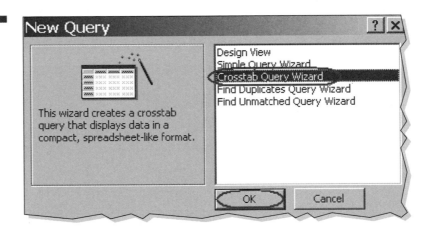

7.3

The first Crosstab Query Wizard dialog box is displayed. You are prompted to specify the table or query that contains the fields that are to appear in the query results. Notice that the dialog box currently lists the two tables in the database.

- **In the list of tables, click on Table: Employee List.**
- **Click on the Next > button.**

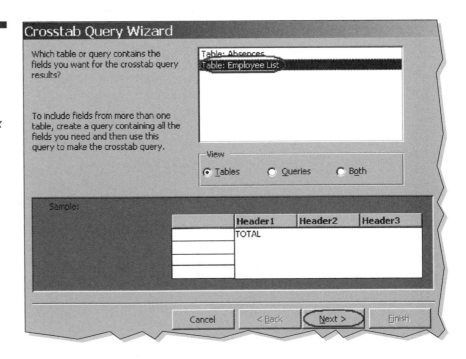

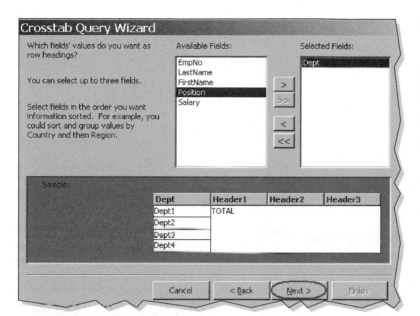

7.4

The next Crosstab Query Wizard dialog box is displayed, and you are prompted to specify the field(s) that contain(s) the values that are to appear as row headings.

- **In the Available Fields box, double-click on Dept.**

The field is added to the field list.

- **Click on the Next > button.**

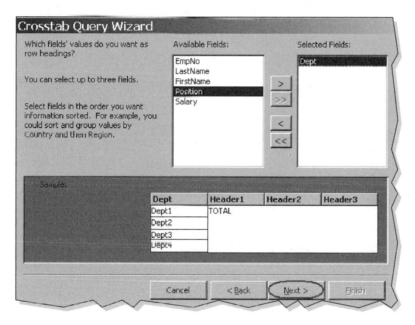

7.5

The next Crosstab Query Wizard dialog box is displayed, and you are prompted to specify the field that contains the values that are to appear as column headings.

- **In the field list, click on Position.**

- **The field is selected.**

- **Click on the Next > button.**

7.6

The next Crosstab Query Wizard dialog box is displayed, and you are prompted to specify the number that is to be calculated for each column and row intersection.

- **In the Fields box, click on Salary. Then, in the Functions box, click on Sum.**

The field and summary function are selected.

- **Click on the Next > button.**

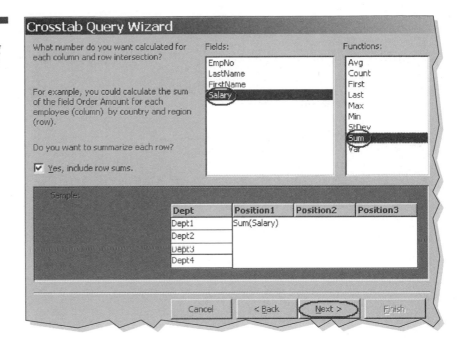

7.7

The last Crosstab Query Wizard dialog box is displayed, and you are prompted to enter a name for the query.

- **Type: Dept/Position Salary Summary**

The query name is entered.

- **Make sure that the View the query option is selected. Then click on the Finish button.**

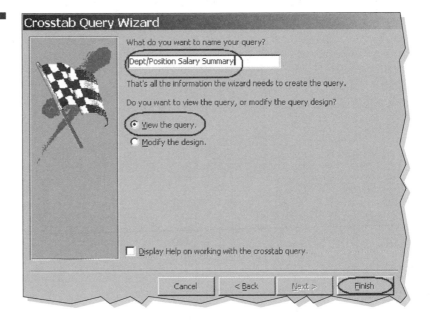

7.8

The query is run, and the query results are displayed. You will now modify the query.

- **Click on the View button.**

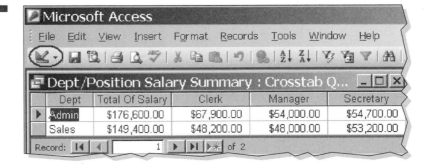

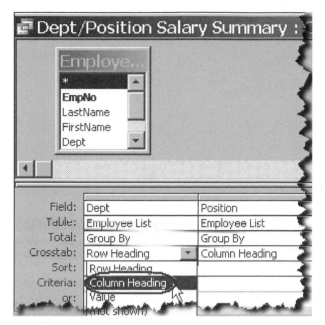

- **Click in the first Crosstab box (under the Dept field). Click on the down arrow that appears. Then click on Column Heading in the list of options.**

The Dept field entries will appear as column headings (instead of as row headings).

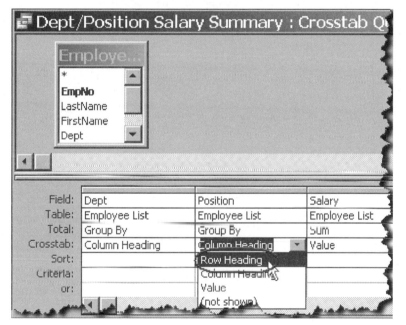

- **Click in the second Crosstab box (under the Position field). Click on the down arrow that appears. Then click on Row Heading in the list of options.**

The Position field entries will appear as row headings (instead of as column headings).

▬7.11▬

- **Click on the Run button.**

The modified query is run, and the query results are displayed.

- **Close the query, without saving the changes.**

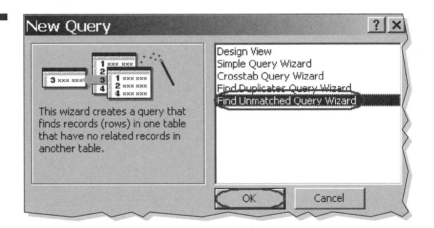

Creating a Query to Find Unmatched Records in a Table

At times, you may wish to find records in one table that do not have a matching record in a related table of the same database. This can be accomplished with the **Find Unmatched Query Wizard**, as demonstrated in the next exercise.

Objective

In this exercise, you will **use the Find Unmatched Query Wizard**.

▬8.1▬

- **Click on the New Object button.**

- **Click on Find Unmatched Query Wizard. Then click on the OK button.**

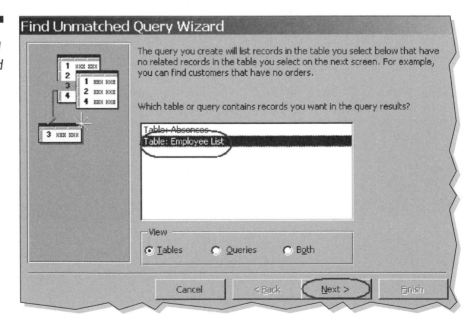

▬8.2▬

The first Find Unmatched Query Wizard dialog box is displayed. You are prompted to specify the table or query that contains the records that are to appear in the query results.

- **In the list of tables, click on Table: Employee List.**

- **Click on the Next > button.**

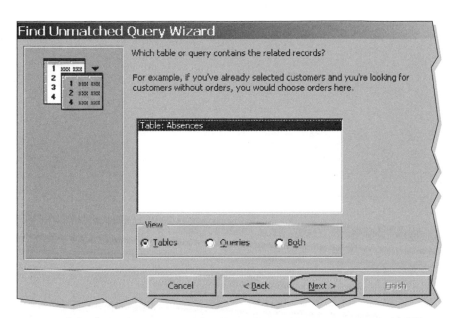

8.3

The next Find Unmatched Query Wizard dialog box is displayed, and you are prompted to specify the table or query that contains the related records. Notice that the related table (Absences) is already selected.

- **Click on the Next > button.**

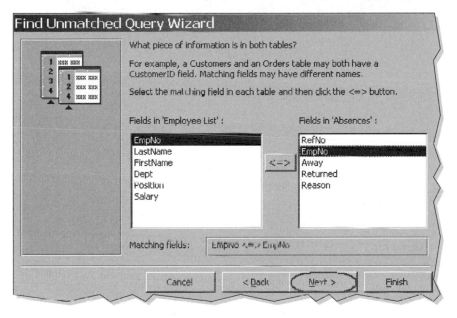

8.4

The next Find Unmatched Query Wizard dialog box is displayed, and you are prompted to specify the piece of information that is in both tables. Notice that the common field (EmpNo) is already selected in each field list.

- **Click on the Next > button.**

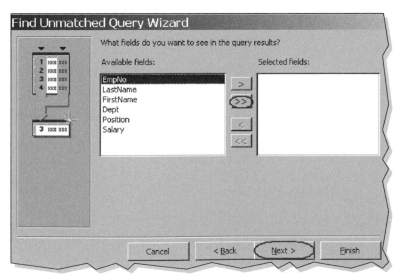

8.5

The next Find Unmatched Query Wizard dialog box is displayed, and you are prompted to specify the fields that are to appear in the query results.

- **Click on the double right arrow button.**

All fields are added to the field list.

- **Click on the Next > button.**

8.6

The last Find Unmatched Query Wizard dialog box is displayed, and you are prompted to enter a name for the query. You will accept the default name.

• **Make sure that the View the results option is selected. Then click on the Finish button.**

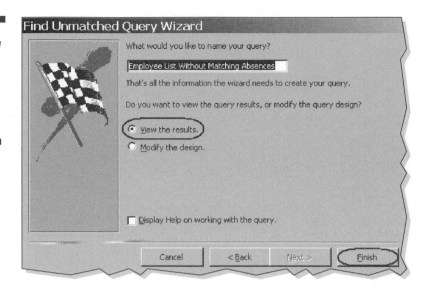

8.7

The query is run, and the query results are displayed.

• **Close the query without saving changes.**

Including Multiple Conditions in a Query

When you include two or more conditions in a query, records are selected on the basis of how those conditions have been entered.

When multiple conditions appear in the same Criteria row, a record is selected only when *all* conditions are satisfied. The criteria, in this case, are called **AND** conditions.

When multiple conditions appear in different Criteria rows, a record is selected if *any* condition is satisfied. The criteria, in this case, are called **OR** conditions.

You can combine AND and OR conditions.

Notes

1. You can also include multiple conditions in an advanced filter (or when using the Filter by Form method for filtering records).
2. In addition to the method illustrated on the previous page, you can specify two OR conditions for the same field by entering both conditions into the same field and by separating them with the **Or** operator (for example, "Admin" Or "Sales").

Objective

In this exercise, you will **create and run a query** that includes both **AND and OR** conditions.

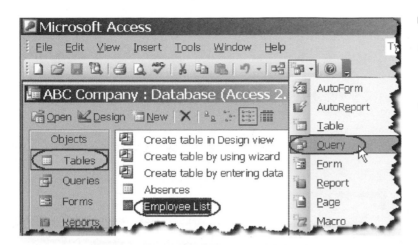

9.1

- **Make sure that the Employee List table is selected in the list of tables.**

- **Expand the New Object button, and click on Query in the list of objects.**

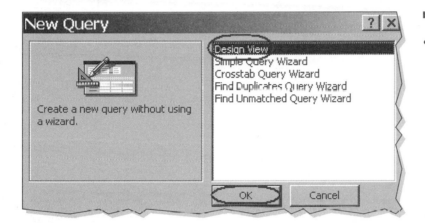

9.2

- **Make sure that the Design View option is selected. Then click on the OK button.**

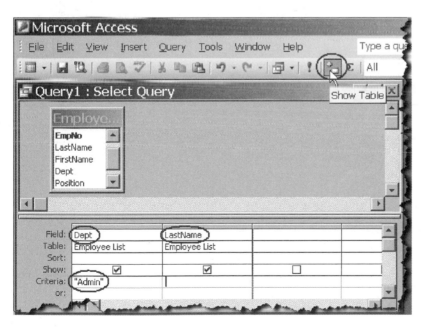

9.3

The Query window is displayed in Design view. You will begin by creating a query that displays the records for Administration department employees who are scheduled for training on or after August 1.

- **In the field list, double-click on the following fields:**

  Dept
  Last Name

- **Click in the first Criteria box (under the Dept field).**

  Type: Admin

- **Press [RIGHT ARROW].**

The first query condition is entered. Notice that the program has automatically enclosed the text in quotation marks. You will now add a second table to the query.

- **Click on the Show Table button on the Application window toolbar.**

9.4

The Show Table dialog box is displayed.

- **Click on Absences. Then click on the Add button.**

The field list for the Absences table is added to the Query window.

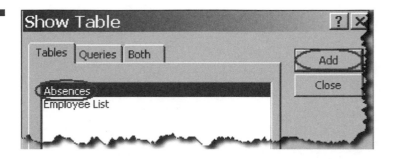

9.5

- **Click on the Close button in the Show Table dialog box.**

The dialog box is closed.

- **In the Absences table field list, double-click on the following fields:**

Away
Reason

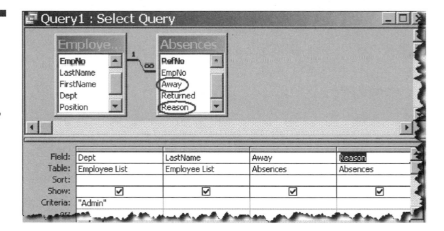

9.6

The additional fields are added to the Field row.

- **Double-click in the second Sort box (under the LastName field).**

The Ascending option is entered into the box.

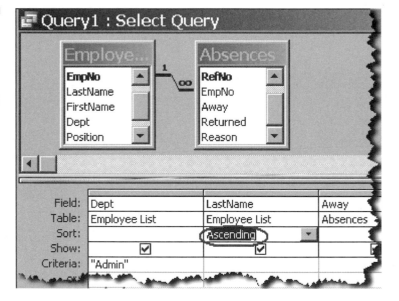

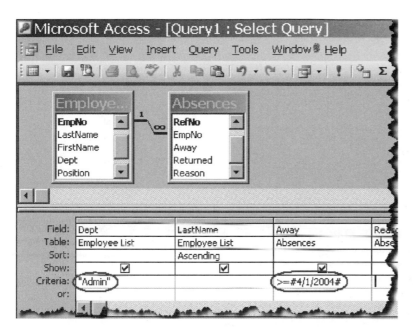

9.7

- **Click in the Criteria box (under the Away field).**

  **Type: >=4/1/2004
  Press [RIGHT ARROW].**

The second query condition is entered. Notice that the program has automatically enclosed the date in pound symbols.

NOTE: *In this case, you have specified two AND conditions. Selected records must contain "Admin" in the Dept field and a date of 4/1/2004 or later in the Away field.*

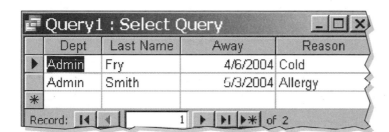

9.8

- **Click on the Run button on the Application window toolbar.**

The query is run, and the selected records are displayed

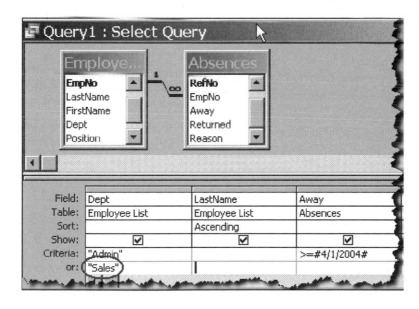

9.9

- **Click on the View button.**

The query is redisplayed in Design view. You will now modify the query to also display the records for Sales department employees who are away on or after April 1 2004.

- **Click in the first or box (under the Dept field).**

  **Type: Sales
  Press [RIGHT ARROW].**

The first query condition is entered.

9.10

- **Double-click in the first Sort box (under the Dept field).**

The Ascending option is entered into the box.

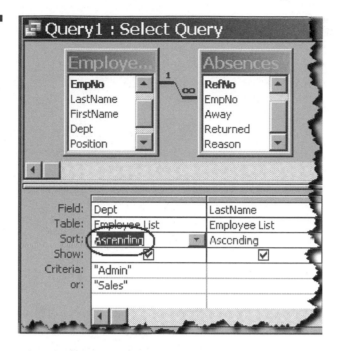

9.11

- **Click in the third or box (under the Away field).**

  Type: >=4/1/04
  Press [RIGHT ARROW].

The second query condition is entered. The Query window should now appear as illustrated in the screen shot.

NOTE: *In this case, you have specified two more AND conditions, as well as two OR conditions. Selected records must now contain either "Admin" in the Dept field and a date of 4/1/2004 or later in the Away field or "Sales" in the Dept field and a date of 4/1/2004 or later in the Away field.*

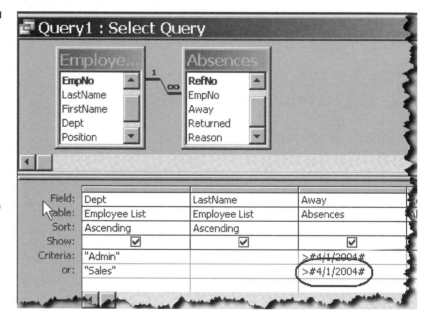

9.12

- **Click on the Run button.**

The selected records are displayed.

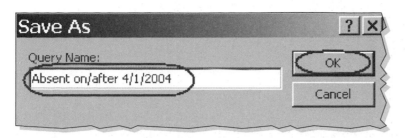

9.13

- **Click on Save button.**
- **On Save As dialog box, type: Absent on/after 4/1/2004 and click OK.**
- **Click on the Close button on the Title bar of the Query window.**

Creating a Parameter Query

A **parameter query** is one that prompts the user for selection criteria when it is run. A prompt displayed by a parameter query appears in a box that is defined when the query is first set up.

To **create a parameter query**:

- With the Query window displayed in Design view, add the necessary **fields** to the Field row.
- Enter an **operator**, along with the desired **prompt(s)** that is/are to appear when the query is run, into the Criteria row for the appropriate field. (See the examples below.)
- Repeat the previous two steps, if necessary.

The following are examples of parameter query criteria:

Between [Enter the first date:] And [Enter the last date:]

Entering the above into the Criteria row for a Date field would display two prompt boxes—the first prompting the user for the first date in a date range and the second prompting the user for the last date in the range. The query would then display those records in which the field contained an entry within the specified date range.

Like [Enter the first character(s) you wish to find:] & "*"

Entering the above into the Criteria row for a Text field would display a single prompt box, prompting the user for one or more characters. The query would then display those records in which the field contained an entry beginning with the specified character(s).

Objective

In this exercise, you will **create and run a parameter query**.

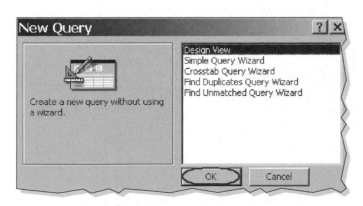

10.1

- **Make sure that the Employees List table is selected in the list of tables.**
- **Click on the New Object button. Then click on the OK button in the New Query dialog box.**

The New Object button should currently display the New Query icon (since Query was the last option selected in the New Object list).

10.2

The Query window is displayed. You will now create a query that displays the records for employees who are scheduled for training within a specific date range.

- **In the field list, double-click on the following fields:**

  Emp No
  Last Name
  Dept

The selected fields are added to the Field row.

- **Click on the Show Table button.**

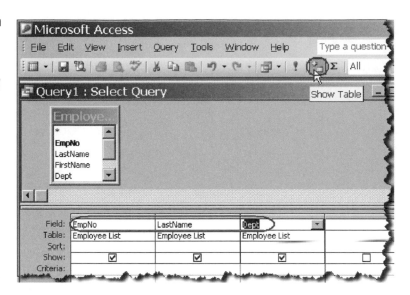

10.3

The Show Table dialog box is displayed.

- **Click on Absences. Then click on the Add button.**

The field list for the Schedule table is added to the Query window.

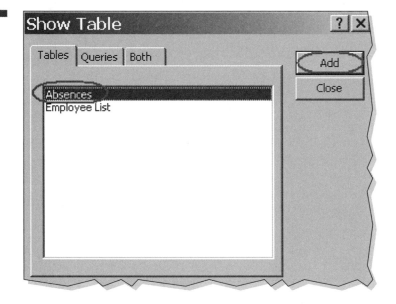

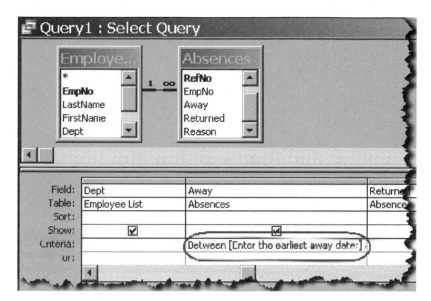

- **Click on the Close button in the Show Table dialog box.**

The dialog box is closed.

- **In the Absences table field list, double-click on the following fields:**

  Away
  Returned
  Reason

The additional fields are added to the Field row.

- **Click in the fourth Criteria box (under the Away field).**

  Type: Between [Enter the earliest away date:] And [Enter the latest start date:]

  Press [TAB].

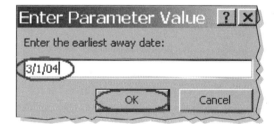

The query condition is entered. You will now run the query and display the records for employees who are scheduled for training during the months of July and August.

- **Click on the Run button.**

A prompt box is displayed.

- **Type: 3/1/04**

*Choose the **OK** button.*

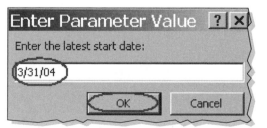

The first date (March 1, 2004) is entered, and another prompt box is displayed.

- **Type: 3/31/04**

*Choose the **OK** button.*

10.7

The second date (March 31, 2004) is entered and the selected records are displayed. Notice that the Start field entry in each record is between July 1, 2004 and August 31, 2004.

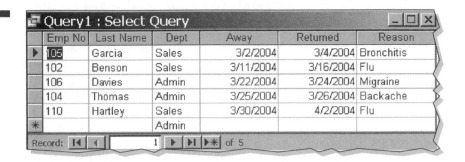

10.8

- **Save the query as Parameter query on Away.**
- **Close the database.**

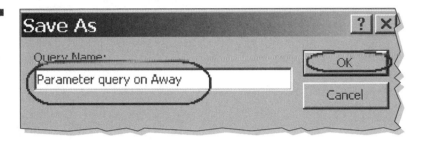

Congratulations! You have completed the Case Study.

Conclusion

You have just completed **Microsoft Office Access 2003—Case Study 2**. In the case study, you were introduced to many techniques. To reinforce your understanding of these techniques, it is recommended that you read and work through it once again.

Further Practice

The following Case Study will give you the opportunity to review and practice many of the Access techniques you have learned.

Assume that you are employed at a university and are responsible for creating and maintaining an Access database. This database, named **Students**, includes two tables—one named **Student List**, which includes a listing of various students, and another named **Grades**, which includes the end-of-semester grades for each of these students.

1. **Create** the **database file** named **Students.mdb**.
2. Create **Student List table** and add the following fields, their respective Data Types and field properties:

   Field Name: **StudentNo**
   Data Type: **Text**
   Field size: **3**
   Caption: **Student No**
   Required: **Yes**

   Click on the **StudentNo** field in the Field Name column and click on the **Primary Key** button on the application window toolbar for this field.

Field Name: **LastName**
Data Type: **Text**
Field size: **15**
Caption: **Last Name**
Required: **Yes**

Field Name: **FirstName**
Data Type: **Text**
Field size: **15**
Caption: **First Name**
Required: **No**

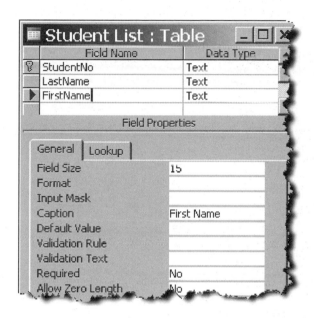

3. Create **Grade table** and add the following fields, their respective Data Types and field properties:

Field Name: **RecordID**
Data Type: **AutoNumber**
Caption: **Record ID**

Click on the **RecordID** field in the Field Name column and click on the **Primary Key** button on the application window toolbar for this field.

Field Name: **Semester**
Data Type: **Text**
Field size: **1**
Required: **No**

Field Name: **StudentNo**
Data Type: **Text**
Field size: **3**
Caption: **Student No**
Required: **No**

Field Name: **History**
Data Type: **Number**
Field size: **Integer**
Decimal Places: **0**

Field Name: **English**
Data Type: **Number**
Field size: **Integer**
Decimal Places: **0**

Field Name: **Math**
Data Type: **Number**
Field size: **Integer**
Decimal Places: **0**

Field Name: **Science**
Data Type: **Number**
Field size: **Integer**
Decimal Places: **0**

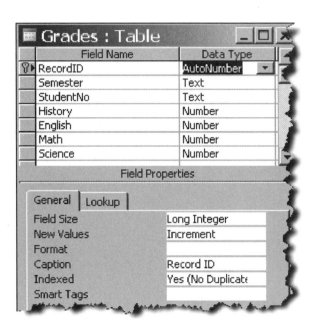

4. Enter the records in **Student List** table as listed below:

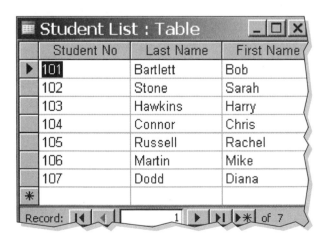

5. Click on the **Save** button and **Close** Student List table.
6. Enter the records in **Grades** table as listed below:

Record ID	Semester	Student No	History	English	Math	Science
1	1	101	77	58	75	89
2	1	102	59	78	68	48
3	1	103	79	86	34	55
4	1	104	87	44	79	52
5	1	105	85	79	90	89
6	1	106	74	87	84	63
7	1	107	32	21	46	37
8	2	101	75	64	63	85
9	2	102	76	73	66	79
10	2	103	47	50	68	76
11	2	104	79	86	65	60
12	2	105	84	89	97	85
13	2	106	60	85	76	54
14	2	107	45	47	58	42
(AutoNumber)						

Record: |◄ ◄   1   ► ►| ►* of 14

7. Click on the **Save** button and **Close** Grades table.
8. **Print** the **datasheet** of each table in the database (**Grades** and **Student List**). Notice that the two tables have a common field, **StudentNo**.
9. **Create** a **one-to-many relationship** between the **Student List table** and the **Grades table**.

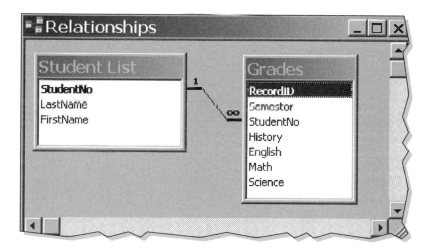

10. In the **Grades table, set** the appropriate **field properties** so that an entry is required in the **Semester** and **StudentNo** fields.
11. Using the **AutoForm Wizard**, create a **form** for the **Grades table. Save** the **form** under the name of **Grades**.

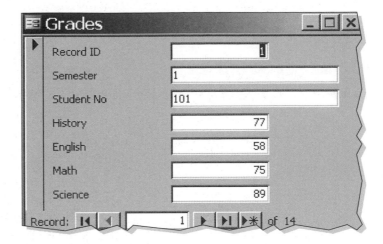

12. Using this **form, enter** the following **records** into the **Grades table:**

Semester	Student No	History	English	Math	Science
3	101	67	73	69	87
3	102	63	61	57	64
3	103	52	42	64	53
3	104	70	59	68	64
3	105	82	93	80	88
3	106	56	79	64	52
3	107	35	49	33	48

13. **Create** a **query** of the records in the **Grades** and **Student List tables** that shows the **third semester History grades** for all students. Include the **student numbers,** along with the **complete name** of each student, in the listing.
14. **Save** the **query** as **Third semester History grades**.
15. **Close** the **query**.

Third Semester History Grades : Selec...			
Student No	Last Name	First Name	History
101	Bartlett	Bob	67
102	Stone	Sarah	63
103	Hawkins	Harry	52
104	Connor	Chris	70
105	Russell	Rachel	82
106	Martin	Mike	56
107	Dodd	Diana	35

Record: 1 of 7

16. **Create** a **query** of the records in the **Grades** and **Student List tables** that shows **both English and History grades below 70** for all students in the **third semester**. Include the **student numbers**, along with the **complete name** of each student, in the listing.
17. **Save** the **query** as **English and History grades below 70**.
18. **Close** the **query**.

English and History grades below 70 : Select Q...				
Student No	Last Name	First Name	History	English
102	Stone	Sarah	63	61
103	Hawkins	Harry	52	42
107	Dodd	Diana	35	49

Record: 1 of 3

19. Create a **query** of the records in the **Grades table** that **prompts the user** for a **range of semesters**. Include the **student numbers**, along with the **complete name** of each student, **History**, **English**, **Math**, and **Science** grades in the listing.
20. **Save** the **query** under the name of **Choose Semester**.
21. **Run** the **query**, and enter appropriate **semesters** in the **prompt boxes** that appear.

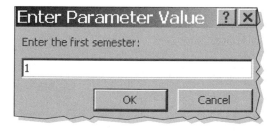

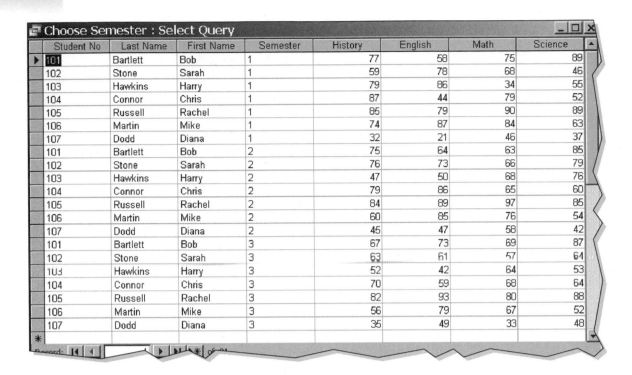

Student No	Last Name	First Name	Semester	History	English	Math	Science
101	Bartlett	Bob	1	77	58	75	89
102	Stone	Sarah	1	59	78	68	46
103	Hawkins	Harry	1	79	86	34	55
104	Connor	Chris	1	87	44	79	52
105	Russell	Rachel	1	85	79	90	89
106	Martin	Mike	1	74	87	84	63
107	Dodd	Diana	1	32	21	46	37
101	Bartlett	Bob	2	75	64	63	85
102	Stone	Sarah	2	76	73	66	79
103	Hawkins	Harry	2	47	50	68	76
104	Connor	Chris	2	79	86	65	60
105	Russell	Rachel	2	84	89	97	85
106	Martin	Mike	2	60	85	76	54
107	Dodd	Diana	2	45	47	58	42
101	Bartlett	Bob	3	67	73	69	87
102	Stone	Sarah	3	63	61	57	64
103	Hawkins	Harry	3	52	42	64	53
104	Connor	Chris	3	70	59	68	64
105	Russell	Rachel	3	82	93	80	88
106	Martin	Mike	3	56	79	67	52
107	Dodd	Diana	3	35	49	33	48

22. **Close** the **query**.

Microsoft Internet Explorer Introduction

After participating in this course, you should be able to:

- Start Internet Explorer
- Customize Internet Explorer toolbar
- Display Help information
- Exit Internet Explorer
- Display a specific Web page
- Navigate through a Web site
- Use the History Explorer bar
- Set a new Home page

- Add a Web page to the Favorites list
- Add an Internet radio station to the Favorites list
- Print a Web page
- Use the Search Companion
- Use the AutoSearch feature
- Use a Major Search engine
- Use security certificates and security zones
- Define your privacy preferences

Getting Started

Introduction

This section **introduces Internet Explorer**. In it, you will learn how to:

- **Start Internet Explorer.**
- **Identify** the **elements** of the **Internet Explorer window**.
- **Customize** the **Internet Explorer toolbar**.
- **Display Help information.**
- **Exit** from **Internet Explorer**.

The section begins with a discussion of **terminology** and **concepts** that are associated with **Internet Explorer**.

What Is the Internet?

The **Internet** is a global network of computers that allows individuals in government, in business, in school and at home to share information. The computers that communicate over the Internet fall into two categories: **servers** and **clients**. A server offers a service of some kind to other computers on the network; a client, on the other hand, requests a particular service from a server.

Some of the more popular Internet services include **File Transfer Protocol** (FTP), which transfers files from one computer to another, **electronic mail** (e-mail), which allows individuals to send messages to other individuals, **newsgroups** (also called **bulletin boards** and **discussion groups**), which allow groups of individuals to post messages to, and respond to messages on, a special news server, and what is probably the most widely used Internet service—the **World Wide Web**.

What Is the World Wide Web?

The **World Wide Web**, also known as simply the **Web**, provides access to a wealth of information stored in **hypertext files** called **Web pages**. A series of related Web pages is called a **Web site**.

All Web pages are written in **Hypertext Markup Language** (HTML), a still-evolving computer language. A single Web page can include text, graphic images, sounds, as well as **hyperlinks** to other Web pages.

The information on the World Wide Web is displayed with a Web client program called a **Web browser**, which requests a particular page from a Web server by specifying its Internet address, or **Uniform Resource Locator** (URL). To communicate, Web browsers and Web servers use a set of rules called **Hypertext Transfer Protocol** (HTTP).

What Is Internet Explorer?

Internet Explorer is one of the leading **Web browser** programs for personal computers. It is, however, much more than simply a means of browsing, or "surfing" the World Wide Web since it can be used for other functions, such as transferring data.

Included with Internet Explorer is **Outlook Express**, a smaller version of Microsoft Outlook. Using Outlook Express, you can send and receive e-mail messages, as well as participate in newsgroups.

The Components of a URL

The **URL**, as mentioned earlier, is the Internet address of a particular Web page. In addition to Web pages, URLs can also point to various other files and locations on the Internet—for example, files on an FTP server and e-mail addresses.

A typical **Web page URL** appears in the following form:

http://network location/path/filename.extension

http: The first component of a URL is the **protocol**, which indicates a particular Internet service. This protocol, **http (HyperText Transfer Protocol)**, identifies a file on a World Wide Web server. Other common protocols include **ftp (File Transfer Protocol)**, which identifies a file on an FTP server, and **mailto**, which identifies an individual's e-mail address.

network location: This component identifies the computer (Internet server) on which the file you wish to access is stored. The component has two or more parts, separated by periods—for example, **www.microsoft.com**. (In this example, "www" indicates the World Wide Web.)

path: This component identifies the folder in which the file you wish to access is stored (if it is stored in a folder other than the root folder)—for example, **business**.

filename.extension: This component identifies the actual file you wish to access—for example, **information.htm**.

Connecting to the Internet

Before you can browse the World Wide Web, you must be connected to the Internet. Internet connection service is sold by companies called **Internet Service Providers (ISPs)**, which provide both access to the Internet as well as the software necessary to use the Internet.

This course assumes that you have the proper connection to the Internet.

Starting Internet Explorer

You start Internet Explorer by **double-clicking** on the **Internet Explorer** icon on the Windows desktop.

Objective

In this exercise, you will **start Internet Explorer**.

- On the Windows desktop, identify the **Internet Explorer** icon.

NOTE: You can also start Internet Explorer by selecting the **All Programs** option on Windows' Start menu, followed by the **Internet Explorer** option on the All Programs submenu, or by simply clicking on the **Internet Explorer** button in the Windows Taskbar.

- **Double-click** on the **Internet Explorer** icon.
- If the **Dial-up Connection dialog box** appears, enter the necessary **user name** and/or **password**, and press **[ENTER]**.

Internet Explorer is started, and the Internet Explorer Home page is displayed.

NOTE: The **Home page** is the main, or starting, page of a Web site. The URL of the default Internet Explorer Home page is http://www.msn.com. On your system, however, the default page may have been reset. If so, a different page will appear on your screen.

The Internet Explorer Window

The elements of the main **Internet Explorer window** are:

Title bar	This displays the **title** of the current Web page, as well as the name of the program (Microsoft Internet Explorer).
Menu bar	This displays the program's menu of **primary commands**. Selecting an option on the Menu bar displays a menu of options for performing specific Internet Explorer operations.
Toolbar	This displays **shortcut buttons** for performing common Internet Explorer operations (for example, moving to the previously-viewed Web page, searching for a particular Web page, and printing a Web page). Clicking on several of these buttons (for example, **Search**, **Favorites**, **History**, **Media**) displays an **Explorer bar** along the left side of the window from which other Web sites can be accessed.

Address bar	This displays the **URL** of the currently-displayed Web page. Clicking on the down arrow at the right side of the Address bar displays a drop-down list of Web sites you have visited recently, allowing you to quickly move back and forth between different sites.
Links bar	This displays predefined **links** to specific Web pages when clicked on. You can add your own links to the Links bar by 1) dragging an icon or hyperlink for the Web page to be linked and by placing it on the bar, and 2) displaying the Web page to be linked, by choosing the **Favorites**, **Add to Favorites** command, by clicking on the **Create in** button in the Add Favorite dialog box, and by selecting the **Links** folder in the Create in box.
Display area	This is the area in which a Web page appears.
Vertical scroll bar	This allows you to scroll forward and backward through a Web page. The window also displays a **Horizontal scroll bar** when a Web page is wider than the width of the window.
Status bar	This displays information relevant to the current Web page, including the amount that has been transferred from the server when a page is being loaded and the associated URL of a hyperlink when you point to that hyperlink.

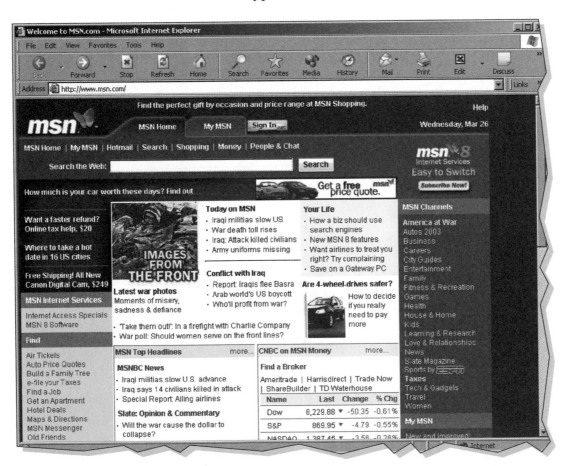

INTERNET EXPLORER WINDOW

Notes

This manual assumes that **Microsoft Windows XP** is your operating system. If you are using earlier versions of Windows, what appears on your screen will vary slightly from what is shown in this manual.

Customizing the Internet Explorer Toolbar

The default Internet Explorer toolbar appears somewhat different from the toolbar displayed in the Internet Explorer Window shown earlier.

By choosing the **View**, **Toolbars**, **Customize** command, toolbar buttons can be added or removed, reordered, or changed to a smaller size. You can also specify whether or not text labels should appear on the toolbar, as well as the position of the labels—to the right of *or* below the button.

To **add buttons to the toolbar**:

- Choose the **View**, **Toolbars**, **Customize** command.
- From the **Available toolbar buttons** list, click on the button to be added.
- Click on the **Add** button in the center of the window.
- Drag the new button at the bottom of the **Current toolbar buttons** list to the desired position in that list.
- Click on the **Close** button.

To **remove buttons from the toolbar**:

- Choose the **View**, **Toolbars**, **Customize** command.
- From the **Current toolbar buttons** list, click on the button to be removed.
- Click on the **Remove** button in the center of the window.
- Click on the **Close** button.

To **display text labels below the toolbar buttons**:

- Choose the **View**, **Toolbars**, **Customize** command.
- Expand the **Text options** box.
- Choose **Show text labels**.
- Click on the **Close** button.

To **reset the toolbar to its default settings**:

- Choose the **View**, **Toolbars**, **Customize** command.
- Click on the **Reset** button.
- Click on the **Close** button.

Displaying Help Information

Internet Explorer provides an extensive **Help system**, which is always ready to provide assistance should you encounter a problem or just need additional information while using the program.

Listing your favorite pages for quick viewing

When you find Web sites or pages that you like, you can keep track of them, so it's easy to open them in the future.

- Add a Web page to your list of favorite pages. Any time you want to open that page, just click the **Favorites** button on the toolbar, and then click the shortcut in the Favorites list.

  Add a page to your list of favorite pages

- If you have a handful of sites or pages that you visit often, add them to your Links bar.

  Add a page to your Links bar

- If there is one page you visit most, you can make it your home page so that it appears every time you start Internet Explorer or click the **Home** button on the toolbar.

  Change your home page

✓ **Note**

- If you forget to add Web pages to your Favorites or Links bar, click the **History** button on the toolbar. The History list shows where you've been—today, yesterday, or a few weeks ago. Click a name from the list to display the page.

HELP INFORMATION

You can access the Help system by choosing the **Help, Contents and Index** command. Doing this opens the Help window, which displays a list of topics in outline format and an index of topics in alphabetical order.

Objective

In this exercise, you will **access and use the Internet Explorer Help system**.

2.1

- **Choose the Help command.**

The Help menu is displayed.

| Contents and Index |
| Tip of the Day |
| For Netscape Users |
| Online Support |
| Send Feedback |
| About Internet Explorer |

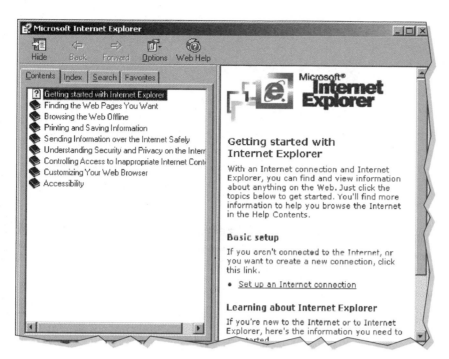

2.2

- **Click on Contents and Index.**

NOTE: *If the Contents panel does not currently appear in this window, click on the **Contents** tab.*

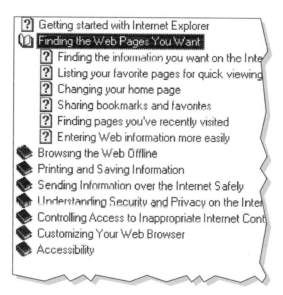

2.3

- **Click on the topic Finding the Web Pages You Want.**

The topic is expanded (as shown in the figure on the left).

2.4

- **Click on Listing your favorite pages for quick viewing.**

Information about listing favorite Web pages is displayed in the right pane of the Help window.

- **In the Help information, click on Add a page to your list of favorite pages (which is marked with an underline).**

Information about adding a page to the Favorites list is displayed.

- **Click on the Back** 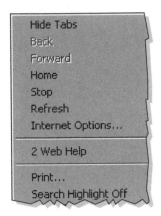 **button on the Toolbar of the Help window.**

Information about listing favorite Web pages is redisplayed.

- **Click on the Forward button on the Toolbar of the Help window.**

Information about adding a page to the Favorites list is redisplayed.

- **Click on the Hide button on the Toolbar of the Help window.**

The left pane of the Help window is hidden.

- **Click on the Show button (which replaced the Hide button).**

The left pane of the Help window is redisplayed.

- **Click on the Options button on the Toolbar of the Help window.**

The Options menu is displayed.

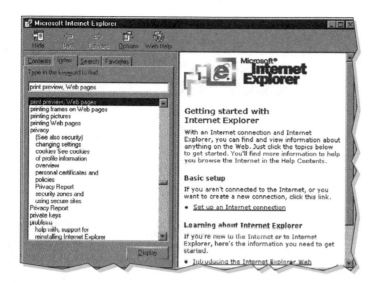

2.5

- **Click on Print.**

The Print Topics dialog box is displayed.

- **Make sure that the Print the selected topic option is selected. Click on the OK button. Then click on the Print button in the Print dialog box, which is displayed.**

The currently-displayed Help information is printed.

- **Click on the Index tab.**

The Index panel of the window is displayed.

- **Type: print**

The list is scrolled to the first topic beginning with the word "print."

- **Click on the topic printing Web pages. Then click on the Display button.**

The Topics Found dialog box is displayed.

- **In the dialog box, click on Print a Web page. Then click on the Display button.**

Information about printing a Web page is displayed.

- **Click on the Close ☒ button on the Title bar of the Help window.**

The window is closed, and the Help system is exited.

Notes

The **Search** panel of the Help window allows you to display a list of topics that include one or more words you have specified.

1. When you are finished, display the **Contents** panel of the Help window.
2. **Exit** from the **Help system**.

Exiting from Internet Explorer

When you are finished using Internet Explorer, you can exit from the program either by choosing the **File, Close** command or by clicking on the **Close** button on the Title bar of the Internet Explorer window.

Objective

In this exercise, you will **exit from Internet Explorer**.

- Make sure that the **Internet Explorer home page** is displayed.
- Choose the **File**, **Close** command.

The Internet Explorer window is closed, and the Windows desktop is redisplayed.

  NOTE: If the Auto Disconnect dialog box appears, click on the **Disconnect Now** button.

Browsing the World Wide Web

This section discusses methods for **accessing information on the World Wide Web**. In it, you will learn how to:

- **Display** a **specific Web page**.
- **Navigate** through a **Web site**.
- **Use** the **History Explorer bar**.
- **Set** a **new Home page**.
- **Add** a **Web page** to the **Favorites list**.
- **Add** an **Internet radio station** to the **Favorites list**.
- **Print** a **Web page**.

Displaying a Specific Web Page

You can easily display any Web page if you know its URL.
  To **display a specific Web page**:

- In the Internet Explorer window, click in the **Address bar**. Doing this selects (highlights) the URL of the current Web page.
- Type the **URL** of the Web page you wish to display.
- Click on the **Go** button next to the Address bar, or press [**ENTER**].

Notes

As you begin typing in the Address bar, Internet Explorer's **AutoComplete** feature displays a list of URLs that are similar to the URL you are entering. If the correct URL appears in this list, you can display the associated page by simply clicking on the URL. Alternatively, you can continue typing and then click on the **Go** button (or press [**ENTER**]) when you have entered the complete URL.

Objective

In this exercise, you will **display the Home page for the White House Web site**.

4.1

- **Make sure that the Internet Explorer Home page is displayed in the Internet Explorer window.**

- **Click in the Address bar.**

The URL of the current page is highlighted.

- **Type: http//www.whitehouse.gov**

NOTE: In this case, entering the protocol, http:// is optional since Internet Explorer assumes the protocol of the current page when no other protocol is specified.

4.2

- **Press [ENTER].**

After a few moments, the White House Home page is displayed.

Navigating Through a Web Site

A Web site usually includes a number of related Web pages. From the Home page, you can display any other page of a particular site by clicking on the **hyperlink** to that page, which is often indicated by underlined text, by text of a different color, or by a picture (graphic) of some kind.

You can move backward and forward through previously-viewed pages of the current Web site (or a previously-visited Web site) by using the **Back** and **Forward** buttons on the Toolbar. (These buttons are demonstrated in the next exercise.)

BACK / FORWARD BUTTONS

Objective

In this exercise, you will **view other pages of the current Web site**.

- Using the **Vertical scroll bar**, **scroll** through the current **page**.
- Point to **History and Tours** (in the list of topics at the top of the page).

The mouse pointer changes to a small hand with an upward-pointing finger, which indicates a hyperlink.

- **Click** the mouse button.

The Web page associated with the selected hyperlink (History and Tours) is displayed.

- Click on **First Ladies** (in the list of topics on the left side of the page).

The Web page associated with the selected hyperlink (First Ladies) is displayed. You will now use the Back and Forward buttons.

- Click on the **Back** button on the Toolbar.

  NOTE: Click on the button itself and not on the down arrow at the right side of the button.
  The History and Tours page is redisplayed.

- Click again on the **Back** button.

The White House Home page is redisplayed.

- Click on the **Forward** button on the Toolbar.

  NOTE: Click on the button itself and not on the down arrow at the right side of the button.
  The History and Tours page is redisplayed.

- Click again on the **Forward** button.

The First Ladies page is redisplayed.

- Click on the **down arrow** at the right side of the **Back** button.

The button is expanded, listing the Web pages you viewed before displaying the current page.

- Click on **Welcome To The White House**.

The selected page is redisplayed.

- Click on the **down arrow** at the right side of the **Forward** button.

The button is expanded, listing the Web pages you viewed after displaying the current page.

- Click on **First Lady's Gallery**.

The selected page is redisplayed.

- Click on the **Home** ⌂ Home button on the Toolbar.

The Internet Explorer Home page is redisplayed. You will now use the Address bar to access the White House Web site.

- Click on the **down arrow** at the right side of the **Address bar**.

A list of previously-visited Web sites is displayed.

NOTE: You may have to click on the up arrow of the vertical scroll bar to see www.whitehouse.gov.

- Click on **http://www.whitehouse.gov**.

The White House Home page is redisplayed.

- Click on the **Home** button.

The Internet Explorer Home page is redisplayed.

Using the History Explorer Bar

The **History Explorer bar**, which is displayed by clicking on the **History** button on the Toolbar of the Internet Explorer window (or choosing the **View**, **Explorer Bar** command, followed by the **History** option on the Explorer Bar submenu), includes links to Web pages you have viewed recently. These pages can be listed by date, by Web site, by most visited and by order visited today.

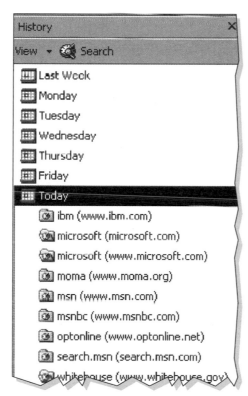

HISTORY EXPLORER BAR

Objective

In this exercise, you will **use the History Explorer bar to redisplay previously-viewed Web pages**.

- Make sure that the **Internet Explorer Home page** is displayed.

- Click on the **History** History button on the Toolbar.

The History Explorer bar is displayed along the left side of the window.

NOTE: If Web sites are not listed by date (the default order), click on the **down arrow** at the right side of the **View** button (at the top of the Explorer bar), and select the **By Date** option in the list that appears.

• In the Explorer bar, click on **whitehouse (www.whitehouse.gov)**.

NOTE: Notice that when you point to a link on the Explorer bar, the complete URL of the associated Web page appears in a pop-up window.

 6.1

The option is expanded, and the relevant pages of the White House Web site (those viewed in the previous exercise) are listed.

• **Click on Life in the White House.**

The selected page is displayed.

• **Click on the down arrow at the right side of the View  button.**

The button is expanded, and a list of view options is displayed.

• **Click on By Site.**

The Explorer bar now lists previously-visited Web sites in ascending alphabetical order.

• **Expand the View button, and click on By Order Visited Today.**

The Explorer bar now lists the Web pages viewed today in the order in which they were displayed.

• **Expand the View button, and click on By Date.**

The default Explorer bar listing is restored.

• **Click on the History button.**

The Explorer bar is closed.

NOTE: *You can also close an Explorer bar by clicking on the **Close** (X) button in the upper-right corner of the bar.*

• **Click on the Home button.**

The Internet Explorer Home page is redisplayed.

Setting a New Home Page

As you know, the first Web page that appears when you start Internet Explorer is the program's Home page. You can, however, have another page displayed when you start the program.

To **set a new Home page**:

• With the appropriate Web page (the page that is to appear when you start Internet Explorer) displayed, choose the **Tools, Internet Options** command.
• On the **General** panel of the Internet Options dialog box, which is subsequently displayed, click on the **Use Current** button.
• Click on the **OK** button.

To **restore the default Internet Explorer Home page**:

- Choose the **Tools, Internet Options** command.
- On the **General** panel of the Internet Options dialog box, click on the **Use Default** button.
- Click on the **OK** button.

Objective

In this exercise, you will set a new Internet Explorer Home page. You will then restore the default Home page.

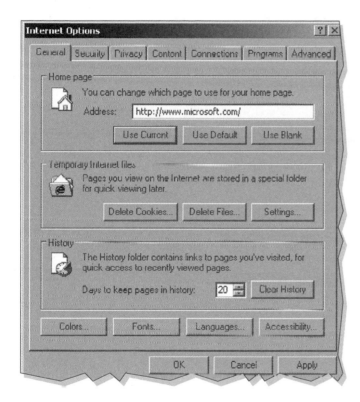

7.1

- **Make sure that the current Internet Explorer Home page is displayed.**

- **Click in the Address bar. Type: www.microsoft.com Press [ENTER].**

The Home page for the Microsoft Corporation Web site is displayed. You will now set this page as the new Internet Explorer Home page.

- **Choose the Tools, Internet Options command.**

The General panel of the Internet Options dialog box is displayed.

- **Under Home page, click on the Use Current button.**

The URL of the current page is entered into the Address box (as illustrated on the left).

- **Click on the OK button.**

The dialog box is closed. You will now test the new Home page.

- **Click on any hyperlink on the current page.**

The associated Web page is displayed.

- **Click on the Home button.**

The Microsoft Corporation Home page is displayed. You will now restore the default Internet Explorer Home page.

- **Choose the Tools, Internet Options command.**

The Internet Options dialog box is redisplayed.

- **Under Home page, click on the Use Default button.**

The Home page is reset.

- **Click on the OK button.**

The dialog box is closed.

- **Click on the Home button.**

The default Internet Explorer Home page is displayed.

Adding a Web Page to the Favorites List

Internet Explorer maintains a **Favorites list**, which includes the URLs of Web pages designated as Favorites, providing quick access to those pages. If you frequently view a particular Web page, you may wish to add it to this list.

FAVORITES EXPLORER BAR SHOWING FAVORITES LIST

To **add a Web page to the Favorites list**:

- With the Web page displayed, choose the **Favorites, Add to Favorites** command.
- In the Add Favorite dialog box, which is subsequently displayed:

    - Enter an optional **new name** for the page.
    - Optionally, select the **Make available offline** option.
    - Click on the **OK** button.

Notes

Selecting the **Make available offline** option in the Add Favorite dialog box allows you to access the current page without being connected to the Internet. You can customize the option (for example, make all pages linked to the current page also available offline) by using the **Customize** button.

To **remove a Web page from the Favorites list**:

- Choose the **Favorites** command.
- On the Favorites menu, which is subsequently displayed, point to the Web page to be removed, and **right-click** the mouse button.
- On the shortcut menu that appears, select the **Delete** option.
- In the prompt box that appears, click on the **Yes** button to confirm the operation.

Notes

You can also remove a Web page from the Favorites list by using the **Favorites, Organize Favorites** command.

Objective

In this exercise, you will **add the Home page for the National Basketball Association Web site** to the **Favorites list**.

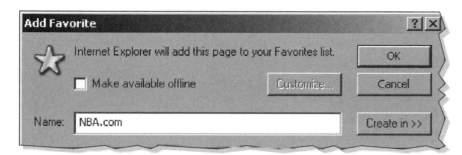

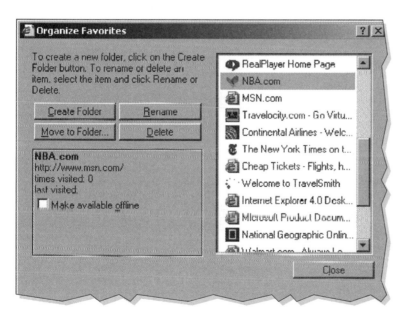

8.1

- **Make sure that the Internet Explorer Home page is displayed.**

- **Click in the Address bar.**

  Type: www.nba.com Press [ENTER].

The National Basketball Association Home page is displayed.

- **Choose the Favorites, Add to Favorites command.**

The Add Favorite dialog box is displayed.

8.2

- **In the Name box, drag the mouse pointer over the current entry.**

The current page name is selected.

- **Type: National Basketball Assn.**

A new page name is entered.

- **Click on Make available offline.**

The option is selected. The page will be available for offline viewing.

- **Click on the OK button.**

The dialog box is closed, and the page is added to the Favorites list.

- **Click on the Home button.**

The Internet Explorer Home page is redisplayed. You will now test the new Favorites link from the Favorites menu.

- **Choose the Favorites command.**

The Favorites menu is displayed.

- **Click on the National Basketball Assn. hyperlink.**

*NOTE: The above hyperlink should appear at the bottom of the Favorites menu. If it does not, click on the **down arrow** at the bottom of the menu to display the remaining entries.*

The National Basketball Association Home page is displayed.

- **Click on the Home button.**

The Internet Explorer Home page is redisplayed. You will now test the new Favorites link from the Favorites bar.

- **Click on the Favorites** Favorites **button on the Toolbar.**

The Favorites Explorer bar is displayed along the left side of the window.

- **Click on National Basketball Assn. hyperlink.**

NOTE: *As with the Favorites menu, you may need to scroll the Explorer bar to display the above hyperlink.*

The National Basketball Association Home page is once again displayed.

- **Click on the Favorites button.**

The Explorer bar is closed.

- **Choose the Favorites, Organize Favorites command.**

The Organize Favorites dialog box is displayed.

Notice that you can manage your Favorites (for example, rename them, move them into different folders, delete them from the Favorites list and make available offline) from this dialog box. In this case, however, you will simply close the dialog box.

- **Click on the Close button.**

The dialog box is closed.

Adding an Internet Radio Station to the Favorites List

Internet Explorer's **Media Bar** allows you to locate and listen to broadcast and Internet radio stations. With the wide variety of music and talk stations available, you might want to add a station to your **Favorites List**.

To **access** and then **add** an **Internet radio station** to the **Favorites List**:

- Click on the **Media button** on the Toolbar of the Internet Explorer window. (If **Windows Media Player** is not installed on your system, you will be asked to download it. If you choose not to download it, you can listen to the station directly from within your browser window).
- Click on the **Radio** hyperlink. A list of **Editor's Picks** and **Featured Stations** will display.
- Click on **More Radio Stations** at the **bottom** of the Media Bar. A complete list of radio stations will appear in the browser window.

- Choose the category of station you would like to listen to (big band, dance, holiday, oldies, sports, talk radio etc.)
- **Right-click** on the station you wish to add to your **Favorites List**. Select **Add to Favorites** from the shortcut menu that appears.
- Click **OK** in the **Add Favorite** window.

THE MEDIA BUTTON

Printing a Web Page

You can produce a hard copy of a Web page by printing it.

To **print a Web page**:

- With the Web page displayed, choose the **File**, **Print** command, or click on the **Print** button on the Toolbar.
- If you click on the Print button, the print operation begins immediately. If you choose the File, Print command, the Print dialog box is displayed. In this case, set any necessary **print options**, and click on the **OK** button.

Objective

In this exercise, you will **print the Internet Explorer Home page**.

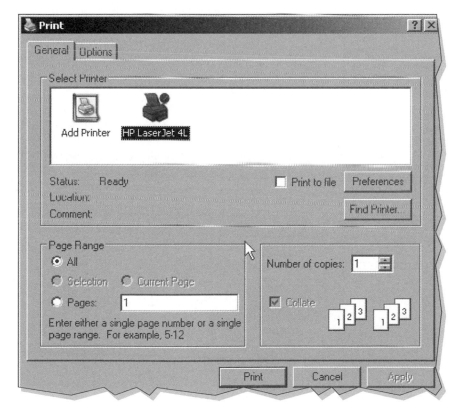

9.1

- **Make sure that the Internet Explorer Home page is displayed.**

- **Choose the File, Print command.**

The Print dialog box is displayed.

- **Under Print range, click on Pages.**

The print range (page 1 only) is set.

- **Click on the OK button.**

The dialog box is closed, and the current page is printed.

Searching the World Wide Web

This section discusses methods for **finding specific information on the World Wide Web**. In it, you will learn how to:

- **Use** the **Search Companion**.
- **Use** the **AutoSearch** feature.
- **Use Google**, a **Major Search Engine**.

The section begins with a discussion of **search services**.

Internet Search Services

With the phenomenal growth of the World Wide Web, it has become necessary to provide a better means of finding specific Web information than simply browsing through hundreds of pages.

To help you quickly locate desired information, Internet Explorer provides access to a number of popular **search services** (also called **search engines**), which search the World Wide Web for pages containing certain words, phrases or other information specified by the user.

Search services generally fall into one of three categories. The categories are as follows:

Crawler-Based: Crawler-based engines "crawl" or "spider" the web and create their listings automatically. Whatever they find goes into an index. The "spider" periodically looks for changes to these sites and subsequently updates the index.

Human-powered directories: Directories of this type depend on humans for their listings. Short descriptions of the site are submitted to the directory. Searches look for matches only in the descriptions submitted. Changes to the web page have no effect on the listing.

Hybrid: Hybrid engines use a combination of both crawler-based results and human-powered listings. One type of listing will be favored over another.

Among these search services are **AllTheWeb**, **AltaVista**, **AskJeeves**, **Dogpile**, **GO**, **Google**, **Lycos**, **Metacrawler**, **MSN Search**, and **Yahoo**.

Using the Search Companion

The **Search Companion** is a suitable starting point for searching for information on the Internet and will help you quickly find Web pages related to almost any topic. It can also be used to find files, folders, printers, people, and other computers on your network.

To **use the Search Companion**:

- Click on the **Search** button on the Toolbar. Doing this displays the Search Explorer bar along the left side of the Internet Explorer window.
- Enter the **search condition** (for example, the topic of the Web pages you wish to view).
- Click on the **Search** button, or press [**ENTER**].
- In the list of search results, click a hyperlink to display the Web page.

Notes

When performing an Internet search, **Search Companion** uses a default search service but also forwards your search request to alternate search services. You can select the default search service by clicking on the **Change preferences** hyperlink in the Search Explorer bar and then clicking on the **Change Internet search behavior** hyperlink.

Objective

In this exercise, you will **use the Search Companion to find Web pages with information about cruises**.

Notes

This exercise assumes that **MSN is the default search service** for finding Web pages.

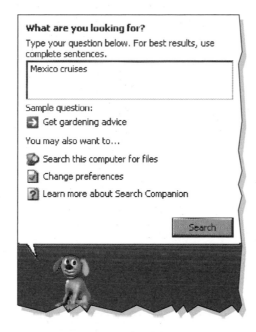

10.1

• **Make sure that the Internet Explorer Home page is displayed.**

• **Click on the Search** [Search] **button on the Toolbar.**

The Search Explorer bar is displayed along the left side of the window.

• **Click in the What are you looking for? box.**

Type: Mexico cruises

The search topic is entered.

• **Press [ENTER].**

The search is performed, and a list of hyperlinks to Web pages found as a result of the search is displayed in the right pane of the window.

• **Observe the list of hyperlinks displayed in the Explorer bar.**

The first few hyperlinks shown under Sponsored Links matches the first few hyperlinks in the right pane of the window.

• **Under Sponsored links in the Explorer bar, click on the first hyperlink.**

The associated page is displayed in the right pane of the window.

• **Click on the Back button on the Internet Explorer toolbar.**

The original search results are displayed. You will now search for a new topic.

- **Click on the Start a new search**

 **hyperlink (at the bottom of the Explorer bar).**

The previous search topic is cleared.

- **Type: Alaska cruises**
  Press [ENTER].

The search is performed, and a list of hyperlinks to Web pages found as a result of the search is displayed. You will now perform the same search using a different search service.

- **Under Sponsored links in the Explorer bar, click on Automatically send your search to other search engines.**

A list of search engines appears.

- **Click on AltaVista search.**

The search is performed using AltaVista search service, and a list of hyperlinks to Web pages found as a result of the search is displayed. You will now explore other search options displayed in the Explorer bar.

- **Under What would you like to do, click on Find Product Information: reviews, tests, news, etc.**

You are asked to indicate a product or service.

- **Type: suntan lotion**
  Press [ENTER].

The search is performed, and the results for ConsumerSearch.com: Product Reviews testing is displayed in the right pane of the window.

- **Click on a hyperlink of your choice.**

The associated page is displayed.

- **Click on the Search button on the Internet Explorer toolbar.**

The Explorer bar is closed.

- **Click on the Home button.**

The Internet Explorer Home page is redisplayed.

Using the Autosearch Feature

In addition to the Search Companion, you can also use Internet Explorer's **AutoSearch** feature to find specific Web pages.

To **use the AutoSearch feature**:

- In the Address bar, type **?**, **go** or **find**, followed by the **search topic**.
- Press [**ENTER**].

Objective

In this exercise, you will use the **AutoSearch feature to find Web pages with information about gardening.**

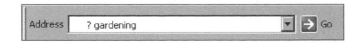

11.1

- **Make sure that the Internet Explorer Home page is displayed.**

- **Click in the Address bar. Type: ? gardening**

- **Press [ENTER].**

The search is performed, and a list of hyperlinks to Web pages found as a result of the search is displayed.

- **Click on a hyperlink of your choice.**

The associated page is displayed.

- **Click on the Back button on the toolbar.**

The original search results are displayed.

- **Click on another hyperlink of your choice.**

The associated page is displayed.

- **Click on the Home button.**

The Internet Explorer Home page is redisplayed.

Using a Major Search Engine

As mentioned earlier, with the wealth of information on the Internet today you can spend hours trying to find the information you are looking for. By utilizing a variety of search engines listed earlier, you can search for a topic by keyword or phrase which then produces a list of Web sites containing information on that topic.

Google a crawler-based search engine, is a top choice today for those searching the World Wide Web and provides access to over **3 billion Web pages**. Using the **tabs** at the **top of the Google Home page**, you can search for:

- Web Pages
- Images
- Newsgroups
- Directories
- News information

Notes

On the Google Home Page, you will find a hyperlink to an **Advanced Search** page which allows you to set more specific search criteria. **From the Advanced page**, you can hyperlink to **All About Google**, a page detailing the specifics of this powerful search engine. You will have access to stock quotes, telephone numbers, street maps and more.

Objective

In this exercise, you will use **Google.com to find Web images of giraffes**. You will then observe **automatic image resizing**.

12.1

- **Make sure that the Internet Explorer Home page is displayed.**

- **Click in the Address bar.**

  Type: www.google.com

  The Google Home page is displayed.

- **Click on the Images tab.**

You are now ready to type the name of the desired image in the Search box.

- **Type: giraffes**

The search topic is entered.

- **Click on Google Search or press [ENTER].**

The search results are displayed.

- **Click on any giraffes image.**

The image appears in the top portion of a screen below which is shown its original context on a Web page.

- **Click on the See full-size image hyperlink directly below the image.**

The image is now full-size in its own window.

- **Place your mouse pointer inside the image.**

■ 12.2 ■

The **Image Toolbar** appears in the upper left corner of the image. It allows you to save, print, and e-mail pictures from your Web page and view all saved pictures in the My Pictures folder.

- **Click on the Restore Down button on the Title bar of the Internet Explorer window.**

The image has been automatically resized to that window.

- **Click on the Maximize button on the Title bar of the Internet Explorer window.**

Once again, the image has been automatically resized.

NOTE: Internet Explorer's Image resizing automatically adjusts pictures to fit the size of the window. Both the picture height and width will be adjusted.

- **Click on the Home button.**

The Internet Explorer Home page is redisplayed.

Security on the Internet

This section discusses methods for **protecting the information sent and received over the Internet as well as methods for protecting your privacy**. In it, you will learn how to:

- **Use security certificates** and **security zones**.
- **Define your privacy preferences**.

The section begins with a discussion of **Internet security concerns**, as well as ways to **protect** your **password** and **e-mail messages**.

Internet Security Concerns

One of the founding principles of the Internet was that information should be free and easily accessible to everyone. This is one of the reasons the Internet has become so popular and is so widely-used.

Because it is an open system, however, the Internet is subject to misuse by unscrupulous individuals. This makes Internet security an important issue.

One Internet security concern is the spread of **computer viruses** and other malicious agents via the network. An infamous example is the Morris Internet Worm of 1988. Although the purpose of this worm was not to cause damage, many millions of dollars were spent on rebuilding systems and removing traces of the program.

Another Internet security concern is **privacy of communications**. When information travels from point A to point B over the Internet, it also travels through other points (computers) between points A and B. This has allowed others with the proper know-how to intercept confidential data, such as credit card numbers.

As the World Wide Web becomes more and more a center of commercial enterprise, offering online banking, online shopping, etc., these and other security concerns are being addressed. As a result, the Internet is becoming an increasingly safer means of exchanging information and doing business. Nevertheless, you should follow certain security guidelines, as well as be aware of available security options and privacy settings, when using the Internet.

Protecting Your Password

Your Internet Service Provider provides you with a password that allows you to connect to the Internet. If another individual acquires this password, he or she can assume your identity on the Internet and gain access to personal information, such as your e-mail messages.

The following is a list of tips for **selecting a password**:

- Do not use an obvious password. To make a password easy to remember, some persons use meaningful words or numbers (for example, their name, their social security number or their birth date). This, however, makes it easy for someone to guess the password of a person he or she knows.
- Do not use a password that is less than six characters in length. Short passwords can sometimes be determined by programs that try every letter and/or number combination until the correct password is found.
- Do not use a password that is listed in a dictionary. Individuals sometime obtain passwords by using words found in online dictionaries. This is one of the ways the Morris Internet Worm of 1988 kept itself alive.
- Do not use the same password for multiple applications. If you need a password to access more than one computer system or if you subscribe to multiple Internet services that require a password, resist the urge to use the same password. This will prevent an unauthorized user from accessing all of your accounts should one of your passwords become known to him or her.
- Use a combination of uppercase and lowercase letters, numbers, and non-alphanumeric characters in a password. Examples of non-alphanumeric characters include the asterisk (*), the dash (-), the dollar sign ($) and the exclamation point (!).
- Change your password often. This will prevent an unauthorized user from having your password for very long should he or she acquire it.

Protecting Your E-mail Messages

E-mail messages, like other information on the Internet, passes through different computers when traveling from its starting point to its destination. If you send sensitive information via e-mail, you can protect that information by using an **encryption program**. Such a program encrypts your data, which can be decrypted only by those individuals to whom you have given a special encryption key.

Using Security Certificates and Security Zones

Internet Explorer provides various means of securing information that travels over the Internet. These include **security certificates** and **security zones**.

Security certificate: A statement that guarantees either the identity of an individual or the security of a Web site. Internet Explorer includes two types of security certificates:

Personal certificates: This type of certificate guarantees that you are who you say you are. In establishing a personal certificate, you identify yourself by specifying such information as your username and password. This information is then sent to Web sites that require verification of your identity.

Web site certificates: This type of certificate guarantees that a particular Web site is secure and genuine. It prevents any other Web site from assuming the identity of the original site.

Security zone: A specific division of the Internet, as defined by Internet Explorer. Each security zone includes a different level of security. The four security zones are as follows:

Local intranet: This zone serves addresses that do not require a proxy server. The default security level for this zone is Medium.

Trusted sites: This zone includes Web sites you trust—for example, sites you know you can download information from without damage to your computer or data. The default security level for this zone is Low.

Restricted sites: This zone includes Web sites you do not trust—for example, sites you are not sure you can download information from without damage to your computer or data. The default security level for this zone is High.

Internet: This zone includes anything that is not on your computer or on an intranet, as well as anything that is not assigned to another zone. The default security level for this zone is Medium.

To **view the security certificates on the current computer**:

- Choose the **Tools, Internet Options** command.
- On the Content panel of the Internet Options dialog box, which is subsequently displayed, use the **Certificates** button.

Notes

Security certificates are issued by independent certification authorities. For information about obtaining a personal certificate, see the Internet Explorer Help system.

To **reset the security level for a security zone**:

- Choose the **Tools, Internet Options** command.
- On the Security panel of the Internet Options dialog box, select the desired **security zone**.
- Click the **Default Level** button.
- Select the **new security level** by **dragging** the **slider up** or **down**.

Notes

You can define a custom security level for a particular security zone by using the **Custom Level** button in the Internet Options dialog box. (The **Default Level** button can be used to subsequently restore the zone to its default security level.)

To **assign a Web site to a security zone**:

- Choose the **Tools**, **Internet Options** command.
- On the Security panel of the Internet Options dialog box, select the appropriate **security zone**.
- Click on the **Sites** button.
- In the dialog box that appears, type the **URL** of the Web site to be added to the specified security zone.
- Click on the **Add** button. Then click on the **OK** button to return to the Internet Options dialog box.

To **remove a Web site from a security zone**:

- Choose the **Tools**, **Internet Options** command.
- On the Security panel of the Internet Options dialog box, select the appropriate **security zone**.
- Click on the **Sites** button.
- In the dialog box that appears, select the **URL** of the Web site to be removed from the specified security zone.
- Click on the **Remove** button. Then click on the **OK** button to return to the Internet Options dialog box.

Objective

In this exercise, you will **assign the National Basketball Association Web site to a different security zone**. You will then **reassign this Web site to its original security zone**.

13.1

- **Make sure that the Internet Explorer Home page is displayed.**

- **Choose the Tools, Internet Options command.**

The Internet Options dialog box is displayed.

- **Click on the Security tab.**

The Security panel of the dialog box is displayed.

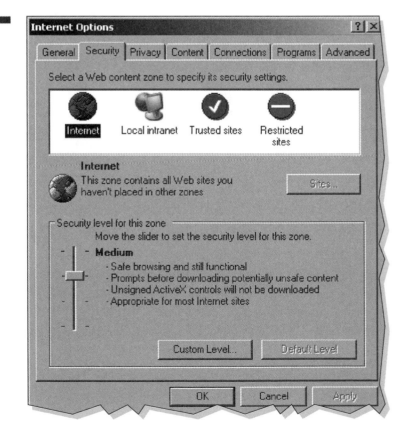

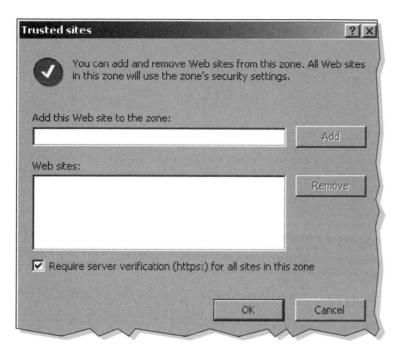

13.2

- **In the list of zones, click on Trusted sites.**

The new security zone is selected.

- **Click on the Sites button.**

The Trusted sites dialog box is displayed.

- **Type: www.nba.com**

The URL of the National Basketball Association Home page is entered.

- **Click on Require server verification (https:) for all sites in this zone (to deselect the option).**

NOTE: *If the above option is already deselected, skip this step.*

- **Click on the Add button.**

The URL is added to the Web sites box.

- **Click on the OK button.**

The Internet Options dialog box is redisplayed.

- **Click on the OK button.**

The dialog box is closed. You will now verify the new security zone for the National Basketball Association Web site.

- **Click in the Address bar.**

  Type: www.nba.com
  Press [ENTER].

The National Basketball Association Home page is displayed. Notice that "Trusted sites" appears at the right side of the Status bar.

- **Click on the Home button.**

The Internet Explorer Home page is redisplayed. You will now reassign the National Basketball Association Web site to its original security zone.

- **Choose the Tools, Internet Options command. Then click on the Security tab in the Internet Options dialog box.**

The Security panel of the Internet Options dialog box is redisplayed.

- **In the list of zones, click on Trusted sites. Then click on the Sites button.**

The Trusted sites dialog box is redisplayed.

- **In the Web sites list, click on www.nba.com. Then click on the Remove button.**

The selected URL is removed from the Web sites list.

- **Click on Require server verification (https:) for all sites in this zone (to select the option and restore it to its original setting).**

- **Click on the OK button.**

The Internet Options dialog box is redisplayed.

- **Click on the OK button.**

The dialog box is closed.

Protecting Your Privacy on the Web

Internet Explorer gives you tools to protect your privacy on the Web by giving you more control over cookies and information on a Web site's privacy policy.

A **cookie** is a text file created by some Web sites and stored on your computer so that the next time you visit the site it can automatically access information about you, such as your name, home address, work address, telephone number, or preferences when visiting that site. Once a cookie is saved on your computer only the Web site that created the cookie can read it. Although the use of cookies is allowed, you can change your privacy preferences for handling cookies to specify that Internet Explorer prompts you before placing a cookie on your computer or you can prevent Internet Explorer from accepting any cookies.

Many Web sites also provide a **privacy policy** that tells you what kind of information the site collects, how it uses the information and to whom it gives the information. Once you define your privacy preferences for handling cookies, Internet Explorer compares your privacy preferences to the Web site's privacy policy (if one exists). The program then decides whether or not to allow cookies or restrict them.

To **view the existing privacy policy of a Web site**:

- With the Web page displayed, choose the **View, Privacy Report** command.
- Select the site from the list and click on **Summary**.

To **change your privacy settings for handling cookies**:

- Choose the **Tools, Internet Options** command.
- On the Privacy panel of the Internet Options dialog box, select the desired **privacy level** by **dragging** the **slider up** or **down**.

To **choose cookie handling preferences for an individual web site**:

- Choose the **Tools, Internet Options** command.
- On the Privacy panel of the Internet Options dialog box, click on the **Edit** button. This is where you can specify which Web sites are always or never allowed to use cookies regardless of their privacy policy.
- Type the address of the web site you want to manage, and then click **Allow** or **Block**.

Notes

Cookie handling preferences for individual web sites can also be chosen from the **Summary window** of the **View, Privacy Report** dialog box.

To **remove cookie handling preferences for an individual web site**:

- Choose the **Tools, Internet Options** command.
- On the Privacy panel of the Internet Options dialog box, click on the **Edit** button.
- Select the name of the web site to be removed from the **List of Managed Sites** and click on the **Remove** button.

To **delete all cookies from your computer**:

- Choose the **Tools, Internet Options** command.
- On the General panel of the Internet Options dialog box, click on the **Delete Cookies** button.

Further Practice

The following **Case Study** will give you the opportunity to review and practice many of the Internet Explorer features you have learned.

1. **Start Internet Explorer.**
2. Display **Microsoft Corporation's Home page** (http://www.microsoft.com).
3. **Print** the above **Web page**.
4. **Navigate** through **Microsoft Corporation's Web site** by clicking on various **hyperlinks**.
5. Using the **Back** and **Forward** buttons, redisplay **previously-visited pages** of **Microsoft Corporation's Web site**.
6. Using the **Search Companion**, search for and display **Web pages** related to **cooking**.
7. **Add two** of the **Web pages** found as a result of the above search to your **Favorites list**. Make **both pages** available for **offline viewing**.
8. Using the **Address bar**, redisplay **Microsoft Corporation's Home page**.
9. From the **Favorites Explorer bar**, redisplay the **Web pages** added to your **Favorites list** in step 7.
10. Display **Web pages** that are available for **offline viewing**.

Congratulations! You have completed the **Case Study**.

XHTML—Case Study I

OBJECTIVES

After successfully completing this case study, you should be able to:

- Create a basic XHTML document using Notepad
- Define the basic rules of XHTML
- Understand DocTypes
- Create a header section containing meta and title tags
- Create body elements
- Add background color in a Web page
- Add horizontal lines in the Web page

- Create paragraphs and line breaks
- Present emphasized and strong text
- Create nested tags
- Create ordered, unordered and definition lists
- Create headers in a Web page
- View web pages in a browser
- Validate Web pages using a Validator tool

Case Study I—XHTML

You are hired as a Teaching Assistant in a University. Your first assignment is to use XHTML to create a web page that includes your name, department, and the name of your University. The page also includes pertinent course information.

Your instructor expects you to adhere to the standards of XHTML. To assure your web page readers that you conform to the XHTML standards, he/she wants you to include a validation icon on your Web page.

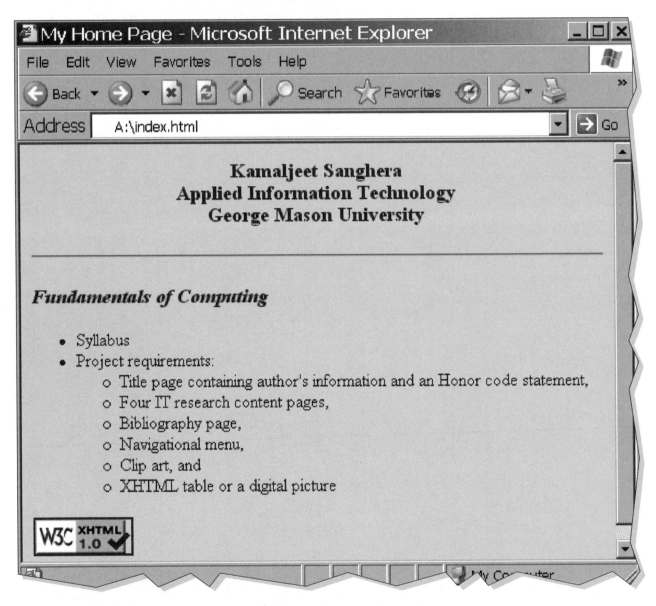

What Is XHTML?

XHTML stands for EXtensible Hypertext Markup Language. It is a cleaner but a stricter standard for making web pages. It is similar to HTML (Hypertext Markup Language) but is based on XML. The goal of XHTML authoring is to make web pages accessible on alternative devices such as Personal Digital Assistants (PDAs), cellular phones, televisions, and aural browsers for visually impaired and blind computer users.

A XHTML document or a Web page is a special text file saved with .htm or .html extension. To open a web page, a user enters a Uniform Resource Locator (URL) in a browser. The browser locates the file, interprets the markups contained in the file, and displays the file in the browser window.

There are several XHTML editors available in the market such as MS FrontPage, Adobe GoLive, and Macromedia DreamWeaver. These tools can quickly generate Web pages. The purpose of this book is not to teach you those tools but to explain the code involved in XHTML.

Creating a Web Page Using Notepad

You will create your first web page using Notepad. To open Notepad, click on the **Start** button on the Windows toolbar, by pointing to **All Programs** (if running Windows XP) or to **Programs** (if you are running Windows 2000), by selecting the **Accessories** option on the All Programs or Programs menu, and by selecting the **Notepad** option on the subsequent submenu.

Objective

In this exercise, you will start **Notepad** and create a **basic XHTML document** template.

1.1

- **Click on the Start button on the Windows taskbar.**

- **Point to All Programs (if you are running Windows XP) or to Programs (if you are running Windows 2000).**

- **Point to Accessories on the menu.**

- **Click on the Notepad on the submenu.**

NOTE: If the Start menu includes a Notepad shortcut icon, you can start the Notepad by simply clicking on the icon. If the Windows desktop includes a Notepad shortcut icon, you can start the Notepad by double-clicking on the icon.

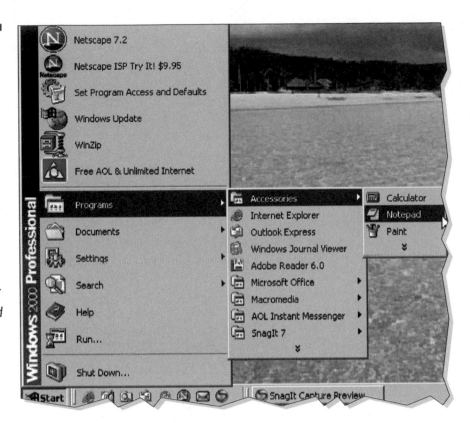

1.2

- **If the Notepad Application window is not maximized, click on the Maximize button on the Title bar of the window.**

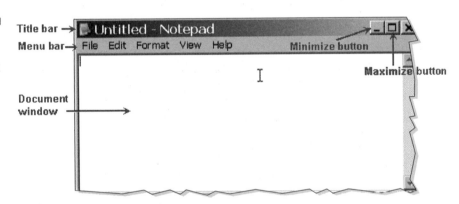

1.3

- **Choose the Format, Word Wrap command. If the Word Wrap command is already selected (check marked), ignore this step and go to the next one.**

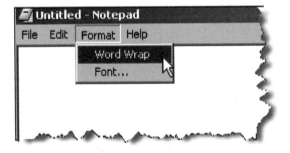

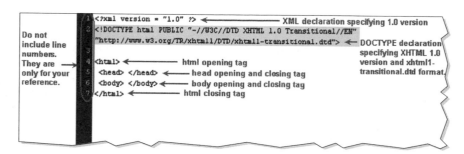

I.4

- **Type XHTML document (without typing line numbers—they are only for your reference) as shown in the figure on the left.**

Lines 1 and 2 are required lines in XHTML document. Line 1 is an xml declaration statement and specifies the xml version. Line 2 has a DOCTYPE declaration and specifies XHTML version and format used in the document. There are three types of DocTypes available: Strict, Transitional, and Frameset. We will follow Transitional Doctype in this text book.

Transitional DocType allows you to use the presentational and deprecated elements such as <font>, <u>, etc.

<!DOCTYPE html PUBLIC "-//W3C//DTD XHTML 1.0 Transitional//EN""http://www.w3.org/TR/xhtml1/DTD/xhtml1-transitional.dtd">

Strict DocType does not allow presentation or deprecated elements. The XHTML presentation elements are included in Cascading Style Sheets (CSS).

<!DOCTYPE html PUBLIC "-//W3C//DTD XHTML 1.0 Strict//EN""http://www.w3.org/TR/xhtml1/DTD/xhtml1-strict.dtd">

Frameset DocType is identical to Transitional DocType but allows you to include frames on your pages.

<!DOCTYPE html PUBLIC "-//W3C//DTD XHTML 1.0 Frameset//EN""http://www.w3.org/TR/xhtml1/DTD/xhtml1-frameset.dtd">

DocType statements are used by the validator to ensure that your document conforms to the specified version and format.

1.5

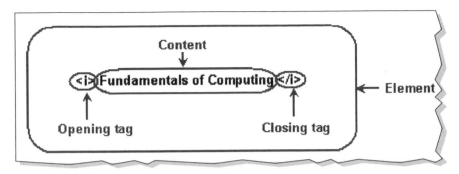

Lines 4–7 contain tags. Browsers interpret XHTML tags in order to format and present text on Web pages. Almost all XHTML tags have an opening tag and a closing tag. The opening tag usually has three main parts—a less than sign (<), name of the tag (e.g. head), and a greater than sign (>). The closing tag has four parts—a less than sign (<), a forward slash (/), name of the tag, and a greater than sign (>). XHTML requires you to write all tags in lower case letters. A text embedded between tags is called the **content** *of the tag.*

An **element** *includes tags and contents.*

XHTML allows empty elements. We will discuss empty elements later in the case study.

Header Section

The header section of an XHTML document includes the **head** element with the **title** and **meta** elements. The **head** element contains information about the document. Both **sub-title** and **meta** elements are parts of the **head** element section.

The **title** element contents appear on the browser's title bar. It is a required element in all XHTML documents. You must include a brief description of your document in the **title** element as it defines the web page in user's bookmarks or favorites.

The **meta** element contains the information about your document and is mainly used by the search engines. The contents of **meta** tag do not appear on the web page. You can include more than one **meta** element in your document. However, each **meta** element must specify a property-value pair. The name attribute identifies the property and the content attribute specifies the property's value. We will discuss attributes later in the case study.

Objective

In this exercise, you will add **meta** and **title** elements in the **head** section.

```
index - Notepad                                    _ □ x
File  Edit  Format  View  Help
<?xml version = "1.0" ?>
<!DOCTYPE html PUBLIC "-//W3C//DTD XHTML 1.0 Transitional//EN"
"http://www.w3.org/TR/xhtml1/DTD/xhtml1-transitional.dtd">

<html>
 <head>
  <meta name = "author" content = "Kamaljeet Sanghera" />
  <meta name = "description" content = "Home page" />
  <title> My Home Page </title>
 </head>

 <body> </body>
</html>
```

2.1

- **Edit your current notepad document by entering the highlighted code in the head section:**

*NOTE: The **meta** elements include the name of the author and a brief description of the current document. The content of title element (My Home Page) will appear on the title bar of the browser window.*

Saving a Document and Viewing in a Browser

To avoid losing what appears on the screen due to an unexpected occurrence, such as a power failure, it is important that you frequently save your documents as you work on them.

Objective

In this exercise, you will **save your new document**.

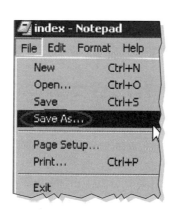

3.1

- **Choose the File, Save As command.**

3.2

- **Save the document as index.html on your floppy (A:) or Removable disk (D:). In Save As dialog box, type index.html for "File Name." Select All Files for "Save as type." Click Save. Remember the location of this file. We will be viewing this file in a browser in the next step.**

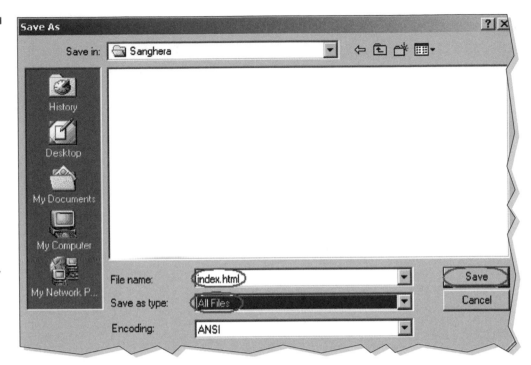

3.3

View your document in an Internet Explorer browser.

- **Click the Start button on the Windows taskbar.**

- **Point to All Programs (if you are running Windows XP) or to Programs (if you are running Windows 2000).**

- **Click on Internet Explorer on the menu.**

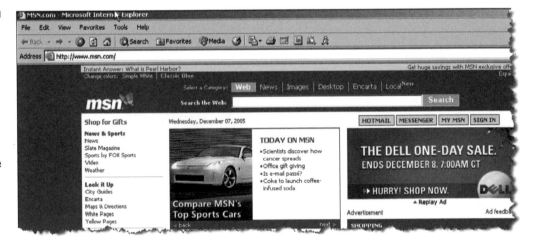

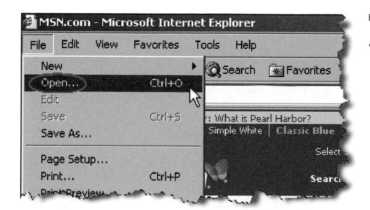

3.4

- **Choose the File, Open command.**

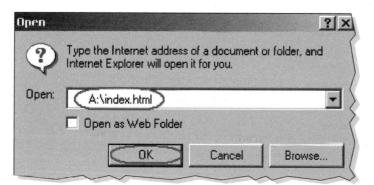

3.5

- **Click on the Browse button and navigate to the appropriate drive where you stored the index.html file.**

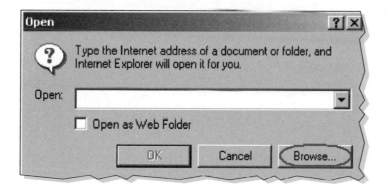

3.6

- **Choose the file index.html, which you saved earlier, and click Open.**
- **Choose the OK button.**

3.7

- **A blank document is displayed on the browser window because the body element in your code does not contain any information. The "My Home Page" in the title bar window is the effect of the title element in the head section.**

- **Minimize the browser window by clicking on the minimize button.**

Effect of title element in the head section ↓

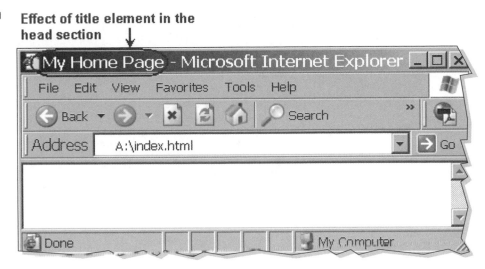

Body Section

The content of the **body** element appears in the browser window. You can use the **body** element attributes to change the appearance of the document. Their possible values, syntax, and usage are listed in the following table:

Attributes of Body Element			
Attribute	**Value**	**Syntax**	**Usage**
background	"URL", e.g. mypic.jpg	`<body background = "URL"> ... </body>`	URL image tiled in the background of the page
bgcolor	"ColorName" or "HexadecimalValue" e.g. yellow, #EAE4EF	`<body bgcolor = "ColorName"> ... </body>`	Sets the background color of the page
link	"ColorName" or "HexadecimalValue" e.g. yellow, #EAE4EF	`<body link = "ColorName"> ... </body>`	Sets the color of hyperlinks in the document
alink	"ColorName" or "HexadecimalValue" e.g. yellow, #EAE4EF	`<body alink = "ColorName"> ... </body>`	Sets the color of active hyperlinks
vlink	"ColorName" or "HexadecimalValue" e.g. yellow, #EAE4EF	`<body vlink = "ColorName"> ... </body>`	Sets the color of visited hyperlinks

An attribute adds information in an opening tag that describes the element. XHTML requires that all attributes be written in lower case letters; they must also have values within the double quotation marks. The name of the attribute is on the left, followed by the equal to sign, and then the value.

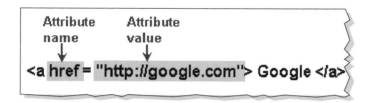

Multiple attributes can be added with a space between them.

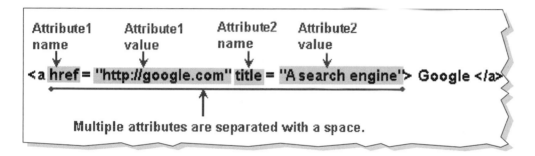

The above example demonstrates a link to Google, a search engine. We will discuss tag and its attributes in the next case study.

XHTML requires the following rules for attributes:

- Must be typed in lower case letters
- Must have value(s)
- Values must be within double quotation marks
- Multiple attributes must be added with a space between them
- One attribute can occur only once in a tag

Objective

In this exercise, you will set the background color and the text color of the document. You will also enter your name for the body of your Web document.

4.1

- **Edit your index.html file in notepad as shown in the figure on the right. Enter your name in place of the author's name, Kamaljeet Sanghera.**

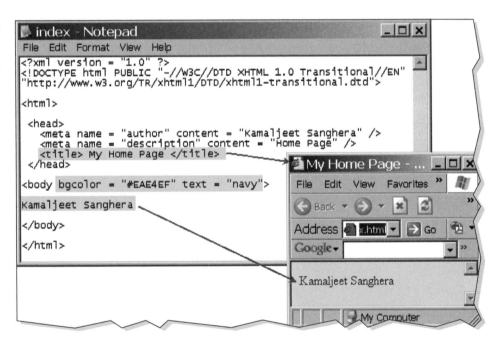

```
index - Notepad
File  Edit  Format  View  Help
<?xml version = "1.0" ?>
<!DOCTYPE html PUBLIC "-//W3C//DTD XHTML 1.0 Transitional//EN"
"http://www.w3.org/TR/xhtml1/DTD/xhtml1-transitional.dtd">

<html>
  <head>
    <meta name = "author" content = "Kamaljeet Sanghera" />
    <meta name = "description" content = "Home page" />
    <title> My Home Page </title>
  </head>

<body bgcolor = "#EAE4EF" text = "navy">        ← Attributes are separated
        Kamaljeet Sanghera   ← Replace with your     with a space.
</body>                            name.
</html>
```

4.2

You have assigned the hexadecimal value (#EAE4EF) of light navy color to the document background. The content of the **body** *will be displayed in a navy color.*

- **Choose File, Save or press Ctrl+S together to save your file.**

- **Switch to the browser window.**

- **Refresh the browser by pressing the F5 function key on your keyboard or by clicking the Refresh icon.**

The document has a very light navy background and a dark navy text. These colors can be different on your screen.

NOTE: *You must be careful in choosing colors for a web page. You should always use a high contrast such as black background with white text or red background with white text. Black background and blue text (or similar contrasts) makes it difficult to read the text.*

```
index - Notepad
File  Edit  Format  View  Help
<?xml version = "1.0" ?>
<!DOCTYPE html PUBLIC "-//W3C//DTD XHTML 1.0 Transitional//EN"
"http://www.w3.org/TR/xhtml1/DTD/xhtml1-transitional.dtd">

<html>

  <head>
    <meta name = "author" content = "Kamaljeet Sanghera" />
    <meta name = "description" content = "Home Page" />
    <title> My Home Page </title>
  </head>

<body bgcolor = "#EAE4EF" text = "navy">

Kamaljeet Sanghera

</body>

</html>
```

```
My Home Page - ...
File  Edit  View  Favorites  »
Back ▾       ▾  ✖  ⟳
Address   xhtml  ▾  → Go
Google ▾
Kamaljeet Sanghera
                    My Computer
```

Document Formatting Tags

XHTML transitional DocType allows the use of document formatting tags. In the strict DocType, these tags must be included in the cascading style sheet (CSS). CSS is not covered in this text book. CSS is usually taught in advanced web development classes.

Line Break

The **br** element forces a line break. The syntax on **br** element is as follows:

It is an empty element i.e. the line break self closes. The ending tag is forbidden in empty elements.

The figure below shows an example of the line break element.

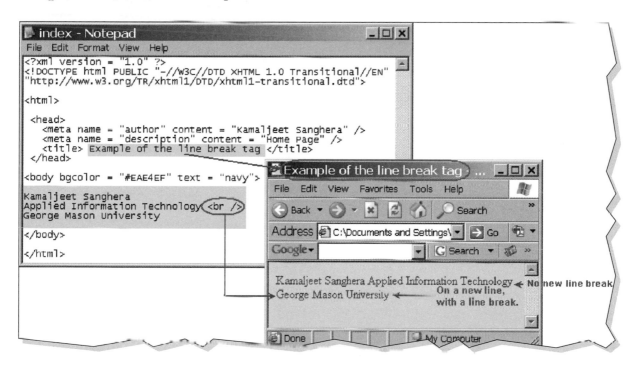

Headers

Headings distinguish text in the document so that information can be easily located. XHTML provides six levels of headings, from <h1> to <h6>. The syntax of these predefined headings is as follows:

<h1> ... </h1>
<h2> ... </h2>
...
<h6> ... </h6>

You must separate document sections using heading tags. The figure below shows an example of the heading elements.

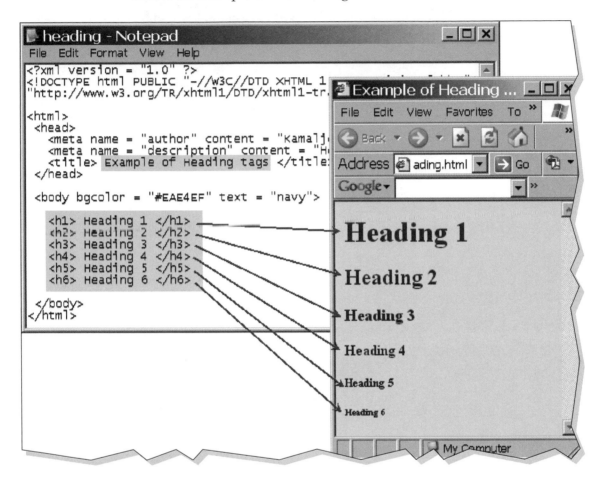

Each of these tags has an align attribute with left (default), right, and center values. The syntax of the heading tag with the align attribute is:

<h1 align = "value"> … </h1>
<h2 align = "value"> … </h2>
…
<h6 align = "value"> … </h6>

The figure below shows an example of an align attribute with left, center, and right values.

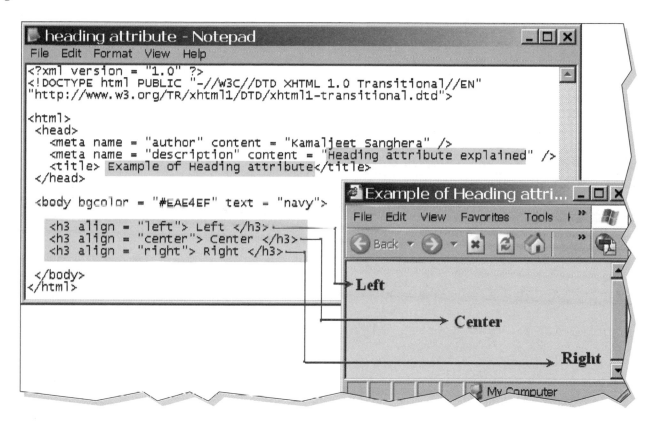

Objective

In this exercise, you will enter your information in the document using both heading tags and line break tags.

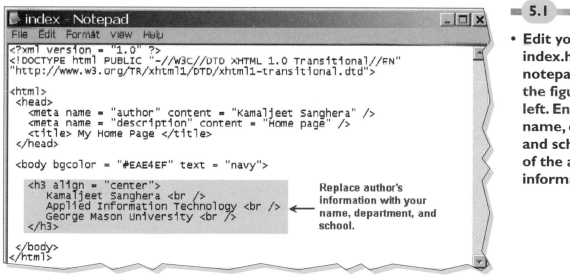

Replace author's information with your name, department, and school.

5.1

- **Edit your index.html file in notepad as shown in the figure on the left. Enter your name, department, and school in place of the author's information:**

5.2

- **Choose File, Save or press Ctrl+S together to save your file.**

- **Switch to the browser window.**

- **Refresh the browser by pressing the F5 function key on your keyboard or by clicking the Refresh icon. Your Web page should look similar to the figure shown on the right.**

Horizontal Rule Tags

The **<hr />** is an empty element and is used to define a horizontal rule. It has align, no shade, size, and width attributes. The possible values, syntax, and usage of these attributes are listed in the following table:

Horizontal Rule <hr />			
Attribute	**Value**	**Syntax**	**Usage**
size	Pixels	<hr size = "value" />	Height of the line. By default, the width of the line is 100%. It runs through the entire browser windows. The align attribute is useful and visible only when the width is reduced.
noshade	noshade	<hr noshade = "noshade" />	Solid bar. No shading.
width	Pixels or percent	<hr width = "value" />	Width in pixels or percentages.
align	right left center	<hr align = "value" />	Aligns the line based on the value.

The figure below shows an example of the horizontal rule along with its attributes:

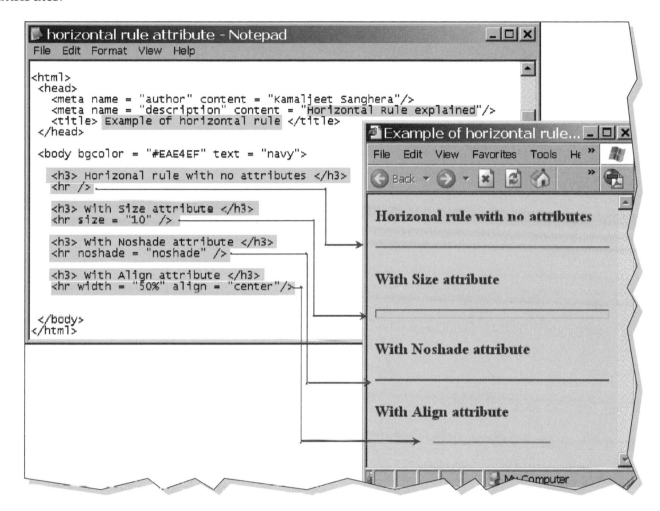

Objective

In this exercise, you will add a horizontal line in the document.

6.1

- **Add the <hr/> element in your index.html file as highlighted in the figure on the left.**

6.2

- **Choose File, Save or press Ctrl+S together to save your file.**

- **Switch to the browser window.**

- **Refresh the browser by pressing the F5 function key on your keyboard or by clicking the Refresh icon. Your Web page should look similar to the page shown on the right.**

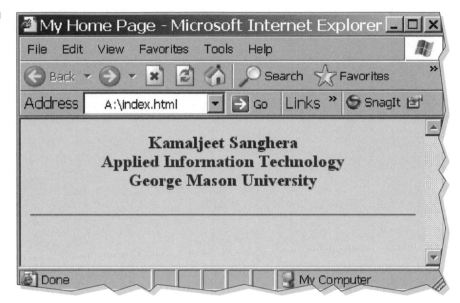

Paragraph

The **p** element defines a text paragraph. The syntax of **p** element is as follows:

<p> ... </p>

It adds one blank line ahead of the text that defines a paragraph. Browsers ignore formatting within the **p** tags. Text within **p** tags is rendered with default font size and type. The figure below shows that paragraph elements ignore extra spaces and formatting within the **p** tags.

```
<?xml version = "1.0" ?>
<!DOCTYPE html PUBLIC "-//W3C//DTD XHTML 1.0 Transitional//EN"
"http://www.w3.org/TR/xhtml1/DTD/xhtml1-transitional.dtd">

<html>
  <head>
    <meta name = "author" content = "Kamaljeet Sanghera"/>
    <meta name = "description" content = "Paragraph explained"/>
    <title> Paragraph formatting ignored</title>
  </head>

<body bgcolor = "#EAE4EF" text = "navy">

    <p> Paragraph tag     ignores          extra spaces
    and formatting
    such as text on the new line here will be displayed on the same line
    in the browser.
    </p>

</body>
</html>
```

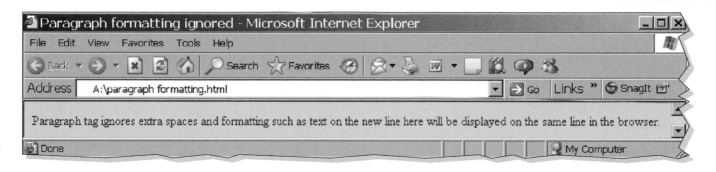

NOTE: The paragraph tag is different from the line break element. The **br** element takes the content to the next line without adding an extra blank line.

The figure below shows the difference between **p** and **br** elements.

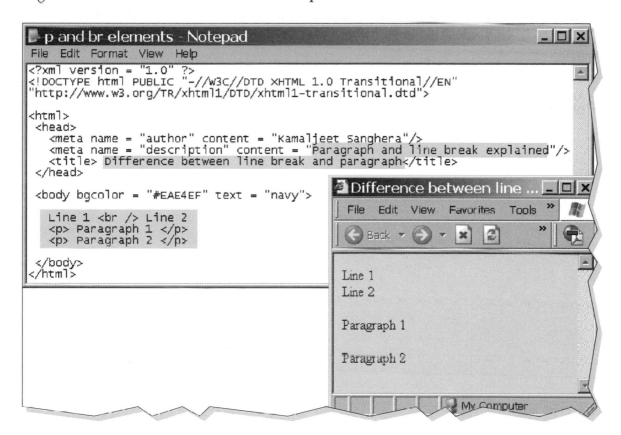

Paragraph tag has only one attribute: **align**. The possible values of align attribute are left (default), right, and center. The syntax of paragraph tag with align attribute is as follows:

<p align = "value"> ... </p>

The example of **p** tag with align attribute is as follows:

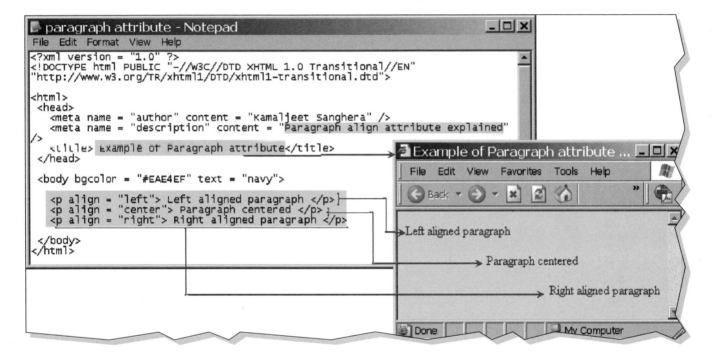

XHTML does not allow you the use of heading tags within **p** tags. However, you can include any of the following elements within the **p** tags to format the entire paragraph's text.

Elements within p Element		
Element	**Syntax**	**Usage**
b	\<b\> ... \</b\>	Bold text.
i	\<i\> ... \</i\>	Italicized text.
strong	\<strong\> ... \</strong\>	Strong font. Browsers usually display boldface text.
em	\<em\> ... \</em\>	Emphasized font. Browsers usually display italicized text.
big	\<big\> ... \</big\>	Bigger in size than the surrounding text.
small	\<small\> ... \</small\>	Smaller in size than the surrounding text.
sup	\<sup\> ... \</sup\>	Superscript (slightly raised) the text.
sub	\<sub\> ... \</sub\>	Subscript (slightly lowered) the text.
del	\<del\> ... \</del\>	Strike out the text.
tt	\<tt\> ... \</tt\>	Teletype or mono spaced text.

The figure below shows an example of the formatting elements.

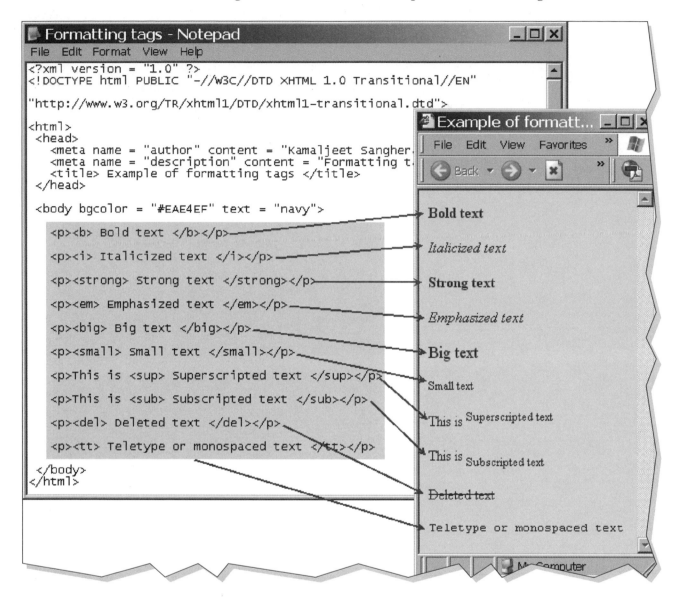

Nested tags contain one or more sets of tags within one tag. You must use nested tags in the opposite sequence from which they were used in the syntax. For example:

<p><b> ... </b></p>

You can apply more than one format tag on a text as illustrated below:

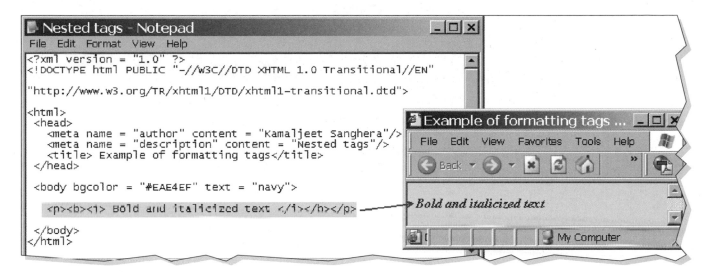

Objective

In this exercise, you will use nested tags.

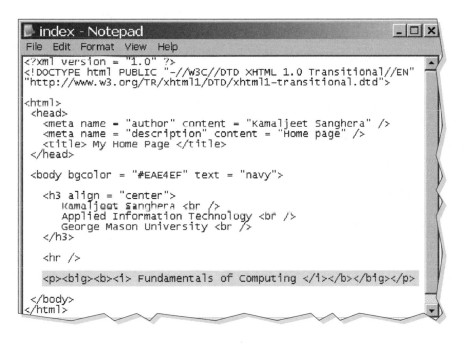

7.1

• **Edit your index.html file in notepad as shown in the figure on the left.**

NOTE: *For a document's well-formedness, you must close tags in the reverse order from which they were opened.*

7.2

- **Choose File, Save or press Ctrl+S together to save your file.**

- **Switch to the browser window.**

- **Refresh the browser by pressing the F5 function key on your keyboard or by clicking the Refresh icon. Your Web page should look similar to the figure shown on the right.**

List Tags

There is a difference between reading on the Web and reading on a paper. People don't like to read much on the Web. Bullets play important roles in clearly stating critical points without adding any superfluous information.

There are three kinds of lists: definition lists, ordered lists, and unordered lists. Their syntax, possible attributes, and examples are as follows:

Three Types of Lists

Definition list defines the list of terms and their definitions.

```
<dl>
  <dt> ... </dt>
  <dd> ... </dd>
  ...
</dl>
```

EXAMPLE OF DEFINITION LIST:

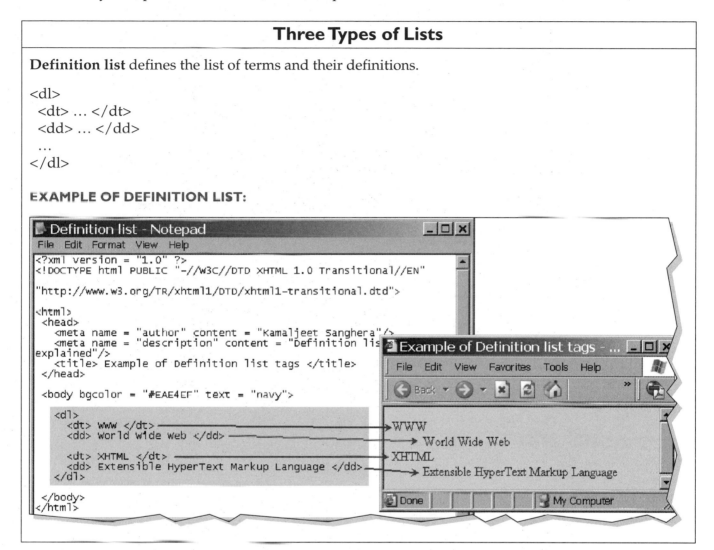

Unordered list begins each item with a bullet. It uses the li element to define each list item.

```
<ul>
  <li> ... </li>
  <li> ... </li>
  ...
  <li> ... </li>
</ul>
```

EXAMPLE OF UNORDERED LIST:

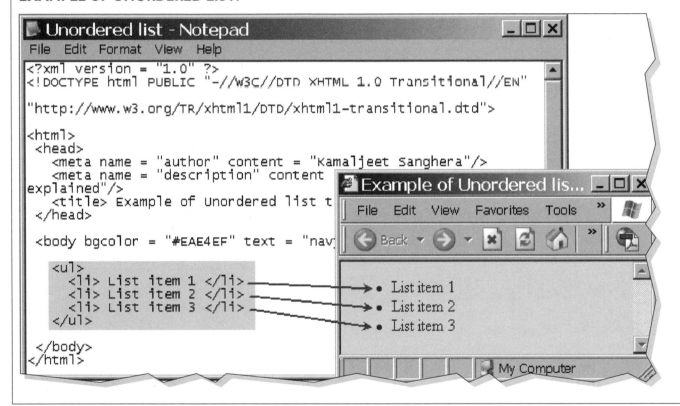

The li element allows the **type** attribute. The possible values of type attribute are disc, square, and circle.

<ul>
  <li type = "value"> … </li>
  <li> … </li>
  …
  <li> … </li>
</ul>

EXAMPLE OF TYPE ATTRIBUTE WITHIN LIST TAGS:

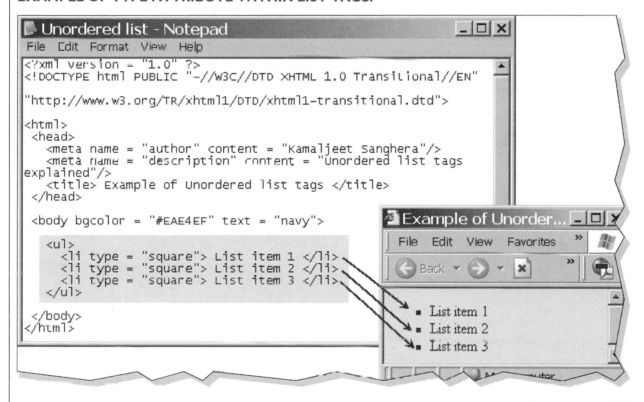

Ordered list begins with a number. The **li** tag is used to define each item of the list.

```
<ol>
 <li> ... </li>
 <li> ... </li>
 ...
 <li> ... </li>
</ol>
```

EXAMPLE OF ORDERED LIST:

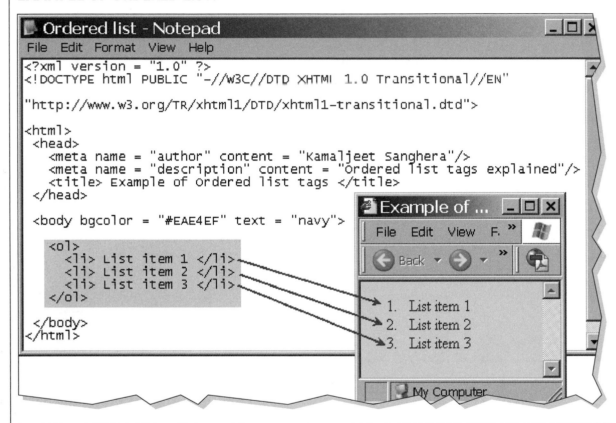

The type attribute of the <li> tag can be used to add different numbering types before the item. The syntax is:

```
<ul>
 <li type = "value"> ... </li>
 <li> ... </li>
 ...
 <li> ... </li>
</ul>
```

The possible values of the type attribute are A (for uppercase letters), a (for lowercase letters), i (for lowercase Roman numbering), I (for uppercase Roman numbering), and 1 (for numbers).

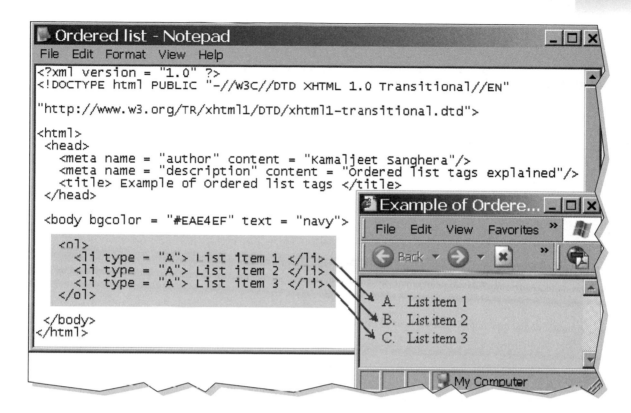

The ordered and unordered lists can be nested in each other. An example of a nested list is as follows:

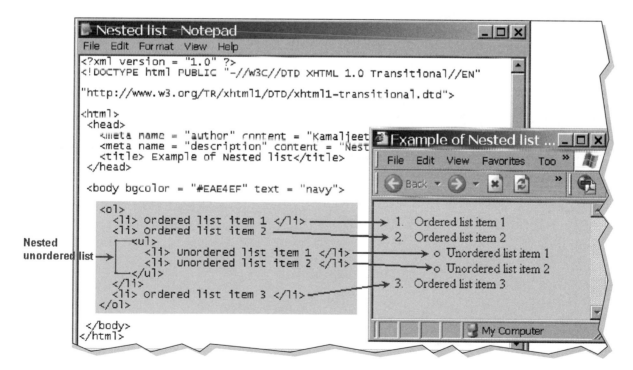

Objective

In this exercise, you will use nested list tags for the course content.

8.1

- **Edit your index.html file in notepad as shown in the figure on the right.**

```
index - Notepad
File  Edit  Format  View  Help

<html>
 <head>
    <meta name = "author" content = "Kamaljeet Sanghera"/>
    <meta name = "description" content = "Home page"/>
    <title> My Home Page </title>
 </head>

<body bgcolor = "#EAE4EF" text = "navy">

  <h3 align = "center">
     Kamaljeet Sanghera <br />
     Applied Information Technology <br />
     George mason University <br />
  </h3>

  <hr />

  <p><big><b><i> Fundamentals of computing </i></b></big></p>

  <ul>
     <li> Syllabus </li>
     <li> Project requirements:
        <ul>
           <li> Title page containing author's information and an Honor code statement, </li>
           <li> Four IT research content pages, </li>
           <li> Bibliography page, </li>
           <li> Navigational menu, </li>
           <li> Clip art, and </li>
           <li> XHTML table or a digital picture </li>
        </ul>
     </li>
  </ul>

 </body>
</html>
```

8.2

- **Choose File, Save or press Ctrl+S together to save your file.**

- **Switch to the browser window.**

- **Refresh the browser by pressing the F5 function key on your keyboard or by clicking the Refresh icon. Your Web page should look similar to the figure on the right.**

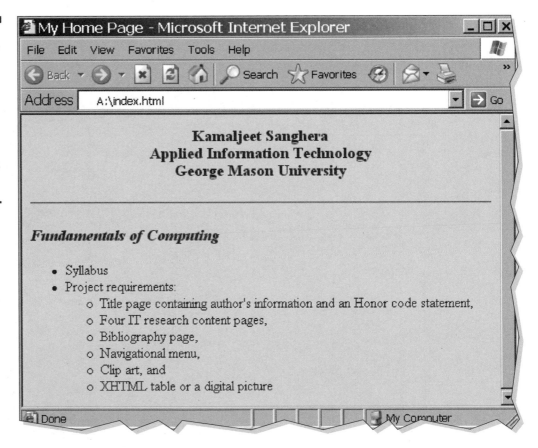

Validating Web Pages

To ensure that your web page follows the rules of XHTML, you will use a tool called Validator. Validator checks your page against formal XHTML standards. It parses your Web document and produces the error list. Once all errors are fixed, you can use a "valid" icon on the page. The "valid" icon shows your Web site user that you have created an interoperable Web page. The icon must link to Validator's site so your page can be revalidated to verify your assertion.

Objective

In this exercise, you will validate your index.html page.

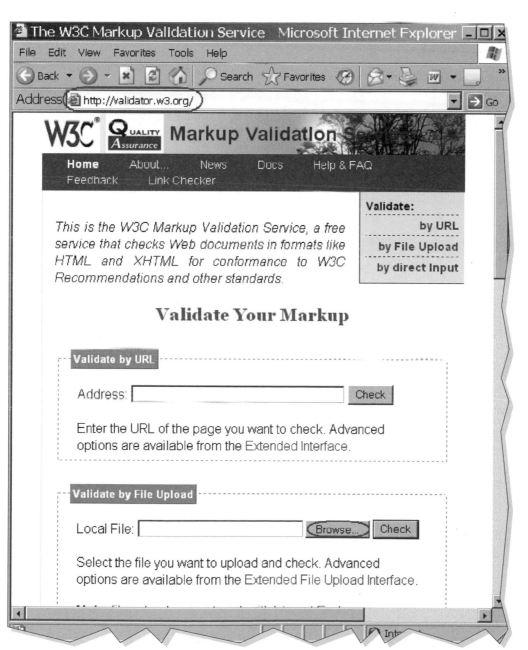

9.1

- **Open Internet Explorer.**

- **Enter the URL: http://validator. w3.org/**

- **Click on the Browse button.**

9.2

• **In the Choose file dialog box, locate the index.html file and click on Open.**

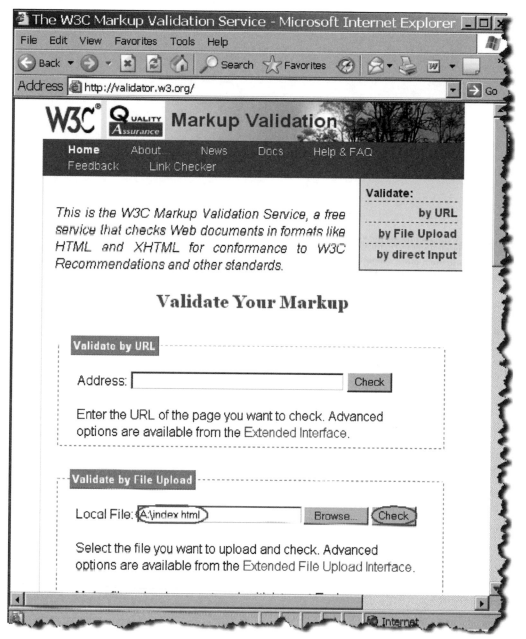

- **Click on the Check button on the Markup Validation Service web page.**

If you get "no character encoding" error, you need to specify character encoding in your document. Character encoding is normally done in the Web server configuration file or administration program.

9.4

- **To specify character encoding in your document, edit index.html with the highlighted code shown in the figure on the right.**

```
index - Notepad
File  Edit  Format  View  Help
<html>
 <head>
   <meta http-equiv="Content-Type" content="text/html; charset=iso-8859-1" />
   <meta name = "author" content = "Kamaljeet Sanghera"/>
   <meta name = "description" content = "Home page"/>
   <title> My Home Page </title>
 </head>

<body bgcolor = "#EAE4EF" text = "navy">

  <h3 align = "center">
    Kamaljeet Sanghera <br />
    Applied Information Technology <br />
    George Mason University <br />
  </h3>

  <hr />

  <p><big><b><i> Fundamentals of computing </i></b></big></p>

  <ul>
      <li> Syllabus </li>
      <li> Project requirements:
         <ul>
           <li> Title page containing author's information and an Honor code statement, </li>
           <li> Four IT research content pages, </li>
           <li> Bibliography page, </li>
           <li> Navigational menu, </li>
           <li> Clip art, and </li>
           <li> XHTML table or a digital picture </li>
         </ul>
      </li>
  </ul>

</body>
</html>
```

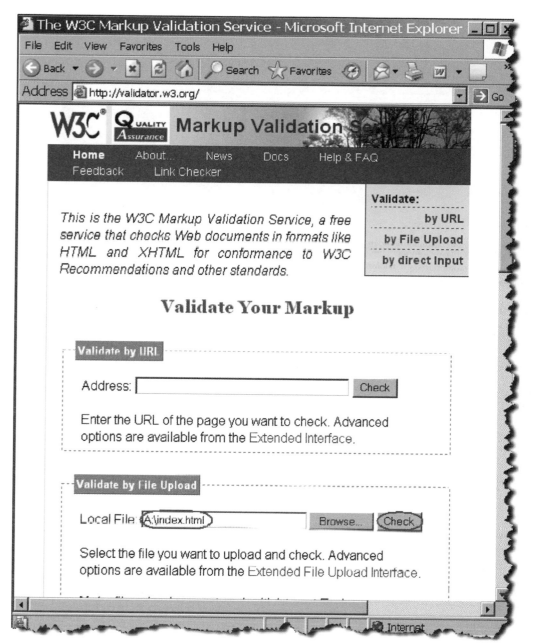

- **Save your file.**

- **Switch to Internet Explorer (XHTML Markup Validation Service). Click on the Back navigation button on the browser.**

- **On the following page, locate your index.html file again and click on Check.**

9.6

- **If you get similar results as shown in the figure on the right, your file is a valid XHTML 1.0 transitional.**

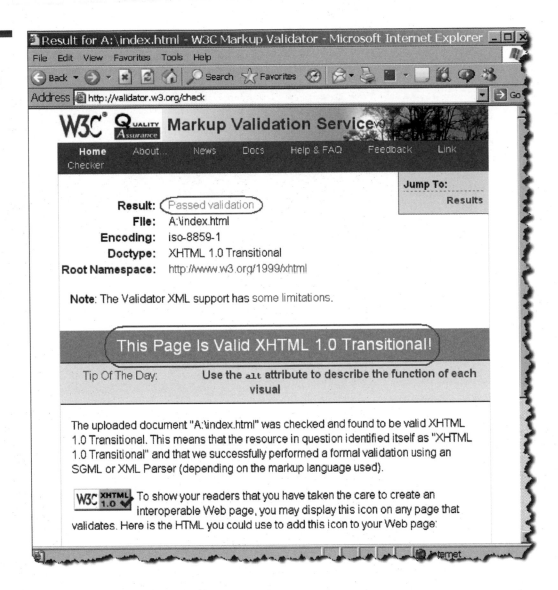

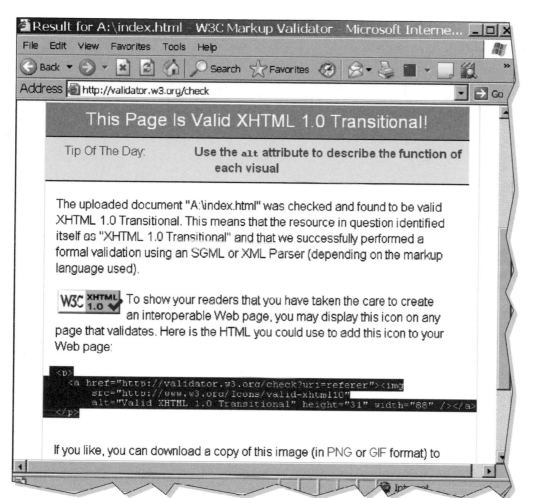

9.7

*Markup Validation Service also provides an icon to be displayed on the page that has successfully been validated. The code to include the icon on the Web page is given on their page. **Select** the code highlighted on the left and **copy** it (CTRL+C).*

9.8

- **Paste the code in your index.html file before the end of the `<body>` tag.**

- **Your index.html file should look similar to the figure on the right.**

```
index - Notepad
File  Edit  Format  View  Help
<!DOCTYPE html PUBLIC "-//W3C//DTD XHTML 1.0 Transitional//EN"
"http://www.w3.org/TR/xhtml1/DTD/xhtml1-transitional.dtd">

<html>
  <head>
    <meta http-equiv="Content-Type" content="text/html; charset=iso-8859-1" />
    <meta name = "author" content = "Kamaljeet Sanghera"/>
    <meta name = "description" content = "Home page"/>
    <title> My Home Page </title>
  </head>

  <body bgcolor = "#EAE4EF" text = "navy">

    <h3 align = "center">
      Kamaljeet Sanghera <br />
      Applied Information Technology <br />
      George mason University <br />
    </h3>

    <hr />

    <p><big><b><i> Fundamentals of computing </i></b></big></p>

    <ul>
        <li> Syllabus </li>
        <li> Project requirements:
            <ul>
                <li> Title page containing author's information and an Honor code statement, </li>
                <li> Four IT research content pages, </li>
                <li> Bibliography page, </li>
                <li> Navigational menu, </li>
                <li> Clip art, and </li>
                <li> XHTML table or a digital picture </li>
            </ul>
        </li>
    </ul>

    <p>
      <a href="http://validator.w3.org/check?uri=referer"><img
         src="http://www.w3.org/Icons/valid-xhtml10"
         alt="Valid XHTML 1.0 Transitional" height="31" width="88" /></a>
    </p>

  </body>
</html>
```

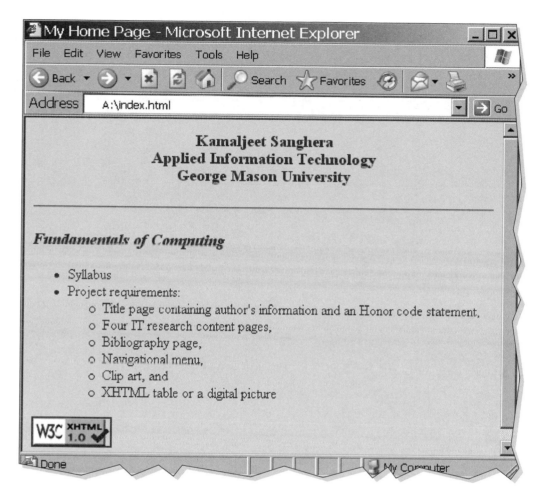

9.9

- **Switch to the Internet Explorer and refresh your web page.**

Conclusion

You have just completed the XHTML—Case Study 1. In this case study, you were introduced to many techniques. To reinforce your understanding of these techniques, it is recommended that you read and work through it once again.

Further Practice

The following Case Study will give you the opportunity to review and practice many of the XHTML features you have learned. It is divided into several steps.

Step 1

Research an IT related topic of your interest.

Step 2

Using Notepad, outline the main ideas and subheadings of your research paper in an XHTML document.

Step 3

Using the techniques learned in this case study, format your page with background and text color. Italicize and bold the text where needed. Add your name, course number, course name, etc. on your web page.

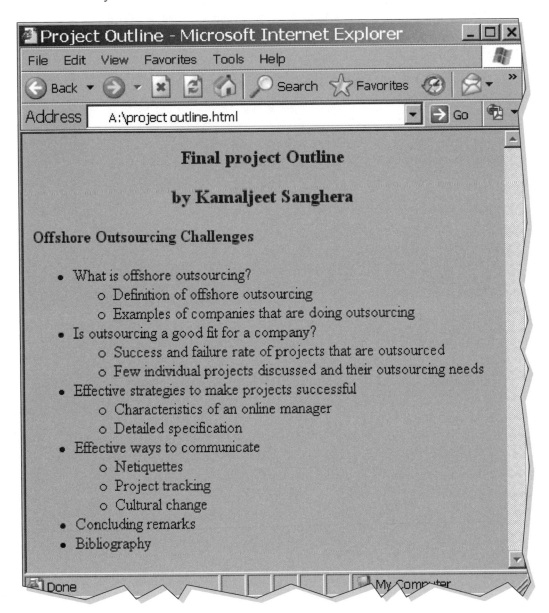

Step 4

Validate your page and include the "valid" icon on your page.

XHTML—Case Study 2

After successfully completing this case study, you should be able to:

- Create hyperlinks in a Web page using both relative and absolute path names
- Create a table in a Web page
- Add rows and columns to the table
- Add caption and summary to the table
- Insert an image from the Internet

- Insert an image from Microsoft applications
- Resize the image
- Cite the sources of images used in the Web site
- View web pages in a browser
- Validate Web pages using a Validator tool

Case Study 2—XHTML

In your last case study, you created an index.html that contained the syllabus and the course project requirements. Your instructor now wants you to create a syllabus web page that includes a clip art image from Microsoft Office. You will cite Microsoft for the clip art on a separate bibliography web page. Finally, you will provide links on each page for easy navigation to other pages. The expected web pages of your new assignment are as follows:

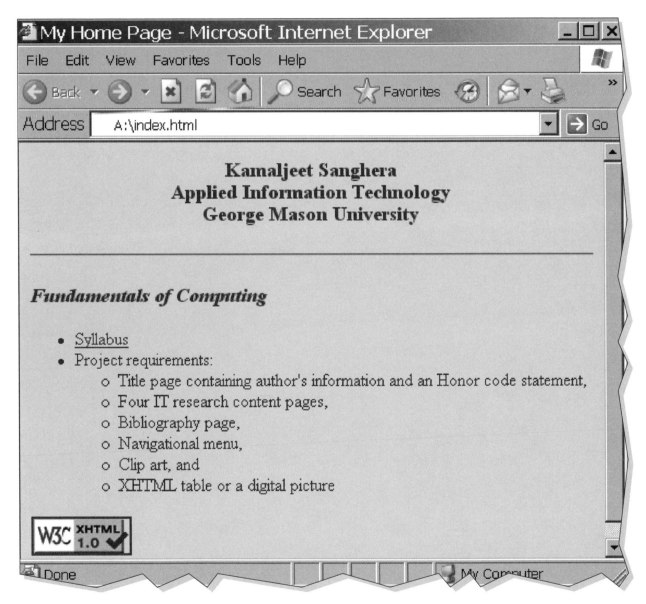

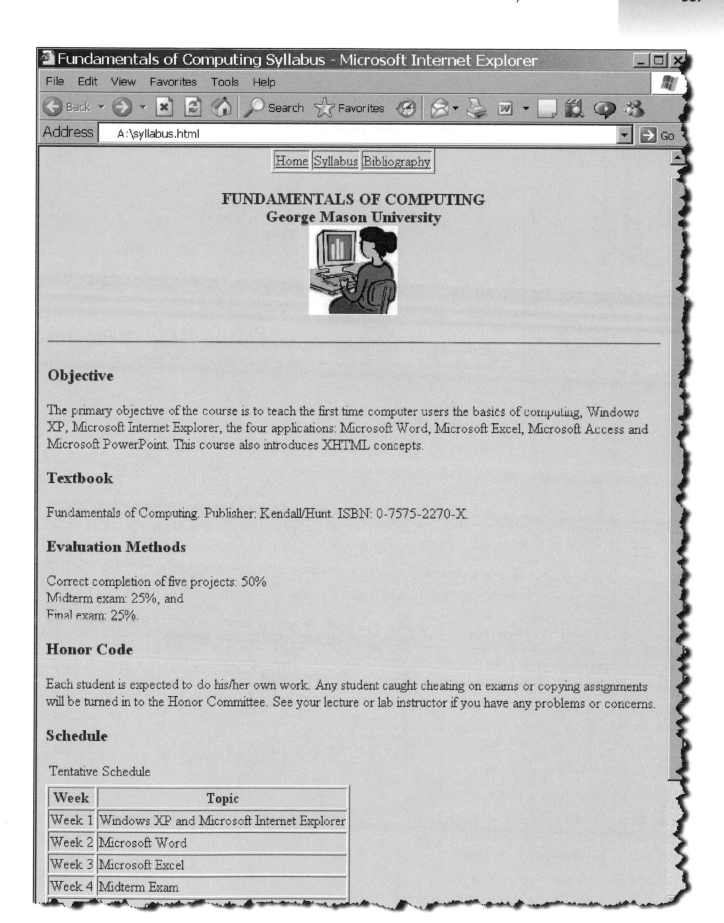

Fundamentals of Computing Syllabus - Microsoft Internet Explorer

File   Edit   View   Favorites   Tools   Help

Address   A:\syllabus.html

Home Syllabus Bibliography

FUNDAMENTALS OF COMPUTING
George Mason University

Objective

The primary objective of the course is to teach the first time computer users the basics of computing, Windows XP, Microsoft Internet Explorer, the four applications: Microsoft Word, Microsoft Excel, Microsoft Access and Microsoft PowerPoint. This course also introduces XHTML concepts.

Textbook

Fundamentals of Computing. Publisher: Kendall/Hunt. ISBN: 0-7575-2270-X.

Evaluation Methods

Correct completion of five projects: 50%
Midterm exam: 25%, and
Final exam: 25%.

Honor Code

Each student is expected to do his/her own work. Any student caught cheating on exams or copying assignments will be turned in to the Honor Committee. See your lecture or lab instructor if you have any problems or concerns.

Schedule

Tentative Schedule

Week	Topic
Week 1	Windows XP and Microsoft Internet Explorer
Week 2	Microsoft Word
Week 3	Microsoft Excel
Week 4	Midterm Exam

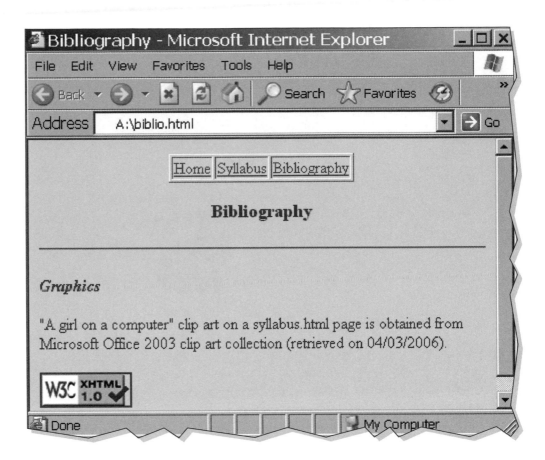

In this case study, we will learn several advanced web page techniques such as hyperlinks and tables. We will start by creating a new file called syllabus.html. We will enhance this file throughout the case study. In the end, the collection of these pages will form your new web site.

Objective

In this exercise, you will create a new file called syllabus.html.

1.1

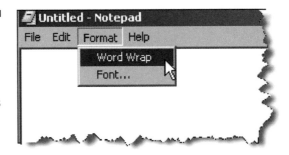

- **Click the Start button on the Windows taskbar.**

- **Point to All Programs (if you are running Windows XP) or to Programs (if you are running Windows 2000).**

- **Point to Accessories on the menu.**

- **Click on the Notepad in the submenu.**

- **If the Notepad Application window is not maximized, click on the Maximize button on the Title bar of the window.**

- **Choose the Format, Word Wrap command. If the Word Wrap command is already selected (is check marked), ignore this step and go to the next one.**

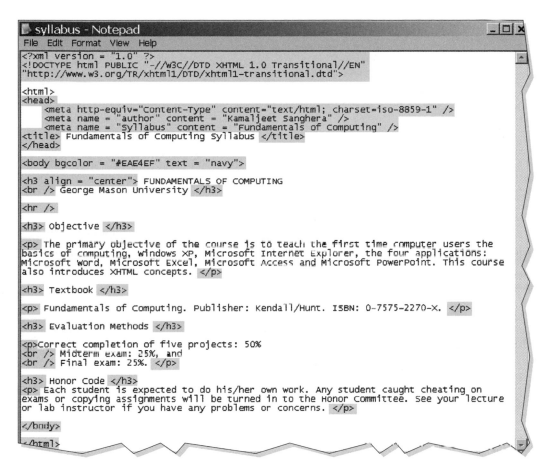

1.2

- **Type the XHTML code as shown in the screen shot. You can also open and edit the index.html file for this step.**

1.3

- **Choose the File, Save As command.**

1.4

- **In Save As dialog box, type syllabus.html for "File Name." Select All Files for "Save as type." Click Save.**

1.5

You will now view your document in an Internet Explorer browser window:

- **Click the Start button on the Windows taskbar.**

- **Point to All Programs (if you are running Windows XP) or to Programs (if you are running Windows 2000).**

- **Click on Internet Explorer on the menu.**

1.6

- **Choose File, Open command.**

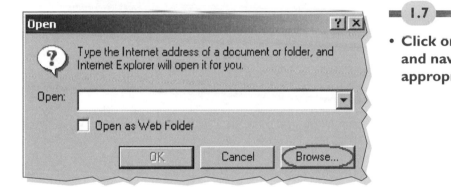

1.7

- **Click on the Browse button and navigate to the appropriate drive.**

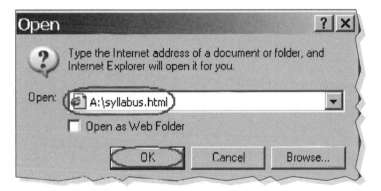

1.8

- **Choose the file syllabus.html, which you saved earlier, and click Open.**
- **Click on the OK button.**

1.9

- **Your page will look similar to the figure shown on the right.**

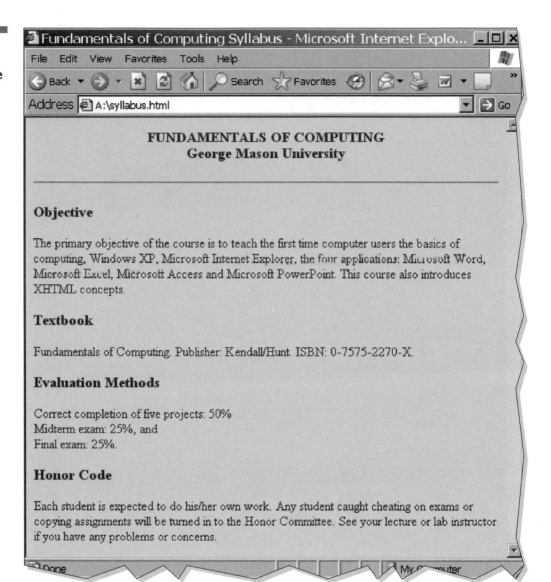

Tables

A table arranges information in rows and columns. An intersection of a row and a column is called a **cell**. The syntax of a table containing one column and one row is as follows:

```
<table>
   <tr>
      <td> ... </td>
   </tr>
</table>
```

The element **tr** stands for table row. It creates a row for a table. The **tr** element is accompanied by the **td** element. The element **td** is for table data. It adds a column in a row.

The figure below contains two and one row:

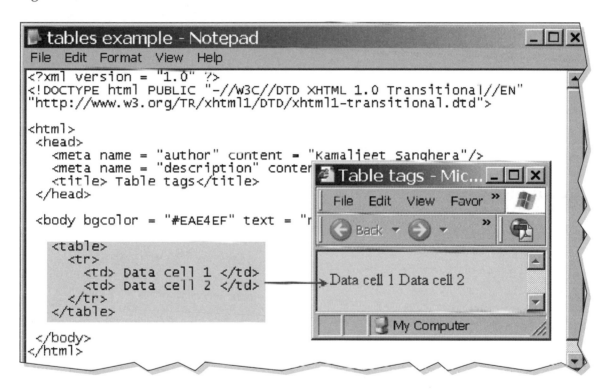

You can have as many **td**s and **tr**s in a table as you want.

By default, tables don't have borders. The figure on the next page shows an example of a table with the border attribute: the **border** attribute applies a **border** to a table. It takes a numerical value for the thickness in pixels of the **border.**

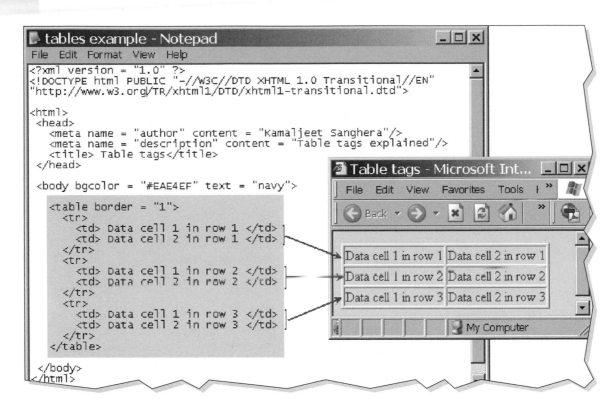

The element **th** stands for table header. It is mainly used for column headings. It is embedded within **tr** tags. Browsers usually center and bold the contents of the **th** element.

The figure below shows an example of a table with the **th** element:

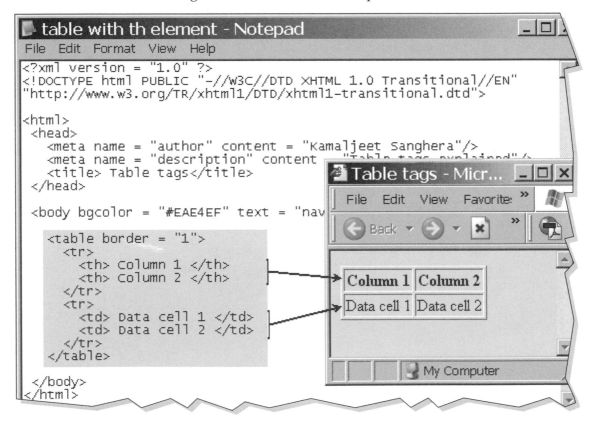

Other common attributes of the table element are **summary** and **width**. The summary attribute provides the summary element of the table. The value of a summary attribute does not appear on the web page. When a visually impaired user accesses the page, the screen reader reads the table summary for him or her. The figure below shows an example of a table with a summary attribute:

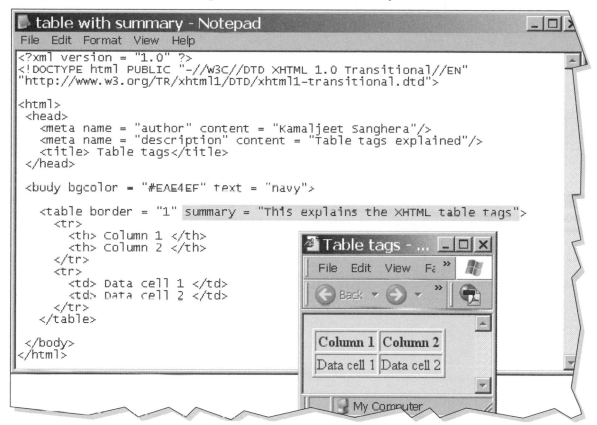

The **align** attribute of a table can be used to right, left, or center the table in the browser window. The figure below shows an example of a table with the **align attribute:**

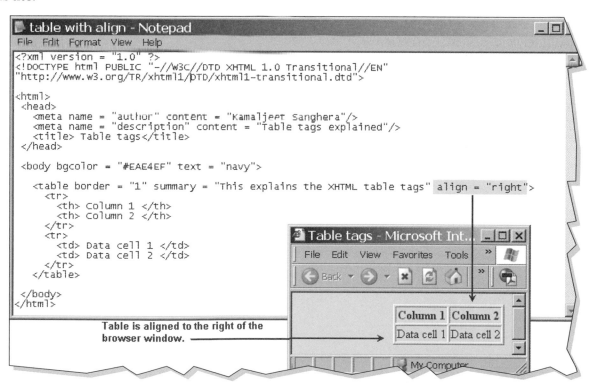

The **width** attribute of the table specifies the width of the table in the browser window. It can be specified in pixels or as a percentage of the browser screen. It is recommended that you specify the percentage for a table width. When a browser window is resized, the percentage of the new window size is calculated and pages are rendered with the new width. For example, 50% width will cover 50% of the client's browser window. This avoids the truncated view that is possible when width is defined in pixels. The figure below shows an example of a table with the **width attribute:**

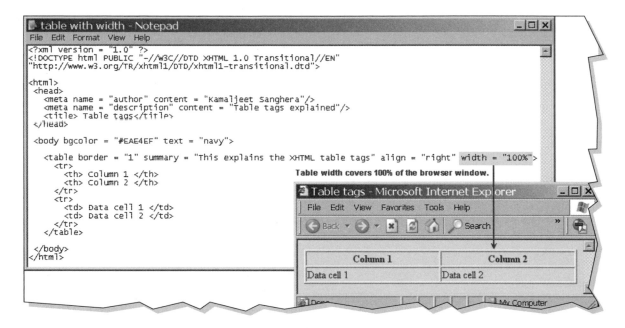

The **cellspacing** attribute specifies the gap between each cell (between one border and the next). The **cellpadding** attribute specifies the space around the content of each cell (space between the content and its border). The values of both cellspacing and cellpadding are specified in pixels. The figure on the next page shows an example of a table with cellspacing and cellpadding attributes:

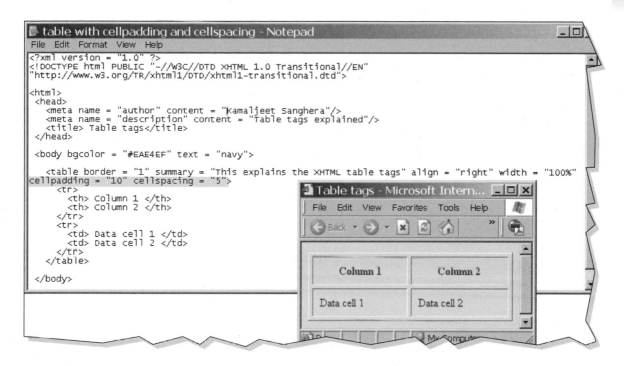

```
table with cellpadding and cellspacing - Notepad
File  Edit  Format  View  Help
<?xml version = "1.0" ?>
<!DOCTYPE html PUBLIC "-//W3C//DTD XHTML 1.0 Transitional//EN"
"http://www.w3.org/TR/xhtml1/DTD/xhtml1-transitional.dtd">

<html>
 <head>
   <meta name = "author" content = "Kamaljeet Sanghera"/>
   <meta name = "description" content = "Table tags explained"/>
   <title> Table tags</title>
 </head>

 <body bgcolor = "#EAE4EF" text = "navy">

   <table border = "1" summary = "This explains the XHTML table tags" align = "right" width = "100%"
cellpadding = "10" cellspacing = "5">
     <tr>
       <th> Column 1 </th>
       <th> Column 2 </th>
     </tr>
     <tr>
       <td> Data cell 1 </td>
       <td> Data cell 2 </td>
     </tr>
   </table>

 </body>
```

The **caption** element creates a caption or headline of a table. The syntax of the **caption** element is as follows:

<caption> … </caption>

The **caption** element can only be included in the **table** element and must be inserted before defining any rows or columns. It has only one attribute: **align**. The possible values of align attribute are left, right, top, and bottom. The syntax of caption element with align attribute is:

<caption align = "value"> … </caption>

The figure below shows an example of a table with the **caption element:**

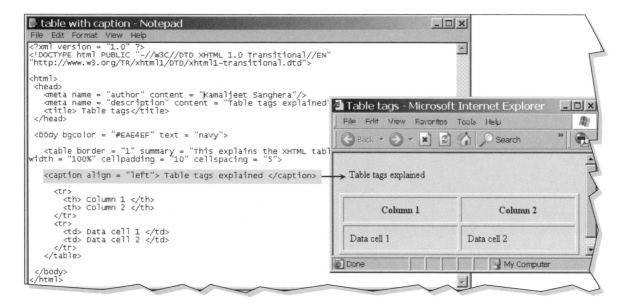

Objective

In this exercise, you will include the course schedule in a table format.

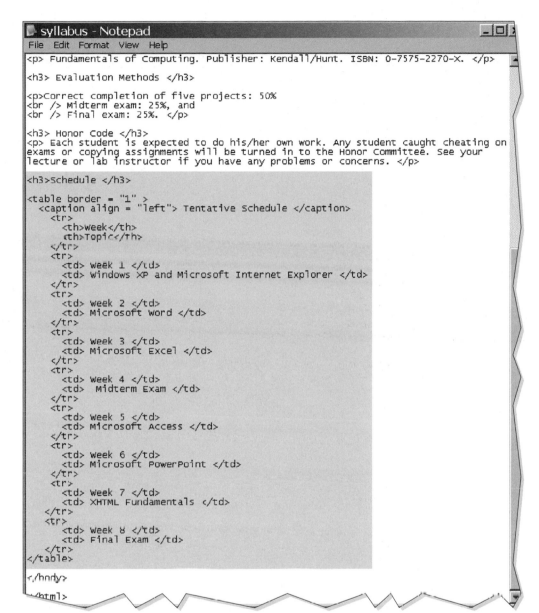

- **Edit syllabus.html file as shown in the screen shot. This will include a "Schedule" header and a table in your web page.**

2.2

- Save your file.
- Switch to Internet Explorer and view the changes. Your page should now include a schedule table as illustrated in the screen shot.

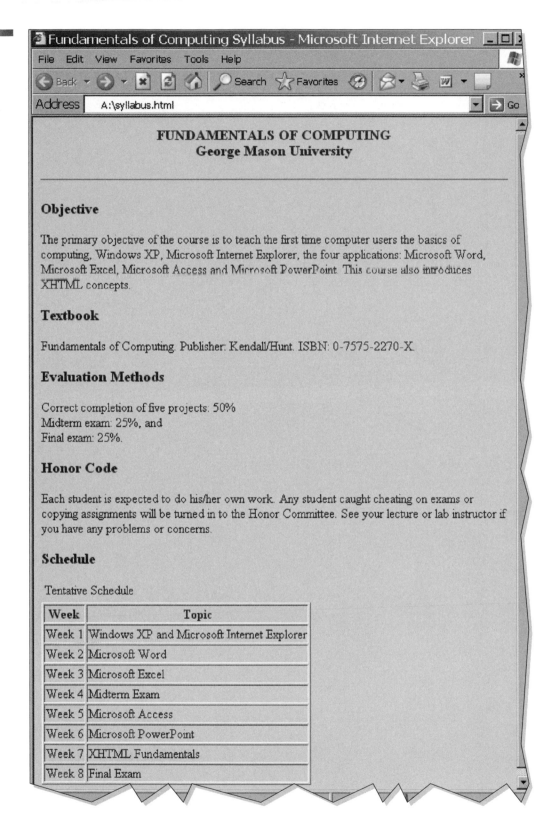

Images

Images have made Web pages interesting and exciting to browse through. The **img** tag is used to insert images in a Web document. It is an empty element and requires **src** and **alt** attributes. The syntax of the **img** element is:

<img src = "source file" alt = "text alternative of an image" />

where source file is the name of the file. The source file name is case sensitive so make sure that you type in the file name exactly as it is saved. The **alt** attribute is short for "alternative." The value of **alt** attribute provides the alternative text of an image. It is useful when the browser is unable to load the image. Also, screen readers read the value of **alt** attribute for visually impaired users. Thus, you must briefly describe the image in the **alt** attribute. If you don't want your page to show the **alt** attribute, exclude text information from the **alt** value, i.e. keep an empty string for an **alt** attribute's value (e.g. alt = " "). The figure below shows an example of inserting an image in a web page:

The following example shows the alternative text when an incorrect file name is entered in the **src** value.

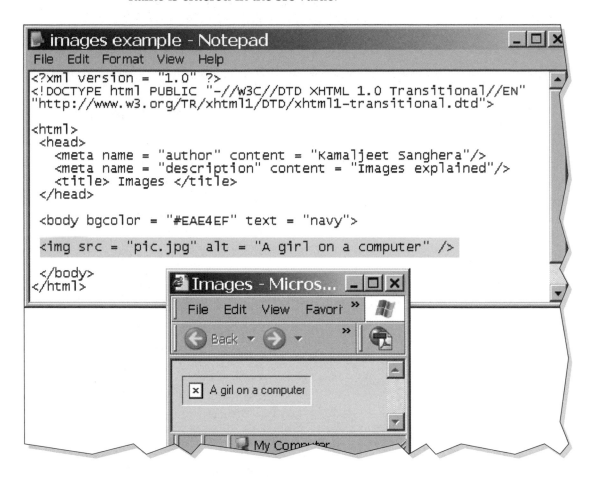

The **height** and **width** attributes define the height and width of the image. Your specified height and width will take over the height and width of the actual image. Note that larger images take more time to download than smaller images. The figure on the next page shows an example of resizing the height and width of an image for a web page.

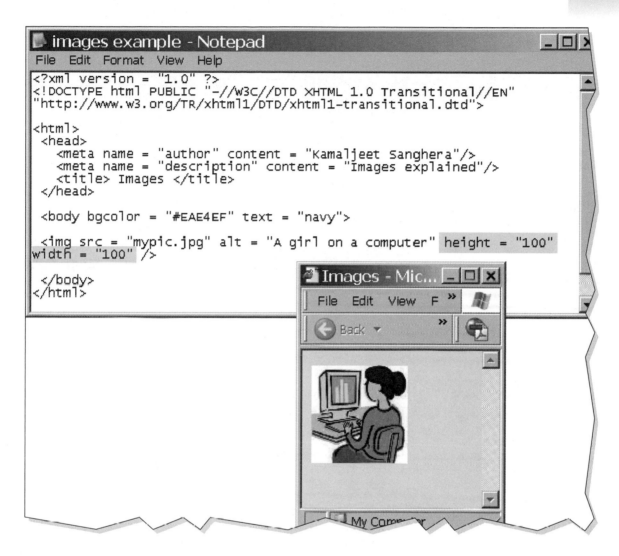

Download an Image from the Web Site

Images on Web pages are not freely available. In this case study, you will insert Microsoft's clipart image in the syllabus html page and then cite the source in the bibliography web page. You must get written permission from the webmaster before using any Internet images for your web site. You can email the webmaster for permission. You should keep the confirmation response until you use the image. You should also give the credit to the creators of the images on your web site.

To save an image from a web page, right click on an image that you would like to download and choose the **Save Picture As command.**

In the Save Picture dialog box, enter a relevant **name** and save the image as **JPEG**.

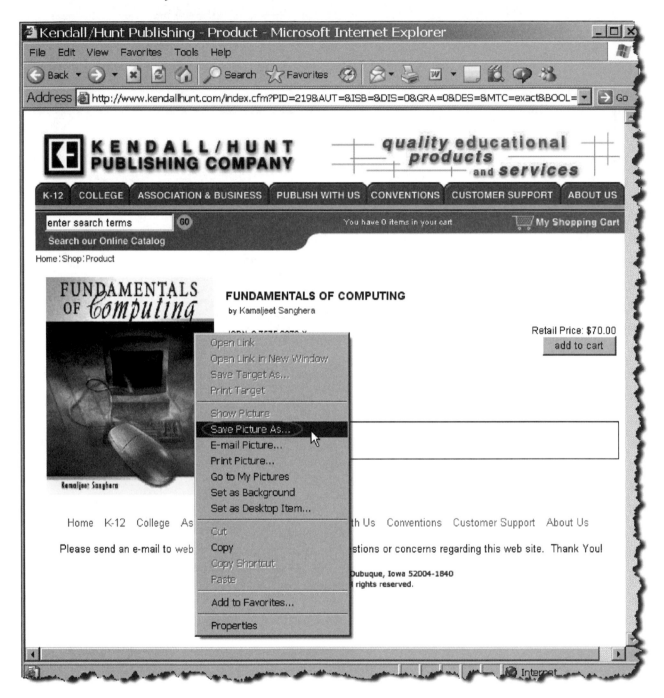

In a Save Picture dialog box, enter a relevant name and save it as JPEG.

The **align** attribute of an **image** element floats an image on left or right. A special line break with **clear** attribute is used to stop the flowing text around an image. This makes new content appear after an image. The syntax is as follows:

<br clear = "value" />

where value can be left or right.

In the following example, <br clear = "left" /> stops <h3> element from wrapping around the image.

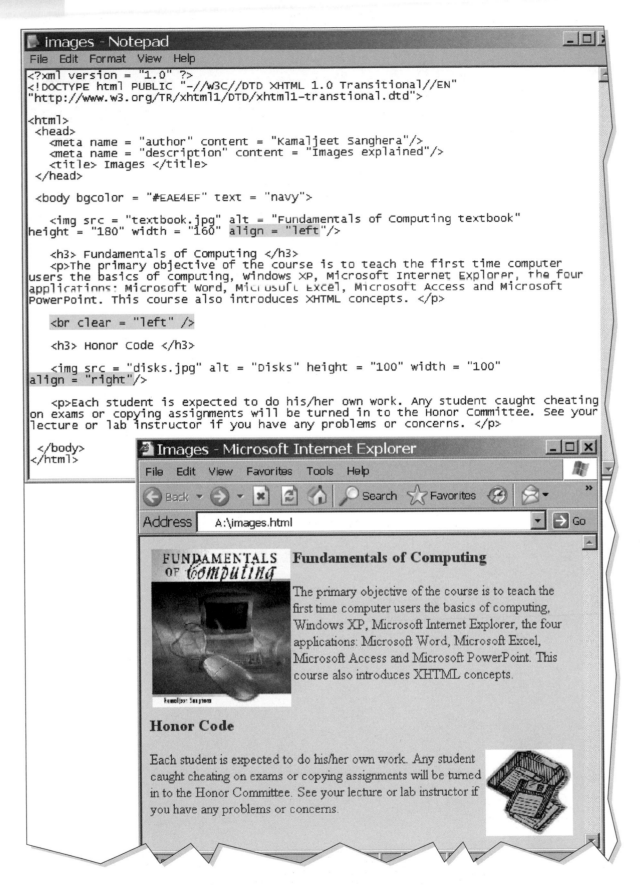

The **border** attribute creates a border around the image. The value of the border can be specified in pixels or as a percentage. The figure on the next page shows an example of applying border around an image:

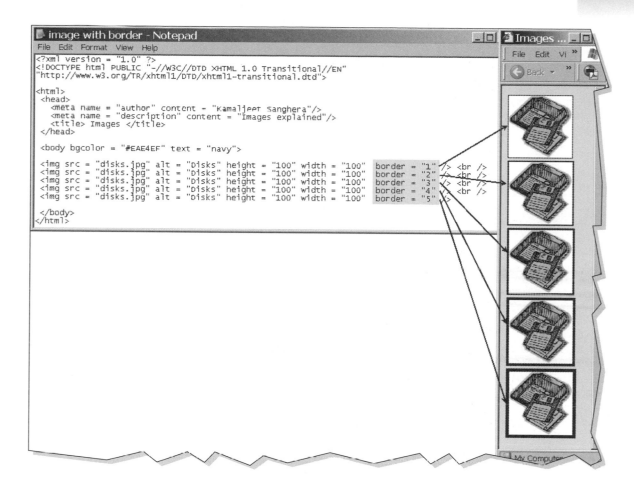

Objective

In this exercise, you will include Microsoft Office clipart in your web page.

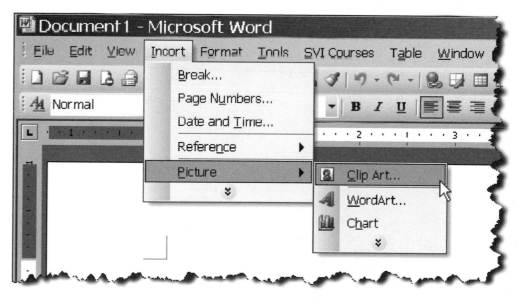

3.1

- **Open MS Word.**

- **Choose Insert, Picture, Clip art.**

3.2

• Enter computers and click **Go** on the **Clip Art** task pane on the right.

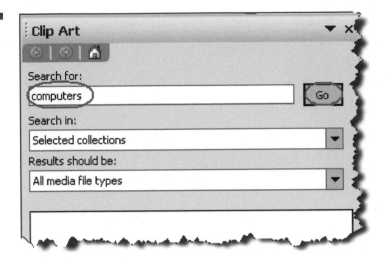

3.3

• Right click on any clip art of your choice and choose copy command by clicking on the arrow to the right of the image.

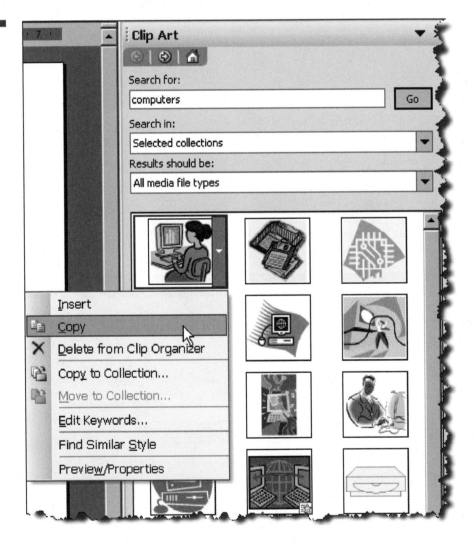

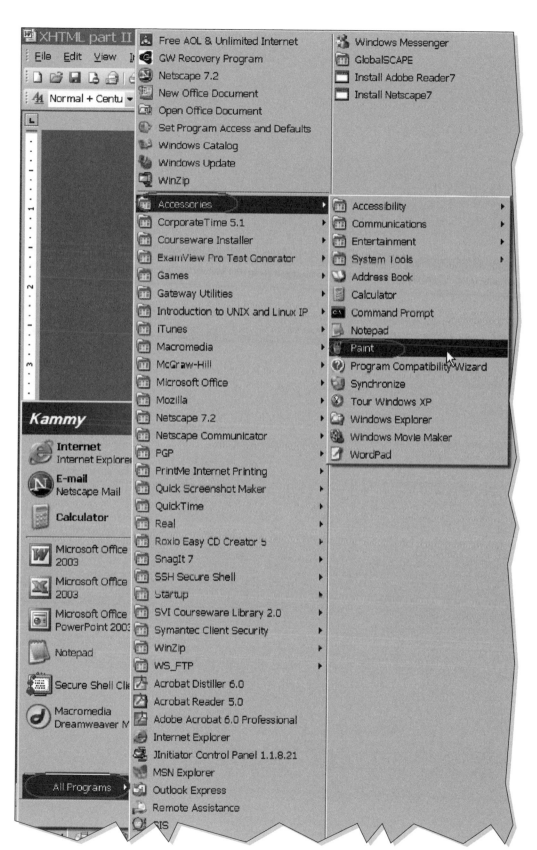

3.4

- **Open MS Paint by choosing All Programs, Accessories, and Paint from the Start menu.**

3.5

- **Choose the Edit and paste command.**

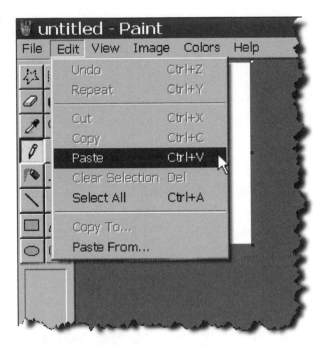

3.6

- **Your screen should be similar to the figure shown on the right.**

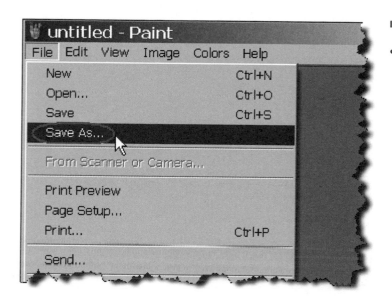

3.7

- **Choose the File, Save As command.**

3.8

- **In a Save As window, select the folder/directory where the syllabus.html file was saved. Select JPEG for the image type and enter computer for the file name. Click on the Save button.**

3.9

- **Edit the syllabus.html file with the highlighted text as shown in the screen shot:**

3.10

- **Save your file.**
- **Switch to Internet Explorer and view the changes. Your page should now include a clipart as illustrated in the figure on the right.**

Since the clipart is not your original work, you must cite the source on its own page or on a separate page. For this case study, you will create a separate web page, biblio.html, and will give credit to Microsoft for the clipart.

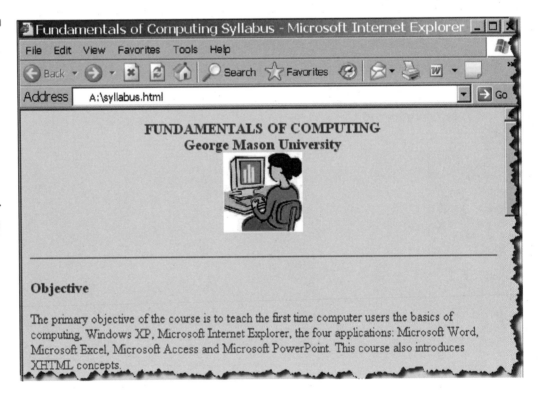

Objective

In this exercise, you will create a new html file called biblio.html and cite the source of the clipart used in the syllabus.html page.

4.1

- **Open a new Notepad.**
- **Copy the code of index.html file and paste it in a new Notepad window.**
- **Edit the file as highlighted in the screen shot.**

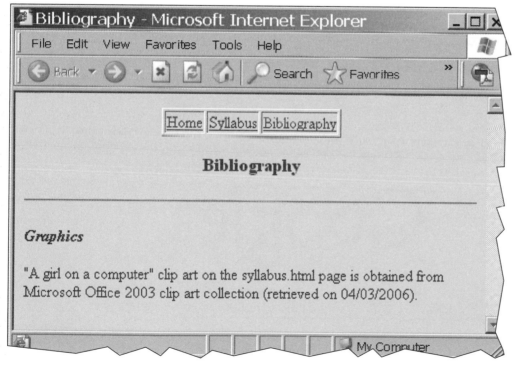

4.2

- **Save the file as biblio.html in the same directory where all other html files (index.html, syllabus.html) are located.**
- **Switch to Internet Explorer.**
- **Open the biblio.html file and view the page. It should be similar to the figure on the left.**

Hyperlinks

Hyperlinks connect web pages on the Internet. They allow you to navigate through Web pages and sites. The **a** element, called anchor, is used for hyperlinks. The syntax of hyperlink is:

<a href = "URL or the name of the file"> Text to appear on your page </a>

The "href" stands for hypertext reference and "a" for anchor. The value of href is the absolute URL such as http:// google.com or the file located on your server, such as index.html file. The figure below shows an example of adding external link on a web page:

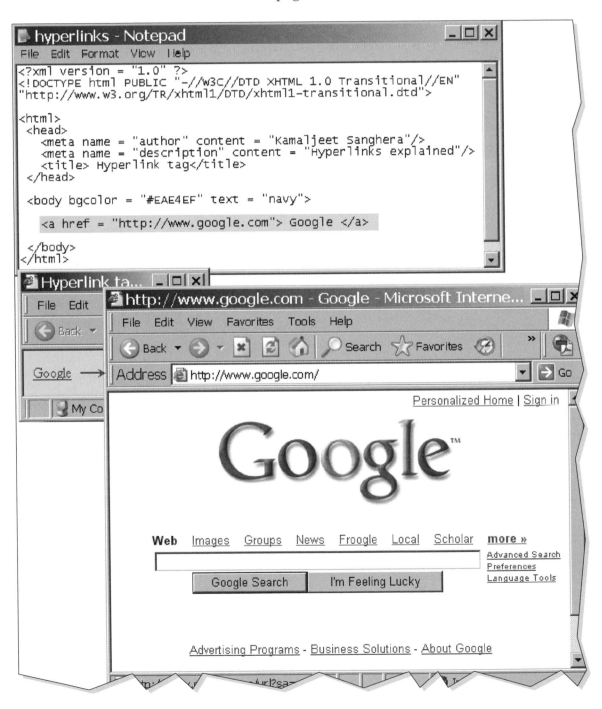

If the file exists in the same directory where the referenced file is located, you only need to provide the name of the file. Notice in the attached view that both hyperlinks.html and index.html files are located under one folder called Examples. In this case, references to each other do not require an absolute pathname.

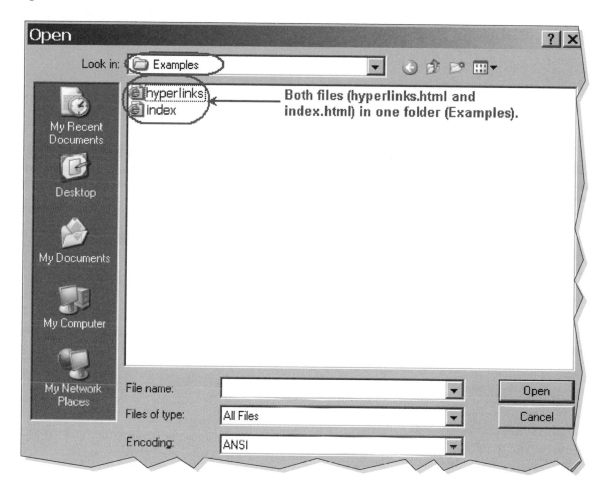

The figure below shows an example of referencing files within the same directory:

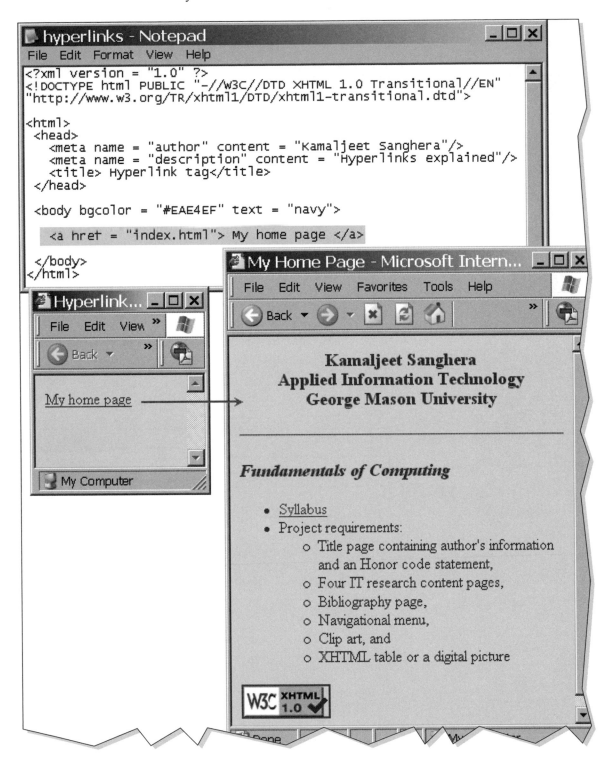

However, if the file does not exist in the current directory, you will specify the path to the file. You can either give the relative pathname or absolute pathname. The relative pathname is relative to the current directory, e.g. ../courses/it100.html, where .. (two dots) represent the parent directory.

In the following example, index.html is located in the Files folder and the hyperlinks.html file is located in the Examples folder.

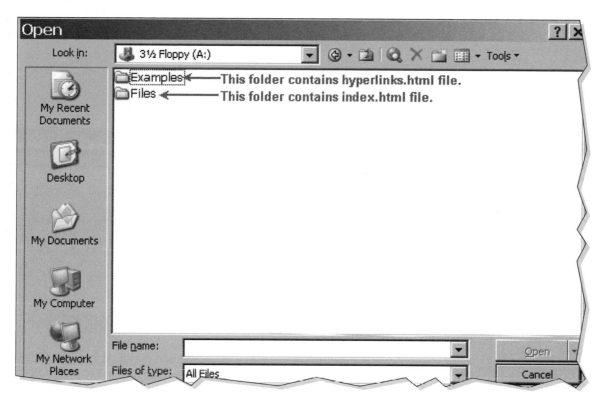

The following hyperlinks.html file is accessing index.html file located in the Files folder:

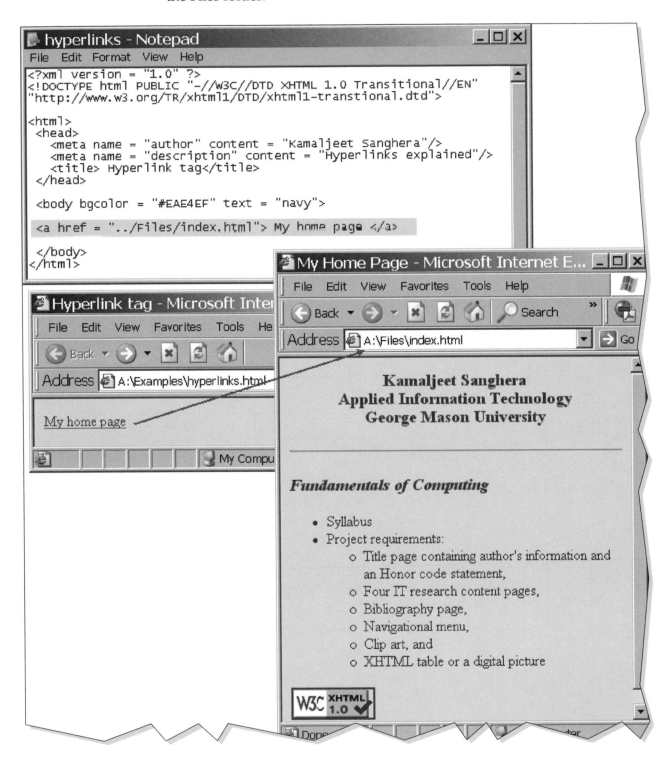

Similarly, if the file exists in the subdirectory of the current directory, the relative pathname will include the subdirectory name and the file name, e.g. images/disks.jpg

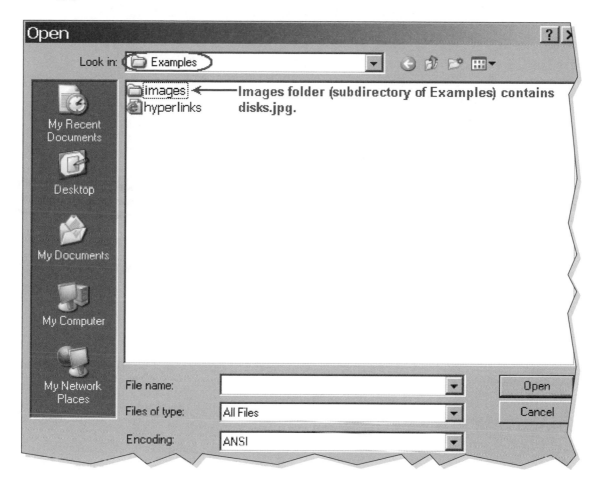

The following example shows how to access the files posted in a subdirectory called "images."

```
hyperlinks - Notepad
File  Edit  Format  View  Help
<?xml version = "1.0" ?>
<!DOCTYPE html PUBLIC "-//W3C//DTD XHTML 1.0 Transitional//EN"
"http://www.w3.org/TR/xhtml1/DTD/xhtml1-transtional.dtd">

<html>
 <head>
   <meta name = "author" content = "Kamaljeet Sanghera"/>
   <meta name = "description" content = "Hyperlinks explained"/>
   <title> Hyperlink tag</title>
 </head>

<body bgcolor = "#EAE4EF" text = "navy">

<a href = "images/disks.jpg"> My home page </a>

</body>
</html>
```

View hyperlinks.html file in Internet Explorer.

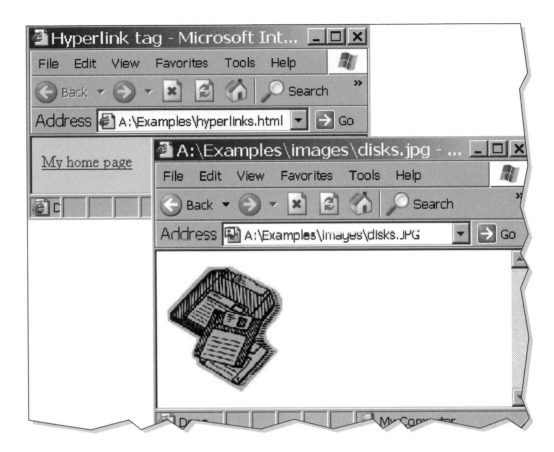

The absolute pathnames are based on the absolute locations of the file name, e.g. /images/disks.html. A forward slash (/) in the beginning of the pathname stands for the root directory. This traces a file from the root to the current directory. In this example, **disks.jpg** file is located under the **images** folder. URLs are also the examples of absolute pathnames.

```
hyperlinks - Notepad
File  Edit  Format  View  Help
<?xml version = "1.0" ?>
<!DOCTYPE html PUBLIC "-//W3C//DTD XHTML 1.0 Transitional//EN"
"http://www.w3.org/TR/xhtml1/DTD/xhtml1-transtional.dtd">

<html>
  <head>
    <meta name = "author" content = "Kamaljeet Sanghera"/>
    <meta name = "description" content = "Hyperlinks explained"/>
    <title> Hyperlink tag</title>
  </head>

  <body bgcolor = "#EAE4EF" text = "navy">

    <a href = "/Examples/images/disks.jpg"> My home page </a>

  </body>
</html>
```

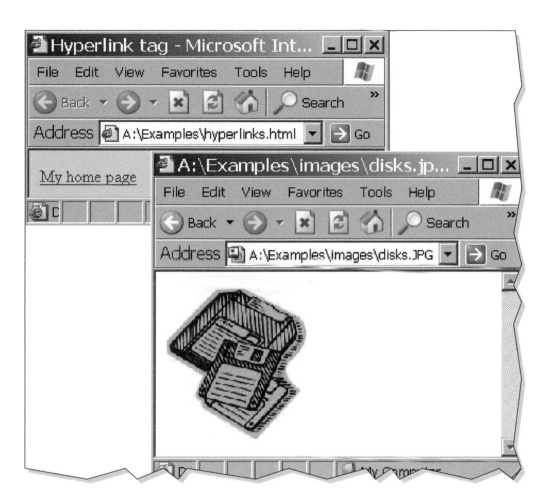

Objective

In this exercise, you will create a link from index.html page to syllabus.html page.

5.1

• **Open the index.html file that you created in XHTML case study I. Edit the index.html file as highlighted in the screen shot.**

```
index - Notepad
File  Edit  Format  View  Help
<?xml version = "1.0" ?>
<!DOCTYPE html PUBLIC "-//W3C//DTD XHTML 1.0 Transitional//EN"
"http://www.w3.org/TR/xhtml1/DTD/xhtml1-transitional.dtd">

<html>
<head>
    <meta http-equiv="Content-Type" content="text/html; charset=iso-8859-1" />
    <meta name = "author" content = "Kamaljeet Sanghera" />
    <meta name = "description" content = "Home page" />
    <title> My Home Page </title>
</head>

<body bgcolor = "#EAE4EF" text = "navy">

    <h3 align = "center">
        Kamaljeet Sanghera <br />
        Applied Information Technology <br />
        George Mason University <br />
    </h3>

    <hr />

    <p><big><b><i> Fundamentals of Computing </i></b></big></p>

    <ul>
        <li> <a href = "syllabus.html"> Syllabus </a> </li>
        <li> Project requirements:
            <ul>
                <li> Title page containing author's information and an Honor code statement, </li>
                <li> Four IT research content pages, </li>
                <li> Bibliography page, </li>
                <li> Navigational menu, </li>
```

5.2

- **Save your file.**
- **Switch to Internet Explorer and view the changes. Your page should now include a link to syllabus.html page.**

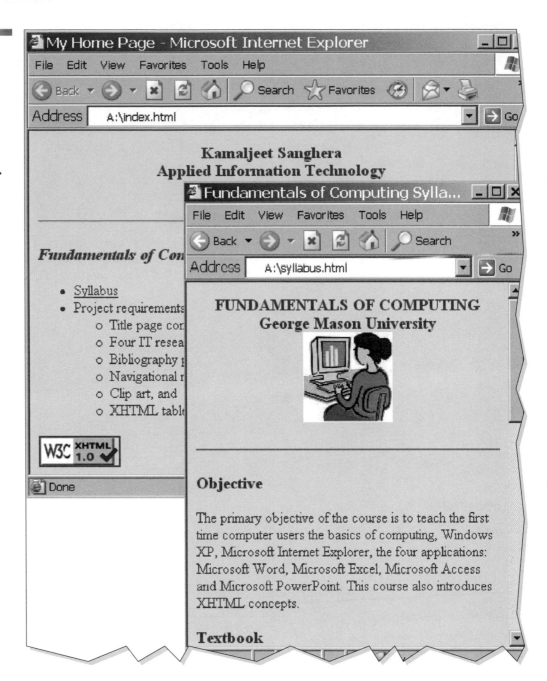

Navigation

Your web site must provide a way to navigate to other web pages. Browsers provide back and forward buttons to go backwards or forward in your search. However, it is not an optimal way to browse through any web site. You should always link your web pages with each other.

Objective

In this exercise, you will add a navigation menu to both syllabus and bibliography web pages.

6.1

- **Open the syllabus.html file.**
- **Edit the syllabus.html file as highlighted in the screen shot.**
- **Save your file.**

6.2

- **Switch to Internet Explorer and view the changes. Your page should now include a navigational table as shown in the figure on the left.**

6.3

- Copy the navigation table html code and paste it in the biblio.html page as shown in the screenshot.

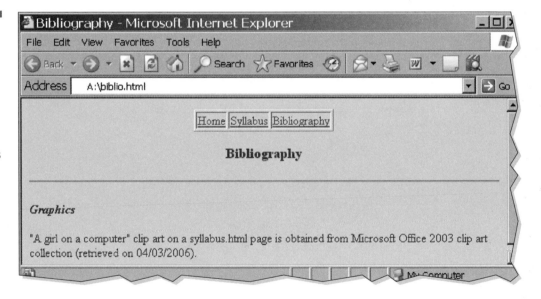

```
biblio - Notepad
File  Edit  Format  View  Help
<?xml version = "1.0" ?>
<!DOCTYPE html PUBLIC "-//W3C//DTD XHTML 1.0 Transitional//EN"
"http://www.w3.org/TR/xhtml1/DTD/xhtml1-transitional.dtd">

<html>
  <head>
    <meta http-equiv="Content-Type" content="text/html;
charset=iso-8859-1" />
    <meta name = "author" content = "Kamaljeet Sanghera" />
    <meta name = "description" content = "Bibliography" />
    <title> Bibliography </title>
  </head>

<body bgcolor = "#EAE4EF" text = "navy">

<table border = "1" summary = "navigation" align = "center">
  <tr>
    <td><a href = "index.html"> Home </a></td>
    <td><a href = "syllabus.html"> Syllabus </a></td>
    <td><a href = "biblio.html"> Bibliography </a></td>
  </tr>
</table>

  <h3 align = "center"> Bibliography </h3>

  <hr />

  <p><b><i> Graphics </i></b></p>
```

6.4

- Save your file.

- Switch to Internet Explorer and view the changes. Your page should now include a navigational table as shown in the figure on the right.

Bibliography - Microsoft Internet Explorer

Address A:\biblio.html

Home | Syllabus | Bibliography

Bibliography

Graphics

"A girl on a computer" clip art on a syllabus.html page is obtained from Microsoft Office 2003 clip art collection (retrieved on 04/03/2006).

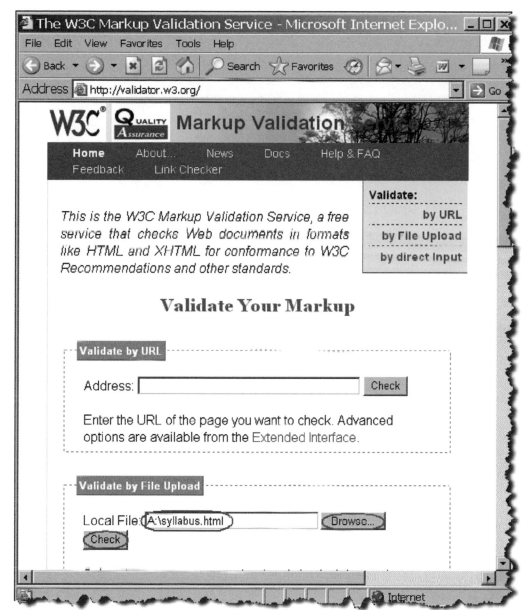

6.5

- **Validate the syllabus.html file by visiting http:// validator.w3.org/ page.**

- **Click on the Browse button.**

- **In a Choose file dialog box, locate the syllabus.html file and click on Open.**

- **Click on Check button on the Markup Validation Service web page.**

6.6

- If you get similar results as shown below, your file is a valid **XHTML 1.0** transitional.

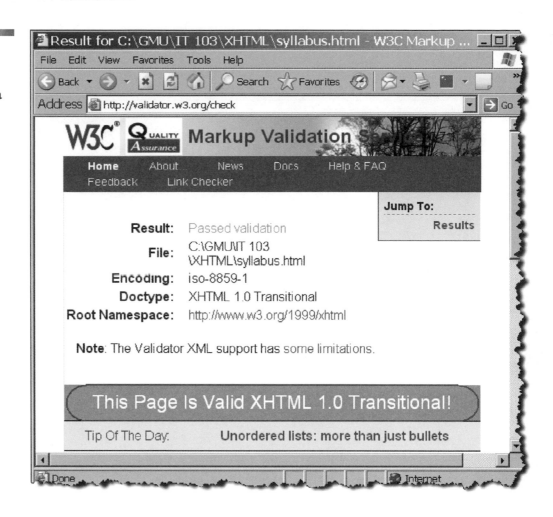

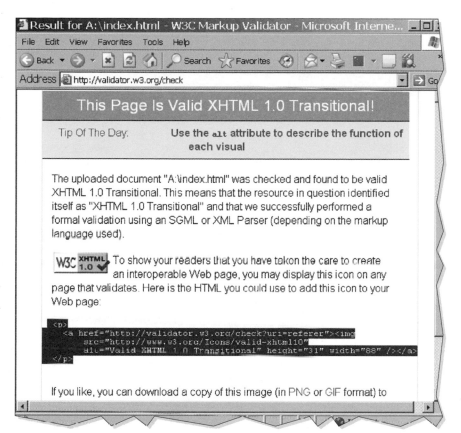

6.7

- **Markup Validation Service also provides an icon to be displayed on a page that has been successfully validated. The code used to include the icon on your Web page is given on the validator page. Select the code highlighted on the left and copy it (CTRL + C).**

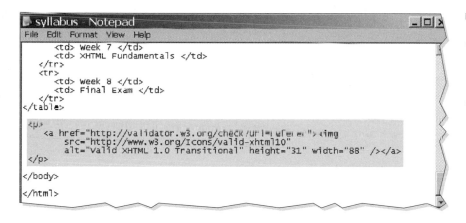

6.8

- **Paste the code in your syllabus.html file before the end of <body> tag.**

- **Your syllabus.html file should look similar to the figure on the left.**

6.9

- **View the modified file in the browser.**

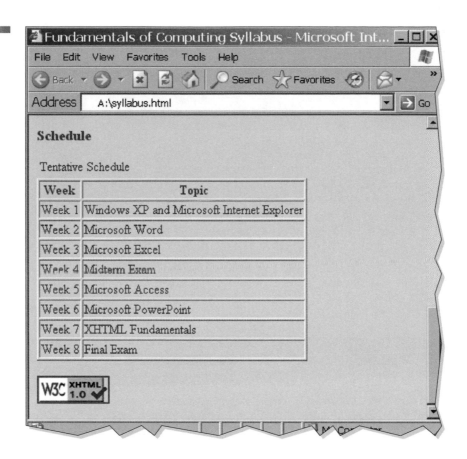

6.10

- **Validate biblio.html file as syllabus.html and include the icon in the page. The biblio.html file will be similar to the screen shot.**

- **View the modified file in a browser.**

Conclusion

You have just completed the XHTML—Case Study 2. In this case study, you were introduced to many advanced techniques. To reinforce your understanding of these techniques, it is recommended that you read and work through it once again.

 Further Practice

The following three exercises will give you the opportunity to review and practice many of the XHTML elements you have learned. It is divided into three steps.

Exercise One

Using Notepad, create an XHTML document that contains links to your favorite web sites. You must include at least four valid links.

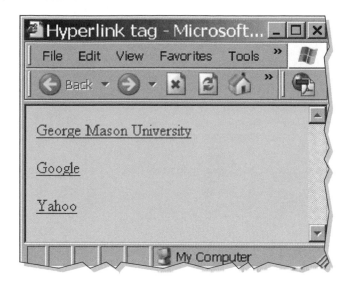

Exercise Two

Using Notepad, create an XHTML document using Notepad that explains allowable XHTML elements within paragraph tags. Present your tags in a table format.

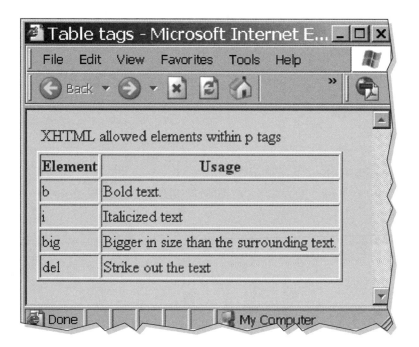

Exercise Three

Insert a Microsoft image or any image from the Internet to your Exercise Two document. Cite your image in a separate bibliography page and link both pages.

Windows XP—Summary of Keyboard and Toolbar Shortcuts

Command/Menu Option	Keyboard Shortcut	Toolbar Shortcut
File, Rename command Rename this file/Rename this folder options (on Windows Explorer's Tasks view menu)	[F2]	
File, Delete command Delete this file/Delete this folder/ Delete the selected items options (on Windows Explorer's Tasks view menu)	[DEL]	
Edit, Undo command	[CTRL] + [Z]	
View, Thumbnails/View, Tiles/View, Icons/View, List/View, Details commands		
View, Go To, Back command	[ALT] + [LEFT ARROW]	
View, Go To, Forward command	[ALT] + [RIGHT ARROW]	
View, Go To, Up One Level command		
View, Explorer Bar, History command	[CTRL] + [H]	
View, Explorer Bar, Favorites command	[CTRL] + [I]	
Help, Help and Support Center command	[F1]	

Internet Explorer— Summary of Keyboard and Toolbar Shortcuts

Command Sequence	Keyboard Shortcut	Toolbar Shortcut
File, Print	[CTRL] + [P]	Print
Tools, Mail and News		Mail
View, Explorer Bar, History	[CTRL] + [H]	History
View, Explorer Bar, Favorites	[CTRL] + [I]	Favorites
View, Explorer Bar, Search	[CTRL] + [E]	Search

MS Word—Summary of Keyboard and Toolbar Shortcuts

Command Sequence	Keyboard Shortcut	Toolbar Shortcut
File, New	[CTRL] + [N]	
File, Open	[CTRL] + [O]	
File, Close	[CTRL] + [W] or [CTRL] + [F4]	
File, Save	[CTRL] + [S]	
File, Print	[CTRL] + [P]	
File, Print Preview		
File, Exit	[ALT] + [F4]	
Edit, Undo	[CTRL] + [Z]	
Edit, Redo	[CTRL] + [Y]	
Edit, Cut	[CTRL] + [X]	
Edit, Copy	[CTRL] + [C]	
Edit, Paste	[CTRL] + [V]	
Edit, Find	[CTRL] + [F]	
Edit, Replace	[CTRL] + [H]	
View, Zoom		100%
Insert, Date and Time	[ALT] + [SHIFT] + [D]	
Insert, Break (to insert page break)	[CTRL] + [ENTER]	
Insert, AutoText, New	[ALT] + [F3]	
Format, Font (to reset font)	[CTRL] + [SHIFT] + [F]	Times New Roman
Format, Font (to reset font size)	[CTRL] + [SHIFT] + [P]	12

Command Sequence	Keyboard Shortcut	Toolbar Shortcut
Format, Font (to turn bold attribute on/off)	[CTRL] + [B]	**B**
Format, Font (to turn italic attribute on/off)	[CTRL] + [I]	*I*
Format, Font (to turn underline attribute on/off)	[CTRL] + [U]	U
Format, Font (to reset font color)		A ▾
Format, Paragraph (to left-align paragraph)	[CTRL] + [L]	☰
Format, Paragraph (to center paragraph)	[CTRL] + [E]	☰
Format, Paragraph (to right-align paragraph)	[CTRL] + [R]	☰
Format, Paragraph (to justify paragraph)	[CTRL] + [J]	☰
Format, Paragraph (to increase left indent of paragraph)	[CTRL] + [M]	☴
Format, Paragraph (to decrease left indent of paragraph)	[CTRL] + [SHIFT] + [M]	☴
Format, Paragraph (to increase hanging indent of paragraph)	[CTRL] + [T]	
Format, Paragraph (to decrease hanging indent of paragraph)	[CTRL] + [SHIFT] + [T]	
Format, Paragraph (to set single-line spacing)	[CTRL] + [1]	☰ ▾
Format, Paragraph (to set double-line spacing)	[CTRL] + [2]	☰ ▾
Format, Paragraph (to set 1.5-line spacing)	[CTRL] + [5]	☰ ▾
Format, Bullets and Numbering (to insert bullet)		☰
Format, Bullets and Numbering (to insert number)		☰
Tools, Spelling and Grammar	[F7]	ABC ✓

Command Sequence	Keyboard Shortcut	Toolbar Shortcut
Format, Borders and Shading		
Format, Columns		
Table, Insert, Table		
Table, Insert, Rows		
Table, Insert, Columns		
Table, Select, Table	[ALT] + [5] (on Numeric Keypad)	
Chart, Chart Type		
File, Print		
Edit, Go To	[CTRL] + [G]	
Help, Microsoft Office Word Help	[F1]	

MS Excel—Summary of Keyboard and Toolbar Shortcuts

Command Sequence	Keyboard Shortcut	Toolbar Shortcut
File, New	[CTRL] + [N]	
File, Open	[CTRL] + [O]	
File, Close	[CTRL] + [W] or [CTRL] + [F4]	
File, Save	[CTRL] + [S]	
File, Print	[CTRL] + [P]	
File, Print Preview		
File, Exit	[ALT] + [F4]	
Edit, Undo	[CTRL] + [Z]	
Edit, Redo	[CTRL] + [Y]	
Edit, Cut	[CTRL] + [X]	
Edit, Copy	[CTRL] + [C]	
Edit, Paste	[CTRL] + [V]	
Edit, Clear, Contents	[DEL]	
Edit, Go To	[CTRL] + [G]	
Insert, Cells	[CTRL] + [SHIFT] + [+]	
Format, Cells	[CTRL] + [1]	
Format, Cells (to left-align entry)		
Format, Cells (to center entry)		
Format, Cells (to right-align entry)		
Format, Cells (to reset font)	[CTRL] + [SHIFT] + [F]	Arial

Command Sequence	Keyboard Shortcut	Toolbar Shortcut
Format, Cells (to reset font size)	[CTRL] + [SHIFT] + [P]	10 ▼
Format, Cells (to turn bold attribute on/off	[CTRL] + [B]	**B**
Format, Cells (to turn italic attribute on/off	[CTRL] + [I]	*I*
Format, Cells (to turn single underline attribute on/off)	[CTRL] + [U]	U
Format, Cells (to apply currency format)	[CTRL] + [SHIFT] + [$]	$
Format, Cells (to apply percent format)	[CTRL] + [SHIFT] + [%]	%
Format, Cells (to apply comma format)		,
Format, Cells (to apply comma/ two decimal places format)	[CTRL] + [SHIFT] + [!]	
Format, Cells (to apply day-month-year date format)	[CTRL] + [SHIFT] + [#]	
Format, Cells (to increase number of decimals)		←.0 .00
Format, Cells (to decrease number of decimals)		.00 →.0
Format, Cells (to add outline border)	[CTRL] + [SHIFT] + [&]	▼
Format, Cells (to remove outline border)	[CTRL] + [SHIFT] + [_]	▼
Format, Cells (to add shading)		▼
Tools, Spelling	[F7]	ABC✓
Help, Microsoft Excel Help	[F1]	?
Edit, Find	[CTRL] + [F]	
Edit, Replace	[CTRL] + [H]	
View, Zoom		100% ▼

Command Sequence	Keyboard Shortcut	Toolbar Shortcut
Insert, Chart		📊
Format, Cells	[CTRL] + [1]	
Format, Row, Hide	[CTRL] + [9]	
Format, Row, Unhide	[CTRL] + [SHIFT] + [(] (left parenthesis)	
Format, Column, Hide	[CTRL] + [0]	
Format, Column, Unhide	[CTRL] + [SHIFT] + [)] (right parenthesis)	
Data, Sort (to sort entries in ascending order)		A/Z↓
Data, Sort (to sort entries in descending order)		Z/A↓

MS PowerPoint—
Summary of Keyboard
and Toolbar Shortcuts

Command Sequence	Keyboard Shortcut	Toolbar Shortcut
File, Open	[CTRL] + [O]	
File, Close	[CTRL] + [W] or [CTRL] + [F4]	
File, Save	[CTRL] + [S]	
File, Print	[CTRL] + [P]	
File, Print Preview		
File, Exit	[ALT] + [F4]	
Edit, Undo . . .	[CTRL] + [Z]	
Edit, Redo . . .	[CTRL] + [Y]	
Edit, Copy	[CTRL] + [C]	
Edit, Paste	[CTRL] + [V]	
View, Slide Sorter		
View, Normal		
View, Slide Show	[F5]	
View, Zoom		67%
Insert, New Slide	[CTRL] + [M]	New Slide
Insert, Table		
Insert, Chart		
Insert, Picture, Clip Art		

Command Sequence	Keyboard Shortcut	Toolbar Shortcut
Insert, Text Box		
Format, Slide Design		
Format, Font (to reset the font)	[CTRL] + [SHIFT] + [F]	Arial
Format, Font (to increase the font size)	[CTRL] + [SHIFT] + [>]	
Format, Font (to decrease the font size)	[CTRL] + [SHIFT] + [<]	
Format, Font (to turn the bold attribute on/off)	[CTRL] + [B]	
Format, Font (to turn the italic attribute on/off)	[CTRL] + [I]	
Format, Font (to reset the font color)		
Format, Alignment, Center (to center a paragraph)	[CTRL] + [E]	
Format, Alignment, Align Left (to left align a paragraph)	[CTRL] + [L]	
Slide Show, Slide Transition		
Tools, Spelling	[F7]	
Help, Microsoft Office PowerPoint Help	[F1]	

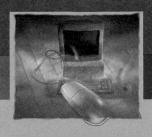

MS Access—Summary of Keyboard and Toolbar Shortcuts

Command Sequence	Keyboard Shortcut	Toolbar Shortcut
File, New	[CTRL] + [N]	
File, Open	[CTRL] + [O]	
File, Close	[CTRL] + [W] or [CTRL] + [F4]	
File, Save	[CTRL] + [S]	
File, Print	[CTRL] + [P]	
File, Print Preview		
File, Exit	[ALT] + [F4]	
Edit, Undo Current Field/Record or Edit, Undo Saved Record	[CTRL] + [Z]	
Edit, Copy	[CTRL] + [C]	
Edit, Paste	[CTRL] + [V]	
Edit, Delete Record	[DEL] or [CTRL] + [-] (minus sign)	
Edit, Find	[CTRL] + [F]	
Edit, Rename	[F2]	
View, Datasheet View		
View, Form View		
View, Design View		
View, Print Preview		
View, Zoom		67%
Insert, New Record	[CTRL] + [+] (plus sign)	

Command Sequence	Keyboard Shortcut	Toolbar Shortcut
Records, Filter, Filter By Selection		
Records, Filter, Filter By Form		
Filter, Apply Filter/Sort		
Records, Remove Filter/Sort		
Records, Sort, Sort Ascending		
Records, Sort, Sort Descending		
Query, Run		
View, Totals		
Tools, Relationships		
Relationships, Show Table		
Edit, Primary Key		
Insert, Rows		
Help, Microsoft Office Access Help	[F1]	

Tags

XHTML Tag Name	XHTML Tag Description
<!-- ...-->	XHTML comments.
A	
<a href = "..."> ... </a>	Links web pages.
B	
<body> ... </body>	Contains presentation and formatting elements for the page content.
<b> ... </b>	Displays bold text.
<big> ... </big>	Big in size than the surrounding text.
 	Forces a line break.
C	
<caption> ... </caption>	Creates a headline of a table.
D	
<del> ... </del>	Strikes out the text.
<dl> ... </dl>	Defines the list of terms and their definitions.
<!DocType>	Defines DocType declaration. Specifies XHTML version and format used in the document.
E	
<em> ... </em>	Displays emphasized font. Browsers usually display italicized text.
H	
<h1> to <h6>	Headings to distinguish text in the document.
<head> ... </head>	Contains information about the web page.
<hr />	Inserts a horizontal rule.
<html> ... </html>	Contains the head and body tags.
I	
<i> ... </i>	Displays italicized text.
<img src = "..." />	Inserts images.
L	
<li> ... </li>	Lists items.

XHTML Tag Name	XHTML Tag Description
M	
`<meta/>`	Contains information about the document and is mainly used for search engines.
O	
`<ol> ... </ol>`	Ordered list. By default, it begins with a number.
P	
`<p> ... </p>`	Defines a text paragraph.
S	
`<strong> ... </strong>`	Strong font. Browsers usually display boldface text.
`<sub> ... </sub>`	Subscript (slightly lowered) text.
`<sup> ... </sup>`	Superscript (slightly raised) text.
T	
`<table> ... </table>`	Arranges information in rows and columns.
`<td> ... </td>`	Adds a column in a table.
`<title> ... </title>`	Contains brief description of web page.
`<tr> ... </tr>`	Adds a row in a table.
U	
`<ul> ... </ul>`	Unordered list. Uses **li** element to define each list item.

Index

A

absolute cell references used in a formula (MS Excel 2003)
  deleting columns, 233
  deleting rows, 233
  inserting columns, 233, 234
  inserting rows, 233, 234
  overview, 231–233
active cell, 166
addition (+), 174
Add Printer Wizard (Windows XP), 21
address bar
  Internet Explorer, 516
  Windows XP, 36
aggregate functions, 487–488
align attribute (XHTML), 560, 564
alignment
  of cell entries, resetting, 181–182
  charts, 145
alink attribute (XHTML), 554
AND conditions in a query, 498
animation effects added to slides, 381–385
anti-virus software programs, 32
Apple Macintosh operating system, 25
application window
  MS Access 2003
    Desktop, 394
    Getting Started task pane, 394
    Menu bar, 393
    Status bar, 394
    Title bar, 393
    toolbar, 393–394
  MS Excel 2003, 165–166
  MS PowerPoint 2003
    Drawing toolbar, 283
    Formatting toolbar, 282
    Getting Started task pane, 282, 285
    Menu bar, 282
    presentation window, 282
    Standard toolbar, 282
    Status bar, 283
    Title bar, 282
    view buttons, 282

area chart, 265
argument function, 237
argument list function, 237
attributes
  applied to text in MS Word 2003, 82–83
  XHTML, 554 555
AutoComplete feature
  Internet Explorer, 522
  MS Excel 2003, 193
AutoContent wizard (MS PowerPoint 2003), 286, 349
AutoCorrect feature
  MS Excel 2003, 193
  MS PowerPoint 2003, 286
  MS Word 2003, 60
AutoFill feature (MS Excel 2003), 194–195
AutoFormat feature (MS Excel 2003), 262–264
AutoForm Wizard (MS Access 2003), 419–420
AutoLayout feature (MS PowerPoint 2003), 286–287
autonumber data type, 401
AutoReport Wizard (MS Access 2003), 451–453
AutoSearch feature (Internet Explorer), 534–535
AutoShapes (MS PowerPoint 2003)
  added to a slide, 312–315
  fill color of object, changing, 312
  line color of object, changing, 313
  line style of object, changing, 313
  repositioning objects, 312
  resizing objects, 312
  shadow added to object, 313
  stacking, 370–374
  text added to, 315–318
AutoSum feature (MS Excel 2003), 238
AVERAGE function, 238, 242
Avg function, 488

B

background attribute (XHTML), 554
background color (XHTML), 556
backups (Windows XP), 42

bar chart, 265

basic XHTML document template, creating, 547–550

bgcolor attribute (XHTML), 554

bibliography page, creation of, 613

blank database
creation of new, 470–472
used for creating a new database, 398

blank presentation (MS PowerPoint 2003), 286, 349

blank worksheet, entering labels and values into a, 170–174

body section (XHTML), 554–556

bold attribute applied to text in MS Word 2003, 82–83

bolding column headings in tables, 127–128

border and shading added to text, 151–152

borders
adding to worksheets, 186–190
modifying table borders, 126, 132–133

bulleted list, creating, 96–98

C

CAD (Computer Aided Design), 32

categories of operating systems, 23–24

category axis, 266

cell pointer
described, 166
moving, 171

cell reference, 166

cells, 166

centering
column headings in tables, 128–129
worksheets, 210

characters inserted into text slides, 294

charts
MS Excel 2003
area chart, 265
bar chart, 265
category axis, 266
Chart Wizard, 266
column chart, 265, 266
cone chart, 265
cylinder chart, 265
data markers, 266
described, 163
doughnut chart, 265
gridlines, 266
legend, 266
line chart, 265
overview, 265–266
pie chart, 265

plotting, 266–271
pyramid chart, 265
title, 266
types of, 265
value axis, 266
xy (scatter) chart, 265
MS PowerPoint 2003
adding PowerPoint chart to a slide, 364–367
modifying components of, 367–370
plotting, 364
MS Word 2003
alignment, 145
color of data marker, changing, 143
inserting into document, 139–141
legend, repositioning, 144
modifying, 141–145
reformatting components, 141
type, changing, 141, 142

Chart Wizard, 266

clients, 513

clip art inserted into slide with Microsoft Clip Organizer, 319–322

closing
database file, 415
MS Word 2003 files, 64
presentation file, 332–333
tables, 415
Windows Explorer, 41

color of data marker, changing, 143

column chart, 265, 266

columns
described, 166
inserting, 134, 136, 197–201, 233, 234
menu system used to adjust column width an exact amount, 190
mouse used to adjust column width an exact amount, 191

column width
in tables, 126, 129–131
in worksheets, 190–191

command-line interface (CLI), 22

common problems associated with working with files in Windows XP, 41–42

comparison of operating systems, 24–25

comparison operators, 244

components of your computer, examining, 35–41

compression software, 32

Computer Aided Design (CAD), 32

computer viruses, 537

conditional formatting applied to worksheets, 249–252

cone chart, 265
consecutive record deletion in MS Access 2003, 430
consecutive worksheets, selecting, 259
consistent look and feel of operating system, 24
contact-management applications, 33
Control Panel (Windows XP)
  described, 9–10
  keyboard settings, 20–21
  mouse settings, 17–20
  printer settings, 21
  screen display, changing, 12–17
  system date and time, changing, 10–12
  themes, applying, 17
cookies, 33, 542–543
copying
  cells, 195–197
  files, 45
  folders, 45
  text, 29
Count function, 488
crawler-based search services, 532
Crosstab Query Wizard (MS Access 2003), 491–496
currency data type, 401
current date and time inserted into document, 70–72
custom animation effects added to slides, 381–385
cut and paste technique, 29, 80–82
cylinder chart, 265

D

database applications, 31
database file, reopening, 416–418
database records (MS Access 2003)
  consecutive record deletion, 430
  deleting records, 430–432
  editing records, 427–430
  entering records in Form view, 425–427
  Find feature used for editing records, 427–430
  single record deletion, 430
  sorting, 436–437
  switching between Form view and Datasheet view, 423–425
database setup (MS Access 2003)
  blank database used for creating a new database, 398
  closing a database file, 415
  closing a table, 415
  creating a new database, 398–400
  Database Wizard used for creating a new database, 398, 470

Datasheet view, entering records in, 408–410
designing a new database, 397
keyboard method of navigating through records, 414
mouse method of navigating through records, 414
navigating through records in Datasheet view, 413–414
printing datasheet of a table, 411–413
table, creating a new, 400–407
databases (MS Access 2003)
  blank database, creation of new, 470–472
  Database Wizard used to create new database, 398, 470
  new database, creation of, 469–472
Database Wizard (MS Access 2003), 398, 470
data entered into cell, 228, 230
data markers, 266
datasheet of table, entering records in, 408–410
Datasheet view, entering records in, 408–410
data types (MS Access 2003)
  autonumber data type, 401
  currency data type, 401
  date/time data type, 401
  hyperlink data type, 401
  Lookup Wizard used to determine, 402
  memo data type, 401
  number data type, 401
  OLE object data type, 401
  overview, 401
  text data type, 401
  yes/no (boolean) data type, 401
date and time functions, 237
date/time data type, 401
definition list tags (XHTML), 569
deleting
  characters in text slides, 294
  columns, 134, 136, 197–198, 233
  files, 41, 47–48
  folders, 47–48
  records, 430–432
  rows, 134, 137, 197–198, 233
  text, 29, 72–74
  words in text slides, 294
"Denied file access" message (Windows XP), 42
designing a new database in MS Access 2003, 397
design templates (MS PowerPoint 2003)
  applying design templates to presentation, 324–327
  described, 286, 324
  footer added to slides, 327–329
  new presentation created from, 349–352

Design view, creating a query in, 447–451
Desktop (MS Access 2003), 394
desktop publishing programs, 32
Details view of folders, 38
disadvantages of operating systems, 24, 26
disk fragmenter software, 32
display area (Internet Explorer), 516
displaying data (MS Access 2003)
    Design view, creating a query in, 447–451
    filtering records in a table, 437–440
    simple query, creating a, 440–446
division (/), 174
document, creating a MS Word 2003, 59–64
document formatting tags (XHTML)
    described, 557
    heading tags, 557–559
    horizontal rule tags, 560–562
    line break tags, 557
    list tags, 568–574
    nested tags, 566–568
    paragraph tags, 562–566
documents
    charts, inserting, 139–141
    tables, inserting, 123–125
doughnut chart, 265
downloading images from Web sites,
        603–607
drag and drop technique
    MS Word 2003, 80–81
    worksheets, 195–197
Drawing toolbar (MS PowerPoint 2003)
    adding text to an AutoShape, 315–318
    AutoShape added to a slide, 312–315
    described, 283
    moving a placeholder, 310–311
    stacking AutoShapes with, 370–374

E

editing
    documents, 65–82
    records, 427–430
    text on text slides, 294–296
    worksheets, 193–208
e-mail programs, 33
encryption programs, 538
entering a formula into worksheets, 174–179
entire worksheet printed on one page, 210
= (equal) operator, 244
existing presentation used for creating text
        slides, 286

exiting
    Internet Explorer, 521–522
    MS Access 2003, 462
    MS Excel 2003, 214–215
    MS Word 2003, 111
exponentiation (^), 174
Extensible Hypertext Markup Language.
        See XHTML

F

Favorites list (Internet Explorer)
    Internet radio station added to, 530–531
    removing a Web page from, 528
fields (MS Excel 2003), 247
file, creating a XHTML, 588–592
file icon (Windows XP), 35
file management in Windows XP, 41–48
filename.extension, 515
File Transfer Protocol (FTP), 514
fill color of object, changing, 312
Filter By Form method used for filtering records
        in tables, 438
Filter By Selection method used for filtering
        records in tables, 437–438
filtering records in tables, 437–440
financial functions, 237
financial software, 33
Find feature used for editing records in MS
        Access 2003, 427–430
finding files (Windows XP), 48
finding text in a MS Word 2003 document, 77–80
Find Unmatched Query Wizard (MS Access
        2003), 496–498
folder icon (Windows XP)
    changing, 43–44
    described, 35
folders
    copying folders, 45
    creating a new folder, 42–44
    deleting folders, 47–48
    Details view, 38
    folder icon, 35
    folder icon, changing, 43–44
    Folders view, 34
    Icons view, 38
    List view, 38
    moving folders, 45–46
    My Documents folder, 39–41
    naming folders, 42
    renaming folders, 46–47

Thumbnails view, 38
Tiles view, 38
Folders view (Windows Explorer), 34
fonts
applying, 84–86
options for cell entries, resetting, 182–185
size, changing, 84
word processing applications, 30
footer
added to slides, 327–329
worksheets, 211–212
formatting
documents, 82–102
tables, 125–133
worksheets, 181–193
Formatting toolbar
MS Excel 2003, 166, 169–170
MS PowerPoint 2003, 282
MS Word 2003, 57–58
forms (MS Access 2003)
AutoForm Wizard used for creating, 419–420
creating, 419–420
described, 396
navigating through records in, 421–422
navigating through records in Form view, 421–422
reopening, 423
Formula bar (MS Excel 2003), 166
formulas
relative cell references, 231
used to link worksheets in a workbook, 255–258
workbooks, 228, 231
worksheets, 171
FTP (File Transfer Protocol), 514
full menus
MS Access 2003, 395
MS Excel 2003, 167–168
MS PowerPoint 2003, 283–284
MS Word 2003, 57
function name, 237
functions (MS Excel 2003)
argument, 237
argument list, 237
AVERAGE function, 238, 242
date and time functions, 237
financial functions, 237
function name, 237
IF function, 243–244
math functions, 237
MAX function, 238, 239–240
MIN function, 238, 240
nesting IF functions, 245

NOW function, 246–247
overview, 237–238
statistical functions, 237
SUM function, 238, 241
TODAY function, 246

G

Getting Started task pane
MS Access 2003, 394
MS Excel 2003, 166, 170
MS PowerPoint 2003, 282, 285
MS Word 2003, 58–59
Google, 535–537
graphical-user interface (GUI), 23
graphics, 30, 31–32
> (greater than) operator, 244
> =(greater than or equal to) operator, 244
gridlines, 212, 266
grouped tabular report, creating, 454–458

H

handouts (MS PowerPoint 2003), 280
hard page break (MS Word 2003), 99–100
headers
reports, 153–155
worksheets, 211
header section (XHTML), 550–551
heading tags (XHTML), 557–559
Help system
Internet Explorer, 517–521
MS Access 2003, 458–461
MS Excel 2003, 215–218
MS PowerPoint 2003, 336–341
MS Word 2003, 107–110
History Explorer bar (Internet Explorer), 525–526
history of operating systems, 22–23
Horizontal ruler used for indenting a paragraph
in MS Word 2003, 87–90
horizontal rule tags (XHTML), 560–562
horizontal scroll bar (MS Excel 2003), 166
HTML (Hypertext Markup Language), 514
HTTP (Hypertext Transfer Protocol), 514
human-powered directories search services, 532
hybrid search services, 532
hyperlink data type, 401
hyperlinks
adding, 621–622
described, 514
Internet Explorer, 523
XHTML, 614–622

Hypertext Markup Language (HTML), 514
Hypertext Transfer Protocol (HTTP), 514

I

Icons view of folders, 38
icons (Windows XP), 3
IF function, 243–244
images (XHTML)
    downloading images from Web sites,
        603–607
    Microsoft Office clipart, 607–612
    overview, 601–603
indenting a paragraph in MS Word 2003,
    87–90
indexes, 30
insertion point, moving, 67, 69
Internet
    described, 513–514
    security
        computer viruses, 537
        cookies, 542–543
        for e-mail messages, 538
        encryption programs, 538
        local intranet, 539
        overview, 537–538
        passwords, 538
        personal certificates, 539
        privacy of communications, 538
        privacy policy, 542
        restricted sites, 539
        security certificates, 539
        security zones, 539–542
        trusted sites, 539
        Web site certificates, 539
Internet Explorer
    address bar, 516
    AutoComplete feature, 522
    AutoSearch feature, 534–535
    commands, 637
    crawler-based search services, 532
    described, 514
    display area, 516
    exiting, 521–522
    Favorites list
        adding a Web page to, 528–530
        Internet radio station added to,
            530–531
        removing a Web from, 528
    Google and, 535–537
    Help system, 517–521
    History Explorer bar, 525–526

human-powered directories search services, 532
hybrid search services, 532
hyperlinks, 523
icon in Windows XP, 3
keyboard shortcuts, 637
links bar, 516
main window, 515–516
Media Bar, 530
menu bar, 515
navigating a Web site, 523–525
new Home page, setting, 526–527
practice exercises, 543
previously viewed Web pages, displaying,
    525–526
printing a Web page, 531
Search Companion, 532–534
search services, 532
specific Web page, displaying, 522–523
starting, 515
status bar, 516
title bar, 515
toolbar
    customizing, 517
    default settings, resetting toolbar to, 517
    described, 515
    removing buttons from, 517
    text labels displayed below toolbar buttons,
        517
toolbar shortcuts, 637
vertical scroll bar, 516
Internet radio station added to Favorites list,
    530–531
ISPs (Internet Service Providers), 515
italic attribute applied to text in MS Word
    2003, 82–83

K

keyboard method used for navigating through
    records in MS Access 2003, 414, 421
keyboard shortcuts
    Internet Explorer, 637
    MS Access 2003, 657–658
    MS Excel 2003, 647–649
    MS PowerPoint 2003, 653–654
    MS Word 2003, 641–643
    Windows XP, 633

L

labels, 171
legend, 144, 266
< (less than) operator, 244

< =(less than or equal to) operator, 244
line break tags (XHTML), 557
line chart, 265
line color of object, changing, 313
line spacing
    in MS Word 2003, 90–93
    of paragraphs on text slides, 307–309
line style of object, changing, 313
link attribute (XHTML), 554
linking worksheets with workbooks,
        253–262
links bar (Internet Explorer), 516
Linux, 25
list, sorting records in a, 247–249
list tags (XHTML)
    definition list tags, 569
    described, 568–569
    nested list tags, 573–574
    ordered list tags, 571–573
    unordered list tags, 570–571
List view of folders, 38
Local Disk (C:), 37
local intranet, 539
location of files (Windows Explorer), 42
logging off Windows XP, 7–8
logging on Windows XP, 1–2
Lookup Wizard (MS Access 2003), 402

M

macros (MS Access 2003), 396
main title on text slides, 286
main window (Internet Explorer), 515–516
many-to-many relationship for multiple
        tables, 478
margin size, 29
margins of document, resetting, 94–96
Markup Validation Service Web page,
        577–581
math functions, 237
MAX function, 238, 239–240, 488
Media Bar (Internet Explorer), 530
memo data type, 401
Menu bar
    Internet Explorer, 515
    MS Access 2003, 393
    MS Excel 2003, 166
    MS PowerPoint 2003, 282
menus
    MS Access 2003, 395
    MS Excel 2003, 167–169
    MS Word 2003, 56–57

menu system
    MS Excel 2003, 167–169
    MS Word 2003, 55–57
    used for indenting a paragraph, 87
    used to adjust column width an exact amount,
        190
meta elements, 550–551
Microsoft Clip Organizer (MS PowerPoint 2003)
    entering additional text into slide with, 322–324
    inserting clip art image into slide with, 319–322
Microsoft Graph, 364
Microsoft Office clipart, 607–612
Microsoft Windows 95/98/ME/XP Home, 25
Microsoft Windows 3.x, 25
MIN function, 238, 240, 488
modifying
    charts, 141–145
    components of PowerPoint chart, 367–370
    Datasheet view of tables, 433–436
    system settings in Windows XP, 9–21
    worksheets, 170–181
modules (MS Access 2003), 396
mouse
    method of navigating through records in MS
        Access 2003, 414, 421
    used to adjust column width an exact
        amount, 191
    used to adjust row height an exact amount, 192
moving
    files, 45–46
    folders, 45–46
    a placeholder, 310–311
    a text block, 80–82
    windows, 5–7
MS Access 2003
    aggregate functions, 487–488
    application window
        Desktop, 394
        Getting Started task pane, 394
        Menu bar, 393
        Status bar, 394
        Title bar, 393
        toolbar, 393–394
    Avg function, 488
    commands, 657–658
    Count function, 488
    database file, reopening, 416–418
    database records
        consecutive record deletion, 430
        deleting records, 430–432
        editing records, 427–430

MS Access 2003—*Continued*
    entering records in Form view, 425–427
    Find feature used for editing records, 427–430
    single record deletion, 430
    sorting, 436–437
    switching between Form view and
      Datasheet view, 423–425
  databases
    blank database, creation of new, 470–472
    Database Wizard used to create new
      database, 470
    new database, creation of, 469–472
  database setup
    blank database used for creating a new
      database, 398
    closing a database file, 415
    closing a table, 415
    creating a new database, 398–400
    Database Wizard used for creating a new
      database, 398
    Datasheet view, entering records in, 408–410
    designing a new database, 397
    keyboard method of navigating through
      records, 414
    mouse method of navigating through
      records, 414
    navigating through records in Datasheet
      view, 413–414
    printing datasheet of a table, 411–413
    table, creating a new, 400–407
  data types
    autonumber data type, 401
    currency data type, 401
    date/time data type, 401
    hyperlink data type, 401
    Lookup Wizard used to determine, 402
    memo data type, 401
    number data type, 401
    OLE object data type, 401
    overview, 401
    text data type, 401
    yes/no (boolean) data type, 401
  described, 396
  displaying data
    Design view, creating a query in, 447–451
    filtering records in a table, 437–440
    simple query, creating a, 440–446
  exiting, 462
  forms
    AutoForm Wizard used for creating, 419–420
    creating, 419–420
    described, 396

    navigating through records in, 421–422
    navigating through records in Form view,
      421–422
    reopening, 423
  full menus, 395
  help system, 458–461
  keyboard shortcuts, 657–658
  Max function, 488
  menus, 395
  Min function, 488
  modules, 396
  multiple tables
    creating a query to extract information from,
      483–487
    creating two new tables and setting their
      primary keys, 472–477
    many-to-many relationship for, 478
    one-to-many relationship for, 477–481
    one-to-one relationship for, 478
    primary keys, setting, 472–477
    relationship between two tables in a
      database, creating, 477–481
    subdatasheets, 481–482
  objects, 396
  overview, 392
  practice exercises, 462–465, 506–512
  primary keys, 404
  queries
    AND conditions, 498
    Crosstab Query Wizard, 491–496
    described, 396
    Design view, creating a query in, 447–451
    Find Unmatched Query Wizard,
      496–498
    multiple conditions included in a query,
      498–503
    multiple tables, creating a query to extract
      information from, 483–487
    OR conditions, 498
    parameter queries, 503–506
    simple query, creating a, 440–446
    Simple Query Wizard, 440–446
    summary information, creating a query to
      generate, 487–491
    unmatched records in a table, creating a
      query to find, 496–498
  reports
    AutoReport Wizard, 451–453
    described, 396
    grouped tabular report, creating, 454–458
    Report Wizard, 454–458
    simple tabular report, creating, 451–453

shortcut menus, 395
short menus, 395
Simple Query Wizard, 440–446
starting, 392
StDev function, 488
Sum function, 488
summary information, 487
tables
   closing, 415
   creating new, 400–407
   datasheet of table, entering records in,
     408–410
   Filter By Form method used for filtering
     records in, 438
   Filter By Selection method used for filtering
     records in, 437–438
   filtering records in, 437–440
   keyboard method used for navigating
     through records in, 421
   modifying Datasheet view of, 433–436
   mouse method used for navigating through
     records in, 421
   navigating through records in, 421–422
   overview, 396
   printing datasheet of a table, 411–413
   reopening, 417–418
   repositioning fields in, 433
   resizing fields in, 433
   sorting records in, 436–437
   Table Wizard used to create new, 401
   unmatched records in a table, creating a
     query to find, 496–498
  toolbar shortcuts, 657–658
  Var function, 488
MS-DOS operating system, 25
MS Excel 2003
  addition (+), 174
  application window, 165–166
  AutoComplete feature, 193
  AutoCorrect feature, 193
  AutoFill feature, 194–195
  AutoFormat feature, 262–264
  AutoSum feature, 238
  charts
    area chart, 265
    bar chart, 265
    category axis, 266
    Chart Wizard, 266
    column chart, 265, 266
    cone chart, 265
    cylinder chart, 265
    data markers, 266

    described, 163
    doughnut chart, 265
    gridlines, 266
    legend, 266
    line chart, 265
    overview, 265–266
    pie chart, 265
    plotting, 266–271
    pyramid chart, 265
    title, 266
    types of, 265
    value axis, 266
    xy (scatter) chart, 265
  commands, 647–649
  comparison operators, 244
  division (/), 174
  exiting, 214–215
  exponentiation (^), 174
  fields, 247
  Formatting toolbar, 166, 169–170
  Formula bar, 166
  full menus, 167–168
  functions
    argument, 237
    argument list, 237
    AVERAGE function, 238, 242
    date and time functions, 237
    financial functions, 237
    function name, 237
    IF function, 243–244
    math functions, 237
    MAX function, 238, 239–240
    MIN function, 238, 240
    nesting IF functions, 245
    NOW function, 246–247
    overview, 237–238
    statistical functions, 237
    SUM function, 238, 241
    TODAY function, 246
  Getting Started task pane, 166, 170
  Help system, 215–218
  horizontal scroll bar, 166
  keyboard shortcuts, 647–649
  list, sorting records in a, 247–249
  Menu bar, 166
  menu system, 167–169
  multiple fields, 247
  multiplication (–), 174
  Name box, 166
  opening a new workbook, 163–165
  operands, 174
  operator precedence, 175

MS Excel 2003—*Continued*
    operators, 174
    overview, 162–163
    Page Setup dialog box
        Header/Footer panel, 209
        Margins panel, 209
        Page panel, 208–209
        Sheet panel, 209
    practice exercises, 219–223, 273–275
    records, 247
    shortcut menus, 168–169
    short menus, 167–168
    single field, 247
    sorting records in list, 247–249
    Spelling Checker, 271–272
    Standard toolbar, 166, 169–170
    starting, 163
    Status bar, 166
    subtraction (-), 174
    task panes, 170
    Title bar, 166
    toolbars, 169–170
    toolbar shortcuts, 647–649
    using absolute cell references in a formula
        deleting columns, 233
        deleting rows, 233
        inserting columns, 233, 234
        inserting rows, 233, 234
        overview, 231–233
    vertical scroll bar, 166
    workbooks
        data entered into cell, 228, 230
        formula entered into worksheet, 228, 231
        linking worksheets with, 253–262
        opening new workbook, 228, 229
        resaving, 180
        saving, 180–181
    Workbook window, 166
    worksheets, 163
        alignment of cell entries, resetting, 181–182
        borders, adding, 186–190
        cell pointer, moving, 171
        centering, 210
        changing data in, 193–194
        column width, adjusting, 190–191
        conditional formatting applied to, 249–252
        consecutive worksheets, selecting, 259
        copying cells, 195–197
        deleting columns, 197–198
        deleting rows, 197–198
        drag and drop technique used for copying cells, 195–197

    editing, 193–208
    entering a formula into, 174–179
    entering labels and values into a blank worksheet, 170–174
    entire worksheet printed on one page, 210
    font options for cell entries, resetting, 182–185
    footer, creating, 211–212
    formatting, 181–193
    formulas, 171
    formulas used to link worksheets in a workbook, 255–258
    gridline included in printout, 212
    header, creating, 211
    inserting columns, 197–201
    inserting rows, 197–201
    labels, 171
    modifying, 170–181
    multiple worksheets formatted in one operation, 259–262
    non-consecutive worksheets, selecting, 259
    number format of cell entries, resetting, 201–208
    page orientation, 213
    page setup options, 208–214
    percentages, formatting cell entries as, 201–208
    print preview, 213–214
    range, selecting a, 186
    renaming, 253–255
    row height, adjusting, 192–193
    shading, adding, 186–190
    values, 171
    workbook, linking worksheets with, 253–262
    worksheet tabs, 166
MS PowerPoint 2003
    animation effects added to slides, 381–385
    Application window
        Drawing toolbar, 283
        Formatting toolbar, 282
        Getting Started task pane, 282, 285
        Menu bar, 282
        presentation window, 282
        Standard toolbar, 282
        Status bar, 283
        Title bar, 282
        view buttons, 282
    AutoContent wizard, 349
    AutoCorrect feature, 286
    AutoLayout feature, 286–287

AutoShapes
   added to a slide, 312–315
   fill color of object, changing, 312
   line color of object, changing, 313
   line style of object, changing, 313
   repositioning objects, 312
   resizing objects, 312
   shadow added to object, 313
   stacking, 370–374
   text added to, 315–318
blank presentation, 349
chart
   adding PowerPoint chart to a slide,
     364–367
   modifying components of, 367–370
   plotting, 364
commands, 653–654
custom animation effects added to slides,
   381–385
design template
   new presentation created from,
     349–352
design templates
   applying design templates to presentation,
     324–327
   described, 324
   footer added to slides, 327–329
Drawing toolbar
   adding text to an AutoShape, 315–318
   AutoShape added to a slide, 312–315
   moving a placeholder, 310–311
   stacking AutoShapes with, 370–374
full menu, 283–284
Getting Started task pane, 285
handouts, 280
Help system, 336–341
keyboard shortcuts, 653–654
Microsoft Clip Organizer
   entering additional text into slide with,
     322–324
   inserting clip art image into slide with,
     319–322
MS PowerPoint 2003, 281–283
new presentation created from design
   template, 349–352
notes, 280
overview, 280
practice exercises, 341–344, 386–387
presentation
   described, 281
   resaving, 353
   saving, 352–354

presentation file
   closing, 332–333
   reopening, 333–334
printing slides, 334–335
running slide shows, 374–379
shortcut menu, 284
short menu, 283–284
Slide Layout task pane, 289
slides, 280
slide shows
   animation effects added to slides, 381–385
   running, 374–379
   transition effects added to slides, 379–380
Spell Checker, 329–332
starting, 281
tables
   adding PowerPoint table to slide, 354–357
   formatting, 357–363
task panes, 285
text slides
   adding new slide to presentation, 288–292
   AutoContent wizard used for creating, 286
   blank presentation, 286
   deleting characters, 294
   deleting words, 294
   design template for, 286
   editing text on, 294–296
   existing presentation used for creating, 286
   inserting characters, 294
   lines pacing of paragraphs on, resetting,
     307–309
   main title, 286
   new presentation, creating, 286–288
   Outline tab, working in, 299–307
   placeholders, 286
   replacing words, 294
   resaving a presentation, 292
   saving a presentation, 292–293
   Slides tab, working in, 296–299
   subtitle, 286
   title slide, 286
toolbar options, 284–285
toolbar shortcuts, 653–654
transition effects added to slides, 379–380
MS Word 2003
   attributes applied to text, 82–83
   AutoCorrect feature, 60
   bold attribute applied to text, 82–83
   bulleted list, creating, 96–98
   charts
     alignment, 145
     color of data marker, changing, 143

MS Word 2003—*Continued*
  inserting into document, 139–141
  legend, repositioning, 144
  modifying, 141–145
  reformatting components, 141
  type, changing, 141, 142
closing a file, 64
columns button, 146
commands, 641–643
current date and time inserted into document,
    70–72
cut and paste technique, 80–82
deleting text from a document, 72–74
described, 52
document, creating a, 59–64
drag and drop technique, 80–81
editing a document, 65–82
entering text into a document, 59–61
exiting, 111
finding text in a document, 77–80
fonts, applying, 84–86
fonts size, changing, 84
formatting a document, 82–102
Formatting toolbar, 57–58
full menus, 57
Getting Started task pane, 58–59
hard page break, inserting, 99–100
Help system, 107–110
Horizontal ruler used for indenting a
    paragraph, 87–90
indenting a paragraph, 87–90
Insert/Break command, 116, 118
inserting text into document, 72–74
insertion point, moving, 67, 69
italic attribute applied to text, 82–83
keyboard shortcuts, 641–643
line spacing, resetting, 90–93
margins of document, resetting, 94–96
menu system, 55–57
menu system used for indenting a
    paragraph, 87
Microsoft Office Word Help button, 107–110
moving a text block, 80–82
multiple fonts, applying, 85–86
multiple-page document, creating, 99–100
multiple-section document, creating, 116–123
New Black Document button, 60
newsletter-style columns, creating, 146–150
numbered list, creating, 96–97
Open dialog box, 66
paragraph spacing, resetting, 90–93
practice exercises, 111–112, 158–160

Print dialog box, 56
printing a document, 63–64
Print Preview button, 122–123
Redo feature, 75–76
reopening a file, 65–66
reports
  border and shading added to text, 151–152
    header/footer added to document, 153–155
    page numbers added to document, 156–158
reversing an edit operation, 75–76
saving a document, 62–63
section breaks, inserting, 116–123
selecting text, 68–70
shortcut menus, 57
short menus, 56 57
Spelling and Grammar Checker, 61
spelling and grammar checker, 102–103
Standard toolbar, 57–58
starting, 52–54
tables
  bolding column headings, 127–128
  borders, modifying, 126, 132–133
  centering column headings, 128–129
  column width, 126, 129–131
  deleting columns, 134, 136
  deleting rows, 134, 137
  formatting, 125–133
  inserting columns, 134, 136
  inserting into document, 123–125
  inserting rows, 133–134, 135
  restoring rows, 137
  row height, 126, 131
  shading cells, 127
  Table AutoFormat feature, 137–138
tables, setting up, 123–138
task panes, 58–59
templates, 103–106
toolbar shortcuts, 641–643
underline attribute applied to text, 82–83
Undo feature, 75–76
wizards, 104
Word Application window, 53–54
zoom level of document, changing, 100–102
multimedia applications, 32
multiple conditions included in a query,
    498–503
multiple fields in MS Excel 2003, 247
multiple fonts in MS Word 2003, 85–86
multiple-page document in MS Word 2003,
    99–100
multiple-section document in MS Word 2003,
    116–123

multiple tables (MS Access 2003)
    creating a query to extract information from, 483–487
    creating two new tables and setting their primary keys, 472–477
    many-to-many relationship for, 478
    one-to-many relationship for, 477–481
    one-to-one relationship for, 478
    primary keys, setting, 472–477
    relationship between two tables in a database, creating, 477–481
    subdatasheets, 481–482
multiple worksheets formatted in one operation, 259–262
multiplication (–), 174
multi-user operating system, 23
My Computer icon (Windows XP), 3
My Computer (Windows Explorer), 37
My Documents folder (Windows Explorer), 39–41
My Documents icon (Windows XP), 3
My Network Places icon (Windows XP), 3

N

Name box (MS Excel 2003), 166
naming
    files, 42
    folders, 42
navigation
    menu, creating, 623–629
    of records in Datasheet view, 413–414
    of records in forms, 421–422
    of records in Form view, 421–422
    of records in tables, 421–422
    of Web sites, 523–525
    XHTML, 622–629
nested list tags (XHTML), 573–574
nested tags (XHTML), 566–568
nesting IF functions, 245
network domain, logging on to a computer that is part of a, 1–2
network location, 514
new database, creation of, 469–472
new Home page, setting, 526–527
new presentation, creating, 286–288
newsletter-style columns, creating, 146–150
<> (not equal to) operator, 244
non-consecutive worksheets, selecting, 259
noshade attribute (XHTML), 560
Notepad used to create a Web page
    background color, setting, 556
    basic XHTML document template, creating, 547–550

    body section, 554–556
    document formatting tags, 557–574
    header section, 550–551
    meta elements, adding, 550–551
    opening Notepad, 548
    saving a new document, 551–552
    text color, setting, 556
    title element, adding, 550–551
    viewing a document, 552–554
notes (MS PowerPoint 2003), 280
Notification area (Windows XP desktop), 3
NOW function, 246–247
number data type, 401
numbered list, creating, 96–97
number format of cell entries, resetting, 201–208

O

objects (MS Access 2003), 396
Office 2003 application, selecting commands in, 28–29
OLE object data type, 401
one-to-many relationship for multiple tables, 477–481
one-to-one relationship for multiple tables, 478
Open dialog box (MS Word 2003), 66
opening a new workbook in MS Excel 2003, 163–165, 228, 229
opening Notepad, 548
operands, 174
operating systems
    Apple Macintosh, 25
    categories of, 23–24
    command-line interface (CLI), 22
    comparison of, 24–25
    consistent look and feel of, 24
    described, 1
    disadvantages of, 24, 26
    graphical-user interface (GUI), 23
    history of, 22–23
    Linux, 25
    Microsoft Windows 95/98/ME/XP Home, 25
    Microsoft Windows 3.x, 25
    MS-DOS, 25
    multi-user operating system, 23
    overview, 22
    PalmOS, 25
    real-time operating system (RTOS), 24
    single-user multi-tasking operating system, 23
    single-user single task operating system, 24
    Unix, 25
    Windows Mobile 2003, 25

operator precedence, 175
operators, 174
OR conditions, 498
ordered list tags, 571–573
Outline tab used for working on text slides, 299–307
Outlook Express, 514

P

page numbers added to document, 156–158
page orientation of worksheets, 213
Page Setup dialog box (MS Excel 2003)
   Header/Footer panel, 209
   Margins panel, 209
   Page panel, 208–209
   Sheet panel, 209
page setup options for worksheets, 208–214
page size, 29
PalmOS, 25
paragraph spacing, resetting, 90–93
paragraph tag (XHTML), 562–566
parameter queries, 503–506
passwords, 538
path, 514
percentages, formatting cell entries as, 201–208
personal certificates, 539
pie chart, 265
placeholders on text slides, 286
plotting charts, 266–271
practice exercises
   Internet Explorer, 543
   MS Access 2003, 462–465, 506–512
   MS Excel 2003, 219–223, 273–275
   MS PowerPoint 2003, 341–344, 386–387
   MS Word 2003, 111–112, 158–160
   XHTML, 583–584, 629–630
presentation applications, 31
presentations (MS PowerPoint 2003)
   closing, 332–333
   described, 281
   reopening, 333–334
   resaving, 353
   saving, 352–354
presentation window (MS PowerPoint 2003), 282
previously viewed Web pages, displaying, 525–526
primary keys (MS Access 2003), 404, 472–477
Print dialog box (MS Word 2003), 56

printing
   datasheet of a table, 411–413
   documents, 63–64
   entire worksheet printed on one page, 210
   print preview for worksheets, 213–214
   slides, 334–335
   Web pages, 531
   word processing applications, 30
privacy of communications, 538
privacy policy, 542
Properties dialog box (Windows XP)
   Customize panel, 39
   General panel, 39
   Sharing panel, 39
pyramid chart, 265

Q

queries (MS Access 2003)
   AND conditions, 498
   Crosstab Query Wizard, 491–496
   described, 396
   Design view, creating a query in, 447–451
   Find Unmatched Query Wizard, 496–498
   multiple conditions included in a query, 498–503
   multiple tables, creating a query to extract information from, 483–487
   OR conditions, 498
   parameter queries, 503–506
   simple query, creating a, 440–446
   Simple Query Wizard, 440–446
   summary information, creating a query to generate, 487–491
   unmatched records in a table, creating a query to find, 496–498

R

RAM (Random Access Memory), 22
range in worksheet, selecting a, 186
real-time operating system (RTOS), 24
records entered in Form view (MS Access 2003), 425–427
records (MS Excel 2003), 247
Recycle Bin icon (Windows XP), 3
Redo feature (MS Word 2003), 75–76
reformatting components in charts, 141
relationship between two tables in a database, creating, 477–481
relative cell references, 231

removing a Web site from Favorites list, 528
renaming
    files, 41–42, 46–47
    folders, 46–47
    worksheets, 253–255
reopening
    database file, 416–418
    files, 65–66
    forms, 423
    presentation file, 333–334
    tables, 417–418
replacing words in text slides, 294
reports
    MS Access 2003
        AutoReport Wizard, 451–453
        described, 396
        grouped tabular report, creating, 454–458
        Report Wizard, 454–458
        simple tabular report, creating, 451–453
    MS Word 2003
        border and shading added to text,
            151–152
        header/footer added to document,
            153–155
        page numbers added to document,
            156–158
Report Wizard (MS Access 2003), 454–458
repositioning fields in tables, 433
repositioning objects, 312
resaving
    presentations, 353
    text slides, 292
    workbooks, 180
resizing
    fields in tables, 433
    objects, 312
    windows, 5–7
restoring rows in tables, 137
restricted sites, 539
reversing an edit operation in MS Word 2003,
        75–76
root directory, 37
root folder, 37
rows
    described, 166
    height of, 126, 131, 192–193
    inserting, 133–134, 197–201
    mouse used to adjust row height an exact
        amount, 192
    tallest entry, adjusting row height to
        accommodate, 192

S

saving
    documents, 62–63
    new documents, 551–552
    presentations, 352–354
    text slides, 292–293
    workbooks, 180–181
search and replace, 30
Search Companion (Internet Explorer), 532–534
search services, 532
section breaks in MS Word 2003, 116–123
security
    computer viruses, 537
    cookies, 542–543
    for e-mail messages, 538
    encryption programs, 538
    local intranet, 539
    overview, 537–538
    passwords, 538
    personal certificates, 539
    privacy of communications, 538
    privacy policy, 542
    restricted sites, 539
    security certificates, 539
    security zones, 539–542
    trusted sites, 539
    Web site certificates, 539
security certificates, 539
security zones, 539–542
selecting text in MS Word 2003, 68–70
servers, 513
shading cells, 127
shading in worksheets, 186–190
shadow added to object, 313
shortcut buttons for Windows XP, 29
shortcut menus
    MS Access 2003, 395
    MS Excel 2003, 168–169
    MS PowerPoint 2003, 284
    MS Word 2003, 57
    Windows Explorer (Windows XP), 36–37
short menus
    MS Access 2003, 395
    MS Excel 2003, 167–168
    MS PowerPoint 2003, 283–284
    MS Word 2003, 56–57
shutting down Windows XP, 8–9
simple query, creating a, 440–446
Simple Query Wizard, 440–446
simple tabular report, creating, 451–453

single field in MS Excel 2003, 247
single record deletion in MS Access 2003, 430
single-user multi-tasking operating system, 23
single-user single task operating system, 24
size attribute (XHTML), 560
Slide Layout task pane (MS PowerPoint 2003), 289
slide shows (MS PowerPoint 2003)
    animation effects added to slides, 381–385
    running, 374–379
    transition effects added to slides, 379–380
slides (MS PowerPoint 2003)
    adding new slide to presentation, 288–292
    animation effects added to slides, 381–385
    AutoShape added to, 312–315
    described, 280
    entering additional text into slide with
        Microsoft Clip Organizer, 322–324
    PowerPoint chart added to a slide, 364–367
Slides tab, working in, 296–299
software
    contact-management applications, 33
    database applications, 31
    e-mail programs, 33
    financial software, 33
    graphics applications, 31–32
    multimedia applications, 32
    Office 2003 application, selecting commands
        in, 28–29
    operating systems, 21–26
    presentation applications, 31
    shortcut buttons, 29
    software application programs, 26–27
    spreadsheet applications, 30–31
    system software, 21–26
    types of, 27
    utility programs, 32
    Web browsers, 33
    Web page authoring programs, 34
    word processing applications, 29–30
sorting records in lists, 247–249
sorting records in tables, 436–437
specific Web page, displaying, 522–523
spell checker
    MS Excel 2003, 271–272
    MS PowerPoint 2003, 329–332
    word processing applications, 30
spelling and grammar checker (MS Word 2003),
    61, 102–103
spreadsheet applications, 30–31
stacking AutoShapes, 370–374
stand-alone computer, logging on to a, 2

Standard toolbar
    MS Excel 2003, 166, 169–170
    MS PowerPoint 2003, 282
    MS Word 2003, 57–58
starting
    Internet Explorer, 515
    MS Access 2003, 392
    MS Excel 2003, 163
    MS PowerPoint 2003, 281
    MS Word 2003, 52–54
    Windows Explorer (Windows XP), 35
Start menu (Windows XP)
    All Programs, 4
    Control Panel, 4
    described, 4
    displaying, 5
    Help and Support, 4
    Log Off, 4
    My Computer, 4
    My Documents, 4
    My Music, 4
    My Pictures, 4
    My Recent Documents, 4
    Printers and Faxes, 4
    Run, 4
    Search, 4
    selecting options on, 5
    Shut Down, 4
    Turn Off Computer, 4
statistical functions, 237
Status bar
    Internet Explorer, 516
    MS Access 2003, 394
    MS Excel 2003, 166
    MS PowerPoint 2003, 283
StDev function, 488
subdatasheets (MS Access 2003), 481–482
subtitles on text slides, 286
subtraction (-), 174
SUM function, 238, 241, 488
summary information, creating a query to
    generate, 487–491
switching between Form view and Datasheet
    view in MS Access 2003, 423–425
syllabus.html file creation (XHTML)
    hyperlinks, adding, 621–622
    Microsoft Office clipart added to, 607–612
    navigation menu, creating, 623–629
    overview, 588–592
    table added to, 598–600
system software, 21–26

T

Table AutoFormat feature (MS Word 2003),
    137–138
table of contents, 30
tables
    MS Access 2003
        closing, 415
        creating new, 400–407
        datasheet of table, entering records in,
            408–410
        Filter By Form method used for filtering
            records in, 438
        Filter By Selection method used for filtering
            records in, 437–438
        filtering records in, 437–440
        keyboard method used for navigating
            through records in, 421
        modifying Datasheet view of, 433–436
        mouse method used for navigating through
            records in, 421
        navigating through records in, 421–422
        overview, 396
        printing datasheet of a table, 411–413
        reopening, 417–418
        repositioning fields in, 433
        resizing fields in, 433
        sorting records in, 436–437
        Table Wizard used to create new, 401
        unmatched records in a table, creating a
            query to find, 496–498
    MS PowerPoint 2003
        adding PowerPoint table to slide, 354–357
        formatting, 357–363
    MS Word 2003
        bolding column headings, 127–128
        borders, modifying, 126, 132–133
        centering column headings, 128–129
        column width, 126, 129–131
        deleting columns, 134, 136
        deleting rows, 134, 137
        formatting, 125–133
        inserting columns, 134, 136
        inserting into document, 123–125
        inserting rows, 133–134, 135
        restoring rows, 137
        row height, 126, 131
        setting up, 123–138
        shading cells, 127
        Table AutoFormat feature, 137–138
    syllabus.html file, added to, 598–600
    XHTML, 593–600

Table Wizard (MS Access 2003), 401
tags (XHTML), 661–662
tallest entry, adjusting row height to
    accommodate, 192
Taskbar (Windows XP desktop), 3
task panes
    MS Excel 2003, 170
    MS PowerPoint 2003, 285
    MS Word 2003, 58–59
Tasks view (Windows Explorer), 34–35
templates (MS Word 2003), 103–106
text
    AutoShape, adding text to, 315–318
    color, setting, 556
    inserting text into MS Word 2003 document,
        59–61, 72–74
text data type, 401
text slides (MS PowerPoint 2003)
    adding new slide to presentation, 288–292
    AutoContent wizard used for creating, 286
    blank presentation, 286
    deleting characters, 294
    deleting words, 294
    design template for, 286
    editing text on, 294 296
    existing presentation used for creating, 286
    inserting characters, 294
    lines pacing of paragraphs on, resetting,
        307–309
    main title, 286
    new presentation, creating, 286–288
    Outline tab, working in, 299–307
    placeholders, 286
    replacing words, 294
    resaving a presentation, 292
    saving a presentation, 292–293
    Slides tab, working in, 296–299
    subtitle, 286
    title slide, 286
thesaurus, 30
Thumbnails view of folders, 38
Tiles view of folders, 38
Title bar
    Internet Explorer, 515
    MS Access 2003, 393
    MS Excel 2003, 166
    MS PowerPoint 2003, 282
title element (XHTML), 550–551
title of chart, 266
title slide, 286
TODAY function, 246

toolbar
  Internet Explorer
    customizing, 517
    default settings, resetting toolbar to, 517
    described, 515
    removing buttons from, 517
    text labels displayed below toolbar buttons, 517
  MS Access 2003, 393–394
  MS Excel 2003, 169–170
  MS PowerPoint 2003, 284–285
toolbar shortcuts
  Internet Explorer, 637
  MS Access 2003, 657–658
  MS Excel 2003, 647–649
  MS PowerPoint 2003, 653–654
  MS Word 2003, 641–643
  Windows XP, 633
trusted sites, 539

U

underline attribute applied to text, 82–83
Undo feature (MS Word 2003), 75–76
Uniform Resource Locator (URL), 514–515
Unix, 25
unmatched records in a table, creating a query to find, 496–498
unordered list tags, 570–571
utility programs
  anti-virus software programs, 32
  compression software, 32
  disk fragmenter software, 32

V

validating Web pages, 575–583
value axis, 266
values in worksheets, 171
Var function, 488
vertical scroll bar
  Internet Explorer, 516
  MS Excel 2003, 166
viewing an XHTML document, 552–554
vlink attribute (XHTML), 554

W

Web browsers, 33, 514
Web page authoring programs, 34
Web pages
  described, 514
  Favorites list, adding a Web page to, 528–530

Markup Validation Service Web page, 577–581
Notepad used to create a Web page
  background color, setting, 556
  basic XHTML document template, creating, 547–550
  body section, 554–556
  document formatting tags, 557–574
  header section, 550–551
  meta elements, adding, 550–551
  opening Notepad, 548
  saving a new document, 551–552
  text color, setting, 556
  title element, adding, 550–551
  viewing a document, 552–554
previously viewed Web pages, displaying, 525–526
printing a Web page, 531
specific Web page, displaying, 522–523
Web site certificates, 539
Web sites, 514
width attribute, 560
Windows Explorer (Windows XP)
  Address bar, 36
  backups, 42
  closing, 41
  common problems associated with working with files, 41–42
  components of your computer, examining, 35–41
  copying files, 45
  copying folders, 45
  creating a new folder, 42–44
  deleting files, 41, 47–48
  deleting folders, 47–48
  "Denied file access" message, 42
  file icon, 35
  file management with, 41–48
  finding files, 48
  folder icon, 35
  folder icon, changing, 43–44
  Folders view, 34
  Local Disk (C:), 37
  location of files, 42
  moving files, 45–46
  moving folders, 45–46
  My Computer, 37
  My Documents folder, 39–41
  naming files, 42
  naming folders, 42
  overview, 34–35
  Properties dialog box, 39
  renaming files, 41–42, 46–47

renaming folders, 46–47
saving your work, 42
shortcut menu, 36–37
starting, 35
Tasks view, 34–35
Views button, 38
Windows Mobile 2003, 25
Windows XP
　Add Printer Wizard, 21
　commands, 633
　Control Panel
　　described, 9–10
　　keyboard settings, 20–21
　　mouse settings, 17–20
　　printer settings, 21
　　screen display, changing, 12–17
　　system date and time, changing, 10–12
　　themes, applying, 17
　Internet Explorer icon, 3
　keyboard shortcuts, 633
　logging off, 7–8
　logging on, 1–2
　modifying system settings, 9–21
　moving windows, 5–7
　My Computer icon, 3
　My Documents icon, 3
　My Network Places icon, 3
　network domain, logging on to a computer
　　that is part of a, 1–2
　Recycle Bin icon, 3
　resizing windows, 5–7
　shortcut buttons, 29
　shutting down, 8–9
　stand-alone computer, logging on to a, 2
　Start menu
　　All Programs, 4
　　Control Panel, 4
　　described, 4
　　displaying, 5
　　Help and Support, 4
　　Log Off, 4
　　My Computer, 4
　　My Documents, 4
　　My Music, 4
　　My Pictures, 4
　　My Recent Documents, 4
　　Printers and Faxes, 4
　　Run, 4
　　Search, 4
　　selecting options on, 5
　　Shut Down, 4
　　Turn Off Computer, 4

system software, 21–26
toolbar shortcuts, 633
Windows Explorer
　Address bar, 36
　closing, 41
　components of your computer, examining,
　　35–41
　file icon, 35
　file management with, 41–48
　folder icon, 35
　Folders view, 34
　Local Disk (C:), 37
　My Computer, 37
　My Documents folder, 39–41
　overview, 34–35
　Properties dialog box, 39
　shortcut menu, 36–37
　starting, 35
　Tasks view, 34–35
　Views button, 38
Windows XP desktop
　described, 2–4
　icons, 3
　Notification area, 3
　Start button, 3
　Taskbar, 3
wizards
　Crosstab Query Wizard, 491–496
　Find Unmatched Query Wizard, 496–498
　MS Word 2003, 104
　Simple Query Wizard, 440–446
word processing applications
　copying text, 29
　cut and paste, 29
　deleting text, 29
　fonts, 30
　graphics, 30
　indexes, 30
　inserting text, 29
　margin size, 29
　overview, 29–30
　page size, 29
　print, 30
　search and replace, 30
　spell checker, 30
　table of contents, 30
　thesaurus, 30
　word wrap, 30
word wrap, 30
workbooks (MS Excel 2003)
　data entered into cell, 228, 230
　formula entered into worksheet, 228, 231

workbooks (MS Excel 2003)—*Continued*
   linking worksheets with, 253–262
   opening new workbook, 228, 229
   resaving, 180
   saving, 180–181
Workbook window (MS Excel 2003), 166
worksheets (MS Excel 2003)
   alignment of cell entries, resetting, 181–182
   borders, adding, 186–190
   cell pointer, moving, 171
   centering, 210
   changing data in, 193–194
   column width, adjusting, 190–191
   conditional formatting applied to, 249–252
   consecutive worksheets, selecting, 259
   copying cells, 195–197
   deleting columns, 197–198
   deleting rows, 197–198
   described, 163
   drag and drop technique used for copying
      cells, 195–197
   editing, 193–208
   entering a formula into, 174–179
   entering labels and values into a blank
      worksheet, 170–174
   entire worksheet printed on one page, 210
   font options for cell entries, resetting, 182–185
   footer, creating, 211–212
   formatting, 181–193
   formulas, 171
   formulas used to link worksheets in a
      workbook, 255–258
   gridline included in printout, 212
   header, creating, 211
   inserting columns, 197–201
   inserting rows, 197–201
   labels, 171
   modifying, 170–181
   multiple worksheets formatted in one
      operation, 259–262
   non-consecutive worksheets, selecting, 259
   number format of cell entries, resetting,
      201–208
   page orientation, 213
   page setup options, 208–214
   percentages, formatting cell entries as, 201–208
   print preview, 213–214
   range, selecting a, 186
   renaming, 253–255
   row height, adjusting, 192–193
   shading, adding, 186–190

values, 171
   workbook, linking worksheets with, 253–262
worksheet tabs, 166
World Wide Web (WWW), 514

X

XHTML
   align attribute, 560, 564
   alink attribute, 554
   attributes, 554–555
   background attribute, 554
   background color, setting, 556
   basic XHTML document template, creating,
      547–550
   bgcolor attribute, 554
   bibliography page, creation of, 613
   body section, 554–556
   document formatting tags
      described, 557
      heading tags, 557–559
      horizontal rule tags, 560–562
      line break tags, 557
      list tags, 568–574
      nested tags, 566–568
      paragraph tags, 562–566
   file, creating a, 588–592
   header section, 550–551
   hyperlinks, 614–622
   images
      downloading images from Web sites,
         603–607
      Microsoft Office clipart, 607–612
      overview, 601–603
   link attribute, 554
   list tags
      definition list tags, 569
      described, 568–569
      nested list tags, 573–574
      ordered list tags, 571–573
      unordered list tags, 570–571
   Markup Validation Service Web page, 577–581
   meta elements, adding, 550–551
   navigation, 622–629
   noshade attribute, 560
   Notepad used to create a Web page
      background color, setting, 556
      basic XHTML document template, creating,
         547–550
      body section, 554–556
      document formatting tags, 557–574

header section, 550–551
meta elements, adding, 550–551
opening Notepad, 548
saving a new document, 551–552
text color, setting, 556
title element, adding, 550–551
viewing a document, 552–554
opening Notepad, 548
overview, 547
practice exercises, 583–584, 629–630
saving a new document, 551–552
size attribute, 560
syllabus.html file creation
hyperlinks, adding, 621–622
Microsoft Office clipart added to, 607–612
navigation menu, creating, 623–629
overview, 588–592
table added to, 598–600

tables, 593–600
tags, 661–662
text color, setting, 556
title element, adding, 550–551
validating Web pages, 575–583
viewing a document, 552–554
vlink attribute, 554
width attribute, 560
xy (scatter) chart, 265

Y

yes/no (boolean) data type, 401

Z

zoom level of document, changing, 100–102